MANAGERIAL ECONOMICS

Fifth Edition

Edwin Mansfield

late of University of Pennsylvania

W. Bruce Allen

The Wharton School
University of Pennsylvania

Neil A. Doherty

The Wharton School
University of Pennsylvania

Keith Weigelt

The Wharton School
University of Pennsylvania

MANAGERIAL ECONOMICS

Theory, Applications, and Cases

Fifth Edition

W. W. NORTON & COMPANY

NEW YORK • LONDON

Dedication:

To Edwin Mansfield, a pioneer of managerial economics

MANAGERIAL ECONOMICS
Theory, Applications, and Cases, Fifth Edition
Edwin Mansfield, W. Bruce Allen, Neil A. Doherty, and Keith Weigelt

The text of this book is composed in Rotis Serif
Composition by Matrix Publishing Services
Manufacturing by RR Donnelley
Book design by Rubina Yeh
Manufacturing director: Roy Tedoff

Library of Congress Cataloging-in-Publication Data
Managerial economics : theory, applications, and cases / Edwin Mansfield . . . [et al.].—5th ed.
   p. cm.
   After original author's death, a group of editors published the 5th ed.
   Includes bibliographical references and index.
   ISBN 0-393-97677-7
   1. Managerial economics. I. Mansfield, Edwin.
   HD30.22.M354 2001
   338.5′024′658—dc21   2001045283
ISBN 0-393-97677-7

W. W. Norton & Company, Inc., 500 Fifth Avenue, New York, N.Y. 10110
   www.wwnorton.com
W. W. Norton & Company Ltd., Castle House, 75/76 Wells Street, London W1T 3QT

4 5 6 7 8 9 0

CONTENTS

Chapter 2   Optimization Techniques   37

Chapter 15   Auctions   565

Chapter 18   Managerial Economics: Taking a
Global View   679

Appendix A Discounting and Present Values A-1

Appendix B The Normal, *t*, and *F* Distributions A-9

Recent thought on culture describes it as the process by which knowledge is passed between generations. Most cultures use two devices to learn, teaching and copying, with both being independent of any genetic influences. We've used both in presenting this Fifth Edition of *Managerial Economics*. It is our vision of the future, based on the wisdom of the past.

Succession is an issue many ponder but few act upon timely. It knows no legal bounds, being faced both by families and corporate entities. In the transfer of intellectual property (i.e., ideas), both groups face succession issues. We feel extremely lucky that both the Mansfield family and W. W. Norton acted in a timely manner and fostered the exchange process. We thank both of them for all their helpful advice.

Professor Mansfield was a true pioneer of managerial economics. Before him, most viewed the field as theory with a "wink and nod" link to application. Though this link differentiates managerial from microeconomics, few ventured more than a cursory link to reality. Mansfield's vision changed this by hard-wiring theory to practice. Today, this standard still differentiates the two fields. (And, if anything, today's micro textbooks are more applied.) Professor Mansfield instilled each chapter with an actual business situation, and then for good measure, sprinkled shorter cases throughout the theory. If you needed an example for class, the Mansfield text was a very reliable source.

This pioneering style was likely fueled by his eclectic nature; for only those who integrate ideas across disciplines can marry theory to practice. Professor Mansfield's knowledge covered economics, operations, technology management, and statistics. The three of us joke about how it has taken three to replace what one covered himself—a fact that attests to Ed's breadth of knowledge.

It is upon this legacy that we present the fifth edition. It, like any generational transfer, builds the future on the past. Some things remain the same, others change. Our criteria for justifying changes was whether it helped us better integrate the Mansfield tradition within the changing landscape of what we call the business world. We see five mainstays of this tradition:

1. to tightly couple practice to theory;
2. to use formal analysis;
3. to use mathematics as a tool, not an end;
4. to update materials to remain current with the changing business landscape; and
5. to listen and learn from the experiences of readers and instructors.

The three of us teach the managerial economics course at The Wharton School. It is required for most MBA students, taken in their first semester. Eight years ago, The Wharton School completely revised its curriculum to better prepare students for the business world. This curriculum change coincided with Wharton's enhanced standing in the rankings of business schools.

Our charge was to develop a class to help students transfer economic principles to the business world, to make economics a decision-making norm (in ten weeks or less), which required impact in both short- and long-term memory. During our six-week run, we could command our share of time and effort as well as any of the other five classes students were taking. So we knew what to expect in the short run. But, what about the long run? When humans process information, they must transfer bytes from short- to long-term memories. Much gets lost in the switch, and that which does never returns unless short-term picks it up again. Ours was the only economics course taken by most students, so our ideas would have to make the switch with seemingly little reinforcing support. In two years, MBA students get bombarded (and often overwhelmed) by millions of information bytes. In school, ideas play the ultimate survivor game— you don't just get voted out, you cease to exist.

To make the memory jump to long-term, we felt the course had to accomplish several goals. One was to establish economics as a decision-making framework, to get students to see past the equations and graphs and understand why, as managers, they want to follow its general percepts, like marginal analysis or backward induction. Another message we wanted to convey was the integrative nature of economics—its ideas permeate all business disciplines. So an understanding of economics now will help the student better understand finance and marketing later.

A third goal was to accomplish the above without sacrificing the formal analysis that underlies rational choice. For without it, knowledge is speculative. The objectivity of mathematics brings focus to a business discussion. After all, most managers realize that demand should increase if prices drop, but fewer are able to quantify the sales increase. We wanted to produce managers that could do the latter. Our final goal was to acknowledge that at times managers can be boundedly rational. We wanted to show students how boundedly rational managers might act and help them to understand how behavior is affected.

We kept these four goals in mind in revising this book, and they will direct our future efforts. This edition represents the path we will follow in the future. Though our contributions to this edition are substantial, they represent a beginning toward our goal of producing a book that students use even after they graduate. The most important changes in the Fifth Edition include:

1. **A New Chapter on Auctions.** Recent years have seen an explosion in the use of auctions. New auction businesses like eBay and Priceline.com have attracted millions of customers, and businesses of various sorts have begun to rely on auctions to purchase materials and to buy and sell equipment. More than ever before, modern managers need to know a few things about auctions. How does the design of an auction affect its outcome? What are the best bidding strategies for different types of auctions? How do auctions compare to other types of markets? Such questions are answered in Chapter 15.

2. **A New Chapter on Moral Hazard and the Principal-Agent Problem.** Businesses are driven by incentives. For instance, in the most simple case, classic economic models look at firms as profit maximizers compelled by competition to minimize costs. But this is only part of the story. What about the incentives of employees, managers, and the owners who employ them? Do employees always focus on the economic goals of the firm, or do factors like personal comfort come into play? Or, what if an owner's economic interest in selling her company bumps into the senior manager's desire for job stability? In the real world of business, incentives can become misaligned in countless ways. Chapter 16 looks at two of the most general incentive problems—moral hazard and the principal-agent problem—with applications to executive compensation, conflicts between shareholders and their creditors, and product liability.

3. **New Cases and Applications.** This textbook has long been viewed as the best expression of Edwin Mansfield's special talents as an economist and business consultant. As one who spent a great deal of time applying microeconomics in the business world, Professor Mansfield believed deeply in the power of example. Accordingly, applications have always been used liberally throughout this book. For the Fifth Edition, we have embraced this tradition by introducing a variety of new applications. They are consistently interwoven into

the main body of the text, and they also appear in a variety boxed inserts. Every step of the way, students are presented with economic ideas and their applications and real instances when the ideas at hand have been critical to solving managerial problems. Multiple cases and applications appear in each chapter of the book (see the endpapers). Many of these cases are new or significantly revised in this edition including:

- Shell Gains by Giving Safe-Driving Advice
- Using Patents to Maintain Market Power
- Verizon Local Calling Plans
- Yield Management at American Airlines
- Japan's Tax Man Leans on Foreign Firms
- The Use of Sophisticated Pricing within an Auction Format
- Auction Design at Freemarkets, Inc.
- The Composition of CEO Pay
- Do Directors Act on Behalf of Shareholders or Managers?

4. **An E-Media Package** which addresses the desire of the business student and the need of the business instructor to integrate electronic media into the curriculum. The Fifth Edition comes complete with a power group of electronic ancillaries, including:

- **Spreadsheet Exercises** This completely new set of exercises—replacing those offered with the Fourth Edition—is available to qualified adopters free of charge. The exercises consist of 40 Microsoft Excel files. Some of the exercises are tutorial in nature, designed to help students work through various principles and models. Others are set up as labs, suitable for use as homework problems. These exercises have been prepared by Stephen Erfle of Dickinson College.
- **Economics News Server** News articles from the *New York Times* will be e-mailed to a list serve to which students and instructors subscribe. The articles will reach the subscriber as an e-mail message, with a brief opening commentary relating the article to material in the textbook. Approximately two articles will be sent out each week of the academic year.
- **XanEdu Course Pack Edition** New for the Fifth Edition, and in partnership with XanEdu.Com, Norton will offer a special XanEdu Edition of *Managerial Economics* (5e). XanEdu.Com, a wing of Proquest Information and Learning, offers electronic course packs for higher education markets, using an archive of articles from thousands of periodicals and content providers. Instructors who order this special edition will provide their students with access to a course pack customized for MEC5. In addition to the specially selected articles, this course pack will include the XanEdu search engine for Proquest's full archive of economics content. Students can search for articles on all sorts of topics related to business and economics.

- **PowerPoint Slides**   All the figures in the textbook will be reproduced for PowerPoint and available for download from the book's Internet site.

5. **New Four-Color Design.** Along with the book's new emphasis, we introduce a new look. The attractive four-color design of our figures makes it easier for students to understand the relevant concepts. It also signals to teachers that our Fifth Edition warrants a fresh evaluation.

The textbook also continues to be accompanied by the *Study Guide and Case-book,* which for this edition was revised by Thomas Donley of DePaul University, and the *Instructor's Manual and Test-Item File* by Kathryn Nantz of Fairfield University.

Finally, teachers familiar with previous editions will note that two chapters, one on linear programming and another on capital budgeting, have been dropped to make room for new material. Surveys of users of the textbook reported a large majority no longer convering these subjects in their classes. Even so, the chapters from the Fourth Edition are available in electronic form and free of charge to any adopter of the Fifth Edition.

In preparing this Fifth Edition, we benefited from the feedback and suggestions of the following reviewers, survey respondents, and colleagues, to whom we offer our thanks: Sheryl B. Ball, Virginia Polytechnic Institute and State University; Thomas Donley, DePaul University; Stephen Erfle, Dickinson College; Maria Gamba, University of Findley; Susan P. Gilbert, Emory University; Walton Padelford, Union University; Richard Sheehan, Notre Dame University; Robert Stewart, Rutgers University; Ali Tarhouni, University of Washington; Peter Touamnoff, Marquette University; and Chun-sheng Zhou, University of California at Riverside.

PART

1

Introduction

Introduction to Managerial Economics

What do Boeing, the Walt Disney Company, and the Toyota Motor Company have in common?

What do Boeing, the Walt Disney Company, and the Toyota Motor Company have in common? All three, like countless other firms, have used the well-established principles of managerial economics to improve their profitability. Managerial economics draws on economic analysis for such concepts as cost, demand, profit, competition, pricing, entry strategy, and market protection strategy. It attempts to bridge the gap between the purely analytical problems that intrigue many economic theorists and the day-to-day decisions that managers face. It now offers powerful tools and approaches for managerial policymaking, like game theory, sophisticated pricing policies such as bundling, and two-part tariffs.

In this opening chapter, we begin our study by presenting several case studies illustrating just some of the problems that managerial economics can help solve. Although they cover only a small sample of the situations in which managerial economics is useful, these illustrative problems should provide a reasonable first impression of the nature of managerial economics and its relevance to real business decisions. To aid in elucidating the application to business decisions, strategically placed highlighted sections called Concepts in Context, Consultant's Corner, and Analyzing Managerial Decisions, will directly point the reader to applications of the adjacent concept in the text. Also, we will examine the relationship between managerial economics and such related disciplines as microeconomics and the decision sciences, including statistics.

Next, we will take up basic models of decision making, as well as the theory of the firm. Since managerial economics is concerned with the ways in which business executives and other policymakers *should* make decisions, it is important at the outset that the nature of this decision-making process be analyzed and that the motivation of firms be discussed. Since profits play so major a role in business decision making, we will proceed to define profit and recognize how the economist's definition of profit differs from that of the accountant. Finally, we will present an overview of the basic principles of demand and supply, a central topic that will be examined much more completely in subsequent chapters.

Boeing's Struggle to Retain Market Leadership

To illustrate the strategic issues managerial economics can help managers solve, consider the world's largest producer of commercial aircraft, the Boeing Company. Beginning in the 1970s Boeing managers mapped out a two-prong approach to retaining market leadership. The company would be the low-cost producer and the technological leader in the industry. By 1980, the company had achieved a market share of 81 percent, a seven-fold lead over its nearest competitor. And, Boeing was able to accomplish this feat while maintaining high profit margins. One industry expert estimated that in 1991, Boeing realized a profit of $45 million on every 747 aircraft it sold for $150 million.

Boeing's principal rival since the 1980s has been Airbus, a joint venture of British, French, German, and Spanish aerospace firms. Starting with the delivery of their first plane in 1974, Airbus quickly moved into the number-two spot behind Boeing. By 1997, Airbus achieved a market share of over 33 percent, while Boeing's share was reduced to under 65 percent.[1] And, not only did Airbus reduce Boeing's market share, the company also assumed the lead in technological advances and challenged Boeing for low-cost leadership. This aggressive move by Airbus also forced Boeing managers to drop prices and rely more heavily on discounts to sell their planes. By 1994, the net earnings of Boeing had fallen 31 percent relative to 1991 levels, primarily due to the increased competition offered by Airbus.

Managerial economics can help us better understand how Airbus was so quickly able to erode Boeing's market domination. Chapter 9 provides some rationale to explain how Airbus was able to reduce its costs to approach those of Boeing. For example, this chapter illustrates how the costs of aircraft produc-

[1]*Wall Street Journal*, April 30, 1997.

tion are affected by the number of planes built. Chapter 8 helps us understand how further cost savings can be realized by reducing the development time of new aircraft models. Finally, Chapter 18 helps us understand how national trade policy may have helped Airbus in their quest to challenge Boeing.

The Disney Corporation: Expansion of the Magic Kingdom

The Disney Corporation has always been known as a mecca for creative talent and energy. However, after its founder, Walt Disney, died in 1966 the company was adrift for decades. Though the company retained high brand recognition, its managers seemed unable to turn this recognition into increased sales and profits. Because of this lack of performance, in the early 1980s, the company was attacked by a series of corporate raiders, including Saul Steinberg and Irwin Jacobs. In desperation, directors hired Michael Eisner as the new CEO.

Eisner and his management team have unlocked the value of the Disney name and positioned the Magic Kingdom for the twenty-first century. In less than twenty years, Eisner's team has increased revenues tenfold to over $23 billion in 1999.[2] Disney now ranks as one of the 100 biggest global firms and the second largest global media company (behind Time-Warner). Disney holdings include the following: ABC television and radio networks; 10 U.S. television and 21 U.S. radio stations; ownership in over 8 cable channels, including ESPN International, the global leader in sports networking (with 24-hour broadcasting in 21 languages to over 165 countries); several major film, video, and television studios including Disney, Miramax, and Buena Vista; several major record labels; theme parks in the United States, Japan, and France; the Disney Cruise Line; controlling interest in two major league sports teams (ice hockey and baseball); and 550 Disney retail stores worldwide.

In expanding their Magic Kingdom, Eisner's team has used analyses that are based on managerial economics principles. For example, after studies indicated that increases in advertising would raise theme park attendance and raise profits, they launched a series of successful advertising campaigns, which will be discussed in Chapter 11.

Eisner's team has also shown its ability to use both simple and sophisticated pricing techniques to improve firm performance. When the Disney animated classic film *Pinocchio* was released on videocassette, it was initially priced at $79.95 (as were most videocassettes). At this price only 100,000 copies were sold in the first two months. Eisner's team decided to drop the price to $29.95, and promptly sold over 300,000 copies. Disney has also been a leader in using sophisticated

[2]1999 Disney Fact Book.

pricing strategies such as bundling. They have bundled together a Disney cruise with a stay at their Disneyworld theme park in Florida, a McDonald kid's meal, and action figures from their movies, and several of their cable channels to cable customers. They also practice price discrimination. Consumers who buy a Disney videocassette will find coupons for merchandise at Disney retail stores. These and other pricing strategies are examined in Chapter 14. With the help of these techniques, Disney has given its shareholders 20 percent annual earnings growth for 14 consecutive years and an annualized return on equity of 18.5 percent.

In What Size Production Runs Should Toyota Produce Its Cars?

Firms must decide how to produce their products. Firms that produce multiple products on an assembly line must decide how much of a given product they should produce in a production run—in essence, the length of the production run. Long production runs lower the costs associated with changing over the production line to produce a different product (set-up costs), while shorter runs lower the costs associated with raw material and final product inventory (inventory carrying charges). More frequent, smaller production runs mean high set-up costs and low inventory costs. Less frequent, larger production runs have just the reverse effect.

Toyota Motor Company (and many other producers) face exactly this problem. What production run is optimal to minimize the combined costs of set-up and inventory? In Chapter 7, we discuss how Toyota's significant decrease in set-up costs enabled them to significantly decrease their optimal production runs and hence to decrease their total costs.

The model used in the Toyota case is called the Economic Order Quantity (EOQ) model. It is the mainstay of supply chain management. Using it (in sophisticated versions), companies determine the optimal amount of a product needed each time they place an order. In the simple model, the firm trades off ordering cost and inventory costs. As the model is expanded, reliability in delivery time plays a major role in determining the optimal EOQ. We'll discuss this model in Chapter 7.

Relationships of Managerial Economics to Other Disciplines

Having considered three case studies illustrating the sorts of problems that managerial economics can help to solve, we can begin to describe how managerial economics is related to other disciplines. As shown in Figure 1.1, managerial

FIGURE
1.1

Relationship between Managerial Economics and Related Disciplines

Managerial economics provides a link between economic theory and the decision sciences in the analysis of managerial decision making.

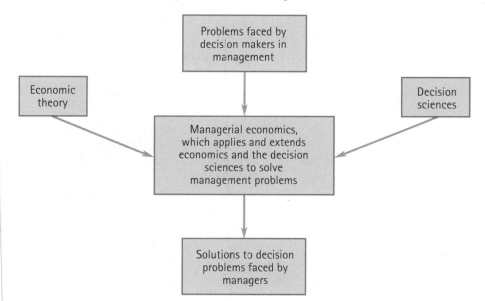

economics provides a link between economic theory and the decision sciences in the analysis of managerial decision making. Traditional economic theory—which consists of microeconomics (focusing on individual consumers, firms, and industries) and macroeconomics (focusing on aggregate output, income, and employment)—contains a considerable amount of material that bears on managerial decision making, the role of microeconomics being particularly important in this regard. Managerial economics draws heavily from microeconomics, as well as from other areas of economic theory.

But managerial economics is quite different from microeconomics. Whereas microeconomics is largely descriptive (that is, it attempts to describe how the economy works without indicating how it should operate), managerial economics is largely prescriptive (that is, it attempts to establish rules and techniques to fulfill specified goals). For example, microeconomics is concerned with the way in which computer manufacturers like IBM price their products, while managerial economics is concerned with how they *should* price their products. Of course, this is a difference of emphasis and degree, not of kind, but it nonetheless is important.

As shown in Figure 1.1, managerial economics draws heavily on the decision sciences, as well as traditional economics. The decision sciences provide ways to analyze the impact of alternative courses of action. Managerial economics uses optimization techniques, such as differential calculus and mathematical programming, to determine optimal courses of action for decision makers. To implement these techniques, statistical methods must be employed to estimate the relationships between relevant variables and to forecast their values. Thus, managerial economics has arisen from a complex mixture of various parts of economics and the decision sciences, including statistics.

Managerial economics plays two important roles in the study of business administration. First, the course in managerial economics, like courses in accounting, quantitative methods, and management information systems, provides fundamental analytical *tools* that can and should be used in other courses, such as marketing, finance, and production. Second, the course in managerial economics, like courses in business policy, can serve an *integrating* role, showing how other areas such as marketing, finance, and production must be viewed as a whole in order to fulfill the goals of the firm.

Although managerial economics is at the heart of the study of business administration, it plays no less a part in the management of nonbusiness organizations such as government agencies, hospitals, and schools. Regardless of whether one manages Eastman Kodak, the Mayo Clinic, or the University of Hawaii, one must pay attention to the efficient allocation of resources. Waste is waste, wherever it occurs. The principles of managerial economics are as important in reducing waste in nonbusiness organizations as they are in firms.

The Basic Process of Decision Making

Both for firms and for nonbusiness organizations, the process of decision making can be divided into five basic steps, as indicated in Figure 1.2. These steps are as follows:[3]

Step 1 Establish or Identify the Objectives

In making any decision, you, as the decision maker, should determine what are the organization's (or individual's) objectives. Unless you know what it is that you are trying to achieve, there is no sensible way to make the decision. For example, consider the managers of Black and Decker, the power tool manufacturer, who had to decide in the 1970s whether the firm's consumer power tools

---

[3]For further discussion, see H. Simon, "The Decision-Making Process," in *Managerial Economics and Operations Research*, ed. E. Mansfield (5th ed.; New York: Norton, 1987).

FIGURE
1.2

Basic Process of Decision Making

This process can be divided into the five basic steps shown above.

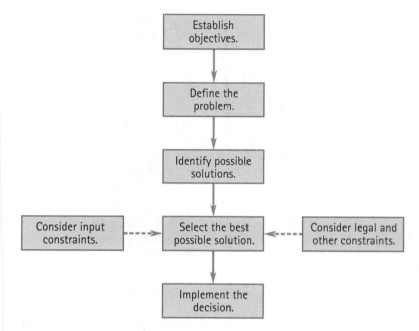

should be redesigned. Their objectives were to bolster the company's profits, to attain a 15 percent annual growth rate, to remain independent, and to service world markets.[4]

Step 2 Define the Problem

One of the most difficult parts of decision making is to determine exactly what the problem is. Frequently executives confront a situation that is judged to be unsatisfactory. For example, Black and Decker's management felt that they had to change their operations drastically if they were to continue to be a domestic manufacturer doing business internationally. To meet this challenge, they had to determine exactly what the problem was, since otherwise they had little chance of solving it. After considerable study, they concluded that the problem was the likelihood of increased foreign competition and the possibility that

[4]A. Lehnerd, "Revitalizing the Manufacture and Design of Mature Global Products," in *Technology and Global Industry*, eds. B. Guile and H. Brooks (Washington, D.C.: National Academy Press, 1987).

double insulation of power tools would be legally required. ("Double insulation" means that an additional insulation barrier is placed in an electric device to protect the user from electric shock if the main insulation system fails.)

Step 3 Identify Possible Solutions

Once the problem is defined, you should try to construct and identify possible solutions. For example, Black and Decker considered a variety of options, including more-effective production and marketing of its products based on existing designs, as well as redesigning its entire product line.

Step 4 Select the Best Possible Solution

Having identified the set of alternative possible solutions, you must evaluate each one and determine which is best, given the objectives of the organization. In the case of Black and Decker, studies indicated that the best solution was to redesign the firm's consumer power tools. Black and Decker's managers "decided that a window of opportunity existed to improve their product lines and manufacturing capability. Moreover, they decided that if they did not take time to do it right the first time, they would never have the time or resources to do it over."[5]

Step 5 Implement the Decision

Once a particular solution has been chosen, it must be implemented in order to be effective. Even organizations as disciplined as armies find it difficult to carry out orders effectively. Since even the best decisions come to naught if they are not carried out, this phase of the decision-making process is of crucial importance. In the case of Black and Decker, the organization of the firm was changed, and a new job—vice president of operations—was created so that manufacturing, product development, and advanced manufacturing engineering were all under one manager. The firm's top management made sure the decision was implemented properly.

The Theory of the Firm

Although managerial economics is not concerned solely with the management of business firms, this is its principal field of application. To apply managerial economics to business management, we need a **theory of the firm**, a theory indicating how firms behave and what their goals are. Firms are complex organizations that vary enormously. Any theory, or model (which means the same

[5]Ibid., p. 50.

as theory), must be a simplification. The trick is to construct a model in such a way that irrelevant and unimportant considerations and variables are neglected, but the essential factors—those that have an important effect on the phenomena the model is designed to illuminate—are included.

The basic model of the business enterprise stems from what economists designate as the theory of the firm. In its most stripped-down version, this theory assumes that the firm tries to maximize its profits. But this version is too stark to be useful in many circumstances, particularly where a problem facing the firm has important dynamic elements and where risk is involved. A richer version of this theory assumes that the firm tries to maximize its wealth or value. At present, this version is the dominant theory used by managerial economists.

To understand this theory, we must spell out what managerial economists mean by the **value** of the firm. Since a firm's value can be defined in a variety of ways,[6] it will prevent confusion if we provide a detailed definition at this point. Put briefly, *a firm's value will be defined here as the present value of its expected future cash flows.* In later chapters, we will learn more about what is meant by "cash flow." For present purposes, we can regard a firm's cash flow as being the same as its profit. (For those who are unfamiliar with the concept of a "present value," or who want to review this concept, a detailed discussion is provided in Appendix A.)

Thus, expressed as an equation, the value of the firm equals

$$\text{Present value of expected future profits} = \frac{\pi_1}{1+i} + \frac{\pi_2}{(1+i)^2} + \cdots + \frac{\pi_n}{(1+i)^n}$$

$$\text{Present value of expected future profits} = \sum_{t=1}^{n} \frac{\pi_t}{(1+i)^t}, \tag{1.1}$$

where π_t is the expected profit in year t, i is the interest rate, and t goes from 1 (next year) to n (the last year in the planning horizon). Because profit equals total revenue (TR) minus total cost (TC), this equation can also be expressed as

$$\text{Present value of expected future profits} = \sum_{t=1}^{n} \frac{TR_t - TC_t}{(1+i)^t}, \tag{1.2}$$

where TR_t is the firm's total revenue in year t, and TC_t is its total cost in year t.

A careful inspection of equation (1.2) suggests how a firm's managers and workers can influence its value. Consider, for example, the Ford Motor Company. Its marketing managers and sales representatives work hard to increase its total revenues, while its production managers and manufacturing engineers strive to reduce its total costs. At the same time, its financial managers play a major role

[6]For example, one could define a firm's value as its book value or liquidating value, among others.

in obtaining capital, and hence influence equation (1.2), while its research and development personnel invent new products and processes that both increase the firm's total revenues and reduce its total costs. All these diverse groups affect Ford Motor's value, defined here as the present value of its expected profits.

The Role of Constraints

To repeat, managerial economists generally assume that managers want to maximize firm value, as defined in equations (1.1) and (1.2). However, this does not mean that managers have complete control over firm value and can set it at any level they choose. On the contrary, managers must cope with the fact that there are many constraints on what they can achieve in this regard.

The constraints that limit the extent to which a firm's value can be increased are of various kinds. For one thing, the amount of certain types of inputs may be limited. In the relevant period of time, managers may be unable to obtain more than a particular amount of specialized equipment, skilled labor, essential materials, or other inputs. Particularly if the period of time is relatively short, these input constraints may be quite severe. For example, because it takes many months to expand the capacity of a steel plant, many short-run problems facing a steel firm must be solved on the basis of the recognition that plant capacity is essentially fixed. However, in dealing with longer-run problems, the firm has more flexibility and can alter (within limits) its capacity.

Another important type of constraint that limits managerial actions is legal or contractual in nature. For example, a firm may be bound to pay wages exceeding a certain level because the minimum wage laws stipulate that it must do so. Also, it must pay taxes in accord with federal, state, and local laws. Further, it must act in accord with its contracts with customers and suppliers—or take the legal consequences. A wide variety of laws (ranging from environmental laws to antitrust laws to tax laws) limit what managers can do, and the contracts and other legal agreements made by them further constrain their actions. As indicated in Figure 1.3, these constraints limit how much profit a firm can make, as well as the value of the firm itself.

Because there are constraints on a firm's actions and behavior, the relevant techniques used to analyze many of a firm's problems are **constrained optimization techniques**, such as Lagrangian multipliers (described in Chapter 2).

What Are Profits?

Throughout previous sections, we have repeatedly encountered the term "profits." Practically all published profit figures are based on the accountants' definition of profits. It is important at the outset to recognize that managerial

FIGURE
1.3

Determinants of the Value of a Firm

A firm's value depends on factors influencing TR_t, TC_t, and i, as well as the constraints it faces.

economists define profits somewhat differently. In particular, when economists speak of **profit**, they mean profit after taking account of the capital and labor provided by the owners. Thus, suppose that the owners of the San Jose Shoe Store, who receive profits but no salary or wages, put in long hours for which they could receive $40,000 in 1999 if they worked for someone else. Also suppose that if they invested their capital somewhere other than in this firm, they could obtain a return of $24,000 on it in 1999. Under these circumstances, if the store's 1999 accounting profit is $60,000, economists would say that the firm's economic profits in 1999 were $60,000 − $40,000 − $24,000, or −$4,000, rather than the $60,000 shown in the store's accounting statements. In other words, the economists' concept of profit includes only what the owners make above and beyond what their labor and capital employed in the business could earn elsewhere. In this case, that amount is negative.

The differences between the concepts used by the accountant and the economist reflect the difference in their functions. The accountant is concerned with controlling the firm's day-to-day operations, detecting fraud or embezzlement, satisfying tax and other laws, and producing records for various interested groups. The economist is concerned primarily with decision making and rational choice among prospective alternatives. While the figures published on profits almost always conform to the accountant's, not the economist's, concept, the economist's is the more relevant one for many kinds of decisions. (And this, of course, is recognized by sophisticated accountants.) For example, suppose the owners of the San Jose Shoe Store are trying to decide whether they should continue in business. If they are interested in making as much money as possible, the answer depends on the firm's profits as measured by the economist, not the accountant. If the firm's economic profits are greater than (or equal to) zero, the firm should continue in existence; otherwise, it should not. Hence, if 1999 is a good indicator of its prospective profitability, the San Jose Shoe Store should not stay in existence.

Reasons for the Existence of Profit

Why do economic profits exist? Three important reasons are innovation, risk, and monopoly power. Suppose that an economy is composed of competitive industries, that entry into these industries is completely free, and that no changes in technology—no new processes, no new products, and no other innovations—are permitted. Moreover, suppose that everyone can predict the future with perfect accuracy. Under these conditions, there will be no profits, because people will enter industries where profits exist, thus reducing these profits eventually to zero, and leave industries where losses exist, thus reducing these negative profits eventually to zero.

But in reality innovations of various kinds are made. For example, Boeing, (recall page 4) introduces its 777 (a new twin-engined wide-bodied jet); or Intel, the California electronics firm, introduces the microprocessor (a computer-on-a-chip). The people who carry out these bold schemes are the **innovators**, those with vision and the daring to back it up. The innovators are not necessarily the inventors of new techniques or products, although in some cases the innovator and the inventor are the same. Often the innovator takes another's invention, adapts it, and introduces it to the market. Profits are a reward earned by successful innovators.

Risk also exists in the real world. Indeed one of the hazards in attempting to be an innovator is the risk involved. Profit is a reward for risk bearing. Assuming that people would like to avoid risk, they will prefer relatively stable, sure earnings to relatively unstable, uncertain earnings—*if the average level of earnings is the same.* Consequently, to induce people to take the risks involved in owning businesses in various industries, a profit—a premium for risk—must be paid to them.

Another reason for the existence of profits is the fact that markets are not perfectly competitive. Under perfect competition, there is a tendency in the long run for economic profits to disappear. But this is not the case if an industry is a monopoly or oligopoly. Instead, profits may well exist in the long run in such imperfectly competitive industries. Monopoly profits are fundamentally the result of "contrived scarcities." The monopolist takes account of the fact that the more it produces, the smaller the price it will receive. In other words, the monopolist realizes that it will spoil the market if it produces too much. Consequently, it pays the monopolist to limit its output, and this contrived scarcity is responsible for the existence of its profits.

Organizational Factors and "Satisficing"

Although managerial economists generally assume that managers want to maximize profit [and hence their value, as defined in equation (1.1)], other assumptions can be made. To see why it sometimes is sensible to make other assumptions, you must recognize that in many firms, particularly big ones, it is hard to know exactly where, how, and by whom decisions are made. Some firms, rather than being run by a single owner-manager, have large numbers of people in middle management, as well as the top brass occupying key management positions, all of whom participate in varying degrees in the formulation of company policy. Various groups within the firm develop their own party lines, and intrafirm politics is an important part of the process determining company policy. For example, if a firm is composed of two divisions (each making a different product), each division may fight to maintain and expand its share of the firm's budget, and each may try to put the other in a subordinate position. Political struggles within the firm may play an important role in determining its objectives.

Under such circumstances, a firm may "satisfice" rather than attempt to maximize profit. In other words, it may aim at a satisfactory rate of profit rather than the maximum figure. A firm's aspiration level is the boundary between unsatisfactory and satisfactory outcomes. For example, the aspiration level might be a particular goal, such as "Our profit for this year should be $5 million." The firm may abandon the attempt to maximize profits because intrafirm politics rule out such a goal—and because the calculations required are too complicated and the available data are too poor. Instead the firm may attempt to attain certain minimal levels of performance.[7]

If the environment facing the firm is relatively constant, the aspiration level may tend to be slightly higher than the firm's performance. If performance is improving, the aspiration level may tend to lag behind actual performance. And if performance is decreasing, the aspiration level may tend to be above actual performance. Of course, if the aspiration level is close to the maximum profit,

---

[7]For example, see H. Simon, "Theories of Decision-Making in Economic and Behavioral Science," reprinted in *Microeconomics: Selected Readings*, ed., E. Mansfield (5th ed.; New York: Norton, 1985).

ANALYZING MANAGERIAL DECISIONS

Shell Gains by Giving Safe-Driving Advice

McDonald's sponsors Ronald McDonald houses so that parents of a sick child can be near the child's hospital and receive support from similarly situated parents. Texaco sponsored the opera. Many corporations sponsor public television. Shell Oil created television ads to notify viewers that it will send them a booklet on safe driving and how to cope with problems on the road. All of this occurs without Shell mentioning its products.

While a cost stream for such behavior is evident (TV ads are expensive—the total campaign cost Shell $50 million), the revenue stream isn't quite so explicit. So why do these companies do it? Is such behavior consistent with profit maximizing? Is it satisficing?

According to a survey by Cone Inc., a strategic marketing consultant, and Roper Starch Worldwide Inc., a poll of 2,000 Americans showed that 80 percent of Americans have a more positive image of companies aligned with social issues, and *two-thirds would probably switch brands to one associated with a good cause.*

While Shell hasn't released the revenue stream impact of its campaign, the above survey results suggest that revenues increase as a result of what is known as "cause branding" and such behavior may be very compatible with the goal of profit maximizing.

Source: Sullivan Allannia, "Advertising: Shell Gains by Giving Safe-driving Advice," *Wall Street Journal*, February 18, 1999, Sec. B, p. 9.

the findings obtained by assuming satisficing are likely to be similar to those obtained by assuming profit maximization.

Managerial Interests and the Principal–Agent Problem

Satisficing is not the only alternative to the assumption of profit maximization. When differences arise between profit maximization and the interests of the management group, executives are likely to follow policies favoring their own interests.[8] Important in this regard is the separation of ownership from control in the large corporation in the United States. The owners of the firm—the stockholders—usually have little detailed knowledge of the firm's operations. Even if the board of directors is made up largely of people other than top management,

[8]See R. Marris, *The Economic Theory of "Managerial" Capitalism* (New York: Free Press, 1964). For a study of intrafirm organization, see O. Williamson, *Markets and Hierarchies: Analysis and Antitrust Implications* (New York: Free Press, 1975).

top management usually has a great deal of freedom as long as it seems to be performing adequately. Consequently, the behavior of the firm may be dictated in part by the interests of the management group, the result being higher pay and more perquisites (and a larger staff) for managers than otherwise would be true.

Economists designate this as the *principal-agent problem.* A firm's managers are *agents* who work for the firm's owners, who are the *principals.* The principal-agent problem is that the managers may pursue their own objectives, even though this decreases the profits of the owners. Consider Joseph Wagner, a manager of a local textile firm. Because the cost of the benefits (large staff, company-paid travel, and so on) that he receives from the firm is borne entirely by the owners, he has an incentive to increase these benefits substantially. Since the owners of the firm find it difficult to distinguish between those benefits which bolster profits and those which do not do so, the manager has some leeway.

To deal with this problem, firms often establish contracts with their managers that give the latter an incentive to pursue objectives that are reasonably close to profit maximization. Thus, the firm's owners might give the managers a financial stake in the success of the firm. Many corporations have adopted stock option plans, whereby managers can purchase shares of common stock at less than market price. These plans give managers an incentive to promote the firm's profits and to act in accord with the owners' interests. There is some evidence that these plans do have an effect. For example, according to one recent study, if managers own between 5 and 20 percent of a firm, the firm is likely to perform better (in terms of profitability) than if they own less than 5 percent. In some firms, managers are being forced in fact to purchase stock, and boards of directors are being compensated in stock.

Demand and Supply: A First Look

Having described the nature of managerial economics, we turn now to an overview of the basic principles of demand and supply. Any manager, whether in Tokyo, Singapore, New York, or Toronto, must understand these basic principles, which are taken up in more detail in subsequent chapters. Our purpose here is to take a preliminary look at this topic, our first task being to define what we mean by a market.

For present purposes, a *market* can be defined as a group of firms and individuals that are in touch with each other in order to buy or sell some good. Of course, not every person in a market has to be in contact with every other person in the market. A person or firm is part of a market even if it is in contact with only a subset of the other persons or firms in the market.

On first inspection, concepts like "market" and "good" seem completely clear, but precise definitions of specific markets and goods can be complicated, for

ANALYZING MANAGERIAL DECISIONS

How Disney Dealt with the Principal-Agent Problem

As you have already seen (on page 5), the Walt Disney Company brought in Michael Eisner, a Paramount executive, as CEO in 1984. The firm's board of directors agreed to pay Eisner a salary of $750,000, plus a $750,000 bonus for signing on, plus an annual bonus equal to 2 percent of the dollar amount by which the firm's net income exceeded a 9 percent return on shareholders' equity. In addition, he received options on 2 million shares of Disney stock, which meant that he could purchase them from the firm at any time during the five-year life of the contract for only $14 per share.*

(a) At the end of 1984, shareholders' equity was about $1.15 billion. How much would Eisner's 1985 bonus have been if Disney's net income that year were $100 million? If it were $200 million? (b) In 1987, the price of Disney stock rose to about $20 per share. How much were Eisner's options worth? (c) Eisner's bonus was $2.6 million in 1986 and $6 million in 1987. Including the stock options he exercised, his compensation in 1988 was about $41 million, a record at that time for any U.S. executive. In 1993, his total compensation was about

$202 million, again a record. Had Disney's owners provided a substantial incentive for Eisner to work hard to increase the firm's profits? (d) A shareholder who invested $100 in Disney stock at the beginning of Eisner's tenure would have seen its value rise to $1,460 in 1994. Was this why there was no substantial outcry from the firm's owners about Eisner's compensation? (e) Eisner is reported to have said: "You've got to . . . pretend you're playing with your own money."

SOLUTION (a) Since 9 percent of $1.15 billion equals $103.5 million, Eisner's bonus would have been zero if Disney's net income were $100 million, and his bonus would have been 0.02 ($200 million − $103.5 million) = $1.93 million if Disney's net income were $200 million. (b) 2 million × ($20 − $14) = $12 million. (c) Yes. (d) Yes. (e) No.[†]

*Flower, *Prince of the Magic Kingdom*, p. 261.
[†]For further discussion, see Flower, *Prince of the Magic Kingdom*; P. Milgrom and J. Roberts, *Economics, Organization, and Management* (Englewood Cliffs, N.J.: Prentice-Hall, 1992); and *Business Week*, April 25, 1994.

interesting reasons. Consider the case of Staples Inc., which in 1997 attempted to merge with Office Depot. As is the case in many large-scale mergers, the United States Federal Trade Commission (FTC) evaluated the proposed merger to be sure the new firm would not command excessive power in the market for office supplies. Staples argued that the combined entity would have less than a 6 percent share of that $185 billion market. Staples argument was that you could buy paper clips at any stationary store, a drug store, Wal-Mart, Kmart, wherever. You could buy computers from a number of bricks and mortar computer stores as well as online. And so on for any other element of office supplies. Thus, argued Staples, what's the problem with a resulting new entity which controlled only 6 percent of the market? The FTC on the other hand viewed the market as one of the "category killers"—a market in which by one stop shopping, one could satisfy all of his office supply needs. With the exception of some local and regional players, the FTC viewed this as a market with three major players—Staples, Office Depot, and Office Max. A merger between Staples and Office Depot would leave only two category killers left. An FTC study showed that when the market had three category killers in it, "prices are significantly lower than in two chain markets."[9]

Thus, one can see that in addition to beauty being in the eye of the beholder, it is also the case that what constitutes a market (or a good) is also in the eye of the beholder. The FTC's view prevailed and Staples gave up its attempt to merge with Office Depot.

Effective business management often requires careful thinking about markets. Consider now the case of Coca-Cola Company. In addition to all the variants of coke (diet, caffeine free, diet caffeine free), they also make Sprite and Minute Maid Orange Juice. Its major competitor in the soft drink business is Pepsi. If one considers the market as brown carbonated cola soft drinks, Coke and Pepsi combined have about an 80 percent share of the market. The same figure holds if the market is all soft drinks.

But how does Coke view its market? According to Douglas Ivester, recently retired CEO of Coke, its "stomach share," that is, Coke's share of potable liquids that a human can put in her stomach, is how Coke views its market. Coke estimates that each person needs to consume an average of 64 ounces of fluids each day to survive. Coke currently accounts for less than 2 ounces of that total. So rather than a 40 percent or so market share, Coke views itself as having about a 3 percent market share—competing with coffee, tea, water (Coke now has a bottled water)—whatever's potable.[10]

A firm that's too myopic may neglect to understand that what consumers want is for a need to be satisfied and not necessarily by the firm's product. If Coke felt that the market was soft drinks, they could find that profits could dissipate rapidly because other potable liquids could fulfill customers' needs.

FedEx determined that customers only cared about their package, good, document, and so on, getting to their destinations within a certain time period. The customer didn't care how it got there, so FedEx went from an airline to a transportation company to a logistics provider—a company that will use whatever mode of transportation or means is available to deliver the item on time. Likewise, UPS has done the same but from the starting base of trucking.

[9]"The FTC, Proudly Ensuring Its Survival at Your Expense," *Wall Street Journal*, April 8, 1997.
[10]"Pop Culture: A Coke and a Perm? Soda Giant Is Pushing Into Unusual Locales," *Wall Street Journal*, May 8, 1997.

Managers must know their current market as they and others perceive it and plan for the future market. In doing so, they must view product competition (other products that substitute for their product in fulfilling consumer needs), geographical competition (spatial separation may insulate you from competitors), and temporal competition (hours of operation and seasonality may influence the market).

Now, let's turn to the model of supply and demand, the economist's most basic tool for analyzing markets.

The Demand Side of a Market

Every market has a demand side and a supply side. The *demand* side can be represented by a *market demand curve*, which shows the amount of the commodity buyers would like to purchase at various prices. Consider Figure 1.4, which shows the demand curve for copper in the world market in the 1990s.[11] The figure shows that about 11.7 million metric tons of copper will be demanded annually if the price is $1.00 per pound, about 11 million metric tons will be demanded annually if the price is $1.10 per pound, and about 10.3 million metric tons will be demanded annually if the price is $1.20 per pound. An important reason why copper is demanded in such substantial amounts is that it is very useful in constructing equipment to generate and transmit electricity.

The demand curve in Figure 1.4 shows the total demand—worldwide—at each price. Any demand curve pertains to a particular period of time, and the shape and position of the demand curve depend on the length of the period. The demand curve for copper slopes downward to the right. In other words, the quantity of copper demanded increases as the price falls. This is true of the demand curves of most commodities: they almost always slope downward to the right. This makes sense; one would expect increases in a good's price to result in a smaller quantity demanded.

Any demand curve is based on the assumption that the tastes, incomes, and number of consumers, as well as the prices of other commodities, are held constant. Changes in any of these factors are likely to shift the position of a commodity's demand curve. Thus, if consumers' tastes shift toward goods that use considerable copper or if consumers' incomes increase (and they therefore buy more goods using copper), the demand curve for copper will shift to the right. In other words, holding the price of copper constant, more copper will be demanded than before. Much more will be said on this score in later sections (and in Chapter 3).

---

[11]We are indebted to officials of the U.S. Bureau of Mines for providing relevant information. Of course, these estimates, based on a variety of studies of the copper industry, are only rough approximations, but they are good enough for present purposes.

FIGURE
1.4

The Market Demand Curve for Copper, World Market

The market demand curve for copper shows the amount of copper that buyers would like to purchase at various prices.

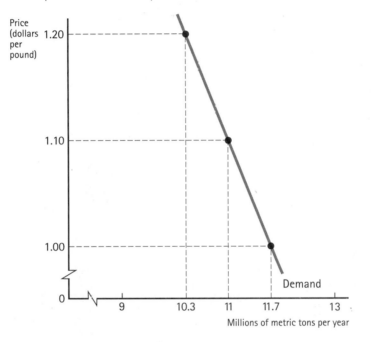

The Supply Side of a Market

The *supply* side of a market can be represented by a *market supply curve* that shows the amount of the commodity that sellers would offer at various prices. Let's continue with the case of copper. Figure 1.5 shows the supply curve for copper in the world market in the 1990s, based on estimates made informally by industry experts.[12] According to the figure, about 9.5 million metric tons of copper would be supplied per year if the price of copper were $1.00 per pound, about 11 million tons if the price were $1.10 per pound, and about 12.5 million tons if the price were $1.20 per pound.

Note that the supply curve for copper slopes upward to the right. In other words, the quantity of copper supplied increases as the price increases. This seems plausible, since increases in price give a greater incentive for firms to

[12]Officials of the U.S. Bureau of Mines provided relevant information. This supply curve is based on a variety of studies and assumptions. While it is only a rough approximation, it is good enough for present purposes.

FIGURE
1.5

The Market Supply Curve for Copper, World Market

The market supply curve for copper shows the amount of copper that sellers would offer at various prices.

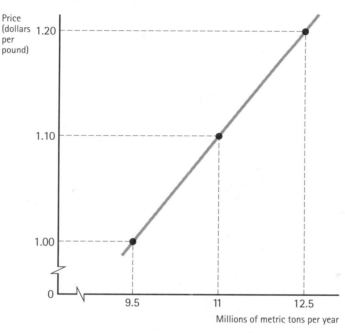

produce copper and offer it for sale. Also, there is more incentive to extract the copper from scrap metal. Empirical studies indicate that the supply curves for a great many commodities share this characteristic of sloping upward to the right.

Any supply curve is based on the assumption that technology, which we define as society's pool of knowledge regarding the industrial arts, is held constant. As technology progresses, it becomes possible to produce commodities more cheaply, so that firms often are willing to supply a given amount at a lower price than formerly. Thus, technological change often causes the supply curve to shift to the right. This certainly has occurred in the case of copper. There have been many important technological innovations in copper production, ranging from very large flotation cells to in-pit crushers of ore and conveyor belts to transport ore to the mill.

The supply curve for a product is also affected by the prices of the resources (labor, capital, and land) used to produce it. Decreases in the prices of these inputs make it possible to produce commodities more cheaply, so that firms may be willing to supply a given amount at a lower price than they formerly would. Thus, decreases in the prices of inputs may cause the supply curve to shift to the right. On the other hand, increases in the prices of inputs may cause it to shift to the left. For example, if the wage rates of workers in the copper industry increase, the supply curve for copper may shift to the left. Much more will be said on this score in Chapter 11.

Equilibrium Price

The two sides of a market, demand and supply, interact to determine the price of a commodity. To illustrate, consider the copper market. Let's put both the demand curve for copper (in Figure 1.4) and the supply curve for copper (in Figure 1.5) together in the same diagram. The result, shown in Figure 1.6, will help us determine the equilibrium price of copper. *An equilibrium price is a*

FIGURE 1.6

Equilibrium Price of Copper, World Market

The equilibrium price is $1.10 per pound, since the quantity demanded equals the quantity supplied at this price.

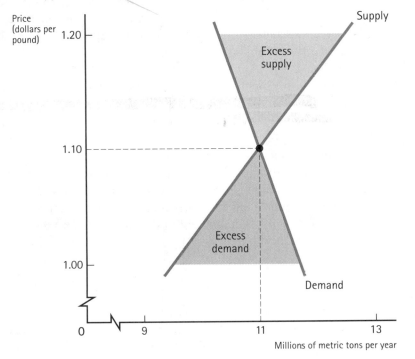

price that can be maintained. Any price that is not an equilibrium price cannot be maintained for long, since there are fundamental factors at work to cause a change in price.

Let's see what would happen if various prices were established in the market. For example, if the price were $1.20 per pound, the demand curve indicates that 10.3 million metric tons of copper would be demanded, while the supply curve indicates that 12.5 million metric tons would be supplied. Thus, if the price were $1.20 per pound, there would be a mismatch between the quantity supplied and the quantity demanded per year, since the rate at which copper is supplied would be greater than the rate at which it is demanded. Specifically, as shown in Figure 1.6, there would be an *excess supply* of 2.2 million metric tons. Under these circumstances, some of the copper supplied by producers could not be sold, and, as inventories of copper built up, suppliers would tend to cut their prices in order to get rid of unwanted inventories. Thus, a price of $1.20 per pound would not be maintained for long—and for this reason, $1.20 per pound is not an equilibrium price.

If the price were $1.00 per pound, on the other hand, the demand curve indicates that 11.7 million metric tons would be demanded, while the supply curve indicates that 9.5 million metric tons would be supplied. Again we find a mismatch between the quantity supplied and the quantity demanded per year, since the rate at which copper is supplied would be less than the rate at which it is demanded. Specifically, as shown in Figure 1.6, there would be an *excess demand* of 2.2 million metric tons. Under these circumstances, some of the consumers who want copper at this price would have to be turned away empty-handed. There would be a shortage. And given this shortage, suppliers would find it profitable to increase the price, and competition among buyers would bid the price up. Thus, a price of $1.00 per pound could not be maintained for long—so $1.00 per pound is not an equilibrium price.

The equilibrium price must be the price where the quantity demanded equals the quantity supplied. Obviously, this is the only price at which there is no mismatch between the quantity demanded and the quantity supplied, and consequently the only price that can be maintained for long. In Figure 1.6, the price at which the quantity supplied equals the quantity demanded is $1.10 per pound, the price where the demand curve intersects the supply curve. Thus $1.10 is the equilibrium price of copper under the circumstances visualized in Figure 1.6, and 11 million metric tons is the equilibrium quantity.

Actual Price

Of course, the price we really are interested in is the *actual price*—the price that really prevails, not the equilibrium price. In general, economists simply assume that the actual price will approximate the equilibrium price, which seems reasonable enough, since the basic forces at work tend to push the actual price to-ward the equilibrium price. Thus, if conditions remain fairly stable for a time, the actual price should move toward the equilibrium price.

To see that this is true, consider the market for copper, as described in Figure 1.6. What if the price somehow is set at $1.20 per pound? As we saw in the previous section, there is downward pressure on the price of copper under these conditions. Suppose the price, responding to this pressure, falls to $1.15 per pound. Comparing the quantity demanded with the quantity supplied at $1.15 per pound, we find that there is still downward pressure on price, since the quantity supplied exceeds the quantity demanded at $1.15 per pound. The price, responding to this pressure, may fall to $1.12 per pound, but comparing the quantity demanded with the quantity supplied at this price, we find that there is still a downward pressure on price, since the quantity supplied exceeds the quantity demanded at $1.12 per pound.

So long as the actual price is greater than the equilibrium price, there will be a downward pressure on price. Similarly, so long as the actual price is less than the equilibrium price, there will be an upward pressure on price. Thus there is always a tendency for the actual price to move toward the equilibrium price. But this movement may not be fast. Sometimes it takes a long time for the actual price to get close to the equilibrium price because by the time it gets close, the equilibrium price changes (because of shifts in either the demand curve or the supply curve or both). All that safely can be said is that the actual price will move toward the equilibrium price. But of course this information is of great value, since frequently all that a manager needs to know is the direction in which a price will change.

What If the Demand Curve Shifts?

Any supply-and-demand diagram like Figure 1.6 is essentially a snapshot of the situation during a particular period of time. The results in Figure 1.6 are limited to a particular period because the demand and supply curves in the figure, like any demand and supply curves, pertain only to a certain period. What happens to the equilibrium price of a product when its demand curve changes? This is an important question because managers must try to anticipate and forecast the changes that will occur in the prices of their products (as well as the prices of their inputs).

To illustrate the effects of a shift to the left of the demand curve, consider the situation in the copper industry during the 1980s. Because of the recession during the early 1980s, and reductions in the growth rate of electric power output, there was a decrease in the demand for copper. Also, due in part to the substitution of fiber optics and other materials for copper, there was a further decrease in copper demand. What this meant, of course, was that the demand

FIGURE 1.7

Effects of Leftward and Rightward Shifts of the Demand Curve on the Equilibrium Price of Copper

A leftward shift of the demand curve results in a decrease in the equilibrium price; a rightward shift results in an increase in the equilibrium price.

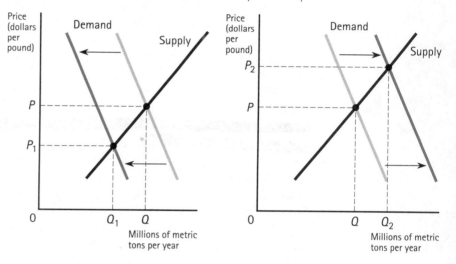

curve for copper shifted *to the left*, as shown in the left-hand panel of Figure 1.7. According to this panel, one would expect that this leftward shift of the demand curve would have resulted in a decrease in the price of copper, from P to P_1.

In fact, there was a very severe drop in the price of copper during this period. In 1980, the price was about $1 per pound; in 1986, it was about $.60 per pound. Thus, our theory predicts exactly what occurred. It is important to recognize how momentous this price drop was—and how important it was for managers to understand why it occurred. Kennecott Copper, the nation's largest copper producer, cut operations at its Utah Copper Division by two-thirds and experienced heavy losses in the mid-1980s. Kennecott's president, G. Frank Joklik, was all too aware of the fact that this drastic price cut was due in part to a leftward shift in the demand curve for copper.[13]

On the other hand, suppose that the market demand curve for copper shifts *to the right*, as in the late 1980s. During this period, there was considerable economic growth in the United States and the demand for copper increased. As

[13]Wheelen and Hunger, *Cases in Strategic Management and Business Policy.*

indicated in the right-hand panel of Figure 1.7, we would expect that such a rightward shift of the demand curve would result in an increase in the price of copper, from P to P_2. In fact, the price of copper did increase during the late 1980s, from about \$.60 per pound in 1986 to about \$1.30 per pound in 1989. Thus, in both the early and late 1980s, the price of copper behaved in accord with our simple demand-and-supply analysis.

What If the Supply Curve Shifts?

What happens to the equilibrium price of a product when its supply curve changes? For example, suppose that, because of technological advances in copper production, firms like Kennecott Copper are willing and able to supply more copper at a given price than they used to, with the result that the supply curve shifts *to the right*, as shown in the right-hand panel of Figure 1.8. What will be the effect on the equilibrium price? Clearly, it will fall from P (where the original supply curve intersects the demand curve) to P_4 (where the new supply curve intersects the demand curve).

On the other hand, suppose that there is a marked increase in the wage rates of copper workers, with the result that the supply curve shifts *to the left*, as

FIGURE
1.8

Effects of Leftward and Rightward Shifts of the Supply Curve on the Equilibrium Price of Copper

A leftward shift in the supply curve results in an increase in the equilibrium price; a rightward shift results in a decrease in the equilibrium price.

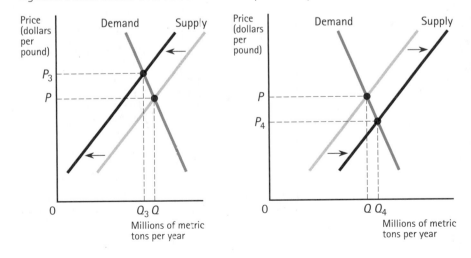

shown in the left-hand panel of Figure 1.8. What will be the effect? The equilibrium price will increase from P (where the original supply curve intersects the demand curve) to P_3 (where the new supply curve intersects the demand curve).

How Russia Glutted the Aluminum Market: A Case Study

The basic principles of supply and demand are useful in understanding many markets, not just the copper market. Consider, for example, the fascinating and interesting case of aluminum (Figure 1.9). Before the breakup of the Soviet Union in 1991, its aluminum industry primarily served military needs. When those needs decreased because of the decline in cold war tensions, Russia and

FIGURE
1.9

Effect of a Shift in the Supply Curve in the Early 1990s on the Equilibrium Price of Aluminum

Because of the rightward shift in the supply curve due to large sales on the world market by Russia and other newly independent states in the former Soviet Union, the equilibrium price fell from about 80 cents to about 47 cents.

CONCEPTS IN CONTEXT

Problems in the Potato Market

The United States is one of the world's leading producers of potatoes. Idaho is a particularly famous source of this product, but other states like Maine, Oregon, and Washington are important too. In 1995, farmers in Idaho and elsewhere planted more potatoes than usual, and growing conditions were unusually favorable. Frost, pests, and diseases were of limited importance. The result was a marked shift to the right of the supply curve for potatoes. The 1996 crop was the largest in U.S. history, almost 49 billion pounds. Consequently, the price of potatoes per 100-pound sack nosedived from about $8 in 1995 to about $1.75 in 1996. According to leading potato producers, farmers lost about $1,000 per acre on the 1996 crop.

Unfortunately, this is not the only problem facing U.S. potato producers. The potato market today is dominated by french fries, which are becoming popular throughout the world. But as demand for french fries grows in various countries, producers of french fries are trying to establish local sources of potatoes. For example, according to the chairman of McCain Foods, the world's leading producer of frozen french fries, "If we're in England, we're buying all of the potatoes we can buy in England."* Obviously, this reduces the export of potatoes by U.S. producers. While U.S. exports of french fries have increased considerably in recent years, there is the feeling that this growth may slow considerably.†

*New York Times, April 12, 1997, p. 35.
†For further discussion, see ibid.

the other newly independent states in the former Soviet Union began selling aluminum on the world market. In four years, Russian exports rose over 600 percent, pushing the supply curve for aluminum to the right. The result, as shown in Figure 1.9, was a severe drop in the price of aluminum, from about 80 cents per pound in 1990 to about 47 cents in November 1993.

Because of the lower price of aluminum, about 20 percent of U.S. aluminum capacity was idled by the end of 1993, and about 5,000 aluminum workers lost their jobs. Aluminum producers in the United States complained strongly to the federal government, which took up the issue with the Russian government. In January 1994, the world's leading aluminum-producing countries met in Brussels to formulate a plan to cope with the enormous glut of aluminum. One outcome was that Russia agreed to cut its annual output by about 15 percent during the next two years. Western producers were also expected to reduce output. The effect was expected to be a shift of the supply curve to the left, which would raise price. In fact, the price rose to 56 cents per pound in February 1994 and soared to about 90 cents per pound in December 1994.

While this was a very unpleasant episode for aluminum producers (and workers), it was a boon to users of aluminum, who paid low prices. Clearly, managers of both aluminum-producing firms and aluminum-using firms have an intense interest in the ups and downs of the aluminum market—and to understand these ups and downs, they need to know the basic principles of demand and supply we have discussed. Managers in other industries must know these principles too. Much more will be said on this score in subsequent chapters.[14] Virtually every issue of the *Wall Street Journal* and the *Financial Times* (in the commodities section) contains a story on a commodity price change due to shifts or anticipated shifts in demand and supply curves. You should test your knowledge of the concepts of demand and supply curves by examining the stories and explaining what happened in the market by drawing demand and supply curves and then shifts.[14]

Summary

1. Managerial economics draws heavily on economics (particularly microeconomics) and the decision sciences. In contrast to microeconomics, which is largely descriptive, managerial economics is prescriptive. Courses in managerial economics provide fundamental analytical tools, as well as play a major integrating role. Managerial economics is at the core of the management of nonbusiness organizations like government agencies, as well as the management of firms.

2. Both for nonbusiness organizations and firms, the process of decision making can be divided into the following five steps: (1) Establish or identify the organization's objectives. (2) Define the problem. (3) Identify possible solutions. (4) Select the best possible solution. (5) Implement the decision.

3. To apply managerial economics to business management, we need a theory of the firm. According to the theory accepted by most managerial economists, the firm tries to maximize its value, defined as the present value of its expected future cash flows (which for now are equated with profits). However, this maximization occurs subject to constraints, since the firm has limited inputs, particularly in the very short run, and must act in accord with a variety of laws and contracts.

4. Managerial economists define profits somewhat differently from the way accountants do. When economists speak of profit, they mean profit over and above what the owners' labor and capital employed in the business could earn elsewhere. To a considerable extent, the differences between the

[14]For further discussion of this case, see *New York Times*, February 13, 1994, and December 6, 1994; *Philadelphia Inquirer*, March 18, 1994; *Business Week*, March 28, 1994; WEFA Group, *Industrial Analysis Service Monthly Update*, February 1994; and *Wall Street Journal*, June 9, 1994.

concepts of profit used by the accountant and the economist reflect the difference in their functions.

5. Three important reasons for the existence of profits are innovation, risk, and monopoly power. Profits and losses are the mainsprings of a free-enterprise economy. They are signals that indicate where resources are needed and where they are too abundant. They are important incentives for innovation and risk taking. They are society's reward for efficiency.

6. Although managerial economists generally assume that firms want to maximize profit (and hence their value), it is recognized that a principal-agent problem arises if managers pursue their own interests, even though this decreases the profits of the owners. To deal with this problem, the owners often give the managers a financial stake in the success of the firm.

7. Every market has a demand side and a supply side. The market demand curve shows the amount of a product that buyers would like to purchase at various prices. The market supply curve shows the amount of a product that sellers would offer at various prices. The equilibrium price is the price where the quantity demanded equals the quantity supplied.

8. Both demand curves and supply curves shift over time; this results in changes in a product's price. Rightward shifts in the demand curve (and leftward shifts in the supply curve) tend to increase price. Leftward shifts in the demand curve (and rightward shifts in the supply curve) tend to decrease price.

Problems

1. In 1991, Bantam Books agreed to pay General Norman Schwarzkopf, who led U.S. forces in the Persian Gulf war against Iraq, $6 million for the rights to his not-yet-written memoirs. According to one leading publisher, Bantam would earn profits of about $1.2 million from the book if it sold 625,000 copies in hardcover. On the other hand, if it sold 375,000 copies in hardcover it would lose about $1.3 million.

   a. Publishing executives stated that it was very hard to sell more than 500,000 copies of a nonfiction hardcover, and very exceptional to sell 1 million copies. Was Bantam taking a substantial risk in publishing this book?

   b. In early 1993, Bantam announced that Schwarzkopf's book, *It Doesn't Take a Hero*, had already sold over 1 million copies and was the second most successful Bantam hardcover ever, behind only *Iacocca*, which sold 2.6 million copies in its hardcover edition. Did Bantam make a profit on this book? If so, was this profit, at least in part, a reward for risk bearing?

2. According to Paul Kagan Associates, a market research firm in Carmel, California, the average price of a combined AM/FM radio station fell from about $6.2 million in 1987 to about $1.8 million in 1990. From the mid-1980s to the early 1990s, the Federal Communications Commission, which regulates the airwaves, approved over a thousand new radio stations. Did this action by the commission help to cause the price decrease? Why or why not?

3. "No self-respecting [top] executive joining a company from the outside these days does so without a front-end, or signing, bonus. And in many cases, the bonus is in the seven figures. At the same time, the entering executive may be given a bonus guarantee; hence, he does not have to worry that if the company's fortunes sag right after he joins, he will lose some or all of his normal bonus. Typically, the bonus guarantee lasts for two or three years, although [sometimes] . . . the guarantee turns out to be for life."[15] Do long-term bonus guarantees help to solve the principal-agent problem, or do they tend to exacerbate it? Why?

4. What are the five basic steps in decision making? After the stock market crash on October 19, 1987, when the Dow-Jones average plummeted about 500 points, Louis Eckhardt, a New York broker, had to decide whether to buy Dow Chemical's stock. In his particular decision-making process, describe each of these five steps.

5. If the interest rate is 10 percent, what is the present value of the Monroe Corporation's profits in the next 10 years?

Number of years in the future	Profit (millions of dollars)
1	8
2	10
3	12
4	14
5	15
6	16
7	17
8	15
9	13
10	10

6. The profits of Du Pont de Nemours and Company in 1997 were about $2.4 billion. Does this mean that Du Pont's economic profit equaled $2.4 billion? Why or why not?

[15]G. Crystal, *In Search of Excess* (New York: Norton, 1991).

7. William Howe must decide whether to start a business renting beach umbrellas at an ocean resort during June, July, and August of next summer.
He believes that he can rent each umbrella to vacationers at $5 a day, and
he intends to lease 50 umbrellas for the three-month period for $3,000. To
operate this business, he does not have to hire anyone (but himself), and
he has no expenses other than the leasing costs and a fee of $3,000 per
month to rent the location of the business. Howe is a college student, and
if he did not operate this business, he could earn $4,000 for the three-month
period doing construction work.
   a. If there are 80 days during the summer when beach umbrellas are de-
       manded, and if Howe rents all 50 of his umbrellas on each of these
       days, what will be his accounting profit for the summer?
   b. What will be his economic profit for the summer?

8. If the demand curve for wheat in the United States is

$$P = 12.4 - 4Q_D,$$

where P is the farm price of wheat (in dollars per bushel) and Q_D is the
quantity of wheat demanded (in billions of bushels), and the supply curve
for wheat in the United States is

$$P = -2.6 + 2Q_S,$$

where Q_S is the quantity of wheat supplied (in billions of bushels), what
is the equilibrium price of wheat? What is the equilibrium quantity of
wheat sold? Must the actual price equal the equilibrium price? Why or
why not?

9. During the 1980s, lumber prices averaged between $195 and $250 per
thousand square feet. In 1993, the price hit $491. According to some ob-
servers, this price increase was due to a boom in housing construction;
according to others, it was because the federal government was reducing
the amount of federal forest open to logging. Did both groups feel that
it was due to a shift in the demand curve for lumber? Did both feel that it
was due to a shift in the supply curve for lumber? If not, which group
emphasized the demand side of the market, and which emphasized the
supply side?

10. From October 1994 to March 1995, the price of cotton increased from $0.65
to over $1 per pound, the highest level since the Civil War. According to
Business Week, "Supplies have dwindled because of poor crops in China,
India, and Pakistan. At the same time, consumers, undeterred by rising costs,

have pumped up demand for cotton-rich casual clothing, as well as home furnishings made from cotton."[16]

a. Was this price increase due to a shift in the demand curve for cotton, a shift in the supply curve for cotton, or both?

b. Did this price increase affect the supply curve for clothing? If so, how?

11. On October 2, 1994, a revival of *Show Boat*, the great Broadway musical by Jerome Kern and Oscar Hammerstein, opened at the Gershwin Theater in New York. While the hit songs (like "Ole Man River" and "Make Believe") were old favorites, the top ticket price of $75 was new. Never before had a regularly priced ticket for an open-ended Broadway run been this high. The show's weekly gross revenues, operating costs, and profits were estimated to be as follows, depending on whether the top ticket price was $75 or $65 (the normal top price prior to this show):

	Top price of $75	Top price of $65
Gross revenues	$765,000	$680,000
Operating costs	600,000	600,000
Profit	165,000	80,000

a. With a cast of 71 people, a 30-piece orchestra, and more than 500 costumes, *Show Boat* cost about $8 million to stage. This investment was in addition to the operating costs (such as salaries and theater rent). How many weeks would it take before the investors got their money back, according to these estimates, if the top price were $65? If it were $75?

b. George Wachtel, director of research for the League of American Theaters and Producers, has said that about one in three shows that have opened on Broadway in recent years has at least broken even. Were the investors in *Show Boat* taking a substantial risk?

c. According to one Broadway producer, "Broadway isn't where you make the money any more. It's where you establish the project so you can make the money. When you mount a show now, you really have to think about where it's going to play later." If so, should the above profit figures be interpreted with caution?

d. If the investors in this revival of *Show Boat* make a profit, will this profit be, at least in part, a reward for risk bearing?

12. In July 1993, the price of a pound of green, or unroasted, coffee was about $0.52. In early 1994, there was concern among coffee traders that Brazil's

---

[16]*Business Week*, March 13, 1995, p. 83.

crop, the world's largest, would be smaller than expected. According to the U.S. Department of Agriculture, Brazil's 1994 crop was expected to be 18 percent below that in 1993 because of severe freezes. Brazil exported about 77 million pounds of coffee in April 1994, the smallest monthly shipment since April 1989. In Colombia, another very important coffee producer, the coffee crop was reduced by worm infestation; and in Java, Indonesia's largest coffee-producing region, heavy rains hampered the harvest. Whereas the price of coffee was $0.52 in July 1993, it rose to about $1.38 in June 1994. Why?

Optimization
Techniques

Carly Fiorina, Chairperson of Hewlett-Packard, recently purchased Compaq Computer Company. Why? Because she and her colleagues felt the acquisition would enhance the performance of Hewlett-Packard. As we learned in Chapter 1, managerial economics is concerned with the ways in which managers make decisions in order to maximize the effectiveness or performance of the organization they manage. To understand how this can be done, you must understand the basic optimization techniques taken up in this chapter.

To begin, we describe the nature of marginal analysis. While simple in concept, marginal analysis is a powerful tool that illuminates many central aspects of decision-making regarding resource allocation. Economists think at the margins. It's intuitive that one would undertake a project if the additional (marginal) benefit one received from undertaking the project exceeded the additional (marginal) cost incurred by undertaking the project. Virtually all of the rules of optimal behavior of firms and individuals that we will study will be driven by this concept.

Next, we examine the basic elements of differential calculus, including the rules of differentiation and the use of a derivative to maximize a function—such as profit—or minimize a function—such as cost. Differentiation tells us what changes will occur in one variable (the dependent variable) when a small (marginal) change is made in another variable (the independent variable). Thus, the marginal analysis first discussed can be implemented by the use of differentiation.

Finally, we take up constrained optimization and include an optional section on Lagrangian multipliers. While we want to maximize the profits of our firm (or minimize the costs of production), such maximization or minimization is often subject to constraints (such as producing a certain amount to adhere to a contract or utilizing a certain amount of labor in a union agreement).

Since Lagrangian multipliers require more mathematical sophistication than the rest of this chapter, the section in which they are discussed can be skipped without loss of continuity.

Functional Relationships

To understand the optimization techniques described in this chapter, you must know how economic relationships are expressed. Frequently, the relationship between two or more economic variables can be represented by a *table* or *graph*. For example, Table 2.1 shows the relationship between the price charged by the Cherry Corporation and the number of units of output the company sells per day. Figure 2.1 represents the same relationship using a graph.

While tables and graphs are extremely helpful, and will be used often in this book, another way of expressing economic relationships is through the use of *equations*. How can the relationship between the number of units sold and the price in Table 2.1 (and Figure 2.1) be expressed in the form of an equation? One way is to use the following functional notation:

$$Q = f(P), \tag{2.1}$$

TABLE
2.1

Relationship between Price and Quantity Sold, Cherry Corporation

Price per unit	Number of units sold per day
$10	150
20	100
30	50
40	0

FIGURE
2.1

Relationship between Price and Quantity Sold, Cherry Corporation

This graph presents the data in Table 2.1.

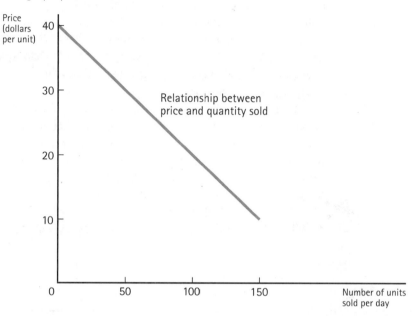

where Q is the number of units sold, and P is price. This equation should be read as: "The number of units sold is a function of price," which means that the number of units sold *depends* on price. In other words, the number of units sold is the *dependent* variable, and price is the *independent* variable.

While equation (2.1) is useful, it does not tell us *how* the number of units sold depends on price. A more specific representation of this relationship is

$$Q = 200 - 5P. \tag{2.2}$$

Comparing this equation with the data in Table 2.1 (and Figure 2.1), you can verify that these data conform to this equation. For example, if the price equals $10, the number of units sold should be $200 - 5(10) = 150$, according to the equation. This is exactly what Table 2.1 (and Figure 2.1) shows. Regardless of what price you choose, the number of units sold is the same, no matter whether you consult Table 2.1, Figure 2.1, or equation (2.2).

Marginal Analysis

Whether economic relationships are expressed as tables, graphs, or equations, marginal analysis has enabled managers to use these relationships more effectively. The **marginal value** of a dependent variable is defined as the *change* in this dependent variable associated with a 1-unit *change* in a particular independent variable. As an illustration, consider Table 2.2, which indicates in columns 1 and 2 the total profit of the Roland Corporation if the number of units produced equals various amounts. In this case, total profit is the dependent variable and output is the independent variable. Thus, the marginal value of profit, called **marginal profit,** is the *change* in total profit associated with a 1-unit *change* in output.

Column 3 of Table 2.2 shows the value of marginal profit. If output increases from 0 to 1 unit, column 2 shows that total profit increases by $100 (from $0 to $100). Thus, marginal profit in column 3 equals $100 if output is between 0 and 1 unit. If output increases from 1 to 2 units, total profit increases by $150 (from $100 to $250). Thus, marginal profit in column 3 equals $150 if output is between 1 and 2 units.

The central point to bear in mind about a marginal relationship of this sort is that the dependent variable—in this case, total profit—is maximized

TABLE 2.2

Relationship between Output and Profit, Roland Corporation

(1) Number of units of output per day	(2) Total profit	(3) Marginal profit	(4) Average profit
0	0		—
1	100	100	100
2	250	150	125
3	600	350	200
4	1,000	400	250
5	1,350	350	270
6	1,500	150	250
7	1,550	50	221.4
8	1,500	−50	187.5
9	1,400	−100	155.5
10	1,200	−200	120

when its marginal value shifts from positive to negative. To see this, consider Table 2.2. So long as marginal profit is positive, the Roland Corporation can raise its total profit by increasing output. For example, if output is between 5 and 6 units, marginal profit is positive ($150); thus, the firm's total profit will go up (by $150) if output is increased from 5 to 6 units. But when marginal profit shifts from positive to negative, total profit will fall, not go up, with any further increase in output. In Table 2.2, this point is reached when the firm produces 7 units of output. If output is increased beyond this point (to 8 units), marginal profit shifts from positive to negative—and total profit goes down (by $50). Thus, as stated above, the dependent variable—in this case, total profit—is maximized when its marginal value shifts from positive to negative.

Since managers are interested in determining how to maximize profit (or other performance measures), this is a very useful result. It emphasizes the importance of looking at marginal values, and the hazards that may arise if average values are used instead. In Table 2.2, **average profit**—that is, total profit divided by output—is shown in column 4. It may seem eminently reasonable to choose the output whose average profit is highest. Countless managers have done so. But this is not the correct decision if one wants to maximize profit. Instead, as stressed in the previous paragraph, one should choose the output where marginal profit shifts from positive to negative.

To prove this, one need only find the output in Table 2.2 at which average profit is highest. Based on a comparison of the figures in column 4, this output is 5 units; and according to column 2, total profit at this output equals $1,350. In the paragraph before last, we found that the output where marginal profit shifts from positive to negative is 7 units; and according to column 2, total profit at this point equals $1,550. Clearly, total profit is $200 higher if output is 7 rather than 5 units. Thus, if the managers of this firm were to choose the output at which average profit is highest, they would sacrifice $200 per day in profits.

It is important to understand the relationship between average and marginal values: because the marginal value represents the change in the total, the average value must *increase* if the marginal value is *greater* than the average value; by the same token, the average value must *decrease* if the marginal value is *less* than the average value. Table 2.2 illustrates these propositions. For the first to fifth units of output, marginal profit is greater than average profit. Since the extra profit from each additional unit is greater than the average, the average is pulled up as more is produced. For the sixth to tenth units of output, marginal profit is less than average profit. Since the extra profit from each additional unit is less than the average, the average is pulled down as more is produced.

Relationships between Total, Marginal, and Average Values

To explore further the relationships between total, marginal, and average values, consider Figure 2.2, which shows the relationships between total, average, and marginal profit, on the one hand, and output, on the other hand, for the Roland Corporation. The relationship between output and profit is exactly the same as in Table 2.2, but rather than using particular numbers to designate output or profit, we use symbols such as Q_0 and Q_1 for output levels and π_0 for a profit level. The results are of general validity, not true for only a particular set of numerical values.

At the outset, note that Figure 2.2 contains two panels. The upper panel (panel A) shows the relationship between total profit and output, while the lower panel (panel B) shows the relationship between average profit and marginal profit, on the one hand, and output, on the other. The horizontal scale of panel A is the same as that of panel B, the result being that a given output like Q_0 is the same distance from the origin (along the horizontal axis) in panel A as in panel B.

In practice, one seldom is presented with data concerning both (1) the relationship between total profit and output and (2) the relationship between average profit and output, because it is relatively simple to derive the latter relationship from the former. How can this be done? Take any output, say Q_0. *At this output, average profit equals the slope of the straight line from the origin to point E, the point on the total profit curve corresponding to output Q_0.* To see that this is the case, note that average profit at this output level equals π_0/Q_0, where π_0 is the level of total profit if output is Q_0. Because the slope of any straight line equals the vertical distance between two points on the line divided by the horizontal distance between them, the slope of the line from the origin to point E equals π_0/Q_0.[1] Thus, the slope of line OE equals average profit at this output. (In other words, K_0 in panel B of Figure 2.2 is equal to the slope of line OE.) To determine the relationship between average profit and output from the relationship between total profit and output, we repeat this procedure for each level of output, not Q_0 alone. The resulting average profit curve is shown in panel B.

Turning to the relationship between marginal profit and output (in panel B), it is relatively simple to derive this relationship too from the relationship between total profit and output (in panel A). Take any output, say Q_1. *At this output, marginal profit equals the slope of the tangent to the total profit curve (in panel A) at the point where output is Q_1.* In other words, marginal profit equals

---

[1]The vertical distance between the origin and point E equals π_0, and the horizontal distance between these two points equals Q_0. Thus, the vertical distance divided by the horizontal distance equals π_0/Q_0.

FIGURE
2.2

Total Profit, Average Profit, and Marginal Profit, Roland Corporation

The average and marginal profit curves in panel B can be derived geometrically from the total profit curve in panel A.

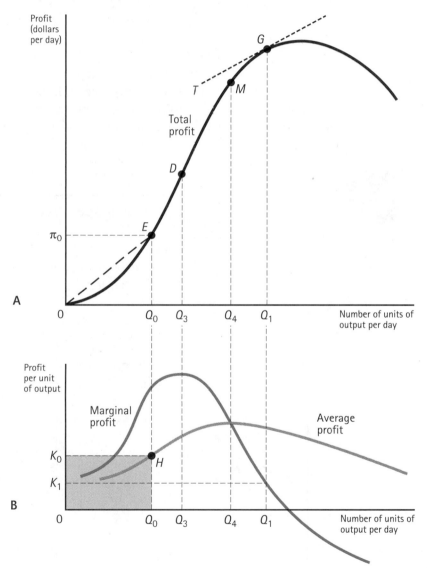

the slope of line T in Figure 2.2, which is tangent to the total profit curve at point G. As a first step toward seeing why this is true, consider Figure 2.3, which provides a magnified picture of the total profit curve in the neighborhood of point G.

Recall that marginal profit is defined as the extra profit resulting from a very small increase (specifically, a 1-unit increase) in output. If output increases from Q_1 to Q_2, total profit increases from π_1 to π_2, as shown in Figure 2.3. Thus, the extra profit per unit of output is $(\pi_2 - \pi_1)/(Q_2 - Q_1)$, which is the slope of the GK line. But this increase in output is rather large. Suppose that we decrease Q_2 so that it is closer to Q_1. In particular, let the new value of Q_2 be Q_2'. If output increases from Q_1 to Q_2', the extra profit per unit of output equals $(\pi_2' - \pi_1)/(Q_2' - Q_1)$, which is the slope of the GL line. If we further decrease Q_2 until the distance between Q_1 and Q_2 is extremely small, the slope of the tangent (line T) at point G becomes a very good estimate of $(\pi_2 - \pi_1)/(Q_2 - Q_1)$. In the limit, for changes in output in a very small neighborhood around

FIGURE
2.3

Marginal Profit Equals the Slope of the Tangent to the Total Profit Curve

As the distance between Q_1 and Q_2 becomes extremely small, the slope of line T becomes a very good estimate of $(\pi_2 - \pi_1)/(Q_2 - Q_1)$.

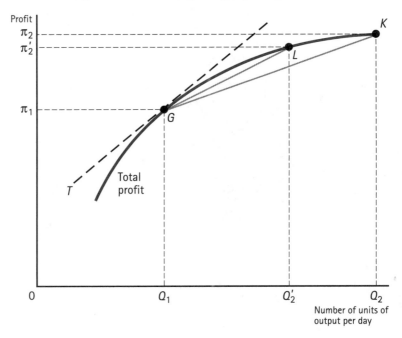

Q_1, the slope of the tangent *is* marginal profit. (This slope equals K_1 in panel B of Figure 2.2.) To determine the relationship between marginal profit and output from the relationship between total profit and output, we repeat this procedure for each level of output, not Q_1 alone. The resulting marginal profit curve is shown in panel B of Figure 2.2.

Sometimes one is given an average profit curve like that in panel B, but not the total profit curve. To derive the latter curve from the former, note that total profit equals average profit times output. Thus, if output equals Q_0, total profit equals K_0 times Q_0, which is the area of the shaded rectangle OK_0HQ_0 in panel B. In other words, π_0 in panel A equals the area of rectangle OK_0HQ_0 in panel B. To derive the relationship between total profit and output from the relationship between average profit and output, we repeat this procedure for each level of output. That is, we find the area of the appropriate rectangle of this sort corresponding to each output, not Q_0 alone. The resulting total profit curve is shown in panel A.

Finally, two further points should be made concerning the total, average, and marginal profit curves in Figure 2.2. First, you should be able to tell by a glance at panel A that marginal profit increases as output rises from zero to Q_3, and that it decreases as output rises further. Why is this so obvious from panel A? Because the slope of the total profit curve increases as one moves from the origin to point D. In other words, lines drawn tangent to the total profit curve become steeper as one moves from the origin to point D. Thus, since marginal profit equals the slope of this tangent, it must increase as output rises from zero to Q_3. To the right of point D, the slope of the total profit curve is decreasing as output increases. That is, lines drawn tangent to the total profit curve become less steep as one moves to the right of point D. Consequently, since marginal profit equals the slope of this tangent, it too must decrease when output rises beyond Q_3.

Second, panel B of Figure 2.2 confirms the following proposition: *The average profit curve must be rising if it is below the marginal profit curve, and it must be falling if it is above the marginal profit curve.* At output levels below Q_4, the average profit curve is below the marginal profit curve; thus, the average profit curve is rising because the higher marginal profits are pulling up the average profits. At output levels above Q_4, the average profit curve is above the marginal profit curve; thus, the average profit curve is falling because the lower marginal profits are pulling down the average profits. At Q_4, the straight line drawn from the origin to point M is just tangent to the total cost curve. Thus average profit and marginal profit are equal at output Q_4.

The Concept of a Derivative

In the case of the Roland Corporation, we used Table 2.2—which shows the relationship between the firm's output and profit—to find the profit-maximizing output level. Frequently, a table of this sort is too cumbersome or inaccurate to be useful for this purpose. Instead, an equation is used to represent the relationship between the variable we are trying to maximize (in this case, profit) and the variable or variables under the control of the decision maker (in this case, output). Given an equation of this sort, the powerful concepts and techniques of differential calculus can be employed to find optimal solutions to the decision maker's problem.

In previous sections, we defined the marginal value as the change in the dependent variable resulting from a 1-unit change in an independent variable. If Y is the dependent variable and X is the independent variable,

$$Y = f(X), \tag{2.3}$$

according to the notation in equation (2.1). Using Δ (called delta) to denote change, a change in the independent variable can be expressed as ΔX, and a change in the dependent variable can be expressed as ΔY. Thus, the marginal value of Y can be estimated by

$$\frac{Change\ in\ Y}{Change\ in\ X} = \frac{\Delta Y}{\Delta X}. \tag{2.4}$$

For example, if a 2-unit increase in X results in a 1-unit increase in Y, $\Delta X = 2$ and $\Delta Y = 1$; this means that the marginal value of Y is about 1/2. That is, the dependent variable Y increases by about 1/2 if the independent variable X increases by 1.[2]

Unless the relationship between Y and X can be represented as a straight line (as in Figure 2.4), the value of $\Delta Y/\Delta X$ is not constant. For example, consider the relationship between Y and X in Figure 2.5. If a movement occurs from point G to point H, a relatively small change in X (from X_1 to X_2) is associated with a big change in Y (from Y_1 to Y_2). Thus, between points G and H, the value of $\Delta Y/\Delta X$, which equals $(Y_2 - Y_1)/(X_2 - X_1)$, is relatively large. On the other hand, if a movement occurs from point K to point L, a relatively large change in X (from X_3 to X_4) is associated with a small change in Y (from Y_3 to Y_4). Consequently, between points K and L, the value of $\Delta Y/\Delta X$, which equals $(Y_4 - Y_3)/(X_4 - X_3)$, is relatively small.

The value of $\Delta Y/\Delta X$ is related to the steepness or flatness of the curve in Figure 2.5. Between points G and H, the curve is relatively *steep*; this means that a *small* change in X results in a *large* change in Y. Consequently, $\Delta Y/\Delta X$ is relatively large. Between points K and L, the curve is relatively *flat;* this means that a *large* change in X results in a *small* change in Y. Consequently, $\Delta Y/\Delta X$ is relatively small.

---

[2]Why do we say that Y increases by about 1/2, rather than by exactly 1/2? Because Y may not be linearly related to X. More is said on this subject in the next paragraph of the text.

FIGURE
2.4

Linear Relationship between Y and X

The relationship between Y and X can be represented as a straight line.

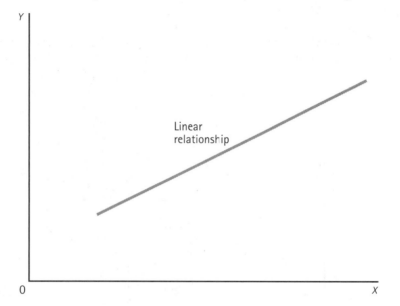

The derivative of Y *with respect to* X *is defined as the limit of* $\Delta Y/\Delta X$ *as* ΔX *approaches zero.* Since the derivative of Y with respect to X is denoted by dY/dX, this definition can be restated as

$$\frac{dY}{dX} = \lim_{\Delta X \to 0} \frac{\Delta Y}{\Delta X}, \tag{2.5}$$

which is read "The derivative of Y with respect to X equals the limit of the ratio $\Delta Y/\Delta X$ as ΔX approaches zero." To understand what is meant by a limit, consider the function $(X - 2)$. What is the limit of this function as X approaches 2? Clearly, as X gets closer and closer to 2, $(X - 2)$ gets closer and closer to zero. What is the limit of this function as X approaches zero? Clearly, as X gets closer and closer to zero, $(X - 2)$ gets closer and closer to -2.

Graphically, the derivative of Y with respect to X equals the *slope* of the curve showing Y (on the vertical axis) as a function of X (on the horizontal axis). To see this, suppose that we want to find the value of the derivative of Y with respect to X when X equals X_5 in Figure 2.6. A rough measure is the

FIGURE
2.5

How the Value of $\Delta Y / \Delta X$ Varies Depending on the Steepness or Flatness of the Relationship between Y and X

Between points G and H, since the curve is steep, $\Delta Y / \Delta X$ is large. Between points K and L, since the curve is flat, $\Delta Y / \Delta X$ is small.

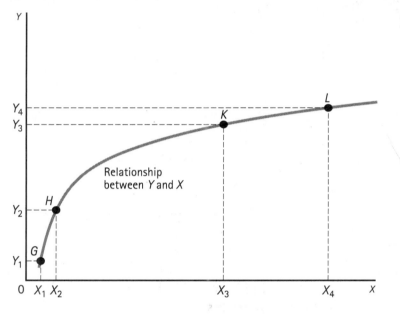

value of $\Delta Y / \Delta X$ when a movement is made from point A to point C; this measure equals

$$(Y_7 - Y_5)/(X_7 - X_5),$$

which is the slope of the AC line. A better measure is the value of $\Delta Y / \Delta X$ when a movement is made from point A to point B; this measure equals

$$(Y_6 - Y_5)/(X_6 - X_5),$$

which is the slope of the AB line. Why is the latter measure better than the former? Because the distance between points A and B is less than the distance between points A and C. What we want is the value of $\Delta Y / \Delta X$ when ΔX is as small as possible. Clearly, *in the limit, as ΔX approaches zero, the ratio $\Delta Y / \Delta X$ is equal to the slope of the line* M, *which is drawn tangent to the curve at point* A.

FIGURE
2.6

Derivative as the Slope of the Curve

When X equals X_5, the derivative of Y with respect to X equals the slope of line M, the tangent to the curve at point A.

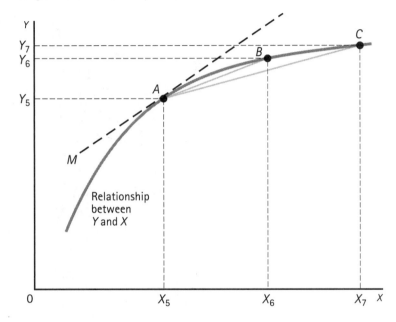

How to Find a Derivative

Managers like John Welch would like to know how to optimize the performance of their organizations. If Y is some measure of organizational performance and X is a variable under a particular manager's control, he or she would like to know the value of X that will maximize Y. To find out, it is very useful, as we shall see in the next section, to know the derivative of Y with respect to X. In this section, we learn how to find this derivative.

Derivatives of Constants

If the dependent variable Y is a constant, its derivative with respect to X is always zero. That is, if $Y = a$ (where a is a constant),

$$\frac{dY}{dX} = 0. \tag{2.6}$$

FIGURE
2.7

Case in Which $Y = 6$

In this case, dY/dX equals zero, since the slope of this horizontal line equals zero.

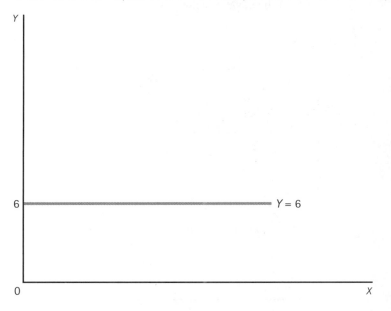

EXAMPLE Suppose that $Y = 6$, as shown in Figure 2.7. Since the value of Y does not change as X varies, dY/dX must be equal to zero. To see how this can also be shown geometrically, recall from the previous section that dY/dX equals the slope of the curve showing Y as a function of X. As is evident from Figure 2.7, this slope equals zero; this means that dY/dX must equal zero.

Derivatives of Power Functions

A power function can be expressed as

$$Y = aX^b,$$

where a and b are constants. If the relationship between X and Y is of this kind, the derivative of Y with respect to X equals b times a multiplied by X raised to the $(b - 1)$ power:

$$\frac{dY}{dX} = baX^{b-1}. \tag{2.7}$$

EXAMPLE Suppose that

$$Y = 3X,$$

which is graphed in panel A of Figure 2.8. Applying equation (2.7), we find that

$$\frac{dY}{dX} = 1 \cdot 3 \cdot X^0 = 3,$$

FIGURE
2.8

Case in Which $Y = 3X$

In this case, dY/dX equals 3, since the slope of the line in panel A equals 3.

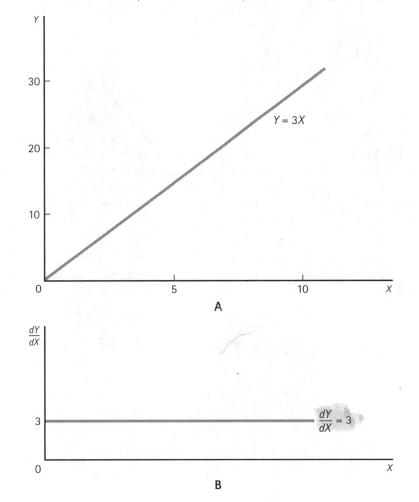

CONCEPTS IN CONTEXT

The Allocation of the TANG Brand Advertising Budget

Managers and analysts use differential calculus to help solve all sorts of problems. Consider the work that Young and Rubicam, the prominent advertising agency, did for one of its General Foods accounts, TANG beverages. TANG is the trademark for an instant breakfast drink with an orange flavor. Young and Rubicam did a study to estimate the effects of advertising expenditures on the sales of TANG and found that the relationships between advertising expenditures and sales in two districts were*

$$S_1 = 10 + 5A_1 - 1.5A_1^2$$

and

$$S_2 = 12 + 4A_2 - 0.5A_2^2$$

where S_1 is the sales of TANG (in millions of dollars per year) in the first district, S_2 is its sales in the second district, A_1 is the advertising expenditure on TANG (in millions of dollars per year) in the first district, and A_2 is the advertising expenditure in the second district.

Young and Rubicam wanted to determine the amount of additional sales that an extra dollar of advertising would generate in each district. To answer this question, the derivative of sales with respect to advertising expenditure was calculated for each district:

$$\frac{dS_1}{dA_1} = 5 - 3A_1$$

$$\frac{dS_2}{dA_2} = 4 - A_2$$

Thus, in each district, the effect on sales of an extra dollar of advertising depended on the amount spent on advertising. Supposing that $.5 million was being spent on advertising in the first district and that $1 million was being spent on advertising in the second district,

$$\frac{dS_1}{dA_1} = 5 - 3(0.5) = 3.5$$

and

$$\frac{dS_2}{dA_2} = 4 - 1 = 3.$$

Consequently, an extra dollar of advertising generated an extra $3.50 of sales in the first district and an extra $3.00 of sales in the second district.

On the basis of these findings, Young and Rubicam made a number of recommendations to General Foods concerning the regional allocation of the TANG brand advertising budget. In particular, it recommended that, if General Foods wanted to boost the total sales of TANG, more should be spent on advertising in the first district, and less should be spent on it in the second district. This would not mean an increase in General Foods's total advertising budget, since the extra advertising expenditure in the first district would be offset by the reduced advertising expenditure in the second district.

How did Young and Rubicam come to this conclusion? The fact that an extra dollar of advertising would result in a greater addition to sales in the first district than in the second indicated that a reallocation of the advertising budget was called for. To see this, consider what would happen if a dollar extra were spent on advertising in the first district and a dollar less spent in the second. The result, as indicated above, would be an extra $3.50 of sales in the first district and a \$3.00 reduction in sales in the second. The overall effect would be a $\$3.50 - \$3.00 = \$.50$ increase in total sales. Thus, if General Foods wanted to increase the sales of TANG beverages, a reallocation of the advertising budget in favor of the first district was to be recommended.[†]

*Although these equations are of the form derived by Young and Rubicam. the numerical coefficients are hypothetical. For present purposes, this is of no consequence. Our purpose here is to describe the general features of this case, and how differential calculus played a role, not the specific numbers. The methods that can be used to estimate such coefficients are described in Chapter 5. Also, note that sales in each district are assumed to depend on the level of advertising in this district only.

[†]F. DeBruicker, J. Quelch, and S. Ward, *Cases in Consumer Behavior* (2d ed; Englewood Cliffs, N.J.: Prentice-Hall, 1986). This case has been simplified in various respects for pedagogical reasons.

since $a = 3$ and $b = 1$. Thus, the value of dY/dX, which is graphed in panel B of Figure 2.8, is 3, regardless of the value of X. This makes sense, since the slope of the line in panel A is 3, regardless of the value of X. Recall once again from the previous section that dY/dX equals the slope of the curve showing Y as a function of X. In this case (as in Figure 2.7), this "curve" is a straight line.

EXAMPLE Suppose that

$$Y = 2X^2,$$

which is graphed in panel A of Figure 2.9. Applying equation (2.7), we find that

$$\frac{dY}{dX} = 2 \cdot 2 \cdot X^1 = 4X,$$

since $a = 2$ and $b = 2$. Thus, the value of dY/dX, which is graphed in panel B of Figure 2.9, is proportional to X. As would be expected, dY/dX is negative when the slope of the curve in panel A is negative, and positive when this slope is positive. Why? Because as we have stressed repeatedly, dY/dX equals this slope.

Derivatives of Sums and Differences

Suppose that U and W are two variables, each of which depends on X. That is,

$$U = g(X) \quad \text{and} \quad W = h(X)$$

The functional relationship between U and X is denoted by g, and that between W and X is denoted by h. Suppose further that

$$Y = U + W.$$

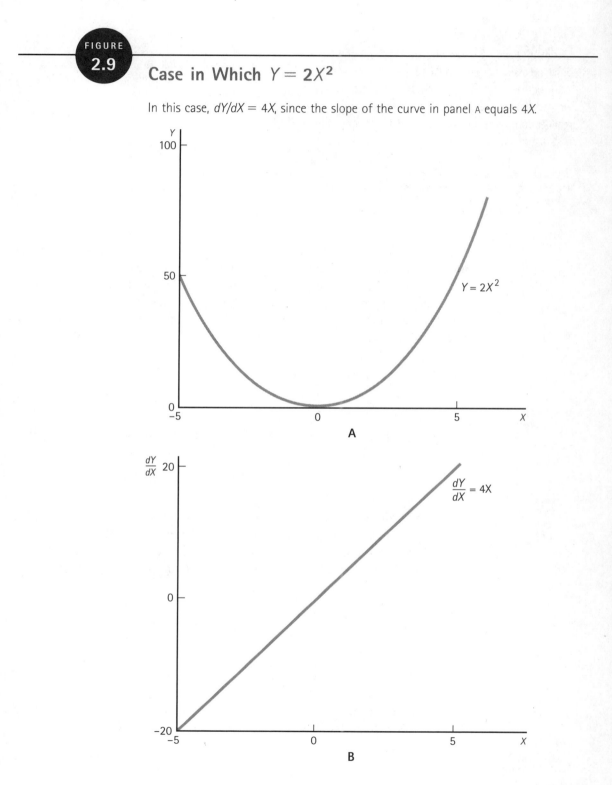

FIGURE 2.9

Case in Which $Y = 2X^2$

In this case, $dY/dX = 4X$, since the slope of the curve in panel A equals $4X$.

$Y = 2X^2$

$\dfrac{dY}{dX} = 4X$

A

B

In other words, Y is the sum of U and W. If so, the derivative of Y with respect to X is equal to the *sum* of the derivatives of the individual terms:

$$\frac{dY}{dX} = \frac{dU}{dX} + \frac{dW}{dX}. \tag{2.8}$$

On the other hand, if

$$Y = U - W,$$

the derivative of Y with respect to X is equal to the *difference* between the derivatives of the individual terms:

$$\frac{dY}{dX} = \frac{dU}{dX} - \frac{dW}{dX}. \tag{2.9}$$

EXAMPLE Consider the case in which $U = g(X) = 3X^3$ and $W = h(X) = 4X^2$. If $Y = U + W = 3X^3 + 4X^2$,

$$\frac{dY}{dX} = 9X^2 + 8X. \tag{2.10}$$

To see why, recall from equation (2.8) that

$$\frac{dY}{dX} = \frac{dU}{dX} + \frac{dW}{dX}. \tag{2.11}$$

Applying equation (2.7),

$$\frac{dU}{dX} = 9X^2 \quad \text{and} \quad \frac{dW}{dX} = 8X.$$

Substituting these values of the derivatives into equation (2.11), equation (2.10) follows.

EXAMPLE Suppose that $Y = U - W$, where $U = 8X^2$ and $W = 9X$. Then

$$\frac{dY}{dX} = 16X - 9,$$

since, according to equation (2.9),

$$\frac{dY}{dX} = \frac{dU}{dX} - \frac{dW}{dX}$$

and, applying equation (2.7),

$$\frac{dU}{dX} = 16X \quad \text{and} \quad \frac{dW}{dX} = 9.$$

Derivatives of Products

The derivative of the product of two terms is equal to the sum of the first term multiplied by the derivative of the second, plus the second term times the derivative of the first. Consequently, if $Y = UW$,

$$\frac{dY}{dX} = U\frac{dW}{dX} + W\frac{dU}{dX}. \tag{2.12}$$

EXAMPLE If $Y = 6X(3 - X^2)$, we can let $U = 6X$ and $W = 3 - X^2$; then

$$\frac{dY}{dX} = 6X\frac{dW}{dX} + (3 - X^2)\frac{dU}{dX}$$

$$= 6X(-2X) + (3 - X^2)(6)$$

$$= -12X^2 + 18 - 6X^2$$

$$= 18 - 18X^2.$$

The first term, $6X$, is multiplied by the derivative of the second term, $-2X$, and the result is added to the second term, $3 - X^2$, times the derivative of the first, 6. As indicated above, the result is $18 - 18X^2$.

Derivatives of Quotients

If $Y = U/W$, the derivative of Y with respect to X equals

$$\frac{dY}{dX} = \frac{W(dU/dX) - U(dW/dX)}{W^2}. \tag{2.13}$$

In other words, the derivative of the quotient of two terms equals the denominator times the derivative of the numerator minus the numerator times the derivative of the denominator—all divided by the square of the denominator.

EXAMPLE Consider the problem of finding the derivative of the expression

$$Y = \frac{5X^3}{3 - 4X}.$$

If we let $U = 5X^3$ and $W = 3 - 4X$,

$$\frac{dU}{dX} = 15X^2 \quad \text{and} \quad \frac{dW}{dX} = -4.$$

Consequently, applying equation (2.13),

$$\frac{dY}{dX} = \frac{(3 - 4X)(15X^2) - 5X^3(-4)}{(3 - 4X)^2}$$

$$= \frac{45X^2 - 60X^3 + 20X^3}{(3 - 4X)^2}$$

$$= \frac{45X^2 - 40X^3}{(3 - 4X)^2}.$$

Derivatives of a Function of a Function (Chain Rule)[3]

Sometimes a variable depends on another variable, which in turn depends on a third variable. For example, suppose that $Y = f(W)$ and $W = g(X)$. Under these circumstances, the derivative of Y with respect to X equals

$$\frac{dY}{dX} = \left(\frac{dY}{dW}\right)\left(\frac{dW}{dX}\right). \tag{2.14}$$

In other words, to find this derivative, we find the derivative of Y with respect to W, and multiply it by the derivative of W with respect to X.

EXAMPLE Suppose that $Y = 4W + W^3$, and $W = 3X^2$. To find dY/dX we begin by finding dY/dW and dW/dX:

$$\frac{dY}{dW} = 4 + 3W^2$$

$$= 4 + 3(3X^2)^2$$

$$= 4 + 27X^4.$$

$$\frac{dW}{dX} = 6X.$$

---

[3]This section can be skipped without loss of continuity.

Then, to find dY/dX, we multiply dY/dW and dW/dX:

$$\frac{dY}{dX} = (4 + 27X^4)(6X)$$
$$= 24X + 162X^5.$$

Using Derivatives to Solve Maximization and Minimization Problems

Having determined how you can find the derivative of Y with respect to X, we now take up the way in which you can determine the value of X that maximizes or minimizes Y. *The central point to recognize is that a maximum or minimum point can occur only if the slope of the curve showing* Y *on the vertical axis and* X *on the horizontal axis equals zero.* To see this, suppose that Y equals the profit of the Monroe Company and X is its output level. If the relationship between Y and X is as shown by the curve in panel A of Figure 2.10, the maximum value of Y occurs when $X = 10$, and at this value of X the slope of the curve equals zero.

Since the derivative of Y with respect to X equals the slope of this curve, it follows that Y can be a maximum or minimum only if this derivative equals zero. To see that Y really is maximized when this derivative equals zero, note that the relationship between Y and X in Figure 2.10 is

$$Y = -50 + 100X - 5X^2, \tag{2.15}$$

which means that

$$\frac{dY}{dX} = 100 - 10X. \tag{2.16}$$

Thus, if this derivative equals zero,

$$100 - 10X = 0$$
$$X = 10.$$

This is the value of X where Y is maximized, as we saw in the previous paragraph. The key point here is that *to find the value of* X *that maximizes or minimizes* Y, *we must find the value of* X *where this derivative equals zero.* Panel B of Figure 2.10 shows graphically that this derivative equals zero when Y is maximized.

However, on the basis of only the fact that this derivative is zero, one cannot distinguish between a point on the curve where Y is maximized and a point where Y is minimized. For example, in Figure 2.11, this derivative is zero both

FIGURE
2.10

Value of the Derivative When Y Is a Maximum

When Y is a maximum (at $X = 10$), dY/dX equals zero.

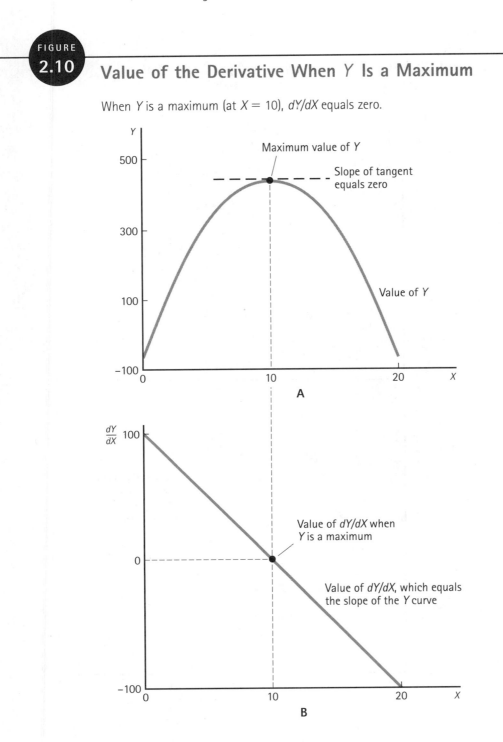

FIGURE
2.11

Using the Second Derivative to Distinguish Maxima from Minima

At maxima (such as $X = 15$), d^2Y/dX^2 is negative; at minima (such as $X = 5$), d^2Y/dX^2 is positive.

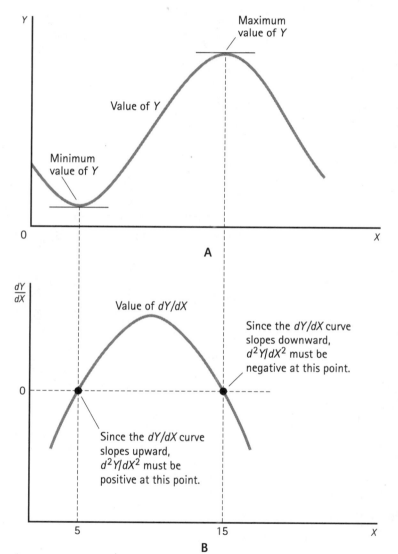

when $X = 5$ and when $X = 15$. In the one case (when $X = 15$), Y is a maximum; in the other case (when $X = 5$), Y is a minimum. To distinguish between a maximum and a minimum, one must find the *second derivative of* Y *with respect to* X, *which is denoted* d^2Y/dX^2, *and which is the derivative of* dY/dX. For example, in Figure 2.10, the second derivative of Y with respect to X is the derivative of the function in equation (2.16); thus, it equals -10.

The second derivative measures the slope of the curve showing the relationship between dY/dX (the first derivative) and X. Just as the first derivative (that is, dY/dX) measures the slope of the Y curve in panel A of Figure 2.11, so the second derivative (that is, d^2Y/dX^2) measures the slope of the dY/dX curve in panel B of Figure 2.11. In other words, just as the first derivative measures the slope of the total profit curve, the second derivative measures the slope of the marginal profit curve. The reason why the second derivative is so important is that it is always *negative* at a point of *maximization* and always *positive* at a point of *minimization*. Thus, *to distinguish between maximization and minimization points, all that we have to do is determine whether the second derivative at each point is positive or negative.*

To understand why the second derivative is always negative at a maximization point and always positive at a minimization point, consider Figure 2.11. When the second derivative is *negative*, this means that the slope of the dY/dX curve in panel B is *negative*. Because dY/dX equals the slope of the Y curve in panel A, this in turn means that the slope of the Y curve decreases as X increases. At a maximum point, such as when $X = 15$, this must be the case. On the other hand, when the second derivative is *positive*, this means that the slope of the dY/dX curve in panel B is *positive*, which is another way of saying that the slope of the Y curve in panel A increases as X increases. At a minimum point, such as when $X = 5$, this must be the case.

EXAMPLE To illustrate how one can use derivatives to solve maximization and minimization problems, suppose that the relationship between profit and output at the Kantor Corporation is

$$Y = -1 + 9X - 6X^2 + X^3,$$

where Y equals annual profit (in millions of dollars), and X equals annual output (in millions of units). This equation is valid only for values of X that equal 3 or less; capacity limitations prevent the firm from producing more than 3 million units per year. To find the values of output that maximize or minimize profit, we find the derivative of Y with respect to X and set it equal to zero.

$$\frac{dY}{dX} = 9 - 12X + 3X^2 = 0 \qquad (2.17)$$

Solving this equation for X, we find that two values of X—1 and 3—result in this derivative's being zero.[4]

To determine whether each of these two output levels maximizes or minimizes profit, we find the value of the second derivative at these two values of X. Taking the derivative of dY/dX, which is shown in equation (2.17) to equal $9 - 12X + 3X^2$ we find that

$$\frac{d^2Y}{dX^2} = -12 + 6X.$$

If $X = 1$

$$\frac{d^2Y}{dX^2} = -12 + 6(1) = -6.$$

Thus, since the second derivative is negative, profit is a maximum (at 3) when output equals 1 million units. If $X = 3$

$$\frac{d^2Y}{dX^2} = -12 + 6(3) = 6.$$

Thus, since the second derivative is positive, profit is a minimum (at -2) when output equals 3 million units.

Marginal Cost Equals Marginal Revenue and the Calculus of Optimization

Once you know how elementary calculus can be used to solve optimization problems, it is easy to see that the fundamental rule for profit maximization—set marginal cost equal to marginal revenue—has its basis in the calculus of optimization. Figure 2.12 shows a firm's total cost and total revenue functions. Since total profit equals total revenue minus total cost, it is equal to the vertical distance between

---

[4]If an equation is of the general quadratic form, $Y = aX^2 + bX + c$, the values of X where Y is 0 are

$$X = \frac{-b \pm (b^2 - 4ac)^{0.5}}{2a}$$

In the equation in the text, $a = 3$, $b = 12$, and $c = 9$. Thus,

$$X = \frac{12 \pm (144 - 108)^{0.5}}{6} = 2 \pm 1$$

Therefore, $Y = 0$ when X equals 1 or 3.

ANALYZING MANAGERIAL DECISIONS

The Optimal Size of a Nursing Home

The nursing home industry takes in about $70 billion a year, and is growing rapidly because of the aging of the U.S. population. According to Peter Sidoti of Nat West Securities Corporation, "Nursing homes are the only area in health care where there is a shortage."[*] A study by Niccie McKay of Trinity University has estimated that the average cost per patient-day of a nursing home (owned by a chain of for-profit homes) is

$$Y = A - 0.16X + 0.00137X^2,$$

where X is the nursing home's number of patient-days per year (in thousands) and A is a number that depends on the region in which the nursing home is located (and other such factors) but not on X.

(a) On the basis of the results of this study, how big must a nursing home be (in terms of patient-days) to minimize the cost per patient-day? (b) Show that your result minimizes, rather than maximizes, the cost per patient-day. (c) Is the number of patient-days a good measure of a nursing home's output? Why or why not?

SOLUTION (a) To find the value of X that minimizes Y, we set the derivative of Y with respect to X equal to zero:

$$= -0.16 + 0.00274X = 0.$$

Thus, $X = 0.16/0.00274 = 58.4$ thousands of days.

(b) Since

$$\frac{d^2Y}{dX^2} = 0.00274,$$

d^2Y/dX^2 is positive. Thus, Y must be a minimum, not a maximum, at the point where $dY/dX = 0$.

(c) It is a crude measure, since some patients require far more complex and intensive care than others.[†]

[*]*New York Times*, February 27, 1994, p. F5.
[†]For further discussion, see N. McKay, "The Effect of Chain Ownership on Nursing Home Costs," *Health Services Research*, April 1991.

the total revenue and total cost curves at any level of output. This distance is maximized at output Q_1, where the slopes of the total revenue and total cost curves are equal. Since the slope of the total revenue curve is marginal revenue and the slope of the total cost curve is marginal cost, this means that profit is maximized when marginal cost equals marginal revenue.

Inspection of Figure 2.12 shows that Q_1 must be the profit-maximizing output. Outputs below Q_0 result in losses (since total cost exceeds total revenue) and obviously do not maximize profit. As output increases beyond Q_0, total revenue rises more rapidly than total cost, so profit must be going up. So long as the slope of the total revenue curve (which equals marginal revenue) exceeds the slope of the total cost curve (which equals marginal cost), profit will continue to rise as output increases. But when these slopes become equal (which means that marginal revenue equals marginal cost), profit will no longer rise but will be at a maximum. Since these slopes become equal at an output of Q_1, this must be the profit-maximizing output. After output Q_1, profit decreases (because marginal cost exceeds marginal revenue).

Using calculus, one can readily understand why firms maximize profit by setting marginal cost equal to marginal revenue. The first thing to note is that

$$\pi = TR - TC,$$

where π equals total profit, TR equals total revenue, and TC equals total cost. Taking the derivative of π with respect to Q (output), we find that

FIGURE
2.12

Marginal-Revenue-Equals-Marginal-Cost Rule for Profit

At the profit-maximizing output of Q_1, marginal revenue (equal to the slope of line R) equals marginal cost (the slope of line S).

CONCEPTS IN CONTEXT

An Alleged Blunder in the Stealth Bomber's Design

Managerial economics is of great use in the aerospace industry, but this does not mean that errors will not occur sometimes. The B-2 "Stealth" bomber has cost billions of dollars to develop. According to Joseph Foa, an emeritus professor of engineering at George Washington University, its design is fundamentally flawed because two aerodynamicists made a mistake: they mistook a minimum point for a maximum point.

The B-2 is basically a jet-powered "flying wing" aircraft. In a secret study for the Air Force, the two aerodynamicists, William Sears and Irving Ashkenas (then at the Northrop Corporation), used mathematical formulas to determine how an aircraft's volume should be proportioned between wing and fuselage in order to maximize its range. Taking the derivative of range with respect to volume, they found that this derivative equaled zero

when the total volume was almost all in the wing. Hence, they concluded that a "flying wing" design would maximize range.

But in a subsequent analysis, Foa showed that the second derivative was positive, not negative, under these circumstances. Thus, the "flying wing" design *minimized* range; it didn't maximize it. In Foa's words, "The flying wing was the aerodynamically worst possible choice of configuration."

This is a very interesting example of how important it is to look at the second derivative to make sure that you do not confuse a maximization point with a minimization point. While the backers of the B-2 bomber claim that it is a good plane despite this error, no one denies that the error is an embarrassment.*

*This discussion is based on W. Biddle, "Skeleton Alleged in the Stealth Bomber's Closet," *Science*, May 12, 1989.

$$\frac{d\pi}{dQ} = \frac{dTR}{dQ} - \frac{dTC}{dQ}.$$

For π to be a maximum, this derivative must be zero, so it must be true that

$$\frac{dTR}{dQ} = \frac{dTC}{dQ}. \tag{2.18}$$

And since marginal revenue is defined as dTR/dQ and marginal cost is defined as dTC/dQ, marginal revenue must equal marginal cost.[5]

[5]Two points should be noted. (1) For profit to be maximized, $d^2\pi/dQ^2$ must be negative. (2) The analysis in this section (as well as earlier sections) results in the determination of a *local* maximum. Sometimes a local maximum is not a global maximum. For example, under some circumstances, the profit-maximizing (or loss-minimizing) output is zero, as we shall see in Chapter 11.

Partial Differentiation and the Maximizations of Multivariable Functions

Up to this point, we have been concerned solely with situations in which a variable depends on only one other variable. Although such situations exist, there are many cases in which a variable depends on a number (often a large number) of other variables, not just one. For example, the Merrimack Company produces two goods, and its profit depends on the amount that it produces of each good. That is,

$$\pi = f(Q_1, Q_2), \tag{2.19}$$

where π is the firm's profit, Q_1 is its output of the first good, and Q_2 is its output of the second good.

To find the value of each of the independent variables (Q_1 and Q_2 in this case) that maximizes the dependent variable (π in this case), we need to know the marginal effect of each independent variable on the dependent variable, *holding constant the effect of all other independent variables*. For example, in this case, we need to know the marginal effect of Q_1 on π when Q_2 is held constant, and we need to know the marginal effect of Q_2 on π when Q_1 is held constant. To get this information, we obtain the partial derivative of π with respect to Q_1 and the partial derivative of π with respect to Q_2.

To obtain the *partial derivative of π with respect to* Q_1, denoted $\partial \pi / \partial Q_1$, one applies the rules for finding a derivative (on pages 45–58) to equation (2.19), but treats Q_2 as a constant. Similarly, to obtain the *partial derivative of π with respect to Q_2*, denoted $\partial \pi / \partial Q_2$, one applies these rules to equation (2.19), but treats Q_1 as a constant.

EXAMPLE Suppose that the relationship between the Merrimack Company's profit (in thousands of dollars) and its output of each good is

$$\pi = -20 + 113.75Q_1 + 80Q_2 - 10Q_1^2 - 10Q_2^2 - 5Q_1Q_2. \tag{2.20}$$

To find the partial derivative of π with respect to Q_1, we treat Q_2 as a constant, and find that

$$\frac{\partial \pi}{\partial Q_1} = 113.75 - 20Q_1 - 5Q_2.$$

ANALYZING MANAGERIAL DECISIONS

The Effects of Advertising on the Sales of TANG

On page 54, we encountered Young and Rubicam's study to estimate the effects of advertising expenditures on the sales of TANG, an instant breakfast drink marketed by General Foods. Specifically, the agency found that the relationship between advertising expenditures and sales in two districts were

$$S_1 = 10 + 5A_1 - 1.5A_1^2$$

and

$$S_2 = 12 + 4A_2 - 0.5A_2^2,$$

where S_1 is TANG's sales (in millions of dollars per year) in the first district, S_2 is its sales in the second district, A_1 is the advertising expenditure (in millions of dollars per year) on TANG in the first district, and A_2 is the advertising expenditure in the second district.

(a) If General Foods wants to maximize TANG's sales in the first district, how much should it spend on advertising? (b) If General Foods wants to maximize TANG's sales in the second district, how much should it spend on advertising? (c) Show that your answers to parts a and b maximize, rather than minimize, sales. (d) Would you recommend that General Foods attempt to maximize TANG's sales? Why or why not?

SOLUTION (a) To find the value of A_1 that maximizes S_1, we set the derivative of S_1 with respect to A_1 equal to zero:

$$\frac{dS_1}{dA_1} = 5 - 3A_1 = 0.$$

Thus $A_1 = 5/3$ million dollars. (b) To find the value of A_2 that maximizes S_2, we set the derivative of S_2 with respect to A_2 equal to zero:

$$\frac{dS_2}{dA_2} = 4 - A_2 = 0.$$

Thus, $A_2 = 4$ million dollars. (c) Since $d^2S_1/dA_1^2 = -3$, S_1 must be a maximum at the point where $dS_1/dA_1 = 0$. Since $d^2S_2/dA_2^2 = -1$, S_2 must be a maximum at the point where $dS_2/dA_2 = 0$. If S_1 and S_2 were minimized, not maximized, the second derivatives would be positive, not negative. (d) No. As stressed in Chapter 1, firms generally are assumed to be interested in maximizing profit, not sales. In general, a firm is unlikely to increase its sales if it means a decrease in its profits. But in some cases, a firm may do this because, although profits may fall in the short run, they may increase in the long run. For example, a firm may make some sales at a loss in order to gain customers who eventually will enhance the firm's profits.*

*See DeBruicker, Quelch, and Ward, *Cases in Consumer Behavior*.

To find the partial derivative of π with respect to Q_2, we treat Q_1 as a constant, and find that

$$\frac{\partial \pi}{\partial Q_2} = 80 - 20Q_2 - 5Q_1.$$

Once we have derived the partial derivatives, it is relatively simple to determine the values of the independent variables that maximize the dependent variable.

All that we have to do is *set all of the partial derivatives equal to zero*. Thus, in the case of the Merrimack Company,

$$\frac{\partial \pi}{\partial Q_1} = 113.75 - 20Q_1 - 50Q_2 = 0 \tag{2.21}$$

$$\frac{\partial \pi}{\partial Q_2} = 80 - 20Q_2 - 5Q_1 = 0. \tag{2.22}$$

Equations (2.21) and (2.22) are two equations in two unknowns. Solving them simultaneously, we find that profit is maximized when $Q_1 = 5.0$ and $Q_2 = 2.75$. In other words, to maximize profit, the firm should produce 5.0 units of the first good and 2.75 units of the second good per period of time. If it does this, its profit will equal \$374.375 thousand per period of time.[6]

To see why all the partial derivatives should be set equal to zero, consider Figure 2.13, which shows the relationship in equation (2.20) between π, Q_1, and Q_2, in the range where π is close to its maximum value. As you can see, this relationship is represented by a three-dimensional surface. The maximum value of π is at point M, where this surface is level. A plane that is tangent to this surface at point M will be parallel to the Q_1Q_2 plane; in other words, its slopes with respect to either Q_1 or Q_2 must be zero. Thus, since the partial derivatives in equations (2.21) and (2.22) equal these slopes, they too must equal zero at the maximum point, M.[7]

Constrained Optimization

As we learned in Chapter 1, managers of firms and other organizations generally face constraints that limit the options available to them. A production manager may want to minimize his or her firm's costs, but may not be permitted to produce less than is required to meet the firm's contracts with its customers. The top managers of a firm may want to maximize profits, but in the short run they may be unable to change its product or augment its plant and equipment.

Constrained optimization problems of this sort can be solved in a number of ways. In relatively simple cases in which there is only one constraint, one can use this constraint to express one of the decision variables—that is, one of the variables the decision maker can choose—as a function of the other decision variables. Then, one can apply the techniques for unconstrained opti-

---

[6]Inserting 5.0 for Q_1 and 2.75 for Q_2 in equation (2.20), we find that

$$\pi = 20 + 113.75(5) + 80(2.75) - 10(5)^2 - 10(2.75)^2 - 5(5)(2.75) = 394.375$$

[7]The second order conditions for distinguishing maxima from minima can be found in any calculus book. For present purposes, a discussion of these conditions is not essential. Also note that the techniques presented in this section result in a local maximum, not necessarily a global maximum (recall footnote 5).

FIGURE

2.13

Relationship between π, Q_1, and Q_2

At M, the point where π is a maximum, the surface representing this relationship is flat; its slope with regard to either Q_1 or Q_2 is zero.

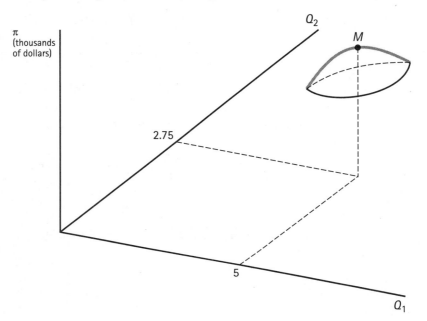

mization described in the previous sections. In effect, what one does is convert the problem to one of unconstrained maximization or minimization.

To illustrate, suppose that the Kloster Company produces two products, and that its total cost equals

$$TC = 4Q_1^2 + 5Q_2^2 - Q_1Q_2, \qquad (2.23)$$

where Q_1 equals its output per hour of the first product, and Q_2 equals its output per hour of the second product. Because of commitments to customers, the number produced of both products combined cannot be less than 30 per hour. Kloster's president wants to know what output levels of the two products will minimize the firm's costs, given that the output of the first product plus the output of the second product equals 30 per hour.

This constrained optimization problem can be expressed as follows:

Minimize $\qquad\qquad TC = 4Q_1^2 + 5Q_2^2 - Q_1Q_2$

subject to $\qquad Q_1 + Q_2 = 30.$

Of course, the constraint is that $(Q_1 + Q_2)$ must equal 30. Solving this constraint for Q_1, we have

$$Q_1 = 30 - Q_2.$$

Substituting $(30 - Q_2)$ for Q_1 in equation (2.23), it follows that

$$
\begin{aligned}
TC &= 4(30 - Q_2)^2 + 5Q_2^2 - (30 - Q_2)Q_2 \\
&= 4(900 - 60Q_2 + Q_2^2) + 5Q_2^2 - 30Q_2 + Q_2^2 \\
TC &= 3600 - 270Q_2 + 10Q_2^2.
\end{aligned}
\tag{2.24}
$$

The methods of unconstrained optimization described above can be used to find the value of Q_2 that minimizes TC. As indicated in earlier sections, we must obtain the derivative of TC with respect to Q_2, and set it equal to zero.

$$
\begin{aligned}
\frac{dTC}{dQ_2} = -270 + 20Q_2 &= 0 \\
20Q_2 &= 270 \\
Q_2 &= 13.5.
\end{aligned}
$$

To make sure that this is a minimum, not a maximum, we obtain the second derivative, which is

$$\frac{d^2TC}{dQ_2^2} = 20.$$

Since this is positive, we have found a minimum.

To find the value of Q_1 that minimizes total cost, recall that the constraint requires that

$$Q_1 + Q_2 = 30,$$

which means that

$$Q_1 = 30 - Q_2.$$

Since we know that the optimal value of Q_2 is 13.5, it follows that the optimal value of Q_1 must be

$$Q_1 = 30 - 13.5 = 16.5.$$

Summing up, if the Kloster Company wants to minimize total cost subject to the constraint that the sum of the output levels of its two products be 30, it should produce 16.5 units of the first product and 13.5 units of the second prod-

uct per hour.[8] (In other words, it should produce 33 uni
and 27 units of the second product every 2 hours.)

Lagrangian Multipliers[9]

If the technique described in the previous section is not feasible because the constraints are too numerous or complex, the method of Lagrangian multipliers can be used. This method of solving constrained optimization problems involves the construction of an equation—the so-called **Lagrangian function**—that combines the function to be minimized or maximized and the constraints. This equation is constructed so that two things are true: (1) When this equation is maximized (or minimized), the original function we want to maximize (or minimize) is in fact maximized (or minimized). (2) All the constraints are satisfied.

To illustrate how one creates a Lagrangian function, consider once again the problem faced by the Kloster Company. As indicated in the previous section, this firm wants to minimize $TC = 4Q_1^2 + 5Q_2^2 - Q_1Q_2$, subject to the constraint that $Q_1 + Q_2 = 30$. The first step in constructing the Lagrangian function for this firm's problem is to restate the constraint so that an expression is formed that is equal to zero:

$$30 - Q_1 - Q_2 = 0. \tag{2.25}$$

Then if we multiply this form of the constraint by an unknown factor, designated λ (lambda), and add the result to the function we want to minimize (in equation (2.23)), we get the Lagrangian function, which is

$$L_{TC} = 4Q_1^2 + 5Q_2^2 - Q_1Q_2 + \lambda(30 - Q_1 - Q_2). \tag{2.26}$$

For reasons specified in the next paragraph, we can be sure that if we find the unconstrained maximum (or minimum) of the Lagrangian function, the solution will be exactly the same as the solution of the original constrained maximization (or minimization) problem. In other words, to solve the constrained optimization problem, all that we have to do is optimize the Lagrangian function. For example, in the case of the Kloster Company, we must find the values of Q_1, Q_2, and λ that minimize L_{TC} in equation (2.26). To do this, we must

---

[8]Substituting 16.5 for Q_1 and 13.5 for Q_2 in equation (2.23), the firm's total cost will equal

$$\begin{aligned} TC &= 4(16.5)^2 + 5(13.5)^2 - (16.5)(13.5) \\ &= 4(272.25) + 5(182.25) - 222.75 \\ &= 1089 + 911.25 - 222.75 \\ &= 1777.5, \quad \text{or} \quad \$1,777.50 \end{aligned}$$

[9]This section can be skipped without loss of continuity.

find the partial derivative of L_{TC} with respect to each of these three variables—Q_1, Q_2, and λ:

$$\frac{\partial L_{TC}}{\partial Q_1} = 8Q_1 - Q_2 - \lambda$$

$$\frac{\partial L_{TC}}{\partial Q_2} = -Q_1 + 10Q_2 - \lambda$$

$$\frac{\partial L_{TC}}{\partial \lambda} = -Q_1 - Q_2 + 30.$$

As indicated in the section before last, we must set all three of these partial derivatives equal to zero in order to minimize L_{TC}. Thus,

$$8Q_1 - Q_2 - \lambda = 0 \qquad (2.27)$$
$$-Q_1 + 10Q_2 - \lambda = 0 \qquad (2.28)$$
$$-Q_1 - Q_2 + 30 = 0. \qquad (2.29)$$

It is important to note that the partial derivative of the Lagrangian function with regard to λ (that is, $\partial L_{TC}/\partial \lambda$), when it is set equal to zero [in equation (2.29)], is the constraint in our original optimization problem. [Recall equation (2.25).] This, of course, will always be true because of the way the Lagrangian function is constructed. Thus, if this derivative is zero, we can be sure that this original constraint is satisfied. And, if this constraint is satisfied, the last term on the right of the Lagrangian function is zero, so the Lagrangian function boils down to the original function that we wanted to maximize (or minimize). Consequently, by maximizing (or minimizing) the Lagrangian function, we solve the original constrained optimization problem.

Returning to the Kloster Company, equations (2.27), (2.28), and (2.29) are three simultaneous equations with three unknowns—Q_1, Q_2, and λ. If we solve this system of equations for Q_1 and Q_2, we get the optimal values of Q_1 and Q_2. Subtracting equation (2.28) from equation (2.27), we find that

$$9Q_1 - 11Q_2 = 0. \qquad (2.30)$$

Multiplying equation (2.29) by 9 and adding the result to equation (2.30), we can solve for Q_2:

$$\begin{aligned}
-9Q_1 - 9Q_2 + 270 &= 0 \\
\underline{9Q_1 - 11Q_2 \qquad\quad = 0} \\
-20Q_2 + 270 &= 0 \\
Q_2 &= 270/20 = 13.5.
\end{aligned}$$

CONSULTANT'S CORNER

Planning to Meet Peak Engineering Requirements*

A leading computer manufacturer, after analyzing the history of its product development projects, found that there were regular patterns of labor-power buildup and phaseout in its projects. Specifically, the number of engineers required to carry out such a project t months after the start of the project could be approximated reasonably well by

$$Y = at - bt^2, \qquad \text{for } 0 \le t \le a/b$$

where Y is the number of engineers required t months after the start of the project, and a and b are numbers that vary from project to project (and that depend on the kind of product being developed).

The computer manufacturer wanted to use these results to estimate when the number of engineers required to carry out a particular product development project would hit its peak, and how great this peak requirement would be. Estimates of this sort would help the firm's managers in planning the allocation and utilization of the firm's engineering staff, and alert them to situations in which its staff might have to be expanded or supplemented. The project for which the firm's managers wanted these estimates was to begin immediately. On the basis of previous experience with projects of this type, the firm's managers estimated that a would be about 18 and b would be about 1 for this project.

If you were a consultant to this firm, how would you make the estimates wanted by the firm's managers?

*This section is based on an actual case, although the equations and the situation have been simplified somewhat for pedagogical purposes.

Thus, the optimal value of Q_2 is 13.5. Substituting 13.5 for Q_2 in equation (2.29), we find that the optimal value of Q_1 is 16.5.

The answer we get is precisely the same as in the previous section: the optimal value of Q_1 is 16.5, and the optimal value of Q_2 is 13.5. In other words, the Kloster Company should produce 16.5 units of the first product and 13.5 units of the second product per hour. But the method of Lagrangian multipliers described in this section is more powerful than that described in the previous section for at least two reasons: (1) It can handle more than a single constraint, and (2) the value of λ provides interesting and useful information to the decision maker.

Specifically λ, called the **Lagrangian multiplier,** measures the change in the variable to be maximized or minimized (TC in this case) if the constraint is relaxed by 1 unit. For example, if the Kloster Company wants to minimize total cost subject to the constraint that the total output of both products is 31 rather than 30, the value of λ indicates by how much the minimum value of TC will increase. What is the value of λ? According to equation (2.27),

$$8Q_1 - Q_2 - \lambda = 0.$$

Thus, since $Q_1 = 16.5$ and $Q_2 = 13.5$,

$$\lambda = 8(16.5) - 13.5 = 118.5.$$

Consequently, if the constraint is relaxed so that total output is 31 rather than 30, total cost will go up by $118.50.

For many managerial decisions, information of this sort is of great value. Suppose that a customer offers the Kloster Company $115 for one of its products, but to make this product, Kloster would have to stretch its total output to 31 per hour. On the basis of the findings of the previous paragraph, Kloster would be foolish to accept this offer, since this extra product would raise its costs by $118.50, which is $3.50 more than the amount the customer offers to pay for it.

Comparing Incremental Costs with Incremental Revenues

Before concluding this chapter, we must point out that many business decisions can and should be made by comparing incremental costs with incremental revenues. Typically, a manager must choose between two (or more) courses of action, and what is relevant is the difference in costs between the two courses of action, as well as the difference in revenues between them. For example, if the managers of a machinery company are considering whether to add a new product line, they should compare the incremental cost of adding the new product line—that is, the extra cost resulting from its addition—with the incremental revenue—that is, the extra revenue resulting from its addition. If the incremental revenue exceeds the incremental cost, the new product line will add to the firm's profits.

Note that *incremental* cost is not the same as *marginal* cost. Whereas marginal cost is the extra cost from a very small (1-unit) increase in output, **incremental cost** is the extra cost from an output increase that may be very substantial. Similarly, **incremental revenue**, unlike marginal revenue, is the extra revenue from an output increase that may be very substantial. For example, suppose that you want to see whether a firm's profits will increase if it doubles its output. If the incremental cost of such an output increase is $5 million and the incremental revenue is $6 million, the firm will increase its profits by $1 million if it doubles its output. Marginal cost and marginal revenue cannot tell you this, because they refer only to a very small increase in output, not to a doubling of it.

While it may seem very easy to compare incremental costs with incremental revenues, there in fact are many pitfalls. One of the most common errors is the failure to recognize the irrelevance of *sunk* costs. Costs incurred in the past often are irrelevant in making today's decisions. Suppose you are going to make a trip and you want to determine whether it will be cheaper to drive your car or to go by plane. What costs should be included if you drive your car? Since the only *incremental* costs that will be incurred will be the gas and oil (and a certain amount of wear and tear on tires, engine, and so on), they are the only costs that should be included. Costs incurred in the past, such as the original price of the car, and costs that will be the same regardless of whether you make the trip by car or plane, such as your auto insurance, should not be included. On the other hand, if you are thinking about buying a car to make this and many other trips, these costs should be included.[10]

To illustrate the proper reasoning, consider the actual case of an airline that has deliberately run extra flights that do no more than return a little more than their out-of-pocket costs. Assume that this airline is faced with the decision of whether to run an extra flight between city *A* and city *B*. Assume that the fully allocated costs—the out-of-pocket costs plus a certain percent of overhead, depreciation, insurance, and other such costs—are $5,500 for the flight. Assume that the out-of-pocket costs—the actual sum that this airline has to disburse to run the flight—are $3,000, and the expected revenue from the flight is $4,100. In such a case, this airline will run the flight, which is the correct decision, since the flight will add $1,100 to profit. The incremental revenue from the flight is $4,100, and the incremental cost is $3,000. Overhead, depreciation, and insurance would be the same whether the flight is run or not. Thus, fully allocated costs are misleading here; the relevant concept of costs is out-of-pocket, not fully allocated costs.

Errors of other kinds can also mar firms' estimates of incremental costs. For example, a firm may refuse to produce and sell some items because it is already working near capacity, and the incremental cost of producing them is judged to be very high. In fact, however, the incremental cost may not be so high because the firm may be able to produce these items during the slack season (when there is plenty of excess capacity), since the potential customers may be willing to accept delivery then.

Also, incremental revenue frequently is misjudged. Take the case of a firm that is considering the introduction of a new product. The firm's managers may estimate the incremental revenue from the new product without taking proper account of the effects of the new product's sales on the sales of the firm's ex-

---

[10]This example is worked out in more detail in the paper by E. Grant and W. Ireson in *Managerial Economics and Operations Research*, Mansfield.

isting products. Whereas they may think that the new product will not cut into the sales of existing products, it may in fact do so, with the result that their estimate of incremental revenue may be too high.

Summary

1. Functional relationships can be represented by tables, graphs, or equations. The marginal value of a dependent variable is defined as the change in this variable associated with a 1-unit change in a particular independent variable. The dependent variable achieves a maximum when its marginal value shifts from positive to negative.

2. The derivative of Y with respect to X, denoted dY/dX, is the limit of the ratio $\Delta Y/\Delta X$ as ΔX approaches zero. Geometrically, it is the slope of the curve showing Y (on the vertical axis) as a function of X (on the horizontal axis). We have provided rules that enable us to find the value of this derivative.

3. To find the value of X that maximizes or minimizes Y, we determine the value of X where dY/dX equals zero. To tell whether this is a maximum or a minimum, we find the second derivative of Y with respect to X, denoted d^2Y/dX^2, which is the derivative of dY/dX. If this second derivative is negative, we have found a maximum; if it is positive, we have found a minimum.

4. A dependent variable often depends on a number of independent variables, not just one. To find the value of each of the independent variables that maximizes the dependent variable, we determine the partial derivative of Y with respect to each of the independent variables, denoted $\partial Y/\partial X$, and set it equal to zero. To obtain the partial derivative of Y with respect to X, we apply the ordinary rules for finding a derivative; however, all independent variables other than X are treated as constants.

5. Managers of firms and other organizations generally face constraints that limit the options available to them. In relatively simple cases in which there is only one constraint, we can use this constraint to express one of the decision variables as a function of the other decision variables, and we can apply the techniques for unconstrained optimization.

6. In more complex cases, constrained optimization problems can be solved by the method of Lagrangian multipliers. The Lagrangian function combines the function to be maximized or minimized and the constraints. To solve the constrained optimization problem, we optimize the Lagrangian function.

7. Many business decisions can and should be made by comparing incremental costs with incremental revenues. Typically, a manager must choose between two (or more) courses of action, and what is relevant is the difference between the costs of the two courses of action, as well as the difference between their revenues.

Problems

1. One very important question facing hospitals is: How big must a hospital be (in terms of patient-days of care) to minimize the cost per patient-day? According to one well-known study, the total cost (in dollars) of operating a hospital (of a particular type) can be approximated by

$$C = 4,700,000 + 0.00013X^2,$$

where X is the number of patient-days.

   a. Derive a formula for the relationship between cost per patient-day and the number of patient-days.

   b. On the basis of the results of this study, how big must a hospital be (in terms of patient-days) to minimize the cost per patient-day?

   c. Show that your result minimizes, rather than maximizes, the cost per patient-day.

2. The Trumbull Company has developed a new product. Trumbull's chairperson estimates that the new product will increase the firm's revenues by $5 million per year, and that it will result in extra out-of-pocket costs of $4 million per year, the fully allocated costs (including a percentage of overhead, depreciation, and insurance) being $5.5 million.

   a. Trumbull's chairperson feels that it would not be profitable to introduce this new product. Is the chairperson right? Why or why not?

   b. Trumbull's vice president for research argues that since the development of this product has already cost about $10 million, the firm has little choice but to introduce it. Is the vice president right? Why or why not?

3. For the Martin Corporation, the relationship between profit and output is the following:

Output (number of units per day)	Profit (thousands of dollars per day)
0	−10
1	−8
2	−5
3	0
4	2
5	7
6	12
7	21
8	22
9	23
10	20

a. What is the marginal profit when output is between 5 and 6 units per day? When output is between 9 and 10 units per day?

b. At what output is average profit a maximum?

c. Should the Martin Corporation produce the output where average profit is a maximum? Why or why not?

4. Determine the first derivative of each of the following functions:

a. $Y = 3 + 10X + 5X^2$

b. $Y = 2X(4 + X^3)$

c. $Y = 3X/(4 + X^3)$

d. $Y = 4X/(X - 3)$

5. The total cost function at the Duemer Company is $TC = 100 + 4Q + 8Q^2$ where TC is total costs, and Q is output.

a. What is marginal cost when output is 10?

b. What is marginal cost when output is 12?

c. What is marginal cost when output is 20?

6. he Bartholomew Company's profit is related in the following way to its output: $\pi = -40 + 20Q - 3Q^2$, where π is total profit and Q is output.

a. If the firm's output equals 8, what is its marginal profit?

b. Derive an equation relating the firm's marginal profit to its output.

c. What output will maximize the firm's profit?

7. Determine the second derivative of the following functions:

a. $Y = 4 + 9X + 3X^2$

b. $Y = 4X(3 + X^2)$

c. $Y = 4X(2 + X^3)$

d. $Y = (4/X) + 3$

8. The Mineola Corporation hires a consultant to estimate the relationship between its profit and its output. The consultant reports that the relationship is

$$\pi = -10 - 6Q + 5.5Q^2 - 2Q^3 + .25Q^4.$$

a. The consultant says that the firm should set Q equal to 1 to maximize profit. Is it true that $d\pi/dQ = 0$ when $Q = 1$? Is π a maximum when $Q = 1$?

b. Mineola's executive vice president says that the firm's profit is a maximum when $Q = 2$. Is this true?

c. If you were the chief executive officer of the Mineola Corporation, would you accept the consultant's estimate of the relationship between profit and output as being correct?

9. Find the partial derivative of Y with respect to X in each of the following cases:

a. $Y = 10 + 3Z + 2X$

b. $Y = 18Z^2 + 4X^3$

c. $Y = Z^{0.2}X^{0.8}$

d. $Y = 3Z/(4 + X)$

10. The Stock Corporation makes two products, paper and cardboard. The relationship between π, the firm's annual profit (in thousands of dollars), and its output of each good is

$$\pi = -50 + 40Q_1 + 30Q_2 - 5Q_1^2 - 4Q_2^2 - 3Q_1Q_2,$$

where Q_1 is the firm's annual output of paper (in tons), and Q_2 is the firm's annual output of cardboard (in tons).

a. Find the output of each good that the Stock Corporation should produce if it wants to maximize profit.

b. If the community in which the firm is located imposes a tax of $5,000 per year on the firm, will this alter the answer to part a? If so, how will the answer change?

11. The Miller Company uses skilled and unskilled labor to do a particular construction project. The cost of doing the project depends on the number of hours of skilled labor and the number of hours of unskilled labor that are used, the relationship being

$$C = 4 - 3X_1 - 4X_2 + 2X_1^2 + 3X_2^2 + X_1X_2,$$

where C is cost (in thousands of dollars), X_1 is the number of hours (in thousands) of skilled labor, and X_2 is the number of hours (in thousands) of unskilled labor.

a. Find the number of hours of skilled labor and the number of hours of unskilled labor that will minimize the cost of doing the project.

b. If the Miller Company has to purchase a license costing $2,000 to do this project (and if the cost of this license is not included in C), will this alter the answer to part a? If so, how will the answer change?

12. Ilona Stafford manages a small firm that produces wool rugs and cotton rugs. Her total cost per day (in dollars) equals

$$C = 7X_1^2 + 9X_2^2 - 1.5X_1X_2,$$

where X_1 equals the number of cotton rugs produced per day, and X_2 equals the number of wool rugs produced per day. Because of commitments to retail stores that sell her rugs to consumers, she must produce ten rugs per day, but any mix of wool and cotton rugs is acceptable.

a. If she wants to minimize her costs (without violating her commitment to the retail stores), how many cotton rugs and wool rugs should she produce per day? (Do *not* use the method of Lagrangian multipliers.)

      b. Does it seem reasonable that she would want to minimize cost in a situation of this sort? Why or why not?

      c. Can she produce fractional numbers of rugs per day?

13. a. Use the method of Lagrangian multipliers to solve problem 12.

      b. Do you get the same answer as you do without using this method?

      c. What does λ equal? What does this mean?

PART

2

Demand and Forecasting

Demand Theory

CHAPTER

3

Introduction

Demand is half of the equation to determine a firm's profits. Managers, therefore, spend enormous amounts of time, energy, and money analyzing the demand for their products. This analysis of demand can be difficult. Intuitively, we know that price will influence the quantity demanded for our product. But many other variables will too: the price of substitute products, the price of complementary products, the state of the economy, disposable personal income, advertising expenditures, the quality of the product, people's tastes, government regulations, and so on.

Some of the variables (endogenous) that influence our demand are under the manager's control, such as price, advertising, and quality, while other variables are exogenous to the manager, such as the prices of substitute and complementary goods, the state of the economy, disposable personal income, and government regulation. The manager wants to understand the impact of these (and other) variables on the product, so that they can make decisions on endogenous variables and so that they can plan a reactive strategy to changes in exogenous variables.

TABLE
3.1

Market Demand Schedule for Personal Computers, 2001

Price per computer (dollars)	Quantity demanded per year (thousands)
3,000	800
2,750	975
2,500	1,150
2,250	1,325
2,000	1,500

Suppose a firm wishes to change its price. What will be the impact on quantity demanded of its product? What will be the impact on the firm's total revenues? The same questions can be asked for a change in any variable listed above. Without knowledge of the firm's demand, the manager cannot answer these important questions.

This chapter introduces market demand functions and discusses how changes in the above variables cause the demand function to shift or cause movements along the function.

A critical application of our marginal analysis called elasticity will be introduced. Elasticity tells us how the percentages of quantity will change given a small (marginal) percentage change in one of the variables listed above. When the changed variable is the firm's price, the elasticity also tells us how total revenue changes. Having estimates of elasticities can help managers make decisions about how to price their products and how to anticipate quantity and revenue changes when uncontrollable variables change.

The Market Demand Curve

The **market demand schedule** for a good is a table that shows the total quantity of the good that would be purchased at each price. For example, suppose that the market demand schedule for personal computers is as shown in Table 3.1.[1] According to this table, 1.5 million personal computers will be demanded per year if the price is $2,000 per computer, 800,000 will be demanded if the price is $3,000, and so on. Another way of presenting the data in Table 3.1 is

---

[1]These numbers are hypothetical, but adequate for present purposes. In subsequent chapters, we shall provide data describing the actual relationship between the price and quantity demanded of various goods. At this point, the emphasis is on the concept of a market demand schedule, not on the detailed accuracy of these numbers.

FIGURE
3.1

Demand Curve for Personal Computers

This demand curve is a graphical representation of the figures in Table 3.1.

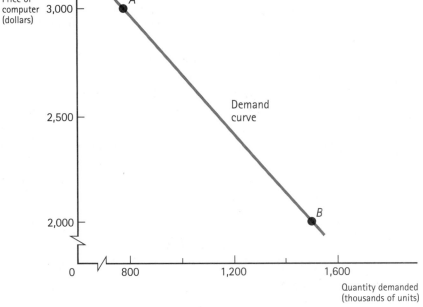

by a **market demand curve,** which is a plot of the market demand schedule on a graph. The vertical axis of the graph measures the price per unit of the good, and the horizontal axis measures the quantity of the good demanded per unit of time. Figure 3.1 shows the market demand curve for personal computers, based on the figures in Table 3.1.

In Chapter 1, we provided an introductory look at the market demand curve. Now we must study this topic in more detail. Three things should be noted concerning Figure 3.1. First, the market demand curve shows the *total* quantity of personal computers demanded at each price, not the quantity demanded from a *particular* firm. We will discuss the demand for a particular firm's product in the next section of this chapter. Second, the market demand curve for personal computers slopes downward to the right. In other words, the quantity of personal computers demanded increases as the price falls. As we pointed out in Chapter 1, this is true of the demand curve for most goods; they almost always slope downward to the right. Third, the market demand curve in Figure 3.1 pertains to a particular period of time: 2001. As you will recall from Chapter 1, any demand curve pertains to some period of time, and its shape and position depend on the length and other characteristics of this period. For example, if we were to estimate the market demand curve for personal computers for the first week in 2001, it would be a different curve from the one in Figure 3.1, which pertains to the whole year. The difference arises partly because consumers can adapt their purchases more fully to changes in the price of personal computers in a year than in a week.

Besides the length of time period, what other factors determine the position and shape of the market demand curve for a good? As indicated in Chapter 1, one important factor is the **tastes of consumers.** If consumers show an increasing preference for a product, the demand curve will shift to the right; that is, at each price, consumers will desire to buy more than they did previously. Alternatively, for each quantity, consumers will be willing to pay a higher price. On the other hand, if consumers show a decreasing preference for a product, the demand curve will shift to the left, since, at each price, consumers will desire to buy less than previously. Alternatively, for each quantity, consumers will only be willing to pay a lower price. For example, as shown in Figure 3.2, if people find that personal computers are more helpful than they thought, and if

FIGURE 3.2

Effect of an Increased Preference for Personal Computers on the Market Demand Curve

The demand curve for personal computers shifts to the right.

Effect of an Increase in Per Capita Income on the
Market Demand Curve for Personal Computers

The demand curve shifts to the right.

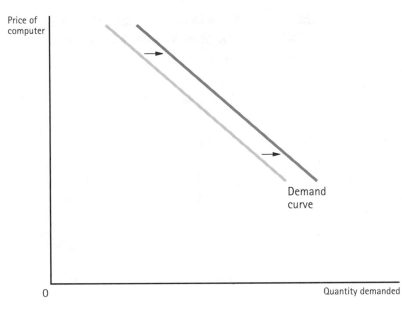

they begin to use them more and give them in larger numbers to their children
and others, the demand curve for personal computers may shift to the right.
The greater the shift in preferences, the farther the demand curve will shift.

Another factor that influences the position and shape of a good's market
demand curve is the **level of consumer incomes.** For some types of products,
the demand curve shifts to the right if per capita income increases, whereas for
other types of commodities, the demand curve shifts to the left if per capita income rises. In the case of personal computers, one would expect that an increase in per capita income would shift the demand curve to the right, as shown
in Figure 3.3. Still another factor that influences the position and shape of a
good's market demand curve is the **level of other prices.** For example, one
would expect that the quantity of personal computers demanded would increase
if the price of software for such computers fell drastically.

Finally, the position and shape of a good's market demand curve is also affected by the size of the population in the relevant market. Thus, if the population increases, one would expect that, if all other factors were held equal, the
quantity of personal computers demanded would increase. Of course, the pop-

ulation generally changes slowly, so this factor often has little effect in the very short run.

Industry and Firm Demand Functions

Building on the results of the previous section, we can define the **market demand function** for a product, which is the relationship between the quantity demanded of the product and the various factors that influence this quantity. Put generally, this market demand function can be written as

$$\text{Quantity demanded of good } X = Q = f(\text{price of } X, \text{ incomes of consumers, tastes of consumers, prices of other goods, population, advertising expenditures, and so forth}).$$

To be useful for analytical and forecasting purposes, this equation must be made more specific. For example, if good X is personal computers, the market demand function might be

$$Q = b_1P + b_2I + b_3S + b_4A, \tag{3.1}$$

where Q equals the number of personal computers demanded in a particular year, P is the average price of personal computers in that year, I is per capita disposable income during that year, S is the average price of software during that year, and A is the amount spent on advertising by producers of personal computers in that year. The assumption in equation (3.1) is, of course, that the relationship is linear. (Also, we assume for simplicity that the population in the relevant market is essentially constant.)

Going a step further, it generally is necessary for managers and analysts to obtain numerical estimates of the bs in equation (3.1). Employing the statistical techniques described in Chapter 5, one usually can estimate these so-called **parameters** of the demand function. To illustrate the sorts of results that might be obtained, we might find that

$$Q = -700P + 200I - 500S + 0.01A. \tag{3.2}$$

According to equation (3.2), a \$1 increase in the price of a personal computer results in a decrease in the quantity demanded of 700 units per year; a \$1 increase in per capita disposable income results in a 200-unit increase in the quantity demanded; a \$1 increase in the price of software reduces the quantity demanded by 500 units per year; and a \$1 increase in advertising raises the quantity demanded by 0.01 unit per year.

It is important to understand the relationship between the market demand function and the demand curve. The market demand curve shows the relationship between Q and P when all other relevant variables are held constant. For example, suppose that we want to know what the relationship between quantity demanded and price would be if per capita disposable income is $13,000, if the average price of software is $400, and if advertising expenditure is $50 million. Since $I = 13,000$, $S = 400$, and $A = 50,000,000$, equation (3.2) becomes

$$Q = -700P + 200(13,000)$$
$$-500(400) + .01(50,000,000), \qquad (3.3)$$

or
$$Q = 2,900,000 - 700P. \qquad (3.4)$$

Solving this equation for P, we obtain

$$P = 4,143 - .001429Q$$

which is graphed in Figure 3.1. This is the demand curve for personal computers, given that I, S, and A are held constant at the stipulated levels.

Given the market demand function, managers and analysts can readily quantify the shifts in the demand curve that will result from changes in the variables other than the product's price. For example, how much of a shift will occur in the demand curve if the price of software falls from $400 to $200? Inserting 200 (rather than 400) for S in equation (3.3), we find that

$$Q = 3,000,000 - 700P. \qquad (3.5)$$

Solving this equation for P, we obtain

$$P = 4,286 - .001429Q, \qquad (3.6)$$

which is graphed (together with the demand curve based on $S = 400$) in Figure 3.4. Clearly, the demand curve has shifted to the right, the quantity demanded being 100,000 more than when $S = 400$ (if P is held constant).

Market demand functions can be formulated for individual firms as well as for entire industries. That is, one can formulate an equation like equation (3.2) to predict the sales of an individual producer of personal computers. In such an equation, the quantity demanded of the firm's good would be inversely related to its price but directly related to the prices charged by its competitors; and it would be directly related to its advertising expenditures but inversely related to the advertising expenditures of its competitors. It is important to distinguish between industry and firm demand functions, since they are quite different. Both are important to managers, because firms often are interested in the effects of

FIGURE
3.4

Demand Curve for Personal Computers

If the price of software falls from $400 to $200, the demand curve shifts to the right by 100,000 units.

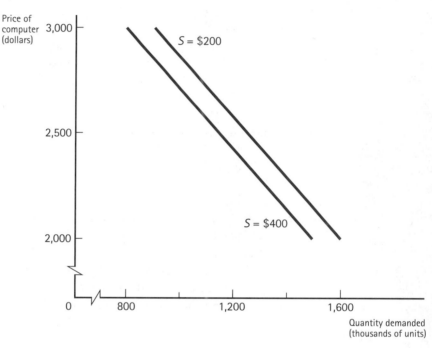

variables like disposable income and advertising on industry sales, as well as on the sales of their own firms—which obviously are of primary significance.

The Price Elasticity of Demand

Market demand curves vary with regard to the sensitivity of quantity demanded to price. For some goods, a small change in price results in a big change in quantity demanded; for other goods, a big change in price results in a small change in quantity demanded. To indicate how sensitive quantity demanded is to changes in price, economists use a measure called the **price elasticity of demand.** The price elasticity of demand is defined to be *the percentage change in quantity demanded resulting from a 1 percent change in price.* More precisely, it equals

$$\eta = \left(\frac{P}{Q}\right)\left(\frac{\partial Q}{\partial P}\right)$$

(3.7)

Suppose that a 1 percent reduction in the price of cotton shirts results in a 1.3 percent increase in the quantity demanded in the United States. If so, the price elasticity of demand for cotton shirts is −1.3. The price elasticity of demand generally will vary from one point to another on a demand curve. For instance, the price elasticity of demand may be higher in absolute value when the price of cotton shirts is high than when it is low. Similarly, the price elasticity of demand will vary from market to market. For example, India may have a different price elasticity of demand for cotton shirts from that of the United States.

The price elasticity of demand for a product must lie between zero and negative infinity. If the price elasticity is zero, the demand curve is a vertical line; that is, the quantity demanded is unaffected by price. If the price elasticity is negative infinity, the demand curve is a horizontal line; that is, an unlimited amount can be sold at a particular price ($15 in Figure 3.5), but nothing can be sold if the price is raised even slightly. Figure 3.5 shows these two limiting cases.

FIGURE 3.5

Demand Curves with Zero and Infinite Price Elasticities of Demand

The demand curve is a vertical line if the price elasticity is zero and a horizontal line if it is negative infinity.

Point and Arc Elasticities

If we have a market demand schedule showing the quantity of a commodity demanded in the market at various prices, how can we estimate the price elasticity of market demand? Let ΔP be a change in the price of the good and ΔQ be the resulting change in its quantity demanded. If ΔP is very small, we can compute the **point elasticity of demand:**

$$\eta = \frac{\Delta Q}{Q} \div \frac{\Delta P}{P}. \tag{3.8}$$

For instance, consider Table 3.2, where data are given for very small increments in the price of a commodity. If we want to estimate the price elasticity of demand when the price is between $0.9995 and $1, we obtain

$$\eta = \frac{20{,}002 - 20{,}000}{20{,}000} \div \frac{99.95 - 100}{100} = -0.2.$$

Note that we used $1 as P and 20,000 as Q. We could have used $0.9995 as P and 20,002 as Q, but it would have made no real difference to the answer.

But if we have data concerning only large changes in price (that is, if ΔP and ΔQ are large), the answer may vary considerably depending on which value of P and Q is used in equation (3.8). Consider the example in Table 3.3. Suppose that we want to estimate the price elasticity of demand in the price range between $4 and $5. Then, depending on which value of P and Q is used, the answer will be

$$\eta = \frac{40 - 3}{3} \div \frac{4 - 5}{5} = -61.67$$

or

$$\eta = \frac{3 - 40}{40} \div \frac{5 - 4}{4} = -3.70.$$

TABLE 3.2

Quantity Demanded at Various Prices (Small Increments in Price)

Price (cents per unit of commodity)	Quantity demanded per unit of time (units of commodity)
99.95	20,002
100.00	20,000
100.05	19,998

TABLE 3.3

Quantity Demanded at Various Prices (Large Increments in Price)

Price (dollars per unit of commodity)	Quantity demanded per unit of time (units of commodity)
3	50
4	40
5	3

The difference between these two results is very large. To avoid this difficulty, it is advisable to compute the **arc elasticity of demand,** which uses the average value of P and Q:

$$\eta = \frac{\Delta Q}{(Q_1 + Q_2)/2} \div \frac{\Delta P}{(P_1 + P_2)/2}$$

$$\eta = \frac{\Delta Q(P_1 + P_2)}{\Delta P(Q_1 + Q_2)}, \qquad (3.9)$$

where P_1 and Q_1 are the first values of price and quantity demanded, and P_2 and Q_2 are the second set. Thus, in Table 3.3,

$$\eta = \frac{40 - 3}{(40 + 3)/2} \div \frac{4 - 5}{(4 + 5)/2} = -7.74.$$

Using the Demand Function to Calculate the Price Elasticity of Demand

As we saw in a previous section, estimates frequently are made of the demand function for particular products. In equation (3.2), we provided the following hypothetical demand function for personal computers:

$$Q = -700P + 200I - 500S + 0.01A.$$

Given such a demand function, how can you calculate the price elasticity of demand?

The first step is to specify the point on the demand curve at which this price elasticity is to be measured. Assuming that per capita disposable income (I) is $13,000, the average price of software (S) is $400, and advertising expenditure

CONCEPTS IN CONTEXT

Fur Demand in Russia

In the past, Russia has been an important exporter of furs like mink, fox, and sable; for example, in 1993, over $60 million worth of pelts was sent abroad. But in 1994, Russia exported only $30 million worth of pelts. "We were taken by surprise at first," said Andrei Nyukhalov, deputy director of Russia's largest fur farm. "We thought nobody was going to buy the fur. Then we realized they were buying it all in Russia."*

In 1995, the fur stores in Moscow were very busy. The high-priced furs were selling well, and the cheaper coats were difficult to keep in stock. Why? Because newly rich Russians, flaunting their new wealth and anxious to keep warm during the tough Russian winter (six months long), were purchasing fur in unprecedented amounts. "The market in Russia is simply exploding," said Jay Mechutan, a New York fur importer.[†]

Given the Russian climate, the substantial demand for fur is understandable. Two-thirds of the Russian land mass stays frozen from October to April. Also, the demand for fur is promoted by a shift from expensive to more moderate priced furs. Russian fur producers seem to be turning their attention from mink and sable to cheaper furs like lambskin, nutria, and some varieties of fox, all of which sell for less than $1,000 per coat.

*"Russia Answers Capitalism: Let the People Have Fur," *New York Times*, October 12, 1995, p. A6.
[†]Ibid., p. A1.

(A) is $50 million, we know from equation (3.4) that the relationship between quantity demanded and price is

$$Q = 2,900,000 - 700P. \tag{3.10}$$

Suppose that we want to measure the price elasticity of demand when price equals $3,000. At this point on the demand curve (point *A* in Figure 3.1),

$$Q = 2,900,000 - 700(3,000)$$
$$= 800,000.$$

Next, we must evaluate the partial derivative of *Q* with respect to *P*. Applying Chapter 2's rules for finding a derivative to equation (3.10), we find that the desired derivative equals

$$\frac{\partial Q}{\partial P} = -700.$$

According to equation (3.7), to obtain the price elasticity of demand, we must multiply $\partial Q/\partial P$ by P/Q. Performing this multiplication, we get

$$-700 \ \frac{3,000}{800,000} = -2.62,$$

which means that the price elasticity of demand equals -2.62.

As a further illustration, let's calculate the price elasticity of demand when price equals \$2,000 rather than \$3,000. At this point on the demand curve (point B in Figure 3.1),

$$Q = 2,900,000 - 700(2,000)$$
$$= 1,500,000.$$

Since $\partial Q/\partial P = -700$,

$$\eta = \left(\frac{\partial Q}{\partial P}\right)\left(\frac{P}{Q}\right) = (-700) \ \frac{2,000}{1,500,000} = -0.93.$$

Thus, the price elasticity of demand equals -0.93.

An important thing to note is that the price elasticity of demand can vary greatly from point to point on a particular demand curve. As we have just seen, on the demand curve in Figure 3.1, the price elasticity of demand is -2.625 at point A, but only -0.93 at point B. For any linear demand curve, the price elasticity of demand will vary from zero to negative infinity, as shown in Figure 3.6. If

$$P = a - bQ,$$

where a is the intercept of the demand curve on the price axis, and b is the slope (in absolute terms) of the demand curve, it follows that

$$Q = \frac{a}{b} - \frac{1}{b}P.$$

Thus, the price elasticity of demand is

$$\left(\frac{\partial Q}{\partial P}\right)\left(\frac{P}{Q}\right) = \frac{-1}{b} \ \frac{a - bQ}{Q}.$$

Clearly, if the demand curve is linear, the price elasticity approaches zero as P ($= a - bQ$) gets very small, and approaches negative infinity as Q gets very small.

FIGURE
3.6

Values of the Price Elasticity of Demand at Various Points along a Linear Demand Curve

The price elasticity increases as price rises, approaching negative infinity as quantity approaches zero.

Price Elasticity and Total Money Expenditure

Managers are interested in questions like: Will an increase in price result in an increase in the total amount spent by consumers on their product? Or will an increase in price result in a decrease in the total amount spent by consumers on their product? The answers depend on the price elasticity of demand, as we show in this section.

Suppose that the demand for the product is **price elastic;** that is, the price elasticity of demand is less than -1. The total amount of money spent by consumers on the product equals the quantity demanded times the price per unit. In this situation, if the price is reduced, the percentage increase in quantity demanded is greater than the percentage reduction in price (since this follows from the definition of the price elasticity of demand). It then follows that a price reduction must lead to an increase in the total amount spent by consumers on the commodity. Similarly, if the demand is price elastic, a price increase leads to a reduction in the amount of money spent on the commodity.

If the demand for the product is **price inelastic** (which means that the price elasticity of demand is greater than −1), a price decrease leads to a reduction in the total amount spent on the commodity, and a price increase leads to an increase in the amount spent on the commodity. If the demand is of **unitary elasticity** (which means that the price elasticity of demand equals −1), an increase or decrease in price has no effect on the amount spent on the commodity.

As an illustration, consider the case shown in Figure 3.7. The demand curve shown there is a rectangular hyperbola, which means that

$$Q = \frac{m}{P},$$ (3.11)

where Q is the quantity demanded of the good, P is its price, and m is some constant. This kind of demand curve is of unitary elasticity at all points. Thus, changes in price have no effect on the total amount spent on the product. It is evident from equation (3.11) that, regardless of the price, the total amount spent on the product will be m ($10 million in Figure 3.7).

FIGURE 3.7

Demand Curve with Unitary Elasticity at All Points

The demand curve is a rectangular hyperbola if the price elasticity of demand is always −1.

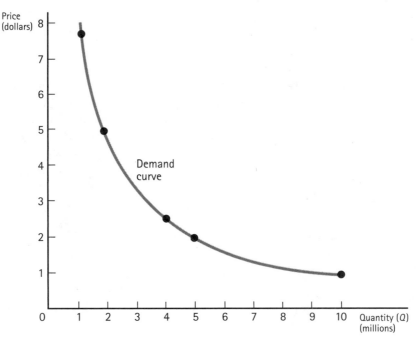

Total Revenue, Marginal Revenue, and Price Elasticity

To its producers, the total amount of money spent on a product equals their total revenue. Thus, to the Ford Motor Company, the total amount spent on its cars (and other products) is its total revenue. Suppose that the demand curve for a firm's product is linear; that is,

$$P = a - bQ, \tag{3.12}$$

where a is the intercept on the price axis, and b is the slope (in absolute terms), as shown in panel A of Figure 3.8. Thus, the firm's total revenue equals

$$
\begin{aligned}
TR &= PQ \\
&= (a - bQ)Q \\
&= aQ - bQ^2. \tag{3.13}
\end{aligned}
$$

An important concept is **marginal revenue,** which, as we know from Chapter 2, is defined as dTR/dQ. In subsequent chapters, we will use this concept repeatedly. In the present case,

$$
\begin{aligned}
MR &= \frac{dTR}{dQ} \\
&= \frac{d(aQ - bQ^2)}{dQ} \\
&= a - 2bQ, \tag{3.14}
\end{aligned}
$$

which is also shown in panel A of Figure 3.8. Comparing the marginal revenue curve with the demand curve, we see that both have the same intercept on the vertical axis (this intercept being a), but that the marginal revenue curve has a slope that (in absolute terms) is twice that of the demand curve.

According to the definition in equation (3.7), the price elasticity of demand, η, equals $(\partial Q/\partial P)(P/Q)$. Thus, since $\partial Q/\partial P = -1/b$ and $P = a - bQ$, it follows that in this case,

$$\eta = \frac{-1}{b} \frac{a - bQ}{Q}. \tag{3.15}$$

Thus, whether η is greater than, equal to, or less than -1 depends on whether Q is greater than, equal to, or less than $a/2b$. As shown in Figure 3.8, demand is price elastic if $Q < a/2b$; it is of unitary elasticity if $Q = a/2b$; and it is price inelastic if $Q > a/2b$.

FIGURE
3.8

Relationship between Price Elasticity, Marginal Revenue, and Total Revenue

If demand is price elastic, marginal revenue is positive, and increases in quantity result in higher total revenue. If demand is price inelastic, marginal revenue is negative, and increases in quantity result in lower total revenue.

ANALYZING MANAGERIAL DECISIONS

The Demand for Newsprint

In early 1995, there was a sharp increase in the price of newsprint, the paper used by newspapers. Since newsprint is the second-largest expense for U.S. newspapers (after salaries), publishers were concerned about the price hike. Suppose that the demand for newsprint can be represented as

$$Q_1 = 17.3 = 0.0092P + 0.0067I,$$

where Q_1 equals the quantity demanded (in kilograms per capita), P is the price of newsprint (in dollars per metric ton), and I is income per capita (in dollars).

(a) If there are 1 million people in the market, and if per capita income equals \$10,000, what is the demand curve for newsprint? (b) Under these circumstances, what is the price elasticity of demand if the price of newsprint equals \$400 per metric ton? (c) According to a 1984 study,* the demand curve for newsprint in the northeastern United States is

$$Q_2 = 2,672 - 0.51P,$$

where Q_2 is the number of metric tons of newsprint demanded (in thousands). What is the price elasticity of demand for newsprint in the northeastern United States if price equals \$500 per metric ton? (d) On the basis of this study, will the 1995

price increase result in an increase or decrease in the amount spent on newsprint in the northeastern United States? Why?

SOLUTION (a) Since there are 1 million people in the market, and since Q_1 equals per capita quantity demanded, the quantity demanded equals 1 million times Q_1. Letting Q_1' be the quantity demanded (in millions of kilograms),

$$Q_1' = 17.3 - 0.0092P$$
$$+ 0.0067(10,000)$$
$$= 84.3 - 0.0092P.$$

(b) Since $dQ_1'/dP = -0.0092$, the price elasticity of demand equals $-0.0092 \, P/Q_1'$. Because $P = 400$ and $I = 10,000$, Q_1' must equal $17.3 -0.0092(400) + 0.0067(10,000) = 80.62$ million kilograms. Thus, the price elasticity of demand equals $-0.0092(400/80.62) = -0.0456$. (c) Since $dQ_2/dP = -0.51$, and since $P = 500$, the price elasticity of demand equals $-0.51(500)/[2,672 - 0.51(500)] = -0.1055$. (d) It will result in an increase in the amount spent on newsprint because the demand for newsprint is price inelastic.

* F. Guder and J. Buongiorno, "An Interregional Analysis of the North American Newsprint Industry," *Interfaces*, September–October 1984, pp. 85–95.

Panel B in Figure 3.8 plots the firm's total revenue against the quantity demanded of its product. As would be expected, at quantities where marginal revenue is positive, increases in quantity result in higher total revenue; at quantities where marginal revenue is negative, increases in quantity result in lower total revenue. Why would this be expected? Because, as pointed out above, marginal revenue is the derivative of total revenue with respect to quantity. Thus, if marginal revenue is positive (negative), increases in quantity must increase (decrease) total revenue.

Another thing to note about Figure 3.8 is that at quantities where demand is price elastic, marginal revenue is positive; at quantities where it is of unitary elasticity, marginal revenue is zero; and at quantities where it is price inelastic, marginal revenue is negative. This is no accident. In general, whether or not the demand curve is linear, this will be the case. To see why, recall that by definition,

$$MR = \frac{dTR}{dQ}.$$

Since total revenue equals price times quantity, it follows that

$$MR = \frac{d(PQ)}{dQ}.$$

Using the rule for differentiating a product (given in Chapter 2),

$$MR = P\frac{dQ}{dQ} + Q\frac{dP}{dQ}.$$

Because $dQ/dQ = 1$,

$$MR = P + Q\frac{dP}{dQ}$$
$$= P\left[1 + \left(\frac{Q}{P}\right)\left(\frac{dP}{dQ}\right)\right].$$

And since the definition of the price elasticity of demand implies that $(Q/P)(dP/dQ) = 1/\eta$,

$$MR = P\left(1 + \frac{1}{\eta}\right). \tag{3.16}$$

Equation (3.16) is a famous result, which shows that if $\eta < -1$, marginal revenue must be positive; if $\eta > -1$, marginal revenue must be negative; and if $\eta = -1$, marginal revenue must be zero. (This is what we set out to prove.) In later chapters, we will use equation (3.16) repeatedly. You should study it carefully, and understand it. To illustrate its meaning, what is the value of marginal revenue if price is $10 and the price elasticity of demand is -2? On the basis of equation (3.16), it equals $10(1 - 1/2) = \$5$.

Using Price Elasticity of Demand: Application to Phillip Morris

In 1993, Phillip Morris cut cigarette prices by 18 percent. Its major competitor (R. J. Reynolds) matched the price cut. Not surprisingly, the quantity sold of Phillip Morris' cigarettes increased (by 12.5 percent). In a June 13, 1994 article referring to the perils of a price cut, *Fortune* reported that Phillip Morris' profits fell by 25 percent—the result of a bad pricing strategy.

While all the information is not available, you shouldn't be surprised by the qualitative fall in profits. A rough estimate of the price elasticity of demand for Phillip Morris' cigarettes ($\%\Delta Q/\%\Delta P$) is 12.5%/-18% = -0.694, or inelastic. As was just demonstrated, cutting price when demand is inelastic will decrease total revenues. Since output increased (by 12.5%), total cost increased. Since profits are total revenue less total cost, and total revenue decreased and total cost increased, profits had to fall.

Using Price Elasticity of Demand: Public Transit

Consider another example where your knowledge of elasticity and its properties will give you a qualitative answer (and with more information, you would have the quantitative answer). The fare (price) elasticity for public transportation service in the United States is about -0.3 (that is, fairly inelastic). All transit systems in the United States lose money. Keeping the deficit under control is a constant battle because typical subsidizers (federal, state, and local governments) are reluctant to fund transit (because of their own deficit problems) in many jurisdictions. Can you guess which transit systems they are?

They tend to be the ones with the high transit fares. Here's where your knowledge of elasticity comes in. How is the general manager of the transit system going to raise the needed revenues? With an inelastic demand, raising fares increases revenues. Raising fares decreased ridership, hence decreasing total cost. Therefore, the bottom line of the transit agency improves as total revenue increases and total cost decreases.

Determinants of the Price Elasticity of Demand

Table 3.4 shows the price elasticity of demand for selected products in the United States. What determines whether the demand for a product is price elastic or price inelastic? Why does the price elasticity of demand for fresh apple products in the United States equal -1.159 while the short-run price elasticity of demand for gasoline in Canada lies between -0.01 and -0.2?

TABLE
3.4

Own Price Elasticities of Demand, Selected Goods, and Services from Global Locations

Good/Service	Elasticity
Agricultural products	
Apples (US)[1]	−1.159
Potatoes (UK)[3]	−0.13
Oranges (US)[2]	−0.62
Lettuce (US)[2]	−2.58
Products from animals/fish	
1 percent milk (US)[5]	−0.54 to −0.74
Cheese (UK)[3]	−1.36
Cheese (US)[6]	−0.595
Meat (China)[4]	−0.06 to −0.18
Beef/veal (UK)[3]	−1.45
Manufactured agricultural products	
Beer and malt beverages (US)[6]	−2.83
Wine (UK/Ireland)[7]	−1.12
Wine and brandy (US)[6]	−0.198
Cigarettes (US)[7]	−0.107
Bread (UK)[3]	−0.26
Energy	
Gasoline—Short run (Canada)[8]	−0.01 to −0.2
Gasoline—Long run (Canada)[8]	−0.4 to −0.8
Transportation	
Domestic cars (US)[12]	−0.78
European cars (US)[12]	−1.09

(*Continued*)

1. The price elasticity of demand for a product depends heavily on the number and closeness of the substitutes that are available. If a product has lots of close substitutes, its demand is likely to be price elastic. If the product's price is increased, a large proportion of its buyers will turn to the close substitutes that are available; if its price is reduced, a great many buyers of substitutes will switch to this product. The extent to which a product has close substitutes depends on how narrowly it is defined. As the definition of the product becomes narrower and more specific, the product would be expected to have more close substitutes, and its demand would be expected to become more price elastic. Hence, the demand for a particular brand of gasoline is likely to be more price elastic than the overall demand for gasoline, and the demand for gasoline is likely to be more price elastic than the demand for all fuels taken as a whole.

TABLE
3.4

Own Price Elasticities of Demand, Selected Goods, and Services from Global Locations (Continued)

Good/Service	Elasticity
Other manufactured goods	
Clothing and footwear (UK/Ireland)[8]	−0.94
Other goods (UK/Ireland)[8]	−0.85
Services	
Childcare (North America)[11]	−0.570
Government healthcare (Kenya)[12]	−0.100

[1]Clyde Elmore, Chapter 10, "Use of 2.4-D in Orchard, Vineyard, and Soft Fruit Production in the United States," Phenoxy Herbicides, December 20, 1998, found at *http://piked.agn.uiuc.edu/piap/assess2/ch10.htm.*

[2]Daniel Suits, "Agriculture," in *The Structure of American Industry,* Tenth edition, Walter Adams and James Brock, eds. (Englewood Cliffs, NJ: Prentice-Hall, 2000).

[3]AEF116: 1.6: Major market response concepts and measures 1: The demand side and its elasticities found at *http://www.staff.ncl.ac.uk/davidharvey/AEF116/1.6/1.6/html.*

[4]Millennium Institute, China Agricultural Project found at *http://www.threshold21.com/chinaag/report/appendix.html.*

[5]A Regional Economic Analysis of Dairy Compacts: Implications for Missouri Dairy Producers, Section IV—Economic Analysis of Dairy Compact, circa 1999, found at *http://agebb.missouri.edu/commag/dairy/bailey/compact/sect4.htm.*

[6]Emilo Pagoulatos and Robert Sorensen, "What Determines the Elasticity of Industry Demand," *International Journal of Industrial Organization,* Vol. 4, 1986.

[7]Cathal O'Donoghue, "Carbon Dioxide, Energy Taxes, and Household Income," Department of Statistics and Social Policy, London School of Economics, October 13, 1998.

[8]"Potential for Fuel Taxes to Reduce Greenhouse Gas Emissions in Transportation," Hagler Bailly Canada for Department of Public Works and Government Services, Hull, Quebec, June 11, 1990 found at *http://www.tc.gc.ca/envaffairs/sub . . . udy1/Final_report/Final_Report. html.*

[9]Patrick McCarthy, "Market Price and Income Elasticities of New Vehicle Demands," *Review of Economics and Statistics,* Vol. 78(3), August 1996, 543–547.

[10]Eric Brynjolfsson, "Some Estimates of the Contribution of Information Technology to Consumer Welfare," MIT Sloan School, Working Paper 3647-094, January 1994.

[11]Duncan Chaplin et al., "The Price Elasticity of Child Care Demand: A Sensitivity Analysis," found at *http://www.cpc.unc.edu/pubs/ppp_papers/1997/chaplin.html.*

[12]Section 4: The Basics of Markets and Health Care Markets: Box 4.4: Demand for Health Care in Kenya found at *http://www.worldbank.org/wbi/healthflagship/learning/module1/box4_4.htm.*

2. The price elasticity of demand for a product may depend on the importance of the product in consumers' budgets. It is sometimes claimed that the demand for products like thimbles, rubber bands, and salt may be quite inelastic, since the typical consumer spends only a very small fraction of his or her income on such goods. In contrast, for products that bulk larger in the typical consumer's budget, like major appliances, the elasticity of demand may tend to be higher, since consumers may be more conscious of, and influenced by,

TABLE 3.5

Elasticities of Demand for Air Tickets between the United States and Europe

Type of ticket	Price elasticity	Income elasticity
First class	−0.45	1.50
Regular economy	−1.30	1.38
Excursion	−1.83	2.37

Source: J. Cigliano, "Price and Income Elasticities for Airline Travel: The North Atlantic Market," *Business Economics,* September 1980.

price changes in the case of goods that require larger outlays. However, although a tendency of this sort is sometimes hypothesized, there is no guarantee that you can count on its being true.

3. The price elasticity of demand for a product is likely to depend on the length of the period to which the demand curve pertains. (As pointed out above, every market demand curve pertains to a certain time interval.) Demand is likely to be more elastic, or less inelastic, over a long period of time than over a short period of time because the longer the period of time, the easier it is for consumers and firms to substitute one good for another. If, for instance, the price of oil should decline relative to other fuels, the consumption of oil in the day after the price decline would probably increase very little. But over a period of several years, people would have an opportunity to take account of the price decline in choosing the type of fuel to be used in new houses and renovated old houses. In the longer period of several years, the price decline would have a greater effect on the consumption of oil than in the shorter period of one day.[2]

Uses of the Price Elasticity of Demand

Managers display an avid interest, and for good reason, in the price elasticity of demand for their products. Consider Table 3.5, which provides estimates of the price elasticity of demand for first-class, regular economy, and excursion air tickets between the United States and Europe. The price elasticity of demand for first-class air tickets is much lower in absolute value than for regular econ-

[2]However, for durable goods like automobiles, the price elasticity of demand may be greater in absolute value in the short run than in the long run. If the price of automobiles goes up, the quantity demanded is likely to fall sharply because many consumers will put off buying a new car. But as time goes on and old cars wear out, the quantity of automobiles demanded will tend to increase.

omy or excursion tickets, owing in part to the fact that the people who fly first class—often business travelers and relatively wealthy people—are unlikely to change their travel plans if moderate increases or decreases occur in the price of an air ticket. Airline executives have studied these data carefully, with an eye toward the pricing of various kinds of tickets. Because the price elasticity of demand for first-class air tickets is relatively low in absolute value, they have nudged up the prices for such tickets.

It is important to recognize that no manager interested in maximizing profit will set price at a point where the demand for his or her product is price inelastic. To see why this is a mistake, recall from equation (3.16) that marginal revenue must be negative if demand is price inelastic (that is, if $\eta > -1$). If marginal revenue is negative, a firm can increase its profit by raising its price and lowering its output. Why? Because its total revenue will increase if it sells less. (This, after all, is what it means to say that marginal revenue is negative.) Since the firm's total cost will not rise if less is sold, its profits will go up if it sells less.

Market researchers are continually engaged in studies to estimate the price elasticity of demand for particular products. The results enable firms to answer questions like: How much of an increase in sales can we expect if we reduce our price by 5 percent? To increase the amount we sell by 10 percent, how much must we reduce price? These are fundamental questions of the sort that firms confront repeatedly.

For example, take the soft drink industry. The price elasticity of demand for Royal Crown Cola has been estimated to be about −2.4, which means that the amount sold is very sensitive to price. A 1 percent reduction in the price of Royal Crown Cola (holding the prices of its competitors constant) results in a 2.4 percent increase in the quantity sold. Coke is even more price elastic, the price elasticity being about −5.5. Thus, a 1 percent reduction in the price of Coke (holding the prices of its competitors constant) results in a 5.5 percent increase in the quantity sold.[3] Clearly, the managers of Royal Crown and Coke need this information to function effectively, and they and their opposite numbers in firms across the country spend plenty to obtain such information.

Price Elasticity and Pricing Policy

To see more specifically how managers use information concerning the price elasticity of demand for their products, let's consider in more detail the important topic of pricing. According to equation (3.16),

$$MR = P\left(1 + \frac{1}{\eta}\right).$$

[3] J. Nevin, "Laboratory Experiments for Estimating Consumer Demand," *Journal of Marketing Research*, August 1974.

From Chapter 2, we know that marginal revenue equals marginal cost if a firm is maximizing profit, which means that

$$MC = P\left(1 + \frac{1}{\eta}\right), \tag{3.17}$$

where MC equals marginal cost. (To obtain equation (3.17), we substitute MC for MR on the left-hand side of equation (3.16).) Solving equation (3.17) for P, we obtain

$$P = MC\left(\frac{1}{1 + 1/\eta}\right). \tag{3.18}$$

While equation (3.18) looks rather innocuous, it is in fact a very powerful and useful result. What it says is that the optimal price of a product depends on its marginal cost and its price elasticity of demand. Suppose that the marginal cost of a particular type of shirt is $10 and that its price elasticity of demand equals -2. According to equation (3.18), its optimal price is

$$P = 10\left(\frac{1}{1 - 1/2}\right)$$
$$= \$20.$$

For present purposes, the central point to note is that the optimal price depends heavily on the price elasticity of demand. Holding constant the value of marginal cost, a product's optimal price is inversely related to its price elasticity of demand. Thus, if the shirt's price elasticity of demand were -5 rather than -2, its optimal price would be

$$P = 10\left(\frac{1}{1 - 1/5}\right)$$
$$= \$12^{1}/_{2}.$$

Given the importance of the price elasticity of demand in determining the optimal price of a product, it is not hard to see why managers are so intent on obtaining at least rough estimates of its value. (In Chapters 10 to 13, we will say much more about optimal pricing policies.)

The Income Elasticity of Demand

As was stressed in previous sections, price is not the only factor that influences the quantity demanded of a product. Another important factor is the level of money income among the consumers in the market. If shoppers have plenty of money to spend, the quantity demanded of men's suits is likely to be greater than it would be if they were poverty-stricken. Or if incomes in a particular city are high, the quantity demanded of cognac is likely to be greater than it would be if incomes were low.

The **income elasticity of demand** for a particular good is defined to be *the percentage change in quantity demanded resulting from a 1 percent change in consumers' income.* More precisely, it equals

$$\eta_I = \left(\frac{\partial Q}{\partial I}\right)\left(\frac{I}{Q}\right),$$
(3.19)

where Q is quantity demanded, and I is consumers' income. For some products, the income elasticity of demand is positive, indicating that increases in consumers' money income result in increases in the amount of the good consumed. For example, one would generally expect luxury items like gourmet foods to have positive income elasticities. Other goods have negative income elasticities, indicating that increases in money income result in decreases in the amount of the good consumed. For example, inferior grades of vegetables and clothing might have negative income elasticities. In calculating the income elasticity of demand, it is assumed that the prices of all commodities are held constant.

Whether the income elasticity of demand for a firm's product is high or low can have a great impact on the firm's opportunities and problems. Firms making products with high income elasticities are likely to grow relatively rapidly as incomes rise in an expanding economy, whereas firms making products with low income elasticities are likely to experience more modest expansion. On the other hand, if the economy is jolted by a serious depression and incomes fall sharply, firms making products with low income elasticities are likely to experience less of a decrease in output than those making products with high income elasticities.

In forecasting the long-term growth of the quantity demanded for many major products, the income elasticity of demand is of key importance. According to studies done by the United States Department of Agriculture, the income elasticity of demand for milk has been about 0.5, which means that a 1 percent increase in disposable income is associated with about a 0.5 percent increase in the quantity demanded of milk. But, in a study done in Britain, the income elasticity of bread has been about -0.17, which means that a 1 percent increase in disposable income is associated with about a -0.17 percent decrease in the quantity demanded of bread. Table 3.5 indicates that the income elasticity of demand for first class air tickets between the United States and Europe is 1.50, which means that a 1 percent increase in disposable income is associated with a 1.50 percent increase in the quantity demanded of such tickets. Table 3.6 shows the income elasticity of demand for other commodities from across the world. In measuring income elasticities, income can be defined as the aggregate income of consumers (as in Table 3.6) or as per capita income (as in the next section), depending on the circumstances.

TABLE 3.6

Income Elasticity of Demand, Selected Commodities, Global

Good	Elasticity
Agricultural products	
Grain (China)[1]	−0.12 to +0.15
Potatoes (UK)[2]	−0.32
Potatoes (US)[3]	+0.15
Oranges (US)[3]	+0.83
Apples (US)[3]	+1.32
Lettuce (US)[3]	+0.88
Animal products	
Meat (China)[1]	+0.1 to +1.2
Milk (UK)[2]	+0.05
Milk (US)[3]	+0.50
Cream (US)[3]	+1.72
Eggs (UK)[2]	−0.21
Eggs (US)[3]	+0.57
Processed food products	
Break (UK)[2]	−0.17
Other cereal products (UK)[2]	+0.18
Automobiles	
Domestic cars (US)[4]	+1.62
European cars (US)[4]	+1.93
Asian cars (US)[4]	+1.65

[1]Millennium Institute, China Agricultural Project found at *http://www.threshold21.com/chinaag/report/appendix.html*.

[2]AEF116: 1.6: Major market response concepts and measures 1: The Demand side and its elasticities found at *http://www.staff.ncl.ac.uk/david.harvey/AEF116/1.6/1.6.html*

[3]Daniel Suits, "Agriculture" in *The Structure of American Industry*, Tenth edition, Walter Adams and James Brock, eds. Englewood Cliffs, NJ: Prentice-Hall, 2000).

[4]Patrick McCarthy, "Market Price and Income Elasticities of New Vehicle Demands," *Review of Economics and Statistics*, Vol. 78(3), August 1996, 543–547.

Using the Demand Function to Calculate the Income Elasticity of Demand

In a previous section, we learned how to calculate the price elasticity of demand, based on a product's demand function. Here we see how the income elasticity of demand can be calculated. Suppose that the demand function for good X is

$$Q = 1,000 - 0.2P_X + 0.5P_Y + 0.04I,$$

where Q is the quantity demanded of good X, P_X is the price of good X, P_Y is the price of good Y, and I is per capita disposable income. The income elasticity of demand is

$$\eta_I = \left(\frac{\partial Q}{\partial I}\right)\left(\frac{I}{Q}\right)$$

$$= 0.04 \, \frac{I}{Q}.$$

If $I = 10,000$ and $Q = 1,600$,

$$\eta_I = 0.04 \left(\frac{10,000}{1,600}\right) = 0.25.$$

Thus, the income elasticity of demand equals 0.25, which means that a 1 percent increase in per capita disposable income is associated with a 0.25 percent increase in the quantity demanded of good X.

Cross Elasticities of Demand

Besides price and income, still another factor influencing the quantity demanded of a product is the price of other commodities. Holding constant the product's own price (as well as the level of money incomes) and allowing the price of another product to vary may result in important effects on the quantity demanded of the product in question. By observing these effects, we can classify pairs of commodities as **substitutes or complements,** and we can measure how close the relationship (either substitute or complementary) is. Consider two commodities, good X and good Y. If good Y's price goes up, what is the effect on Q_X, the quantity of good X that is demanded? The **cross elasticity of demand** is defined as *the percentage change in the quantity demanded of good X resulting from a 1 percent change in the price of good Y.* Expressed in terms of derivatives,

$$\eta_{XY} = \left(\frac{\partial Q_X}{\partial P_Y}\right)\left(\frac{P_Y}{Q_X}\right). \tag{3.20}$$

Goods X and Y are classified as substitutes if the cross elasticity of demand is positive. For instance, an increase in the price of wheat, when the price of corn remains constant, will tend to increase the quantity of corn demanded; thus, η_{XY} is positive, and wheat and corn are classified as substitutes. On the other hand, if the cross elasticity of demand is negative, goods X and Y are classified as complements. Thus, an increase in the price of software may tend to decrease the purchase of personal computers when the price of personal computers remains constant; thus, η_{XY} is negative, and software and personal computers are classified as complements.

CONSULTANT'S CORNER

Estimating the Demand for Rail Passenger Business by Amtrak

Amtrak (the national passenger railroad in the United States) has used its aggregate demand model to obtain its forecasts of system-wide passenger revenues. The first part of its model was a multivariate, linear regression that forecasts its system-wide passenger miles—the dependent variable (a passenger mile is one passenger moved one mile). Explanatory variables are: disposable personal income; Amtrak's average fare; the ratio of Amtrak's average fare to the airlines' average fare; retail gasoline price; dummy variables to reflect such events as weather, holidays, strikes, derailments, etc.; and dummy variables to reflect seasonal variation.

The most important determinant of rail passenger miles was disposable personal income (a proxy variable for the strength of the U.S. economy). From the regression, a 1 percent increase in disposable personal income was expected to yield a 1.8 percent increase in system-wide passenger miles.

(a) Explain the rationale for each of the explanatory variables appearing in the model and what signs (positive or negative) you expect for their regression coefficients. (b) How did Amtrak use this forecast of system-wide passenger miles to obtain their estimate of system-wide passenger revenues? (c) What is Amtrak's estimate of income elasticity of demand for passenger service (based on income level of the economy as a whole)? If U.S. disposable personal income per capita increased from $24,000 to $25,000, what's your prediction for the increase in train passenger miles in the new situation (all other independent variables remaining constant)? Will this prediction be 100 percent accurate? Why or why not? (d) Despite the fact that disposable personal income has been rising throughout the 1990s, Amtrak's market share of intercity passenger miles has been decreasing. Can you explain this?

To illustrate the calculation of cross elasticities, suppose once again that the demand function for good X is

$$Q_X = 1,000 - 0.2P_X + 0.5P_Y + 0.04I,$$

where Q_X is the quantity demanded of good X, P_X is the price of good X, P_Y is the price of good Y, and I is per capita disposable income. The cross elasticity of demand between goods X and Y is

$$\eta_{XY} = \left(\frac{\partial Q_X}{\partial P_Y}\right)\left(\frac{P_Y}{Q_X}\right)$$

$$= 0.5 \frac{P_Y}{Q_X}$$

Although the value of the cross elasticity will depend on the values of P_Y and Q_X, the goods will always be substitutes, since η_{XY} must be positive, regardless of the values of P_Y and Q_X. If $P_Y = 500$ and $Q_X = 2,000$,

$$\eta_{XY} = 0.5\left(\frac{500}{2,000}\right) = 0.125.$$

The cross elasticity of demand is of fundamental importance to firms because they continually must do their best to anticipate what will happen to their own sales if their rivals change *their* prices. To do so, they need information concerning the cross elasticities of demand. Table 3.7 shows the cross elastici-

TABLE
3.7

Cross Elasticity of Demand, Selected Pairs of Commodities, Global

Change of price of good	Change of quantity of good	Cross price elasticity
European/Asian cars	US domestic cars	+0.28[1]
European/US domestic cars	Asian cars	+0.61[1]
US domestic/Asian cars	European cars	+0.76[1]
Australian public transit	Australian auto ownership	+0.1 to +0.3[2]
Irish coal	Irish natural gas	+0.4[3]
Irish coal	Irish oil	+0.7[3]
Kenyan government Provided healthcare	Mission or private sector Provided healthcare in Kenya	+0.023[4]
US durum wheat	US hard red spring wheat	+0.04[5]
US hard red winter wheat	US white wheat	+1.80[5]
UK beef/veal	UK pork	0.00[6]
UK mutton/lamb	UK beef/veal	+0.25[6]

[1]Patrick McCarthy, "Market Price and Income Elasticities of New Vehicle Demand," *Review of Economics and Statistics,* Vol. 78 (3), August 1996, 543–547.

[2]J. Luk and S. Hepburn, "A Review of Australian Travel Demand Elasticities," Working Document No.: TE 93/004, 1993, Australian Road Research Board.

[3]Competition Authority Decision of 30 January 1998, relating to a proceeding under Section 4 of the Competition Act 1991: Notification No. CA/15/97—Statoil Ireland Ltd./Clare Oil Company Ltd.—Share Purchase Agreement and Service Employment Agreement. Decision No. 490 found at *http://www.irlgov.ie/compauth/dec490.htm.*

[4]Section 4: The Basics of Markets and Health Care Markets: Box 4.4: Demand for Health Care in Kenya found at *http://www.worldbank.org/wbi/heathflagship/learning/module1/box4_4.htm.*

[5]Wheat Yearbook, March 30, 1998, Economic Research Services, United States Department of Agriculture, Washington, DC 20036-5831.

[6]AEF116: 1.6: Major market response concepts and measures 1: The demand side and its elasticities found at *http://www.staff.ncl.ac.uk/david.harvey/AEF116/1.6/1.6.html.*

ties of demand for selected pairs of commodities. In Chapter 5, we will take up some of the statistical techniques used to estimate them.

The Advertising Elasticity of Demand

Although the price elasticity, income elasticity, and cross elasticities of demand are the most frequently used elasticity measures, they are not the only ones. For example, firms sometimes find it useful to calculate the **advertising elasticity of demand.** Suppose that the demand function for a particular firm's product is

$$Q = 500 - 0.5P + 0.01I + 0.82A,$$

where Q is the quantity demanded of the product, P is its price, I is per capita disposable income, and A is the firm's advertising expenditure. The advertising elasticity is defined as *the percentage change in the quantity demanded of the product resulting from a 1 percent change in advertising expenditure.* More precisely, it equals

$$\eta_A = \left(\frac{\partial Q}{\partial A}\right)\left(\frac{A}{Q}\right). \tag{3.21}$$

Thus, in this case, since $\partial Q / \partial A = 0.82$,

$$\eta_A = 0.82 \, \frac{A}{Q}.$$

If A/Q—the amount of advertising per unit of the product demanded—is $2,

$$\eta_A = 0.82(2) = 1.64.$$

This elasticity is useful because it tells the firm's managers that a 1 percent increase in advertising expenditure results in a 1.64 percent increase in the quantity demanded. In later chapters, we shall see how information of this sort can be used to help guide major managerial decisions.

The Constant-Elasticity Demand Function

In previous sections of this chapter, we generally have assumed that the demand function is linear. That is, the quantity demanded of a product has been assumed to be a linear function of its price, the prices of other goods, consumer income, and other variables. Another mathematical form that is frequently used is the **constant-elasticity demand function.** If the quantity demanded (Q) depends only on the product's price (P) and consumer income (I), this mathematical form is

$$Q = aP^{-b_1}I^{b_2}. \tag{3.22}$$

Thus, if $a = 200$, $b_1 = 0.3$, and $b_2 = 2$,

$$Q = 200P^{-0.3}I^2.$$

An important property of this demand function is that the price elasticity of demand equals $-b_1$, regardless of the value of P or I. (This accounts for its being called the constant-elasticity demand function.) To see this, let's differentiate Q with respect to price:

$$\frac{\partial Q}{\partial P} = -b_1 aP^{-b_1-1}I^{b_2}$$

$$= \frac{-b_1}{P} aP^{-b_1}I^{b_2}$$

$$= \frac{-b_1}{P} Q.$$

Thus,

$$\left(\frac{P}{Q}\right)\left(\frac{\partial Q}{\partial P}\right) = -b_1 \tag{3.23}$$

Since the left-hand side of equation (3.23) is defined to be the price elasticity of demand, it follows that the price elasticity of demand equals $-b_1$, a constant whose value does not depend on P or I.

Similarly, the income elasticity of demand equals b_2, regardless of the value of P or I. To prove this, differentiate Q with respect to income:

$$\frac{\partial Q}{\partial I} = b_2 aP^{-b_1}I^{b_2-1}$$

$$= \frac{b_2}{I} aP^{-b_1}I^{b_2}$$

$$= \frac{b_2}{I} Q.$$

Thus,

$$\left(\frac{\partial Q}{\partial I}\right)\left(\frac{I}{Q}\right) = b_2. \tag{3.24}$$

ANALYZING MANAGERIAL DECISIONS

Price Cutting at the *London Times*

The *London Times*, owned by Rupert Murdoch, is one of the leading newspapers in the world. In September 1993, the *London Times* lowered its price from 45 pence to 30 pence, while the prices of its rivals remained unchanged. The numbers of newspapers sold by the *London Times* and its rivals in August 1993 and May 1994 were as follows:

	August 1993	May 1994
London Times	355,000	518,000
Daily Telegraph	1,024,000	993,000
Independent	325,000	277,000
Guardian	392,000	402,000

(a) Based on these figures, what was the price elasticity of demand for the *London Times*? (b) Was the cross electricity of demand between the *Daily Telegraph* and the *London Times* positive or negative? Would you expect it to be positive or negative? Why? (c) Did this price reduction increase or decrease the *London Times*'s total revenue from newspaper sales? (d) On the basis of newspaper sales alone, was this price reduction profitable? (e) Peter Stothard, editor of the *London Times*, pointed out that "the increase in circulation . . . made the paper a more attractive vehicle for advertisers."* If so, could this price reduction be profitable?

SOLUTION (a) Based on these figures, the arc elasticity was

$$\eta = \frac{518,000 - 355,000}{(355,000 + 518,000)/2} \div \frac{30 - 45}{(45 + 30)/2} = -0.9336$$

This assumes that the demand curve did not shift between August 1993 and May 1994. (b) Positive, since a cut in the price of the *London Times* reduced the quantity sold of the *Daily Telegraph*. It would be expected to be positive since the *London Times* and the *Daily Telegraph* are substitutes. (c) Total revenue from newspaper sales fell from 355,000 × 45 pence = 15,975,000 pence to 518,000 × 30 pence = 15,540,000 pence. This is to be expected since price was cut when demand was inelastic. (d) No. Since total revenue fell and total cost did not fall (because the output of papers increased), profits went down. (e) If the increase in advertising revenue due to the newspaper's higher circulation were large enough, it could offset the decline in profit from newspaper sales. Only time will tell whether this occurs.[†]

New York Times, June 13, 1994, p. D7.
[†]For further discussion, see ibid.

Since the left-hand side of equation (3.24) is defined to be the income elasticity of demand, it follows that the income elasticity of demand equals b_2, another constant whose value does not depend on P or I.

The constant-elasticity demand function is often used by managers and managerial economists, for several reasons. First, in contrast to the linear demand function, this mathematical form recognizes that the effect of price on quantity depends on the level of income, and that the effect of income on quantity depends on the level of price. The multiplicative relationship in equation (3.22) is often more realistic than the additive relationship in equation (3.1). Second, like the linear demand function, the constant-elasticity demand function is relatively easy to estimate. If we take logarithms of both sides of equation (3.22),[4]

$$\log Q = \log a - b_1 \log P + b_2 \log I. \qquad (3.25)$$

Since this equation is linear in the logarithms, the parameters—a, b_1, and b_2—can readily be estimated by regression analysis. In Chapter 5, we will learn how such estimates can be made.

Summary

1. The market demand curve for a product shows how much of the product will be demanded at each price. The market demand curve shifts in response to changes in tastes, incomes, the prices of other products, and the size of the population.

2. The market demand function for a product is an equation showing how the quantity demanded depends on the product's price, the incomes of consumers, the prices of other products, advertising expenditure, and additional factors. Holding all factors other than the product's price constant, one can derive the market demand curve for the product from the market demand function. Market demand functions can be formulated for individual firms as well as for entire industries.

3. The price elasticity of demand is the percentage change in quantity demanded resulting from a 1 percent change in price; more precisely, it equals $(\partial Q/\partial P)(P/Q)$. Whether a price increase (or decrease) results in an increase in the total amount spent by consumers on a product depends on the price elasticity of demand.

4. Marginal revenue is the change in total revenue resulting from a 1-unit increase in quantity; that is, it equals the derivative of total revenue with respect to quantity. Marginal revenue equals $P(1 + 1/\eta)$, where P is price and η is the price elasticity of demand.

5. The price elasticity of demand for a product tends to be elastic if the product has a large number of close substitutes. Also, it often tends to be more elastic in the long run than in the short run. It is sometimes asserted that

---

[4]A review of some basic points regarding logarithms may be of use. To begin with, X equals the logarithm of Y (that is, $\log Y$) if $10^X = Y$. Thus, the logarithm of the product of two variables (say Y_1 and Y_2) equals the sum of the logarithms of these variables; that is, $\log (Y_1 Y_2) = \log Y_1 + \log Y_2$. Also, the logarithm of Y^C equals $C \log Y$.

the demand for a product is relatively price inelastic if the product accounts for a very small percentage of the typical consumer's budget, but this need not be the case.

6. The optimal price for a product depends on its price elasticity of demand, as well as on its marginal cost. To maximize profit, a firm should set its price equal to $MC[1/(1 + 1/\eta)]$, where MC is marginal cost, and η is the price elasticity of demand.

7. The income elasticity of demand is the percentage change in quantity demanded resulting from a 1 percent increase in consumer income; that is, it equals $(\partial Q/\partial I)(I/Q)$, where I is the income of consumers. The income elasticity of demand may be positive or negative. Like the price elasticity of demand, it is of major importance in forecasting the long-term growth of the quantity demanded for many major products.

8. The cross elasticity of demand is the percentage change in the quantity demanded of product X resulting from a 1 percent increase in the price of product Y; in other words, it equals $(\partial Q_X/\partial P_Y)(P_Y/Q_X)$. If X and Y are substitutes, it is positive; if they are complements, it is negative. This elasticity is important for managers, because they must try to understand and forecast the effects of changes in other firms' prices on their own firm's sales.

9. If a demand curve is linear, the price elasticity of demand varies from point to point on the demand curve. As price approaches zero, the price elasticity of demand also approaches zero. As quantity demanded approaches zero, the price elasticity approaches negative infinity. In contrast, for a constant-elasticity demand function, the price elasticity of demand is the same, regardless of the product's price. Both linear demand functions and constant-elasticity demand functions are used frequently by managers and managerial economists.

Problems

1. The Dolan Corporation, a maker of small engines, determines that in 1999 the demand curve for its product is

$$P = 2,000 - 50Q,$$

where P is the price (in dollars) of an engine, and Q is the number of engines sold per month.

a. To sell 20 engines per month, what price would Dolan have to charge?
b. If it sets a price of $500, how many engines will Dolan sell per month?
c. What is the price elasticity of demand if price equals $500?
d. At what price, if any, will the demand for Dolan's engines be of unitary elasticity?

2. The Johnson Robot Company's marketing officials report to the company's chief executive officer that the demand curve for the company's robots in 2001 is

$$P = 3{,}000 - 40Q,$$

where P is the price of a robot, and Q is the number sold per month.
   a. Derive the marginal revenue curve for the firm.
   b. At what prices is the demand for the firm's product price elastic?
   c. If the firm wants to maximize its dollar sales volume, what price should it charge?

3. After a careful statistical analysis, the Chidester Company concludes that the demand function for its product is

$$Q = 500 - 3P + 2P_r + 0.1I,$$

where Q is the quantity demanded of its product, P is the price of its product, P_r is the price of its rival's product, and I is per capita disposable income (in dollars). At present, $P = \$10$, $P_r = \$20$, and $I = \$6{,}000$.
   a. What is the price elasticity of demand for the firm's product?
   b. What is the income elasticity of demand for the firm's product?
   c. What is the cross elasticity of demand between its product and its rival's product?
   d. What is the implicit assumption regarding the population in the market?

4. The Haas Corporation's executive vice president circulates a memo to the firm's top management in which he argues for a reduction in the price of the firm's product. He says that such a price cut will increase the firm's sales and profits.
   a. The firm's marketing manager responds with a memo pointing out that the price elasticity of demand for the firm's product is about -0.5. Why is this fact relevant?
   b. The firm's president concurs with the opinion of the executive vice president. Is he correct?

5. According to J. Fred Bucy, former president of Texas Instruments, his firm continually made detailed studies of the price elasticity of demand for each of its major products in order to determine how much its sales would increase if it changed its price by a particular amount.[5] For example, Texas Instruments had to estimate the effect of a 10 percent reduction in the price

---

[5]See his paper in J. Backman and J. Czepiel, eds., *Changing Marketing Strategies in a New Economy* (Indianaplis: Bobbs-Merrill, 1977).

of the TI-55, a hand calculator that the company produced, and whether such a price reduction would increase sales by a large enough amount to be profitable. In 1982, Texas Instruments reduced the price of its 99/4A home computer from $299 to $199, and its rivals followed suit. If the price elasticity of demand was less than minus 1, did the price cut increase the amount spent on such computers?

6. The Hanover Manufacturing Company believes that the demand curve for its product is

$$P = 5 - Q,$$

where P is the price of its product (in dollars) and Q is the number of millions of units of its product sold per day. It is currently charging a price of $1 per unit for its product.
   a. Evaluate the wisdom of the firm's pricing policy.
   b. A marketing specialist says that the price elasticity of demand for the firm's product is -1.0. Is this correct?

7. On the basis of historical data, Richard Tennant has concluded: "The consumption of cigarettes is . . . [relatively] insensitive to changes in price. . . . In contrast, the demand for individual brands is highly elastic in its response to price. . . . In 1918, for example, Lucky Strike was sold for a short time at a higher retail price than Camel or Chesterfield and rapidly lost half its business."
   a. Explain why the demand for a particular brand is more elastic than the demand for all cigarettes. If Lucky Strike raised its price by 1 percent in 1918, was the price elasticity of demand for its product greater than -2?
   b. Do you think that the demand curve for cigarettes is the same now as it was in 1918? If not, describe in detail the factors that have shifted the demand curve, and whether each has shifted it to the left or right.

8. According to S. Sackrin of the U.S. Department of Agriculture, the price elasticity of demand for cigarettes is between -0.3 and -0.4, and the income elasticity of demand is about 0.5.
   a. Suppose the federal government, influenced by findings that link cigarettes and cancer, were to impose a tax on cigarettes that increased their price by 15 percent. What effect would this have on cigarette consumption?
   b. Suppose a brokerage house advised you to buy cigarette stocks because if incomes rose by 50 percent in the next decade, cigarette sales would be bound to spurt enormously. What would be your reaction to this advice?

9. Using the PIMS (Profit Impact of Market Strategies) survey of major U.S. firms, Michael Hagerty, James Carman, and Gary Russell estimated that, on

the average, the advertising elasticity of demand was only about 0.003. Doesn't this indicate that firms spend too much on advertising?

10. Market researchers at the Lawrence Corporation estimate that the demand function for the firm's product is

$$Q = 50P^{-1.5}I^{0.5},$$

where Q is the quantity demanded, P is the product's price, and I is per capita disposable income. The marginal cost of the firm's product is estimated to be $10. Population is assumed to be constant.

a. Lawrence's price for its product is $20. Is this the optimal price? Why or why not?

b. If it is not the optimal price, write a brief memorandum indicating what price might be better, and why.

11. The McCauley Company hires a marketing consultant to estimate the demand function for its product. The consultant concludes that this demand function is

$$Q = 100P^{-3.1}I^{2.3}A^{0.1},$$

where Q is the quantity demanded per capita per month, P is the product's price (in dollars), I is per capita disposable income (in dollars), and A is the firm's advertising expenditures (in thousands of dollars).

a. What is the price elasticity of demand?

b. Will increases in price result in increases or decreases in the amount spent on McCauley's product?

c. What is the income elasticity of demand?

d. What is the advertising elasticity of demand?

e. If the population in the market increases by 10 percent, what is the effect on the quantity demanded if P, I, and A are held constant?

12. The Schmidt Corporation estimates that its demand function is

$$Q = 400 - 3P + 4I + 0.6A,$$

where Q is the quantity demanded per month, P is the product's price (in dollars), I is per capita disposable income (in thousands of dollars), and A is the firm's advertising expenditures (in thousands of dollars per month). Population is assumed to be constant.

a. During the next decade, per capita disposable income is expected to increase by $5,000. What effect will this have on the firm's sales?

b. If Schmidt wants to raise its price enough to offset the effect of the increase in per capita disposable income, by how much must it raise its price?

c. If Schmidt raises its price by this amount, will it increase or decrease the price elasticity of demand? Explain. Make sure your answers reflect the fact that elasticity is a negative number.

13. The marketing manager of the Summers Company must formulate a recommendation concerning the price to be charged for a new product. According to the best available estimates, the marginal cost of the new product will be $18, and the price elasticity of demand for this product will be −3.0.

a. What recommendation should she make, if Summers wants to maximize profit?

b. If her recommendation is accepted, what will be the new product's marginal revenue?

Consumer Behavior and
Rational Choice

Market demand was discussed in Chapter 3. But market demand for a product is just the aggregate of individual demands. How do individual consumers form their demands for products? How do the variables discussed in Chapter 3 (prices, income, advertising, tastes) influence an individual consumer's demand for a product? Firms need to understand what consumers' tastes and preferences are and how they will be influenced by changes in variables that influence consumer behavior that managers can or cannot control.

We will assume that our consumer is rational and wishes to maximize her well-being. Her well-being will be a function of the goods she consumes. However, the amount of goods she can consume will be constrained by her income. Thus, using the techniques of constrained maximization from Chapter 2, we'll show how a consumer's demand curve is derived from the rational behavior of an individual who maximizes their well-being given the prices of goods, given their tastes and preferences for goods, and given their income. We'll develop the concepts of utilify functions, indifference curves, and budget lines. Using them, we'll derive the consumer's demand curve for a good (food). We'll show how the consumer's demand curve shifts when income changes and how consumption is related to an income and a substitution effect.

Many firms use focus groups of consumers to help them understand what variables influence consumer demands and how consumers tradeoff one variable versus another. For instance, Isuzu has run focus groups in which customers estimate how much they'd pay for a given function.

Firm's often use market research firms to survey consumers in person or over the telephone or send them questionnaires—all designed to assess consumer demand characteristics.

Indifference Curves

To make things as simple as possible, we assume that there are only two goods—food and clothing. This assumption can easily be relaxed. To understand the theory of consumer behavior, you must know what an indifference curve is. *An indifference curve contains points representing market baskets among which the consumer is indifferent.* To illustrate, consider Joan Ewing, a consumer in Houston, Texas. Certain market baskets—that is, certain combinations of food and clothing (the only commodities)—will be equally desirable for her. For example, she may be indifferent between a market basket containing 50 pounds of food and 5 pieces of clothing and a market basket containing 100 pounds of food and 2 pieces of clothing. These two market baskets can be represented by two points, *K* and *L* in Figure 4.1. In addition, other market baskets—each of which can be represented by a point in Figure 4.1—are just as desirable to Ms. Ewing as those represented by points *K* and *L*. If we connect all these points, we get a curve that represents market baskets that are equally desirable to the consumer. In our case, Ms. Ewing is indifferent among all the market baskets represented by points on curve I_1 in Figure 4.1. Curve I_1 is therefore called an **indifference curve.**

Three important things should be noted about any consumer's indifference curves:

1. *A consumer has many indifference curves, not just one.* If Ms. Ewing is indifferent among all the market baskets represented by points on I_2 in Figure 4.1, I_2 is another of her indifference curves. Moreover, one thing is certain. She prefers any market basket on I_2 to any market basket on I_1, since I_2 includes market baskets with as much clothing as and more food than (or as much food as and more clothing than) the market baskets on I_1. (Of course, consumers sometimes become so satiated with a commodity that they prefer less of it to more, but we assume for simplicity that this is not the case here.) Consequently, it must be true that market baskets on higher indifference curves like I_2 must be preferred to market baskets on lower indifference curves like I_1.

2. *Every indifference curve must slope downward and to the right,* so long as the consumer prefers more of each commodity to less. If one market bas-

FIGURE 4.1

Two of Ms. Ewing's Indifference Curves

The curves I_1 and I_2 are two of Ms. Ewing's indifference curves. Each shows market baskets that are equally desirable to Ms. Ewing.

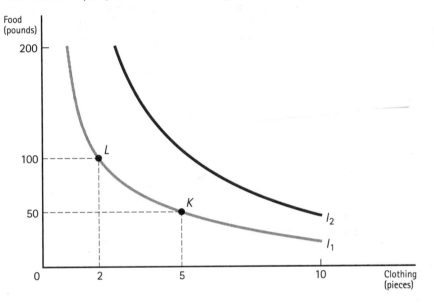

ket has more of one commodity than a second market basket, it must have less of the other commodity than the second market basket—assuming that the two market baskets are to yield equal satisfaction to the consumer. This must be true so long as more of each commodity is preferred over less by the consumer.

3. *Indifference curves cannot intersect.* If they did, this would contradict the assumption that more of a commodity is preferred to less. For example, suppose that I_1 and I_2 in Figure 4.2 are two indifference curves and that they intersect. If this is the case, the market basket represented by point D is equivalent in the eyes of the consumer to the one represented by point C, since both are on indifference curve I_1. Moreover, the market basket represented by point E is equivalent in the eyes of the consumer to the one represented by point C, since both are on indifference curve I_2. And this means that the market basket represented by point E must be equivalent in the eyes of the consumer to the one represented by point D. But this is impossible because market basket E contains the same amount of food and two more pieces of clothing than does market basket D. Since we are as-

Intersecting Indifference Curves: A Contradiction

Indifference curves cannot intersect. If they did, the consumer would be indifferent between D and C, since both are on indifference curve I_1, and between E and C, since both are on indifference curve I_2. But this implies that he or she must be indifferent between C and E, which is impossible since E contains the same amount of food and two more pieces of clothing than D, and we are assuming more of a commodity is preferred to less.

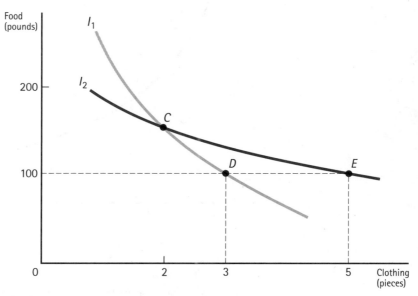

suming more of a commodity is preferred to less, market basket E must be preferred to market basket D.

The Marginal Rate of Substitution

Some consumers value an extra unit of a particular good highly; they would be willing to give their eye teeth to get an extra unit of it. Other consumers do not value an extra unit of this good at all highly; they wouldn't give up much of anything to get an extra unit of it. Obviously, in studying consumer behavior, it is useful to have a measure of the relative importance attached by the consumer to the acquisition of another unit of a particular good. The measure that economists use is called the **marginal rate of substitution**.

The marginal rate of substitution of good X *for good* Y *is defined as the number of units of good* Y *that must be given up if the consumer, after receiv-*

ing an extra unit of good X, *is to maintain a constant level of satisfaction.* Obviously, the larger the number of units of good Y that the consumer is willing to give up to get an extra unit of good X, the more important good X is (relative to good Y) to the consumer. To measure the marginal rate of substitution, we can obtain the slope of the consumer's indifference curve and multiply this slope by -1. This will give us the number of units of good Y that the consumer is willing to give up for an extra unit of good X.

To illustrate, consider consumer preferences with regard to the characteristics of automobiles. Two of the key characteristics of an automobile are stylishness and performance (for example, speed, gasoline mileage, and handling). Some consumers are willing to trade off a lot of stylishness for a little extra performance. For these consumers, the indifference curves in Figure 4.3 are relatively steep, as in the left-hand panel of Figure 4.3. The marginal rate of substitution of performance for stylishness is relatively high, since the slope of the indifference curves (times -1) is relatively large. On the other hand, other consumers are willing to trade off a lot of performance for a little extra stylishness. For these consumers, the indifference curves in Figure 4.3 are relatively

Indifference Curves of Consumers with High and Low Marginal Rates of Substitution of Performance for Stylishness

The left-hand panel shows the indifference curves of consumers who are willing to trade off a lot of stylishness for a little extra performance. The right-hand panel shows the indifference curves of consumers who are willing to trade off a lot of performance for a little extra stylishness.

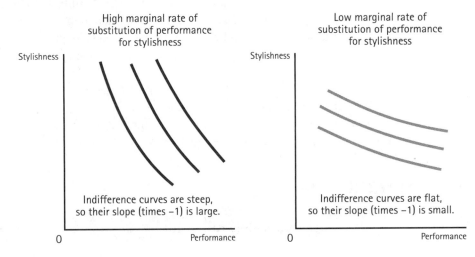

flat, as in the right-hand panel of Figure 4.3. The marginal rate of substitution of performance for stylishness is relatively low, since the slope of the indifference curves (times −1) is relatively small.

The Concept of Utility

As we have seen, the consumer's indifference curves are a representation of his or her tastes. Given all the indifference curves of a particular consumer, we attach a number, a **utility**, to each of the market baskets that might confront him or her. *This utility indicates the level of enjoyment or preference attached by this consumer to this market basket.* More specifically, it summarizes the preference ranking of market baskets. Since all market baskets on a given indifference curve yield the same amount of satisfaction, they would have the same utility. Market baskets on higher indifference curves would have higher utilities than market baskets on lower indifference curves.

The reason why we attach these utilities to market baskets is that once this is done, we can tell at a glance which market baskets the consumer would prefer over other market baskets. If the utility attached to one market basket is higher than that attached to another market basket, the consumer will prefer the first over the second. If the utility attached to the first market basket is lower than the second, he or she will prefer the second over the first. If the utility attached to the first market basket equals the second, he or she will be indifferent between the two market baskets.

How should we pick these utilities? Any way will do as long as market baskets on the same indifference curve receive the same utility and market baskets on higher indifference curves receive higher utilities than market baskets on lower indifference curves. For example, if the consumer prefers market basket R to market basket S, and market basket S to market basket T, the utility of market basket R must be higher than the utility of market basket S, and the utility of market basket S must be higher than the utility of market basket T. But any set of numbers conforming to these requirements is an adequate measure of utility. Thus, the utility of market baskets R, S, and T may be 30, 20, and 10, or 6, 5, 4, respectively. Both are adequate utility measures, since all that counts is that the utility of market basket R be higher than that of market basket S, which in turn should be higher than that of market basket T. Put differently, both provide a correct ordering or ranking of market baskets in terms of levels of consumer satisfaction.

The Budget Line

The consumer would like to maximize his or her utility, which means that he or she wants to achieve the highest possible indifference curve. But whether a particular indifference curve is attainable depends on the consumer's money income and on commodity prices. Exactly what constraints are imposed on the consumer by the size of his or her money income and the nature of commodity prices? To make things concrete, let's return to Joan Ewing. Suppose that her total income is $600 per week and that she can spend this amount on only two commodities, food and clothing. Needless to say, it is unrealistic to assume that there are only two commodities in existence, but, to repeat what was said earlier, this simplification makes it easier to present the model, and the results can easily be generalized to cases where more than two commodities exist.

Under these circumstances, the answer to how much of each commodity Ms. Ewing can buy depends on the price of a pound of food and the price of a piece of clothing. Suppose the price of a pound of food is $3 and the price of a piece of clothing is $60. Then if she spent all her income on food, she could buy 200 pounds of food per week. On the other hand, if she spent all her income on clothing, she could buy 10 pieces of clothing per week. Or she could, if she wished, buy some food and some clothing. There are a large number of combinations of amounts of food and clothing that she could buy, and each such combination can be represented by a point on the line in Figure 4.4. This line is called her **budget line**. *A consumer's budget line shows the market baskets*

FIGURE
4.4

Ms. Ewing's Budget Line

The consumer's budget line shows the market baskets that can be purchased, given the consumer's income and prevailing commodity prices. This budget line assumes that Ms. Ewing's income is $600 per week, that the price of a pound of food is $3, and that the price of a piece of clothing is $60.

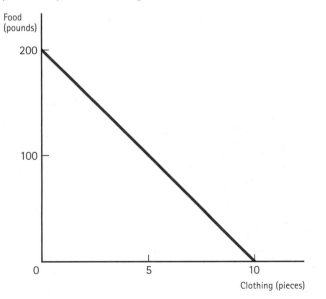

that he or she can purchase, given the consumer's income and prevailing market prices.

To obtain the equation for Joan Ewing's budget line, note that

$$YP_f + XP_c = I, \tag{4.1}$$

where Y is the amount she buys of food, X is the amount she buys of clothing, P_f is the price of food, P_c is the price of clothing, and I is her income. The left-hand side of equation (4.1) equals the total amount she spends on food and clothing; what equation (4.1) says is that this amount must equal her income. For simplicity, we assume that she saves nothing. (This assumption can be relaxed.) Solving equation (4.1) for Y, we obtain

$$Y = \frac{I}{P_f} - \frac{P_c}{P_f} X, \tag{4.2}$$

which is the equation for her budget line.

A shift will occur in the consumer's budget line if changes occur in the consumer's money income or in commodity prices. In particular, an increase in money income means that the budget line rises, and a decrease in money income means that the budget line falls (parallel to the original line since a change in I does not affect the slope). This is illustrated in Figure 4.5, which shows Ms.

FIGURE 4.5

Ms. Ewing's Budget Line at Money Incomes of $300, $600, and $900 per Week

The higher the consumer's money income, the higher the budget line. Holding commodity prices constant, the budget line's slope remains constant.

FIGURE
4.6

Ms. Ewing's Budget Line at Food Prices of $3 and $6 per Pound

Holding constant Ms. Ewing's money income at $600 per week and the price of a piece of clothing at $60, the budget line cuts the vertical axis farther from the origin when the price of food is $3 than when it is $6.

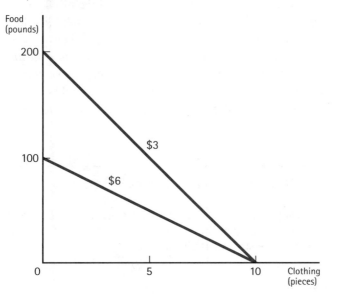

Ewing's budget line at money incomes of $300, $600, and $900 per week. Her budget line moves upward as her income rises.

Also, commodity prices affect the budget line. A decrease in a commodity's price causes the budget line to cut this commodity's axis at a point farther from the origin. Figure 4.6 shows Ms. Ewing's budget line when the price of a pound of food is $3 and when it is $6. You can see that the budget line cuts the vertical, or food, axis farther from the origin when the price of food is $3 per pound. This is because the change in the price of food alters the slope of the budget line, which equals $-P_c/P_f$ [as shown in equation (4.2)].

The Equilibrium Market Basket

Given the consumer's indifference curves and budget line, we are in a position to determine the consumer's equilibrium market basket—the market basket that, among all those that the consumer can purchase, yields the maximum utility.

The first step is to combine the indifference curves with the budget line on the same graph. Figure 4.7 brings together Ms. Ewing's indifference curves (from Figure 4.1) and her budget line (from Figure 4.4). On the basis of the information assembled in Figure 4.7, it is a simple matter to determine her equilibrium market basket. *Her indifference curves show what she wants:* specifically, she wants to attain the highest possible indifference curve. Thus, she would rather be on indifference curve I_2 than on indifference curve I_1, and on indifference curve I_3 than on indifference curve I_2. But, as we have emphasized, she cannot choose any market basket she likes. *The budget line shows which market baskets her income and commodity prices permit her to buy.* Consequently, she must choose some market basket on her budget line.

Clearly, *the consumer's choice boils down to choosing that market basket on the budget line that is on the highest indifference curve. That is the equilibrium market basket.* For example, Ms. Ewing's equilibrium market basket is at point H in Figure 4.7; it consists of 100 pounds of food and 5 pieces of clothing per

Equilibrium Market Basket

Ms. Ewing's equilibrium market basket is at point H, containing 100 pounds of food and 5 pieces of clothing. This is the point on her budget line that is on the highest indifference curve she can attain, I_2.

CONCEPTS IN CONTEXT

Effect of a Time Constraint on Consumer Behavior

For consumers, time can be as important as money. For example, suppose that Mildred Evans, an avid sports fan who goes regularly to baseball and football games, decides that she can devote no more than 24 hours per month to attending such games and that she can spend no more than $120 per month on baseball and football tickets. Since she lives much closer to the local baseball stadium than to the nearest football stadium, it takes 4 hours to see a baseball game but 6 hours to see a football game. The price of each baseball ticket is $10, and the price of each football ticket is $40.

Let B be the number of baseball games and F be the number of football games she attends per month. If she spends a total of $120 per month on tickets,

$$40F + 10B = 120. \qquad (4.3)$$

Why? Because $40F$ is the amount spent on football tickets, and $10B$ is the amount spent on baseball tickets, so $40F + 10B$ is the total amount spent per month on baseball and football tickets, which must equal $120. From equation (4.3), it follows that

$$F = 3 - B/4. \qquad (4.4)$$

This is the equation for the *budget line*, plotted in the graph below.

But this ignores the time constraint. If she spends a total of 24 hours per month at baseball and football games,

$$6F + 4B = 24. \qquad (4.5)$$

Why? Because $6F$ equals the number of hours spent at football games and $4B$ equals the num-

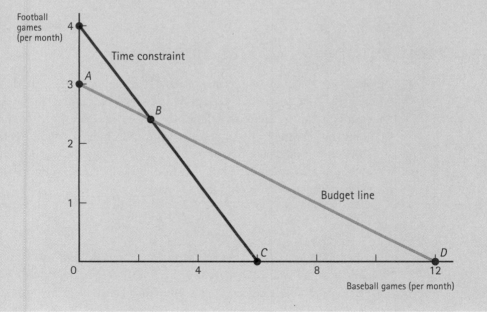

ber of hours spent at baseball games, so $6F + 4B$ equals the total number of hours spent at baseball and football games, which must equal 24. From equation (4.5), it follows that

$$F = 4 - 2B/3 \qquad (4.6)$$

This is the equation for the time constraint, plotted in the graph on page 133.

To keep within both the time and expenditure constraints, she must pick a market basket on line segment AB or line segment BC in the figure on page 133. Note that the time constraint cuts down on the number of feasible market baskets. Given that she wants to devote only 24 hours per month

to attending baseball and football games, she must be content with market baskets along line segment BC rather than line segment BD, which would be available if there were no time constraint.

week. This is her equilibrium market basket because any other market basket on the budget line is on a lower indifference curve than point H is. But will a consumer like Ms. Ewing choose this market basket? Admittedly, it may take some time for the consumer to find out that this is the best market basket for him or her under the circumstances, but eventually one would expect a consumer to come very close to acting in the predicted manner.

Maximizing Utility: A Closer Look

Let's look more closely at the market basket at point H, the one that Ms. Ewing chooses. Clearly, this market basket is at the point where the budget line is tangent to an indifference curve. Since the slope of the indifference curve equals -1 times the marginal rate of substitution of clothing for food (see page 126) and since the slope of the budget line is $-P_c/P_f$ (see page 129), it follows that Ms. Ewing, if she maximizes utility, will choose in equilibrium to allocate her income between food and clothing so that

$$\text{MRS} = P_c/P_f \qquad (4.7)$$

where MRS is the marginal rate of substitution of clothing for food.

To understand what this means, recall that the marginal rate of substitution is the rate at which the consumer is *willing* to substitute clothing for food, holding his or her total level of satisfaction constant. Thus, if the marginal rate of substitution is 4, the consumer is willing to give up 4 pounds of food in order to obtain 1 more piece of clothing. On the other hand, the price ratio, P_c/P_f, is the rate at which the consumer is *able* to substitute clothing for food. Thus, if P_c/P_f is 3, he or she *must* give up 3 pounds of food to obtain 1 more piece of clothing.

What equation (4.7) is saying is: The rate at which the consumer is willing to substitute clothing for food (holding satisfaction constant) must equal the rate at which he or she is able to substitute clothing for food. Otherwise it is always possible to find another market basket that will increase the consumer's satisfaction. And this means, of course, that the present market basket is not the one that maximizes consumer satisfaction.

To illustrate, suppose that Ms. Ewing has chosen a market basket for which the marginal rate of substitution of clothing for food is 4. Suppose that the price ratio, P_c/P_f, is 3. If this is the case, Ms. Ewing can obtain an extra piece of clothing if she buys 3 less pounds of food, since the price ratio is 3. But an extra piece of clothing is worth 4 pounds of food to Ms. Ewing, since the marginal rate of substitution is 4. Thus, she can increase satisfaction by substituting clothing for food—and this will continue to be the case so long as the marginal rate of substitution exceeds the price ratio. Conversely, if the marginal rate of substitution is less than the price ratio, Ms. Ewing can increase satisfaction by substituting food for clothing. Only when the marginal rate of substitution equals the price ratio does her market basket maximize her utility.

Corner Solutions

While Ms. Ewing chooses in this case the market basket where the budget line is tangent to an indifference curve (the market basket at point H in Figure 4.7), this is not always true. In particular, the consumer may consume *none* of some goods because even tiny amounts of them (or the minimum amount of them that can be bought) are worth less to the consumer than they cost. For example, although your money income may be big enough so that you can buy some Beluga caviar (which you would enjoy), you may not purchase any because even a bit would be worth less to you than it would cost.

Figure 4.8 shows the situation graphically. For simplicity, we assume that there are only two goods, Beluga caviar and pizza. Given the position of your indifference curves, you will maximize utility by choosing market basket W, which contains all pizza and no Beluga caviar at all. This market basket maximizes your utility because it is on a higher indifference curve than any other market basket on the budget line. It is a *corner solution,* in which the budget line touches the highest achievable indifference curve along an axis (in this case, the vertical axis).

If the consumer purchases some of both commodities, the marginal rate of

Corner Solution

The market basket that maximizes your utility is *W*, which lies on the vertical axis.

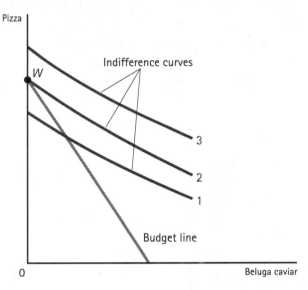

substitution must equal the price ratio if utility is maximized. This was shown in the previous section. But if the consumer does not purchase both commodities, this is not the case.

Representing the Process of Rational Choice

Of what practical use is the theory of consumer behavior? Later in this chapter we shall describe how this theory helps us to interpret and analyze demand curves, but for now we want to emphasize that, apart from its usefulness as a theoretical tool, it can be applied to practical decision making. Many problems people and organizations face are of the following type: *the person or organization has a certain amount of money to spend, and must decide how much to allocate to a number of different uses.* For example, a person may have a certain money income, and the problem is how much to spend on various goods and services. Or a philanthropic foundation like the Ford Foundation must determine how much of its money to allocate each year to various kinds of research and educational purposes.

Faced with a problem of this sort, the economist's model of consumer behavior can be of some help. All these problems are basically the same as that facing the consumer, and the economist's model of consumer behavior shows the rational approach to their solution. Thus, this model does not apply only to consumers. It can be useful in any situation where a person or organization must allocate a fixed amount of money among alternative uses. *This model is much more than a theory of consumer behavior; it is a theory of rational choice.* That is, it is a theory which indicates how one should go about making choices.

A model like this is useful because it shows what factors are important to the decision maker, and how these factors should be combined to come to a decision. At first glance, this statement may not mean much, but put yourself in the position of the people making a decision. There are lots of factors that they might weigh and try to measure in coming to a decision. There is a good chance that they will look at the wrong factors, or give some factors improper weight. The economist's model of consumer behavior can be useful in indicating which factors are relevant and how they should be used.

In subsequent chapters, we will explain in detail how this model can be applied to help improve managerial decision making. For now, you may want to try problem 11 on page 147. See if you can figure out how this model sheds light on a state's choice between mass transit and highways. (The answer is provided in the Appendix.)

Deriving the Individual Demand Curve

A consumer's individual demand curve shows how much he or she will purchase of the good in question at various prices of this good (when other prices and the consumer's income are held constant). In this section, we show how our theory can be used to derive the consumer's demand curve. In particular, let's return to the case of Ms. Ewing and show how her demand curve for food can be derived.

Assuming that food and clothing are the only goods, that Ms. Ewing's weekly income is $600, and that the price of clothing is $60 per piece of clothing, Ms. Ewing's budget line is budget line 1 in Figure 4.9 when the price of food is $3 per pound. Thus, as we saw in Figure 4.7, Ms. Ewing will buy 100 pounds of food per week under these circumstances.

But if the price of food increases to $6 per pound, and her income and the price of clothing remain constant, her budget line will be budget line 2 in Figure 4.9, and she will attain her highest indifference curve I_1 by choosing the market basket corresponding to point K, a market basket containing 50 pounds of food per week. Thus, if the price of food is $6 per pound, she will buy 50 pounds of food per week.

We have derived two points on Ms. Ewing's individual demand curve for food—those corresponding to food prices of $3 and $6 per pound. Figure 4.10 shows these two points, U and V. To obtain more points on her individual de-

Effect of a Change in Price on Ms. Ewing's Equilibrium Market Basket

If the price of a pound of food is $3, Mrs. Ewing's budget line is such that her equilibrium market basket is at point *H*, where she buys 100 pounds of food per week. If the price of a pound of food is $6, Mrs. Ewing's budget line is such that her equilibrium market basket is at point *K*, where she buys 50 pounds of food per week.

mand curve for food, all we have to do is assume a particular price of food, construct the budget line corresponding to this price (holding her income and the price of clothing constant), and find the market basket on this budget line that is on her highest indifference curve. Plotting the amount of food in this market basket against the assumed price of food, we obtain a new point on her individual demand curve for food. Connecting all these points, we get her complete individual demand curve for food, shown in Figure 4.10. (In this situation, the amount of clothing consumed was the same under both pricing scenarios for food. This does not have to be the case.)

FIGURE
4.10

Ms. Ewing's Individual Demand Curve for Food

Ms. Ewing's individual demand curve for food shows the amount of food she will buy at various prices.

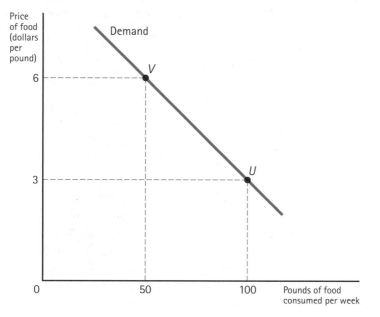

Deriving the Market Demand Curve

We have just described how each consumer's individual demand curve for a commodity can be derived, given the consumer's tastes and income, as well as the prices of other commodities. Suppose that we have obtained the individual demand curve for each of the consumers in the market. How can these individual demand curves be used to derive the market demand curve?

The answer is easy. *To derive the market demand curves, we obtain the horizontal sum of all the individual demand curves.* In other words, to find the total quantity demanded in the market at a certain price, we add up the quantities demanded by all the individual consumers at that price.

Table 4.1 shows the individual demand curves for food of four families: the Millers, Sarafians, Chases, and Grubers. For simplicity, suppose that these four families constitute the entire market for food. (This assumption can easily be relaxed; it just makes things simple.) Then the market demand curve for food

TABLE 4.1

Individual Demand Curves and Market Demand Curve for Food

Price of food (dollars per pound)	Individual demand (hundreds of pounds per month)				Market Demand
	Miller	Sarafian	Chase	Gruber	
3.00	51.0	45.0	5.0	2.0	103
3.20	43.0	44.0	4.2	1.8	93
3.40	36.0	43.0	3.4	1.6	84
3.60	30.0	42.0	2.6	1.4	76
3.80	26.0	41.4	2.4	1.2	71
4.00	21.0	41.0	2.0	1.0	65

is shown in the last column of Table 4.1. Figure 4.11 shows the families' individual demand curves for food, as well as the resulting market demand curve. To illustrate how the market demand curve is derived from the individual demand curves, suppose that the price of food is $3 per pound. Then the total quantity demanded in the market is 103 hundreds of pounds per month, since this is the sum of the quantities demanded at this price by the four families. (As shown in Table 4.1, this sum equals 51.0 + 45.0 + 5.0 + 2.0, or 103 hundreds of pounds.)

Consumer Surplus

One of the most important lessons of our analysis of demand is that individual consumers may value a good above its market price. This is a simple, but powerful idea. An individual's demand curve tells us the unit price (P_r) that the individual is willing to pay to purchase a given number of units of a product (say, X). Because the demand curve (usually) is downward sloping, the curve indicates that the consumer values goods $X - 1$, $X - 2$, etc., at a greater amount than the value of the Xth good purchased (say at values P_{X-1}, P_{X-2}, etc.). The price value for each number of units demanded is called the **consumer's reservation price** for that particular unit of good.

The difference between what an individual is willing to pay and what an individual has to pay for a good is called **consumer surplus.** Alternatively, consumer surplus is the actual price paid subtracted from the reservation price.

When a market price is determined, in a market context, the last individual (or set of individuals) to purchase the good will be the individual whose reser-

FIGURE 4.11

Individual Demand Curves and Market Demand Curve for Food

The market demand curve is the horizontal sum of all the individual demand curves.

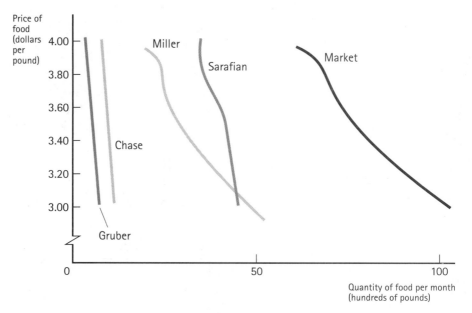

vation price just equals the market price. All other purchasers of the good have reservation prices exceeding the market price. Hence, all of these individuals have "gained" a consumer surplus since they paid less for the good than they were willing to pay. If we aggregate all the individuals' consumer surpluses, we have the consumer surplus for the good at that price. Simply put, the consumer surplus for a good is the area below the demand curve but above the price charged. This is area *A* in Figure 4.12.

We will have more to say about consumer surplus in later chapters, when we introduce the analogous idea pertaining to the production side of the market, called producer surplus, and the summation of consumer and producer surplus, called total surplus. Economists use these concepts to describe the efficiency of markets and the social benefits of market transactions. But for now we will draw a simpler observation. As a business manager, so long as the demand curve for your good or service is downward sloping, you would generate more revenue for your firm if you could charge each consumer his reservation price, or if you could simply charge higher prices to groups of consumers who value the good more highly than others. Relative to charging a single market price,

FIGURE
4.12

The Consumer Surplus for a Price of P_x

Consumer surplus for an individual is the area under the demand curve but above the price (P_x) paid (area A). The same definition would hold for a market demand curve.

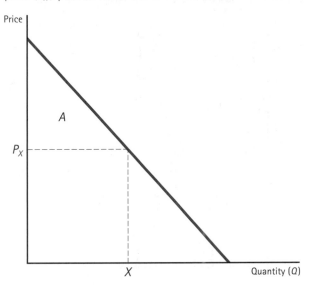

such a policy would amount to capturing some of the consumer surplus for the benefit of your firm. Though there are various legal, practical, and economic constraints that limit the extent to which firms can charge different prices for the same good, beyond these constraints, the practice is widespread. Examples include airline tickets, automobiles sold at dealerships where haggling is the norm, and goods and services offered at discounts through coupon systems and other special offers.

Summary

1. An indifference curve contains points representing market baskets among which the consumer is indifferent. If the consumer prefers more to less of both commodities, an indifference curve must have a negative slope.
2. Market baskets on higher indifference curves provide more satisfaction than those on lower indifference curves. Utility is a number that indexes the level of satisfaction derived from a particular market basket. Market baskets with higher utilities are preferred over market baskets with lower utilities.

CONSULTANT'S CORNER

The Trade-off Between Risk and Return

Ms. Jackson has $1 million, which she must allocate between U.S. government securities and common stocks. If she invests it all in U.S. government securities, she will receive a return of 5 percent, and there is no risk. If she invests it all in common stock, she expects to receive a return of 10 percent, and there is considerable risk. If she invests half in U.S. government securities and half in common stocks, she expects to receive a return of 7.5 percent, and there is some risk. Line RT in the figure below shows the expected return and extent of risk from all possible allocations of the $1 million between these two types of securities.

Investors differ in how much risk they will accept in order to obtain a higher expected return. This investor's indifference curves are shown below.

Why do these indifference curves slope *upward* to the right, whereas the other indifference curves in this chapter slope *downward* to the right? How should this investor allocate the $1 million between U.S. government securities and common stocks? (Much more will be said about problems of this sort in Chapter 14.)

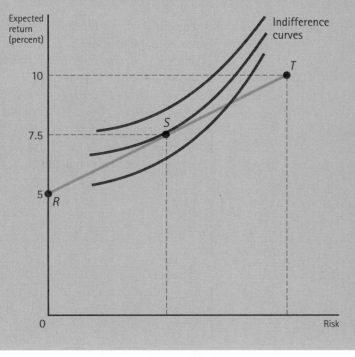

3. The marginal rate of substitution shows how many units of one good must be given up if the consumer, after getting an extra unit of another good, is to maintain a constant level of satisfaction. To obtain the marginal rate of substitution, multiply the slope of the indifference curve by -1.

4. The budget line contains all the market baskets that the consumer can buy, given his or her money income and the level of each price. Increases in income push the budget line upward and parallel to the old budget line; changes in the price ratio alter the budget line's slope.

5. To attain the highest level of satisfaction that is compatible with the budget line, the consumer must choose the market basket on the budget line that is on the highest indifference curve. This market basket is at a point where the budget line is tangent to an indifference curve (unless there is a corner solution).

6. If the consumer maximizes utility, he or she will choose in equilibrium to allocate his or her income so that the marginal rate of substitution of one good for another good equals the ratio of the prices of the two goods (unless there is a corner solution).

7. The theory of consumer behavior is often used to represent the process of rational choice. Frequently, a person or organization has a certain amount of money to spend, and must decide how much to allocate to a number of different uses. This theory indicates how such decisions should be made.

8. A consumer's demand curve shows how much the consumer will purchase of the good in question at various prices of the good when other prices and the consumer's income are held constant. The theory of consumer behavior can be used to derive the consumer's demand curve, and the market demand curve can be obtained by summing the individual demand curves horizontally.

Problems

1. In the market for athletic shoes, there was a big shift in the early 1990s, as sales of hiking shoes increased by over 27 percent, while those of other types of athletic shoes grew much more slowly (or declined). According to Jim Reid of the Coleman Company, "The baby boomers are getting to an age where they are more interested in doing things with families rather than individual sports."[1]

   a. If the typical baby boomer regards each pair of hiking shoes as equally desirable as two pairs of jogging shoes, what do his or her indifference curves (between hiking shoes and jogging shoes) look like? Assume that

[1]*New York Times,* February 13, 1994, p. 6F.

this is true regardless of how many pairs of each type of athletic shoes he or she has.

b. Do they have the typical shape of indifference curves? Why or why not?

2. In recent years, fresh bagel sales have been growing at about 30 percent per year. Once considered an ethnic food to be eaten only with cream cheese and lox, bagels now "have become the new doughnut to bring to the office," according to Michael Goldstein of Goldstein's Bagel Bakery in Pasadena, California.[2] But one problem with bagels is that they get stale fast. In the words of Ray Lahvic, editor emeritus of *Bakery Production and Marketing*, "the worst thing in the world is a day-old bagel."[3] If a market researcher asserts that the slope of the typical consumer's indifference curves between fresh bagels and day-old bagels is −1, would you agree with this assertion? Why or why not?

3. On a piece of graph paper, plot the quantity of lamb consumed by Ms. Turner along the vertical axis and the quantity of rice she consumes along the horizontal axis. Draw the indifference curve that includes the following market baskets. Each of these market baskets gives equal satisfaction.

Market basket	Lamb (pounds)	Rice (pounds)
1	2	8
2	3	7
3	4	6
4	5	5
5	6	4
6	7	3
7	8	2
8	9	1

4. In the previous question, what is the marginal rate of substitution of rice for lamb? How does the marginal rate of substitution vary as Ms. Turner consumes more lamb and less rice? Is this realistic?

5. Suppose that Richard has an after-tax income of $500 per week and that he must spend it all on food or clothing. If food is $5 per pound and clothing is $10 per piece, draw his budget line on a piece of graph paper, where the amount of food is measured along the vertical axis and the amount of clothing is measured along the horizontal axis.

6. In the previous problem, what will be the budget line if Richard's weekly income increases to $600? What will be the budget line if his income is

[2] *Philadelphia Inquirer*, December 28, 1993.
[3] Ibid.

$500, but the price of food increases to $10 per pound? What will be his budget line if his income is $500, but the price of clothing increases to $20 per piece? Draw each of these budget lines on the piece of graph paper used in the previous problem.

7. Maria has budgeted a total of $9 to spend on two goods, chips and salsa. She likes to consume a unit of chips in combination with a unit of salsa. Any unit of chips that she cannot consume in combination with a unit of salsa is useless. Similarly, any unit of salsa that she cannot consume in combination with chips is useless. If the price of a unit of chips is 50 cents and the price of a unit of salsa is 10 cents, how many units of each good will she purchase?

8. In the diagram below, we show one of Jane's indifference curves and her budget line.
   a. If the price of good X is $100, what is her income?
   b. What is the equation for her budget line?
   c. What is the slope of the budget line?
   d. What is the price of good Y?
   e. What is her marginal rate of substitution in equilibrium?

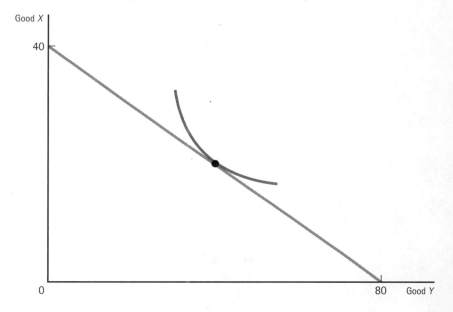

9. Sarah has $300 to allocate between opera tickets and movie tickets. The price of each opera ticket is $60, and the price of each movie ticket is $6. Her marginal rate of substitution of opera tickets for movie tickets equals 5, regardless of what market basket she chooses. How many opera tickets will she purchase?

10. Suppose that Milton has $50 to be divided between corn and beans and that the price of beans is $0.50 per pound. What will be the relationship

between the price of corn and the amount of corn he will buy if $U = \log Q_c + 4 \log Q_b$, where U is his utility, Q_c is the quantity of corn he consumes (in pounds), and Q_b is the quantity of beans he consumes (in pounds)?

11. In 1993, the state of New York received $3 billion (from federal sources and a state petroleum tax) to be spent during the mid-1990s on highways and/or mass transit (subways, buses, and urban rail lines), both of which could be used to meet the transportation needs of the state's population.

   a. If each mile of mass transit costs $20 million, what is the maximum number of miles of mass transit that these funds would have enabled the state to construct?

   b. If each mile of highway costs $10 million, what is the maximum number of miles of highways that these funds would have enabled the state to construct?

   c. If the number of miles of mass transit constructed is put on the vertical axis of a graph, and if the number of miles of highways constucted is put on the horizontal axis, can a budget line (showing the maximum number of miles of mass transit that could be constructed, given each number of miles of highways constructed) be drawn for the state? If so, what is the slope of this budget line? (Assume that the $3 billion is the only source of funds for mass transit or highway construction.)

   d. If the public and the state government agree that every extra mile of mass transit adds three times as much to the state's transportation capability as an extra mile of highways, how much of the $3 billion should be spent on mass transit (if the objective is to maximize transportation capability)?

Estimating Demand
Functions

Sergio Zyman, marketing chief of Coca-Cola, once indicated that his company, one of the world's biggest advertisers, would put less emphasis on traditional newspaper, magazine, and TV ads and more emphasis on new marketing techniques like special programs on cable TV and product tie-ins with movies. All firms, not just Coke, must constantly re-evaluate and adjust their marketing strategies. As has been stressed repeatedly in previous chapters, an effective manager must have a good working knowledge of the demand function for his or her firm's products.

The previous two chapters were concerned with the theory of demand; now we learn how you can estimate a product's demand function. Consumer surveys and market experiments can be useful in providing such information, but the technique most frequently used to estimate demand functions is regression analysis. Since regression analysis will be used repeatedly in subsequent chapters to estimate production functions and cost functions and for forecasting, we must devote considerable attention to this basic statistical technique.

While managers use some or all of the above techniques (we mentioned the Isuzu use of focus groups in Chapter 4), the technique most frequently used to estimate demand functions is regression analysis (even much of the data gathered by questionnaire and focus group is analyzed by regression). In Chapter 3, we showed how Amtrak estimated their demand function with regression analysis. Since regression analysis will be used repeatedly in subsequent chapters to estimate production functions and cost functions and for forecasting, we will devote considerable attention to this basic technique in this chapter.

The Identification Problem

While it is very important that managers have reasonably accurate estimates of the demand functions for their own (and other) products, this does not mean that it is always easy to obtain such estimates. One problem that may arise in estimating demand curves should be recognized at the outset. Given the task of estimating the demand curve for a particular product, you might be inclined to plot the quantity demanded of the product in 1999 versus its 1999 price, the quantity demanded in 1998 versus its 1998 price, and so forth. If the resulting plot of points for 1997 to 1999 were as shown in Figure 5.1, you might be tempted to conclude that the demand curve is *DD'*.

Price Plotted against Quantity, 1997–1999

The curve *DD'* is unlikely to be a good estimate of the demand curve.

FIGURE
5.2

Estimated Demand Curve Contrasted with Actual Demand Curves

The estimated demand curve DD' is not at all similar to the actual demand curves.

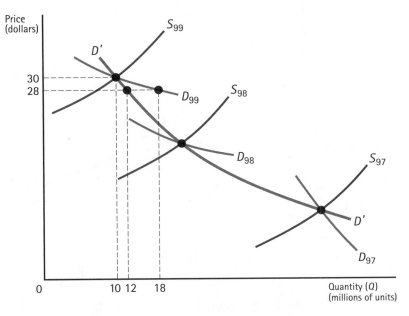

Unfortunately, things are not so simple. Price, as we saw in Chapter 1, is determined by both the demand and supply curves for this product if the market is competitive. Specifically, the equilibrium value of price is at the level where the demand and supply curves intersect. The important point to note is that the demand and supply curves for this product may have been different each year. Thus, as shown in Figure 5.2, the supply curve may have shifted (from S_{97} in 1997 to S_{98} in 1998 to S_{99} in 1999), and the demand curve may have shifted (from D_{97} in 1997 to D_{98} in 1998 to D_{99} in 1999). As indicated in Figure 5.2, DD' is not even close to being a good approximation to the demand curve for this product in any of these three years.

In the situation in Figure 5.2, if you were to conclude that DD' was the demand curve, you would underestimate (in absolute value) the price elasticity of demand for this product in 1999 and 1998 and overestimate it (in absolute value) in 1997. In 1999, you would think that if price were lowered from $30 to $28, the quantity demanded would increase from 10 to 12 million units per year. In fact, as shown in Figure 5.2, such a price reduction would result in an

FIGURE
5.3

Fixed Demand Curve and Shifting Supply Curve

In this special case, *DD'* does represent the actual demand curve.

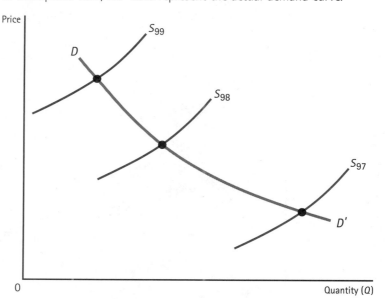

increase of the quantity demanded to 18, not 12, million units per year. This is a mammoth error in anyone's book.

The point is that because we are not holding constant a variety of nonprice variables like consumer tastes, incomes, the prices of other goods, and advertising, we cannot be sure that the demand curve was fixed during the period when the measurements were made. If the demand curve was fixed, and if only the supply curve changed during the period, we could be confident that the plot of points in Figure 5.1 represented the demand curve. As shown in Figure 5.3, the shifts in the supply curve would trace out various points on the demand curve we want to measure.

How can we estimate a demand curve if it has not remained fixed in the past? There are many ways, some simple, some very complex. Econometric techniques recognize that price and quantity are related by both the supply curve and the demand curve, and that both these curves shift in response to nonprice variables. Some basic econometric techniques, such as regression analysis, are presented later in this chapter; others are too complex to be taken up here.[1]

---

[1]See J. Johnston, *Econometric Methods* (3d ed.; New York: McGraw-Hill, 1984); J. Kmenta, *Elements of Econometrics* (2d ed.; New York: Macmillan Co., 1986); or E. Berndt, *The Practice of Econometrics* (Reading, Mass.: Addison-Wesley, 1991).

Consumer interviews and market experiments are also widely used, as indicated in the next three sections.

Consumer Interviews

To obtain information concerning the demand function for a particular product, firms frequently interview consumers and administer questionnaires concerning their buying habits, motives, and intentions. Firms may also run focus groups in an attempt to discern consumers' tastes. For example, a firm might ask a random sample of consumers how much more gasoline they would purchase if its price were reduced by 5 percent. Or a market researcher might ask a sample of consumers whether they liked a new type of perfume better than a leading existing brand, and if so, how much more they would be willing to pay for it (than for the existing brand).

Unfortunately, consumer surveys of this sort have many well-known limitations. The direct approach of simply asking people how much they would buy of a particular commodity at particular prices often does not seem to work very well. Frequently, the answers provided by consumers to such a hypothetical question are not very accurate. However, more subtle approaches can be useful. Thus, interviews indicated that most buyers of a particular baby food selected it on their doctor's recommendation, and that most of them knew very little about prices of substitutes. This information, together with other data, suggested that the price elasticity of demand was quite low in absolute value.[2]

Despite the limitations of consumer interviews and questionnaires, many managers believe that such surveys can reveal a great deal about how their firms can serve the market better. For example, the Campbell Soup Company's researchers contacted close to 110,000 people to talk about the taste, preparation, and nutritional value of food. On the basis of these interviews, Campbell changed the seasonings in five Le Menu dinners and introduced a line of low-salt soups (called Special Request). Some of the factors influencing the quality of survey results can be quite subtle. For example, according to research findings, there are sometimes advantages in respondents' keypunching answers, rather than verbalizing them, because the respondents tend to answer emotional questions more honestly this way.[3]

---

[2]J. Dean, "Estimating the Price Elasticity of Demand," in E. Mansfield, ed., *Managerial Economics and Operations Research* (4th ed.; New York: Norton, 1980).
[3]*New York Times*, November 8, 1987, p. 4F. Also, see W. Baumol, "The Empirical Determination of Demand Relationships," in *Managerial Economics and Operations Research*, Mansfield.

Market Experiments

Another method of estimating the demand curve for a particular commodity is to carry out direct market experiments. The idea is to vary the price of the product while attempting to keep other market conditions fairly stable (or to take changes in other market conditions into account). For example, a manufacturer of ink conducted an experiment some years ago to determine the price elasticity of demand for its product. It raised the price from 15 cents to 25 cents in four cities and found that demand was quite inelastic. Attempts were made to estimate the cross elasticity of demand with other brands as well.

Controlled laboratory experiments can sometimes be carried out. Consumers are given money and told to shop in a simulated store. The experimenter can vary the prices, packaging, and location of particular products, and see the effects on the consumers' purchasing decisions. While this technique is useful, it suffers from the fact that consumers participating in such an experiment know that their actions are being monitored. For that reason, their behavior may depart from what it normally would be.

Before carrying out a market experiment, you should weigh the costs against the benefits. Direct experimentation can be expensive or risky because customers may be lost and profits cut by the experiment. For example, if the price of a product is raised as part of an experiment, potential buyers may be driven away. Also, since they are seldom really controlled experiments and since they are often of relatively brief duration and the number of observations is small, experiments often cannot produce all the information that is needed. Nonetheless, market experiments can be of considerable value, as illustrated by the following actual case.

L'eggs: A Market Experiment

L'eggs Products, a subsidiary of the Hanes Corporation, markets L'eggs Pantyhose, the first major nationally branded and advertised hosiery product distributed through food and drug outlets. According to some estimates, it has been the largest-selling single brand in the hosiery industry. Jack Ward, group product manager of the firm, was interested in determining the effect on sales of four temporary promotion alternatives: a 40-cent price reduction for a package containing two pairs, a 25-cent price reduction for a package containing two pairs, a 20-cent price reduction per pair, and a coupon mailed to homes worth 25 cents off if a pair was purchased.[4]

---

[4]The material in this section is based on DeBruicker, Quelch, and Ward, *Cases in Consumer Behavior.*

To test these four promotion alternatives, Jerry Clawson, director of marketing research, decided that each would be implemented in a carefully chosen test market, and the results would be compared with another market where no unusual promotion was carried out. Specifically, there was a 40-cent reduction (for two pairs) in Syracuse, New York; a 25-cent reduction (for two pairs) in Columbus, Ohio; a 20-cent reduction (for one pair) in Denver, Colorado; and a 25-cent coupon in Cincinnati, Ohio. The results in these markets were compared with those in Boise, Idaho, where no special promotion occurred.

According to the firm's sales research group, the results were as follows: "The 2 for 40¢-off promotion (Syracuse) was the most effective with a net short-term cumulative increase in sales of 53% felt over 6 weeks. The 20¢ price-off promotion (Denver) was the second most effective, with a net cumulative short-term increase of 20% felt over 8 weeks. . . . The 25¢ coupon promotion (Cincinnati) was the least effective with a 3% short-term increase in sales felt over 8 weeks."[5]

This is an example of how firms go about obtaining information concerning their market demand functions. In this case, the firm's managers were interested in the effects of both the form and size of the price cut, and they were concerned only with a temporary price cut. In other cases, firms are interested in the effects of more long-term price changes or of changes in product characteristics or in advertising. But regardless of these differences, marketing research of this sort can play an important role in providing data for the estimation of demand functions.

Regression Analysis

Although consumer interviews and direct market experiments are important sources of information concerning demand functions, they are not used as often as regression analysis. Suppose that a firm's demand function is:

$$Y = A + B_1 X + B_2 P + B_3 I + B_4 P_r,$$ \hfill (5.1)

where Y is the quantity demanded of the firm's product, X is the selling expense (such as advertising) of the firm, P is the price of its product, I is the disposable income of consumers, and P_r is the price of the competing product sold by its rival. What we want are estimates of the values of A, B_1, B_2, B_3, and B_4.

---

[5]Ibid., p. 335. The validity of these results is discussed there also.

Regression analysis enables us to obtain them from historical data concerning Y, X, P, I, and P_r.

In the rest of this chapter, we describe the nature and application of regression analysis, a statistical technique that can be used to estimate many types of economic relationships, not just demand functions. We begin with the simple case in which the only factor influencing the quantity demanded is the firm's selling expense, and then turn to the more complicated (and realistic) case in which the quantity demanded is affected by more than one factor, as it is in equation (5.1).

Regression analysis describes the way in which one variable is related to another. (As we will see later in this chapter, regression techniques can handle more than two variables, but only two are considered at present.) Regression analysis derives an equation that can be used to estimate the unknown value of one variable on the basis of the known value of the other variable. For example, suppose that the Miller Pharmaceutical Company is scheduled to spend $4 million next year on selling expense (for promotion, advertising, and related marketing activities), and that it wants to estimate how much its next-year's sales will be, on the basis of the data in Table 5.1 regarding its sales and selling expense in the previous nine years. In this case, although the firm's selling expense next year is known, its next year's sales are unknown. Regression analysis describes the way in which the firm's sales are historically related to its selling expense.

TABLE 5.1

Selling Expense and Sales, Miller Pharmaceutical Company, Sample of Nine Years

Selling expense (millions of dollars)	Sales (millions of units)
1	4
2	6
4	8
8	14
6	12
5	10
8	16
9	16
7	12

Simple Regression Model

As you will recall from Chapter 1, a **model** is a simplified or idealized representation of the real world. In this section, we describe the model—that is, the set of simplifying assumptions—on which regression analysis is based. Let's begin by visualizing a population of all relevant pairs of observations of the independent and dependent variables. For instance, in the case of the Miller Pharmaceutical Company, we visualize a population of pairs of observations concerning sales and selling expense. This population would include all the levels of sales corresponding to all the levels of selling expense in the history of the firm.

The mean of a variable equals the sum of its values divided by their number. Thus, the mean of a variable that assumes four values, 3, 2, 1, and 0, is $(3 + 2 + 1 + 0)/4$, or 1.5. Regression analysis assumes that *the mean value of* Y, *given the value of* X, *is a linear function of* X. In other words, the mean value of the dependent variable is assumed to be a linear function of the independent variable, the equation of this line being $A + BX$, as shown in Figure 5.4. This straight line is called the **population regression line** or the **true regression line**.

FIGURE 5.4

Regression Model

The mean value of Y, given the value of X, falls on the population regression line.

Put differently, regression analysis assumes that

$$Y_i = A + BX_i + e_i, \qquad (5.2)$$

where Y_i is the ith observed value of the dependent variable, and X_i is the ith observed value of the independent variable. Essentially, e_i is an **error term,** that is, a random amount that is added to $A + BX_i$ (or subtracted from it if e_i is negative). Because of the presence of this error term, the observed values of Y_i fall around the population regression line, not on it. Thus, as shown in Figure 5.4, if e_1 (the value of the error term for the first observation) is -1, Y_1 will lie 1 below the population regression line. And if e_2 (the value of the error term for the second observation) is $+1.50$, Y_2 will lie 1.50 above the population regression line. Regression analysis assumes that the values of e_i are independent and that their mean value equals zero.[6]

Although the assumptions underlying regression analysis are unlikely to be met completely, they are close enough to the truth in a sufficiently large number of cases that regression analysis is a powerful technique. Nonetheless, it is important to recognize at the start that if these assumptions are not at least approximately valid, the results of a regression analysis can be misleading.

Sample Regression Line

The purpose of a regression analysis is to obtain the mathematical equation for a line that describes the average relationship between the dependent and independent variable. This line is calculated from the sample observations and is called the **sample** or **estimated regression line.** It should not be confused with the population regression line discussed in the previous section. Whereas the population regression line is based on the entire population, the sample regression line is based only on the sample.

The general expression for the sample regression line is

$$\hat{Y} = a + bX,$$

where $\hat{Y}$ is the value of the dependent variable predicted by the regression line, and a and b are estimators of A and B, respectively. (An estimator is a function of the sample observations that is used to estimate an unknown parame-

---

[6]The values of e_1 and e_2 are independent if the probability distribution of e_1 does not depend on the value of e_2 and if the probability distribution of e_2 does not depend on the value of e_1. Regression analysis also assumes that the variability of the values of e_i is the same, regardless of the value of X. Many of the tests described subsequently assume too that the values of e_i are normally distributed. For a description of the normal distribution, see Appendix B.

ter. For example, the sample mean is an estimator that is often used to estimate the population mean.) Since this equation implies that $\hat{Y} = a$ when
$X = 0$, it follows that a is the value of $\hat{Y}$ at which the line intersects the Y axis.
Thus, a is often called the Y **intercept** of the regression line. And b, which
clearly is the slope of the line, measures the change in the predicted value of
Y associated with a 1-unit increase in X.

Figure 5.5 shows the estimated regression line for the data concerning sales
and selling expense of the Miller Pharmaceutical Company. The equation for
this regression line is

$$\hat{Y} = 2.536 + 1.504X,$$

where $\hat{Y}$ is sales in millions of units, and X is selling expense in millions of
dollars. What is 2.536? It is the value of a, the estimator of A. What is 1.504?
It is the value of b, the estimator of B. For the moment, we are not interested
in how this equation was determined; what we want to consider is how it should
be interpreted.

FIGURE
5.5

Sample Regression Line

This line is an estimate of the population regression line.

At the outset, note the difference between Y and $\hat{Y}$. Whereas Y denotes an *observed* value of sales, $\hat{Y}$ denotes the *computed* or *estimated* value of sales, based on the regression line. For example, the first row of Table 5.1 shows that in the first year, the actual value of sales was 4 million units when selling expense was \$1 million. Thus, $Y = 4.0$ millions of units when $X = 1$. In contrast, the regression line indicates that $\hat{Y} = 2.536 + 1.504(1)$, or 4.039 millions of units when $X = 1$. In other words, while the regression line predicts that sales will equal 4.039 millions of units when selling expense is \$1 million, the actual sales figure under these circumstances (in the first year) was 4 million units.

It is essential to be able to identify and interpret the Y intercept and slope of a regression line. What is the Y intercept of the regression line in the case of the Miller Pharmaceutical Company? It is 2.536 millions of units. This means that if the firm's selling expense is zero, the estimated sales would be 2.536 millions of units. (As shown in Figure 5.5, 2.536 millions of units is the value of the dependent variable at which the regression line intersects the vertical axis.) What is the slope of the regression line in this case? It is 1.504. This means that the estimated sales go up by 1.504 millions of units when selling expense increases by \$1 million.

Method of Least Squares

The method used to determine the values of a and b is the so-called method of least squares. Since the deviation of the ith observed value of Y from the regression line equals $Y_i - \hat{Y}_i$, the sum of these squared deviations equals

$$\sum_{i=1}^{n} (Y_i - \hat{Y}_i)^2 = \sum_{i=1}^{n} (Y_i - a - bX_i)^2, \tag{5.3}$$

where n is the sample size.[7] Using the minimization technique presented in Chapter 2, we can find the values of a and b that minimize the expression in

[7]As pointed out in Chapter 1, Σ is the mathematical summation sign. What does ΣX_i mean? It means that the numbers to the right of the summation sign (that is, the values of X_i) should be summed from the lower limit on i (which is given below the Σ sign) to the upper limit on i (which is given above the Σ sign). Thus,

$$\sum_{i=1}^{n} X_i$$

means the same thing as $X_1 + X_2 + \cdots + X_n$.

equation (5.3) by differentiating this expression with respect to a and b and by setting these partial derivatives equal to zero:

$$\frac{\partial \sum_{i=1}^{n} (Y_i - \hat{Y}_i)^2}{\partial a} = -2 \sum_{i=1}^{n} (Y_i - a - bX_i) = 0 \qquad (5.4)$$

$$\frac{\partial \sum_{i=1}^{n} (Y_i - \hat{Y}_i)^2}{\partial b} = -2 \sum_{i=1}^{n} X_i(Y_i - a - bX_i) = 0. \qquad (5.5)$$

Solving equations (5.4) and (5.5) simultaneously, and letting $\overline{X}$ equal the mean value of X in the sample and $\overline{Y}$ equal the mean value of Y, we find that

$$b = \frac{\sum_{i=1}^{n} (X_i - \overline{X})(Y_i - \overline{Y})}{\sum_{i=1}^{n} (X_i - \overline{X})^2} \qquad (5.6)$$

$$a = \overline{Y} - b\overline{X}. \qquad (5.7)$$

The value of b in equation (5.6) is often called the **estimated regression coefficient**.

From a computational point of view, it frequently is easier to use a somewhat different formula for b than the one given in equation (5.6). This alternative formula, which yields the same answer as equation (5.6), is

$$b = \frac{n \sum_{i=1}^{n} X_i Y_i - \left(\sum_{i=1}^{n} X_i\right)\left(\sum_{i=1}^{n} Y_i\right)}{n \sum_{i=1}^{n} X_i^2 - \left(\sum_{i=1}^{n} X_i\right)^2}.$$

In the case of the Miller Pharmaceutical Company, Table 5.2 shows the calculation of $\sum X_i Y_i$, $\sum X_i^2$, $\sum X_i$, and $\sum Y_i$. Based on these calculations,

$$b = \frac{9(638) - (50)(98)}{9(340) - 50^2} = 1.504.$$

Thus, the value of b, the least-squares estimator of B, is 1.504, which is the result given in the previous section. In other words, an increase in selling expense of $1 million results in an increase in estimated sales of about 1.504 millions of units.

TABLE
5.2

Computation of ΣX_i, ΣY_i, ΣX_i^2, ΣY_i^2, and $\Sigma X_i Y_i$

	X_i	Y_i	X_i^2	Y_i^2	$X_i Y_i$
	1	4	1	16	4
	2	6	4	36	12
	4	8	16	64	32
	8	14	64	196	112
	6	12	36	144	72
	5	10	25	100	50
	8	16	64	256	128
	9	16	81	256	144
	7	12	49	144	84
Total	50	98	340	1,212	638

$\overline{X} = 50/9 = 5.556$
$\overline{Y} = 98/9 = 10.889$

Having calculated b, we can readily determine the value of a, the least-squares estimator of A. According to equation (5.7),

$$a = \overline{Y} - b\overline{X}$$

where $\overline{Y}$ is the mean of the values of Y, and $\overline{X}$ is the mean of the values of X. Since, as shown in Table 5.2, $\overline{Y} = 10.889$ and $\overline{X} = 5.556$, it follows that

$$a = 10.889 - 1.504(5.556)$$
$$= 2.536$$

Thus, the least-squares estimate of A is 2.536 millions of units, which is the result given in the previous section.

Having obtained a and b, it is a simple matter to specify the average relationship in the sample between sales and selling expense for the Miller Pharmaceutical Company. This relationship is

$$\hat{Y} = 2.536 + 1.504X. \tag{5.8}$$

where $\hat{Y}$ is measured in millions of units, and X is measured in millions of dollars. As we know, this line is often called the sample regression line, or the regression of Y on X. It is the line that we presented in the previous section and that we plotted in Figure 5.5. Now we have seen how this line is derived. (However, a computer usually does the calculations.)

To illustrate how a regression line of this sort can be used, suppose that the managers of the firm want to predict the firm's sales if they decide to devote $4 million to selling expense. Using equation (5.8), they would predict that its sales would be

$$2.536 + 1.504(4) = 8.55. \tag{5.9}$$

Since sales are measured in millions of units, this means that sales would be expected to be 8.55 millions of units.

Coefficient of Determination

Once the regression line has been calculated, one wants to know how well this line fits the data. There can be huge differences in how well a regression line fits a set of data, as shown in Figure 5.6. Clearly, the regression line in panel F of Figure 5.6 provides a much better fit than the regression line in panel B of the same figure. How can we measure how well a regression line fits the data?

The most commonly used measure of the goodness of fit of a regression line is the coefficient of determination. For present purposes, it is not necessary to know the formula for the coefficient of determination because it is seldom calculated by hand. It is a particular item—often designated by R^2, or R-sq on a computer printout, as we shall see in the section after next.

The value of the coefficient of determination varies between 0 and 1. *The closer it is to 1, the better the fit; the closer it is to 0, the poorer the fit.* In the case of the Miller Pharmaceutical Company, the coefficient of determination between sales and selling expense is 0.97, which indicates a very good fit. To get a feel for what a particular value of the coefficient of determination means, look at the six panels of Figure 5.6. Panel A shows that if the coefficient of determination is 0, there is no relationship at all between the independent and dependent variables. Panel B shows that if the coefficient of determination is 0.2, the regression line fits the data rather poorly. Panel C shows that if it is 0.4, the regression line fits better, but not very well. Panel D shows that if it is 0.6, the fit is reasonably good. Panel E shows that if it is 0.8, the fit is good.

FIGURE
5.6

Six Regression Lines: Coefficient of Determination Equals 0, 0.2, 0.4, 0.6, 0.8, and 1.0*

*When there is only one independent variable, the coefficient of determination is often designated by r^2, rather than R^2, but computer printouts generally use R^2, regardless of the number of independent variables. We use R^2 here, even though there is only one independent variable. See footnote 8.

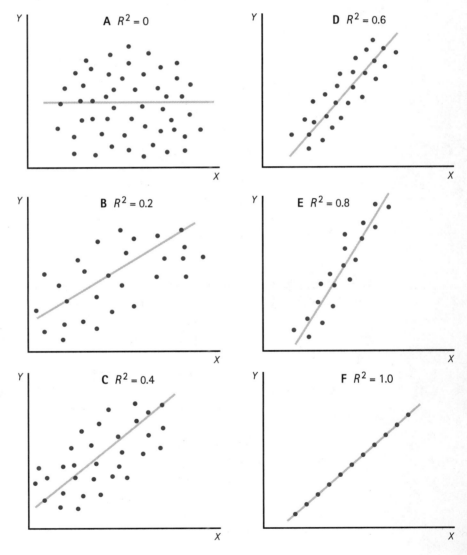

Finally, panel F shows that if it is 1.0, the fit is perfect.[8] (A fuller discussion of the coefficient of determination is provided in the appendix to this chapter.)

Multiple Regression

In previous sections of this chapter, we discussed regression techniques in the case in which there is only one independent variable. In practical applications of regression techniques, it frequently is necessary and desirable to include two or more independent variables. Now we will extend our treatment of regression to the case in which there is more than one independent variable.

Whereas a **simple regression** includes only one independent variable, a **multiple regression** includes two or more independent variables. Multiple regressions ordinarily are carried out on computers with the aid of statistical software packages like Minitab, SAS, or SPSS. Thus, there is no reason for you to learn how to do them by hand. The first step in multiple regression analysis is to identify the independent variables, and to specify the mathematical form of the equation relating the mean value of the dependent variable to these independent variables.

In the case of the Miller Pharmaceutical Company, suppose that the firm's executives feel that its sales depend on its price, as well on its selling expense. More specifically, they assume that

$$Y_i = A + B_1 X_i + B_2 P_i + e_i, \qquad (5.10)$$

where X_i is the selling expense (in millions of dollars) of the firm during the ith year, and P_i is the price (in dollars) of the firm's product during the ith year (measured as a deviation from \$10, the current price). Of course, B_2 is assumed

---

[8]If one is doing the calculations by hand, a convenient formula for the coefficient of determination is

$$r^2 = \frac{\left[n\sum_{i=1}^{n} X_i Y_i - \left(\sum_{i=1}^{n} X_i \right)\left(\sum_{i=1}^{n} Y_i \right) \right]^2}{\left[n\sum_{i=1}^{n} X_i^2 - \left(\sum_{i=1}^{n} X_i \right)^2 \right]\left[n\sum_{i=1}^{n} Y_i^2 - \left(\sum_{i=1}^{n} Y_i \right)^2 \right]}.$$

Table 5.2 contains the quantities to be inserted in this formula.

Note too that the square root of r^2, called the **correlation coefficient,** is also used to measure how well a simple regression equation fits the data. (The sign of the square root is the same as that of b.)

As pointed out in footnote * of Figure 5.6, computer printouts generally refer to the coefficient of determination as R^2, although statisticians often call it r^2 when there is only one independent variable.

CONSULTANT'S CORNER

Marketing Plans at the Stafford Company*

The Stafford Company developed a new type of electric drive. When the design engineering for this machine was finished, Stafford's managers began to make long-range plans concerning the marketing of this product. By means of field surveys and the analysis of published information, the firm's market research personnel estimated that about 10,000 electric drives of this general sort would be sold per year. The share of the total market that Stafford's new product would capture depended on its price. According to the firm's market research department, the relationship between price and market share was as follows:

Price	Market share
$ 800	11.0
900	10.2
1,000	9.2
1,100	8.4
1,200	7.5
1,300	6.6
1,400	5.6

Stafford's managers wanted advice in setting the price for their new drive, and, to help determine the optimal price, they wanted a simple equation expressing the annual quantity demanded of the new product as a function of its price. They also wanted whatever information could readily be provided concerning the reliability of this equation. In particular, they were interested in whether they could safely use this equation to estimate the quantity demanded if price were set at $1,500 or $1,600.

Prepare a brief report supplying the information requested. (Note that the figures on market share in the table are expressed in percentage points. Thus, if the price of Stafford's new product is set at $800, it will capture 11.0 percent of the market for electric drives of this general sort, according to the market research department.)

* This section is based on an actual case, although the numbers and situation are disguised somewhat.

to be negative. This is a different model from that in equation (5.2). Here it is assumed that Y_i—the firm's sales in the ith year—depends on two independent variables, not one. Of course, there is no reason why more independent variables cannot be added, so long as data are available concerning their values, and so long as there is good reason to expect them to affect Y_i. But to keep matters simple, we assume that the firm's executives believe that only selling expense and price should be included as independent variables.[9]

---

[9]As in the case of simple regression, it is assumed that the mean value of e_i is zero, and that the values of e_i are statistically independent (recall footnote 6).

The object of multiple regression analysis is to estimate the unknown constants A, B_1, and B_2 in equation (5.10). Just as in the case of simple regression, these constants are estimated by finding the value of each that minimizes the sum of the squared deviations of the observed values of the dependent variable from the values of the dependent variable predicted by the regression equation. Suppose that a is an estimator of A, b_1 is an estimator of B_1, and b_2 is an estimator of B_2. Then the value of the dependent variable Y_i predicted by the estimated regression equation is

$$\hat{Y}_i = a + b_1 X_i + b_2 P_i,$$

and the deviation of this predicted value from the actual value of the dependent variable is

$$Y_i - \hat{Y}_i = Y_i - a - b_1 X_i - b_2 P_i.$$

Thus, if these deviations are squared and summed, the result is

$$\sum_{i=1}^{n} (Y_i - \hat{Y}_i)^2 = \sum_{i=1}^{n} (Y_i - a - b_1 X_i - b_2 P_i)^2, \tag{5.11}$$

where n is the number of observations in the sample. As pointed out above, we choose the values of a, b_1, and b_2 that minimize the expression in equation (5.11). These estimates are called least-squares estimates, as in the case of simple regression.

Computer programs, described in the following section, are available to calculate these least-squares estimates. Based on the data in Table 5.3, the computer output shows that $b_1 = 1.758$, $b_2 = -0.352$, and $a = 2.529$. Consequently, the estimated regression equation is

$$Y_i = 2.529 + 1.758 X_i - 0.352 P_i \tag{5.12}$$

The estimated value of B_1 is 1.758, as contrasted with our earlier estimate of B, which was 1.504. In other words, a \$1 million increase in selling expense results in an increase in estimated sales of 1.758 millions of units, as contrasted with 1.54 millions of units in the simple regression in equation (5.8). The reason these estimates differ is that the present estimate of the effect of selling expense on sales holds constant the price, whereas the earlier estimate did not

TABLE
5.3

Sales, Selling Expense, and Price, Miller Pharmaceutical Company, Sample of Nine Years

Selling expense (millions of dollars)	Sales (millions of units)	Price (less $10)
2	6	0
1	4	1
8	16	2
5	10	3
6	12	4
4	8	5
7	12	6
9	16	7
8	14	8

hold this factor constant. Since this factor affects sales, the earlier estimate is likely to be a biased estimate of the effect of selling expense on sales.[10]

Software Packages and Computer Printouts

With few exceptions, regression analyses are carried out on computers, not by hand. Thus it is important that you know how to interpret computer printouts showing the results of regression calculations. Because there is a wide variety of "canned" programs for calculating regressions, there is no single format or list of items that are printed out. However, the various kinds of printouts are sufficiently similar so that it is worthwhile looking at two illustrations—Minitab and SAS—in some detail.

Figure 5.7 shows the Minitab printout from the multiple regression of the Miller Pharmaceutical Company's sales (designated as C1) on its selling expense (C2) and price (C3). According to this printout, the regression equation is

$$C1 = 2.529 + 1.758C2 - 0.352C3,$$

[10]Of course, this regression is only supposed to be appropriate when X_i and P_i vary in a certain limited range. If P_i is large and X_i is small, the regression would predict a negative value of sales, which obviously is inadmissible. But as long as the regression is not used to make predictions for values of X_i and P_i outside the range of the data given in Table 5.3, this is no problem. For simplicity, we assume in equation (5.10) that the effect of price on the mean value of sales (holding selling expense constant) can be regarded as linear in the relevant range. Alternatively, we could have assumed that it was quadratic, or the constant-elasticity demand function discussed in Chapter 3 might have been used.

FIGURE
5.7

Minitab Printout of Results of Multiple Regression

```
MTB > regress c1 on 2 predictors in c2 and c3

The regression equation is
C1 = 2.53 + 1.76 C2 - 0.352 C3

Predictor            Coef        Stdev      t-ratio         p
Constant           2.5294       0.2884         8.77     0.000
C2                1.75805       0.06937        25.34     0.000
C3               -0.35187       0.07064        -4.98     0.002

s = 0.3702          R-sq = 99.4%     R-sq(adj) = 99.2%

Analysis of Variance

SOURCE        DF           SS          MS          F        p
Regression     2      144.067      72.033     525.72    0.000
Error          6        0.822       0.137
Total          8      144.889

SOURCE        DF       SEQ SS
C2             1      140.667
C3             1        3.399
```

The column headed "Coef" shows the estimated regression coefficient of each independent variable (called a "Predictor" on the printout). The intercept of the regression is the top figure in this vertical column (the figure in the horizontal row where the "Predictor" is "Constant"). The coefficient of determination (called R-sq) is shown in the middle of the printout. For a multiple regression, the coefficient of determination is often called the *multiple coefficient of determination*.[11]

Figure 5.8 shows the SAS printout for the same regression. To find the intercept of the equation, obtain the figure (2.529431) in the horizontal row labeled "INTERCEP" that is in the vertical column called "Parameter Estimate." To find the regression coefficient of selling expense, obtain the figure (1.758049) in the horizontal row labeled "C2" that is in the vertical column called "Parameter Estimate." To find the regression coefficient of price, obtain the figure (−0.351870) in the horizontal row labeled "C3" that is in the vertical column called "Parameter Estimate." The multiple coefficient of determination is the figure (0.9943) to the right of "R-square."

---

[11]The positive square root of the multiple coefficient of determination is called the multiple correlation coefficient and is denoted R. It too is sometimes used to measure how well a multiple regression equation fits the data.

The *unadjusted* multiple coefficient of determination—R-sq in Figure 5.7—can never decrease as another independent variable is added; a related measure without this property is the *adjusted* multiple coefficient of determination—R-sq (adj.) in Figure 5.7. The latter is often denoted $\bar{R}^2$.

How the Japanese Motorcycle Makers Used the Coefficient of Determination

In late 1982, Harley-Davidson asked the International Trade Commission (ITC), a federal agency that investigates possible injuries to U.S. firms and workers from imports, for relief from Japanese imports of heavyweight motorcycles. According to Harley-Davidson, the Japanese were selling their motorcycles at prices too low for it to meet. On the basis of Section 201 of the 1974 Trade Act, the ITC can impose tariffs or quotas on imported goods to provide "additional time to permit a seriously injured domestic industry to become competitive. . . . " But to receive such tariff or quota relief, the industry must demonstrate that the injuries it suffers are due to increased imports, not some other cause such as bad management or a recession.

Harley-Davidson's petition to the ITC was contested by the major Japanese motorcycle makers: Honda, Kawasaki, Suzuki, and Yamaha. One of their arguments was that general economic conditions, not Japanese imports, were the principal cause of Harley-Davidson's declining share of the market. In other words, they attributed Harley-Davidson's problems to the recession of the early 1980s. They pointed out that heavyweight motorcycles, which cost about $7,000, were a "big-ticket luxury consumer product" and that their sales would be expected to fall in a recession.

To back up this argument, John Reilly of ICF, Inc., the Japanese firms' chief economic consultant, calculated a regression, where Harley-Davidson's sales were the dependent variable and the level of blue-collar employment (a measure of general economic conditions) was the independent variable. He showed that the coefficient of determination was about 0.73. Then he calculated a regression where Harley-Davidson's sales were the dependent variable, and the level of sales of Japanese motorcycles was the independent variable. He

showed that the coefficient of determination was only about 0.22. From this comparison of the two coefficients of determination, he concluded that Harley-Davidson's sales were much more closely related to general economic conditions than to the level of sales of Japanese motorcycles.

Of course, this analysis tells us nothing about the effects of the price of Japanese motorcycles on Harley-Davidson's sales and profits. From many points of view, what was needed was an estimate of the market demand function for Harley-Davidson's motorcycles. Such an analysis would have related Harley-Davidson's sales to the price of Harley-Davidson's motorcycles, the price of Japanese motorcycles, the level of disposable income, and other variables discussed in Chapter 3. In any event, despite the evidence cited, the Japanese motorcycle manufacturers did not prevail. On the contrary, the ITC supported Harley-Davidson's petition, and on April 1, 1983, President Ronald Reagan imposed a substantial tariff (almost 50 percent) on imported (large) motorcycles.*

*See "Revving Up for Relief: Harley-Davidson at the ITC," a case in the Study Guide accompanying this textbook. For further discussion, see J. Gomez-Ibanez and J. Kalt, *Cases in Microeconomics* (Englewood Cliffs, N.J.: Prentice-Hall, 1990); Reid, *Well Made in America;* and *New York Times,* July 20, 1997.

FIGURE
5.8

SAS Printout of Results of Multiple Regression

```
Dependent Variable: C1

Analysis of Variance

                         Sum of        Mean
Source            DF     Squares       Square      F Value    Prob>F

Model              2    144.06678     72.03339     525.718    0.0001
Error              6      0.82211      0.13702
C Total            8    144.88889

      Root MSE      0.37016      R-square      0.9943
      Dep Mean     10.88889      Adj R-sq      0.9924
      C.V.          3.39944

Parameter Estimates

                      Parameter      Standard      T for H0:
Variable      DF      Estimate         Error      Parameter=0   Prob > |T|

INTERCEP       1      2.529431      0.28842968        8.770      0.0001
C2             1      1.758049      0.06937127       25.343      0.0001
C3             1     -0.351870      0.07064425       -4.981      0.0025
```

Interpreting the Computer Printout

The following additional statistics are also of considerable importance: the standard error of estimate, the *F* statistic, and the *t* statistic. Each is discussed briefly below. For more detailed discussions of each, see any business statistics textbook.[12]

The Standard Error of Estimate

A measure that is often used to indicate the accuracy of a regression model is the standard error of estimate, which is *a measure of the amount of scatter of individual observations about the regression line.* The standard error of estimate is denoted by s in the Minitab printout in Figure 5.7 and by ROOT MSE in the SAS printout in Figure 5.8. A comparison of these printouts shows that in the Miller Pharmaceutical multiple regression, the standard error is about 0.37 million units of sales. Of course, the answer will always be the same, no matter which package we use.

[12]For example, E. Mansfield, *Statistics for Business and Economics* (5th ed.; New York: Norton, 1994).

FIGURE
5.9

Four Regression Lines: Standard Error of Estimate Equals 1.5, 1.0, 0.5, and 0.25

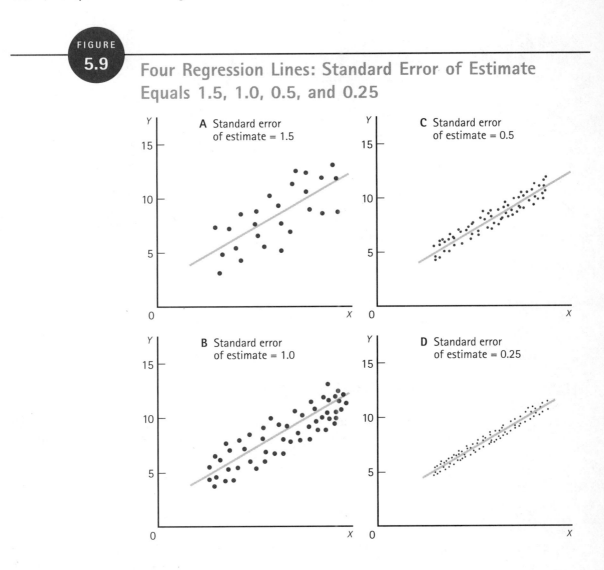

To illustrate what the standard error of estimate measures, consider Figure 5.9. In panel A, the standard error of estimate is 1.5, which is much higher than in panel D, where it is 0.25. This is reflected in the fact that there is a much greater amount of scatter of the points around the regression line in panel A than in panel D. As pointed out above, what the standard error of estimate measures is the amount of such scatter. Clearly, the amount of scatter decreases as we move from panel A to panel B to panel C to panel D. Similarly, the standard error of estimate decreases as we move from panel A to panel B to panel C to panel D.

Color Balance and Shelf-Life Performance of Polaroid Film

Regression analysis is important in many aspects of managerial economics, not just in estimating demand functions. For example, this technique helps the Polaroid Corporation, a leading manufacturer of cameras and film, to supply film at the peak of its usefulness. An extremely important consideration to Polaroid is how well films maintain their sensitivity, and whether they provide satisfactory photographic results and for how long. Information of this sort, together with data concerning average elapsed time between the purchase and utilization of film, enables Polaroid to make manufacturing adjustments to help consumers get good performance from Polaroid film.

One important characteristic of film is color balance—its ability to produce color. To see the effects of film age on color balance, Polaroid took 14 separate samples at monthly intervals, up to 13 months after manufacture. For each sample, the change in blue balance was measured. As shown in the graph below, the color balance becomes bluer (that is, "cooler," not as "warm") as the film ages.

Using the techniques described in this chapter, Polaroid estimated the regression line:

$$\hat{Y} = 8.194 + 6.756X,$$

where Y is the change in blue balance, and X is the age (in months) of the film. The coefficient of determination was 0.966, which indicates a close fit to the data.

According to Polaroid officials, this application of regression analysis has been important. Together with data regarding consumer purchase and use patterns, it enabled "Polaroid to manufacture film that will have shifted those characteristics which determine picture quality to their optimum setting by the time the film is being used. In essence, Polaroid has the information to compensate in its manufacturing process for crucial alterations in film performance that happen as a result of the aging process."*

*D. Anderson, D. Sweeney, and T. Williams, *Statistics for Business and Economics* (3d ed.; St. Paul, Minn.: West, 1987), p. 523.

ANALYZING MANAGERIAL DECISIONS

How Good are *Ward's* Projections of Auto Output?

The automobile industry and its suppliers, as well as other industries and government agencies, try in a variety of ways to forecast auto output in the United States. Each month, *Ward's Automotive Reports* asks eight U.S. automakers to state their domestic production plans for the next three to eight months. The figure below shows actual domestic auto production and Ward's projections made at the beginning of each quarter. The average error is about a half-million cars per year, or about 6 percent.

To obtain a more precise estimate of the relationship between *Ward's* projections and actual output, Ethan Harris regressed actual output (Y) on

Source: Various issues of *Ward's Automotive Reports* (1973–1985) and unpublished data from the Bureau of Economic Analysis.

The standard error of estimate is useful in constructing prediction intervals, that is, intervals within which there is a specified probability that the dependent variable will lie. If this probability is set at 0.95, a very approximate prediction interval is

$$\hat{Y} \pm 2s_e, \qquad (5.13)$$

where $\hat{Y}$ is the predicted value of the dependent variable based on the sample regression, and s_e is the standard error of estimate. For example, if the predicted

Ward's projection *(X)* and the error in Ward's projection during the previous quarter *(E)*, the result being

$$Y = 0.275 + 0.909X + 0.277E.$$

The multiple coefficient of determination equals 0.838.

(a) If *Ward's* projection is 1 million cars higher in one quarter than in another, would you expect actual output to be 1 million cars higher? Why or why not? (b) If *Ward's* projection was 100,000 cars too high in the previous quarter, is it likely that actual output will be higher than if the projection had been 100,000 cars too low in the previous quarter? (c) Does the regression provide a good or poor fit to the data?

SOLUTION (a) No. According to the equation, if *X* increases by 1 million, *Y* would be expected to increase by 0.909 times 1 million, or 909,000 (if *E* remains the same). (b) Under these circumstances, it is likely that actual output will be higher than it would if the projection had been 100,000 cars too low in the previous quarter. To see this, note that the regression coefficient of *E* in the regression equation is positive. Thus, increases in *E* tend to be associated with increases in *Y*. (c) The fact that the multiple coefficient of determination is about 0.8 indicates that the fit is good (about like that in panel E of Figure 5.6).*

*For further discussion, see E. Harris, "Forecasting Automobile Output," *Federal Reserve Bank of New York Quarterly Review,* Winter 1985–86, reprinted in *Managerial Economics and Operations Research,* Mansfield.

value of the Miller Pharmaceutical Company's sales is 11 million units, the probability is about 0.95 that the firm's sales will be between 10.26 (= $11 - 2 \times 0.37$) million units and 11.74 (= $11 + 2 \times 0.37$) million units. However, it is important to note that equation (5.13) is a good approximation only if the independent variable is close to its mean; if this is not true, more complicated formulas must be used instead.[13]

[13]The formula for the standard error of estimate is

$$\left(\sum_{i=1}^{n} (Y_i - \hat{Y}_i)^2 / (n - k - 1) \right)^{0.5}$$

where k is the number of independent variables.

If the error term is normally distributed (see Appendix B for a description of the normal distribution), the exact prediction interval (with 0.95 probability) is

$$\hat{Y} \pm t_{0.025} s_e \left(\frac{n+1}{n} + \frac{(X^* - \bar{X})^2}{\sum_{i=1}^{n} X_i^2 - \left(\sum_{i=1}^{n} X_i \right)^2 / n} \right)^{0.5}$$

where $t_{0.025}$ is the value of a variable with the t distribution with $(n - 2)$ degrees of freedom that is exceeded with probability of 0.025, X^* is the value of the independent variable, and n is the sample size. (The t distribution is taken up in Appendix B.) This assumes that there is only one independent variable. For further discussion, see Mansfield, *Statistics for Business and Economics.*

The *F* Statistic

Frequently, the analyst wants to know whether any of the independent variables really influences the dependent variable. Thus, in the case of the Miller Pharmaceutical Company, the marketing director may ask whether the data indicate that either selling expense or price really influences the firm's sales. To answer such a question, one utilizes the *F* statistic, which is also included in the computer printout. The value of *F* is provided in the fifth horizontal row from the bottom of figures in the Minitab printout (see Figure 5.7) and in the top horizontal row of figures in the SAS printout (Figure 5.8). Both printouts indicate that the value of *F* in the Miller Pharmaceutical case equals about 525.72.

Large values of *F* tend to imply that at least one of the independent variables has an effect on the dependent variable. Tables of the *F* distribution, a probability distribution named (or initialed) after the famous British statistician R. A. Fisher, are used to determine *the probability that an observed value of the F-statistic could have arisen by chance, given that none of the independent variables has any effect on the dependent variable* (see Appendix B). This probability too is shown in the computer printout. It is denoted by "p" (immediately to the right of F) in the Minitab printout, and by "Prob > F" (immediately to the right of F VALUE) in the SAS printout. The value of this probability is 0.0001 (SAS) or 0.000 (Minitab); the difference is due to rounding.

Having this probability in hand, it is easy to answer the marketing director's question. Clearly, the probability is extremely small—only about 1 in 10,000—that one could have obtained such a strong relationship between the dependent and independent variables sheerly by chance. Thus, the evidence certainly suggests that selling expense or price (or both) really influences the firm's sales.

The *t* Statistic

Managers and analysts often are interested in whether a particular independent variable influences the dependent variable. For example, the president of the Miller Pharmaceutical Company may want to determine whether the amount allocated to selling expense really affects the firm's sales. As we know from equation (5.12), the least-squares estimate of B_1 is 1.758, which suggests that selling expense has an effect on sales. But this least-squares estimate will vary from one sample to another, and by chance it may be positive even if the true value of B_1 is zero.

To test whether the true value of B_1 is zero, we must look at the *t* statistic of B_1, which is presented in the printout. For Minitab, recall that B_1 is the regression coefficient of C2, since selling expense is denoted by C2. Thus, to find the *t* statistic for B_1, we must locate the horizontal row of figures in the printout where the "Predictor" is C2, and obtain the figure in the vertical column called "t-ratio." If SAS is used, find the horizontal row of figures where the "Variable" is C2, and obtain the figure in the vertical column called "T for H0: Parameter = 0." If the error terms in the regression (that is, e_i) are normally distributed, the t statistic has a well-known probability distribution—the t distribution (see Appendix B).

All other things equal, the bigger the value of the t statistic (in absolute terms), the smaller the probability that the true value of the regression coefficient in question really is zero. Based on the t distribution, it is possible to calculate *the probability, if the true value of the regression coefficient is zero, that the* t *statistic will be as large (in absolute terms) as we observe.* This probability too is presented in the computer printout. For both Minitab and SAS, this probability is immediately to the right of the t statistic. For Minitab, it is in the vertical column labeled "p"; for SAS, it is in the vertical column labeled "Prob > |T|." Regardless of whether Minitab or SAS is used, this probability is shown to be about 0.0001 (see Figures 5.7 and 5.8).

Given this probability, we can readily answer the question put forth by the president of the Miller Pharmaceutical Company. Recall that the president wanted to know whether the amount allocated to selling expense really affects the firm's sales. Given the results obtained in the previous paragraph, it seems extremely likely that the amount allocated to selling expense really does affect sales. After all, according to the previous paragraph, the probability is only about 1 in 10,000 that chance alone would have resulted in as large a t statistic (in absolute terms) as we found, based on the firm's previous experience.[14]

---

[14]Note that this is a *two-tailed test* of the hypothesis that selling expense has no effect on sales. That is, it is a test of this hypothesis against the alternative hypothesis that the true regression coefficient of selling expense is either positive or negative. In many cases, a *one-tailed test*—for example, in which the alternative hypothesis states that the true regression coefficient is positive only—may be more appropriate.

Frequently, a manager would like to obtain an interval estimate for the true value of a regression coefficient. In other words, he or she wants an interval that has a particular probability of including the true value of this regression coefficient. To find an interval that has a probability equal to $(1 - \alpha)$ of including this true value, you can calculate

$$b_1 \pm t_{\alpha/2} s_{b1}, \tag{5.14}$$

where s_{b1} is the standard error of b_1 (in the horizontal row labeled "C2" and the vertical column labeled "Stdev" in the Minitab printout, or in the horizontal row labeled "C2" and the vertical column labeled "Standard Error" in the SAS printout) and where $t_{\alpha/2}$ is the $\alpha/2$ point on the t distribution with $(n - k - 1)$ degrees of freedom (see Appendix B). If α is set equal to 0.05, you obtain an interval that has a 95 percent probability of including B_1. Thus, in the case of the Miller Pharmaceutical Company, since, $B_1 = 1.758$, $s_{b1} = 0.069$, and $t_{0.025} = 2.447$ it follows that a 95 percent confidence interval for B_1 is

$$1.758 \pm 2.447 \ (0.069),$$

or 1.589 to 1.927. For further discussion, see any business statistics textbook.

Multicollinearity

One important problem that can arise in multiple regression studies is **multicollinearity**, which is a situation in which two or more independent variables are very highly correlated. In the case of the Miller Pharmaceutical Company, suppose that there had been a perfect linear relationship in the past between the firm's selling expense and its price. In a case of this sort, it is impossible to estimate the regression coefficients of both independent variables (X and P) because the data provide no information concerning the effect of one independent variable, holding the other independent variable constant. All that can be observed is the effect of both independent variables together, given that they both move together in the way they have in previous years.

Regression analysis estimates the effect of each independent variable by seeing how much effect this one independent variable has on the dependent variable when other independent variables are held constant. If two independent variables move together in a rigid, lockstep fashion, there is no way to tell how much effect each has separately; all that we can observe is the effect of both combined. If there is good reason to believe that the independent variables will continue to move in lockstep in the future as they have in the past, multicollinearity does not prevent us from using regression analysis to predict the dependent variable. Since the two independent variables are perfectly correlated, one of them in effect stands for both, and we therefore need to use only one in the regression analysis. However, if the independent variables cannot be counted on to continue to move in lockstep, this procedure is dangerous, since it ignores the effect of the excluded independent variable.

In reality, you seldom encounter cases in which independent variables are perfectly correlated, but you often encounter cases in which independent variables are so highly correlated that, although it is possible to estimate the regression coefficient of each variable, these regression coefficients cannot be estimated at all accurately. To cope with such situations, it sometimes is possible to alter the independent variables in such a way as to reduce multicollinearity. Suppose that a managerial economist wants to estimate a regression equation where the quantity demanded per year of a certain good is the dependent variable, and the average price of this good and disposable income of U.S. consumers are the independent variables. If disposable income is measured in money terms (that is, without adjustment for changes in the price level), there may be a high correlation between the independent variables. But if disposable income is measured in real terms (that is, with adjustment for changes in the price level), this correlation may be reduced considerably. Thus, the managerial economist may decide to measure disposable income in real rather than money terms in order to reduce multicollinearity.

If techniques of this sort cannot reduce multicollinearity, there may be no alternative but to acquire new data that do not contain the high correlation among the independent variables. Whether you (or your board of directors) like it or not, there may be no way to estimate accurately the regression coefficient of a particular independent variable that is very highly correlated with some other independent variable.

Serial Correlation

Besides multicollinearity, another important problem that can occur in regression analysis is that the error terms (the values of e_i) are not independent; instead, they are serially correlated. For example, Figure 5.10 shows a case in which if the error term in one period is positive, the error term in the next period is almost always positive. Similarly, if the error term in one period is neg-

FIGURE
5.10

Serial Correlation of Error Terms

If the error term in one year is positive, the error term in the next year is almost always positive. If the error term in one year is negative, the error term in the next year is almost always negative.

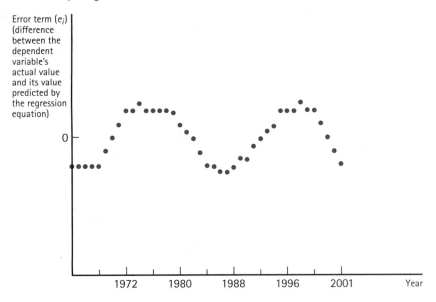

ative, the error term in the next period almost always is negative. In such a situation, we say that the errors are serially correlated (or autocorrelated, which is another term for the same thing).[15] Because this violates the assumptions underlying regression analysis, it is important that we be able to detect its occurrence. (Recall that regression analysis assumes that the values of e_i are independent.)

To see whether serial correlation is present in the error terms in a regression, we can use the Durbin-Watson test. Let $\hat{e}_i$ be the difference between Y_i and $\hat{Y}_i$, the value of Y_i predicted by the sample regression. To apply the Durbin-Watson test, we (or in most cases, the computer) must calculate

$$ d = \frac{\sum\limits_{i=2}^{n} (\hat{e}_i - \hat{e}_{i-1})^2}{\sum\limits_{i=1}^{n} \hat{e}_i^2} \tag{5.15} $$

Durbin and Watson have provided tables that show whether d is so high or so low that the hypothesis that there is no serial correlation should be rejected. (Note that d is often called the Durbin-Watson statistic.)

Suppose we want to test this hypothesis against the alternative hypothesis that there is **positive** serial correlation. (Positive serial correlation would mean that e_i is directly related to e_{i-1}, as in Figure 5.10.) If so, we should reject the hypothesis of no serial correlation if $d < d_L$ and accept this hypothesis if $d > d_u$. If $d_L \leq d \leq d_u$, the test is inconclusive. The values of d_L and d_u are shown in Appendix Table 7. (Note that these values depend on the sample size n and on k, the number of independent variables in the regression.) On the other hand, suppose that the alternative hypothesis is that there is **negative** serial correlation. (Negative serial correlation would mean that e_i is inversely related to e_{i-1}.) If so, we should reject the hypothesis of no serial correlation if $d > 4 - d_L$ and accept this hypothesis if $d < 4 - d_u$. If $4 - d_u \leq d \leq 4 - d_L$, the test is inconclusive.[16]

One way to deal with the problem of serial correlation, if it exists, is to take first differences of all the independent and dependent variables in the regression. For example, in the case of the Miller Pharmaceutical Company, we might

---

[15]This is a case of positive serial correlation. (It is the sort of situation frequently encountered in managerial economics.) If the error term in one period tends to be positive (negative) and if the error term in the previous period is negative (positive), this is a case of negative serial correlation. More is said about this subsequently.

[16]For a two-tailed test of both positive and negative serial correlation, reject the hypothesis of no serial correlation if $d < d_L$ or if $d > 4 - d_L$, and accept this hypothesis if $d_u < d < 4 - d_u$. Otherwise, the test is inconclusive. For a two-tailed test, the significance level is double the significance level shown in Appendix Table 7.

use the change in sales relative to the previous year (rather than the level of sales) as the dependent variable. And the change in selling expense relative to the previous year (rather than the level of selling expense) and the change in price relative to the previous year (rather than the level of price) might be used as the independent variables in the regression.[17]

Further Analysis of the Residuals

In the previous section, we used $\hat{e}_i$—the difference between the actual value of Y_i and its value predicted by the sample regression—to test for serial correlation. Since it is a measure of the extent to which Y_i *cannot* be explained by the regression, $\hat{e}_i$ is often called the **residual** for the ith observation. Now we describe additional ways in which the residuals—that is, the values of $\hat{e}_i$—can be used to test whether the assumptions underlying regression analysis are met. We begin by plotting the value of each residual against the value of the independent variable. (For simplicity, we suppose that there is only one independent variable.) That is, we plot $\hat{e}_i$ against X_i, which is the independent variable.

Suppose that the plot is as shown in Figure 5.11. As you can see, the values of the residuals are much more variable when X_i is large than when it is small. In other words, the variation in $\hat{e}_i$ increases as X_i increases. Since regression analysis assumes that *the variation in the error terms is the same, regardless of the value of the independent variable,* the plot in Figure 5.11 indicates that this assumption is violated. Two ways to remedy this situation are to use a weighted least-squares regression or to change the form of the dependent variable. For example, we might use log Y rather than Y as the dependent variable.[18]

If the plot of $\hat{e}_i$ against X_i looks like Figure 5.12, this is an indication that the relationship between the dependent and independent variables is not linear. When X is very low and very high, the linear regression *overestimates* the dependent variable, as shown by the fact that the residuals tend to be negative. When X is of medium size, the linear regression underestimates the dependent variable, as shown by the fact that the residuals tend to be positive. It appears

---

[17]The use of first differences, while useful in some cases, is not always appropriate. For further discussion, see Johnston, *Econometric Methods.*

It is also important to avoid specification errors, which result when one or more significant explanatory variables are not included in the regression. If specification errors arise, the estimated regression coefficients may be biased, and the regression equation may not predict very well. Also, problems can arise if the independent variables in a regression contain substantial measurement errors, since the regression coefficients of these variables often tend to be biased toward zero.

[18]For further details, see Johnston, *Econometric Methods.*

FIGURE
5.11

Residuals Indicating That the Variation in the Error Terms Is Not Constant

As you can see, the residuals vary less when X is small than when it is large.

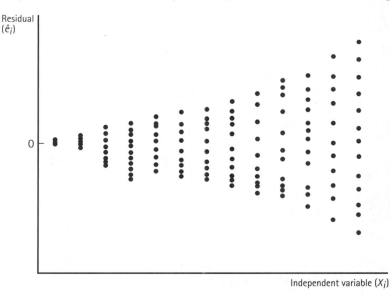

that a quadratic relationship fits the data better than a linear one. Thus, rather than assume that equation (5.2) holds, we should assume that

$$Y_i = A + B_1 X_i - B_2 X_i^2 + e_i.$$

Using the multiple regression techniques described above, the values of A, B_1, and B_2 can be estimated.

Summary

1. An identification problem may occur if price in various periods is plotted against quantity demanded, and the resulting relationship is used to estimate the demand curve. Because nonprice variables are not held constant, the demand curve may have shifted over time. Nonetheless, sophisticated econometric methods may be used to estimate the demand function. Also, market experiments and consumer interviews may be of value. For example, firms sometimes vary price from one city or region to another, and see what

FIGURE
5.12

Residuals Indicating That the Relationship between the Dependent and Independent Variables Is Nonlinear, Not Linear

The residuals are negative when X is very small or very large, and positive when X is of medium size.

the effects are on quantity demanded. An actual illustration of this sort was the evaluation of the four promotion alternatives by L'eggs Products.

2. Regression analysis is useful in estimating demand functions and other economic relationships. The regression line shows the average relationship between the dependent variable and the independent variable. The method of least squares is the standard technique used to fit a regression line to a set of data. If the regression line is $\hat{Y} = a + bX$, and if a and b are calculated by least squares,

$$b = \frac{\sum_{i=1}^{n} (X_i - \overline{X})(Y_i - \overline{Y})}{\sum_{i=1}^{n} (X_i - \overline{X})^2}$$

and $\qquad\qquad a = \overline{Y} - b\overline{X}.$

This value of b is often called the estimated regression coefficient.

ANALYZING MANAGERIAL DECISIONS

How Fed Economists Forecast Auto Output

Since purchases by the auto industry account for more than half of the rubber and lead consumed in this country, as well as a major portion of the steel, aluminum, and a variety of other materials, it is obvious that many firms and government agencies, as well as the auto firms themselves, are interested in forecasting auto output. The Federal Reserve Bank of New York has published an article describing how the regression techniques described in this chapter have been used for this purpose. According to the author, Ethan Harris, the quantity of autos produced quarterly depends on five variables: (1) real disposable income, (2) the ratio of retail auto inventories to sales, (3) the average price of new cars (relative to the overall consumer price index), (4) the price level for nonauto durable goods, and (5) the prime rate (the interest rate banks charge their best customers).

The regression results are shown below. The probability that the t statistic for each of the regression coefficients will be as large (in absolute terms) as it is here, if the true value of the regression coefficient is zero, is less than 0.01, except for the case of the nonauto price.

The value of the adjusted multiple coefficient of determination is 0.862, the standard error of estimate is 532, and the Durbin-Watson statistic (d) is 2.26. According to Ethan Harris, this regression equation has predicted auto output with a mean (absolute) error of about 6.9 percent.

(a) Would you expect the regression coefficient of the inventory-sales ratio to be negative? If so, why? (b) Can we be reasonably sure that the true value of the regression coefficient of the inventory-sales ratio is nonzero? Why or why not? (c) Is there evidence of positive serial correlation of the error terms? (d) Can we use this regression as an estimate of the demand curve for autos? Why or why not?

SOLUTION (a) Yes. If inventories are large relative to sales, one would expect auto firms to produce less than they would if inventories were small. (b) Yes. According to the discussion above, the probability that the t statistic for the regression coefficient of the inventory-sales ratio would be as great as 6.1 (in absolute terms) would be less than 0.01 if the true regression coefficient were zero. Thus, if this true regression coefficient were zero, it is exceedingly unlikely that the t statistic (in absolute terms) would equal its observed value or more. (c) No. Since the value of n is approximately 50 and $k = 5$, Appendix Table 7 shows that $d_L = 1.26$ and $d_u = 1.69$ if the significance level equals 0.025. The observed value of the Durbin-Watson statistic (2.26) is greater than d_u (1.69); this means that we should accept the hypothesis that there is no positive serial correlation. (d) No. One important indication that this is true is the fact that the regression coefficient of the auto price is positive. Clearly, this regression equation cannot be used as an estimate of the demand curve for autos.

Variable	Regression coefficient	t statistic
Constant	−22,302	−4.5
Disposable income	12.9	6.6
Prime rate	−97.8	−3.2
Inventory-sales ratio	−19.9	−6.1
Auto price	230	5.0
Nonauto price	6.0	2.1

3. Whereas a simple regression includes only one independent variable, a multiple regression includes more than one independent variable. An advantage of multiple regression over a simple regression is that you frequently can predict the dependent variable more accurately if more than one independent variable is used. Also, if the dependent variable is influenced by more than one independent variable, a simple regression of the dependent variable on a single independent variable may result in a biased estimate of the effect of this independent variable on the dependent variable.

4. The first step in multiple regression analysis is to identify the independent variables, and then to specify the mathematical form of the equation relating the mean value of the dependent variable to the independent variables. For example, if Y is the dependent variable and X and P are identified as the independent variables, one might specify that

$$Y_i = A + B_1 X_i + B_2 P_i + e_i,$$

where e_i is an error term. To estimate B_1 and B_2 (called the true regression coefficients of X and P) as well as A (the intercept of this true regression equation), we use the values that minimize the sum of squared deviations of Y_i from $\hat{Y}_i$, the value of the dependent variable predicted by the estimated regression equation.

5. In a simple regression, the coefficient of determination is used to measure the closeness of fit of the regression line. In a multiple regression, the multiple coefficient of determination, R^2, plays the same role. The closer R^2 is to 0, the poorer the fit; the closer it is to 1, the better the fit.

6. The F statistic can be used to test whether any of the independent variables has an effect on the dependent variable. The standard error of estimate can help to indicate how well a regression model can predict the dependent variable. The t statistic for the regression coefficient of each independent variable can be used to test whether this independent variable has any effect on the dependent variable. Computer printouts show the probability that the t statistic would be as big (in absolute terms) as we have observed, given that this independent variable has no effect on the dependent variable.

7. A difficult problem that can occur in multiple regression is multicollinearity, a situation in which two or more of the independent variables are highly correlated. If multicollinearity exists, it may be impossible to estimate accurately the effect of particular independent variables on the dependent variable. Another frequently encountered problem arises when the error terms in a regression are serially correlated. The Durbin-Watson test can be carried out to determine whether this problem exists. Plots of the residuals can help to detect cases in which the variation of the error terms is not constant or where the relationship is nonlinear, not linear.

Problems

1. The Klein Corporation's marketing department, using regression analysis, estimates the firm's demand function, the result being

$$Q = -104 - 2.1P + 3.2I + 1.5A + 1.6Z,$$
$$R^2 = 0.89 \quad \text{and} \quad \text{standard error of estimate} = 108,$$

where Q is the quantity demanded of the firm's product (in tons), P is the price of the firm's product (in dollars per ton), I is per capita income (in dollars), A is the firm's advertising expenditure (in thousands of dollars), and Z is the price (in dollars) of a competing product. The regression is based on 200 observations.

a. According to the computer printout, the probability is 0.005 that the t statistic for the regression coefficient of A would be as large (in absolute terms) as it is in this case if in fact A had no effect on Q. Interpret this result.

b. If $I = 5,000$, $A = 20$, and $Z = 1,000$, what is the Klein Corporation's demand curve?

c. If $P = 500$ (and the conditions in part b hold), estimate the quantity demanded of the Klein Corporation's product.

d. How well does this regression equation fit the data?

2. Since the Hawkins Company's costs (other than advertising) are essentially all fixed costs, it wants to maximize its total revenue (net of advertising expenses). According to a regression analysis (based on 124 observations) carried out by a consultant hired by the Hawkins Company,

$$Q = -23 - 4.1P + 4.2I + 3.1A,$$

where Q is the quantity demanded of the firm's product (in dozens), P is the price of the firm's product (in dollars per dozen), I is per capita income (in dollars), and A is advertising expenditure (in dollars).

a. If the price of the product is $10 per dozen, should the firm increase its advertising?

b. If the advertising budget is fixed at $10,000, and per capita income equals $8,000, what is the firm's marginal revenue curve?

c. If the advertising budget is fixed at $10,000, and per capita income equals $8,000, what price should the Hawkins Company charge?

3. The 1980 sales and profits of seven steel companies were as follows:

Firm	Sales	Profit
	(billions of dollars)	
Armco	5.7	0.27
Bethlehem	6.7	0.12
Bundy	0.2	0.00
Carpenter	0.6	0.04
Republic	3.8	0.05
U.S. Steel (now USX)	12.5	0.46
Westran	0.5	0.00

a. Calculate the sample regression line, where profit is the dependent variable and sales is the independent variable.

b. Estimate the 1980 average profit of a steel firm with 1980 sales of $2 billion.

c. Can this regression line be used to predict a steel firm's profit in 2002? Explain.

4. The Cherry Manufacturing Company's chief engineer examines a random sample of ten spot welds of steel. In each case, the shear strength of the weld and the diameter of the weld are determined, the results being as follows:

Shear strength (pounds)	Weld diameter (thousandths of an inch)
680	190
800	200
780	209
885	215
975	215
1,025	215
1,100	230
1,030	250
1,175	265
1,300	250

a. Does the relationship between these two variables seem to be direct or inverse? Does this accord with common sense? Why or why not? Does the relationship seem to be linear?

b. Calculate the least-squares regression of shear strength on weld diameter.

c. Plot the regression line. Use this regression line to predict the average

shear strength of a weld 1/5 inch in diameter. Use the regression line
to predict the average shear strength of a weld 1/4 inch in diameter.

5. The Kramer Corporation's marketing manager calculates a regression, where
the quantity demanded of the firm's product (designated as C1) is the dependent variable and the price of the product (designated as C2) and consumers' disposable income (designated as C3) are independent variables. The
Minitab printout for this regression is shown below:

```
MTB > regress c1 on 2 predictors in c2 and c3
The regression equation is
C1 = 40.8 - 1.02 C2 + 0.00667 C3

Predictor          Coef         Stdev      t-ratio           p
Constant         40.833         1.112        36.74       0.000
C2              -1.02500       0.06807       -15.06       0.000
C3              0.006667      0.005558         1.20       0.244

s=1.361                    R-sq=91.6%              R-sq(adj)=90.8%
Analysis of variance

SOURCE              DF           SS          MS          F           p
Regression           2       422.92      211.46      114.11       0.000
Error               21        38.92        1.85
Total               23       461.83

SOURCE              DF       SEQ SS
C2                   1       420.25
C3                   1         2.67
```

a. What is the intercept of the regression?
b. What is the estimated regression coefficient of the product's price?
c. What is the estimated regression coefficient of disposable income?
d. What is the multiple coefficient of determination?
e. What is the standard error of estimate?
f. What is the probability that the observed value of the F statistic could
have arisen by chance, given that neither of the independent variables
has any effect on the dependent variable?
g. What is the probability, if the true value of the regression coefficient
of price is zero, that the t statistic will be as large (in absolute terms)
as we observe?
h. What is the probability, if the true value of the regression coefficient
of disposable income is zero, that the t statistic will be as large (in absolute terms) as we observe?
i. Describe briefly what this regression means.

6. Railroad executives must understand how the costs incurred in a freight
yard are related to the output of the yard. The two most important services
performed by a yard are switching and delivery, and it seems reasonable
to use the number of cuts switched and the number of cars delivered during a particular period as a measure of output. (A **cut** is a group of cars

that rolls as a unit onto the same classification track; it is often used as a unit of switching output.) A study of one of the nation's largest railroads assumed that

$$C_i = A + B_1 S_i + B_2 D_i + e_i,$$

where C_i is the cost incurred in this freight yard on the ith day, S_i is the number of cuts switched in this yard on the ith day, D_i is the number of cars delivered in this yard on the ith day, and e_i is an error term. Data were obtained regarding C_i, S_i, and D_i for 61 days. On the basis of the procedures described in this chapter, these data were used to obtain estimates of A, B_1, and B_2. The resulting regression equation was

$$\hat{C}_i = 4{,}914 + 0.42S_i + 2.44D_i,$$

where $\hat{C}_i$ is the cost (in dollars) predicted by the regression equation for the ith day.[19]

a. If you were asked to evaluate this study, what steps would you take to determine whether the principal assumptions underlying regression analysis were met?

b. If you were satisfied that the underlying assumptions were met, of what use might the above regression equation be to the railroad? Be specific.

c. Before using the study's regression equation, what additional statistics would you like to have? Why?

d. If the Durbin-Watson statistic equals 2.11, is there evidence of serial correlation in the residuals?

7. Mary Palmquist, a Wall Street securities analyst, wants to determine the relationship between the nation's gross domestic product (GDP) and the profits (after taxes) of the General Electric Company. She obtains the following data concerning each variable:

---

[19]For a much more detailed account of this study, see E. Mansfield and H. Wein, "A Managerial Application of a Cost Function by a Railroad," a case in the *Study Guide* accompanying this textbook.

Year	Gross domestic product (billions of dollars)	General Electric's profits (millions of dollars)
1965	688	355
1966	753	339
1967	796	361
1968	868	357
1969	936	278
1970	982	363
1971	1,063	510
1972	1,171	573
1973	1,306	661
1974	1,407	705
1975	1,529	688
1976	1,706	931

a. What are the least-squares estimates of the intercept and slope of the true regression line, where GE's profits are the dependent variable and GDP is the independent variable?

b. On the average, what effect does a $1 increase in gross domestic product seem to have on the profits of GE?

c. If Ms. Palmquist feels that next year's GDP will be $2 trillion, what forecast of GE's profits will she make on the basis of the regression?

d. What is the coefficient of determination between the nation's gross domestic product and GE's profits?

e. Do the results obtained in previous parts of this problem prove that changes in GE's profits are caused by changes in the gross domestic product? Can we be sure that GE's profit is a linear function of the GDP? What other kinds of functions might be as good or better?

f. If you were the financial analyst, would you feel that this regression line was an adequate model to forecast GE's profits? Why or why not?

8. In the manufacture of cloth, the weft packages should not disintegrate unduly during weaving. A direct measure of the tendency to disintegrate exists, but it is very laborious and uneconomical to carry out. In addition, there are indirect measures based on laboratory tests. The Brockway Textile Company would like to determine the extent to which one of these indirect measures is correlated with the direct measure. If the correlation is high enough, the firm believes that it may be able to use the indirect measure instead of the direct measure.

An experiment was carried out in which both the direct and indirect measures of the tendency to disintegrate were calculated for 18 lots of packages. The results were as shown on the next page:

| | Measure | |
Lot	Direct	Indirect
1	31	6.2
2	31	6.2
3	21	10.1
4	21	8.4
5	57	2.9
6	80	2.9
7	35	7.4
8	10	7.3
9	0	11.1
10	0	10.7
11	35	4.1
12	63	3.5
13	10	5.0
14	51	4.5
15	24	9.5
16	15	8.5
17	80	2.6
18	90	2.9

a. What is the coefficient of determination between the two measures?

b. What is the linear regression line you would use to predict the value of the direct measure on the basis of knowledge of the indirect measure?

c. On the basis of your findings, write a brief report indicating the factors to be weighed in deciding whether to substitute the indirect measure for the direct measure.

9. The Kingston Company hires a consultant to estimate the demand function for its product. Using regression analysis, the consultant estimates the demand function to be

$$\log Q = 2.01 - 0.148 \log P + 0.258 \log Z,$$

where Q is the quantity demanded (in tons) of Kingston's product, P is the price (in dollars per ton) of Kingston's product, and Z is the price (in dollars per ton) of a rival product.

a. Calculate the price elasticity of demand for Kingston's product.

b. Calculate the cross elasticity of demand between Kingston's product and the rival product.

c. According to the consultant, $\bar{R}^2 = 0.98$ and the standard error of estimate is 0.001. If the number of observations is 94, comment on the goodness of fit of the regression.

10. During the 1960s, the Boston and Maine Railroad conducted an experiment in which it reduced fares by about 28 percent for approximately a year in order to estimate the price elasticity of demand. This large fare reduction resulted in essentially no change in the railroad's revenues.

    a. What problems exist in carrying out an experiment of this sort?

    b. Taken at face value, what seemed to be the price elasticity of demand?

11. Because of a shift in consumer tastes, the market demand curve for high-quality red wine has shifted steadily to the right. If the market supply curve has remained fixed (and is upward sloping to the right), there has been an increase over time in both the price of such wine and in the quantity sold.

    a. If one were to plot price against quantity sold, would the resulting relationship approximate the market demand curve?

    b. If not, what would this relationship approximate?

12. The Brennan Company uses regression analysis to obtain the following estimate of the demand function for its product:

$$\log Q = 2 - 1.2 \log P + 1.5 \log I,$$

where Q is quantity demanded, P is price, and I is consumers' disposable income.

    a. Brennan's president is considering a 5 percent price reduction. He argues that these results indicate that it will result in a 6 percent increase in the number of units sold by the firm. Do you agree? Why or why not?

    b. The firm's treasurer points out that, according to the computer printout, the probability that the t statistic of $\log P$ would be as large (in absolute value) as it is, given that $\log P$ has no real effect on $\log Q$, is about 0.5. He says that the estimate of the price elasticity is unreliable. Do you agree? Why or why not?

    c. How can the firm obtain a more accurate estimate of the price elasticity of demand?

Appendix: The Coefficient of Determination and the Concept of Explained Variation

In this appendix, we provide a fuller explanation of what the coefficient of determination is and how it can be interpreted. To begin with, we must discuss the concept of variation, which refers to a sum of squared deviations. The total variation in the dependent variable Y equals

$$\sum_{i=1}^{n} (Y_i - \overline{Y})^2. \tag{5.16}$$

In other words, the total variation equals the sum of the squared deviations of Y from its mean.

To measure how well a regression line fits the data, we divide the total variation in the dependent variable into two parts: the variation that *can* be explained by the regression line, and the variation that *cannot* be explained by the regression line. To divide the total variation in this way, we must note that for the ith observation,

$$(Y_i - \overline{Y}) = (Y_i - \hat{Y}_i) + (\hat{Y}_i - \overline{Y}), \qquad (5.17)$$

where $\hat{Y}_i$ is the value of Y_i that would be predicted on the basis of the regression line. In other words, as shown in Figure 5.13, the discrepancy between Y_i and the mean value of Y can be split into two parts: the discrepancy between Y_i and the point on the regression line directly below (or above) Y_i, and the discrepancy between the point on the regression line directly below (or above) Y_i and $\overline{Y}$.

FIGURE
5.13

Division of $(Y_i - \overline{Y})$ into Two Parts: $(Y_i - \hat{Y}_i)$ and $(\hat{Y}_i - Y)$

This division is carried out to measure how well the regression line fits the data.

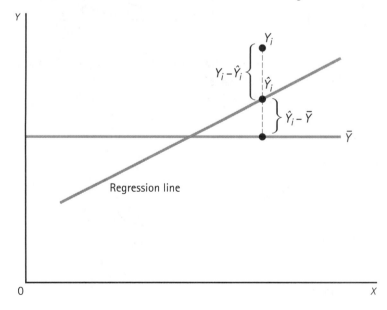

It can be shown that[20]

$$\sum_{i=1}^{n} (Y_i - \overline{Y})^2 = \sum_{i=1}^{n} (Y_i - \hat{Y}_i)^2 + \sum_{i=1}^{n} (\hat{Y}_i - \overline{Y})^2. \qquad (5.18)$$

The term on the left-hand side of this equation shows the *total variation* in the dependent variable. The first term on the right-hand side measures the *variation in the dependent variable that is not explained by the regression*. This is a reasonable interpretation of this term, since it is the sum of squared deviations of the actual observations from the regression line. Clearly, the larger the value of this term, the poorer the regression equation fits the data. The second term on the right-hand side of the equation measures the *variation in the dependent variable that is explained by the regression*. This is a reasonable interpretation of this term, since it shows how much the dependent variable would be expected to vary on the basis of the regression alone.

To measure the closeness of fit of a simple regression line, we use the **coefficient of determination,** which equals

$$1 - \frac{\displaystyle\sum_{i=1}^{n} (Y_i - \hat{Y}_i)^2}{\displaystyle\sum_{i=1}^{n} (Y_i - \overline{Y})^2}. \qquad (5.19)$$

In other words, the coefficient of determination equals

$$1 - \frac{\text{variation not explained by regression}}{\text{total variation}}$$
$$= \frac{\text{variation explained by regression}}{\text{total variation}}. \qquad (5.20)$$

Clearly, the coefficient of determination is a reasonable measure of the closeness of fit of the regression line, since it equals the proportion of the total variation in the dependent variable that is explained by the regression line. The closer it is to 1, the better the fit; the closer it is to 0, the poorer the fit.

---

[20]To derive this result, we square both sides of equation (5.17) and sum the result over all values of *i*. We find that

$$\sum_{i=1}^{n} (Y_i - \overline{Y})^2 = \sum_{i=1}^{n} [(Y_i - \hat{Y}_i) + (\hat{Y}_i - \overline{Y})]^2$$
$$= \sum_{i=1}^{n} (Y_i - \hat{Y}_i)^2 + \sum_{i=1}^{n} (\hat{Y}_i - \overline{Y})^2 + 2 \sum_{i=1}^{n} (Y_i - \hat{Y}_i)(\hat{Y}_i - \overline{Y}).$$

The last term on the right-hand side equals zero, so equation (5.18) follows.

When a multiple regression is calculated, the multiple coefficient of determination is used to measure the goodness of fit of the regression. The multiple coefficient of determination is defined as

$$R^2 = 1 - \frac{\sum\limits_{i=1}^{n} (Y_i - \hat{Y}_i)^2}{\sum\limits_{i=1}^{n} (Y_i - \overline{Y})^2}, \tag{5.21}$$

where $\hat{Y}_i$ is the value of the dependent variable that is predicted from the regression equation. Thus, as in the case of the simple coefficient of determination covered earlier,

$$R^2 = \frac{\text{variation explained by regression}}{\text{total variation}}; \tag{5.22}$$

this means that R^2 *measures the proportion of the total variation in the dependent variable that is explained by the regression equation.*

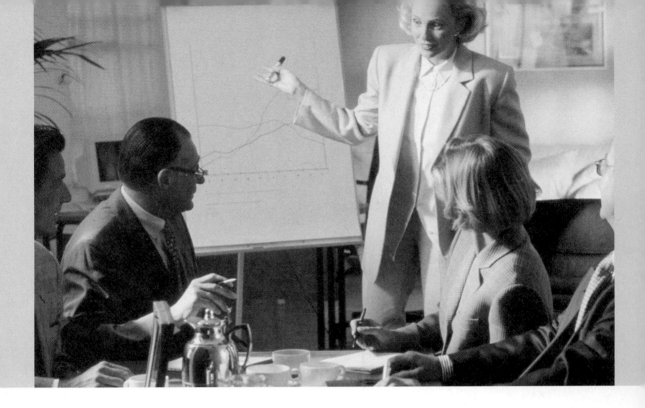

Business and Economic Forecasting

CHAPTER 6

Many corporations have corporate economists or hire consulting firms to forecast their sales or profits. These forecasts can be done on a short-term basis, for example, next quarter, or on a longer-term basis, for the next year, five years, or ten years. Security analysts forecast quarterly and yearly earnings, and one can hear their consensus via First Call before earnings are about to be released. Popular business press publications, like *Business Week*, the *Wall Street Journal,* offer similar results. The Federal Reserve and the Department of Commerce also conduct business forecasts as do trade associations for their industries.

Managers of all sorts are routinely involved in decision making that is informed by forecasts. Sales forecasts, for instance, may dictate raw material ordering, production run scheduling, and hiring decisions. An organization's mid-level managers are likely to make these decisions. On the other hand, long-term growth forecasts for an industry may entail capital expansion or disinvestments of assets, decisions likely to be made by higher level managers within the organization—most likely with the Board of Directors' approval.

In this chapter we take up the techniques used by many business and economic forecasters. As you work through these subjects, keep in mind that economic forecasting is not an exact science. Too many variables exist to precisely model the economic system or even a small part of it. Even so, most corporations prefer rigorous data to intuition or hunch (and, in fact, managers have a fiduciary responsibility to the owners of the firm to practice due diligence in following rational procedures for decision making). Recently, dot.coms and other new economy businesses were started with virtually no business plans and no concept of the market. While some success stories exist, most ventures failed, and after an initial "love affair" with internet startups, the financial community has now declared that "red is dead," that is, they will not throw funding at firms that cannot project a profit within a reasonable period of time.

As we shall see, regression—which we studied in Chapter 5—plays a major role in many of these forecasting techniques, including the econometric models that are the staple of the leading private and public economic forecasters.

Survey Techniques

One of the simplest forecasting devices is to survey firms or individuals and to determine what they believe will occur. Consider the surveys carried out to forecast firms' expenditures. For example, the U.S. Department of Commerce and the Securities and Exchange Commission conduct surveys of business intentions to buy plant and equipment. Still other surveys are aimed at measuring consumer intentions. The Survey Research Center at the University of Michigan and other such groups provide information on planned purchases of automobiles, appliances, and housing. Also, they indicate the extent of consumer confidence in the economy, which is an important factor influencing consumers' spending decisions. Surveys of this type are of value in forecasting the sales of many products. They provide a wealth of information to the forecaster.

At least two types of information can be obtained from surveys. First, they can provide us with the respondent's forecast of some variable over which he or she has no control. For example, the University of Michigan obtains data from consumers concerning their forecasts of the rate of inflation. Second, surveys can provide us with information concerning what people or firms believe they will do. For example, the National Federation of Independent Business surveys firms to determine whether, and to what extent, they plan to increase their prices.[1]

Suppose a survey is used to forecast some variable, such as the sales of a particular firm. How can we determine how reliable this forecasting technique

---

[1]See W. Dunkelberg, "The Use of Survey Data in Forecasting," in *Managerial Economics and Operations Research*, Mansfield.

seems to be? One commonly used measure of the size of the forecast error is the **root-mean-squared forecast error**, which is defined as

$$E = \left(\sum_{i=1}^{n} (Y_i - F_i)^2 / n \right)^{0.5},$$

where F_i is the ith forecast, Y_i is the corresponding actual value, and n is the number of forecasts for which we have data concerning the size of the forecast errors. Thus, if the forecasts for 1999, 2000, and 2001 are $110 million, $120 million, and $130 million, and if the actual values are $105 million, $122 million, and $127 million, respectively, the root-mean-squared forecast error equals

$$\sqrt{\frac{(105 - 110)^2 + (122 - 120)^2 + (127 - 130)^2}{3}} = 3.56,$$

or $3.56 millions of dollars. This measure of forecast error is used to evaluate forecasts, no matter whether they are based on surveys or other techniques. Clearly, the lower the root-mean-squared forecast error, the better the forecasting technique.

Taking Apart a Time Series

Although surveys are of considerable use, most major firms seem to base their forecasts in large part on the quantitative analysis of economic time series. The classical approach to economic forecasting, devised primarily by economic statisticians, was essentially descriptive. It assumed that an economic time series could be decomposed into four components: trend, seasonal variation, cyclical variation, and irregular movements. More specifically, it assumed that the value of an economic variable at a certain time could be represented as the product of each of these four components. For example, the value of a company's sales in January 2002 was viewed as equal to

$$Y = T \times S \times C \times I, \tag{6.1}$$

where T is the trend value of the firm's sales during that month, S is the seasonal variation attributable to January, C is the cyclical variation occurring that month, and I is the irregular variation that occurred then.[2] Each of these components is defined below.

---

[2]In some versions of this model, the components are added rather than multiplied. That is, it is assumed that

$$Y = T + S + C + I,$$

where Y is the value of the time series.

FIGURE
6.1

Civilian Labor Force of the United States, 1947–2001

This series exhibits a strong upward trend.

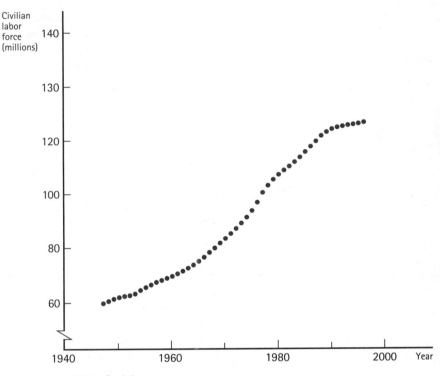

Source: Bureau of Labor Statistics.

Trend

A trend is a relatively smooth long-term movement of a time series. For instance, the civilian labor force of the United States increased rather steadily between 1947 and 2000, as shown in Figure 6.1. Thus, there has been an upward trend in the U.S. civilian labor force. Of course, not all trends are upward. The trend in farm employment in the United States has generally been downward, as shown in Figure 6.2.[3] Whether upward or downward, the trend of a time series is represented by a smooth curve. In equation (6.1), *T* is the value of the firm's sales that would be predicted for January 2002, on the basis of such a curve.

---

[3]In still other cases, the trend is horizontal; that is, there is no upward tendency or downward tendency in the time series. In these cases, it is often said that there is no trend.

FIGURE
6.2

Farm Employment in the United States, 1947–2000

This series exhibits a strong downward trend.

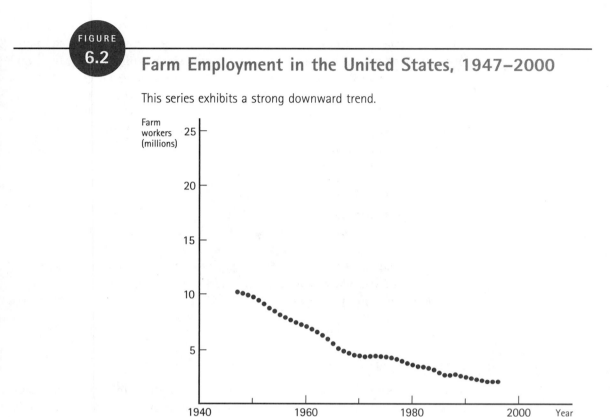

Source: USDA economies and statistics.

Seasonal Variation

In a particular month, the value of an economic variable is likely to differ from what would be expected on the basis of its trend, because of seasonal factors. For example, consider the sales of a firm that produces Christmas trees. Since the demand for Christmas trees is much higher in the winter than in the summer, one would expect that the monthly time series of the firm's sales would show a pronounced and predictable seasonal pattern. Specifically, sales each year would tend to be higher in December than during the rest of the year. As we shall see, it is possible to calculate *seasonal indexes* that estimate how much each month departs from what would be expected on the basis of its trend. In equation (6.1), we must multiply the trend value T by the seasonal index S to allow for the effect of this seasonal variation.

Cyclical Variation

Another reason why an economic variable may differ from its trend value is that it may be influenced by the so-called business cycle. The general tempo of economic activity in our society has exhibited a cyclical nature, with booms being followed by recessions, and recessions being followed by expansions. These cycles have not been regular or consistent (which is one reason why many economists prefer the term "business fluctuations" to "business cycles"); but unquestionably there has been a certain cyclical ebb and flow of economic activity, which has been reflected in a great many time series. For this reason, $T \times S$ is multiplied by C, which is supposed to indicate the effect of cyclical variation on the firm's sales in equation (6.1).

Irregular Variation

Once it has been multiplied by both S and C, the trend value T has been altered to reflect seasonal and cyclical forces. But besides these forces, *a variety of short-term, erratic forces is also at work.* Their effects are represented by I. Essentially, I reflects the effects of all factors other than the trend, seasonal variation, and cyclical variation. According to the classical model, these irregular forces are too unpredictable to be useful for forecasting purposes.

How to Estimate a Linear Trend

Managerial economists have carried out many studies to estimate the trend, seasonal variation, and cyclical variation in particular economic time series. In this and the following sections of this chapter, we will encounter the methods used to estimate a trend; in subsequent sections, we will take up seasonal and cyclical variation. First, we consider the case in which the long-term overall movement of the time series seems to be fairly close to linear. For example, this seems true for the sales of the ABC Corporation during the period 1986 to 2000. (These sales are plotted in Figure 6.3.) In a case in which the trend seems to be linear, analysts frequently use the method of least squares to calculate the trend. In other words, they assume that if the long-term forces underlying the trend were the only ones at work, the time series would be approximately linear. Specifically, they assume that

$$Y_t = A + Bt, \qquad (6.2)$$

where Y_t is the trend value of the variable at time t. (Note that t assumes values like 2000 or 2001 if time is measured in years.) The **trend value** is the value of the variable that would result if only the trend were at work. The deviation of Y, the actual value of the variable, from the trend value is the **deviation from trend.**

To illustrate the calculation of a linear trend, let's examine the ABC Corporation's annual sales from 1986 to 2000. Since sales in year t is the dependent

FIGURE
6.3

Linear Trend in Sales, ABC Corporation, 1986–2000

The ABC Corporation's sales have risen rather steadily throughout the period.

variable and t is the independent variable, it follows from our discussion in Chapter 5 that

$$b = \frac{\sum\limits_{t=t_0}^{t_0+n-1} (S_t - \bar{S})(t - \bar{t})}{\sum\limits_{t=t_0}^{t_0+n-1} (t - \bar{t})^2} \qquad (6.3)$$

and

$$a = \bar{S} - b\bar{t}, \qquad (6.4)$$

where S_t is sales (in billions of dollars) in year t, t_0 is the earliest year in the time series (that is, 1986), $t_0 + n - 1$ is the latest year in the time series (that is, 2000), b is an estimate of B, and a is an estimate of A.

Inserting the data underlying Figure 6.3 into equations (6.3) and (6.4), we find that the trend line is

$$S_t = -11,593 + 5.875t. \qquad (6.5)$$

This trend line is plotted in Figure 6.3.

How to Estimate a Nonlinear Trend

Many time series do not exhibit linear trends. In some such cases, a quadratic function of time provides an adequate trend. Such a trend can be represented as

$$Y_t = A + B_1 t + B_2 t^2.$$

To estimate A, B_1, and B_2, we can use the multiple regression techniques described in Chapter 5. As indicated there, standard computer programs are available to make these computations. The regression contains two independent variables: t and t^2. Whether a quadratic trend is more appropriate than a linear trend can be determined by seeing whether it fits the data significantly better than a linear trend.

For many variables, an exponential curve provides a better-fitting trend than a quadratic curve. The equation for such a trend (shown in Figure 6.4) is

$$Y_t = \alpha \beta^t, \tag{6.6}$$

where Y_t is the trend value of the time series at time t. A trend of this sort seems to fit many business and economic time series. It represents a situation

---

FIGURE
6.4

Exponential Trend, Assuming $\beta = 1.5$, $\alpha = 1$

Many time series have exponential trends.

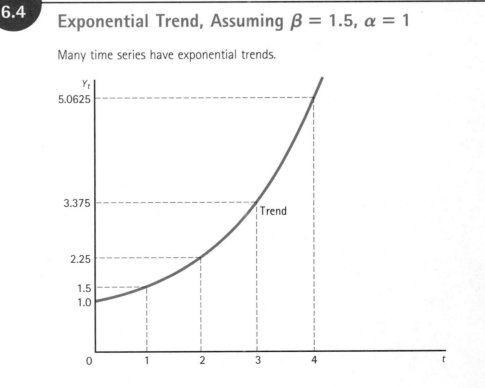

in which the variable grows at a constant percentage rate per year. Thus, if a firm's sales grow at about 5 percent per year, they are likely to exhibit an exponential trend.

If there is an exponential trend, we can take logarithms of both sides of equation (6.6).

$$\log Y_t = A + Bt, \tag{6.7}$$

where $A = \log \alpha$, and $B = \log \beta$. Since equation (6.7) is linear, we can estimate A and B by the method of least squares. Then we can take antilogs of A and B to estimate α and β, the unknown coefficients in equation (6.6). (The average rate of increase of Y_t equals $\beta - 1$.)[4] In this way, we can estimate the nonlinear trend shown in equation (6.6).

Seasonal Variation

Many time series consist of monthly or quarterly rather than annual data. For such time series, managerial economists and decision makers must recognize that seasonal variation is likely to be present in the series. Seasonal variation in many economic time series is due to the weather. For example, sales of soft drinks are higher in the summer than in the winter. In other cases, such as sales of Christmas trees, seasonal variation is due to the location of a specific holiday (Christmas) on the calendar. Still other reasons for seasonal variation are the fact that some industries tend to grant vacations at a particular time of year, that taxes have to be paid at certain times of the year, or that schools tend to open at particular times of the year.

Managerial economists have devised methods for estimating the pattern of seasonal variation in a particular time series. In other words, they can determine the extent to which a particular month or quarter is likely to differ from what would be expected on the basis of the trend and cyclical variation in the same series. [In terms of the traditional model in equation (6.1), they can determine the value of S for each month or quarter.] For example, the marketing vice president for a manufacturer of soft drinks may tell the company's board

---

[4]If Y grows at a constant rate of $100r$ percent per year,

$$Y_t = Y_0(1 + r)^t,$$

where Y_0 is the value of Y in some base year (say 1990), and Y_t is its value t years after the base year. Taking logarithms of both sides of this equation,

$$\log Y_t = \log Y_0 + [\log (1 + r)]t.$$

Thus, $\log (1 + r)$ equals B, and the antilog of B—which is β—equals $(1 + r)$. Consequently, $r = \beta - 1$. In other words, as stated in the text, the average rate of increase of Y_t—which is r—equals $\beta - 1$. (Mathematical review: If X is the logarithm of Y, Y is called the antilog of X.)

of directors that U.S. production of soft drinks tends in June to be 5.9 percent higher than what the trend and cyclical variation in soft drink production would indicate. Or she may tell them that U.S. production of soft drinks in December tends to be 7.0 percent lower than the trend and cyclical variation would indicate.

The seasonal variation in a particular time series is described by a figure for each month, the **seasonal index,** *which shows the way in which that month tends to depart from what would be expected on the basis of the trend and cyclical variation in the time series.* For example, Table 6.1 shows the seasonal variation in U.S. production of soft drinks. January's production tends to be about 93.4 percent of the amount expected on the basis of trend and cyclical variation; February's production tends to be about 89.3 percent of this amount; March's production tends to be about 90.7 percent of this amount; and so on. Figures of this sort can be used in a number of ways. *One important application is to forecast what the time series will be in the future.* For example, suppose that on the basis of the trend and cyclical variation, it appears likely that about 30 million gallons of soft drinks will be produced next January. If this is the case, a reasonable forecast of actual January production is 0.934(30 million) = 28.02 million gallons, since January's production tends to be 93.4 percent of the amount expected based on trend and cyclical variation.

Calculation of Seasonal Variation

One way of calculating the seasonal variation in a time series is to use the regression techniques described in Chapter 5. Suppose, for example, that a business analyst has a time series composed of quarterly values; that is, each observation pertains to the first, second, third, or fourth quarter of a year. If

TABLE 6.1

Seasonal Variation in Production of Soft Drinks in the United States

Month	Seasonal index	Month	Seasonal index
January	93.4	July	112.4
February	89.3	August	113.4
March	90.7	September	108.3
April	94.9	October	103.9
May	99.0	November	95.8
June	105.9	December	93.0

the analyst believes that the time series has a linear trend, he or she may assume that the value of the observation at time t equals

$$Y = A + B_1 t + B_2 Q_1 + B_3 Q_2 + B_4 Q_3 + e_t, \qquad (6.8)$$

where Q_1 equals 1 if time t is the first quarter and 0 otherwise, Q_2 equals 1 if time t is the second quarter and 0 otherwise, Q_3 equals 1 if time t is the third quarter and 0 otherwise, and e_t is an error term.

It is important to understand the meaning of B_1, B_2, B_3, and B_4 in equation (6.8). Clearly, B_1 is the slope of the linear trend, but what are B_2, B_3, and B_4? The answer is that B_2 is *the difference between the expected value of an obser-vation in the first quarter and the expected value of an observation in the fourth quarter when the effects of the trend are removed.* (The **expected value** of an observation is its long-term mean value. To find its expected value, one multiplies each possible value of the observation by the probability of this value, and sums up the results.) To see that this is true, note that if an observation pertains to time t, the first quarter of a particular year, its expected value equals

$$A + B_1 t + B_2,$$

according to equation (6.8). Similarly, if an observation pertains to time $t + 3$, the fourth quarter of the same year, its expected value equals

$$A + B_1(t + 3),$$

according to equation (6.8). Thus, the difference between the expected value of an observation in the first quarter and the expected value of an observation in the fourth quarter equals

$$(A + B_1 t + B_2) - [A + B_1(t + 3)] = B_2 - 3B_1.$$

And if we remove the effects of the trend (which is responsible for the last term on the right, $3B_1$), this difference equals B_2; this is what we set out to prove. When the effects of the trend are removed, one can show in the same way that B_3 is *the difference between the expected value of an observation in the second quarter and the expected value of an observation in the fourth quarter,* and B_4 is *the difference between the expected value of an observation in the third quarter and the expected value of an observation in the fourth quarter.*

Consequently, if equation (6.8) is valid, the analyst can represent the seasonal variation in the time series by the three numbers B_2, B_3, and B_4. To estimate each of these numbers, ordinary multiple regression techniques can be used. The dependent variable is Y, and the independent variables are t, Q_1, Q_2, and Q_3. The latter three independent variables—Q_1, Q_2, and Q_3—are dummy vari-

ANALYZING MANAGERIAL DECISIONS

Forecasting the Demand for Blood Tests

North Carolina Memorial Hospital (now part of University of North Carolina Hospitals) has been interested in forecasting the number of blood tests it will perform. A simple model has been constructed that assumes that the number of tests per month increases according to a linear trend, and that the seasonal variation can be represented in the way described in equation (6.9). In other words, it is assumed that

$$Q = A + B_1 t + B_2 M_1 + B_3 M_2 + \cdots + B_{12} M_{11} + e_t,$$

where Q is the number of blood tests performed at the hospital in month t, M_1 equals 1 if month t is January and 0 otherwise, ..., M_{11} equals 1 if month t is November and 0 otherwise, and e_t equals an error term. Thus, B_2 is the difference between January and December in the expected number of tests, B_3 is the difference between February and December in the expected number of tests, and so on (when the effects of the trend are removed).

(a) Indicate how one can estimate the values of A, B_1, B_2, ..., B_{12}. (b) Potential patients are reluctant to seek medical care during the Christmas holidays. Would you expect B_2 to be positive or negative? Why? (c) According to the hospital, the model forecasts "are being used to plan vacation schedules for ... employees and to order supplies for the tests."* Why would forecasts of this sort be useful for these purposes? (d) Forecasts based on this simple model have been reported to be "excellent." Forecasting errors have averaged only about 4.4 percent. On the other hand, forecasts based on exponential smoothing (a technique described in the chapter appendix) did not perform so well. Do you think that a model of this sort will always outperform exponential smoothing?

SOLUTION (a) The values of these parameters can be estimated by calculating a multiple regression, where Q is the dependent variable and t, M_1, M_2, ..., M_{11} are the independent variables. (b) Positive, because B_2 is the difference between January and December in the expected number of tests when the effects of the trend are removed. Because patients tend not to want such tests during the holidays, December would be expected to be below January in this regard. (c) If one can forecast the demand for blood tests, it is possible to estimate the number of employees and the quantity of supplies needed at various times. Clearly, this information is useful in scheduling vacations and purchases, among other things. (d) No. In some cases, one forecasting technique works well; in others, it works less well. No technique is universally better than the others discussed in this chapter.

*E. Gardner, "Box-Jenkins vs. Multiple Regression: Some Adventures in Forecasting the Demand for Blood Tests," *Interfaces*, August 1979, pp. 49–54.

ables. (A **dummy variable** is defined as a variable that can assume only two values: 0 or 1.) Using the regression methods described in Chapter 5, the constants in equation (6.8)—A, B_1, B_2, B_3, and B_4—can be estimated by the ordinary least-squares technique.

When using this procedure, the analyst assumes that seasonal effects are *added* to the trend value, as shown in equation (6.8). This differs from the traditional model in equation (6.1), where it is assumed that seasonal effects *multiply* the trend value (see footnote 2). The former assumption is appropriate in some cases, whereas the latter assumption is appropriate in others. Techniques based on both assumptions are useful.[5]

To illustrate how this regression procedure can be used to estimate the seasonal variation in monthly data, suppose you have monthly data concerning the sales of a particular firm. If there is a linear trend, you can assume that

$$Y = A + B_1 t + B_2 M_1 + B_3 M_2 + \cdots + B_{12} M_{11} + e_t, \tag{6.9}$$

where Y is the firm's sales in month t, M_1 equals 1 if month t is January and 0 otherwise, M_2 equals 1 if month t is February and 0 otherwise, . . . , M_{11} equals 1 if month t is November and 0 otherwise, and e_t equals an error term. Using ordinary multiple regression techniques, you can estimate A, B_1, B_2, . . . , B_{12}. The estimates of B_2, B_3, . . . , B_{11}, and B_{12} indicate the seasonal variation in the firm's sales. In particular, B_2 is the difference between January and December in the expected value of sales, B_3 is the difference between February and December in the expected value of sales, and so on, until B_{12} is the difference between November and December in the expected value of sales (when the effects of the trend are removed).

Cyclical Variation

Time series in business and economics frequently exhibit cyclical variation, such variation often being termed the **business cycle.** To illustrate what we mean by the business cycle or **business fluctuations,** let's look at how national output has grown in the United States since 1929. Figure 6.5 shows the behavior of gross domestic product (GDP) in constant dollars in the United States since 1929. Clearly, output has grown considerably during this period; indeed, GDP is more than five times what it was sixty years ago. But this growth has not been steady. While the long-term trend has been upward, there have been periods, such as 1929–1933, 1937–1938, 1944–1946, 1948–1949, 1953–1954, 1957–1958, 1969–

---

[5]To calculate the seasonal variation based on the latter assumption, a 4-quarter—or 12-month if the data are monthly—moving average can be used. For the details, see any business statistics book.

FIGURE
6.5

Gross Domestic Product (GDP) (1987 Dollars), United States, 1929–2000 (Excluding World War II)

National output has fluctuated considerably.

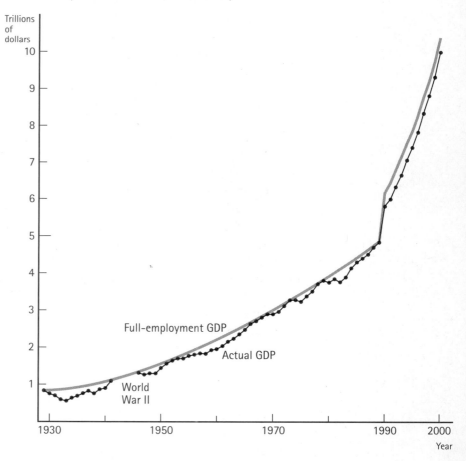

1970, 1973–1975, 1980, 1981–1982, and 1990–1991, when national output has declined.

The **full-employment level** of GDP is defined as the total amount of goods and services that could have been produced if there had been full employment. Figure 6.5 shows that national output tends to rise and approach (and perhaps exceed)[6] its full-employment level for a while, then falters and falls below this level, then rises to approach it once more, then falls below it again, and so on.

[6]During a period of inflationary pressure, national output may exceed its full-employment level.

FIGURE
6.6

Four Phases of Business Fluctuations

The peak occurs when national output is highest relative to its full-employment value; the trough occurs when national output is lowest relative to its full-employment value.

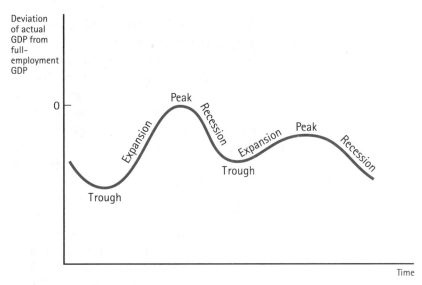

For example, output fell far below the full-employment level in the depressed 1930s, but rose again to this level once we entered World War II. This movement of national output is sometimes called the business cycle, but it must be recognized that these "cycles" are far from regular or consistent.

Each cycle can be divided by definition into four phases, as shown in Figure 6.6. *The **trough** is the point where national output is lowest relative to its full-employment level. **Expansion** is the subsequent phase during which national output rises. The **peak** occurs when national output is highest relative to its full-employment level. Finally, **recession** is the subsequent phase during which national output falls.*[7]

Many business and economic time series go up and down with the business cycle. For example, industrial output tends to be above its trend line at the peak of the business cycle and tends to fall below its trend line at the trough. Similarly, such diverse series as the money supply, industrial employment, and stock prices reflect the business cycle. However, not all series go up and down at exactly the same time. Some turn upward before others at a trough, and some

---

[7]The peak and trough may also be defined in terms of deviations from the long-term trend of GDP rather than in terms of deviations from the full-employment level of GDP.

turn downward before others at a peak. As we shall see below, the fact that some time series tend to precede others in cyclical variation sometimes is used to forecast the pace of economic activity.

Elementary Forecasting Techniques

In general, all forecasting techniques are extremely fallible, and all forecasts should be treated with caution. Nonetheless, businesses and government agencies have no choice but to make forecasts, however crude. Since firms, governments, and private individuals must continually make decisions that hinge on what they expect will happen, they must make implicit forecasts even if they do not make explicit ones. Thus, the central question is how best to forecast, not whether to forecast. In this section, we present some elementary forecasting techniques that are commonly applied. Even among small firms, recent evidence indicates that about three-quarters of the firms use techniques of this sort.[8] However, these techniques should be viewed as crude first approximations rather than as highly sophisticated methods. More sophisticated techniques are taken up subsequently.

The simplest type of forecasting method is a straightforward extrapolation of a trend. For example, let's return to the ABC Corporation. At the end of 2000, suppose that ABC Corporation managers wanted to forecast its 2001 sales. During the period 1986–2000, we know from our earlier discussion that the firm's sales could be represented (approximately) by the trend line

$$S_t = -11,593 + 5.875t,$$

where t equals the year in question. To forecast its 2001 sales, the ABC Corporation could simply insert 2000 for t in the above equation. Thus, the forecast for 2001 is

$$-11,593 + 5.875(2001) = 162.9,$$

or 162.9 billions of dollars. As shown in Figure 6.7, this forecast is a simple extension, or extrapolation, of the trend line into the future.

Decision makers often need forecasts of monthly rather than annual amounts. In such cases, it is necessary to recognize that seasonal variation, as well as trend, is likely to affect the value for a particular month. To see how a forecast can be made under such circumstances, consider a clothing manufacturer that wants to forecast its sales during each month of 2002. On the basis of data

[8]R. Coccari, "How Quantitative Business Techniques Are Being Used," *Business Horizons,* July 1989.

FIGURE
6.7

Simple Trend Extrapolation to Forecast 2001 Sales of the ABC Corporation

The forecast is $139.4 billion.

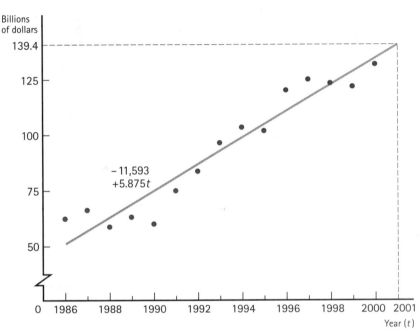

for each month during the period 1973 to 2001, the firm determines that its sales seem to conform to the trend

$$S_t = 12{,}030 + 41t,$$

where S_t is the trend value of the firm's monthly sales (in thousands of dollars), and t is time measured in months from January 2001. Thus, if this trend continues, the expected sales for each month in 2002 would be as shown in the second column of Table 6.2. But this ignores whatever seasonal variation exists in the firm's sales. In order to include seasonal variation, suppose that the clothing manufacturer's marketing manager analyzes past sales data and finds that the monthly seasonal index for sales is as shown in the third column of Table 6.2. (Seasonal effects here are multiplicative, not additive.) Thus, if this seasonal pattern continues in 2002 as in the past, we would expect that actual sales each month would equal the trend value (in the second column) times the seasonal index (in the third column) divided by 100. The result, which is shown

TABLE
6.2

Forecast of Sales of Clothing Manufacturer, 2002

Month	Forecast trend value of sales[a]	Seasonal index	Forecast sales (reflecting both trend and seasonal variables)[a]
January	12,522	90	11,270
February	12,563	80	10,050
March	12,604	80	10,083
April	12,645	90	11,380
May	12,686	110	13,955
June	12,727	120	15,272
July	12,768	80	10,214
August	12,809	110	14,090
September	12,850	120	15,420
October	12,891	100	12,891
November	12,932	100	12,932
December	12,973	120	15,568

[a]Expressed in units of $1,000.

in the fourth column of Table 6.2, is a forecast that includes both the trend and the seasonal variation.

Needless to say, this entire procedure is simply a mechanical extrapolation of the firm's sales data into the future. The assumption is made that the past trend and the past seasonal variation will continue. Moreover, it is assumed that the trend and seasonal variation are the predominant factors that will determine sales in the coming months. The validity of this assumption depends on many considerations, including the extent to which the time series in question (in this case, sales) is affected by cyclical factors and the extent to which the economy is likely to change its cyclical position. In the next section, we turn our attention to a particular method of forecasting business fluctuations.

How Leading Indicators Are Used

Managers and analysts want to modify their forecasts in order to reflect prospective overall changes in economic activity. For example, if the president of the clothing firm in Table 6.2 is convinced that a serious depression will occur in 2002, he is likely to modify the forecasts in Table 6.2 accordingly. But how does the president of the clothing firm—or anyone else—predict whether there is going to be a depression? There are a variety of ways of doing this, all of which are very imperfect. In this section, we discuss an essentially empirical approach, reserving a discussion of more sophisticated techniques for a later section.

One of the simplest ways to forecast business fluctuations is to use **leading indicators,** which are certain economic series that typically go down or up before gross domestic product does. The National Bureau of Economic Research has carried out detailed and painstaking examinations of the behavior of various economic variables over a long period of time, and has attempted to find out whether each variable turns downward before, at, or after the peak of the business cycle, and whether it turns upward before, at, or after the trough. Variables that go down before the peak and up before the trough are called **leading series.** Variables that go down at the peak and up at the trough are called **coincident series.** Variables that go down after the peak and up after the trough are called **lagging series.**

According to the bureau, some important leading series are new orders for durable goods, the average workweek, building contracts, stock prices, certain wholesale prices, and claims for unemployment insurance. These are the variables that tend to turn downward before the peak and upward before the trough.[9] Coincident series include employment, industrial production, corporate profits, and gross domestic product, among many others. Some typical lagging series are retail sales, manufacturers' inventories, and personal income.

These leading series—or leading indicators, as they often are called—are used frequently as forecasting devices. There are sound economic reasons why these series turn downward before a peak or upward before a trough: in some cases, leading series indicate changes in spending in strategic areas of the economy, while in others, they indicate changes in managers' and investors' expectations. In order to guide business executives in their planning, it is important to try to spot turning points—peaks and troughs—in advance. This, of course, is the toughest part of economic forecasting. Economists sometimes use leading indicators as evidence that a turning point is about to occur. If a large number of leading indicators turn down, this is viewed as a sign of a coming peak. The upturn of a large number of leading indicators is thought to signal an impending trough.

Experience with leading indicators has been only partially successful. The economy has seldom turned downward in recent years without a warning from these indicators, but unfortunately these indicators have turned down on a number of occasions—in 1952 and 1962, for example—when the economy did *not* turn down subsequently. Thus, leading indicators sometimes provide false signals. Also, in periods of expansion, they sometimes turn downward too far ahead of the real peak. And in periods of recession, they sometimes turn up-

---

[9] Of course, claims for unemployment insurance turn upward before the peak and downward before the trough.

CONSULTANT'S CORNER

Deciding Whether to Finance the Purchase of an Oil Field*

In 1985, a leading bank was deciding whether to approve a loan application from an oil and gas company. This loan was to finance the purchase of an oil and gas field. The bank projected the oil and gas company's most likely production levels and profits, and estimated how much money the company would have available to meet its debt. To make these estimates, it was necessary to forecast the price of crude oil. In the bank's view, the oil industry had very good prospects for returning to the prosperity of the 1970s.

The 15-year forecast of the oil price that was provided by the bank's head office for the purpose of evaluating this loan was as follows:

Year	Price (par barrel)	Year	Price (per barrel)
1986	$25	1994	$41
1987	27	1995	43
1988	29	1996	45
1989	31	1997	47
1990	33	1998	49
1991	35	1999	51
1992	37	2000	53
1993	39		

You've now got the benefit of hindsight, but even in 1985 you should have been suspicious of the bank's forecast. If the bank hired you to evaluate its forecasting procedure in this case, what comments would you make?

*This section is based on an actual case, although the numbers and situation are simplified somewhat.

ward only a very short while before the trough, so that we've turned the corners before anything can be done. Nonetheless, leading indicators are not worthless; they are watched closely and used to supplement other, more sophisticated forecasting techniques.[10]

Students interested in learning more about these leading indicators should visit the website of The Conference Board (www.conference-board.org). The Con-

[10]See R. Ratti, "A Descriptive Analysis of Economic Indicators," in *Managerial Economics and Operations Research,* Mansfield.

ference Board is a nonprofit organization that provides economic reports and data about business issues and sponsors the business cycle indicators website. The website not only shows a time series for the leading indicators, but also discusses their implications for the U.S. economy. In addition, the site reports the leading indicators for other countries.

How Econometric Models Are Used

Managers and analysts have tended in recent years to base their forecasts more and more on multiple regression techniques and multiequation models. Increased emphasis has been put on the construction and estimation of an equation or system of equations to show the effects of various independent variables on the variable or variables one wants to forecast. For example, one may want to estimate the quantity of automobiles produced by U.S. auto firms next quarter. According to a study published by the Federal Reserve Bank of New York (which was described on page 184), the following regression equation is useful for this purpose:[11]

$$A = -22{,}302 + 12.9D - 97.8I - 19.9R + 230P + 6.0N,$$

where A is the quantity of autos produced quarterly, D is real disposable income, I is the prime interest rate, R is the inventory-sales ratio, P is the auto price, and N is the nonauto price level. To forecast the quantity of autos produced quarterly, one estimates the values of the independent variables and inserts them into this equation.

Multiequation models have been used to forecast many variables, such as gross domestic product. The Wharton model, a pioneer in this field, contained hundreds of equations variously intended to explain the level of expenditures by households, the level of business investment, aggregate output and employment, and wages, prices, and interest rates. The forecasts produced by the Wharton model (and other large models like it) have been followed closely by major business firms and government agencies. Indeed, some firms (like General Electric) have constructed their own multiequation models. Of course, this does not mean that these large models have an unblemished forecasting record; on the contrary, they, like all other forecasting techniques, are quite fallible. However, these models continue to be used in business and government.

Both the single-equation model used to forecast the quantity of autos produced and the Wharton model, with its hundreds of equations, are examples of econometric models. An **econometric model** is a system of equations (or a single equation) estimated from past data that is used to forecast economic and

---

[11]E. Harris, "Forecasting Automobile Output," *Federal Reserve Bank of New York Quarterly Review*, Winter 1985–86, reprinted in *Managerial Economics and Operations Research*, Mansfield.

ANALYZING MANAGERIAL DECISIONS

Forecasting Shipments of Cement by CEMCO

CEMCO is a small cement producer that has used an econometric model to forecast its sales and profits. According to this model, national cement shipments depend on the amount of residential construction and business fixed investment. Assuming its price is unchanged, CEMCO's shipments of cement are assumed to depend on national cement shipments. Holding national cement shipments constant, CEMCO can increase its shipments by reducing its price. However, its rivals are likely to meet such a price cut, whereas they are less likely to match a price increase.

This year, CEMCO shipped 453,000 tons of cement. Based on this model, and alternative assumptions concerning the firm's future price, the forecasted shipments for next year and the year after next were as follows (in thousands of tons):

Assumed future change in CEMCO's price	Next year	Year after next
No price change	468	457
10 percent price increase	306	296
10 percent price decrease	473	459

(a) As stated above, the firm's model assumes that (1) national cement shipments depend on the amount of residential construction and business

fixed investment, and (2) its shipments depend on national cement shipments (if its price does not change). Does it appear that the company expected both residential construction and business fixed investment to be higher in the year after next than in next year? Why or why not? (b) With regard to increases in price, does the demand for the firm's cement seem to be price elastic or price inelastic? Explain. (c) Does the price elasticity of demand seem to be lower for price decreases than for price increases? Is this reasonable? Why or why not?

SOLUTION (a) No. If the company had expected both residential construction and business fixed investment to be higher in the year after next than in next year, it would have forecasted an increase in national cement shipments, which in turn would have implied an increase in CEMCO's cement shipments (assuming no price change). In fact, as shown in the table on the left, it forecasted that its cement shipments would be lower in the year after next than in next year. (b) Price elastic. A 10 percent increase in price seems to reduce shipments by about one-third. (c) Yes. It seems reasonable if, as stated above, the firm's rivals are likely to meet a price reduction, but unlikely to meet a price increase.*

*F. G. Adams, *The Business Forecasting Revolution* (New York: Oxford University Press, 1986), pp. 219–36. A couple of numbers have been changed for pedagogical reasons.

business variables. The essence of any econometric model is that it blends economic theory with modern statistical methods.

John Hancock and Timberland: A Case Study

The John Hancock Mutual Life Insurance Company manages timberland for investors, who reap gains when either the timber or the land is sold at a profit.

Hancock's holdings include 1.8 million acres of forests, mostly in the Southeast and the Pacific Northwest. The firm uses econometric models to estimate future demand for timber, as well as changes in wood and paper prices. On the basis of these estimates, Hancock executives decide what kinds of trees to plant, how to manage their growth, and when to harvest them.

In early 1994, Hancock's economists were predicting rising prices in the next three or four years as the national economy grew and the supply of commercial timber declined. Investors in timberland were getting returns of 20 to 30 percent per year from their investment, but Hancock recognized that the profit rate was likely to decline over time to a 9 to 15 percent rate. Econometric models were used to try to maintain the profit rate at a high level.[12]

The Purvere Corporation: A Numerical Example

To illustrate the nature of multiequation econometric models, consider the Purvere Corporation, a seller of aircraft. Purvere's total revenues come from three sources: the sale of the equipment, the servicing of the equipment, and the sale of accessories to customers who buy equipment or have it serviced. On the basis of regression analysis, Purvere's managers have found that its revenues from each of these sources can be represented by the following three equations:

$$E_t = 100 - 4P_t + 0.02\ G_t \qquad (6.10)$$
$$S_t = 10 + 0.05\ E_{t-1} \qquad (6.11)$$
$$A_t = 25 + 0.1\ Y_t, \qquad (6.12)$$

where E_t is the company's revenue from equipment sales in year t, P_t is the price of its equipment, G_t is gross domestic product (in billions of dollars), S_t is its revenue from servicing its equipment, A_t is its revenue from accessory sales, and Y_t is its total sales (which equal $E_t + S_t + A_t$). The values of E_t, S_t, A_t, and P_t are expressed in millions of dollars.

According to equation (6.10), Purvere's equipment sales are inversely related to its price and directly related to gross domestic product. According to equation (6.11), its service revenues are directly related to its equipment sales during the previous year (because the equipment is serviced about a year after it is bought). According to equation (6.12), its revenue from accessory sales is directly related to its total sales.

Purvere's president wants to use this model to forecast next year's total sales, which equal (in year t)

$$Y_t = E_t + S_t + A_t = (100 + 10 + 25) - 4P_t + 0.02G_t + 0.05E_{t-1} + 0.1\ Y_t.$$

[12]*New York Times*, February 20, 1994.

Thus,
$$(1 - 0.1)Y_t = 135 - 4P_t + 0.02G_t + 0.05E_{t-1},$$

or
$$Y_t = \frac{1}{0.9}(135 - 4P_t + 0.02G_t + 0.05E_{t-1}). \qquad (6.13)$$

This equation can be used to forecast next year's value of Y if we know the price of Purvere's equipment next year, the value of GDP next year, and the firm's revenues from equipment sales this year. Suppose that price will be 10 and that this year's equipment sales will be 100. Then

$$Y_t = \frac{1}{0.9}(135 - 4 \times 10 + 0.05 \times 100 + 0.02G_t)$$

$$= \frac{1}{0.9}(100 + 0.02G_t).$$

To forecast Y_t, we must know G_t, the value of gross domestic product next year. Obviously, the best we can do is to utilize the best available forecast of next year's GDP. Suppose that Purvere's president decides to rely on the forecast of a large econometric model (like Wharton's), which is that GDP next year will be about $6,250 billion. If so, his sales forecast for next year will be

$$Y_t = \frac{1}{0.9}(100 + 0.02 \times 6,250) = \frac{1}{0.9}(225) = 250,$$

or $250 million.

Note that Purvere's president is linking his company model in equations (6.10) to (6.12) to the large econometric model, which is providing the forecasted value of G_t. This is frequently the way managers have used the forecasts of macroeconomic models like the Wharton model.

Before leaving this example, it is important to recognize that it is highly simplified. Firms frequently use multiequation models containing many variables, not just the handful contained in equations (6.10) to (6.12). Some of these additional variables utilized to forecast company sales were identified and discussed in Chapter 3. General Electric, for example, has used an iterative process "in which the initial values are obtained from individual economic relationships but the final results are strongly influenced by the experience, 'feel,' and intuition of business economists. This procedure has the advantage of 'taking everything into account' along with the disadvantage of being time consuming. The GE group, like the large model forecasters, forecasts more than a hundred economic variables, including items of special interest to the company such as total appliance sales and electric power generation."[13]

[13]S. McNees, "The Recent Record of Thirteen Forecasters," *New England Economic Review*, September 1981, p. 291.

"Study Your Residuals"

Before concluding this chapter, it is important to consider Nobel laureate Paul A. Samuelson's well-known statement: "To the scientific forecaster I say, 'Always study your residuals.'" What Samuelson meant was that in evaluating any forecasting technique, it is useful to calculate the difference between each observation and what the technique predicts this observation will be. These differences—or residuals (defined in Chapter 5)—are very useful in indicating whether your forecasting technique excludes some important explanatory variables and whether its assumptions are valid.

To illustrate, suppose you are using an econometric model to forecast your firm's sales, and the difference between each year's sales and what this model predicts these sales to be is as shown in Figure 6.8. To improve this technique, you should think hard about why the model made the errors that it did. Based on Figure 6.8, it might occur to you, for example, that many of the years when the residuals were large and positive were years when your firm had an un-

FIGURE
6.8

Residuals from Sales Forecasting Model

The years (1989 and 1997) when the residuals are large and negative are ones when the sales force was small; the years (1993 and 2000) when they are large and positive are ones when the sales force was large.

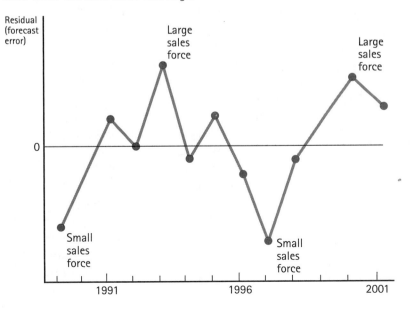

usually large sales force, and that many of the years when the residuals were large and negative were years when your firm had an unusually small sales force. If the size of your firm's sales force is not included as an independent variable in your model, there may be good reason to include it.

By continually studying your forecasting errors, and improving your forecasting techniques, significant progress can be made. Although it generally is unrealistic to expect business and economic forecasts to be very precise, they are likely to be considerably more trustworthy than forecasts that are not based on the principles of managerial economics.

Summary

1. Although surveys are of considerable use, most major firms seem to base their forecasts in large part on the quantitative analysis of economic time series. The classical approach to business forecasting assumes that an economic time series can be decomposed into four components: trend, seasonal variation, cyclical variation, and irregular movements.

2. If the trend in a time series is linear, simple regression may be used to estimate an equation representing the trend. If it seems to be nonlinear, a quadratic equation may be estimated by multiple regression, or an exponential trend may be fitted. An exponential trend is appropriate when the variable increases at a relatively constant percentage rate per year. To fit such a trend, we use the logarithm of the variable, not the variable itself, as the dependent variable in the regression.

3. The seasonal variation in a particular time series is described by a figure for each month (the seasonal index) that shows the extent to which that month's value typically departs from what would be expected on the basis of trend and cyclical variation. Such seasonal indexes, together with the trend, can be useful for forecasting. Regression analysis, including dummy variables, can be employed to estimate seasonal indexes.

4. Cyclical variation, as well as trend and seasonal variation, is reflected in many time series. Variables that go down before the peak and up before the trough are called leading indicators. If a large number of leading indicators turn downward, this is viewed as a sign of a coming peak. If a large number turn upward, this is thought to signal an impending trough. Although these indicators are not very reliable, they are watched closely and are used to supplement other, more-sophisticated forecasting techniques.

5. The simplest kind of forecasting method is a straightforward extrapolation of a trend. To allow for seasonal variation, either multiplicative or additive seasonal effects can be included. This entire procedure is simply a mechanical extrapolation of the time series into the future.

6. In recent years, managerial economists have tended to base their forecasts less on simple extrapolations and more on equations (or systems of equations) showing the effects of various independent variables on the variable (or variables) one wants to forecast. These equations (or systems of equations), which are estimated using the techniques described in Chapter 5, are called econometric models. Examples are the models used by CEMCO and General Electric, as well as the model of auto output published by the Federal Reserve Bank of New York.

Problems

1. The following seasonal index was calculated for the room occupancy of a motel located on a major interstate highway in the Southeast. The motel's customers are largely tourists and commercial truckers who regularly travel this highway. This index is based on actual data.[14]

January	74.8	July	116.8
February	79.8	August	117.4
March	92.9	September	105.4
April	108.8	October	103.7
May	107.5	November	100.3
June	112.0	December	80.6

a. Is there pronounced seasonal variation in this motel's business? All other things equal, by what percentage, on the average, does room occupancy in the peak month exceed that in the lowest month?

b. What factors would you expect to be responsible for the observed seasonal variation? In calculating the seasonal index, it was assumed that the index for a particular month like January was the same from year to year. Some observers have questioned whether this assumption is correct, given that a recession occurred in 1990 and 1991. Why might the recession have changed the pattern of seasonal variation?

c. If you were the motel's manager, how might a seasonal index of this sort be of use? Be specific.

[14]B. Bettegowda, "Calculation of Seasonal Index for Motel Room Occupancy," National Technological University.

2. The Union Carbide Corporation's sales during the period 1960 to 1975 are given below.

Year	Sales (billions of dollars)	Year	Sales (billions of dollars)
1960	1.5	1968	2.7
1961	1.6	1969	2.9
1962	1.6	1970	3.0
1963	1.7	1971	3.0
1964	1.9	1972	3.3
1965	2.1	1973	3.9
1966	2.2	1974	5.3
1967	2.5	1975	5.7

   a. Fit a linear trend line to these data.
   b. Fit an exponential trend line to these data.
   c. In 1980, Union Carbide's sales were $9.994 billion. Suppose that in 1976, both the linear trend line and the exponential trend line had been used to forecast the firm's 1980 sales. Which forecast would have been more accurate?
   d. In 1984, Union Carbide's sales were $9.508 billion. Suppose that in 1976, both the linear trend line and the exponential trend line had been used to forecast the firm's 1984 sales. Which forecast would have been more accurate?

3. The Milton Company's statistician calculates a seasonal index for the firm's sales; the results are shown in the second column below. The firm's monthly 2001 sales are shown in the third column.

Month	Seasonal index	2001 sales (millions of dollars)
January	97	2.5
February	96	2.4
March	97	2.7
April	98	2.9
May	99	3.0
June	100	3.1
July	101	3.2
August	103	3.1
September	103	3.2
October	103	3.1
November	102	3.0
December	101	2.9

a. If one divides each month's sales figure by its seasonal index (divided by 100), it is said to be "deseasonalized." That is, the seasonal element is removed from the data. Why is this true?
b. Calculate deseasonalized sales figures for 2001.
c. Why would the managers of the Milton Company want deseasonalized sales figures?

4. The equation describing the sales trend of the Secane Chemical Company is

$$S_t = 21.3 + 1.3t,$$

where S_t is the sales (in millions of dollars per month) of the firm, and t is time measured in months from January 1995. The firm's seasonal index of sales is

January	103	May	101	September	121
February	80	June	104	October	101
March	75	July	120	November	75
April	103	August	139	December	78

a. Construct a monthly sales forecast for the firm for 2001.
b. Why would the managers of the Secane Chemical Company want monthly sales forecasts of this kind?

5. On October 4, 1994, the U.S. Department of Commerce announced that the index of leading indicators rose 0.6 percent in August 1994.
a. During August, the average workweek rose. Is the average workweek among the leading indicators? If so, did its increase help to raise the index?
b. During August, stock prices rose. Is the level of stock prices among the leading indicators? If so, did its increase help to raise the index?

6. The Allen Company's monthly sales have the following trend:

$$C_t = 4.12 + 0.32t,$$

where C_t is the sales (in millions of dollars per month) of the firm, and t is time measured in months from July 1994. The firm's seasonal index of sales is

January	81	May	137	September	79
February	98	June	122	October	101
March	102	July	104	November	74
April	76	August	101	December	125

a. Construct a monthly sales forecast for the firm in 2002.
b. The firm's president feels strongly that a recession will occur in late 2002. Would this influence your answer to part a? If so, how?

7. The sales of Sears, Roebuck were as follows during 1978 to 1990:

Year	Sales (billions of dollars)	Year	Sales (billions of dollars)
1978	22.9	1985	40.7
1979	24.5	1986	42.3
1980	25.2	1987	45.9
1981	27.4	1988	50.3
1982	30.0	1989	53.8
1983	35.9	1990	56.0
1984	38.8		

   a. Calculate a linear trend based on these data.

   b. Sears, Roebuck's sales in 1991 were about $57.2 billion. If you had used a least-squares trend line based on 1978 to 1990 data to forecast its 1991 sales, how big a forecasting error would have resulted?

   c. In 1992, Sears, Roebuck's sales were $52.3 billion. If you had used a least-squares trend line based on 1978 to 1990 data to forecast its 1992 sales, how big a forecasting error would have resulted?

8. In the Wharton econometric model, housing starts (divided by the number of households) were specified to be a function of (1) the mortgage rate, (2) a consumer sentiment index, (3) capacity utilization, (4) the occupancy rate, and (5) deposit inflows into savings intermediaries.

   a. Indicate why each of these five variables might be expected to influence the number of housing starts.

   b. What factors influence these five variables? What sort of multiequation system might be constructed for forecasting purposes?

9. The General Electric Corporation's sales from 1950 to 1976 were as follows:

Year	Sales (billions of dollars)	Year	Sales (billions of dollars)
1950	2.2	1964	4.9
1951	2.6	1965	6.2
1952	3.0	1966	7.2
1953	3.5	1967	7.7
1954	3.3	1968	8.4
1955	3.5	1969	8.4
1956	4.1	1970	8.8
1957	4.3	1971	9.6
1958	4.2	1972	10.5
1959	4.5	1973	11.9
1960	4.2	1974	13.9
1961	4.5	1975	14.1
1962	4.8	1976	15.7
1963	4.9		

    a. Using the method of least squares, derive a linear trend.

    b. Plot General Electric's sales against time. Also, plot the trend line derived in part a against time. (Time here is the year to which the sales figure pertains.)

    c. Does a visual inspection of how well the linear trend fits suggest that an exponential trend would do better? That a quadratic trend would do better?

    d. Using this linear trend, what would have been the sales forecast for General Electric in 1994? How accurate would it have been?

10. The SAS printout of the regression of the IBM Corporation's annual sales (designated Y) on the year to which the sales figure pertains (designated YEAR) is shown below. This regression is based on data for 1974 to 1986.

    a. If you had used this regression as a linear trend in 1986, what would have been your forecast of IBM's 1987 sales, based on this trend?

    b. IBM's actual sales in 1987 were $54.2 billion. How accurate would your forecast have been?

Appendix: Exponential Smoothing and Forecasting

One frequently used method of calculating a trend is to use **exponential smoothing.** According to this method, *the trend value at time* t *is a weighted average of all available previous values, where the weights decline geometrically as one goes backward in time.* As an illustration, suppose that a firm has been in existence for five years and that its sales have been $2 million, $6 million, $6 million, $4 million, and $8 million (see Figure 6.9). Then, the trend value in the fifth year would be a weighted average of $2 million, $6 million, $6 million, $4 million, and $8 million, where the weights decline geometrically as we go backward in time. Specifically, the weight attached to the observation at time t equals θ, the weight attached to the observation at time $t - 1$ equals $(1 - \theta)\theta$, the weight attached to the observation at time $t - 2$ equals $(1 - \theta)^2\theta$, the weight attached to the observation at time $t - 3$ equals $(1 - \theta)^3\theta, \ldots$, and the weight attached to the observation at the earliest relevant time (time 0) equals $(1 - \theta)^t$. Clearly, the weights decline geometrically as one goes backward in time; that is, the weight attached to the observation at time $t - 1$ is $(1 - \theta)$ times the weight attached to the observation at time t; the weight attached to the observation at time $t - 2$ is $(1 - \theta)$ times the weight attached to the observation at time $t - 1$; and so on.

    To calculate an exponentially smoothed time series, you must choose a value of θ, which is designated the **smoothing constant.** If we choose a value of 0.5

FIGURE
6.9

Sales of Firm, Actual and Exponentially Smoothed

Year 1 is the firm's first year in existence, year 2 is its second year, and so on.

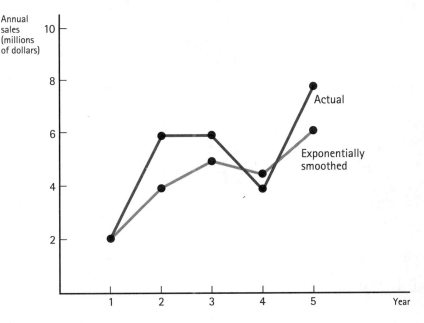

for θ, the exponentially smoothed value of the firm's sales in each of the five years is:

$$S_0 = 2$$

$$S_1 = (0.5)(6) + (1 - 0.5)(2) = 4$$

$$S_2 = (0.5)(6) + (1 - 0.5)(0.5)(6) + (1 - 0.5)^2(2) = 5$$

$$S_3 = (0.5)(4) + (1 - 0.5)(0.5)(6)$$
$$+ (1 - 0.5)^2(0.5)(6) + (1 - 0.5)^3(2) = 4.5$$

$$S_4 = (0.5)(8) + (1 - 0.5)(0.5)(4) + (1 - 0.5)^2(0.5)(6)$$
$$+ (1 - 0.5)^3(0.5)(6) + (1 - 0.5)^4(2) = 6.25,$$

where S_0 is the exponentially smoothed value of the firm's sales in the first year of its existence, S_1 is this value in the second year, S_2 the value in the third year, and so on. Figure 6.9 shows both the original time series and the exponentially smoothed time series.

To compute the value of such a smoothed time series at time t, all you really need is the value of the smoothed time series at time $t - 1$ and the actual value of the time series at time t. This is because the smoothed value of the time series at time t is a simple weighted average of the smoothed value at time $t - 1$ and the actual value at time t. If S_t is the smoothed value at time t,

$$S_t = \theta Y(t) + (1 - \theta)S_{t-1}, \qquad (6.14)$$

where $Y(t)$ is the value of the time series at time t.[15] Thus, to calculate an exponentially smoothed time series, you do not need to keep all the previous values of the actual time series; *all you need to keep is the value of the exponentially smoothed series in the previous period.* From this information alone (together with the current value of the series and the smoothing constant), you can calculate the smoothed value of the series in the current period. For instance, consider the firm in the previous paragraph. If the firm's sales in its sixth year of existence are $10 million, the smoothed value of sales for the sixth year is

$$(0.5)(10) + (1 - 0.5)(6.25) = 8.125,$$

or $8.125 million.

In choosing the value of the smoothing constant θ, you must pick a number between 0 and 1. (In other words, $0 \leq \theta \leq 1$.) If θ is close to 1, past values of the time series are given relatively little weight (compared with recent values) in calculating smoothed values. If θ is close to 0, past values of the time series are given considerable weight (as compared with recent values) in calculating smoothed values. If the time series contains a great deal of random variation, it is often advisable to choose a relatively small value of θ, since this results in relatively little weight being put on $Y(t)$, which is more influenced than S_{t-1} by this variation. On the other hand, if one wants the smoothed time series to reflect relatively quickly whatever changes occur in the average level of the time series, the value of θ should be set at a high level.

---

[15]Let's prove that equation (6.14) is true. If $Y(t)$ is the actual value of the time series at time t, then equation (6.14) implies that

$$
\begin{aligned}
S_t &= \theta Y(t) + (1 - \theta)S_{t-1} \\
&= \theta Y(t) + (1 - \theta)[\theta Y(t - 1) + (1 - \theta)S_{t-2}] \\
&= \theta Y(t) + (1 - \theta)\theta Y(t - 1) + (1 - \theta)^2[\theta Y(t - 2) + (1 - \theta)S_{t-3}] \\
&\;\;\vdots \\
&= \theta Y(t) + (1 - \theta)\theta Y(t - 1) + (1 - \theta)^2\theta Y(t - 2) + \cdots + (1 - \theta)^t Y(0).
\end{aligned}
$$

Since the right-hand side of the last line is equivalent to the definition of an exponentially smoothed time series in the first paragraph of this appendix, it follows that equation (6.14) is true.

MANAGERIAL ECONOMICS IN CONTEXT

How to Forecast the Sales of Paper, According to McKinsey*

Bill Barnett of McKinsey and Company, a leading management consulting firm, has described how a management team constructed a forecast of the sales of uncoated white paper in the United States. The first step was to divide the total demand into more homogeneous components. Then in each of these end-use categories, the analysts tried to identify, understand, and forecast the factors influencing demand.

To illustrate, take the case of reprographics paper. The management team, using existing data, divided reprographics paper into two types: plain-paper copy paper and nonimpact page printer paper. With regard to plain-paper copy paper, there was evidence that sales tended to be directly related to the level of business activity (as measured by macroeconomic variables like gross domestic product). Holding the level of business activity constant, it appeared that the quantity of plain-paper copy paper demanded was related to the average cost (including labor time, equipment, and paper) of making a copy. As indicated in the graph on the

right, the analysts found an inverse relationship between the average cost per copy and the quantity demanded.

Because further declines in cost per copy seemed unlikely, the management team forecasted a slowing in the growth of sales of plain-paper copy paper. Since 1983, there seemed to be a decrease in the rate of growth of sales of this product; the team forecasted that this decrease would continue. (In addition, the analysts looked carefully at how sensitive their conclusions were to alternative assumptions regarding the rate of growth of gross domestic product and the rate of reduction of cost per copy.) According to Barnett, this sort of approach to sales forecasting is frequently very effective.

a. Can regression techniques be used to estimate the relationship between cost per copy and the

*The material on which this was based comes from F. W. Barnett, "Four Steps to Forecast Total Market Demand," *Harvard Business Review*.

Forecasting Based on Exponential Smoothing

Exponential smoothing is also used for forecasting purposes. When used in this way, the basic equation for exponential smoothing is

$$F_t = \theta A(t - 1) + (1 - \theta)F_{t-1}, \qquad (6.15)$$

where $A(t - 1)$ is the actual value of the time series at time $(t - 1)$, and F_t is the forecast for time t. Because the forecast is being made at time $(t - 1)$, the actual value of the time series at this time is known. The forecast for time t is simply a weighted average of the actual value at time $(t - 1)$ and the *forecasted* value for time $(t - 1)$, where the actual value is weighted by θ and the forecasted value is weighted by $(1 - \theta)$. It can readily be demonstrated that the

d. During the relevant period, the quantity demanded of plain-paper copy paper grew at an average annual rate of 7 percent. Does this mean that an exponential curve provides the best representation of the trend in quantity demanded?

e. Does the procedure described above to forecast demand result in a seasonal index for sales of plain-paper copy paper? If not, how might such a seasonal index be calculated? Of what use might it be?

f. How might this forecasting procedure utilize the results of econometric models?

End-use category	Percent of total sales
Business forms	25
Commercial printing	25
Reprographics	20
Envelopes	10
Other converting	5
Stationery and tablet	5
Books	5
Other	5
Total	100

quantity demanded of plain-paper copy paper? If so, how?

b. What statistic would you use to measure how strong this relationship is?

c. Can one calculate the elasticity of demand for plain-paper copy paper with respect to cost per copy? Of what use might it be?

forecast for time t is the weighted sum of the actual values prior to time t, where the weight attached to each value declines geometrically with the age of the observation.

To see how exponential smoothing can be used for forecasting purposes, let's return to the firm in Figure 6.9, which had been in existence for five years. Sales during the first year were $2 million, and we assume that the firm's sales forecast for the first year was also $2 million. What will be its sales forecast for the second year? To make such a forecast, the firm begins by choosing a value for the smoothing constant θ. (Values of 0.3 or less are often used.) Suppose that a value of 0.2 is chosen. Then the forecast for the second year is $0.2(2) + 0.8(2) = 2$, or $2 million. Since the firm's actual sales in the second year turn out to be $6 million, its sales forecast for the third year will be $0.2(6) + 0.8(2) = 2.8$, or $2.8 million. Since the firm's actual sales in the third year turn out to be $6 million, its sales forecast for the fourth year will be $0.2(6) +$

0.8(2.8) = 3.44, or \$3.44 million. And so on. Exponential smoothing is often used in this way to make forecasts, particularly where there is a need for a cheap, fast, and rather mechanical method to make forecasts for a large number of items. For example, to implement various kinds of inventory control models, demand forecasts for hundreds or thousands of items may be required.

Problem

The Dickson Corporation wants to calculate an exponentially smoothed time series from the following data:

1989	2	1994	28
1990	4	1995	38
1991	8	1996	50
1992	12	1997	70
1993	20	1998	90

a. Calculate an exponentially smoothed time series, letting the smoothing constant equal 1/4.
b. Calculate an exponentially smoothed time series, letting the smoothing constant equal 1/2.
c. Calculate an exponentially weighted time series, letting the smoothing constant equal 3/4.

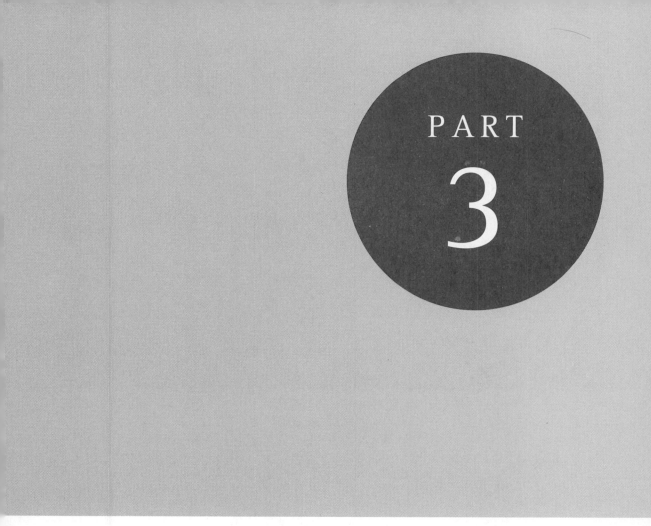

PART

3

Production
and Cost

Production Theory

Once managers determine the demand for the firm's product or service, their job is far from over. Now, they must choose the most profitable way to use the firm's resources to produce the good or service. They must ask many questions, including: What is the optimal level of output? How should managers decide between (among) alternative manufacturing processes? How will investment in manufacturing equipment affect labor costs? Will building a new plant increase or decrease costs?

To answer these (and other) questions, managers must understand the production process. Simply stated, production issues are concerned with how scarce resources (inputs) are used to produce the firm's product or service (output). A production function simply specifies the efficient relationship between inputs and outputs.

Good managers realize that production refers to more than the physical transformation of inputs into outputs. Production involves all activities associated with providing the goods and services, such as employment practices, acquisition of capital resources, and product distribution. Indeed, as much of the economy becomes more services oriented, the transformation of inputs into outputs (which had more of a "blue collar" tone in the "old economy") now has more of a "white collar" tone. Consulting and investment banking and the dis-immediation of the links between manufacturing and the ultimate consumer use the inputs of data, computers, and brainpower to produce output—buy or sell the stock, IPO the stock at 35, or ponder the consultant's recommendation. This is as much of a production process as taking coal, iron ore, massive plants, and blue collar labor to manufacture steel.

To maximize profits, managers must strive to produce the good or service efficiently and at minimal cost by constantly keeping abreast of new methods and by comparing their production performance with that of their rivals (benchmarking).

The study (and understanding) of the production process is fundamental to gaining insights into cost analysis. While demand analysis gave us the total revenue portion of the profit equation, cost analysis will give us total cost the other required portion of the profit equation. But costs evolve from the production process. One cannot understand cost unless one understands the production process.

Production analysis also enables managers to understand the integrated nature of the firm—the relationships among the various factors employed by the firm and among the functional units.

The Production Function with One Variable Input

For any product, the **production function** is a table, a graph, or an equation showing the maximum output rate of the product that can be achieved from any specified set of usage rates of inputs. The production function summarizes the characteristics of existing technology at a given time; it shows the technological constraints that the firm must reckon with. In this chapter, we assume that the firm takes the production function as given; in the next chapter, when we analyze the process of technological change, we study the firm's attempts to change the production function.

Consider the simplest case—in which there is one input whose quantity is fixed and one input whose quantity is variable. Suppose that the fixed input is the service of five machine tools, the variable input is labor, and the product is a metal part. Suppose that John Thomas, owner of the Thomas Machine Company, a very small machine shop, decides to find out what the effect on annual output will be if he applies various numbers of units of labor during the year to the five machine tools (and if he maximizes output). He discovers that one full-time laborer can make 49 hundred parts per year on the machines. But Thomas can make more parts per year by hiring more workers, as we see in Table 7.1. The results in Table 7.1 can be regarded as the production function

TABLE
7.1

Output of Metal Parts When Various Amounts of Labor Are Applied to Five Machine Tools, Thomas Machine Company

Amount of labor (L)	Amount of capital (# of machines)	Output of parts (Q, hundreds per year)
0	5	0
1	5	49
2	5	132
3	5	243
4	5	376
5	5	525
6	5	684
6.67	5	792.59
7	5	847
8	5	1,008
9	5	1,161
10	5	1,300
11	5	1,419
12	5	1,512
13	5	1,573
14	5	1,596
15	5	1,575

in this situation if the Thomas Machine Company is maximizing the output of the labor and machines it uses. Alternatively, the curve in Figure 7.1, which presents exactly the same results, can be regarded as the production function. In fact, the numbers in Table 7.1 (and Table 7.2) are derived from the relationship $Q = 30L + 20L^2 - L^3$.

The production function provides basic information concerning the nature of a firm's production technology; it shows us the maximum *total output* that can be realized by using each combination of quantities of inputs. Two other important concepts are the average product and the marginal product of an input. The **average product** of an input is total product (that is, total output) divided by the amount of the input used to produce this amount of output. The **marginal product** of an input is the addition to total output resulting from the

FIGURE
7.1

Relationship between Total Output and Amount of Labor Used on Five Machine Tools, Thomas Machine Company

Total output increases as labor increases at an increasing rate (up to 6.67 units of labor) and increases at a decreasing rate (until slightly more than 14 units of labor). Thereafter, output decreases as more units of labor are deployed. Managers will never willfully deploy labor in the latter circumstance. The production function shows the relationship between output (in this case, number of parts produced) and input (in this case, units of labor).

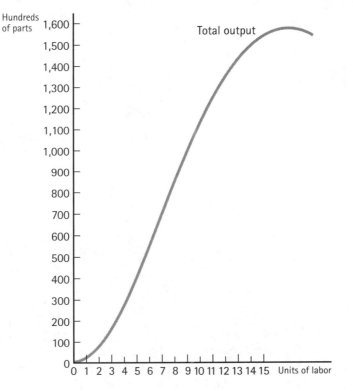

addition of the last unit of the input when the amounts of other inputs used are held constant.[1]

Returning to the Thomas Machine Company, we can calculate the average product and the marginal product of labor, based on the production function

---

[1]More precisely, the marginal product of an input is the derivative of output with regard to the quantity of the input. That is, if Q is output and x is the quantity of the input, the marginal product of the input equals dQ/dx if the quantity of all other inputs is fixed.

TABLE
7.2

Average and Marginal Products of Labor, Thomas Machine Company

Amount of labor (units)	Amount of capital (number of machines)	Output of parts (Q, hundreds of parts)	Average product (Q/L)	Marginal product ($\Delta Q/\Delta L)^a$	Marginal product ($dQ/dL)^a$
0	5	0	–	–	–
1	5	49	49	49	67
2	5	132	66	83	98
3	5	243	81	111	123
4	5	376	94	133	142
5	5	525	105	149	155
6	5	684	114	159	162
6.67	5	792.59	118.89	162.89	<u>163.33</u>
7	5	847	121	<u>163</u>	163
8	5	1,008	126	161	158
9	5	1,161	129	153	147
10	5	1,300	<u>130</u>	139	<u>130</u>
11	5	1,419	129	119	107
12	5	1,512	126	93	78
13	5	1,573	121	61	43
14	5	1,596	114	23	2
15	5	1,575	105	− 19	− 45

^{a}The figures in the $\Delta Q/\Delta L$ column pertain to the interval between the indicated amount of labor and one unit less than the indicated amount of labor. The figures in the dQ/dL column are the continuous marginal product, i.e., $dQ/dL = MPL = 30 + 40L − 3L^2$.

in Table 7.1. Both the average product and the marginal product of labor will vary, of course, depending on how much labor is used. If $Q(L)$ is the total output rate when L units of labor are used per year, the average product of labor when L units of labor are used per year is $Q(L)/L$. And the marginal product of labor when between L and $(L − 1)$ units of labor are used per year is $Q(L) − Q(L − 1)$. Hence, the average product of labor is 49 hundred parts per unit of labor when 1 unit of labor is used, and the marginal product of labor is 83 hundred parts per unit of labor when between 1 and 2 units of labor are used. The results for other amounts of labor are shown in Table 7.2.

The average product curve for labor is shown in Figure 7.2; the numbers are taken from Table 7.1. As is often (but not always) the case for production processes, the average product of labor (which is the only variable input in this

FIGURE
7.2

Average and Marginal Product Curves for Labor

Marginal product exceeds average product when the latter is increasing, and is less than average product when the latter is decreasing. (Output per unit of labor is measured in hundreds of parts.)

case) rises, reaches a maximum (at $L = 10$ and $Q/L = 130$), and then falls. Figure 7.2 also shows the marginal product of labor. These numbers are taken from the last column of Table 7.2. The marginal product of labor also rises, reaches a maximum (at $L = 6.67$ and marginal product $= 163.33$), and then falls. This too is typical of many production processes. Figure 7.2 shows that marginal product equals average product when the latter reaches a maximum, that is, $MP = AP = 130$, when $L = 10$.

Note that we have two definitions of marginal product. The first ($\Delta Q/\Delta L$) assumes that we can employ labor only in discrete units, as in a laborer or a labor-hour. This may be due to employment laws or negotiated contracts with labor. The second (dQ/dL) assumes that we can employ labor continuously, as

ANALYZING MANAGERIAL DECISIONS

Shaquille O'Neal Goes to Los Angeles

In 1996, the Los Angeles Lakers entered into what was then the richest sports contract ever signed: a seven-year, $120 million contract with Shaquille O'Neal, a 7-foot 1-inch, 320-pound center. As soon as the contract was announced, sports commentators speculated about whether the contract was economically sensible. How could the Lakers hope to get enough extra revenue from O'Neal's presence to pay this huge tab? According to the *New York Times,* O'Neal could have a big impact on the Lakers' revenues.

First, consider annual tickets sales. "If all the Lakers' 41 home games sell out this season, with average ticket prices at about $38.50, and the team makes it through a round of playoffs, it could take

in roughly $40 million at the gate."* Second, the Lakers should earn about $15 million per year from national broadcasting contracts and merchandising business. Third, revenues from local broadcasts and from concessions at the arena are estimated at $25 million to $30 million a year.

On the basis of these estimates, the *New York Times* concludes that the annual revenues of the Los Angeles Lakers might increase by about $15 million, which would be about equal to the increase in annual cost due to this record-breaking contract.

*"The Real Deal on O'Neal," *New York Times*, August 23, 1996, p. D1. © Bill Baptist/NBAPhotos

in 1.25 workers or 1.33 workers. This could occur by using part-time workers or workers who work more or less time than in a standard day's work. Which one you use depends on the situation you are in: Are you constrained to an integer number of workers or can you employ fractions of a worker (or worker hour)?

To see why MP equals AP when AP is maximized, let's apply the calculus techniques presented in Chapter 2. If x is the amount of the variable input that is used, and Q is the output rate, then the average product of the variable input is Q/x, and the marginal product of the variable input is dQ/dx (see footnote 1). From Chapter 2, we know that

$$\frac{d(Q/x)}{dx} = \frac{x(dQ/dx) - Q(dx/dx)}{x^2}$$

$$= \frac{1}{x}\left(\frac{dQ}{dx} - \frac{Q}{x}\right).$$

When average product is a maximum, $d(Q/x)/dx$ equals zero. Thus,

$$\frac{d(Q/x)}{dx} = \frac{1}{x}\left(\frac{dQ}{dx} - \frac{Q}{x}\right) = 0,$$

which means that dQ/dx must equal Q/x when the average product is a maximum. But since dQ/dx is the marginal product and Q/x is the average product, this proves the proposition in the previous paragraph: When the average product is a maximum, the average product equals the marginal product.

The Law of Diminishing Marginal Returns

Having defined the production function and the average and marginal products of an input, we are ready to present one of the most famous laws of managerial economics—the law of **diminishing marginal returns.** This law states that *if equal increments of an input are added, and the quantities of other inputs are held constant, the resulting increments of product will decrease beyond some point; that is, the marginal product of the input will diminish.* This law is illustrated by Table 7.2; beyond 7 (6.67 if labor is treated as a continuous input) units of labor, the marginal product of labor decreases.

Three things should be noted concerning the law of diminishing marginal returns. First, this law is an empirical generalization, not a deduction from physical or biological laws. Second, it is assumed that technology remains fixed. The law of diminishing marginal returns cannot predict the effect of an additional unit of input when technology is allowed to change. Third, it is assumed that there is at least one input whose quantity is being held constant. The law of diminishing marginal returns does not apply to cases where there are increases in all inputs.

It is not hard to see why the law of diminishing marginal returns holds true. Take, for example, the case of the Thomas Machine Company, which has a fixed number of machine tools. If this firm hires more and more workers, the marginal product of a worker will eventually begin to decrease, because workers will have to wait in line to use the machine tools, and because the extra workers will have to be assigned to less and less important tasks.

The Optimal Level of Utilization of an Input

If a firm has one fixed input and one variable input, how much of the variable input should it utilize? This is a very important question for the managers of business firms, large or small. To answer it, we must define the marginal revenue product of the variable input and the marginal expenditure on the variable input. These two concepts must be understood if we are to answer the question.

The **marginal revenue product** is the amount that an additional unit of the variable input adds to the firm's total revenue. That is, letting MRP_Y be the marginal revenue product of input Y,

$$MRP_Y = \frac{\Delta TR}{\Delta Y},$$ (7.1)

where ΔTR is the change in total revenue resulting from a change of ΔY in the amount of input Y used by the firm.[2] It can easily be proved that the marginal revenue product of input Y equals input Y's marginal product times the firm's marginal revenue. To see this, note that marginal revenue (MR) equals $\Delta TR / \Delta Q$, where ΔQ is the change in the firm's output, and that

$$MRP_Y = \frac{\Delta TR}{\Delta Y} = \left(\frac{\Delta TR}{\Delta Q} \right) \left(\frac{\Delta Q}{\Delta Y} \right).$$

Thus, since $\Delta Q / \Delta Y$ equals input Y's marginal product (MP_Y), it follows that

$$MRP_Y = MR(MP_Y), \tag{7.2}$$

which is what we set out to prove.

The **marginal expenditure** is the amount that an additional unit of the variable input adds to the firm's total costs. That is, letting ME_Y be the marginal expenditure on input Y,

$$ME_Y = \frac{\Delta TC}{\Delta Y}, \tag{7.3}$$

where ΔTC is the change in total cost resulting from a change of ΔY in the amount of input Y used by the firm.[3] If the firm can buy all it wants of input Y at a price of \$10 a unit, ME_Y will equal \$10. In some cases, however, the firm must raise the price of input Y in order to get more of it; in such cases, ME_Y will exceed the price of input Y. Note that $\Delta TC / \Delta Y$ can be written as $(\Delta TC / \Delta Q)(\Delta Q / \Delta Y)$, where $\Delta TC / \Delta Q$ is the change in the firm's total cost (ΔTC) divided by the firm's change in output (ΔQ). Like $\Delta TR / Q$ is marginal revenue, $\Delta TC / \Delta Q$ is the firm's marginal cost (MC), or the change in the firm's total cost as its output is changed by a small amount.

To maximize its profits, the firm should utilize the amount of input Y where the marginal revenue product equals the marginal expenditure. In other words, the firm should set

$$MRP_Y = ME_Y. \tag{7.4}$$

This follows from our discussion of marginal analysis in Chapter 2. To maximize profit, a firm should expand any activity as long as the marginal benefits exceed the marginal costs. It should stop expanding it when the marginal benefit (in this case, MRP_Y) equals the marginal cost (in this case, ME_Y).

---

[2]More precisely, $MRP_Y = dTR/dY$.
[3]More precisely, $ME_Y = dTC/dY$.

To generalize this further, rewrite (7.4) as

$$(\Delta TR/\Delta Q)(\Delta Q/\Delta Y) = (\Delta TC/\Delta Q)([\Delta Q/\Delta Y),$$

or

$$\Delta TR/\Delta Q = \Delta TC/\Delta Q,$$

or

$$MR = MC.$$

We have thus derived one of the most important rules of managerial economics—the firm should stop expending its output when marginal revenue equals marginal cost (more on this in a later discussion).

The Rondo Corporation: A Numerical Example

To illustrate, consider the case of the Rondo Corporation, a producer of pocket calculators that has a fixed amount of plant and equipment, but that can vary the number of workers it hires per day. The relationship between the number of calculators produced per day (Q) and the number of workers hired per day (L) is

$$Q = 98L - 3L^2. \tag{7.5}$$

The Rondo Corporation can sell all the calculators it can produce (with its current plant and equipment) for $20 per calculator, so its marginal revenue equals $20. It can also hire as many workers as it likes for $40 per day. How many workers should it hire per day?

To apply the results of the previous section, we must determine the marginal revenue product of labor (MRP_L) and the marginal expenditure on labor (ME_L) in this firm. Using equation (7.2),

$$MRP_L = 20MP_L,$$

since the firm's marginal revenue equals $20. Since $MP_L = dQ/dL$,

$$MRP_L = 20 \frac{d(98L - 3L^2)}{dL} = 20(98 - 6L).$$

Thus, if MRP_L is to equal ME_L, the number of workers hired must be such that

$$20(98 - 6L) = 40,$$

since the firm's marginal expenditure on labor equals $40. Solving this equation, we find that L must equal 16. So, if the Rondo Corporation wants to maximize profit, it should hire 16 workers per day.

ANALYZING MANAGERIAL DECISIONS

How to Determine the Optimal Horsepower for an Oil Pipeline

Crude oil is carried by pipelines from oil fields and storage areas over hundreds of miles to urban and industrial centers. The output of such a pipeline is the amount of oil carried per day, and the two principal inputs are the diameter of the pipeline and the horsepower applied to the oil carried. Leslie Cookenboo of the Exxon Corporation estimated the production function for a pipeline with a 10-inch diameter to be as follows:

$$Q = 286H^{0.37},$$

where Q is the amount of crude oil carried per day, and H is horsepower.

(a) Derive a formula for the marginal product of horsepower. (b) Do increases in horsepower result in diminishing marginal returns? (c) Derive a formula for the average product of horsepower. (d) If the marginal revenue from an extra unit of crude oil carried per day is $2, what is the marginal revenue product of horsepower? (e) If an oil-pipeline firm can add all the horsepower it wants at a price of $30 per unit of horsepower, what is the marginal expenditure on horsepower? (f) Under the circumstances described above, what is the amount of horsepower that an oil-pipeline firm should use?

SOLUTION (a) The marginal product of horsepower equals $dQ/dH = 0.37(286)H^{-0.63} = 105.82H^{-0.63}$. (b) Yes. The marginal product of horsepower decreases as horsepower increases, as shown by the formula in the answer to part a. Specifically, $dMP_H/dH = -0.2331H^{-1.63} < 0$. (c) The average product of horsepower equals $Q/H = 286H^{-0.63}$. (d) Using equation (7.2), the marginal revenue

product of horsepower equals $2 times $(105.82H^{-0.63}) = $211.64H^{-0.63}$. (e) $30. (f) Using equation (7.4), the firm should set the marginal revenue product of horsepower equal to marginal expenditure. Thus,

$$211.64H^{-0.63} = 30$$
$$H^{-0.63} = 0.14175$$
$$H = 22.22.$$

The optimal amount of horsepower is 22.22 units.*

*For further discussion, see L. Cookenboo, "Production Functions and Cost Functions in Oil Pipelines," in the *Study Guide* accompanying this textbook.

The Production Function with Two Variable Inputs

Up to this point, we have been concerned with the case where there is only one variable input. Now we take up the more general case where there are two variable inputs. These variable inputs can be thought of as working with one or more fixed inputs, or they may be thought of as the only two inputs (in which case the situation is the long run, since all inputs are variable). In either case, it is easy to extend the results to as many inputs as we like.

When we increase the number of variable inputs from one to two, the production function becomes slightly more complicated, but it is still the relationship between various combinations of inputs and the maximum amount of output that can be obtained from them. Really, the only change is that output is a function of two variables rather than one. To illustrate, suppose that the Monroe Machine Company, which produces a metal part (different from that produced by the Thomas Machine Company), can vary the quantities of both machine tools and labor. Its production function is given in Table 7.3. The average product of either machine tools or labor can be computed simply by dividing the total output by the amount of either machine tools or labor that is used. The marginal product of each input can be obtained by holding the other input constant. For example, the marginal product of a machine tool when 4 units of labor are used and when between 3 and 4 machine tools are used is 51 hundred parts per machine tool; the marginal product of labor when 4 machine tools are used and when between 3 and 4 units of labor are used is 21

TABLE 7.3

Production Function, Two Variable Inputs, Monroe Machine Company

| Amount of labor (units) | Number of machine tools | | | |
| | 3 | 4 | 5 | 6 |
	(hundreds of parts produced per year)			
1	5	11	18	24
2	14	30	50	72
3	22	60	80	99
4	30	81	115	125
5	35	84	140	144

FIGURE
7.3

Production Function, Two Variable Inputs

The production surface, *OAQB*, shows the amount of total output that can be obtained from various combinations of quantities of machine tools and labor.

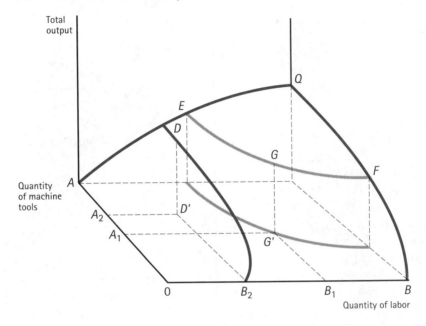

hundred parts per unit. If X_1 is the amount of the first input and X_2 is the amount of the second input, the production function is

$$Q = f(X_1, X_2), \tag{7.6}$$

where Q is the firm's output rate. The marginal product of the first input is $\partial Q/\partial X_1$; the marginal product of the second input is $\partial Q/\partial X_2$.

One can also represent the production function by a surface, like that in Figure 7.3. The production surface is *OAQB*.[4] The height of a point on this surface denotes the quantity of output. Dropping a perpendicular down from a point on the production surface to the "floor" and seeing how far the resulting point is from the labor and machine tool axes indicates how much of each input is required to produce this much output. For example, to produce $G'G$ units

[4]This surface is not meant to represent the numerical values in Table 7.3, but is a general representation of how a production surface of this sort is likely to appear.

ANALYZING MANAGERIAL DECISIONS

How Nucor Stays on the Production Function

Nucor is one of the largest steel firms in the United States, though it did not focus on steel production until the 1960s. By 1990 the company had achieved sales of over $4 billion and had never recorded a loss in over thirty-five years. More remarkably, its performance has far outstripped that of more traditional steel manufacturers like U.S. Steel. For example, when the average integrated steel company in the United States produced 400 tons of steel per employee, Nucor produced about 980 tons per employee. What actions have Nucor's managers implemented to achieve this superior performance?

One difference is that Nucor is a "minimill," not an integrated steel firm. The minimills have a different production function from that of the integrated mills. They use electric arc furnaces to make steel products from scrap metal. In 1999, Nucor was the nation's largest steel recycler, as it used over 10 million tons of scrap steel in its steel production.

Another reason for Nucor's outstanding performance is the company's focus on the efficient use of resources. Management has executed strategies that keep the company on an efficient production function. As pointed out on page 246, the production function includes only efficient input combinations. For example, if a unit of output can be produced with 3 units of labor and 3 units of capital, an input combination containing 4 units of labor and 3 units of capital should not be used because it is more costly. Firms that are inefficient are off the production function. They produce less output than is possible given their input combinations. Hence, they have higher costs.

Efficient production does not occur because of random luck. It is clearly governed by managerial decisions and requires an integrated set of policies. In Nucor's case, they employ over 7,000 people. So, how does management keep employees focused on efficient production?

Nucor uses the following multi-prong approach:

1. They maintain a simple, streamlined organizational structure that encourages decentralized decision making. Most divisions use only three layers of management. Each division is treated as a profit center and is expected to earn a 25 percent return on total assets.

2. The company acts as the general contractor in building new plants. They locate in rural areas where land is cheap (and unions are weak). Also, each plant is located near water and is served by at least two railroad lines to keep freight rates low. Nucor recruits employees to help build the plant. This allows them to observe the working habits of individuals. Those with good working habits are recruited to work in the plant when it opens. They also bring workers from other plants (who have already built plants) to joint the constuction team. Using these methods Nucor is able to build a plant at a lower cost and in about 33 percent less time than competitors.

3. All employees are subject to performance-related compensation plans. For example, production employees are paid weekly bonuses based on the productivity of their work group. Using this team approach, Nucor is able to lower its monitoring costs because employees monitor each other. Bonuses are based on the capabilities of the equipment, and average 80 percent to 150 percent of an employee's base pay. The more output a team produces, the higher are the bonuses.

4. Nucor treats all employees equally. Benefits are the same regardless of organizational position. There are no company cars, executive dining rooms, or corporate jets.

5. The firm's focus on output does not mean that quality suffers. Employees are committed to providing the highest quality steel at a competitive price. To reinforce this commitment to quality, most of Nucor's divisions are ISO 9000 Certified.[5]

6. Finally, Nucor regards itself as a technological leader. It was the first firm to produce thin-slab casting at a minimill, and searches worldwide for new developments in steel production. This emphasis on innovation is reinforced by the firm's flat organizational structure. Decisions can be made and implemented quickly because of it.

of output requires OB_1 $(= A_1 G')$ units of labor and OA_1 $(= B_1 G')$ machine tools. Conversely, one can take any amounts of machine tools and labor, say OA_2 machine tools and OB_2 units of labor, and find out how much output they will produce by measuring the height of the production surface at D', the point where labor input is OB_2 and machine tool input is OA_2. According to Figure 7.3, the answer equals $D'D$.

The production function does not include many of the different ways in which a given output can be produced because it includes only *efficient* combinations of inputs. For example, if 2 units of labor and 3 units of capital can produce 1 unit of output, this combination of inputs and output will not be included in the production function if it is also possible to produce 1 unit of output with 2 units of labor and 2 units of capital. The former input-output combination is clearly inefficient, since it is possible to obtain the result with the same amount of labor and less capital.

Isoquants

An **isoquant** is a curve showing all possible (efficient) combinations of inputs that are capable of producing a certain quantity of output. If we know the production function, we can readily derive the isoquant pertaining to any level of output. In Figure 7.3, suppose we want to find the isoquant corresponding to an output of $G'G$. All we need to do is to cut the production surface at the height of $G'G$ parallel to the base plane, the result being EGF, and to drop per-

[5]ISO 9000 is a set of quality standards. To receive ISO 9000 certification, managers must fulfill various quality assurance requirements and be audited by an external registrar. If a firm's quality assurance system is approved by this registrar, the firm is awarded an ISO 9000 certification and is allowed to advertise it to all customers.

pendiculars from *EGF* to the base. Clearly, this results in a curve that includes all efficient combinations of machine tools and labor that can produce $G'G$ metal parts. Using the notation in equation (7.6), an isoquant shows all combinations of X_1 and X_2 such that $f(X_1, X_2)$ equals a certain output rate.

Several isoquants, each pertaining to a different output rate, are shown in Figure 7.4. The two axes measure the quantities of inputs that are used. In contrast to the previous diagrams, we assume that labor and capital—not labor and machine tools (a particular form of capital)—are the relevant inputs in this case. The curves show the various combinations of inputs that can produce 100, 200, and 300 units of output. For example, consider the isoquant pertaining to 100 units of output per period of time. According to this isoquant, it is possible to attain this output rate if L_0 units of labor and K_0 units of capital are used per period of time. Alternatively, this output rate can be attained if L_1 units of labor and K_1 units of capital—or L_2 units of labor and K_2 units of capital—are used per period of time.

FIGURE 7.4

Isoquants

These three isoquants show the various combinations of capital and labor that can produce 100, 200, and 300 units of output.

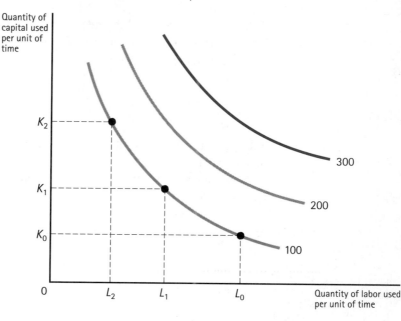

The Marginal Rate of Technical Substitution

As we have just seen, there ordinarily are a number of efficient ways that a particular output can be produced. The **marginal rate of technical substitution** shows the rate at which one input can be substituted for another input if output remains constant. If, as in equation (7.6), the quantity of output produced by a firm is a function of the amounts of two inputs used,

$$Q = f(X_1, X_2),$$

the marginal rate of technical substitution is

$$MRTS = -\frac{dX_2}{dX_1}, \tag{7.7}$$

given that Q is held constant (and X_2 is on the y-axis of the isoquant graph and X_1 is on the x-axis).

Geometrically, the marginal rate of technical substitution is -1 times the slope of the isoquant. This makes sense, since dX_2/dX_1 is the slope of the isoquant. Note that the marginal rate of technical substitution equals MP_1/MP_2, where MP_1 is the marginal product of input 1, and MP_2 is the marginal product of input 2. To show why, it is useful to point out that

$$dQ = \frac{\partial Q}{\partial X_1}\, dX_1 + \frac{\partial Q}{\partial X_2}\, dX_2.$$

Since output is maintained at a constant level, $dQ = 0$, which means that

$$\frac{\partial Q}{X_1}\, dX_1 + \frac{\partial Q}{\partial X_2}\, dX_2 = 0.$$

Thus,
$$\frac{dX_2}{dX_1} = \frac{-(\partial Q/\partial X_1)}{\partial Q/\partial X_2} = -\frac{MP_1}{MP_2}. \tag{7.8}$$

Since $MRTS = -dX_2/dX_1$, it follows that $MRTS = MP_1/MP_2$.

There are vast differences among inputs in how readily they can be substituted for one another. For example, in some production processes, one kind of labor can easily be substituted for another; in others, this is not true at all. In extreme cases, no substitution among inputs is possible; to produce a unit of output, a fixed amount of each input is required. In other words, inputs must be used in fixed proportions. Figure 7.5 shows the firm's isoquants in such a case; as you can see, they are right angles. Very few production processes al-

FIGURE
7.5

Isoquants in the Case of Fixed Proportions

If inputs must be used in fixed proportions, the isoquants are right angles.

low no substitution among inputs at all, but in some cases the amount of substitution is very limited. If perfect substitutability of inputs were possible, isoquants would be straight lines connecting the two axes.

While no substitution is a limiting assumption, in the short run, it may approximate many firms' situations. Assuming that no substitution exists, Leontief collected information from firms in a given industrial sector on how much of each input (measured in dollars) they used to produce their output (in dollars). He then aggregated the output and input data for all firms in a given industrial sector by type. The amount spent on the various inputs was then summed and subtracted from the value of the output (giving a residual or profit for the industry). He did this for many industrial sectors. The dollar value of each input in each industry was then divided by the dollar value of the output of that industry. The result is a production function in terms of the cents of each input required to produce a dollar's worth of output for each industry. This is the fixed (no substitution of inputs) input-output production function.

Consider a highly simplified production function for the steel industry.

$$\text{Iron Ore} = 0.5$$
$$\text{Coal} = 0.4$$
$$\text{Labor} = 0.1$$

Therefore, it takes 40 cents of coal to make a dollar's worth of steel.

The use of this production function (which, in addition to assuming no substitutability of inputs for each other, also does not assume that inputs are used efficiently—it merely measures what is currently being done in the industry) is called input-output analysis and won Leontief the Nobel Prize in Economics in 1973.

To illustrate how it is used, consider a $1 million increase in the demand for steel. The Leontief model would state that $500,000 more iron ore would be required or 0.5 × $1,000,000, $400,000 more coal would be required or 0.4 × $1,000,000 and $100,000 more labor would be required or 0.1 × $1,000,000. All of these dollar figures can be divided by unit prices to get units of iron ore, units of coal, and units of labor required.

Furthermore, since a production function for coal exists, say

| Machine | 0.6 |
| Labor | 0.4 |

then a $1 million increase in steel demand and the subsequent $400,000 increase in coal demand mean that there will be a $240,000 increase or 0.6 × $400,000 increase in machinery demand.

But since machinery also has a production function which undoubtedly involves steel, an increase in steel demand will entail yet a further increase in steel demand. Thus, Leontief's analysis (actually Walras', 1874) shows the interdependence of the economy through the production functions (since the output of one sector is the input to other sectors).

Many governments, like the United States and the Japanese governments, and many private sector institutions have developed and used very large and sophisticated input-output models to aid in their policy and managerial decision making.

Isoquants may also have positively sloped segments, or bend back on themselves, as shown in Figure 7.6. Above OU and below OV, the slope of the isoquants is positive, which implies that increases in both capital and labor are required to maintain a certain output rate. If this is the case, the marginal product of one or the other input must be negative. Above OU, the marginal product of capital is negative; thus, output will increase if less capital is used while the amount of labor is held constant. Below OV, the marginal product of labor

FIGURE
7.6

Economic Region of Production

No profit-maximizing firm will operate at a point outside the ridge lines, *OU* and *OV.*

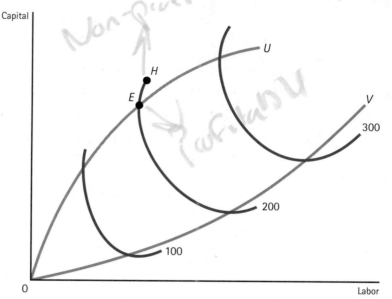

is negative; thus, output will increase if less labor is used while the amount of capital is held constant. The lines *OU* and *OV* are called **ridge lines.**

No profit-maximizing firm will operate at a point outside the ridge lines, since it can produce the same output with less of both inputs, which must be cheaper. Consider point *H* in Figure 7.6. Because this is a point where the iso-quant is positively sloped—and thus outside the ridge lines—it requires a greater amount of both labor and capital than some other point (for example, point *E*) on the same isoquant. Since both capital and labor have positive prices, it must be cheaper to operate at point *E* than at point *H*. The moral is: Don't operate at a point outside the ridge lines if you want to maximize profit.

The Optimal Combination of Inputs

If a firm wants to maximize profit, it will try to minimize the cost of produc-ing a given output or maximize the output derived from a given level of cost.[6]

---

[6]The conditions for minimizing the cost of producing a given output are the same as those for maximizing the output from a given cost. This is shown in the present section. Thus, we can view the firm's problem in either way.

Suppose that the firm takes input prices as given, and that there are two inputs, capital and labor, that are variable in the relevant time period. What combination of capital and labor should the firm choose if it wants to maximize the quantity of output derived from the given level of cost?

To begin to answer this question, let's determine the various combinations of inputs that the firm can obtain for a given expenditure. For example, if capital and labor are the inputs and the price of labor is P_L per unit and the price of capital is P_K per unit, the input combinations that can be obtained for a total outlay of M are such that

$$P_L L + P_K K = M, \tag{7.9}$$

where L is the amount of the labor input, and K is the amount of the capital input. Given M, P_L, and P_K, it follows that

$$K = \frac{M}{P_K} - \frac{P_L L}{P_K}. \tag{7.10}$$

Thus, the various combinations of capital and labor that can be purchased, given P_L, P_K, and M, can be represented by a straight line like that shown in Figure 7.7. (Capital is plotted on the vertical axis; labor is plotted on the horizontal.) This line, which has an intercept on the vertical axis equal to M/P_K and a slope of $-P_L/P_K$, is called an **isocost curve.**

If we superimpose the relevant isocost curve on the firm's isoquant map, we can determine graphically which combination of inputs will maximize the output for the given expenditure. The firm should pick the point on the isocost curve that is on the highest isoquant, for example, R in Figure 7.8. This is a point where the isocost curve is tangent to the isoquant. Thus, since the slope of the isocost curve is the negative of P_L/P_K and the slope of the isoquant is the negative of MP_L/MP_K (as we pointed out in the previous section), it follows that the optimal combination of inputs is one where $MP_L/MP_K = P_L/P_K$. Or put differently, the firm should choose an input combination where $MP_L/P_L = MP_K/P_K$.

If there are more than two inputs, the firm will maximize output by distributing its expenditures among various inputs in such a way that the marginal product of a dollar's worth of any one input is equal to the marginal product of a dollar's worth of any other input used. Thus, the firm will choose an input combination such that

$$\frac{MP_a}{P_a} = \frac{MP_b}{P_b} = \cdots = \frac{MP_n}{P_u}, \tag{7.11}$$

where MP_a, MP_b, ..., MP_n are the marginal products of inputs $a, b, \ldots, n$, and P_a, P_b, ..., P_n are the prices of inputs $a, b, \ldots, n$. (For further proof of the decision rule in equation (7.11), see the chapter appendix.)

FIGURE
7.7

Isocost Curve

The isocost curve shows the combinations of inputs that can be obtained for a total outlay of M.

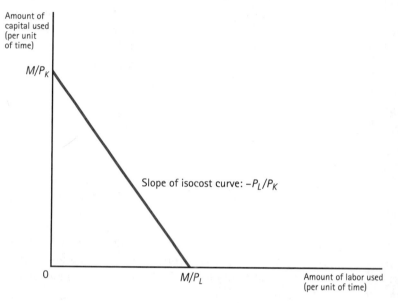

FIGURE
7.8

Maximization of Output for a Given Cost

To maximize output for a given cost, the firm should choose the input combination at point R.

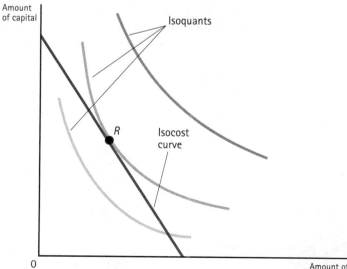

FIGURE 7.9

Minimization of Cost for a Given Output

To minimize the cost of producing the amount of output corresponding to this isoquant, the firm should choose the input combination at point S.

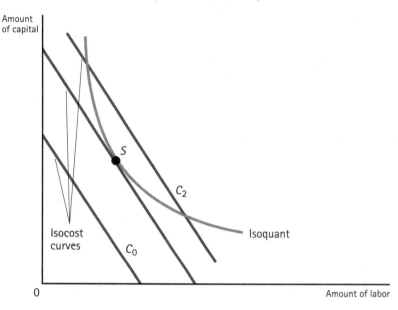

To determine the input combination that will minimize the cost of producing a given output, we use a graph similar to Figure 7.8. Moving along the isoquant corresponding to the stipulated output level, we must find the point on the isoquant that lies on the lowest isocost curve, for example, S in Figure 7.9. Input combinations on isocost curves like C_0 that lie below S are cheaper than S, but they cannot produce the desired output. Input combinations on isocost curves like C_2 that lie above S will produce the desired output but at a higher cost than S. It is obvious that the optimal point, S, is a point where the isocost curve is tangent to the isoquant. Thus, to minimize the cost of producing a given output or to maximize the output from a given cost outlay, the firm must equate MP_L/MP_K and P_L/P_K; this means that $MP_L/P_L = MP_K/P_K$. And if more than two inputs are needed, the firm must satisfy equation (7.11).

The Beiswanger Company: A Numerical Example

To illustrate how the technique presented in the previous section can be used, consider the Beiswanger Company, a small firm engaged in engineering analysis. Beiswanger's president has determined that the firm's output per month (Q) is related in the following way to the number of engineers used (E) and the number of technicians used (T):

$$Q = 20E - E^2 + 12T - 0.5T^2. \tag{7.12}$$

The monthly wage of an engineer is \$4,000, and the monthly wage of a technician is \$2,000. If Beiswanger allots \$28,000 per month for the total combined wages of engineers and technicians, how many engineers and technicians should it hire?

On the basis of the previous section, if the Beiswanger Company is to maximize output, it must choose a combination of engineers and technicians such that

$$\frac{MP_E}{P_E} = \frac{MP_T}{P_T}, \tag{7.13}$$

where MP_E is the marginal product of an engineer, MP_T is the marginal product of a technician, P_E is the wage of an engineer, and P_T is the wage of a technician. Taking partial derivatives of Q in equation (7.12) with respect to E and T, we find that

$$MP_E = \frac{\partial Q}{\partial E} = 20 - 2E \tag{7.14a}$$

and

$$MP_T = \frac{\partial Q}{\partial T} = 12 - T. \tag{7.14b}$$

Inserting these expressions for MP_E and MP_T into equation (7.13), and noting that $P_E = 4,000$ and $P_T = 2,000$, it follows from equation (7.13) that

$$\frac{20 - 2E}{4,000} = \frac{12 - T}{2,000}$$

$$\frac{2,000(20 - 2E)}{4,000} = 12 - T$$

$$10 - E = 12 - T$$

$$T = E + 2.$$

Since Beiswanger will spend \$28,000 per month on the total combined wages of engineers and technicians,

$$4,000E + 2,000T = 28,000.$$

Substituting $(E + 2)$ for T,

$$4{,}000E + 2{,}000(E + 2) = 28{,}000;$$

this means that $E = 4$ (and $T = 6$). Thus, to maximize the output from the $28{,}000 outlay on wages, Beiswanger should hire 4 engineers and 6 technicians.

The Miller Company: Another Numerical Example

To show how the analysis in the section before last can be used to determine the input combination that will minimize the cost of producing a given output, consider the Miller Company, for which the relationship between output per hour (Q) and the number of workers (L) and the number of machines (K) used per hour is:

$$Q = 10(LK)^{0.5}$$

The wage of a worker is $8 per hour, and the price of a machine is $2 per hour. If the Miller Company produces 80 units of output per hour, how many workers and machines should it use?

According to equation (7.11), the Miller Company should choose an input combination such that

$$\frac{MP_L}{P_L} = \frac{MP_K}{P_K},$$

where MP_L is the marginal product of a worker, MP_K is the marginal product of a machine, P_L is the wage of a worker, and P_K is the price of using a machine. Since $Q = (LK)^{0.5}$

$$MP_L = \frac{\partial Q}{\partial L} = 5\left(\frac{K}{L}\right)^{0.5}$$

and

$$MP_K = \frac{\partial Q}{\partial K} = 5\left(\frac{L}{K}\right)^{0.5}$$

Thus, if $MP_L/P_L = MP_K P_K$,

$$\frac{5\left(\frac{K}{L}\right)^{0.5}}{8} = \frac{5\left(\frac{K}{K}\right)^{0.5}}{2}.$$

Multiplying both sides of this equation by $\left(\frac{K}{L}\right)^{0.5}$ we get

$$\frac{5K}{8L} = \frac{5}{2},$$

which means that $K = 4L$. And since $Q = 80$,

$$10(LK)^{0.5} = 80$$
$$10[L(4L)]^{0.5} = 80$$
$$L = 4.$$

Thus, to minimize cost, the Miller Company should hire 4 workers and use 16 machines.

Optimal Lot Size

In previous sections, we have described how a firm's managers can find the input combination that minimizes the cost of producing a particular quantity of output. In this section, we extend our analysis to include more than one time period, and recognize that many firms produce goods in lots or batches, which are produced intermittently. A central question for such firms is: What is the optimal lot size? Managerial economists have devoted considerable attention to this question. By using the optimization techniques described in earlier chapters, this question can readily be answered, thus extending our analysis in previous sections.

Suppose that the Monarch Company, a manufacturer of trucks, has to produce 100,000 parts of a particular type, since each of its trucks requires such a part. Each time the firm begins to produce this type of part, it incurs a setup cost of $20,000 because it has to devote considerable labor time to setting up the equipment that produces this part. The advantage of producing large lots is that this cuts the total setup cost incurred during the year. If the firm were to produce its annual requirement of 100,000 parts in one huge lot, it would only have to set up the equipment once, the result being that its total setup cost for the year would be $20,000. If it produced its annual requirement of 100,000 parts in two lots (each of 50,000), it would have to set up the equipment twice, the result being that the total setup cost for the year would be $40,000. The relationship between the size of a lot and the annual total setup cost is shown in Figure 7.10.

The reason why firms often do not produce large lots is that they result in large inventories that are expensive to maintain and finance. If, for example, the firm produces all 100,000 of the parts in one huge lot at the beginning of the year, its inventory equals 100,000 parts at the beginning of the year and

FIGURE
7.10

Relationship between the Size of Lot and Annual Setup Cost

The larger the lot size, the lower the annual setup cost.

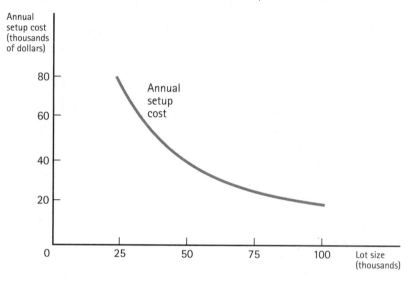

zero parts at the end of the year. Its average inventory is 50,000 parts, as shown in the left-hand panel of Figure 7.11. On the other hand, if the firm produces the annual requirement of 100,000 parts in two lots (each of 50,000 units), its inventory equals 50,000 parts at the beginning of the year and zero parts at the end of six months; then after the second lot is produced, its inventory jumps back up to 50,000 parts, after which it declines once again to zero parts at the end of the year. Thus, its average inventory is 25,000 parts, as shown in the right-hand panel of Figure 7.11.

If the annual cost of holding inventory is proportional to the average inventory, the relationship between the size of a lot and the annual cost of holding inventory is shown in Figure 7.12.[7] Adding the annual setup cost for each lot size (taken from Figure 7.10 and reproduced in Figure 7.12) to the inventory cost, we obtain the total annual cost for each lot size. Under the conditions shown in Figure 7.12, the optimal lot size is 25,000, where the total annual costs are a minimum.

---

[7]Delaney estimates that the cost of carrying a dollar's worth of inventory for a year is 21 cents.

FIGURE
7.11

Size of Inventory during the Year

Average inventory is 50,000 parts if the lot size equals 100,000 and 25,000 parts if the lot size equals 50,000.

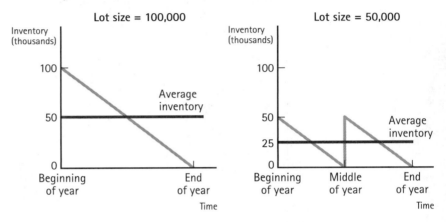

In general, how can we determine the optimal lot size? Total annual setup cost equals $20,000Q/L$ dollars, where Q is the total annual requirement of the relevant part, and L is the number of identical parts of this sort produced in a lot. If $6.40 is the annual cost of holding each identical part of this sort in inventory for a year, the annual cost of holding inventory equals $6.4L/2$ dollars. Adding the annual setup cost and the annual cost of holding inventory, we obtain the following expression for the total annual cost:

$$C = 6.4L/2 + 20,000Q/L.$$

To minimize total annual cost, we set

$$\frac{dC}{dL} = 3.2 - \frac{20,000Q}{L^2} = 0.$$

Solving for L, we find that to minimize total annual cost, L should equal

$$\left(\frac{20,000Q}{3.2}\right)^{0.5} \tag{7.15}$$

More generally, the optimal lot size equals $(\frac{2SQ}{b})^{0.5}$ where S is the cost per setup, and b is the annual cost of carrying each good of this sort in inventory.

FIGURE
7.12

Relationship between Size of Lot and Total Annual Cost

Setup cost decreases as lot size increases because fewer setups occur. The cost of carrying inventory increases as lot size increases, because supply exceeds demand more often and goods remain in inventory for a long time period. Total costs are the vertical summation of the two costs. The optimal lot size (which minimizes total cost) is where the two cost curves intersect. Total cost is the sum of the cost-of-carrying inventory and the setup cost. Thus, the total cost curve is the vertical sum of the cost-of-carrying-inventory curve and the setup cost curve. For example, if the optimal lot size is 25,000, annual setup cost equals OH, as does annual inventory carrying cost and total annual cost equals $2OH = OK$.

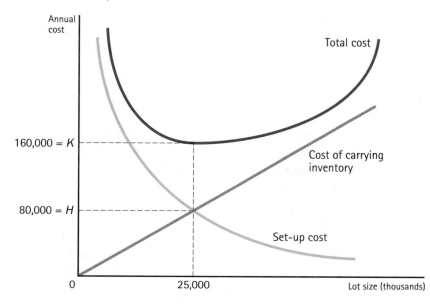

Note that this optimal lot size occurs when inventory holding costs equal setup costs, or $\dfrac{6.4L}{2} = \dfrac{20,000Q}{L}$, or $3.2L^2 = 20,000Q$, which gives the same result as equation 7.15. It can also be shown that the optimal (minimum) total cost is $(2b5Q)^{0.5}$.

In the case of the Monarch Company described above, Q equals 100,000. Thus, to minimize total annual cost, L should equal $[20,000(100,000)/3.2]^{0.5} =$ (625 million)$^{0.5} = 25,000$. In other words, the optimal lot size is 25,000, which means that 25,000 identical parts of this sort should be produced in each lot. (Of course, there is no reason for the number of setups per year to be an inte-

TABLE 7.4 Reductions in Time Required to Set Up Selected Machines, Japanese Firms

Firm	Machine	Initial setup time	New setup time
Toyota	Bolt maker	8 hours	1 minute
Mazda	Ring gear cutter	6.5 hours	15 minutes
Mazda	Die casting machine	1.5 hours	4 minutes
Mitsubishi	8-arbor boring machine	24 hours	3 minutes

Source: J. Blackburn, *Time-Based Competition* (Homewood, II.: Business One Irwin, 1991), p. 178.

ger number. For example, one could have five setups during each two-year period, or two and a half setups per year.)[8]

What Toyota Taught the World

The Japanese have taught the rest of the world a great deal about production. For one thing, they have succeeded in lowering the cost per setup, thus reducing the optimal lot size. For example, in the late 1970s, Toyota Motor Company's workers took about 10 minutes to set up the 800-ton presses used in forming auto hoods and fenders, whereas this took about 6 hours in the United States (see Table 7.4 for other cases). To see that such a reduction in the cost per setup will reduce the optimal lot size, consider the Monarch Company, discussed in the previous section. If this firm can reduce the cost per setup from \$20,000 to \$5,000, the optimal lot size will be $(5,000Q/3.2)^{0.5}$, not $(20,000Q/3.2)^{0.5}$, which means that the optimal lot size will be cut in half to 12,500 (holding Q constant).

A big advantage of reducing lot sizes is that less inventory has to be held. At least one senior Japanese manager has stated that "inventory is the root of all evil." Toyota's famous just-in-time production system calls for every part's arrival just when it is needed, or just when a machine is available. This can result in a great increase in efficiency. Less work-in-process inventory cuts the cost of holding inventory, as well as speeds up the production cycle time, and makes it simpler to monitor the progress of work through the factory.[9] Note

[8]See J. Magee, "Guides to Inventory Policy: Functions and Lot Sizes," in *Managerial Economics and Operations Research,* Mansfield.

[9]R. Hayes and S. Wheelwright, *Restoring Our Competitive Edge* (New York: Wiley, 1984). Also, see National Research Council, "The Japanese Cost and Quality Advantages in the Auto Industry," in *Managerial Economics and Operations Research,* Mansfield.

TABLE
7.5

Cost of Producing a Forklift Truck (European Cost = 100)

	Factory	
	West European	Toyota
Number of product families	20	6
Cost per truck		
Materials	75	65
Direct labor	4	2
Overhead	21	14
Total cost	100	81

Source: Abegglen and Stalk, *Kaisha.*

above that as S goes to zero, L goes to 0, and hence $L/2$ (average inventory held) goes to 0. Thus, Toyota's lowering of setup costs enabled them to follow a policy of virtually no inventory.

Many U.S. firms have come to use just-in-time production systems. The results have sometimes been stunning. For example, consider Northern Telecom's plant in Santa Clara, California, which makes printed circuit boards. Managers report that output increased by 25 percent, without additional workers, and that inventories were reduced by over 80 percent.

Another technique adopted by the Japanese is focused manufacturing. For example, Toyota, in making forklift trucks, restricted its production to a comparatively narrow line of 6 families of trucks in its factory in Nagoya. In this way, it reduced the complexity of its production operations, which in turn decreased the number of parts, the level of inventories, the required amount of supervision, and the number of errors and defects. Table 7.5 compares the average cost of producing a forklift truck at Toyota with that at a West European factory that produced 20 families of trucks in its factory. As you can see, Toyota's cost was about 20 percent lower than the West European firm's.[10]

European, U.S., and other firms have responded by adopting similar techniques. For example, the West European manufacturer of forklift trucks in Table 7.5 reduced the number of product families made in its plant from 20 to 6. The result was about the same as in Japan: cost per truck fell by 19 percent.[11] One

[10]J. Abegglen and G. Stalk, *Kaisha: The Japanese Corporation* (New York: Basic Books, 1985). Of course, from a marketing point of view, there can be disadvantages in reducing the variety of products produced. They must be balanced against the cost reductions.
[11]Ibid.

important point that this illustrates is that Japanese firms have no monopoly on production knowledge and expertise. Indeed, many of the ideas that the Japanese have utilized with great success—for example, quality control techniques—originated in the United States.

Returns to Scale

In previous sections, we learned how technology in a particular industry can be represented by a production function and described the characteristics of production functions (and of related concepts like the marginal and average product) that seem to hold in general for production processes. However, one important characteristic of production functions has not been described: how output responds in the long run to changes in the *scale* of the firm. In other words, suppose we consider a long-run situation in which all inputs are variable, and suppose the firm increases the amount of all inputs by the same proportion. What will happen to output?

Clearly, there are three possibilities: First, output may increase by a larger proportion than each of the inputs. For example, a doubling of all inputs may lead to more than a doubling of output. This is the case of **increasing returns to scale.** Second, output may increase by a smaller proportion than each of the inputs. For example, a doubling of all inputs may lead to less than a doubling of output. This is the case of **decreasing returns to scale.** Third, output may increase by exactly the same proportion as the inputs. For example, a doubling of all inputs may lead to a doubling of output. This is the case of **constant returns to scale.**

It may seem that production functions must necessarily exhibit constant returns to scale. If two factories are built with the same plant and the same types of workers, it may appear obvious that twice as much output will result than if one such plant is built. But things are not so simple. If a firm doubles its scale, it may be able to use techniques that could not be used at the smaller scale. Some inputs are not available in small units; for example, we cannot install half a robot. Because of indivisibilities of this sort, increasing returns to scale may occur. Thus, although one could double a firm's size by simply building two small factories, this may be inefficient. One large factory may be more efficient than two smaller factories of the same total capacity because it is large enough to use certain techniques and inputs that the smaller factories cannot employ.

Increasing returns to scale also arise because of certain geometrical relations. Since the volume of a box that is $2 \times 2 \times 2$ feet is 8 times as great as the volume of a box that is $1 \times 1 \times 1$ foot, the former box can carry 8 times as much as the latter box. But since the area of the six sides of the $2 \times 2 \times 2$-

CONSULTANT'S CORNER

Choosing the Size of an Oiltanker

Over 60 percent of crude oil output is transported by oil tankers. The product is the largest commodity in transocean trade, accounting for 40 percent of all ocean shipments, by weight. Oil tankers can be regarded as a large cylinder. The surface area of a cylinder is not proportional to its volume; instead, as a cylinder's volume increases, its surface area goes up less than proportionately. Thus, a tanker that can carry 300,000 deadweight tonnes is only about twice as broad, long, and deep as one that can carry 30,000 tonnes.

Since the 1970s, the size of oil tankers has increased, as indicated below:

Year	Average oil tanker size (thousands of deadweight tonnes)
1973	64.0
1978	103.0
1985	146.0
2000	220.0

The oil tanker business is cyclical in nature. It is characterized by periods of overcapacity (and low prices) and undercapacity (and high prices). For example, in 1999, Standard & Poor's either lowered ratings or downwardly revised outlooks for twenty-three of the thirty-four public shipping companies they cover.

In the fall of 2000, some analysts believed that pricing conditions in the oil tanker market would improve because of a strong U.S. economy and strong economies in Asia. If you were a consultant to a shipping company that was interested in building a new tanker, would you advise the company to build a tanker of 200,000 tonnes or 20,000 tonnes?

Sources: www.eagibson.co.uk/posidonia; www.standardandpoors.com/ratings/corporates/shipping.htm; www.europa.eu.int/scadplus/leg (Maritime safety communications of 21 March 2000 to Parliament).

foot box is 24 square feet and the area of the six sides of the $1 \times 1 \times 1$-foot box is 6 square feet, the former box only requires 4 times as much wood as the latter. Greater specialization also can result in increasing returns to scale: as more workers and machines are used, it is possible to subdivide tasks and allow various inputs to specialize. Also, economies of scale may arise because of probabilistic considerations: for example, because the aggregate behavior of a bigger number of customers tends to be more stable, a firm's inventory may not have to increase in proportion to its sales.

Why do decreasing returns to scale occur? The most frequently cited reason is the difficulty of coordinating a large enterprise. It can be difficult even in a small firm to obtain the information required to make important decisions; in a large firm, the difficulties tend to be greater. It can be difficult even in a small firm to be certain that management's wishes are being carried out; in a larger firm, these difficulties too tend to be greater. Although the advantages of a large organization are obvious, there are often very great disadvantages. For example, in certain kinds of research and development, there is evidence that large engineering teams tend to be less effective than smaller ones and that large firms tend to be less effective than small ones.

Whether there are constant, increasing, or decreasing returns to scale in a particular situation is an empirical question that must be settled case by case. There is no simple, all-encompassing answer. In some industries, the available evidence may indicate that increasing returns are present over a certain range of output. In other industries, decreasing or constant returns may be present. Moreover, it is important to note that the answer is likely to depend on the level of output that is considered. There may be increasing returns to scale at small output levels and constant or decreasing returns to scale at larger output levels.

The Output Elasticity

To measure whether there are increasing, decreasing, or constant returns to scale, the **output elasticity** can be computed. The *output elasticity is defined as the percentage change in output resulting from a 1 percent increase in all inputs.* If the output elasticity exceeds 1, there are increasing returns to scale; if it equals 1, there are constant returns to scale; and if it is less than 1, there are decreasing returns to scale.

As an illustration, consider the Lone Star Company, a maker of aircraft parts, which has the following production function:

$$Q = 0.8L^{0.3}K^{0.8},$$

where Q is the number of parts produced per year (measured in millions of parts), L is the number of workers hired, and K is the amount of capital used. This is a Cobb-Douglas production function (named after Charles Cobb and Paul Douglas, who pioneered in its application), which will be discussed in more detail in the section after next.

To calculate the output elasticity at the Lone Star Company, let's see what happens to Q if we multiply both inputs (L and K) by 1.01. Clearly, the new value of Q, that is, Q', equals

$$\begin{aligned}
Q' &= 0.8(1.01L)^{0.3}(1.01K)^{0.8}, \\
&= 0.8(1.01)^{1.1}L^{0.3}K^{0.8} \\
&= (1.01)^{1.1}(0.8L^{0.3}K^{0.8}) \\
&= (1.01)^{1.1}Q, \\
&= 1.011005484Q
\end{aligned}$$

Thus, if the quantity of both inputs increases by 1 percent, output increases by slightly more than 1.1 percent; this means that the output elasticity is approximately 1.1. It is exactly 1.1 for an infinitesimal change in input use (of both inputs). Since a 1 percent change is larger than infinitesimal, the increase in output is slightly larger than 1.1.

How Firms Obtain Information About the Production Function: Competitive Benchmarking at Xerox

Having discussed at length the key role of the production function in managerial decision making, we must look carefully at how managers obtain information concerning the production function. How does Hewlett-Packard or Merck or ExxonMobil find out how to get the most out of a particular combination of inputs, and what the maximum output obtainable from this input combination is? One way that firms try to solve this problem is by sending out teams of engineers and technicians to visit other firms to obtain information concerning best-practice methods and procedures. In this way, they try to determine whether they are operating on the industry production function—or whether they are inefficient relative to other firms. This practice, known as **competitive benchmarking,** has produced valuable results for many companies, such as the Xerox Corporation.

In 1979, Xerox, confronted with a falling share of the market and reduced profitability of its basic copier business, began a searching examination of its methods. Starting with an engineering study of rival products, including an examination of Fuji Xerox, its partly owned subsidiary in Japan, Xerox's executives found strong evidence that it was not as efficient as its major Japanese rivals.[12]

Interestingly, Xerox found that it could learn a great deal from firms in seemingly unrelated fields. For example, Xerox executives, intent on improving their warehousing operations, searched for a firm to study in this regard. After looking in trade journals and discussing warehousing systems with consultants, they decided to visit L. L. Bean, the Maine apparel and footwear seller, which had acquired a strong reputation for customer service and which had distribution problems similar to Xerox's.

[12]This section is based largely on R. Hayes, S. Wheelwright, and K. Clark, *Dynamic Manufacturing* (New York: Free Press, 1988).

TABLE
7.6

Comparison of Warehouse Operations

Measure of output per worker per day	L. L. Bean	Xerox
Orders per worker per day	550	117
Lines per worker per day[a]	1,440	497

[a]A line is a standard measure of travel distance for one trip to a storage bin.

Source: Hayes, Wheelwright, and Clark, *Dynamic Manufacturing.*

Xerox's managers found that although L. L. Bean's warehouse operations were largely manual, it had achieved a high degree of output per worker. Table 7.6 compares output per worker in L. L. Bean's warehouse operation with that in a proposed operation at Xerox. In large part, Bean's superiority could be attributed to differences in methods; it arranged materials so that big-selling items were closer to stock pickers, and it chose storage locations to minimize forklift travel distance.

In this way, Xerox learned what the production function was for this type of warehousing operation. On the basis of these findings, it modernized its own warehousing operations. Competitive benchmarking is a very important technique and is applicable in a wide variety of areas. Xerox's top managers felt that it was responsible for much of the improvement in the firm's performance during the 1980s. Many other firms swear by the effectiveness and significance of this technique.

Measurement of Production Functions

Although techniques like competitive benchmarking are valuable, they generally can provide only part of the information managers need concerning production functions. Thus, managerial economists have devised other methods, based largely on the regression techniques described in Chapter 5, to measure production functions. As we will see in subsequent sections of this chapter, the results often have proved very useful. One of the first steps in estimating a production function is to choose the mathematical form of the production function. If labor and capital are the only inputs used, one possible mathematical form is the following cubic equation:

$$Q = aLK + bL^2K + cLK^2 - dL^3K - eLK^3, \tag{7.16}$$

where Q is output, L is the quantity of labor input, and K is the quantity of capital input. This mathematical form exhibits first increasing and then decreasing returns to scale. Also, the marginal product of each input first increases and then decreases as more and more of the input is used. To see that this is true, consider the marginal product of labor, which equals

$$\frac{\partial Q}{\partial L} = (aK + cK^2 - eK^3) + 2bKL - 3dKL^2.$$

Clearly, the marginal product of labor is a quadratic function of the amount of labor used; it increases at first if $(b/3d > L)$ and then decreases (as $L > b/3d$) as more and more labor is employed.

Another mathematical form that is more commonly used is the Cobb-Douglas form, which we encountered in the section before last. With only two inputs, this form is

$$Q = aL^b K^c. \tag{7.17}$$

One advantage of this form is that the marginal productivity of each input depends on the level of all inputs employed, which is often realistic. Consider the marginal product of labor, which equals

$$\frac{\partial Q}{\partial L} = baL^{b-1}K^c = b\left(\frac{Q}{L}\right) = b \times AP_L$$

Obviously, the marginal product of labor depends on the values of both L and K. Another advantage is that if logarithms are taken of both sides of equation (7.17),

$$\log Q = \log a + b \log L + c \log K. \tag{7.18}$$

Thus, the regression techniques in Chapter 5 can be used to estimate b and c (as well as $\log a$). If we regress $\log Q$ on $\log L$ and $\log K$, the regression coefficients are these estimates.

Note that if the Cobb-Douglas production function is used, we can easily estimate the returns to scale. If the sum of the exponents (that is, $b + c$) exceeds 1, increasing returns to scale are indicated; if the sum of the exponents equals 1, constant returns to scale prevail; and if the sum of the exponents is less than 1, decreasing returns to scale are indicated. This is because, if the Cobb-Douglas production function prevails, the output elasticity equals the sum of the exponents. For example, in the section before last, the output elasticity of the Lone Star Company was 1.1, which equaled the sum of the exponents (0.3 and 0.8).

There is no cut-and-dried way to determine which mathematical form is best, since the answer depends on the particular situation. Frequently, a good procedure is to try more than one mathematical form and see which one fits the data best. The important thing is that the chosen form provide a faithful representation of the actual situation. To determine whether this is the case, it often is useful to see how well a particular estimated production function can forecast the quantity of output resulting from the combination of inputs actually used.

Three Types of Statistical Analysis

Having chosen a mathematical form for the production function, there remains the question of which of three types of data to use. One possibility is to use time-series data concerning the amount of various inputs used in various periods in the past and the amount of output produced in each period. For example, you might obtain data concerning the amount of labor, the amount of capital, and the amount of various raw materials used in the steel industry during each year from 1958 to 2001. On the basis of such data and information concerning the annual output of steel during 1958 to 2001, you might estimate the relationship between the amounts of the inputs and the resulting output, using regression techniques like those discussed in Chapter 5.

The second possibility is to use cross-section data concerning the amount of various inputs used and output produced in various firms or sectors of the industry at a given time. For example, you might obtain data concerning the amount of labor, the amounts of capital, and the amount of various raw materials used in various firms in the steel industry in 2001. On the basis of such data and information concerning the 2001 output of each firm, you might use regression techniques to estimate the relationship between the amounts of the inputs and the resulting output.

The third possibility is to use technical information supplied by the engineer or the agricultural scientist. This information is collected by experiment or from experience with the day-to-day workings of the technical process. There are advantages to be gained from approaching the measurement of the production function from this angle because the range of applicability of the data is known, and, unlike time-series and cross-section studies, we are not restricted to the narrow range of actual observations.[13]

Regardless of which approach you use, it is important to recognize that the data may not always represent technically efficient combinations of inputs and output. For example, because of errors or constraints, the amount of inputs used

[13]For an illustration of this approach, see Cookenboo, "Production Functions and Cost Functions in Oil Pipelines," in the *Study Guide* accompanying this textbook.

by the steel industry in 2001 may not have been the minimum required to produce the 2001 output of the steel industry. Since the production function theoretically includes only efficient input combinations, a case of this sort should be excluded if our measurements are to be pristine pure. In practice, however, such cases are not always excluded (or recognized), and the resulting estimate of the production function contains errors on this account.

Another important difficulty is the measurement of capital input. The principal problem stems from the fact that the stock of capital is composed of various types and ages of machines, buildings, and inventories. Combining them into a single measure—or a few measures—is not easy. In addition, errors can arise because various data points that are assumed to be on the same production function are in fact on different ones. Moreover, biases can occur because of identification problems somewhat similar to those discussed on pages 149 to 152.

With regard to the engineering approach, it is difficult to combine the results for the processes for which engineers have data into an overall plant or firm production function. Since engineering data generally pertain to only a part of the firm's activities, this is often a very hard job. For example, engineering data tell us little or nothing about the firm's marketing or financial activities.

The Telephone Industry in Canada: A Case Study

Despite these difficulties, estimates of production functions have proved of considerable interest and value. To illustrate the empirical results that have been obtained, A. Dobell, L. Taylor, L. Waverman, T. Liu, and M. Copeland found that the production function in the telephone industry in Canada was

$$Q = AL^{0.70}K^{0.41}, \tag{7.19}$$

where A is the level of output when both L and K equal 1.[14] On the basis of this equation, it appears that a 1 percent increase in labor (holding the amount of capital constant) will result in approximately a 0.70 percent increase in output. To prove that this is true, note that

$$\frac{\partial Q}{\partial L} = 0.70AL^{-0.30}K^{0.41}$$

$$= 0.70\,\frac{Q}{L}.$$

[14]A. Dobell, L. Taylor, L. Waverman, T. Liu, and M. Copeland, "Communications in Canada," *Bell Journal of Economics and Management Science,* 1972.

Thus,

$$\left(\frac{\partial Q}{\partial L}\right)\left(\frac{L}{Q}\right) = 0.70.$$ (7.20)

Since $(\partial Q/\partial L)(L/Q)$ is (approximately) equal to the percentage increase in output resulting from a 1 percent increase in labor, a 1 percent increase in labor will result in an approximate 0.70 percent increase in output.

On the basis of the estimated production function in equation (7.19), one can also determine the effect on output of a 1 percent increase in capital. Because

$$\frac{\partial Q}{\partial K} = 0.41AL^{0.70}K^{-0.59}$$

$$= 0.41\frac{Q}{K},$$

it follows that a 1 percent increase in capital will raise the output of the telephone industry by approximately 0.41 percent. Why? Because $(\partial Q/\partial K)(K/Q) = 0.41$.

In addition, equation (7.19) provides valuable information concerning returns to scale in the Canadian telephone industry. Because the production function is of the Cobb-Douglas form, the output elasticity equals the sum of the exponents; that is, it equals $0.70 + 0.41 = 1.11$ (recall our discussion on pages 270 and 271). Since the output elasticity is the percentage change in output resulting from a 1 percent increase in all inputs, this means that a 1 percent increase in all inputs would result in approximately a 1.11 percent increase in output. Clearly these results indicate increasing returns to scale.

Estimated production functions of this sort are of enormous value to managers and analysts, since they enable the manager or analyst to estimate the marginal product of each input, and to determine whether there are increasing, decreasing, or constant returns to scale. As we have stressed in this chapter, information of this kind is of fundamental importance in deciding how to minimize a firm's costs. In a world where competition is intense and costs matter greatly, it is no wonder that firms find estimated production functions valuable.

Poultry Production in the United States: Another Case Study

As a further illustration, consider the production of broiler chickens, which is a big industry in the United States (1997 production value: $14.2 billion). To estimate the production function, an experiment was carried out in which broilers were fed various amounts of corn and soybean oilmeal, and the gain in weight of each broiler was carefully measured.[15] On the basis of regression analysis of the sort described in Chapter 5, it was found that

$$G = 0.03 + 0.48C + 0.64S - 0.02C^2 - 0.05S^2 - 0.02CS, \qquad (7.21)$$

where G is the gain in weight (in pounds per broiler), C is pounds of corn per broiler, and S is pounds of soybean oilmeal per broiler. The multiple coefficient of determination (R^2) is very high, about 0.998.

Using equation (7.21), we can obtain isoquants for poultry production. Suppose that we want to obtain the isoquant pertaining to a weight gain of 1 pound. In other words, we want to find the various combinations of amounts of corn per broiler and soybean oilmeal per broiler that will result in a weight gain per broiler of 1 pound. To find these combinations, we set $G = 1$.

$$1 = 0.03 + 0.48C + 0.64S - 0.02C^2 - 0.05S^2 - 0.02CS. \qquad (7.22)$$

Then we set C equal to various values and see what each resulting value of S is. For example, suppose that $C = 1$. Then

$$1 = 0.03 + 0.48(1) + 0.64S - 0.02(1^2) - 0.05S^2 - 0.02(1)S,$$

or

$$1 = 0.03 + 0.48 - 0.02 + (0.64 - 0.02)S - 0.05S^2$$

Solving $0.05S^2 - 0.62S + 0.51 = 0$ by the quadratic formula yields

$$\begin{aligned} S &= (0.62 \pm (0.62^2 - 4(0.05)(0.51))^{0.5})/2(0.05) \\ &= (0.62 \pm (0.3844 - 0.0102)^{0.5})/0.1 \\ &= (0.62 \pm (0.2824)^{0.5})/0.1 \\ &= (0.62 \pm 0.5314)/0.1. \end{aligned}$$

Thus, $S = 1.1514/0.1 = 11.514$, or $S = 0.08858/0.1 = 0.886$.

Consequently, if a broiler is to gain 1 pound of weight, it must be fed 0.886 pounds of soybean oilmeal, as well as 1 pound of corn.[16]

---

[15]Organization for Economic Cooperation and Development, *Interdisciplinary Research in Input/Output Relationships and Production Functions to Improve Decisions and Efficiency for Poultry Production*, Paris, 1966.

[16]To obtain this expression for S, we use the formula in footnote 4, Chapter 2 (see page 62). There is another possible value of S, which corresponds to the use of the plus sign (rather than the minus sign) before $(b^2 - 4ac)^{0.5}$ in this formula, but this other value is not relevant here.

FIGURE
7.13

Isoquant for 1-Pound Weight Gain for a Broiler and Isocost Curve If Corn Price Is 3/4 of Soybean Oilmeal Price

The optimal input combination is 1.35 pounds of corn and 0.61 pounds of soybean oilmeal.

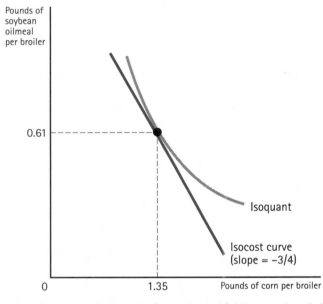

Source: Organization for Economic Cooperation and Development, *Interdisciplinary Research.*

If we let $C = 1.1$, we can find the corresponding value of S by substituting 1.1 for C in equation (7.22) and solving for S. If we let $C = 1.2$, we can find the corresponding value of S by substituting 1.2 for C in equation (7.22) and solving for S. Proceeding in this way, we can find more and more points on the isoquant corresponding to a weight gain of 1 pound. The resulting isoquant is shown in Figure 7.13. Isoquants of this sort are of great importance to managers. Coupled with data regarding input prices, they can be used to determine how much of each input should be used to minimize costs (recall Figure 7.9).

In fact, poultry producers have used the isoquant in Figure 7.13 to determine how much corn and soybean oilmeal to feed a broiler if they want a 1-pound weight gain. To see how they have done this, suppose that the price of a pound of corn is three-quarters of the price of a pound of soybean oilmeal. Then the slope of each isocost curve in Figure 7.13 equals $-3/4$, since, as pointed out in Figure 7.7, the slope equals -1 times the price of the input on the horizontal axis (corn) divided by the price of the input on the vertical axis (soybean oilmeal). For the cost of the weight gain to be a minimum, the isocost curve should be tangent to the isoquant; this means that the slope of the isoquant should also equal $-3/4$. As shown in Figure 7.13, this occurs when 1.35 pounds of corn and 0.61 pounds of soybean oilmeal are used. Thus, this is the optimal input combination if the price of a pound of corn is three-quarters the price of a pound of soybean oilmeal.

Summary

1. The production function is the relationship between the quantities of various inputs used per period of time and the maximum quantity of the good that can be produced per period of time. Given the production function for a particular firm, one can calculate the average product of an input and the marginal product of an input.

2. To determine how much of a particular input to utilize, a firm should compare the marginal revenue product of the input with the marginal expenditure on the input. To maximize profit, the firm should utilize the amount of the input that results in making the marginal revenue product equal to the marginal expenditure.

3. An isoquant is a curve showing all possible (efficient) combinations of inputs that are capable of producing a particular quantity of output. The marginal rate of technical substitution shows the rate at which one input can be substituted for another input if output remains constant. No profit-maximizing firm will operate at a point where the isoquant is positively sloped.

4. To minimize the cost of producing a particular output, a firm should allocate its expenditures among various inputs in such a way that the ratio of the marginal product to the input price is the same for all inputs used. Graphically, this amounts to choosing the input combination where the relevant isoquant is tangent to an isocost curve.

5. Many firms produce goods in lots. The optimal lot size equals $\left(\dfrac{2SQ}{b}\right)^{0.5}$ where S is the cost per setup, Q is the total annual requirement of the relevant good, and b is the annual cost of holding each good of this sort in inventory. It is important that firms produce lots of approximately optimal size; otherwise, their costs will be higher than is necessary or desirable.

6. If the firm increases all inputs by the same proportion and output increases by more (less) than this proportion, there are increasing (decreasing) returns to scale. Increasing returns to scale may occur because of indivisibility of inputs, various geometrical relations, or specialization. Decreasing returns to scale can also occur; the most frequently cited reason is the difficulty of man-

aging a huge enterprise. Whether there are constant, increasing, or decreasing returns to scale is an empirical question that must be settled case by case.

7. Competitive benchmarking is frequently used to obtain information concerning the production function. Also, using techniques of the sort described in Chapter 5, business analysts, engineers, and others have estimated production functions in many firms and industries. Statistical analyses of time-series and cross-section data, as well as engineering data, have been carried out. For example, many studies have fit the Cobb-Douglas production function to the data. The results have proved of considerable value to managers, here and abroad.

Problems

1. In the Elwyn Company, the relationship between output (Q) and the number of hours of skilled labor (S) and unskilled labor (U) is:

$$Q = 300S + 200U - 0.2S^2 - 0.3U^2.$$

The hourly wage of skilled labor is $10, and the hourly wage of unskilled labor is $5. The firm can hire as much labor as it wants at these wage rates.

   a. Elwyn's chief engineer recommends that the firm hire 400 hours of skilled labor and 100 hours of unskilled labor. Evaluate this recommendation.

   b. If the Elwyn Company decides to spend a total of $5,000 on skilled and unskilled labor, how many hours of each type of labor should it hire?

   c. If the price of a unit of output is $10 (and does not vary with output), how many hours of unskilled labor should the company hire?

2. On the basis of a regression analysis like those in Chapter 5, the Washington Company finds that its production function is

$$\log Q = 1.50 + 0.76 \log L + 0.24 \log K,$$

where Q is its daily output, L is the number of workers employed per day, and K is the number of machines used per day. The Washington Company's product is sold in a competitive market, the price per unit being $10. The firm cannot influence the wage of workers or the price of machines.

   a. If the wage of a worker is $30 per day, how many workers per unit of output should the firm hire?

   b. What percentage of the firm's revenues will be spent on labor? Why?

   c. Will this percentage vary depending on the daily wage of a worker? Why or why not?

3. A consulting firm specializing in agriculture determines that the following combinations of hay and grain consumption per lamb will result in a 25-pound gain on a lamb:

Pounds of hay	Pounds of grain
40	130.9
50	125.1
60	120.1
70	115.7
80	111.8
90	108.3
110	102.3
130	97.4
150	93.8

   a. The firm's president wants to estimate the marginal product of a pound of grain in producing lamb. Can he do so on the basis of these data?

   b. The firm's president is convinced that constant returns to scale prevail in lamb production. If this is true, and if hay and grain consumption per lamb are the only inputs, how much gain will accrue if the hay consumption per lamb is 100 pounds and the grain consumption per lamb is 250.2 pounds?

   c. What is the marginal rate of technical substitution of hay for grain when between 40 and 50 pounds of hay (and between 130.9 and 125.1 pounds of grain) are consumed per lamb?

   d. A major advance in technology occurs that allows farmers to produce a 25-pound gain on a lamb with less hay and grain than the table above indicates. If the marginal rate of technical substitution (at each rate of consumption of each input) is the same after the technological advance as before, can you draw the new isoquant corresponding to a 25-pound gain on a lamb?

4. The Ascot Corporation, which produces stationery, hires a consultant to estimate its production function. The consultant concludes that

$$Q = 0.9P + 0.06L,$$

where Q is the number of pounds of stationery produced by Ascot per year, L is the number of hours of labor per year, and P is the number of pounds of paper used per year.

   a. Does this production function seem to include all the relevant inputs? Explain.

   b. Does this production function seem reasonable if it is applied to all pos-
      sible values of *L*? Explain.
   c. Does this production function exhibit diminishing marginal returns?
5. A Cobb-Douglas production function was estimated for six types of farms.
   There were five inputs in the production function: (1) land, (2) labor, (3)
   equipment, (4) livestock and feed, and (5) other resource services. The ex-
   ponent of each input was as shown below.

			Exponent		
Farm type	Land	Labor	Equipment	Livestock and feed	Other resource services
Crop farms	0.24	0.07	0.08	0.53	0.02
Hog farms	0.07	0.02	0.10	0.74	0.03
Dairy farms	0.10	0.01	0.06	0.63	0.02
General farms	0.17	0.12	0.16	0.46	0.03
Large farms	0.28	0.01	0.11	0.53	0.03
Small farms	0.21	0.05	0.08	0.43	0.03

   a. Do there appear to be increasing returns to scale in any of these six
      types of farms?
   b. In what type of farm does a 1 percent increase in labor have the largest
      percentage effect on output?
   c. On the basis of these results, would you expect that output would in-
      crease if many of the farms included in this sample were merged?
6. According to the chief engineer at the Zodiac Company, $Q = AL^{\alpha}K^{\beta}$, where
   Q is the output rate, L is the rate of labor input, and K is the rate of
   capital input. Statistical analysis indicates that $\alpha = 0.8$ and $\beta = 0.3$. The owner
   of the firm claims that there are increasing returns to scale in the plant.
   a. Is the owner correct?
   b. If β were 0.2 rather than 0.3, would she be correct?
   c. Does output per unit of labor depend only on α and β? Why or why
      not?
7. On the basis of data obtained by the U.S. Department of Agriculture, the
   relationship between a cow's total output of milk and the amount of grain
   it is fed is as follows:

Amount of grain (pounds)	Amount of milk (pounds)
1,200	5,917
1,800	7,250
2,400	8,379
3,000	9,371

(This relationship assumes that forage input is fixed at 6,500 pounds of hay.)

   a. Calculate the average product of grain when each amount is used.

   b. Estimate the marginal product of grain when between 1,200 and 1,800 pounds are fed, when between 1,800 and 2,400 pounds are fed, and when between 2,400 and 3,000 pounds are fed.

   c. Does this production function exhibit diminishing marginal returns?

8. The owner of the Hughes Car Wash believes that the relationship between the number of cars washed and labor input is

$$Q = -0.8 + 4.5L - 0.3L^2,$$

where Q is the number of cars washed per hour, and L is the number of people employed per hour. The firm receives $5 for each car washed, and the hourly wage rate for each person employed is $4.50. The cost of other inputs like water is trivial, and hence they are ignored.

   a. How many people should be employed to maximize profit?

   b. What will be the firm's hourly profit?

   c. Is the above relationship between output and labor input valid for all values of L? Why or why not?

9. An electronics plant's production function is $Q = 5LK$, where Q is its output rate, L is the amount of labor it uses per period of time, and K is the amount of capital it uses per period of time. The price of labor is $1 per unit of labor, and the price of capital is $2 per unit of capital. The firm's vice president for manufacturing hires you to determine which combination of inputs the plant should use to produce 20 units of output per period.

   a. What advice would you give him?

   b. Suppose that the price of labor increases to $2 per unit. What effect will this have on output per unit of labor?

   c. Is this plant subject to decreasing returns to scale? Why or why not?

10. In its Erie, Pennsylvania, plant, General Electric has installed a flexible manufacturing system to produce locomotives. Flexible manufacturing systems, which are very sophisticated forms of factory automation, operate with a minimum of manual intervention. They are integrated systems of machines under full programmable control. According to General Electric, the new system compares as follows with the old one:

	Old system	New system
Number of machines	29	9
Number of workers	86	16
Annual output	4,100	5,600

   a. Does the new system increase the average product of labor?

    b. Does it increase the average product of machines?

    c. According to a study by Harvard's Ramchandran Jaikumar, U.S. firms generally do not exploit flexible manufacturing systems as well as they might. For one thing, the percentage of time that such systems are actually functioning, rather than awaiting adjustments or repair, seems to be relatively low. He believes that U.S. firms should invest more in skilled engineering personnel. Can steps of this sort result in shifts of the production function?

    d. How can a firm determine whether such steps are worthwhile?[17]

11. The Arbor Company produces metal fasteners. The cost per setup is $8,000, and the annual cost of holding each fastener in inventory for a year is $40. What is the optimal lot size if the Arbor Company produces each of the following annual outputs?

    a. 1,000

    b. 10,000

    c. 100,000

12. A. B. Volvo, the Swedish auto firm, opened a new car-assembly plant at Udevalla in 1988. The idea was to have a small team of highly skilled workers build an entire car. According to the proponents, it would reduce the tedium associated with the conventional assembly line and cut absenteeism and turnover among workers. In 1991, there were reports that it takes 50 hours of labor to assemble a car at Udevalla, in contrast to 25 hours at Volvo's conventional assembly plant at Ghent, Belgium. If you were Volvo's chief executive officer, what questions would you ask Udevalla's managers, and what steps would you take?

13. Porsche, the German producer of sports cars, almost went bankrupt in 1992. It then remade itself, on the basis of Japanese manufacturing techniques. Several measures of the changes in the efficiency of its manufacturing process are given below.

	Manufacturing area (square yards)	Manufacturing time (hours)	Manufacturing flaws (per car)	Inventory levels (parts)	Managers
Before	765	120	6	8,490	328
After	514	72	3	1,600	226

Source: *New York Times*, January 20, 1996.

[17]For further discussion, see S. Miller, *Impacts of Industrial Robotics* (Madison: University of Wisconsin Press, 1988); R. Jaikumar, "Postindustrial Manufacturing," *Harvard Business Review*, November–December 1986; and E. Mansfield, "Flexible Manufacturing Systems: Economic Effects in Japan, United States, and Western Europe," *Japan and the World Economy*, 4 (1992): 1–16.

   a. Why was it desirable to reduce the manufacturing area?
   b. Why was it desirable to reduce the manufacturing time?
   c. Why was it desirable to reduce inventory levels?
14. During the 1950s and 1960s, the Toyota Motor Company originated and developed the just-in-time system of production, which has had an enormous effect in Japan and elsewhere. According to this system, materials, parts, and components are produced and delivered just before they are needed. One advantage is that inventories of parts and of work in process are reduced considerably, but this is only part of the story. In addition, the time and cost required to change from the production of one part or model to another are reduced; this cuts setup costs and enables the firm to produce small lots economically.

   A careful comparison of an automobile plant using the just-in-time system with an automobile plant not using it resulted in the following data:*

	Plant using just-in-time system	Plant not using just-in-time system
Cars produced per day	1,000	860
Total factory workers	1,000	2,150
Workers per car per day		
Direct labor	0.79	1.25
Overhead personnel	0.21	1.25
Total	1.00	2.50

   a. On the basis of this comparison, does it appear that the average product of labor is higher with the just-in-time system than without it?
   b. Does such a system increase the average product of overhead personnel to a greater extent than it does the average product of direct labor?
   c. If changeovers from one part or model to another require a great deal of time, the required planning and management effort is greater than it would be if such changeovers could be accomplished quickly. Does this help to explain why the average product of overhead personnel increases so much?
   d. According to James Abegglen and George Stalk, "Many Japanese companies by adopting the just-in-time system doubled the productivity of their factory labor forces and almost doubled the productivity of the assets they employed." Did this result in a shift in these firms' isoquants, or a movement along fixed isoquants?

*Abegglen and Stalk, *Kaisha.*

Appendix: Lagrangian Multipliers and Optimal Input Combinations

In this chapter, we stated that equation (7.11) must be satisfied if a firm is to maximize output for a given expenditure level, or if it is to minimize the cost of producing a specified amount of output. In this appendix, we show how the decision rule in equation (7.11) can be derived using the method of Lagrangian multipliers (discussed in Chapter 2). To simplify matters, the firm is assumed to employ only two inputs.

Maximizing Output from a Specified Expenditure Level Suppose that a firm's production function is

$$Q = f(X_1, X_2),$$

where Q is output, X_1 is the amount used of the first input, and X_2 is the amount used of the second input. The firm's total expenditure on both inputs is specified to equal E^*. Thus,

$$X_1 P_1 + X_2 P_2 = E^*,$$

where P_1 is the price of the first input, and P_2 is the price of the second input. The firm wants to maximize the quantity of output from this specified level of expenditure. Thus, the firm wants to maximize Q, where

$$Q = f(X_1, X_2), \tag{7.23}$$

subject to the constraint that

$$E^* - X_1 P_1 - X_2 P_2 = 0. \tag{7.24}$$

Following the procedure described in Chapter 2, we can use the method of Lagrangian multipliers to solve this problem. The first step is to construct the Lagrangian function, which is the right-hand side of equation (7.23) plus λ times the left-hand side of equation (7.24):

$$L_1 = f(X_1, X_2) + \lambda(E^* - X_1 P_1 - X_2 P_2),$$

where λ is the Lagrangian multiplier. Taking the partial derivatives of L_1 with respect to X_1, X_2, and λ, and setting them all equal to zero, we obtain

$$\frac{\partial L_1}{\partial X_1} = \frac{\partial f(X_1, X_2)}{\partial X_1} - \lambda P_1 = 0 \tag{7.25}$$

$$\frac{\partial L_1}{\partial X_2} = \frac{\partial f(X_1,\ X_2)}{\partial X_2} - \lambda P_2 = 0 \tag{7.26}$$

$$\frac{\partial L_1}{\partial \lambda} = E^* - X_1 P_1 - X_2 P_2 = 0. \tag{7.27}$$

These are the conditions for output maximization subject to the expenditure constraint.

Letting MP_1 be the marginal product of the first input and MP_2 be the marginal product of the second input, the following is true (by definition):

$$\frac{\partial f(X_1,\ X_2)}{\partial X_1} = \frac{\partial Q}{\partial X_1} = MP_1$$

$$\frac{\partial f(X_1,\ X_2)}{\partial X_2} = \frac{\partial Q}{\partial X_2} = MP_2.$$

Thus, equations (7.25) and (7.26) can be restated:

$$MP_1 - \lambda P_1 = 0$$
$$MP_2 - \lambda P_2 = 0,$$

which implies that
$$MP_1 = \lambda P_1 \tag{7.28}$$

$$MP_2 = \lambda P_2. \tag{7.29}$$

Dividing each side of equation (7.28) by the corresponding side of equation (7.29), we find that

$$\frac{MP_1}{MP_2} = \frac{P_1}{P_2},$$

or
$$\frac{MP_1}{P_1} = \frac{MP_2}{P_2}, \tag{7.30}$$

which is the decision rule in equation (7.11) when there are only two inputs. Thus, we have proved what we set out to prove—that this decision rule can be derived using the method of Lagrangian multipliers when the object is to maximize output subject to an expenditure constraint.

Minimizing the Cost of a Specified Amount of Output Suppose this firm is committed to produce a specified quantity of output, Q^*, which means that

$$f(X_1,\ X_2) = Q^*.$$

The firm's problem is to minimize its costs, which equal

$$C = X_1 P_1 + X_2 P_2, \tag{7.31}$$

subject to the constraint that

$$Q^* - f(X_1, X_2) = 0 \tag{7.32}$$

Following the procedure described in Chapter 2, we can use the method of Lagrangian multipliers to solve this problem. The first step is to construct the Lagrangian function, which is the right-hand side of equation (7.31) plus λ times the left-hand side of equation (7.32):

$$L_2 = X_1 P_1 + X_2 P_2 + \lambda [Q^* - f(X_1, X_2)],$$

where λ is the Lagrangian multiplier. Taking the partial derivatives of L_2 with respect to X_1, X_2, and λ, and setting them all equal to zero, we obtain

$$\frac{\partial L_2}{\partial X_1} = P_1 - \lambda \frac{\partial f(X_1, X_2)}{\partial X_1} = 0 \tag{7.33}$$

$$\frac{\partial L_2}{\partial X_2} = P_2 - \lambda \frac{\partial f(X_1, X_2)}{\partial X_2} = 0 \tag{7.34}$$

$$\frac{\partial L_2}{\partial \lambda} = Q^* - f(X_1, X_2) = 0. \tag{7.35}$$

These are the conditions for cost minimization subject to the output constraint.

Substituting MP_1 for $\partial f(X_1, X_2)/\partial X_1$ and MP_2 for $\partial f(X_1, X_2)/\partial X_2$ in equations (7.33) and (7.34), we get:

$$P_1 - \lambda MP_1 = 0$$
$$P_2 - \lambda MP_2 = 0,$$

which implies that

$$P_1 = \lambda MP_1 \tag{7.36}$$
$$P_2 = \lambda MP_2. \tag{7.37}$$

Dividing each side of equation (7.36) by the corresponding side of equation (7.37), we find that

$$\frac{P_1}{P_2} = \frac{MP_1}{MP_2}$$

or
$$\frac{MP_1}{P_1} = \frac{MP_2}{P_2},$$

which is the decision rule in equation (7.11) when there are only two inputs. Thus, we have proved what we set out to prove—that this decision rule can be derived using the method of Lagrangian multipliers when the object is to minimize cost subject to an output constraint.

Technological Change
and Industrial
Innovation

The United States is generally viewed as having the highest labor productivity (output per labor hour) in the world. Our high standard of living is strongly correlated with this high labor productivity. However, in recent years, the rate of growth of labor productivity has fallen below that of other nations. For example, between 1947 and 1973, productivity in the United States grew annually at an average of 2.8 percent. This average growth rate dropped to 1.1 percent between 1973 and 1998. Hence, the question facing the United States is whether we will be able to sustain our productivity lead over other developed nations. Since output depends on all inputs, the level of capital inputs (both private and public) and the improvement in the quality of labor (via education) will certainly impact productivity growth in the United States.

Companies in the United States have traditionally been at the forefront in using new technologies. Their long-term profitability and market successes are often based on new products or processes. Most of these advances in products or processes are the result of an active commitment to devoting resources to research and development. After all, increases in productivity don't occur haphazardly, but are the result of active management of the research and development process. This management not only includes the initial development of a product or process but also the implementation issues involved in getting new products to market.

In this chapter we discuss various models and techniques for measuring productivity and examine several research and developmental models. These models have proven useful both in helping managers oversee research and development programs and in bringing new products to market.

Technological Change

Technological change—the advance of technology—often takes the form of new methods of producing existing products and new techniques of organization, marketing, and management. Technological change results in a change in the production function. If the production function were readily observable, a comparison of the production function at two different times would provide the manager with a simple measure of the effect of technological change during the intervening period. If there were only two inputs, labor and capital, and if there were constant returns to scale, the characteristics of the production function at a given date could be captured fully by a single isoquant.[1] One could simply look at the changing position of this isoquant to see the effects of technological change. If this isoquant shifted from position A to position B in Figure 8.1 during a certain period of time, technological change had less impact during this period than it would have had if the curve had shifted to position C.

Technological change may also result in the availability of new products. Videocassette recorders, for example, did not exist several decades ago; now they are commonplace. Palm pilots and laptop computers didn't exist a decade ago. Today, many managers rely on them. Nylon was first brought to markets in the 1930s; today it is hard to imagine what life would be like without it. In many cases, the availability of new products can be regarded as a change in the production function, since they are merely more efficient ways of meeting old wants if these wants are defined with proper breadth. This is particularly true in the case of new goods used by firms, which may result in little or no change in the final product shipped to consumers. In other cases, however, the availability of new products cannot realistically be viewed as a change in the production function, since the new products represent an important difference in kind.

---

[1]Recall from Chapter 7 that if there are constant returns to scale, an x percent increase in all inputs results in an x percent increase in output. Thus, if there are constant returns to scale, there is at a given time a unique relationship between capital input per unit of output and labor input per unit of output. This relationship holds for any output and completely summarizes the efficient input combinations.

FIGURE
8.1

Change over a Period of Time in the Position of an Isoquant

If the isoquant shifted from position *A* to position *B*, technological change had less impact than it would have had if it had shifted to position *C*.

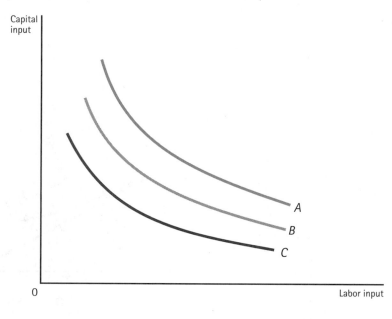

Labor Productivity

Managers have long been interested in productivity—the ratio of output to input. The oldest and most commonly studied productivity measure is labor productivity, output per hour of labor. One determinant of the rate of growth of labor productivity is the rate of technological change, a high rate of technological change being likely to result, all other things being equal, in a high rate of growth of labor productivity. However, the rate of technological change is not the sole determinant of the rate of growth of labor productivity; as a consequence, although labor productivity is often used to measure the rate of technological change, it is in fact an incomplete measure.

Figure 8.2 shows how changes in labor productivity can produce false signals concerning the rate of technological change. Suppose the relevant isoquant is II′ and the input prices at the beginning of the period are such that the isocost curves are *A, B, C,* and so on. The least-cost combination of inputs is L_1 of labor and C_1 of capital. Now suppose that input prices change, and labor be-

FIGURE
8.2

Productivity Increase without Technological Change

Because labor becomes more expensive relative to capital, labor productivity increases.

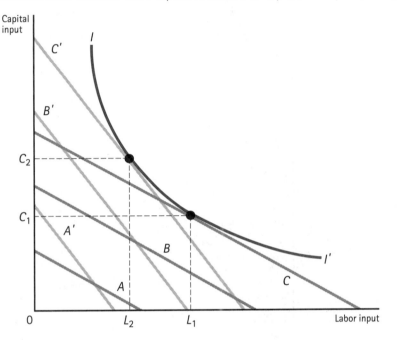

comes more expensive relative to capital, the result being that the isocost curves shift to A', B', C', and so on. Under these new circumstances, the least-cost combination of inputs to produce the same output is L_2 of labor and C_2 of capital. Since output remains constant and labor input decreases, labor productivity increases as a result of the change in input prices. But this productivity increase is not an indication of technological change, there being no change at all in the production function.

Total Factor Productivity

A better measure of the rate of technological change is **total factor productivity,** which relates changes in output to changes in both labor and capital inputs, not changes in labor inputs alone. Assume that the production function is of the simple form

$$Q = \alpha(bL + cK), \tag{8.1}$$

where Q is the quantity of output, L is the quantity of labor, K is the quantity of capital, and b and c are constants. Dividing both sides of equation (8.1) by $(bL + cK)$,

$$\frac{Q}{bL + cK} = \alpha, \tag{8.2}$$

which is total factor productivity. In this simple case, changes in total factor productivity measure changes in efficiency.

If a firm uses more than two inputs, total factor productivity equals

$$\frac{Q}{a_1 I_1 + a_2 L_2 + \cdots + a_n L_n} \tag{8.3}$$

where I_1 is the amount of the first input used, I_2 is the amount of the second input used, . . . , and I_n is the amount of the nth input used. In calculating total factor productivity, firms often let a_1 equal the price of the first input, a_2 equal the price of the second input, . . . , and a_n equal the price of the nth input in some base period, as we shall see below. The principal advantage of total factor productivity over labor productivity is its inclusion of more types of inputs, not labor alone. It otherwise shares many of the limitations of labor productivity. Note that $\Sigma_i P_i X_i$, where P_i is unit input cost and X_i is amount of input used, is just the firm's total cost. Then Q/TC is just the inverse of the firm's average total cost. To maximize productivity, minimize *ATC*. But firms want to maximize profits. That won't often occur when firms minimize *ATC*.

Firms calculate total factor productivity in order to measure changes over time in the efficiency of their operations. It is important for a firm's managers to be aware of the extent to which productivity has increased in response to new techniques and other factors. For example, consider flexible manufacturing systems, a major innovation in industries like machinery (recall page 281). According to Messerschmidt, a leading German firm, the flexible manufacturing system that it installed at its Augsburg facility reduced the labor requirements to produce a given output by over 50 percent and reduced the capital investment required by 10 percent.[2]

To calculate the changes in total factor productivity for a firm or plant over a period of time, managers must obtain data concerning the quantity of output and the quantities of inputs utilized in each period. For example, suppose that the Landau Company uses three inputs—labor, energy, and raw materials. In 1999, it uses 10,000 hours of labor, 100,000 kilowatt-hours of energy, and 5,000 pounds of materials to produce 400,000 pounds of output. In 2001, it

---

[2]National Research Council, *Toward a New Era in Manufacturing* (Washington, D.C.: National Academy Press, 1986), p. 118.

uses 12,000 hours of labor, 150,000 kilowatt-hours of energy, and 6,000 pounds of materials to produce 700,000 pounds of output. What is total factor productivity in each year?

As a first step toward answering this question, we must get data concerning the price of each input in some base period, say 1999. Suppose that the price of labor is $8 per hour, the price of a kilowatt-hour of energy is $.02, and the price of a pound of materials is $3. Then, inserting these figures into the expression in (8.3), we find that total factor productivity in 1999 is

$$\frac{400,000}{8(10,000) + 0.02(100,000) + 3(5,000)} = 4.12,$$

and total factor productivity in 2001 is

$$\frac{700,000}{8(12,000) + 0.02(150,000) + 3(6,000)} = 5.98.$$

Thus, from 1999 to 2001, total factor productivity increases by 45 percent—from 4.12 to 5.98.

Note that the base-year input prices are used for all years, not just the base year. For example, the 1999 input prices would be used for all years, not just 1999, in the case of the Landau Company. In this way, we hold constant input prices and do not let changes in them over time affect our results.[3]

Using Total Factor Productivity to Track Factory Performance

To illustrate how changes in total factor productivity can be used to track factory performance, consider a manufacturing plant studied by Harvard's Robert Hayes, Steven Wheelwright, and Kim Clark.[4] Figure 8.3 shows the behavior of total factor productivity in this plant during a 10-year period. As you can see, total factor productivity increased at a healthy pace up to 1976. This was the period during which the plant was started up. Because it takes time for a factory to operate properly, one would expect that total factor productivity would increase substantially in this start-up phase.

---

[3]Of course, this does not mean that the value of total factor productivity is not affected by the base-year prices. For example, if the price of labor in the base period were $10 (rather than $8) per hour, our results would be different. But changes *over time* in input prices are not allowed to influence our results.

[4]Hayes, Wheelwright, and Clark, *Dynamic Manufacturing*.

FIGURE 8.3

Total Factor Productivity, Actual Manufacturing Plant

Total factor productivity increased up to 1976, but in 1982 was only slightly higher than in 1976.

Source: Hayes, Wheelwright, and Clark, *Dynamic Manufacturing*.

From 1977 to 1983, there was no evidence of any strong, persistent increase in total factor productivity. Instead, there was an increase in 1977 to 1979, a fall in 1979 to 1980, and an increase in 1981 to 1982. In 1982, total factor productivity was only somewhat higher than in 1976. The data in Figure 8.3 indicate that this factory experienced little in the way of technological change from 1977 to 1983. Hayes, Wheelwright, and Clark report that these data triggered an investigation of the causes for this poor performance which indicated that it was due in considerable part to the way the factory managed equipment introductions.[5] Obviously, this information was of use to the firm's top managers.

In passing, note that the fact that total factor productivity fell during 1979 to 1980 does not mean that there was *negative* technological change then. If the factory's sales decreased during this period, perhaps because of cyclical factors (recall Chapter 6), this could cause such a decline in total factor produc-

[5]Ibid.

tivity. Also, it sometimes takes time for new equipment to reach its full efficiency. When equipment is first used, productivity may fall temporarily because of "teething" problems.

Research and Development: A Learning Process

Particularly in science-based industries like electronics and chemicals, a firm's success depends on the extent and nature of the research and development that it carries out. Research and development encompasses work of many kinds. Basic research is aimed purely at the creation of new knowledge, applied research is expected to have a practical payoff, and development is aimed at the reduction of research findings to practice. Inventions can occur in either the research phase or the development phase of organized research and development activity.

Chance plays a crucial role in research and development, and a long string of failures frequently occurs before any kind of success is achieved. A research or development project can be regarded as a process of uncertainty reduction, or learning. Suppose, for example, that a firm that is trying to fabricate a part can use one of two alloys and that it is impossible to use standard sources to determine their characteristics. Suppose that strength is of paramount importance and that the firm's estimates of the strengths of the alloys, alloy X and alloy Y, are represented by the probability distributions in part A of Table 8.1. If the firm were forced to make a choice immediately, it would probably choose

TABLE 8.1

Subjective Probability Distribution of Strength of Alloys X and Y

Extent of strength	Probabilities			
	A before test		B after test	
	Alloy X	Alloy Y	Alloy X	Alloy Y
Exceptionally high	0.20	0.30	0.10	0.10
Very high	0.40	0.50	0.20	0.80
High	0.20	0.10	0.60	0.10
Medium	0.10	0.05	0.10	0.00
Low	0.10	0.05	0.00	0.00
Total	1.00	1.00	1.00	1.00

alloy *Y*, since it believes that there is better than a 50-50 chance that alloy *Y* will turn out to be stronger than alloy *X*.

However, there is a good chance that this decision might turn out to be wrong, with the consequence that the part would be weaker than if alloy *X* had been used. Thus, the firm may decide to perform a test prior to making the selection. On the basis of the test results, the firm will formulate new estimates, represented by the probability distributions in part B of Table 8.1. These probability distributions show less dispersion than the distributions in part A; in other words, the firm believes it is able to pinpoint more closely the strength of each alloy in part B than in part A. Because of the tests, the firm feels more certainty concerning which alloy will prove to be stronger.

Parallel Development Efforts

Research and development is more risky than most other economic activities. Many development projects use parallel efforts to help cope with uncertainty. For example, in the development of the atomic bomb, there were several methods of making fissionable materials, and no consensus existed among scientists as to which of these alternatives was most promising. To make sure that the best one was not discarded, all methods were pursued in parallel. The wisdom of this decision was borne out by the fact that the method that was first to produce appreciable quantities of fissionable material was one that had been considered relatively unpromising early in the development program's history.

How can a firm's managers tell whether it is optimal to run parallel research and development efforts? What factors determine the optimal number of parallel efforts? Suppose that a firm can select *x* approaches, spend *C* dollars on each one over a period of *n* months, choose the one that looks most promising at the end of the period, and carry it to completion, dropping the others. Suppose that the only relevant criterion is the extent of the development costs, the usefulness of the result and the development time being assumed to be the same regardless of which parallel effort is pursued. For further simplification, suppose that all approaches look equally promising. Under these circumstances, the optimal value of *x*—the number of parallel research and development efforts— is inversely related to *C* and directly related to the amount learned in the next *n* months. As the cost of running each effort increases, the optimal number of parallel efforts decreases. As the prospective amount of learning increases, the optimal number of parallel efforts goes up.

To illustrate why it is sometimes cheaper to run parallel development efforts, consider a case in which each approach has a 50-50 chance of costing $5 million and a 50-50 chance of costing $8 million. Since we assume that all approaches are equally promising, these probabilities are the same for all approaches. The expected total cost of development is the sum of the total costs of development if each possible outcome occurs times the probability of the occurrence of this outcome. If a single approach is used, the expected total costs of development are

$$0.5(\$5 \text{ million}) + 0.5(\$8 \text{ million}) = \$6.5 \text{ million}, \qquad (8.4)$$

since there is a 0.5 probability that total costs with any single approach will be $5 million and a 0.5 probability that they will be $8 million.

If two approaches are run in parallel and if the true cost of development using each approach can be determined after C dollars are spent on each approach, the expected total costs of development are

$$0.25(\$8 \text{ million}) + 0.75(\$5 \text{ million}) + C = \$5.75 \text{ million} + C \qquad (8.5)$$

if each approach is carried to the point at which C dollars have been spent on it, and if the cheaper approach is chosen at that point (and the other approach is dropped). Why? Because there is a 0.25 probability that total costs with the better of the two approaches will be $8 million and a 0.75 probability that they will be $5 million. In addition, there is the certainty that a cost of C will be incurred for the approach that is dropped. (The C dollars spent on the project that is not dropped are included in its total costs, given above.) The reason why there is a 0.25 chance that total costs with the better of the two approaches is $8 million is that this will occur only when the total cost of both approaches turns out to be $8 million—and the probability that this will occur is 0.5 times 0.5, or 0.25. Comparing equation (8.4) with equation (8.5), it is obvious that the expected total cost of development is lower with two parallel approaches than with a single approach if C is less than $750,000.

More generally, if the probability is P that the development cost will be C_1 and $(1 - P)$ that it will be C_2 (where $C_2 < C_1$), the expected cost if a single approach is used is

$$PC_1 + (1 - P)C_2.$$

If two approaches are run in parallel, the expected cost is

$$P^2C_1 + (1 - P^2)C_2 + C,$$

which is less than the cost of a single approach if

$$C < (1 - P)(P)(C_1 - C_2). \qquad (8.6)$$

Thus, if the inequality in (8.6) holds, two parallel approaches will result in a lower expected cost than a single approach.[6]

What Makes for Success?

Even companies in the same industry may differ markedly in their ability to make R and D pay off commercially. During a four-year period, for instance, three evenly matched chemical companies found the proportion of their R and D expenditures that earned a profit to be 69 percent, 54 percent, and 39 percent, respectively. These differences are too large to be attributed to errors of measurement or definition. What can explain them?[7]

An R and D project's likelihood of economic success is the product of three separate factors: (1) the probability of technical success, (2) the probability of commercialization (given technical success), and (3) the probability of economic success (given commercialization). One econometric study shows that all three of these probabilities are directly related to how quickly an R and D project is evaluated for its economic, as opposed to technical, potential. Also, in those companies whose R and D staff members do not work closely or responsively with marketing staff, the integration of R and D activity with market realities is haphazard, belated, or both. Commercially successful innovation depends on just this sort of integration. Numerous case studies of successful and unsuccessful innovation come to the same conclusion: the closer the link between marketing and R and D, the greater the probability of commercialization (given technical completion).

Consider, by way of illustration, the experience of three chemical companies of roughly the same size and level of R and D expenditure that underwent reorganization at roughly the same time. In two of them, the reorganization produced a closer integration of R and D with marketing by improving the channels of communication between them as well as by noticeably increasing marketing's input to R and D decision making. In the third, however, integration decreased; R and D paid even less attention to marketing than it had before the reorganization.

[6]See R. Nelson, "Uncertainty, Learning, and the Economics of Parallel Research and Development Efforts," *Review of Economics and Statistics*, 1961, for an early paper on this topic. Also, see B. Dean and J. Goldhar, eds., *Management of Research and Innovation*, vol. 15 of *Studies in the Management Sciences* (Amsterdam: North-Holland, 1980).
[7]For references and sources of information for the data presented in this and the next three sections, see E. Mansfield, "How Economists See R and D," *Harvard Business Review*, November–December 1981. Also, see K. Clark and T. Fujimoto, *Product Development Performance* (Boston: Harvard Business School Press, 1991); R. Stobaugh, *Innovation and Competition* (Boston: Harvard Business School Press, 1988); and E. Mansfield, *Innovation, Technology, and the Economy* (Aldershot, U.K.: Elgar, 1995).

CONCEPTS IN CONTEXT
Parallel Development Efforts at IBM

The IBM Corporation, which spends billions of dollars per year on research and development, is one of the world's leading high-technology companies. Nonetheless, IBM, like other firms, must face the fact that R and D is a risky activity, and that it is not able to predict with confidence whether a particular R and D project will be successful. Recognizing this fact, parallel development efforts have played a major role in IBM's history, as indicated by the following quotation from one IBM manager: *Parallel projects are crucial—no doubt of it. When I look back over the last dozen products we've introduced, I find in well over half the instances the big development project that we "bet on" via the system came a cropper somewhere along the way. In every instance—and we've gone back and taken a look and I do mean every—there were two or three* *(about five once) other small projects, you know, four-to-six person groups, two people in one instance, who had been working on parallel technology or parallel development efforts. It had been with scrounged time and bodies. But that's a time-honored thing. We wink at it. It pays off. Looking at the projects where the initial bets failed, the subsequently developed project came in ahead of the original schedule in three instances. It's just amazing what a handful of dedicated people can do when they are really turned on. Of course they had an advantage. Since they were so resource-constrained, they had to design a simple product in the first place.**

*Bartlett, *Cases in Strategic Management.*

Data on the probability of commercialization (given technical completion) of 330 R and D projects in these companies—projects carried out anywhere from three to seven years before reorganization to five to eight years after it—are highly suggestive. They show an increase of about 20 percentage points for the two companies that more closely linked R and D with marketing and a decrease of about 20 percentage points for the third.

More generally, a substantial portion of a company's R and D efforts may lie fallow because other parts of the company do not make proper use of them. One survey of executive opinion has noted the widely held belief that the economic success rate of R and D projects would increase by half if marketing and production people fully exploited them. If this figure is anywhere close to the truth, the faulty interface between R and D and the other functions has a very serious effect on the productivity of industrial R and D.

Project Selection

However well-founded the fears of excessively detailed control, some managerial oversight of R and D is essential. To make effective use of its R and D capacity, a company must first spell out its business objectives and then communicate them to its scientists and engineers. Research, after all, makes sense only when undertaken in areas relevant to economic goals.

Simply taking on a team of scientists and allowing them to do research in their favorite fields may produce novel results—but results that are unlikely to have much immediate commercial value. Most companies, therefore, have found it worthwhile to make economic evaluations of both project proposals and continuing projects. Without question, these evaluations have been useful, since they have forced managers to make their assumptions explicit. Research suggests that the sooner such evaluations are carried out, the greater a project's chances of ultimate commercial success.

The nature of these evaluations is different for a research as opposed to a development project. As a project moves from the laboratory toward the market, it receives more intensive scrutiny from both a technical and an economic angle. In the early research phase, the screening of proposals will probably be quick and informal, since costs at this stage are still low and predicting outcomes is very difficult. But as projects enter the development phase, where costs and predictability are higher, they require a far more detailed process of economic evaluation.

Managerial economists have developed a number of more or less sophisticated models to help solve these problems of evaluation. Some employ relatively straightforward adaptations of capital budgeting techniques. For example, the net present value or internal rate of return (concepts developed in a basic course in finance) of each project may be calculated and compared. Others, described in Chapter 10, use mathematical programming techniques (concepts developed in a basic course in decision science). The more complicated versions of these models have not found extensive use, for the following reasons: (1) Many of the models fail to recognize that R and D is essentially a process of buying information, that unsuccessful projects can provide valuable information, and that as a result the real task is to facilitate sequential decision making under conditions of uncertainty. (2) Application of the more-sophisticated models is not cheap. (3) Perhaps most important, the models often rest on overly optimistic estimates that are not very reliable—estimates that reflect both the uncertainty of the undertaking and the desire by researchers and others to "sell" projects to top management.

Innovation

An invention, when applied for the first time, is called an **innovation.** The distinction between an invention and an innovation becomes somewhat blurred in cases like Du Pont's nylon, in which the inventor and the innovator are the same firm. In these circumstances, the final stages of development may entail at least a partial commitment to a market test. However, in many cases, the firm that is the inventor is not in a position to—and does not want to—apply its invention, because its business is invention, not production; because it is a supplier, not a user, of the equipment embodying the innovation; or for some other reason. In these cases, the distinction remains relatively clear-cut.

Regardless of whether the break between invention and innovation is clean, innovation is a key stage in the process leading to the full evaluation and utilization of an invention. The innovator—the firm that is first to apply the invention—must be willing to take the risks involved in introducing a new and untried process, good, or service. In many cases these risks are high. Although R and D can provide a great deal of information regarding the technical characteristics and cost of production of the invention—and market research can provide considerable information regarding the demand for it—there are many areas of uncertainty that can be resolved only by actual production and marketing of the invention. By obtaining needed information regarding the actual performance of the invention, the innovator plays a vital social role.

Time-Cost Trade-offs

For a particular innovator, there is likely to be a time-cost trade-off function, like that in Figure 8.4. If the firm cuts the total time taken to develop and introduce the innovation, it incurs higher costs. As the development schedule is shortened, more tasks must be carried out concurrently rather than sequentially, and since each task provides information that is useful in carrying out the others, there are more false starts and wasted designs. Also, diminishing returns set in as more and more technical workers are assigned simultaneously to the project.

Faced with this time-cost trade-off function, how quickly should the firm develop and introduce the innovation? Clearly, the answer depends on the relationship between the present value of profit (gross of innovation cost) from the innovation and how quickly the firm develops and introduces it. (For a detailed discussion of the concept of present value, see Appendix A.) If $R(t)$ is the present value of gross profit if the duration of the project is t years, and if the time-cost trade-off function is $C(t)$, profit equals

$$\pi(t) = R(t) - C(t), \tag{8.7}$$

and the first-order condition for profit maximization is

$$\frac{dC}{dt} = \frac{dR}{dt}. \tag{8.8}$$

FIGURE
8.4

Time–Cost Trade-off Function and Optimal Duration of the Project

The optimal duration of the project is t^* years.

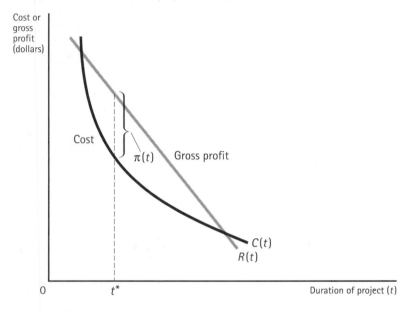

Thus, in Figure 8.4, the optimal duration of the project is t^* years, since $\pi(t)$—which is the vertical difference between $R(t)$ and $C(t)$—is greatest when this is the duration of the project.

To illustrate, consider the Hanover Company, which wants to develop a new plastic. Its vice president for research and development believes that the time-cost trade-off function for this project is

$$C = 520 - 100t + 5t^2,$$

where C is cost (in thousands of dollars), and t is the duration of the project (in years). This equation assumes that $t \geq 1$, since it is believed that the project cannot be carried out in less than a year. Hanover's president believes that

$$R = 480 - 20t,$$

where R is the present value of profit (gross of innovation cost) from the innovation (in thousands of dollars). Since

$$\frac{dC}{dt} = \frac{d(520 - 100t + 5t^2)}{dt} = -100 + 10t$$

and

$$\frac{dR}{dt} = \frac{d(480 - 20t)}{dt} = -20,$$

it follows from equation (8.8) that the firm should choose t so that

$$-100 + 10t = -20$$
$$t = 8.$$

In other words, the Hanover Company should carry out the project in about eight years.

The Learning Curve

In many industries, technological change is due in considerable part to the learning and on-the-job experience that occurs as a firm produces more and more of a given item. Thus, holding the firm's output rate constant, its average cost declines with increases in its cumulative total output (that is, the total number of items of this sort that it has produced in the past). For example, production of the first hundred machine tools of a particular type may require about 50 percent more hours of labor than production of the second hundred machine tools of this type, even though the number of machine tools produced per month remains about the same. Thus, the average cost of this machine tool falls substantially as cumulative total output grows.

One should distinguish between cost reductions that are due to *learning* and those that are due to greater current output. Holding constant the number of these machine tools produced by this firm in the past, it is quite possible that the average cost of producing such a machine tool during the current period declines as more of them are produced. But this is different from learning. Holding constant the number of such machine tools produced currently, if the average cost is inversely related to the firm's previous total output of this machine tool, this is due to learning.

Managers, economists, and engineers often use the **learning curve** to represent the extent to which the average cost of producing an item falls in response to increases in its cumulative total output. Figure 8.5 shows the learning curves for two actual products: a piece of optical equipment (produced by Optical Equipment Company) and a portable turbine (produced by Solar Interna-

FIGURE
8.5

Learning Curves

Average cost declines with increases in cumulative total output.

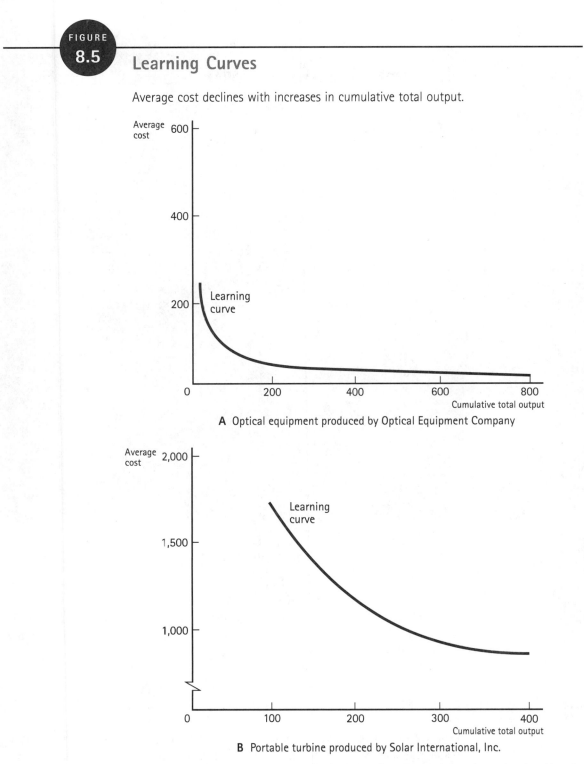

A Optical equipment produced by Optical Equipment Company

B Portable turbine produced by Solar International, Inc.

Source: Hayes and Wheelwright, *Restoring Our Competitive Edge.* The cost data are incomplete, but this makes no difference for present purposes.

ANALYZING MANAGERIAL DECISIONS

The Time-Cost Trade-off Function for Airliners

Keith Hartley of the University of York and W. Corcoran of the University of Newcastle (both British universities) have estimated the time-cost trade-off function for the development of airliners (like the Boeing 707 or McDonnell Douglas DC-10) in the United States and the United Kingdom. Their results are shown in the graph below.

(a) If an aircraft manufacturer in the United Kingdom decides to reduce the duration of a development project by 10 percent, by about how much will the cost of the project increase? (b) Holding the duration of a development project constant, does the cost of the project tend to be different in the United States from that in the United Kingdom? (c) What factors may account for this difference between the United States and the United Kingdom in the time-cost trade-off function for airliners?

SOLUTION (a) The cost will increase by about 15 percent. To see this, let $t' = 0.9t$. Then according to the formula in the graph, $C(t') = A(t')^{-1.3} = A(0.9t)^{-1.3} = 0.9^{-1.3} At^{-1.3} = 0.9^{-1.3}C(t) =$ 1.15$C(t)$, since $0.9^{-1.3} = 1.15$. Thus, C increases by about 15 percent when t is reduced by 10 percent (to $0.9t$). (b) Yes. The cost tends to be less in the United States than in the United Kingdom. (c) Hartley and Corcoran suggest that one factor may be that U.S. aircraft manufacturers benefit from defense contracts to a greater extent than their British counterparts do. Thus, the U.S. manufacturers can develop a commercial airliner more cheaply (holding the duration of the development project constant) than can the British firms. (More will be said on this score in Chapter 18.)*

*For further discussion, see K. Hartley and W. Corcoran, *Journal of Industrial Economics*, March 1978.

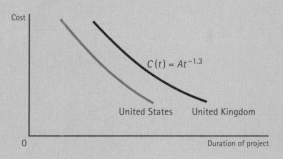

$C(t) = At^{-1.3}$

United States   United Kingdom

Cost

0   Duration of project

tional, Inc.). As you can see, learning results in major reductions in the average cost of both products. Of course, these cost reductions are not automatic: they occur only if workers and managers strive for increased efficiency. But for many products of this sort, a doubling of cumulative output tends to produce about a 20 or 30 percent reduction in average cost.

Applications of the Learning Curve

Many firms have adopted pricing strategies based on the learning curve. Consider the case of Texas Instruments, a major producer of semiconductor chips and other electronic products. When the semiconductor industry was relatively young, Texas Instruments priced its product at less than its then-current average costs in order to increase its output rate and its cumulative total output. Believing that the learning curve was relatively steep, it hoped that this would reduce its average costs to such an extent that its product would be profitable to produce and sell at this low price. This strategy was extremely successful. As Texas Instruments continued to cut price, its rivals began to withdraw from the market, its output continued to go up, its costs were reduced further, and its profits rose.[8]

The learning curve is expressed as:

$$C = aQ^b, \tag{8.9}$$

where C is the input cost of the Qth unit of output produced. If this relationship holds exactly, a is the cost of the first unit produced. The value of b is negative, since increases in cumulative total output reduce cost. If the absolute value of b is large, cost falls more rapidly with increases in cumulative total output than it would if the absolute value of b were small. Taking logarithms of both sides of equation (8.9),

$$\log C = \log a + b \log Q. \tag{8.10}$$

In this logarithmic form, b is the slope of the learning curve.

To estimate the learning curve from historical data concerning cost and cumulative output, one can use the regression techniques in Chapter 5. As shown in equation 8.10, $\log C$ is a linear function of $\log Q$. Thus, to estimate a and b, we can regress $\log C$ on $\log Q$. (In other words, $\log C$ is the equivalent of Y in Chapter 5, and $\log Q$ is the equivalent of X.) Of course, the values of a and b will vary from product to product and from firm to firm.

To illustrate how the learning curve can be used in specific cases, suppose that the controller of the Killian Company, a maker of a particular type of machine tool, finds that for her firm the learning curve (in logarithmic form) is

$$\log C = 4.0 - 0.30 \log Q,$$

where C is expressed in dollars. (That is, $\log a = 4.0$ and $b = -0.30$.) From this equation, she can estimate how much the cost per unit will go down in the fu-

---

[8]For a classic paper concerning learning curves, see K. Arrow, "The Economic Implications of Learning by Doing," *Review of Economic Studies,* June 1962. The Boston Consulting Group was a leading advocate of their application to corporate planning.

ture. For example, if she wants to estimate the cost of the 100th machine tool of a particular type, the answer is

$$\log C = 4.0 - 0.30 \log 100 = 4.0 - 0.30(2) = 3.4.$$

Since the antilog of 3.4 is 2,512, the answer is that the cost will be $2,512.

Henry Ford's Model T and Douglas Aircraft's DC-9

The learning curve is nothing new. Between 1908 and 1923, the price of Henry Ford's famous Model T automobile fell from over $3,000 to under $1,000, owing in considerable measure to cost reductions that were due to learning. Ford worked hard to push costs down in this way. Standardization was increased. His product line was less diverse than those of his competitors, and model improvements occurred less frequently. The production throughput time was reduced, and the division of labor was increased.

However, not all firms have been as successful as the Ford Motor Company in reducing costs in this way. In cases in which labor turnover is high or in which a firm cannot obtain workers with the necessary skills, expected cost reductions that are due to learning may not materialize. For example, when Douglas Aircraft planned the production of the DC-9 airframe, it anticipated little problem in getting qualified workers. But when the time came, the labor market was so tight in Los Angeles that Douglas soon lost 12,000 of the 35,000 workers it hired. The result was that, contrary to the firm's expectations, costs did not fall as a result of learning, substantial losses were incurred, and the firm was forced into a merger (resulting in McDonnell Douglas, which is now part of Boeing).[9]

Diffusion Models

Another type of technological forecasting technique is based on the use of econometric diffusion models, which analyze the rate at which an innovation spreads. Although these models forecast the diffusion of new processes and products that are already in existence rather than the occurrence of future inventions, this limitation may be less important than it seems, since the inventions that have already occurred are sometimes all that really matter in the short and the intermediate run. In part, this is because it frequently takes a long time for an invention to be commercially introduced. For example, it took about

[9]J. Macklin, "Douglas Aircraft's Stormy Flight Path," *Fortune,* December 1966.

nine years before catalytic cracking, a major innovation in oil refining, was first used.

The diffusion process, like the earlier stages in the creation and assimilation of new processes and products, is essentially a learning process. However, rather than being confined to a research laboratory or to a few firms, the learning takes place among a considerable number of users and producers. When the innovation first appears, potential users are uncertain of its nature and effectiveness, and they tend to view its purchase as an experiment. Sometimes considerable additional research and development is required before the innovation is successful; sometimes, despite attempts at redesign and improvement, the innovation never is a success. Information regarding the existence, characteristics, and availability of the innovation is circulated by the producers through advertisements and sales representatives; information regarding the reaction of users to the innovation tends to be circulated informally and through the trade press.

Figure 8.6 illustrates an important aspect of the process by which new techniques spread throughout an industry. The figure shows that the probability that a firm not using an innovation will adopt it in the next few months is influ-

FIGURE
8.6

Relation between Probability of a Nonuser's Adopting a Process Innovation and the Proportion of Firms Already Using the Innovation

This relationship tends to be direct.

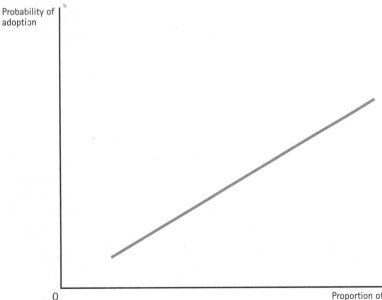

Probability of adoption

0

Proportion of firms using the innovation

enced by the proportion of firms in the industry that already are using it. Specifically, as the number of firms adopting an innovation increases, the probability of its adoption by a nonuser increases. This is because the risks associated with its introduction grow smaller, competitive pressures mount, and bandwagon effects increase as experience and information regarding an innovation accumulate.

Other important aspects of the diffusion process are brought out by Figure 8.7. Panel A shows that the probability that a nonuser will adopt the innovation is higher for more profitable innovations than for less profitable innovations, holding constant the proportion of firms in the industry that are already using it. The more profitable the investment in an innovation promises to be, the greater will be the probability that a firm's estimate of its potential profitability will compensate for the risks involved in its installation.

Panel B of Figure 8.7 shows that the probability that a nonuser will adopt the innovation is higher for innovations requiring fairly small investments, holding constant the proportion of firms in the industry that are already using it (and the profitability of the innovation). This is because firms will be more cautious before committing themselves to large, expensive projects, and they will have more difficulty in financing them.

FIGURE 8.7

Effect of Profitability of the Innovation and Size of Investment Required to Adopt the Innovation on Probability of Adoption

This probability tends to be directly related to profitability and inversely related to the size of the investment.

A

B

FIGURE
8.8

Growth over a Period of Time in the Proportion of Firms Using the Innovation

Both growth curves L and M are S-shaped.

If the relationship in Figure 8.6 holds, it can be shown that $P(t)$, the proportion of firms using the innovation, will increase in accord with the S-shaped growth curve shown in Figure 8.8. The formula for this growth curve (often called the logistic curve) is

$$P(t) = \frac{1}{1 + e^{-(A+Bt)}} \qquad (8.11)$$

where A and B are parameters that vary from innovation to innovation. Whether the diffusion process goes on slowly, as in curve L in Figure 8.8, or quickly, as in curve M, depends on the profitability of the innovation and the size of the investment it requires. This model has much in common with the models used by epidemiologists to represent the spread of contagious diseases. Firms in a wide variety of industries have found that it has been able to explain reasonably well the available data concerning the diffusion process.[10]

[10]See E. Mansfield, *Industrial Research and Technological Innovation* (New York: Norton, 1968); E. Mansfield et al., *The Production and Application of New Industrial Technology* (New York: Norton, 1977); V. Mahajan and Y. Wind, eds., *Innovation Diffusion Models of New Product Acceptance* (Cambridge, Mass.: Ballinger, 1986); and E. Mansfield, "Contributions of New Technology to the Economy," in *Technology, R and D, and the Economy*, eds., Bruce Smith and Claude Barfield (Washington, D.C.: Brookings Institution and American Enterprise Institute, 1996).

How Robots Spread in Japan and the United States

One of the most important manufacturing innovations of recent decades is the industrial robot. In Japan and the United States, the growth over time of the proportion of firms that have begun to use robots in each country can be approximated reasonably well by the logistic function in equation (8.11). In this function, let b_{ij} be the least-squares estimate of B_{ij}, the value of B in the ith industry (autos, machinery, metals, or electrical) in the jth country (Japan or the United States).

Let π_{ij} be the average rate of return from robots (divided by the required rate of return) in the ith industry in the jth country, and let D_{ij} be the number of years from the first introduction of robots in 1961 to their first use in the ith industry in the jth country. If we regress b_{ij}, which is a mea-

sure of the rate of diffusion of robots in the ith industry in the jth country, on π_{ij} and D_{ij}, we find that

$$b_{ij} = \left\{ \begin{matrix} -0.341 \\ -0.234 \end{matrix} \right\} + 0.25\pi_{ij}$$
$$+ 0.031D_{ij}, \qquad (8.12)$$

where the top figure in brackets pertains to Japan, and the bottom figure pertains to the United States.* Does this equation indicate that the rate of diffusion of robots tended to be higher in Japan than in the United States? Indicate what this equation means and what its limitations are.

*E. Mansfield, "The Diffusion of Industrial Robots in Japan and the United States," *Research Policy*, 1989.

Forecasting the Rate of Diffusion of Numerically Controlled Machine Tools

To illustrate the use of diffusion models for forecasting purposes, consider a study carried out for the Small Business Administration to forecast the percentage of firms in the tool and die industry that would be using numerically controlled machine tools two years after the time of the study.[11] When the study was carried out, about 20 percent of the firms in the National Tool, Die, and Precision Machining Association were using numerically controlled machine tools. To use the model described in the previous section, data were obtained, both from a mail survey and from an interview study, of the past growth over time in the percentage of tool and die firms using such machine tools. Based on these data, and using the regression techniques in Chapter 5, estimates of A and B in equation (8.11) were made. To see how these estimates were calculated, note that equation (8.11) implies that

$$\ln \{P(t)/[1 - P(t)]\} = A + Bt. \tag{8.13}$$

Thus, A and B can be estimated by regressing $\ln \{P(t)/[1 - P(t)]\}$ on t.[12] (The natural logarithm of any number—say Y—is designated as $\ln Y$. Recall footnote 20, Chapter 5.)

Given estimates of A and B, equation (8.11) can be used to forecast $P(t)$ for future values of t. On the basis of interview data, the model forecasted that about 33 percent of the firms would be using numerically controlled machine tools. On the basis of mail-survey data, the model forecasted that about 37 percent of the firms would be using them.

To see how these forecasts compared with those obtained on the basis of other methods, two alternative types of forecasts were made. First, the firms—both in interviews with a carefully selected sample of industry executives and in the mail survey of the industry—were asked whether they planned to begin using numerical control in the next two years. Since there was considerable lead time required in obtaining numerical control, it seemed reasonable to suppose that their replies would have some forecasting value. The results of the interviews indicated that about 16 percent of nonusers planned to use numerical control; the results of the mail survey indicated that this was the case for 28 percent of the nonusers. Thus, the forecast was 33 percent, based on the interview data, or 43 percent, based on the mail survey.

Second, forecasts were obtained from the machine tool builders, the firms that presumably are closest to and best informed about the market for nu-

---

[11]See Mansfield et al., *New Industrial Technology*.
[12]This is only a rough estimation technique, but it is adequate for present purposes.

ANALYZING MANAGERIAL DECISIONS

The Development and Introduction of Canon's Personal Copier

In 1980, Canon, the Japanese copier firm, began work on the development of a small model for the home or office that would be virtually service-free. The copy speed—six, eight, or ten copies per minute—didn't matter much, but it was felt that its cost should be less than $1,000. About 140 top R and D personnel were recruited from various parts of the firm, and worked in great secrecy for two and a half years to achieve this result. The project cost Canon about $8 million. To field-test the resulting machines, Canon employees used them in their homes. Until a day before the announcement of the new copier, practically no one knew the characteristics of the new machine, the Canon PC-10.*

(a) This new machine cost Canon less than $300 to manufacture because it was so well designed for automatic assembly. Thus, it was sold to U.S. dealers for $400 to $420. The cartridge unit could be assembled totally by robots without human hands touching it. Were both product and process innovations involved in this project? (b) Canon de-voted $15 million to advertising this new copier in 1983. Jack Klugman, star of TV's *The Odd Couple* and *Quincy* series, appeared in television ads in the United States. What sorts of potential customers were these marketing efforts aimed at? (c) By the end of 1983, sales reached 10,000 per month; by 1985, they were more than 30,000 per month. To speed up delivery, Canon began shipping machines in cargo jets. What sorts of techniques might have been used to forecast the sales of this copier?

SOLUTION (a) Yes. The new copier was a product innovation; the new methods used to produce it were process innovations. (b) Klugman seemed to represent small retailers, executives, and the several million Americans who have offices in their homes. These were some of the most important potential customers. (c) The diffusion models described in this chapter might have been useful in this regard.

*G. Jacobson and J. Hillkirk, *Xerox: American Samurai* (New York: Macmillan Co., 1987).

merically controlled machine tools. About 25 of the 150 members of the National Machine Tool Builders Association provided forecasts. The results showed a considerable amount of variation, but the median forecast was about 30 percent.

How accurate were these forecasts? Which forecasting approach was most accurate? Table 8.2 shows that the model's forecast based on the data from the mail survey was almost precisely correct and that the model's forecast based on the interview data was off by only 4 percentage points. Regardless of whether we look at results based on the interview data or the mail survey data, the model forecasts better than the other two techniques. Moreover, it forecasts bet-

TABLE
8.2

Alternative Two-Year Forecasts of the Percentage of Firms in the U.S. Tool and Die Industry Using Numerical Control, and the Actual Percentage

Type of forecast	Based on interview data	Based on mail survey
	(percent)	
Model	33	37
Plans of tool and die firms	33	43
Median forecast by machine tool builders	30	30
Actual percentage	37	37

ter than simple extrapolation by "naive" models.[13] Certainly, this is encouraging. On the basis of these and other results, it appears that this simple model may be of use in forecasting the rate of diffusion. Of course, this does not mean that it is anything more than a crude device—or that it can be applied in situations in which its basic assumptions do not hold. But it does mean that, used with caution, the model may perform at least as well as other commonly used forecasting devices.

Summary

1. Technological change is the advance of technology; it often results in a change in the production function for an existing product or in a new product. The rate of technological change is often measured by changes in productivity. Changes in total factor productivity are often used by firms to measure changes in efficiency.

2. Research and development can be regarded as a process of uncertainty reduction, or learning. Chance plays a large role in research and development, and many projects use parallel efforts to help cope with uncertainty. Techniques are presented in this chapter to indicate when parallel efforts should be used.

[13]Specifically, the model forecast better than naive models that assumed that the increase in the percentage of firms using numerical control would be the same amount, in absolute or relative terms, during the next two years as it had been during the previous two years.

3. An R and D project's likelihood of economic success is the product of three separate factors: (a) the probability of technical success, (b) the probability of commercialization (given technical success), and (c) the probability of economic success (given commercialization). All three seem to be directly related to how quickly an R and D project is evaluated for its economic, as opposed to only technical, potential.

4. To promote successful R and D, there must be a strong linkage between R and D and marketing personnel, and project selection techniques must be effective. However, this does not mean that the more complicated quantitative selection techniques need be used.

5. For a particular innovation, there is likely to be a time-cost trade-off function. If the firm cuts the total time taken to develop and introduce the innovation, it incurs higher costs. Time-cost trade-off functions vary from firm to firm, because some firms are more adept and experienced than others in developing and introducing a particular innovation. The optimal duration of the project is the time interval where the discounted gross profits exceed the discounted cost by the maximum amount.

6. In many industries, there is a learning curve, which shows the extent to which the average cost of producing an item falls in response to increases in its cumulative total output. This learning curve plays an important role in pricing. For example, Texas Instruments successfully priced its product at less than its then-current average cost to move quickly down the learning curve. Regression techniques can be applied to estimate the learning curve for a particular product.

7. As the number of firms adopting a new process increases, the probability of its adoption by a nonuser increases. Also, the probability that a nonuser will adopt the innovation is higher for more profitable innovations than for less profitable innovations, and for innovations requiring small investments than for those requiring large investments. A model based on these propositions can sometimes be of use in forecasting the rate of diffusion of an innovation.

Problems

1. The Monroe Corporation uses three inputs: labor, energy, and materials. In 2000, it uses 20,000 hours of labor, 50,000 kilowatt-hours of energy, and 10,000 pounds of materials to produce 200,000 pounds of output. In 2001, it uses 30,000 hours of labor, 100,000 kilowatt-hours of energy, and 14,000 pounds of materials to produce 300,000 pounds of output. In 2000, the price of labor is $10 per hour, the price of a kilowatt-hour of energy is $0.02, and the price of a pound of materials is $5.
   a. What is total factor productivity in 2000?

b. What is total factor productivity in 2001?

c. What is the base year in the above calculations?

2. The chief scientist at the Roosevelt Laboratories estimates that the cost (in millions of dollars) of developing and introducing a new type of anti-ulcer drug equals

$$C = 100 - 19t + 0.5t^2, \qquad \text{for } 1 \le t \le 6,$$

where t is the number of years taken to develop and introduce the new drug. The discounted profit (gross of innovation cost) from a new drug of this type (in millions of dollars) is estimated to equal

$$R = 110 - 15t, \qquad \text{for } 1 \le t \le 6.$$

a. The managers of the Roosevelt Laboratories are committed to develop and introduce this new drug within six years, and it is impossible to develop and introduce it in less than one year. What project duration would minimize cost?

b. Why does R decline as t increases?

c. What is the optimal project duration? Why?

3. The Flynn Company produces a particular type of commercial truck. Its chief engineer regresses the logarithm of the input cost of the Qth truck produced on the logarithm of Q, the result being

$$\log C = 5.1 = 0.25 \log Q,$$

where C is input cost (in dollars).

a. What is the estimated input cost of the 100th truck produced?

b. What is the estimated input cost of the 200th truck produced?

c. By what percentage does unit input cost decline if output is doubled (from 100 to 200 trucks)?

4. The Martin Company's president wants to estimate the proportion of chemical firms that will be using a particular new process in 2001. One of her assistants regresses $\ln \{m(t)/[n - m(t)]\}$ on t where $m(t)$ is the number of chemical firms using this process in year t, and n is the total number of chemical firms that can use this process. Measuring t in years from 1986, the regression is

$$\ln\left[\frac{m(t)}{n - m(t)}\right] = -4.0 + 0.22t.$$

a. Prove that if the proportion of chemical firms using the new process increases in accord with the logistic curve in equation 8.11, $\ln \{m(t)/[n - m(t)]\}$ will be a linear function of t.

b. On the basis of the above regression, can you estimate A and B [the parameters of the logistic curve in equation (8.11)]? If so, how?

c. Forecast the percentage of chemical firms using the new process in 2001.

5. In the aircraft industry, many studies indicate that a doubling of cumulative output results in about a 20 percent reduction in cost. If the cost of the 30th unit produced of a particular aircraft is $12 million, what is the cost of the 60th unit produced? Of the 120th unit produced?

6. The Bureau of Labor Statistics has produced data showing that output per hour of labor in blast furnaces using the most up-to-date techniques has sometimes been about twice as large as the industry average.

a. How can such large differences exist at a given time? Why don't all firms continually adopt the most up-to-date techniques?

b. Should firms always adopt techniques that maximize output per hour of labor? Why or why not?

c. Should firms adopt techniques that maximize output per dollar of capital? Why or why not?

7. The Russell Corporation is trying to develop an improved engine that will emit fewer pollutants. There are two possible approaches to this technical problem. If either one is adopted, there is a 50-50 chance that it will cost $2 million to develop the engine and a 50-50 chance that it will cost $1 million to do so.

a. If the firm chooses one of the approaches and carries it to completion, what is the expected cost of developing the engine?

b. If the two approaches are run in parallel and if the true cost of development using each approach can be determined after $150,000 has been spent on each approach, what is the expected cost of developing the engine? (Note that the total cost figure for each approach, if adopted, includes the $150,000.)

c. Should parallel approaches be used?

8. To help decide whether particular R and D projects should be carried out, some firms compare the estimated cost of each project with the estimated profits it will earn. To carry out such an analysis, the firm's personnel must estimate how much the R and D project would cost if it were carried out. In one major drug firm, the frequency distribution of 49 projects by the ratio of actual to estimated cost is as shown below:

Actual cost divided by estimated cost	Number of projects
Less than 1.01	6
1.01 and under 2.01	24
2.01 and under 3.01	16
3.01 and under 4.01	3

    a. If this firm were using this technique to help determine whether particular R and D projects should be carried out, what problems would be encountered?

    b. How might the firm try to cope with these problems?

9. The Monroe Corporation wants to develop a new process that will reduce its costs by 10 percent. There are two ways to go about developing such a process. If the first way is adopted, there is a 0.6 probability that it will cost $5 million to develop the process, and a 0.4 probability that it will cost $3 million to do so. If the second way is adopted, there is a 0.7 probability that it will cost $3 million, and a 0.3 probability that it will cost $5 million.

    a. If the first way is adopted, what is the expected cost of developing the new process?

    b. If the second way is adopted, what is the expected cost?

    c. If the two approaches can be run in parallel, and if the true cost of development using each approach can be determined after $500,000 has been spent on each approach, what is the expected cost? (Assume that the outcomes of the two approaches are independent. Also, note that the total cost figure for each approach, if adopted, includes the $500,000.)

10. On the basis of past growth of the percentage of firms in the machinery industry using robots, this percentage can be approximated by:

$$P(t) = \frac{1}{1 + e^{-(-6.1 + 0.41t)}},$$

where $P(t)$ is this percentage, and t is measured in years from 1970.

    a. During which year did about 25 percent of the firms in the machinery industry use robots?

    b. During which year did 50 percent of the firms in this industry use robots?

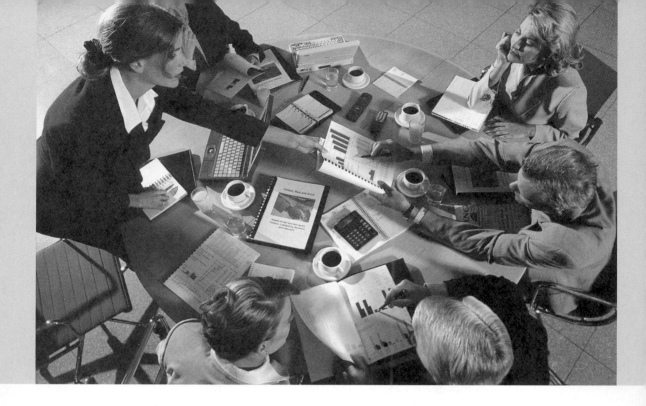

The Analysis
of Costs

CHAPTER 9

Introduction

Even if a manager fully understands the physical relationship between inputs and outputs, she still cannot make optimal (profit-maximizing) decisions without cost information. The key question managers must ponder is how are costs related to output? A full understanding of costs is a necessary managerial characteristic since virtually all business decisions require a comparison between costs and benefits. The marginal analysis of Chapter 2 highlights this importance. A manager wants to undertake an action if the additional (marginal) revenue attributable to that action exceeds the additional (marginal) cost attributable to that action. As we will see, to maximize profit, a manager wishes to produce when the marginal revenue equals the marginal cost. Obviously, this is not obtainable without a knowledge of costs.

Cost is a complex concept. As managers, you will find that what seems like a simple cost concept will often provoke controversy over the nature of costs, how they are defined, and the scope and attribution of relevant costs for the decision (and hence the basis for a core course in cost accounting in virtually every MBA program). This means that a thorough understanding of cost is necessary for a variety of basic managerial decisions—pricing output, transfer pricing within and among divisions of a firm, cost control, and planning for future production needs. Thus, costs have both a short- and a long-run component, and management decisions will differ in the short run and the long run in similar situations given the nature of costs.

This chapter includes the basics of cost analysis, examines the results of empirical studies relating costs and output for various firms and industries, and describes the nature and usefulness of breakeven analysis, which is commonly used by managers to analyze the effects of variation in price or output on their profits and to decide whether to enter a market or not.

Opportunity Costs

Managerial economists define the cost of producing a particular product as the value of the other products that the resources used in its production could have produced instead. For example, the cost of producing locomotives is the value of the goods and services that could be obtained from the labor, equipment, and materials used currently in locomotive production. The costs of inputs to a firm are their values in their most valuable alternative uses. These costs, together with the firm's production function (which indicates how much of each input is required to produce various amounts of the product), determine the cost of producing the product. This is called the **opportunity cost doctrine.**

The opportunity cost of an input may not equal its **historical cost,** which is defined to be the amount the firm actually paid for it. For example, if a firm invests $1 million in a piece of equipment that is quickly outmoded and is too inefficient relative to new equipment to be worth operating, its value is clearly not $1 million. Although conventional accounting rules place great emphasis on historical costs, managerial economists emphasize that historical costs can be misleading.

There are two types of costs, both of which are generally important. The first type is **explicit costs,** which are the ordinary items that accountants include as the firm's expenses. They are the firm's payroll, payments for raw materials, and so on. The second type is **implicit costs,** which include the costs of resources owned and used by the firm's owner. Unfortunately, accountants and managers, in calculating the costs of the firm, often omit the second type of costs.

Implicit costs arise because the opportunity cost doctrine must be applied to the inputs supplied by the owner of the firm. Consider John Harvey, the proprietor of a firm who invests his own labor and capital in the business. These inputs should be valued at the amount he would have received if he had used these inputs in another way. If he could have received a salary of $25,000 if he worked for someone else, and if he could have received dividends of

CONCEPTS IN CONTEXT

How Harley-Davidson Has Reduced Costs

Harley-Davidson Motor Company, a producer of motorcycles, has experienced very tough competition, particularly from Japanese rivals. Faced with a decreasing share of the market and lower profits, it took a number of major steps to increase manufacturing efficiency and reduce costs. For one thing, it phased out many of its machining operations and began to purchase its metal from steel service centers, which are companies that supply steel products and provide just-in-time delivery.

According to Harley-Davidson officials, this program reduced its work-in-process inventory by nearly $24 million. This meant a substantial cost reduction. Why? Because it costs money to house inventories, to tie up capital in inventories, and to hire people to move materials in and out of inventory. If a firm can reduce its inventories, it can cut these costs significantly.

Specifically, suppose that Harley-Davidson had borrowed the money to finance its work-in-process inventory and that the interest rate on its

loan was 15 percent. By reducing the amount that it had to borrow by $24 million (the amount of the reduction in its work-in-process inventory), Harley-Davidson reduced its annual costs by $0.15 \times 24 = \$3.6$ million.

To some extent, Harley-Davidson has adopted the sort of just-in-time system pioneered by Toyota and other Japanese firms (recall page 264). As pointed out by one Harley-Davidson executive, "The plant doesn't have enough real estate to physically accommodate the larger mill orders. Timely service center deliveries have enabled us to make more productive use of our floor space."* This story also illustrates the importance of fostering and maintaining good working relationships between firms and their suppliers. Often economies can be realized if relationships of this sort are improved.

*A. Sharkey, "Making Industry More Competitive," *Chicago Purchasor*, November–December 1986, pp. 11–12. Also, see "Revving Up for Relief: Harley-Davidson at the ITC," a case in the *Study Guide* accompanying this textbook.

$20,000 if he invested his money in someone else's firm, he should value his labor and his capital at these rates. To exclude these implicit costs can be a serious mistake.

Short-Run Cost Functions

Given the firm's cost of producing each level of output, we can define the firm's **cost functions,** which play a very important role in managerial economics. A firm's cost functions show various relationships between its costs and its output rate. The firm's production function and the prices it pays for inputs determine the firm's cost functions, which can pertain to the short run or the long run.

The **short run** is a time period so short that the firm cannot alter the quantity of some of its inputs. As the length of the time period increases, the amounts of more and more inputs become variable. Any time span between one where the quantity of no input is variable and one where the quantity of all inputs is variable could reasonably be called the short run. However, a more restrictive definition is generally employed: we say that the short run is the time interval so brief that the firm cannot alter the quantities of plant and equipment. These are the firm's **fixed inputs,** and they determine the firm's **scale of plant.** Inputs like labor, which the firm can vary in quantity in the short run, are the firm's **variable inputs.**

Three concepts of total cost in the short run must be considered: total fixed cost, total variable cost, and total cost. **Total fixed costs** are the total costs per period of time incurred by the firm for fixed inputs. Since the amount of the fixed inputs is fixed (by definition), the total fixed costs will be the same regardless of the firm's output rate. Examples of fixed costs may be depreciation of plant and equipment and property taxes. Table 9.1 shows the costs of the Media Corporation, a producer of sofas. According to Table 9.1, this firm's total fixed costs are $100 per day; the firm's total fixed cost function is shown graphically in Figure 9.1. The values in Table 9.1 (and in Table 9.2) come from the total cost relationship

$$TC = 100 + 50Q - 11Q^2 + Q^3$$

TABLE
9.1

Fixed, Variable, and Total Costs, Media Corporation

Units of output Q	Total fixed cost (dollars per day) TFC	Total variable cost (dollars per day) TVC	Total cost (dollars per day) TC
0	100	0	100
1	100	40	140
2	100	64	164
3	100	78	178
4	100	88	188
5	100	100	200
5.5	100	108.625	208.625
6	100	120	220
6.64	100	139.6	239.6
7	100	154	254
8	100	208	308
9	100	288	388
10	100	400	500

FIGURE
9.1

Fixed, Variable, and Total Costs, Media Corporation

Fixed costs do not vary with output and so the fixed cost curve is a horizontal line. Variable costs at first increase with output at a decreasing rate and then increase with output at an increasing rate. The total cost curve is the vertical summation of the fixed cost curve and the average variable cost curve. The total cost function and the total variable cost function have the same shape, since they differ by only a constant amount, which is total fixed cost.

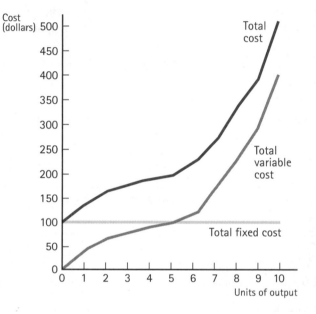

Total variable costs are the total costs incurred by the firm for variable inputs. They go up as the firm's output rate rises, since higher output rates require higher variable input rates, which mean bigger variable costs. For example, the larger the product of a woolen mill, the larger the quantity of wool that must be used, and the higher the total cost of the wool. The Media Corporation's total variable cost schedule is shown in Table 9.1. Figure 9.1 shows the corresponding total variable cost function. Up to a particular output rate (4 units of output), total variable costs are shown to rise at a decreasing rate; beyond that output level, total variable costs rise at an increasing rate. This characteristic of the total variable cost function follows from the law of diminishing marginal returns. At low levels of output, increases in the variable inputs may result in increases in their productivity, with the result that total variable costs increase with output, but at a decreasing rate. (More will be said on this score on page 328.)

Finally, **total costs** are the sum of total fixed costs and total variable costs. To derive the total cost column in Table 9.1, add total fixed cost and total variable cost at each output. The total cost function for the Media Corporation is shown in Figure 9.1. The total cost function and the total variable cost function have the same shape, since they differ by only a constant amount, which is total fixed cost.

Average and Marginal Costs

While the total cost functions are of great importance, managers must be interested as well in the average cost functions and the marginal cost function. There are three average cost functions, corresponding to the three total cost functions. **Average fixed cost** is total fixed cost divided by output. Average fixed cost declines with increases in output; mathematically, the average fixed cost function is a rectangular hyperbola. Table 9.2 and Figure 9.2 show the average fixed cost function for the Media Corporation.

TABLE
9.2

Average and Marginal Costs, Media Corporation

Units of output Q	Average fixed cost (dollars) TFC/Q	Average variable cost (dollars) TVC/Q	Average total cost (dollars) TC/Q	Marginal cost (dollars) $\Delta TC/\Delta Q$[a]	Marginal cost (dollars) dTC/dQ[a]
0	–	–	–	–	–
1	100	40	140	40	31
2	50	32	82	24	18
3	33.33	26	59.33	14	11
4	25	22	47	10	10
5	20	20	40	12	15
5.5	18.18	<u>19.75</u>	37.93		<u>19.75</u>
6	16.67	20	36.67	20	26
6.64	15.06	21.04	<u>36.11</u>		<u>36.11</u>
7	14.29	22	36.29	34	43
8	12.5	26	38.5	54	66
9	11.11	32	43.11	80	95
10	10	40	50	112	130

[a]The figures in the $\Delta TC/\Delta Q$ column pertain to the interval between the indicated amount of quantity and one unit less than the indicated amount of quantity. The figures in the dTC/dQ column are the continuous marginal cost, i.e., $dTC/dQ = MC = 50 - 22Q + 3Q^2$.

FIGURE
9.2

Average and Marginal Cost Curves, Media Corporation

Average fixed cost continually decreases as output increases. Average variable cost and average total cost at first decrease, reach a minimum, and then increase as output increases. The minimum of the average total cost occurs at a higher output than the minimum of the average variable cost. The average total cost curve is the vertical summation of the average fixed cost and the average variable cost curves. Marginal cost passes through the minimum of both average cost curves and when marginal cost is below the average cost, average cost falls and vice versa. Average total cost achieves its minimum at a higher output rate (6.64) than average variable cost (5.5), because the increases in average variable cost are up to a point more than offset by decreases in average fixed cost.

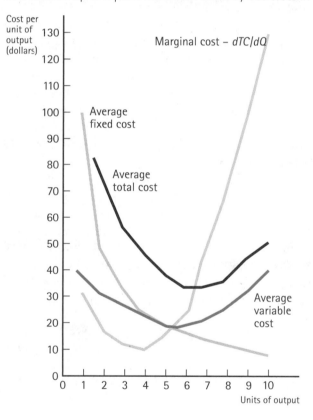

Average **variable cost** is total variable cost divided by output. For the Media Corporation, the average variable cost function is shown in Table 9.2 and Figure 9.2. At first, output increases result in decreases in average variable cost, but beyond a point, they result in higher average variable cost. The theory of production in Chapter 7 leads us to expect this curvature of the average variable cost function. If AVC is the average variable cost, TVC is the total variable cost, Q is the quantity of output, U is the quantity of the variable input, and W is the price of the variable input, it must be true that

$$AVC = \frac{TVC}{Q} = W\frac{U}{Q}.$$

Consequently, since Q/U is the average product of the variable input (AVP),

$$AVC = W\frac{1}{AVP}. \tag{9.1}$$

Hence, since AVP generally rises and then falls with increases in output and since W is constant, AVC must decrease and then go up with increases in output.

Average total cost is total cost divided by output. For the Media Corporation, the average total cost function is shown in Table 9.2 and Figure 9.2. Average total cost equals the sum of average fixed cost and average variable cost, which helps to account for the shape of the average total cost function. For those levels of output where both average fixed cost and average variable cost decrease, average total cost must decrease too. However, average total cost reaches its minimum after average variable cost, because the increases in average variable cost are for a time more than offset by decreases in average fixed cost.

Marginal cost is the addition to total cost resulting from the addition of the last unit of output. That is, if $C(Q)$ is the total cost of producing Q units of output, the marginal cost between Q and $(Q-1)$ units of output is $C(Q) - C(Q-1)$. For the Media Corporation, the marginal cost function is shown in Table 9.2 and Figure 9.2. At low output levels, marginal cost may decrease (as it does in Figure 9.2) with increases in output, but after reaching a minimum, it goes up with further increases in output. The reason for this behavior is found in the law of diminishing marginal returns. If ΔTVC is the change in total variable costs resulting from a change in output of ΔQ and if ΔTFC is the change in total fixed costs resulting from a change in output of ΔQ, marginal cost equals

$$\frac{\Delta TVC + \Delta TFC}{\Delta Q}.$$

But ΔTFC is zero because fixed costs are fixed; thus marginal cost equals

$$\frac{\Delta TVC}{\Delta Q}.$$

Moreover, if the price of the variable input is taken as given by the firm, $\Delta TVC = W(\Delta U)$, where ΔU is the change in the quantity of the variable input resulting from the increase of ΔQ in output. Consequently, marginal cost equals

$$MC = W\frac{\Delta U}{\Delta Q} = W\frac{1}{MP}, \tag{9.2}$$

where *MP* is the marginal product of the variable input. Because *MP* generally increases, attains a maximum, and declines with increases in output, marginal cost normally decreases, attains a minimum, and then increases.[1]

If the total cost function is continuous, marginal cost is defined as dTC/dQ, where *TC* is total cost (recall Chapter 2). Suppose, for example, using the Media Corporation's total cost function:

$$TC = 100 + 50Q - 11Q^2 + Q^3$$

where *TC* is expressed in thousands of dollars, and *Q* is expressed in units of output. This firm's marginal cost function will be

$$MC = \frac{\partial TC}{\partial Q} = 50 - 22Q + 3Q^2$$

Consider the above definitions with the product function of the Thomas Machine Company ($Q = 30L + 20L^2 - L^3$) from Chapter 7. If the wage rate is 390, then Table 9.3 shows the relationship between average variable product and average variable cost, and between marginal product and marginal cost. As you can see, when *AVP* is maximized, *AVC* is minimized. Likewise, it can be seen that marginal cost equals average variable cost when average variable cost is minimized. This is to be expected because marginal product equaled average variable product when average variable product was maximized. Average variable product is maximized when 10 units are labor employed (at 130); and average variable cost is minimized when 10 units of labor are employed (at 3); and marginal cost is also equal to 3 when 10 units of labor are employed.

Note that marginal cost always equals average variable cost when the latter is a minimum. If *AVC* is this firm's average variable cost,

$$AVC = \frac{TVC}{Q} = 50 - 11Q + Q^2$$

Taking the derivative of *AVC* with respect to *Q*, and setting it equal to zero, we find the value of *Q* where *AVC* is a minimum:

$$\frac{\partial AVC}{\partial Q} = -11 + 2Q = 0$$

$$Q = 5.5$$

When *Q* equals 5.5, both marginal cost and average variable cost equal 19.75 thousand dollars. (Substitute 5.5 for *Q* in the above equations for *MC* and *AVC*, and see for yourself that this is true.) Thus, as pointed out above, marginal cost

[1]However, this is not always true, as indicated in Figure 9.6, in which short-run marginal cost always rises as output increases.

Relationship of Average Variable Product and Marginal Product to Average Variable Cost and Marginal Cost for the Thomas Machine Company

L	Q	AVP_L	$MP_L =$ dQ/dL	W	$AVC =$ W/AVP_L	$MC =$ W/MP_L
0	0	–	–	390	–	–
1	49	49	67	390	7.96	5.82
2	132	66	98	390	5.91	3.98
3	243	81	123	390	4.81	3.17
4	376	94	142	390	4.15	2.75
5	525	105	155	390	3.71	2.52
6	684	114	162	390	3.42	2.41
6.67	792.6	118.9	163.33	390	3.28	2.388 ← MP_L max,
7	847	121	163	390	3.22	2.393 so MC min
8	1008	126	158	390	3.10	2.47
9	1161	129	147	390	3.02	2.65
10	1300	130	130	390	3.00	3.00 ← AVP_L max,
11	1419	129	107	390	3.02	3.64 so AVC min
12	1512	126	78	390	3.10	5.00
13	1573	121	43	390	3.22	9.07
14	1596	114	2	390	3.42	195.00
15	1575	105	−45	390	3.71	–

equals average variable cost when the latter is a minimum. Note also that marginal cost equals average total cost when the latter is at a minimum. The firm's average total cost is:

$$ATC = (100/Q) + 50 - 11Q + Q^2$$

Taking the derivative of ATC with respect to Q, and setting it equal to zero, we find the value of Q where ATC is a minimum:

$$dATC/dQ = (-100/Q^2) - 11 + 2Q = 0$$
$$\text{or } 2Q^3 - 11Q^2 - 100 = 0$$

This can be solved for $Q = 6.64$. Substituting 6.64 into the ATC and MC equations yields $MC = ATC = 36.11$.

The Effects of Output on the Cost of Producing Aircraft

The National Research Council made a study of the U.S. aircraft industry that stressed the importance to airplane manufacturers of serving the entire world market. As evidence, the council presented the graph below.*

(a) As indicated in this graph, the cost per airplane of producing 525 aircraft of a particular type is about 10 percent higher than the cost per airplane of producing 700 aircraft of this type. Assuming that this graph pertains to the short run, by what percentage does average fixed cost increase if 525 rather than 700 aircraft are produced? (b) If average fixed cost is 30 percent of average total cost if 700 aircraft are produced and 36 percent of average total cost if 525 aircraft are produced, is it true that average total cost is about 10 percent higher if 525 rather than 700 aircraft are produced? (c) According to the council, "If a

*National Research Council, *The Competitive Status of the U.S. Civil Aviation Manufacturing Industry* (Washington, D.C.: National Academy Press, 1985).

foreign government elected to incur a cost penalty in order to establish a domestic [aircraft] industry that serves 25 percent of the world market, the effect would be to dramatically change the pricing and thus the profit prospects for a privately funded U.S. manufacturer." What sorts of changes in pricing and profit prospects would occur? Why? (d) The council goes on to say "With the opportunity for profit reduced or destroyed due to a split market, the U.S. firm might well choose not to enter, and the foreign competitor would then have the total market available." Why?

SOLUTION (a) If the number of aircraft produced is 525 rather than 700, average fixed cost is $TFC/525$ rather than $TFC/700$, where TFC equals total fixed cost. Thus, average fixed cost increases by 33 percent. (b) For 700 aircraft, average total cost equals $X/0.30 = 3.33X$, where X is average fixed cost when 700 aircraft are produced. For 525 aircraft, average total cost equals $1.33X/0.36 = 3.69X$, since average fixed cost equals $1.33X$ when

525 aircraft are produced. Thus, average total cost increases by about 11 percent (from 3.33X to 3.69X) if 525 rather than 700 aircraft are produced. (c) Because U.S. airplane manufacturers would be shut out of part of the market, they would be likely to sell fewer airplanes, the result being that their average total cost would be higher. Thus, their profits would be reduced, or their prices would have to go up, or both. (d) If the U.S. airplane manufacturer felt that it was shut out of so large a part of the market that its average cost would be too high to enable it to make a reasonable profit, it would not build the airplane in question.

Note that we have two definitions of marginal cost. The first ($\Delta TC/\Delta Q$) assumes that we can only produce in discrete units, like a car or a cake. The second (dTC/dQ) assumes that we can produce on a continuous basis, as in 3.14 tons of grain or 10.33 gallons of gasoline. Which one you use depends on the situation you are in: Are you constrained to an integer number of the product or can you produce fractions of the product?

Long-Run Cost Functions

In the **long run,** all inputs are variable, and a firm can build any scale or type of plant that it wants. There are no fixed cost functions (total or average) in the long run, since no inputs are fixed. A useful way to look at the long run is to consider it a **planning horizon.** While operating in the short run, the firm must continually be planning ahead and deciding its strategy in the long run. Its decisions concerning the long run determine the sort of short-run position the firm will occupy in the future. For example, before the IBM Corporation makes the decision to add a new type of product to its line, the firm is in a long-run situation, since it can choose among a wide variety of types and sizes of equipment to produce the new product. But once the investment is made, IBM is confronted with a short-run situation, since the type and size of equipment are, to a considerable extent, frozen.

Assume it is possible for a firm to construct only three alternative scales of plant; the short-run average cost function for each scale of plant is represented by G_1G_1', G_2G_2', and G_3G_3' in Figure 9.3. In the long run, the firm can build (or convert to) any one of these possible scales of plant. Which scale is most profitable? Obviously, the answer depends on the long-run output rate to be produced, since the firm will want to produce this output at a minimum average cost. For example, if the anticipated output rate is Q, the firm should pick the smallest plant, since it will produce Q units of output per period of

FIGURE
9.3

Short–Run Average Cost Functions for Various Scales of Plant

The long-run average cost function is the solid portion of the short-run average cost functions, G_1DEG_3'.

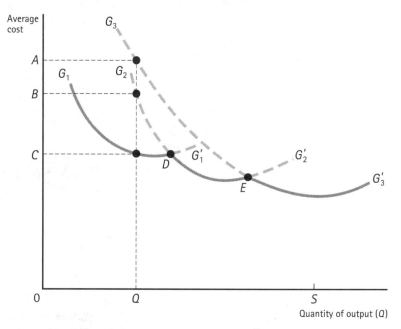

time at a cost per unit, C, which is smaller than what the medium-sized plant (its cost per unit being B) or the large plant (its cost per unit being A) can do. However, if the anticipated output rate is S, the firm should pick the largest plant.

The **long-run average cost function** shows the minimum cost per unit of producing each output level when any desired scale of plant can be built. In Figure 9.3, the long-run average cost function is the solid portion of the short-run average cost functions, G_1DEG_3'. The broken-line segments of the short-run functions are not included since they are not the lowest average costs, as is obvious from the figure.

Now, we must abandon the simplifying assumption that there are only three alternative scales of plant. In fact, there are many alternative scales, so the firm is confronted with a host of short-run average cost functions, as shown in Figure 9.4. The minimum cost per unit of producing each output level is given by

FIGURE
9.4

Long–Run Average Cost Function

The long-run average cost function, which shows the minimum long-run cost per unit of producing each output level, is the envelope of the short-run functions.

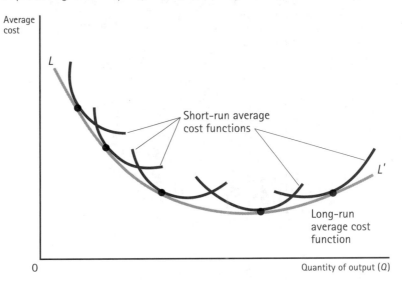

the long-run average cost function, *LL'*. The long-run average cost function is tangent to each of the short-run average cost functions at the output where the plant corresponding to the short-run average cost function is optimal. (Mathematically, the long-run average cost function is the envelope of the short-run functions.)

If you have the long-run average cost of producing a given output, you can readily derive the long-run total cost of the output, since the latter is simply the product of long-run average cost and output. Figure 9.5 shows the relationship between long-run total cost and output; this relationship is called the **long-run total cost function.** Given the long-run total cost function, you can readily derive the **long-run marginal cost function,** which shows the relationship between output and the cost resulting from the production of the last unit of output if the firm has time to make the optimal changes in the quantities of all inputs used. Of course, long-run marginal cost must be less than long-run average cost when the latter is decreasing, equal to long-run average cost when the latter is a minimum, and greater than long-run average cost when the latter is increasing. It can also be demonstrated that when the firm has built the

FIGURE
9.5

Long-Run Total Cost Function

The long-run total cost of a given output equals the long-run average cost (given in Figure 9.4) times output.

optimal scale of plant for producing a given level of output, long-run marginal cost will be equal to short-run marginal cost at that output.[2]

---

[2]Suppose that the long-run average cost of producing an output rate of Q is $L(Q)$ and that the short-run average cost of producing this output with the ith scale of plant is $A_i(Q)$. Let $M(Q)$ be the long-run marginal cost and $R(Q)$ be the short-run marginal cost with the ith scale of plant. If the firm is maximizing profit, it is operating where short-run and long-run average costs are equal; in other words, $L(Q) = A_i(Q)$. Also, the long-run average cost function is tangent to the short-run average cost function; this means that

$$\frac{dL(Q)}{dQ} = \frac{dA_i(Q)}{dQ} = \text{and } Q\frac{dL(Q)}{dQ} = Q\frac{dA_i(Q)}{dQ}.$$

From these conditions, it is easy to prove that the long-run marginal cost, $M(Q)$, equals the short-run marginal cost, $R_i(Q)$.

$$M(Q) = \frac{d[QL(Q)]}{dQ} = L(Q) + \frac{QdL(Q)}{dQ}.$$
$$R_i(Q) = \frac{d[QA(Q)]}{dQ} = A_iQ + \frac{QdA_i(Q)}{dQ}.$$

Since we know from the previous paragraph that $L(Q) = A_i(Q)$ and $QdL(Q)/dQ = QdA_i(Q)/dQ$, it follows that $R_i(Q)$ must equal $M(Q)$.

The Crosby Corporation: A Numerical Example

To illustrate the relationship between a firm's long-run and short-run cost functions, consider the Crosby Corporation, a hypothetical producer of flashlights. Crosby's engineers have determined that the firm's production function is

$$Q = 4(KL)^{0.5} \qquad (9.3)$$

where Q is output (in thousands of flashlights per month), K is the amount of capital used per month (in thousands of units), and L is the number of hours of labor employed per month (in thousands). Because Crosby must pay $8 per hour for labor and $2 per unit for capital, its total cost (in thousands of dollars per month) equals

$$TC = 8L + 2K = \frac{Q^2}{2K} + 2K, \qquad (9.4)$$

since equation (9.3) implies that

$$L = \frac{Q^2}{16K}.$$

In the short run, which is a time period so brief that a firm cannot vary the quantity of its plant and equipment, K is fixed. Because the Crosby Corporation has 10 thousand units of capital, $K = 10$. Substituting 10 for K in equation (9.4), the short-run cost function is

$$TC_S = \frac{Q^2}{20} + 20, \qquad (9.5)$$

where TC_S is short-run total cost. Thus, the short-run average total cost function is

$$AC_S = \frac{TC_S}{Q} = \frac{Q}{20} + \frac{20}{Q},$$

and the short-run marginal cost function is

$$MC_S = \frac{dTC_S}{dQ} = \frac{Q}{10}.$$

ANALYZING MANAGERIAL DECISIONS

Should We Continue to Make Autos from Steel?

In recent years, auto makers have begun to substitute synthetic materials for steel. Engineers at the Materials Systems Laboratory of the Massachusetts Institute of Technology have made careful studies of the costs of producing an automobile fender. Assuming that the annual production volume of the fender is 100,000, the average cost of a fender is as shown below if sheet steel or four alternative plastics fabrication technologies (injection moulding, compression moulding, reaction injection moulding, and thermoplastic sheet stamping) are used to make the fender:

Cost	Sheet steel	Injection moulding	Compression moulding	Reaction injection moulding	Thermo- plastic sheet
Materials	$4.25	$8.50	$4.84	$4.89	$5.75
Labor	0.24	0.42	0.63	0.83	0.52
Capital	0.66	2.62	1.57	1.40	2.18
Tooling	2.57	0.86	0.71	0.57	0.71
Total[a]	$7.71	$12.39	$7.75	$7.70	$9.17

[a]Figures do not sum to totals because of rounding errors.

If the annual production volume is 200,000, rather than 100,000, the cost per fender, if sheet metal is used in its production, is less than $7—and less than the cost if any of the plastics fabrication technologies are used at this production volume.

(a) If 100,000 fenders are made per year, does the cost per fender differ significantly if sheet steel is used from the cost if reaction injection moulding (or compression moulding) is used? (b) Compared with reaction injection moulding (or compression moulding), sheet steel uses less (or less costly) materials, labor, and capital. Why then doesn't it have lower average total costs? (c) If sheet steel is used, are there economies of scale in fender production? (d) Steel is commonly thought to be the most advantageous material for high-volume production of auto fenders. Does this seem to be true?

SOLUTON (a) No. The cost is $7.71 for sheet steel versus $7.70 for reaction injection moulding (and $7.75 for compression moulding). (b) Sheet steel has much higher tooling costs per fender than does reaction injection moulding (or compression moulding). (c) Yes. Whereas the cost per fender is $7.71 when 100,000 fenders are produced per year, it is less than $7 when 200,000 are produced per year. (d) Yes. For a production volume of 200,000 per year, sheet steel, according to the figures quoted, has a lower average cost than any of the plastics fabrication techniques.*

*For further discussion, see G. Amendola, "The Diffusion of Synthetic Materials in the Automobile Industry," Research Policy, 1990.

In the long run, no input is fixed. To determine the optimal amount of capital input to be used to produce an output of Q units per month, Crosby's managers should minimize total cost. On the basis of equation (9.4),

$$\frac{dTC}{dK} = -\frac{Q^2}{2K^2} + 2.$$

Setting this derivative equal to zero, we find that the cost-minimizing value of K is

$$K = \frac{Q}{2}.$$

Substituting $Q/2$ for K in equation (9.4), we see that the long-run cost function is

$$TC_L = 2Q, \tag{9.6}$$

where TC_L is long-run total cost. Thus, since $TC_L/Q = 2$, long-run average cost equals \$2 per flashlight.

Figure 9.6 shows the relationship between the Crosby Corporation's short-run average and marginal costs and its long-run average costs. As is always the case (recall page 329), the short-run marginal cost function intersects the short-run average cost function at its minimum point—where $Q = 20$ and $AC_S = 2$, in this case. Because it is horizontal (owing to constant returns to scale), the long-run average cost function is tangent to the short-run average cost function at the latter's minimum point. Note that the fact that the long-run average cost function is horizontal is unusual. Instead, as illustrated in the following section, there are economies of scale (over at least some range of output) in a wide variety of industries.

Economies of Scale in Nursing Homes

A long-run average cost curve is important for practical decision making by managers because it shows whether, and to what extent, larger plants have cost advantages over smaller ones. In cases in which this occurs, we often say that there are *economies of scale*. To illustrate, consider nursing homes, which are a huge industry with annual sales of over \$70 billion. Figure 9.7 shows the long-run average cost curve for a nursing home, based on Texas data.

As you can see, there are substantial economies of scale. If a nursing home provides only 10,000 patient-days of service per year, the cost per patient-day is almost \$29; if it provides about 50,000 patient-days of service per year, the cost per patient-day is under \$26. Curves like Figure 9.7 are constructed by en-

FIGURE
9.6

Short-Run Average and Marginal Costs and Long-Run Average Cost, Crosby Corporation

Because the long-run average cost function is horizontal, it is tangent to the short-run average cost function at the latter's minimum point.

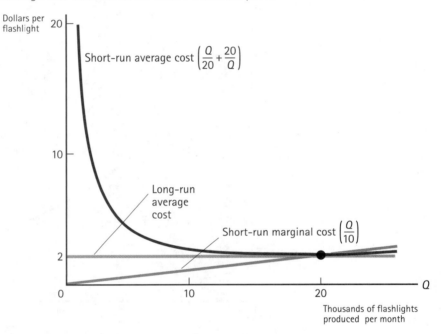

gineers and economists for a wide variety of plants and industrial processes. Without such information, managers could not make rational decisions concerning the size of plant they should build.

In many industries, firms can operate more than one plant, and there may be economies of scale at the *firm* (in contrast to the *plant*) level. In other words, holding the size of each plant constant, average cost may fall in response to increases in the number of plants operated by the firm. This seems to be true in the nursing home industry. Because of advantages due to centralized purchasing of inputs and a more specialized staff, firms with many nursing homes seem to have lower costs than those with only one nursing home.[3]

Beyond nursing homes, other examples of economies of scale exist. Mergers are happening in many industries. The oil industry has recently seen merg-

[3]N. McKay, *Health Services Research,* April 1991. The average cost curve in Figure 9.7 is based on the assumption that a variety of factors influencing nursing home costs are held constant.

Long-Run Average Cost Curve for Texas Nursing Homes

For nursing homes with under 60,000 patient-days, there seem to be substantial economies of scale.

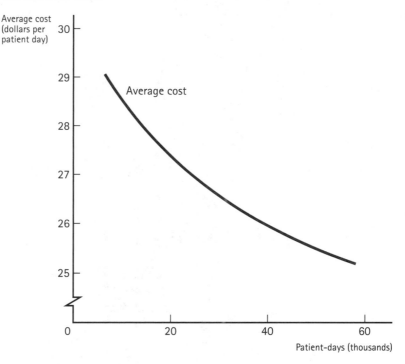

ers with BP Amoco and ExxonMobil, among others. DaimlerChrysler, Ford and Volvo, Renault and Nissan, and GM and Fiat are among the numerous automobile company mergers. United Airlines and US Airways have proposed a merger, talks have occurred between British Airways and KLM, and Sabena and Swiss Air have also come together. After a series of large rail mergers, the Burlington Northern and Canadian National systems have proposed North America's first transcontinental railroad.

While there are many reasons for firms to merge, one may be economies of scale—by becoming larger, average costs may become smaller. Consider the following three examples:

1. Cruise ships: The economies of scale created by the advent of huge ships have put pressure on smaller cruise lines prompting rapid industry consolidation in recent years.[4]

---

[4]"Carnival Sails into Dominant Position in Cruise Holidays" *Financial Times*, March 19, 1998.

2. UniDanmark: The merger of UniDanmark and Tryg-Baltica (banking and insurance companies) in Denmark is expressed as a merger to exploit economies of scale.[5]
3. DaimlerChrysler: The creation of DaimlerChrysler is described as forcing the other auto companies to assess their previous assumptions about optimal size and economies of scale.[6]

Managers must understand their cost relationships to know whether economies of scale exist. If scale exists, managers must then decide how to attain scale either by making it (through expansion of output and plant) or by acquiring it (through a merger).

Measurement of Short-Run Cost Functions: The Choice of a Mathematical Form

To analyze many important problems, managers must estimate cost functions—or **cost curves,** as they are often called—in particular firms and industries. One of the initial steps in estimating a cost function is to choose the mathematical form of the relationship between output and cost. As a first approximation, managers often assume that short-run total cost is a linear function of output, which means that marginal cost tends to be constant in the relevant output range (see Figure 9.8). In fact, as we shall see below, a linear function often fits the data for particular firms and plants quite well in the short run. To some extent, this may reflect the fact that some empirical studies are biased toward constant marginal cost by the nature of accounting data and the statistical methods used. Also, the data used in these studies often do not cover periods when the firm was operating close to the peak of its capacity, which is when marginal cost would be expected to increase substantially. Although marginal costs may well be relatively constant over a wide range, it is inconceivable that they do not eventually increase with increases in output. Thus, a linear function is likely to be appropriate for only a restricted range of output.

It is also possible to assume that total cost is a quadratic or cubic function of output. If the quadratic form is chosen, marginal cost increases with output, as shown in Figure 9.9. If the cubic form is chosen (and if c is large enough), marginal cost first decreases and then increases with output, as shown in Figure 9.10. Whether these forms are better than the linear form depends on whether they fit the data better. In many cases, they seem to do no better in this regard than the linear form. However, before deciding that the linear form is satisfactory, you should be careful to inspect the residuals from the estimated cost func-

[5]"Merger Aims to Exploit Economies of Scale," *Financial Times,* May 19, 1999.
[6]"End of the Road for Independence?" *Financial Times,* February 5, 1999.

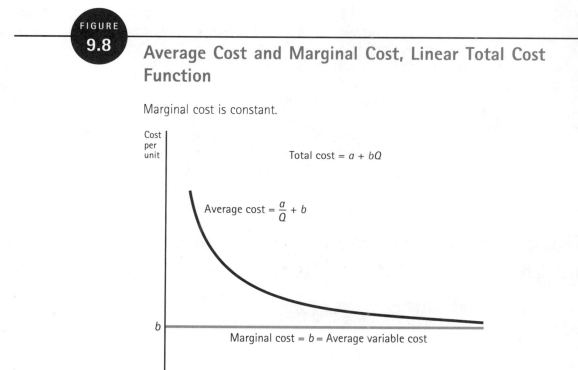

FIGURE
9.8

Average Cost and Marginal Cost, Linear Total Cost Function

Marginal cost is constant.

Cost per unit

Total cost = $a + bQ$

Average cost = $\dfrac{a}{Q} + b$

b

Marginal cost = b = Average variable cost

0

Quantity of output (Q)

tion to see whether there is evidence of departures from linearity. (Recall our discussion on pages 181 to 182 of the appropriate inspection procedure.)

Nature and Limitations of Available Data

Having chosen a mathematical form, one must decide on the type of data to be used in estimating a cost function. One possibility is to use time-series data, and relate the total cost of a firm in each time period to its output level in that period. Regression analysis (described in Chapter 5) is frequently used to estimate this relationship. Another possibility is to use cross-section data, and relate the total costs of a variety of firms (during the same period of time) to their output levels. Figure 9.11 plots the 1999 output of eight firms in a given industry against their 1999 total costs. Here too, regression analysis can be used to estimate the relationship. A third possibility is to use engineering data to construct cost functions.

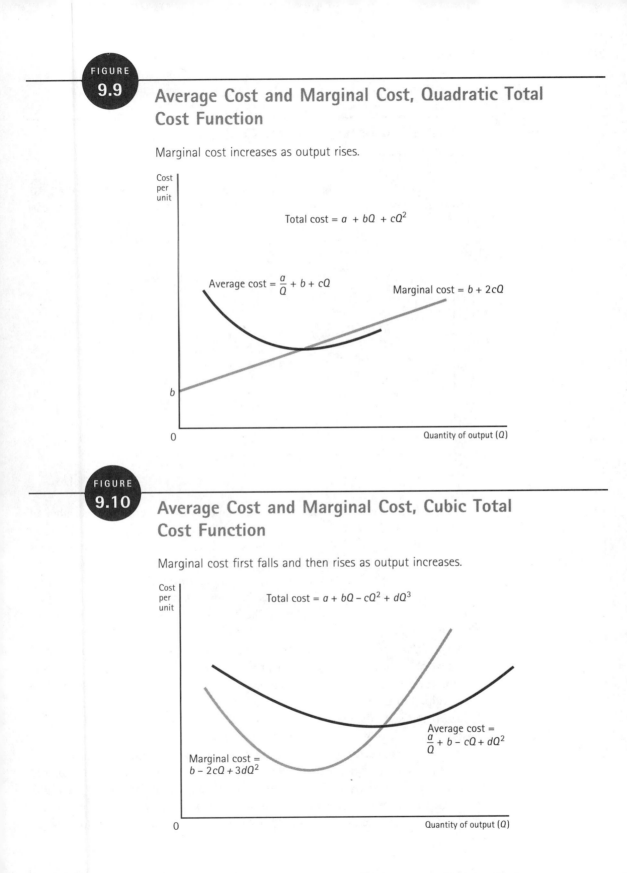

FIGURE 9.9

Average Cost and Marginal Cost, Quadratic Total Cost Function

Marginal cost increases as output rises.

Cost per unit

Total cost $= a + bQ + cQ^2$

Average cost $= \dfrac{a}{Q} + b + cQ$

Marginal cost $= b + 2cQ$

b

0 Quantity of output (Q)

FIGURE 9.10

Average Cost and Marginal Cost, Cubic Total Cost Function

Marginal cost first falls and then rises as output increases.

Cost per unit

Total cost $= a + bQ - cQ^2 + dQ^3$

Average cost $= \dfrac{a}{Q} + b - cQ + dQ^2$

Marginal cost $= b - 2cQ + 3dQ^2$

0 Quantity of output (Q)

FIGURE
9.11

Relationship between Total Cost and Output, Cross Section

Each firm's level of cost during 1999 is plotted against its output level during that year. Such a relationship generally is only a very rough approximation to the relevant cost function.

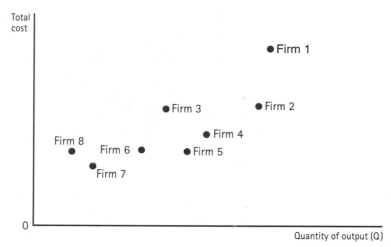

Regardless of which of these types of data is used, there are a number of important difficulties in estimating cost functions. Accounting data, which are generally the only cost data available, suffer from a number of deficiencies when used for this purpose. The time period used for accounting purposes generally is longer than the economist's short run. Accountants often use arbitrary allocations of overhead and joint costs. The depreciation of an asset over a period of time is determined largely by the tax laws rather than economic criteria. Many inputs are valued at historical, rather than opportunity, cost.

Engineering data also suffer from important limitations. Engineering data, like cost accounting data, relate to processes within the firm. There is an inevitable arbitrariness involved in allocating costs that are jointly attached to the production of more than one product in multiproduct firms. Also, a problem in using such data to estimate cost functions for an entire firm is that the costs of various processes may affect one another and may not be additive.

If you are considering the use of cross-section data, it is important to watch out for the so-called regression fallacy. Because the output produced and sold by a firm is only partly under its control, actual and expected output often differ. When firms are classified by actual output, firms with very high output levels may be producing at an unusually high level, and firms with very low output levels may be producing at an unusually low level. Since firms producing at an unusually high level of output may be producing at lower average costs than firms producing at an unusually low level of output, cross-section studies may be biased, the observed cost of producing various output levels being different from the minimum cost of producing these output levels.

Key Steps in the Estimation Process

Having chosen a mathematical form and having decided on the type of data to be used, the following six steps should be carried out before using the regression techniques described in Chapter 5 to estimate a short-run cost function.

1. **Definition of Cost** As pointed out at the beginning of this chapter, the relevant concept of cost for managerial decision making ordinarily is opportunity cost, not cost based on accounting data. You must be careful to ensure that the accounting data—or engineering data, for that matter—on which an estimated cost function is based are reasonably indicative of opportunity costs. If not, they should be adjusted. For example, suppose that historical data regarding a firm's depreciation costs are based on the tax laws, rather than on opportunity costs of the relevant equipment. To remedy this problem, the cost data should be revised to reflect opportunity costs, not tax conventions.

2. **Correction for Price Level Changes** When using time-series data to estimate cost functions, it is important that changes over time in the prices of all inputs be recognized and measured. What we want is a cost function based on next year's input prices if next year is the period to which the analysis pertains. Since our historical data are based on input prices at various times in the past, we need a price index that will allow us to adjust our historical cost data for changes in the prices of various inputs. Moreover, since various inputs may experience quite different rates of inflation, we frequently must obtain or construct a separate price index for each of a number of major types of inputs. Using these price indexes, we must convert the available historical cost data into cost data reflecting next year's input prices, not those in the past.

3. **Relating Cost to Output** If an estimated cost function is to be reasonably accurate, it is important that our cost data distinguish properly between costs that vary with output and those that do not. For many types of equipment, as well as other assets, depreciation depends on both the passage of time and the extent to which they are used, the result being that it is very difficult, if not impossible, to determine solely from accounting data how much the depreciation cost varies with output alone. Also, some costs do not vary with output so long as output does not exceed some critical level.

But above this critical level, these costs may increase considerably. For example, up to some output level, a firm may be able to get along with one machine tool of a particular type, but beyond that output level, it may have to get an additional machine tool.

4. **Matching Time Periods** Major errors sometimes occur because the cost data do not pertain to the same time periods as the output data. To see what mayhem this can cause, suppose that we were to plot a firm's 1999 cost against its 1998 output, its 1998 cost against its 1997 output, and so on. Would the resulting plot of points be a good estimate of the firm's cost function? Of course not. Instead, we should relate a firm's costs in a particular period to its level of output *in that same period*. However, this rule must be modified in cases in which some of the costs of producing output in one period do not arise until subsequent periods. These delayed costs must be recognized, measured, and charged against the period in which the output occurred. Thus, costs of maintenance and repairs, when they are delayed, should be treated in this way.

5. **Controlling Product, Technology, and Plant** As was stressed earlier in this chapter, when we estimate a firm's cost function, we do so on the basis of a fixed definition of the firm's product, as well as on a fixed level of technology and (for short-run cost functions) a fixed scale of plant. This means that we must be careful to ensure that the product mix of the firm does not change over time if we are carrying out a time-series analysis. Also, the observations used in the analysis should not cover so long a period of time that they pertain to different levels of technology (or different scales of plant).

6. **Length of Period and Sample Size** Since there are important advantages in having a reasonably large number of observations extending over a period that is not so long that technology has changed greatly, many analyses are based on observations of monthly cost and output. Often there are about thirty or forty such observations. However, one problem with the use of monthly data is that one month's output may result in costs that occur in subsequent months. There is no simple rule that can be used to specify the best length of period. Like so many aspects of this subject, the answer depends in considerable part on the quality and level of detail of the firm's accounting records.

A Hosiery Mill's Short-Run Cost Functions

If a conscientious effort is made to carry out each of the steps described in previous sections, and if one is careful to avoid the pitfalls cited above, it generally is possible to estimate cost functions that are of considerable use in promoting better managerial decisions. To illustrate how cost functions have

TABLE
9.4

Regressions of Combined Cost and Its Components on Output, Hosiery Mill

	Combined cost	Productive labor cost	Nonproductive labor cost	Overhead cost
	(Monthly observations)			
Simple regression equation	$TC = 2935.59$ $+ 1.998Q$	$TC = -1695.16$ $+ 1.780Q$	$TC = 992.23$ $+ 0.097Q$	$TC - 3638.30$ $+ 0.121Q$
Standard error of estimate	6109.83	5497.09	399.34	390.58
Correlation coefficient (r)	0.973	0.972	0.952	0.970

Source: Dean, "Statistical Cost Functions of a Hosiery Mill."

been estimated, let's consider a pioneering study by the late Joel Dean of Columbia University of the cost behavior of a hosiery knitting mill that was a part of a large silk-hosiery manufacturing firm.[7] This mill began with the wound silk and carried the work up to the point at which the stockings were ready to be sent to other plants for dyeing and finishing. Thus, this mill's operations were carried on by skilled labor and highly mechanized equipment.

Besides studying total cost, Dean obtained cost functions for productive labor cost, nonproductive labor cost, and overhead cost. As a first step, he plotted each kind of monthly cost against monthly output. Then he fitted a simple regression equation of the form $TC = a + bQ$ to the observations for combined (that is, total) cost and its three components. The resulting regression equations are shown in Table 9.4. (Total cost is in dollars, and output is in dozens of pairs of stockings.)

The regression equation for combined cost is illustrated graphically in Figure 9.12. As you can see, the linear form of the equation fits quite well. The regression line is $TC = 2,935.59 + 1.998Q$. The slope of the regression line equals 1.998, which indicates that marginal cost was $1.998. Average cost (in dollars) was

$$AC = 1.998 + \frac{2,935.59}{Q}.$$

[7]J. Dean, "Statistical Cost Functions of a Hosiery Mill," *Studies in Business Administration,* vol. 14, no. 3 (Chicago: University of Chicago Press, 1941).

FIGURE
9.12

Regression of Total Cost on Output, Hosiery Mill

In the output range covered by these data, the total cost function seems to be approximately linear.

Total cost (thousands of dollars)

Total combined cost

Output (thousands of dozens)

Using this equation, the firm's managers could estimate average costs for any output level in the range covered by the data. For example, if they planned to produce 20,000 dozen pairs of stockings next month, their estimate of the total cost per dozen pairs of stockings would be

$$1.998 + \frac{2,935.59}{20,000} = 2.145$$

or about $2.15.

A Transportation Firm's Short-Run
Cost Functions

In the six decades since Joel Dean's pioneering study of the hosiery mill, a great many studies of this sort have been carried out, and statistical and economic techniques have advanced considerably. Nonetheless, the basic approach has not changed very much. To illustrate, consider one of the largest road passenger transport firms in the United Kingdom. Jack Johnston, a well-known econometrician, estimated this firm's cost functions.[8] To begin with, he broke down

[8] J. Johnston, *Statistical Cost Analysis* (New York: McGraw-Hill, 1960).

the firm's expenses into six categories: (1) vehicle operating expense, (2) maintenance and depreciation of vehicles and equipment, (3) other traffic costs, (4) maintenance and renewal of structures, (5) vehicle licenses, and (6) general expenses.

The largest and most important element of cost is the vehicle operating expense, which consists of the wages, clothing, and national insurance of drivers and conductors, gasoline and fuel oil, tires, and lubricants. The second element of cost—maintenance and depreciation of vehicles and equipment—is also important. Maintenance cost, which consists of expenditure on labor and materials, varies directly with the number of car-miles run by the firm. The third element of cost—other traffic costs—consists of the wages of traffic staff, bus cleaning, tickets, cost of tolls, insurance of vehicles, and other such miscellaneous expenses. These three categories account for over 90 percent of the firm's costs.

Figure 9.13 shows the relationship between the firm's total costs and its output, as measured by the number of car-miles. (Each point pertains to a four-

FIGURE 9.13

Relationship between Total Costs and Car-Miles, Road Passenger Transportation Firm

As in Figure 9.12, the total cost function seems to be approximately linear.

$$TC = 0.6558 + 0.4433Q$$

Total expenses (tens of thousands of pounds)

Car-miles (millions)

Source: Johnston, *Statistical Cost Analysis.*

week period.) Using more sophisticated statistical methods than were available to Dean, Johnston estimated the firm's total cost function; this estimate is included in Figure 9.13. The equation for this cost function is

$$TC = 0.6558 + 0.4433Q,$$

where TC is total cost (in tens of thousands of British pounds), and Q is car-miles (in millions).

For values of car-miles ranging from 3.2 to 4.0 million, a 10 percent increase in the firm's output is associated with an increase of about 7 percent in its total cost. Thus, the short-run average cost function is downward sloping to the right, a 10 percent increase in output being associated, on the average, with about a 3 percent decrease in average cost per unit of output. Empirical results of this sort are of basic importance to a firm's managers. Any manager, to be effective, must have a good working knowledge of his or her firm's short-run cost structure.

Long-Run Statistical Cost Estimation

The same sorts of regression techniques used by Dean or Johnston to estimate short-run cost functions can also be used to estimate long-run cost functions. However, it is very difficult to find cases in which the scale of a firm has changed but technology and other relevant variables have remained constant. Thus, it is hard to use time-series data to estimate long-run cost functions. Generally, regression analyses based on cross-section data have been used instead. Specifically, a sample of firms (or plants) of various sizes is chosen, and a firm's (or plant's) total cost is regressed on its output, as well as other independent variables, such as regional differences in wage rates or other input prices.

Cross-section analysis of this sort, while useful, faces a number of difficulties, some of which have been noted above. (1) Firms may use different accounting methods, with the result that their cost data are not comparable. Thus, the true relationship between cost and output may be obscured. (2) Firms in different regions of the country may pay quite different wage rates (and other input prices may differ considerably among regions). Unless input prices are held constant (by including them as independent variables in the regression), the estimated relationship between cost and output may be biased. (3) Whereas the long-run cost function is based on the assumption that firms are minimizing cost, the actual data used in the statistical analysis may pertain to firms that are not operating efficiently. Thus, the estimated cost function may exaggerate how much it would cost an efficient firm to produce a particular output.

Despite these difficulties, a great many valuable studies of long-run cost functions have been carried out. In general, these studies have found that there are very significant economies of scale at low output levels, but that these economies of scale tend to diminish as output increases, and that the long-run average cost function eventually becomes close to horizontal at high output levels. In contrast to the U-shaped curve in Figure 9.4, which often is postulated in microeconomic theory, the long-run average cost curve tends to be L-shaped, as in Figure 9.14.

Given that this is the case, managers and others are particularly interested in estimating the **minimum efficient scale** of plant or firm in a particular industry. The minimum efficient scale of plant is defined as the smallest output at which long-run average cost is a minimum. If the long-run average cost curve is as shown in Figure 9.14, the minimum efficient scale of plant is Q_m. One reason why managers are so interested in the minimum efficient scale is that plants below this size are at a competitive disadvantage, since their costs are higher than those of their larger rivals. Table 9.5 shows, for various industries, the cost disadvantage of plants that are 50 percent of minimum efficient scale. In synthetic rubber, such plants have average costs that are 15 percent higher than those of plants of minimum efficient scale.

The minimum efficient scale of plant or firm in a particular industry can be estimated from the long-run average cost function, which, as we have seen, can be approximated on the basis of the regression techniques described above. Another way to estimate the minimum efficient scale of plant or firm is through

---

FIGURE
9.14

Typical Long-Run Average Cost Curve

Its shape is L-shaped, not U-shaped (as in Figure 9.4). The minimum efficient scale is Q_m.

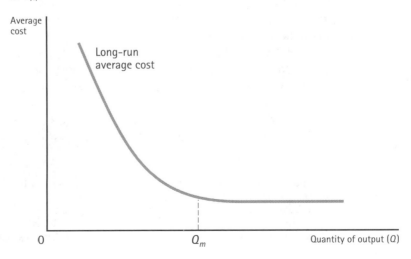

| TABLE 9.5 | Cost Disadvantage of Plants That Are 50 Percent of Minimum Efficient Scale |

Industry	Cost disadvantage (percent)	Industry	Cost disadvantage (percent)
Flour mills	3.0	Synthetic rubber	15.0
Bread baking	7.5	Detergents	2.5
Paper printing	9.0	Bricks	25.0
Sulphuric acid	1.0	Machine tools	5.0

Source: F. M. Scherer, *Industrial Market Structure and Economic Performance* (2d ed; Chicago: Rand McNally, 1980).

engineering analysis. Using their knowledge of the relevant production technology, engineers can determine the optimal input combination to produce each quantity of output. The long-run total cost function can then be estimated by multiplying the optimal quantity of each input by its price and summing to obtain the total cost. From the long-run total cost function, we can readily obtain the long-run average cost function, from which the minimum efficient scale can be determined.[9]

The Long-Run Average Cost Function for Electric Power: A Case Study

To illustrate the estimation of long-run cost functions, consider the study made by Laurits Christenson and William Greene of the U.S. electric power industry.[10] Using cross-section data for all investor-owned utilities with more than $1 million in revenues, they employed the regression techniques described in Chapter 5 to estimate the long-run average cost functions prevailing in 1955 and 1970, the results being shown in Figure 9.15. In accord with the previous section, the long-run cost curve in both years appears to have been L-shaped, not U-shaped.

The minimum efficient scale of firm seems to have been at an output of about 12 billion kilowatt-hours in 1970. Figure 9.15 shows that there was a

[9]For a case study, see Cookenboo, "Production Functions and Cost Functions in Oil Pipelines," in the *Study Guide* accompanying this textbook.

[10]L. Christenson and W. Greene, "Economies of Scale in U.S. Electric Power Generation," *Journal of Political Economy*, 1976. The mathematical form used in this study is the translog cost function, which is a more general (and more complex) relationship than those discussed above.

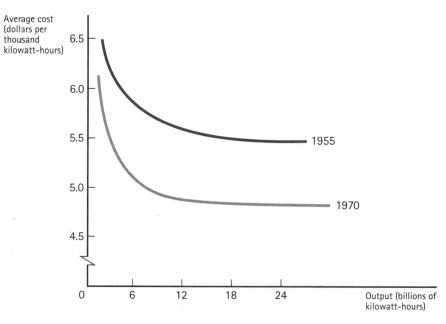

FIGURE 9.15

Long-Run Average Cost Function, Electric Power

Between 1955 and 1970, the average cost function fell considerably. The minimum efficient scale of firm seemed to have been at an output of about 12 billion kilowatt-hours in 1970.

substantial reduction in average costs between 1955 and 1970, as indicated by the fact that the 1970 average cost curve is well below the 1955 curve. In considerable part, this cost reduction was due to technological change of the sort we studied in Chapter 8.

The Survivor Technique

Still another way to estimate the minimum efficient scale is to use the **survivor technique** pioneered by the late Nobel laureate George Stigler. To use this technique, we classify the firms in an industry by size and compute the percentage of the industry output coming from each size class at various times. If the share of one size class diminishes over time, it is assumed to be relatively inefficient, whereas if its share increases, it is assumed to be relatively efficient. Thus, if firms or plants below a particular size tend to account for a smaller share of industry output, this may indicate that they are below the minimum efficient scale. However, because of the effects of regulation, barriers to entry, collusion,

FIGURE
9.16

Long-Run Average Cost Function, Steel Ingot Production

Firms with less than about $2\frac{1}{2}$ and more than 25 percent of the market seem to have had relatively high average costs.

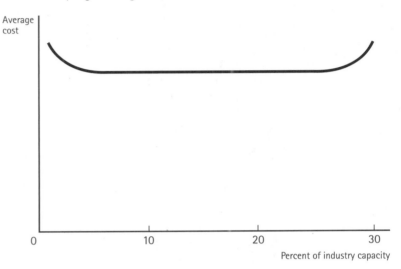

and a variety of other factors, average cost may not be as closely linked to survival as the survivor technique assumes. Thus, this technique should be viewed with appropriate caution.

In Figure 9.16, we show Stigler's estimate of the long-run average cost function for ingot steel production. Apparently, firms with less than about $2\frac{1}{2}$ percent and greater than about 25 percent of the market had relatively high average costs. Firms in these size categories declined (as a percentage of industry output) during the period he studied. As you can see, one of the major limitations of the survivor technique is that it tells us nothing about the *extent* of the cost differentials among firms of different sizes. This is reflected in the fact that there is no scale on the vertical axis in Figure 9.16.

To illustrate the use of the survivor technique, consider the question of whether efficiencies might arise from common ownership of multiple radio stations within a market. Economists at the Federal Trade Commission have carried out an analysis based on the survivor technique to see whether AM-FM radio combinations have increased in number relative to independently owned and operated stations. According to their results, this has been the case. They interpret these findings as suggesting that common ownership may result in significant economies.[11]

[11]K. Anderson and J. Woodbury, "Do Government-Imposed Ownership Restrictions Inhibit Efficiency?" Bureau of Economics, Federal Trade Commission, December 1988.

The Importance of Flexibility

On the basis of the measurement techniques described in previous sections, one can derive for various types of plants the relationship between output and average total cost. Suppose that the Marion Manufacturing Company is faced with the task of deciding which of two types of plant (type 1 or type 2) to build. The nature and quality of the output of one type of plant do not differ from the nature and quality of the output of the other type of plant. The average total cost function for each type of plant is shown in panel A of Figure 9.17. Suppose the executives of the Marion Manufacturing Company believe that they will want to produce about 10,000 units of output per month. Which of the two types of plant should they build?

The answer depends on how certain they are of the output of the plant. Suppose that the probability distribution of the plant's output is distribution C (in panel B of Figure 9.17). In this case, a type 1 plant probably is preferable because it is very likely that the plant will be called on to produce 9,000 to 11,000 units per month, and in that range the type 1 plant produces at lower average cost than the type 2 plant does. However, if the probability distribution of output is distribution D (in panel B of Figure 9.17), the type 2 plant is likely to be preferable, because it is very likely that the plant will be called on to produce fewer than 9,000 or more than 11,000 units, and in those ranges the type 2 plant produces at lower average cost than the type 1 plant does.

This case illustrates the importance of flexibility. While the type 1 plant is more economical if output is close to 10,000 units, the type 2 plant is more flexible. If output is likely to depart greatly from 10,000 units, the type 2 plant is the better choice.

Economies of Scope

Firms commonly produce more than one product. Oil firms like ExxonMobil and BP Amoco produce both petroleum and chemical products; drug firms like Merck and Smith-Kline Beecham produce both vaccines and tranquilizers; and publishers like Random House and Simon and Schuster produce both mysteries and biographies. In many cases, a firm obtains production or cost advantages when it produces a combination of products rather than just one. These advantages sometimes arise because certain production facilities used to make one product can also be used to make another product, or because by-products resulting from the making of one product are useful in making other products.

Economies of scope exist when the cost of producing two (or more) products jointly is less than the cost of producing each one alone. For example, suppose that the Martin Company produces 1,000 milling machines and 500 lathes per year at a cost of $15 million, whereas if a firm produced 1,000 milling machines only, the cost would be $12 million, and if it produced 500 lathes only,

FIGURE
9.17

Average Cost Function, Type 1 and Type 2 Plants, and Two Probability Distributions of Output (C and D)

If the probability distribution of output is D, a type 2 plant is likely to be preferable to a type 1 plant.

CONCEPTS IN CONTEXT

Economies of Scope in Advertising Agencies

In recent years, there has been considerable controversy over the extent to which there are economies of scope in the advertising industry. An advertising agency can provide many products. According to Alvin Silk and Ernst Berndt of MIT, these products (that is, types of advertising) can be categorized into the following nine categories: (1) network television, (2) spot television, (3) general magazines, (4) special print media (such as business publications), (5) newspapers, (6) direct response advertising, (7) radio, (8) outdoor and media services, and (9) nonmedia services. To what extent are an advertising agency's costs reduced by producing a mix of these products rather than producing them separately?

On the basis of a statistical analysis, Silk and Berndt estimated that the percentage cost reduction from joint production for 401 advertising agencies was as follows:

As you can see, the cost saving from joint production of these products ranged from essentially zero to about 86 percent, depending on which advertising agency is considered. On the average, this cost saving was about 26 percent.

Clearly, there are very substantial economies of scope in advertising. However, it is important to recognize that they are much more important for small advertising agencies than for large ones. For the handful of very large agencies with gross annual incomes of $100 million or more, economies of scope seem to be virtually nonexistent, according to the estimates provided by Silk and Berndt. But for small agencies with gross annual incomes of a few million dollars, economies of scope are very significant.*

*For further discussion, see A. Silk and E. Berndt, "Scale and Scope Effects on Advertising Agency Costs," Working Paper No. 3463, National Bureau of Economic Research, October 1990.

the cost would be $6 million. In this case, the cost of producing both the milling machines and the lathes is less than the total cost of producing each separately. Thus, there are economies of scope.

To gauge the extent of economies of scope, the following measure is sometimes calculated:

$$S = \frac{C(Q_1) + C(Q_2) - C(Q_1 + Q_2)}{C(Q_1 + Q_2)}, \qquad (9.7)$$

where S is the degree of economies of scope, $C(Q_1)$ is the cost of producing Q_1 units of the first product alone, $C(Q_2)$ is the cost of producing Q_2 units of the second product alone, and $C(Q_1 + Q_2)$ is the cost of producing Q_1 units of the first product in combination with Q_2 units of the second product. If there are economies of scope, S is greater than zero because the cost of producing both products together—$C(Q_1 + Q_2)$—is less than the cost of producing each alone—$C(Q_1) + C(Q_2)$. Clearly, S measures the percentage saving as a result of producing them jointly rather than individually. Thus, in the case of the Martin Company,

$$S = \frac{\$12 \text{ million} + \$6 \text{ million} - \$15 \text{ million}}{\$15 \text{ million}} = 0.20,$$

which means that there is a 20 percent saving of this sort. The larger the value of S, the bigger the economies of scope.

To managers, it is very important that economies of scope be recognized and exploited. For example, a small airline may find that its regularly scheduled passenger service can be profitably supplemented by providing cargo services, since the cost of flying both passengers and cargo is much less than that of specializing in either passenger or cargo services. Similarly, in the trucking industry, there are substantial economies, particularly for small firms, in combining short hauls, intermediate hauls, and long hauls. A firm's managers must constantly be alert to the potential profitability of extending its product line, or of adding new product lines. Thus, when the Xerox Corporation introduced its 9700 electronic printer, it had to consider whether and to what extent this new product line complemented its existing copier business, and whether there were economies of scope.

Break-Even Analysis

An analytical tool frequently employed by managerial economists is the break-even chart, an important application of cost functions. Generally, a break-even chart assumes that the firm's average variable costs are constant in the relevant output range; hence, the firm's total cost function is assumed to be a straight line. Since average variable cost is constant, the extra cost of an extra unit—marginal cost—must be constant too, and equal to average variable cost. In Figure 9.18, we assume that the Carson Company's fixed costs are $600,000 per month and that its variable costs are $2 per unit of output per month.

To construct a break-even chart, you plot the firm's total revenue curve on the same chart with its total cost function. Typically, it is assumed that the price the firm receives for its product will not be affected by the amount it sells, with the result that total revenue is proportional to output. Consequently, the total revenue curve is a straight line through the origin. Figure 9.18 shows the Carson Company's total revenue curve, assuming that the price of the product will be $3 per unit. The break-even chart, which combines the total cost function and the total revenue curve, shows the monthly profit or loss resulting from each sales level. For example, Figure 9.18 shows that if the Carson Company

FIGURE
9.18

Break-Even Chart, Carson Company

The break-even point, the output level that must be reached if the firm is to avoid losses, is 600,000 units of output per month.

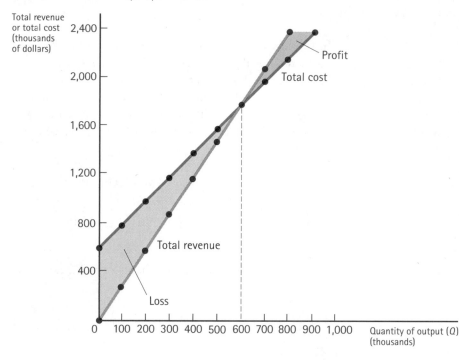

sells 300,000 units per month, it will make a loss of $300,000 per month. The chart also shows the **break-even point,** the output level that must be reached if the firm is to avoid losses; in Figure 9.18, the break-even point is 600,000 units of output per month. In effect, a break-even chart can be regarded as a simplified version of Figure 2.12 for output levels up to about Q_0.

Under the right conditions, break-even charts can produce useful projections of the effect of the output rate on costs, receipts, and profits. For example, a firm may use a break-even chart to determine the effect of a projected decline in sales on profits. Or it may use it to determine how many units of a particular product it must sell in order to break even. However, break-even charts must be used with caution, since the assumptions underlying them may be inappropriate. If the product price is highly variable or if costs are difficult to predict, the estimated total cost function and the estimated total revenue curve may be subject to substantial errors.

Break-even charts are used extensively. It is worth noting that although the total cost function generally is assumed to be a straight line in break-even charts, this assumption can easily be dropped and a curvilinear total cost function can be used instead. But for fairly small changes in output, a linear approximation is probably good enough in many cases. Also, as was pointed out above, empirical studies suggest that the total cost function is often close to linear, as long as the firm is not operating at or close to capacity.

Algebraic Break–Even Analysis

In the previous section, we showed how a break-even analysis can be carried out geometrically; now let's see how such an analysis can be carried out algebraically. Let P be the price of the good, Q be the quantity produced and sold, AVC be the average variable cost, and TFC be the firm's total fixed cost. The break-even point is the output, Q_B, at which total revenue equals total cost. Thus, since total revenue equals PQ and total cost equals $TFC + AVC \cdot Q$, it follows that

$$PQ_B = TFC + AVC \cdot Q_B,$$
$$(P - AVC)Q_B = TFC$$
$$Q_B = \frac{TFC}{P - AVC}. \tag{9.8}$$

In the case of the Carson Company, $P = \$3$, $AVC = \$2$, and $TFC = \$600,000$. Consequently

$$Q_B = \frac{600,000}{3 - 2} = 600,000$$

Mr. Martin Gets Chewed Out by the Boss*

John Martin, an accountant at a small company that manufactures and sells three types of desks, constructed a break-even chart for the company as a whole. He used as a measure of output the total number of desks produced during each year. To obtain an estimate of the average variable cost of a desk, he took the mean of the average variable costs of the three types of desks. To obtain an estimate of the price of a desk, he took the mean of the prices of the three types of desks. Using these figures, he constructed a break-even chart (based on linear total cost and total revenue curves) that indicated that the company was operating at an output well above the break-even point and that profit would increase rapidly as output increased.

When Mr. Martin presented these findings, the company's president, Susan Rogers, said that they were misleading because the analysis lumped together the three types of desks. For one type, the plant was operating at capacity, and marginal cost would increase substantially if output were increased. For another type of desk, it had become increasingly obvious that the price was too high, and it was about to be reduced. For the third type of desk, only a few were produced, so it was incorrect to weight it as heavily as the other two types in the analysis. Ms. Rogers also pointed out that as the firm's output increased, the first and second types accounted for bigger and bigger shares of total output.

If you were a consultant to this company, which of the points raised by Ms. Rogers would you regard as relevant, and why?

*This section is based on an actual case, although the numbers and situation have been disguised somewhat.

which agrees with our finding based on Figure 9.18. Of course, this algebraic procedure will always produce the same results as the geometric procedure in the previous section.

Profit Contribution Analysis

In making short-run decisions, firms often find it useful to carry out various types of profit contribution analysis. The profit contribution is the difference between total revenue and total variable cost; on a per-unit basis, it is equal to price minus average variable cost. Thus, in the case of the Carson Company, where price is $3 and average variable cost is $2, the per-unit profit contribution is $3 − $2, or $1. This profit contribution can be used to help pay the firm's fixed costs, and, once these costs are met, to build up the firm's profits.

To illustrate how profit contribution analysis can be used, suppose that the Carson Company wants to determine how many units of output it will have to produce and sell to earn a profit of $1 million per month. The required sales equals

$$Q = \frac{\text{total fixed cost} + \text{profit target}}{\text{profit contribution (per unit)}}$$

$$= \frac{\$600,000 + \$1,000,000}{\$1}$$

$$= 1,600,000 \text{ units.}$$

As another example, suppose that the Carson Company is selling only 500,000 units per month, which means that it is losing $100,000 per month. The firm's marketing director hopes to land an order for 50,000 units of the firm's product. How much will this order reduce the firm's loss? To find out, one can multiply the order size (50,000 units) by the per-unit profit contribution ($1) to get the increase in profit (or reduction in loss, which is the case here); the result is $50,000.

Summary

1. Managerial economists define the cost of producing a particular product as the value of the other products that the resources used in its production could have produced instead. This is the product's opportunity cost, and it may differ from historical cost, which is generally the basis for accounting statements.

2. In the short run, it is important to distinguish between a firm's fixed and variable costs. The firm's total and average costs, total and average fixed costs, and total and average variable costs can all be plotted against output. So can the firm's marginal cost. The resulting cost functions, or cost curves (as they are often called), show how changes in output will affect the firm's costs, a major concern of any firm.

3. The long-run average cost function shows the minimum cost per unit of producing each output level when any desired scale of plant can be built. The long-run average cost function is tangent to each of the short-run average cost functions at the output where the plant corresponding to the short-run average cost function is optimal. The long-run average cost curve is important to managers because it shows the extent to which larger plants have cost advantages over smaller ones.

4. Many studies based on the statistical analysis of cross-section and time-series data, as well as engineering studies, have been carried out to estimate the cost functions of particular firms. The regression techniques described in Chapter 5 have played an important role here. Both short- and long-run cost functions can be estimated, as illustrated by the many examples we have considered. A detailed account of the relevant procedures and problems has been given.

5. In choosing among plants, a major consideration is flexibility if the output of the plant is highly uncertain. Some plants, while they have higher costs than others at the most likely output, have lower costs than the others over a wide range of output. If one cannot predict output reasonably well, flexible plants of this sort may be best.

6. Economies of scope occur when the cost of producing two (or more) products jointly is less than the cost of producing them separately. Such economies may arise because production facilities used to make one product can also be used to make another product, or because by-products resulting from the making of one product can be useful in making other products.

7. Break-even analysis compares total revenue and total cost, graphically or algebraically. A break-even chart combines the total cost function and the total revenue curve, both of which are generally assumed to be linear, and shows the profit or loss resulting from each sales level. The break-even point is the sales level that must be achieved if the firm is to avoid losses. Firms often find it useful to carry out various types of profit contribution analysis. The profit contribution is the difference between total revenue and total variable cost; on a per-unit basis, it is equal to price minus average variable cost.

Problems

1. In 1985, the National Academy of Engineering, using data developed at the Massachusetts Institute of Technology, estimated the costs of producing steel with three different technologies: (1) coke, blast furnace, basic oxygen furnace, ingots, and finishing mills, (2) coke, blast furnace, basic oxygen furnace, continuous casting, and finishing mills, and (3) steel scrap, electric arc furnace, continuous casting, and finishing mills. Under reasonable assumptions concerning input prices, the estimated average costs per ton were as follows:

Cost category	Coke, blast furnaces, basic oxygen furnace, ingots, finishing mills	Coke, blast furnaces, basic oxygen furnace, continuous casting, finishing mills	Steel scrap, electric arc furnace, continuous casting, finishing mills
Process materials	$148.34	$136.19	$122.78
Energy	21.15	15.98	41.58
Direct labor	83.43	75.09	67.43
Capital	102.06	99.93	54.08
Other	46.74	41.67	24.47
Total	$401.73	$368.86	$310.34

a. The academy's report concludes that "unless significant changes occur in other technologies, the electric-furnace continuous-casting route will dominate domestic production." Why?

b. At the same time, the report notes that the price of scrap (which is used in this route) "could increase as electric furnace production expands because of the increased demand." Why is this relevant?

c. The academy also concludes that, regardless of which of these technologies is used, cost per ton is about 25 to 30 percent higher if wages are $26 per hour rather than $2 per hour. What does this imply concerning the competitiveness of U.S. steel producers relative to producers in other countries that pay wages far below U.S. levels?

d. If the above cost figures are long-run average costs, under what circumstances would they also equal long-run marginal costs?

2. The Haverford Company is considering three types of plants to make a particular electronic device. Plant A is much more highly automated than plant B, which in turn is more highly automated than plant C. For each type of plant, average variable cost is constant so long as output is less than capacity, which is the maximum output of the plant. The cost structure for each type of plant is as follows:

	Plant A	Plant B	Plant C
Average Variable Costs			
Labor	$1.10	$2.40	$3.70
Materials	0.90	1.20	1.80
Other	0.50	2.40	2.00
Total	$2.50	$6.00	$7.50
Total fixed costs	$300,000	$75,000	$25,000
Annual capacity	200,000	100,00	50,000

a. Derive the average cost of producing 100,000, 200,000, 300,000, and 400,000 devices per year with plant A. (For outputs exceeding the capacity of a single plant, assume that more than one plant of this type is built.)

b. Derive the average cost of producing 100,000, 200,000, 300,000, and 400,000 devices per year with plant B.

c. Derive the average cost of producing 100,000, 200,000, 300,000, and 400,000 devices per year with plant C.

d. Using the results of parts a through c, plot the points on the long-run average cost curve for the production of these electronic devices for outputs of 100,000, 200,000, and 400,000 devices per year.

3. The Abner Corporation, a retail seller of television sets, wants to determine how many television sets it must sell in order to earn a profit of $10,000

per month. The price of each television set is $300, and the average variable cost is $100.

   a. What is the required sales volume if the Abner Corporation's monthly fixed costs are $5,000 per month?

   b. If the firm were to sell each television set at a price of $350 rather than $300, what would be the required sales volume?

   c. If the price is $350, and if average variable cost is $85 rather than $100, what would be the required sales volume?

4. According to a statistical study, the following relationship exists between an electric light and power plant's fuel costs (C) and its eight-hour output as a percent of capacity (Q):

$$C = 16.68 + 0.125Q + 0.00439Q^2.$$

   a. When Q increases from 50 to 51, what is the increase in the cost of fuel for this electric plant?

   b. Of what use might the result in part a be to the plant's managers?

   c. Derive the marginal (fuel) cost curve for this plant, and indicate how it might be used by the plant's managers.

5. The following table pertains to the Lincoln Company. Fill in the blanks:

Output	Total cost	Total fixed cost	Total variable cost	Average fixed cost	Average variable cost
0	50	____	____	____	____
1	75	____	____	____	____
2	100	____	____	____	____
3	120	____	____	____	____
4	135	____	____	____	____
5	150	____	____	____	____
6	190	____	____	____	____
7	260	____	____	____	____

6. The Deering Manufacturing Company's short-run average cost function in 1999 is

$$AC = 3 + 4Q,$$

where AC is the firm's average cost (in dollars per pound of the product), and Q is its output rate.

   a. Obtain an equation for the firm's short-run total cost function.

   b. Does the firm have any fixed costs? Explain.

   c. If the price of the Deering Manufacturing Company's product (per pound) is $3, is the firm making profits or losses? Explain.

   d. Derive an equation for the firm's marginal cost function.

7. The president of the Tacke Corporation believes that statistical research by his staff shows that the firm's long-run total cost curve can be represented as:

$$TC = \alpha_0 Q^{\alpha_1} P_L^{\alpha_2} P_K^{\alpha_3}$$

where TC is the firm's total cost, Q is its output, P_L is the price of labor, and P_K is the price of capital.

a. Tacke's president says that α_1 measures the elasticity of cost with respect to output—that is, the percentage change in total cost resulting from a 1 percent change in output. Is he correct? Why or why not?

b. He also says that if $\alpha_1 < 1$, economies of scale are indicated, whereas if $\alpha_1 > 1$, diseconomies of scale are indicated. Is he correct? Why or why not?

c. According to Tacke's president, the αs can be estimated by regressing log (TC/P_K) on log Q and log (P_L/P_K). Is he correct? Why or why not?

8. Engineers sometimes rely on the "0.6 rule," which states that the increase in cost is given by the increase in capacity raised to the 0.6 power; that is,

$$C_2 = C_1 (X_2/X_1)^{0.6},$$

where C_1 and C_2 are the costs of two pieces of equipment, and X_1 and X_2 are their respective capacities.

a. Does the 0.6 rule suggest economies of scale?

b. Some experts have stated that in the chemical and metal industries, the 0.6 rule can be applied to entire plants rather than individual pieces of equipment. If so, will the long-run average cost curve in these industries tend to be negatively sloped?

c. Can you think of a way to test whether this rule is correct?

9. The Dijon Company's total variable cost function is:

$$TVC = 50Q - 10Q^2 + Q^3,$$

where Q is the number of units of output produced.

a. What is the output level where marginal cost is a minimum?

b. What is the output level where average variable cost is a minimum?

c. What is the value of average variable cost and marginal cost at the output specified in the answer to part b?

10. The Berwyn Company is considering the addition of a new product to its product line. The firm has plenty of excess manufacturing capacity to produce the new product, and its total fixed costs would be unaffected if the new product were added to its line. Nonetheless, the firm's accountants decide that a reasonable share of the firm's present fixed costs should be allocated to the new product. Specifically, they decide that a $300,000 fixed

charge will be absorbed by the new product. The variable cost per unit of making and selling the new product is $14, which is composed of the following:

Direct labor	$8.20
Direct materials	1.90
Other	3.90
Total	$14.00

a. Should the Berwyn Company add the new product to its line if it can sell about 10,000 units of this product at a price of $25?

b. Should it add the new product if it can sell about 10,000 units at a price of $20?

c. Should it add the new product if it can sell about 10,000 units at a price of $15?

d. What is the minimum price (that the firm can get for the new product) that will make it worthwhile to add the new product to its line?

11. The Jolson Corporation produces 1,000 wood cabinets and 500 wood desks per year, the total cost being $30,000. If the firm produced 1,000 wood cabinets only, the cost would be $23,000. If the firm produced 500 wood desks only, the cost would be $11,000.

a. Calculate the degree of economies of scope.

b. Why do economies of scope exist?

12. The Smith Company made and sold 10,000 metal tables last year. When output was between 5,000 and 10,000 tables, its average variable cost was $24. In this output range, each table contributed 60 percent of its revenue to fixed costs and profits.

a. What was the price per table?

b. If the Smith Company increases its price by 10 percent, how many tables will it have to sell next year to obtain the same profit as last year?

c. If the Smith Company increases its price by 10 percent, and if its average variable cost increases by 8 percent as a result of wage increases, how many tables will it have to sell next year to obtain the same profit as last year?

Appendix: Break–Even Analysis and Operating Leverage

Managers must continually make comparisons among alternative systems of production. Should one type of plant be replaced by another? How does your plant stack up against your competitor's? Break-even analysis can be extended to help make such comparisons more effective. In this appendix, we show how you can analyze how total costs and profits vary with output, depending on how automated or mechanized the plant may be. This is an important topic, since top-level managers often have to make such comparisons.

At the outset, it is essential to recognize that some plants, because they are much more mechanized than others, have relatively high fixed costs but relatively low average variable costs. Consider firms I, II, and III in Figure 9.19. Firm I's plant has fixed costs of $100,000 per month, which are much higher than those of the plants operated by firm II or III; however, its average variable cost of $2 is much lower than that of firm II or III. Essentially, firm I has substituted capital for labor and materials. It has built a highly automated plant with high fixed costs, but low average variable cost.

At the opposite extreme, firm III has built a plant with low fixed costs but high average variable cost. Because it has not invested a great deal in plant and equipment, its total fixed costs are only $25,000 per month, which is much less than for firm I or II. However, because of the relatively low level of mechanization at its plant, firm III's average variable cost is $4, considerably higher than at the other two firms. Relative to firm I, firm III uses more labor and materials and less capital.

Firm II's plant occupies a middle position (between firms I and III) in this regard. Its total fixed cost of $60,000 is less than firm I's but more than firm III's, and its average variable cost of $3 is greater than firm I's but less than firm III's. It has not automated its plant to the extent that firm I has, but it has done more in this regard than firm III.

In comparing these plants, one of the important things to consider is the **degree of operating leverage,** which is defined as the percentage change in profit resulting from a 1 percent change in the number of units of product sold. Specifically,

$$\text{Degree of operating leverage} = \frac{\text{percentage change in profit}}{\text{percentage change in quantity sold}}$$

$$= \frac{\Delta\pi/\pi}{\Delta Q/Q}$$

$$= \frac{\Delta\pi}{\Delta Q}\left(\frac{Q}{\pi}\right) \quad \text{or} \quad \frac{d\pi}{dQ}\left(\frac{Q}{\pi}\right), \tag{9.9}$$

where π is the firm's profits, and Q is the quantity sold.

The degree of operating leverage, because it measures how a given change in sales volume affects profits, is of great importance. If firm I is selling 40,000 units per month, and if we let $\Delta Q = 10,000$ units, the degree of operating leverage equals

$$\frac{\Delta\pi}{\Delta Q}\left(\frac{Q}{\pi}\right) = \frac{\$50,000 - \$20,000}{10,000}\left(\frac{40,000}{\$20,000}\right) = 6,$$

FIGURE
9.19

Break-Even Analysis and Operating Leverage

Firm I has relatively high fixed costs and low variable costs; firm III has relatively low fixed costs and high variable costs; and firm II is in the middle.

Firm I

Total fixed cost = $100,000
Average variable cost = $2
Selling price = $5

Quantity sold	Total revenue	Total cost	Total profit
10,000	$ 50,000	$120,000	$-70,000
20,000	100,000	140,000	-40,000
30,000	150,000	160,000	-10,000
40,000	200,000	180,000	20,000
50,000	250,000	200,000	50,000

Firm II

Total fixed cost = $60,000
Average variable cost = $3
Selling price = $5

Quantity sold	Total revenue	Total cost	Total profit
10,000	$ 50,000	$ 90,000	$-40,000
20,000	100,000	120,000	-20,000
30,000	150,000	150,000	0
40,000	200,000	180,000	20,000
50,000	250,000	210,000	40,000

Firm III

Total fixed cost = $25,000
Average variable cost = $4
Selling price = $5

Quantity sold	Total revenue	Total cost	Total profit
10,000	$ 50,000	$ 65,000	$-15,000
20,000	100,000	105,000	-5,000
30,000	150,000	145,000	5,000
40,000	200,000	185,000	15,000
50,000	250,000	225,000	25,000

since Figure 9.19 shows that if $\Delta Q = 10{,}000$ units, $\Delta\pi = \$50{,}000 - \$20{,}000$. (Why? Because if Q changes from 40,000 to 50,000 units, π changes from $20,000 to $50,000.) Thus, a 1 percent increase in quantity sold results in a 6 percent increase in profits.

If both the total revenue curve and the total cost function are linear, as in Figure 9.19, a simple way to calculate the degree of operating leverage when output equals Q is to use the following formula:

$$\text{Degree of operating leverage} = \frac{Q(P - AVC)}{Q(P - AVC) - TFC}, \qquad (9.10)$$

where P equals selling price, AVC equals average variable cost, and TFC equals total fixed cost. It can be shown that if both the total revenue curve and the total cost function are linear, equation (9.10) yields the same result as equation (9.9). Thus, for firm I, if $Q = 40{,}000$, equation (9.10) says that the degree of operating leverage equals

$$\frac{Q(P - AVC)}{Q(P - AVC) - TFC} = \frac{\$40{,}000(\$5 - \$2)}{40{,}000(\$5 - \$2) - \$100{,}000}$$

$$= \frac{\$120{,}000}{\$120{,}000 - \$100{,}000} = 6$$

since P equals $5, AVC equals $2, and TFC equals $100,000. The result is the same as in the previous paragraph. (In both cases, it is 6.)

It is interesting and important to compare the degree of operating leverage of the three firms, since this comparison reveals a great deal about how these plants differ. If $Q = 40{,}000$, the degree of operating leverage for firm II equals

$$\frac{Q(P - AVC)}{Q(P - AVC) - TFC} = \frac{\$40{,}000(\$5 - \$3)}{40{,}000(\$5 - \$3) - \$60{,}000} = 4.$$

For firm III, it equals

$$\frac{Q(P - AVC)}{Q(P - AVC) - TFC} = \frac{\$40{,}000(\$5 - \$4)}{40{,}000(\$5 - \$4) - \$25{,}000} = 2.67.$$

Thus, a 1 percent increase in sales volume results in a 6 percent increase in profit at firm I, a 4 percent increase in profit at firm II, and a 2.67 percent increase in profit at firm III. Clearly, firm I's profits are much more sensitive to changes in sales volume than firm III's profits; firm II is in the middle in this regard.

PART

4

Market Structure,
Strategic Behavior,
and Pricing

Perfect Competition, Monopoly, and Monopolistic Competition

Texaco is one of the giants of U.S. industry; it produces oil. Two central decisions that Glenn Tilton, chairman of the company, and his colleagues have to make are: What should be the firm's output rate? What price should it charge? Regardless of whether a firm is high-tech or low-tech, young or old, its executives must address these same questions, and the answers depend on the structure of the market. In this chapter, we take up the results for three market structures: perfect competition, monopoly, and monopolistic competition. (In the next chapter, we will study the fourth market structure—oligopoly.) Besides considering how firms should price their products and set their output rates, we also take up the way in which they should determine their advertising expenditures. Although the model presented here is a simple one, it should provide some useful insights into this difficult and important problem.

Market Structure

As was pointed out in Chapter 1, a **market** consists of a group of firms and individuals who are in touch with each other in order to buy or sell some good or service. Economists have generally found it useful to classify markets into four broad types: **perfect competition, monopoly, monopolistic competition, and oligopoly.** In perfect competition and monopolistic competition, there are *many* sellers, each of which produces only a small part of the industry's output. In monopoly, on the other hand, the industry consists of only a *single* seller. Oligopoly is an intermediate case where there are a *few* sellers. Thus, Baltimore Gas and Electric, if it is the only supplier of electricity in a particular market, is a monopoly. And since there are only a small number of automobile manufacturers, the market for automobiles is an oligopoly.

Market structures vary substantially in the extent to which an individual firm controls its price. A firm under perfect competition has *no control* over price. For example, a farm producing corn (which for present purposes can be regarded as a perfectly competitive firm) has no control over the price of corn. On the other hand, a monopolist is likely to have *considerable control* over price. In the absence of public regulation, Baltimore Gas and Electric would have considerable control over the price of electricity in Baltimore. A firm under monopolistic competition or oligopoly is likely to have *less* control over price than a monopolist and *more* control over price than a perfectly competitive firm.

These market structures also vary in the extent to which the firms in an industry produce standardized (that is, identical) products. Firms in a perfectly competitive market all produce *identical* products. Thus, one farmer's wheat is essentially the same as another farmer's. In a monopolistically competitive industry like shirt manufacturing, firms produce *somewhat different* products. One firm's shirts differ in style and quality from another firm's shirts. In an oligopoly, firms *sometimes,* but not always, produce identical products. And in a monopoly, there can be *no difference* among firms in their products, since the industry contains only one firm.

How easily firms can enter the industry differs from one market structure to another. In perfect competition, **barriers to entry** are *low.* Thus, only a small investment is required to enter many parts of agriculture. Similarly, there are *low* barriers to entry in monopolistic competition. But in oligopolies such as auto manufacturing and oil refining, there tend to be *very considerable* barriers to entry because it is so expensive to build an auto plant or an oil refinery (and for many other reasons too). In monopoly, entry is *blocked;* once entry occurs, the monopoly no longer exists.

Market structures also differ in the extent to which firms compete on the basis of advertising and differences in product characteristics, rather than price. In perfect competition, there is *no* nonprice competition. (If every farmer produces identical corn, and has to take the market price, why devote some of the proceeds to advertising?) In monopolistic competition, there is *considerable emphasis* on nonprice competition. Thus, shirt manufacturers compete by trying to develop better styles and by advertising to accentuate the advantages of their product lines. Oligopolies also tend to rely *heavily* on nonprice competition. For

TABLE 10.1

Characteristics of Perfect Competition, Monopolistic Competition, Oligopoly, and Monopoly

Market structure	Examples	Number of producers	Type of product	Power of firm over price	Barriers to entry	Nonprice competition
Perfect competition	Parts of agriculture are reasonably close	Many	Standardized	None	Low	None
Monopolistic competition	Retail trade	Many	Differentiated	Some	Low	Advertising and product differentiation
Oligopoly	Computers, oil, steel	Few	Standardized or differentiated	Some	High	Advertising and product differentiation
Monopoly	Public utilities	One	Unique product	Considerable	Very high	Advertising

example, computer firms try to increase their sales by building better computers and by advertising. Monopolists also engage in advertising, although this advertising is directed not at capturing the sales of other firms in the industry, since no other firms exist, but rather at increasing total market demand.

Table 10.1 provides a summary of many of the key features of each market structure. Be sure to look this table over before proceeding further.

Market Price under Perfect Competition

In a perfectly competitive industry, market price, as we saw in Chapter 1, is determined by the market demand and supply curves. There is a market demand curve, which shows the total amount that individual buyers of the commodity will purchase, and a market supply curve, which shows the total amount that individual suppliers of the commodity will supply. Figure 10.1 shows the market demand and supply curves for a good produced in a perfectly competitive market. As is ordinarily the case, the market supply curve slopes upward to the right. That is, increases in price generally result in higher industry output because managers find it profitable to expand production. Also, in accord with Chapters 1 and 3, the market demand curve slopes downward to the right. That is, increases in price generally result in less of the product's being demanded.

FIGURE
10.1

Determination of Price in a Perfectly Competitive Market

Equilibrium price is $10, and equilibrium quantity is 24 thousand units.

To determine the equilibrium price, which is the price that will eventually prevail in this market, we must find the price where market supply equals market demand.[1] The demand curve in Figure 10.1 is

$$P = 22 - 0.5Q_D,\qquad(10.1)$$

where P is the price (in dollars) of this good, and Q_D is the quantity demanded (in thousands of units). The supply curve in Figure 10.1 is

$$P = 4 + 0.25Q_S,\qquad(10.2)$$

where Q_S is the quantity supplied. Since the equilibrium price is at the level where Q_D (the quantity demanded) equals Q_S (the quantity supplied),

$$22 - 0.5Q = 4 + 0.25Q$$
$$18 = 0.75Q$$
$$Q = 24.$$

[1]Recall from Chapter 1 that an equilibrium price is a price that can be maintained. If conditions do not change, the actual price tends to equal the equilibrium price.

Substituting 24 for Q_D in equation (10.1), we find that $P = \$10$. [If we substitute 24 for Q_S in equation (10.2), we get the same result.] Thus, as shown in Figure 10.1, price would be expected to equal $10, and output would be expected to equal 24 thousand units.

While Figure 10.1 shows that both total quantity demanded and total quantity supplied depend on price, this does not mean that an individual firm can affect price. According to the market demand curve in equation (10.1),

$$P = 22 - 0.5Q_D.$$

If there are 1,000 firms in this market, each produces, on the average, only 24 units of the product. Even if an individual firm doubles its output (from 24 to 48 units), the effect on price is minuscule. Specifically, an increase in output of 24 units results in a price reduction of only 1.2 cents—or about 0.1 percent.[2] What this means is that the demand curve for the output of an individual firm under perfect competition is essentially *horizontal*. Thus, whereas the demand curve for the output of the entire industry slopes downward to the right (as shown in Figure 10.1), the demand curve for the output of any single firm can be regarded as horizontal.

Shifts in Supply and Demand Curves

Shifts in the market supply or demand curves result in changes in price (recall Chapter 1). For example, if the supply curve in Figure 10.1 shifts to the left, the price would be expected to rise. Shifts in market supply and demand curves are of the utmost significance to managers, who must try to anticipate their occurrence and their effects—and respond to them as best they can. Consider the case of the Coca-Cola Company, which buys about 10 percent of all sugar sold in the United States. Because of shifts in sugar's supply and demand curves (which resulted in worldwide shortages), the price of beet and cane sugar rose from 19 cents per pound in September 1978 to 26 cents per pound in January 1979. The effect on Coca-Cola was particularly severe, since a change of 1 cent per pound in sugar prices can cause a $20 million swing in the firm's operating profits. Its managers responded (in accord with the principles set forth in Chapter 7) by switching from sugar to high-fructose corn sweeteners, which are cheaper than sugar.

For present purposes, the point is that managers must understand the factors affecting the supply and demand curves of products they buy and sell.

---

[2]If output increases by 24 units, Q increases by 0.024, since Q is measured in thousands of units. If Q increases by 0.024, P falls by $0.5(0.024) = 0.012$, according to the demand curve in equation (10.1). Since P is measured in dollars, this amounts to 1.2 cents.

There is no need here to dwell at length on the factors causing shifts in demand curves, since they have been discussed in Chapter 3. But it is worth recalling from Chapter 1 that two of the most important factors causing shifts in supply curves are improvements in technology (discussed in Chapter 8) and changes in input prices. Improvements in technology tend to shift a product's supply curve to the right, since they permit firms to reduce their costs. On the other hand, increases in input prices tend to shift a product's supply curve to the left, since they push up the firms' costs. For agricultural products, the supply curve also shifts in response to weather conditions. For example, in 1986, a drought in Brazil cut the coffee crop by about 60 percent; this caused a significant shift to the left of the supply curve for coffee.

The Output Decision of a Perfectly Competitive Firm

How much output should a perfectly competitive firm produce? As we saw in the section before last, a perfectly competitive firm cannot affect the market price of its product, and it can sell any amount of its product that it wants (within its capabilities) at the market price. To illustrate the firm's situation, consider the example in Table 10.2. The market price is $20 a unit, and the firm can produce as much as it chooses. Hence, the firm's total revenue at various output rates is given in column 3 of Table 10.2. The firm's total fixed cost, total variable cost, and total cost are given in columns 4, 5, and 6 of Table 10.2. Finally, the last column shows the firm's total profit.

TABLE 10.2

Cost and Revenue, Perfectly Competitive Firm

Units of output per period	Price (dollars)	Total revenue (dollars)	Total fixed cost (dollars)	Total variable cost (dollars)	Total cost (dollars)	Total profit (dollars)
0	20	0	24	0	24	−24
1	20	20	24	4	28	−8
2	20	40	24	6	30	10
3	20	60	24	10	34	26
4	20	80	24	16	40	40
5	20	100	24	26	50	50
6	20	120	24	46	70	50
7	20	140	24	76	100	40
8	20	160	24	138	162	−2

FIGURE
10.2

Relationship between Total Cost and Total Revenue, Perfectly Competitive Firm

The output rate that will maximize the firm's profits is either 5 or 6 units per time period. At either of these output rates, profit (total revenue minus total cost) equals $50.

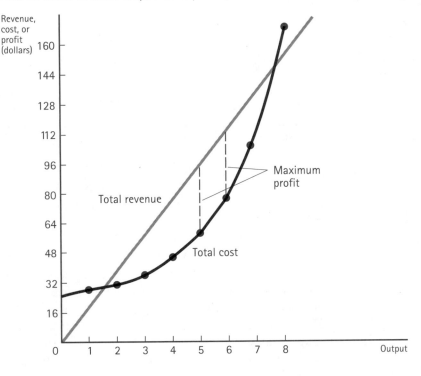

Figure 10.2 shows the relationship between total revenue and total cost, on the one hand, and output, on the other. The vertical distance between the total revenue curve and the total cost curve is the profit at the corresponding output rate. Below 2 units of output and above 7 units of output, this distance is negative. Since the firm can sell either large or small volumes of output at the same price per unit, the total revenue curve is a straight line through the origin. (Specifically, total revenue = price times quantity, so since price is constant, total revenue is proportional to quantity.) Since a perfectly competitive firm takes the price as given, this will always be true under perfect competition.

Both Table 10.2 and Figure 10.2 show that the output rate that will maximize the firm's profits is either 5 or 6 units per time period. These are the out-

TABLE
10.3

Marginal Revenue and Marginal Cost, Perfectly Competitive Firm

Output per period	Marginal revenue (dollars)	Marginal cost[a] (dollars)
1	20	4
2	20	2
3	20	4
4	20	6
5	20	10
6	20	20
7	20	30
8	20	62

[a]This is the marginal cost between the indicated output level 1 unit less than this output level.

put rates where the profit figure in the last column of Table 10.2 is the highest and where the vertical distance between the total revenue and total cost curves in Figure 10.2 is the largest.[3]

It is worthwhile to present the marginal revenue and marginal cost curves, as well as the total revenue and total cost curves. Table 10.3 shows marginal revenue and marginal cost at each output rate. Figure 10.3 shows the resulting marginal revenue and marginal cost curves. Because the firm takes the price as a given, which is constant for all units that it may wish to sell, marginal revenue equals price, since the change in total revenue resulting from a 1-unit change in sales necessarily equals the price. (If the price of a bushel of wheat is $3, then the extra revenue from selling one more bushel is $3.) Thus the marginal revenue curve is the same as the firm's demand curve, which (for reasons discussed above) is horizontal.

The central point to note is that the maximum profit is achieved at the output rate where *price (= marginal revenue) equals marginal cost.* Both the figures in Table 10.3 and the curves in Figure 10.3 indicate that price equals marginal cost at an output rate of between 5 and 6 units, which we know from Table 10.2 or Figure 10.2 to be the profit-maximizing outputs.

[3]If the firm can produce a fractional number of units per time period and if the firm's total cost curve is linear between outputs of 5 and 6 units per time period, profits will be maximized if the firm produces 5 or 6 units per time period—or any output in between.

FIGURE
10.3

Marginal Revenue and Marginal Cost, Perfectly Competitive Firm

When output is at the profit-maximizing level of 5 or 6 units, price (= marginal revenue) equals marginal cost.

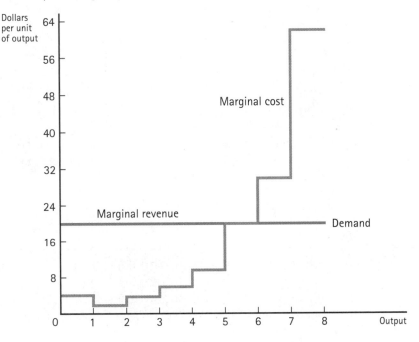

Setting Marginal Cost Equal to Price

In general, the optimal output for a perfectly competitive firm will be the one where marginal cost equals price. To prove that this is the case, let the total cost be *TC*. The equation for total profit per period of time is

$$\pi = PQ - TC,$$

where *P* is the price of the product, and *Q* is the output of the firm. If π is at a maximum, then its derivative with respect to *Q* equals zero. In other words,

$$\frac{d\pi}{dQ} = \frac{d(PQ - TC)}{dQ} = 0.$$

Because $dPQ/dQ = P$, it follows that

$$P - \frac{dTC}{dQ} = 0, \tag{10.3}$$

which means that price must equal marginal cost (since dTC/dQ is marginal cost). This is what we set out to prove. In addition, it is worth noting that the second-order condition for a maximum is

$$\frac{d^2TC}{dQ^2} > 0,$$

which means that marginal cost must be rising. (This must be true because $d^2\pi/dQ^2$ must be negative if this is a maximum, and if $d^2\pi/dQ^2$ is negative, d^2TC/dQ^2 must be positive.)

Even if a firm is doing its best, it may not be able to earn a profit. If the price is P_2 in Figure 10.4, short-run average costs exceed the price at all pos-

FIGURE
10.4

Short–Run Average and Marginal Cost Curves

If price is P_0, the firm will produce an output of X; if price is P_2, it will produce an output of Y; and if price is less than P_3, it will produce nothing.

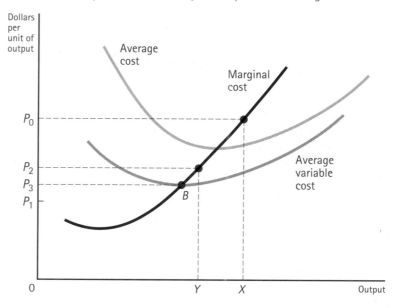

sible outputs. Because the short run is too short (by definition) to permit the firm to alter the scale of its plant, it cannot liquidate its plant in the short run. All the firm can do is to produce at a loss or discontinue production. Its decision should depend on whether the price of the product will cover average variable costs. If there exists an output rate at which price exceeds average variable costs, it will pay the firm to produce, despite the fact that price does not cover average total costs. If there does not exist an output rate at which price exceeds average variable costs, the firm is better off producing nothing at all. Hence, if the average variable cost curve is as shown in Figure 10.4, the firm will produce if the price is P_2, but not if it is P_1.

To see why this is so, it is essential to recognize that if the firm produces nothing, it must still pay its fixed cost. Thus, if the loss resulting from production is less than the firm's fixed cost (the loss from shutting down), it is more profitable (in the sense that losses are smaller) to produce than not to produce. On a per-unit basis, this implies that it is better to produce than to discontinue production if the loss per unit of production is less than average fixed cost, that is, if $ATC - P < AFC$, where ATC is average total cost, P is price, and AFC is average fixed cost. But this will be so if $ATC < AFC + P$, since P has merely been added to both sides of the inequality. Subtracting AFC from both sides, this will be so if $ATC - AFC < P$. But $ATC - AFC$ is average variable cost, which means that we have shown what we set out to show: that it is better to produce than to discontinue production if price exceeds average variable cost.

To summarize, if the firm maximizes profit or minimizes loss, it sets its output rate so that short-run marginal cost equals price. But this proposition, like most others, has an exception: if the market price is below the firm's average variable costs at every conceivable output rate, the firm will minimize losses by discontinuing production.

As an illustration, consider the Green Company, a perfectly competitive firm with the following total cost function:

$$TC = 800 + 6Q + 2Q^2,$$

where TC is total cost (in dollars), and Q is the firm's output per day. If the price of its product equals $30, the firm should set its output so that

$$MC = \frac{dTC}{dQ} = 6 + 4Q = 30. \tag{10.4}$$

In other words, it should set marginal cost equal to price ($30). Solving equation (10.4) for Q, we find that the firm should set output equal to 6 units per day. To make sure that price is no less than average variable cost at this out-

CONSULTANT'S CORNER

Forecasting the Price of Salmon*

A major producer of consumer goods set out to forecast the price of fresh salmon three years ahead. Such a forecast was needed in deciding whether the firm should enter the business of supplying salmon. Its analysts estimated the quantity of fresh salmon that would be supplied three years ahead. Because of substantial plans to expand the production of farmed Atlantic and Pacific salmon in Canada, Chile, Japan, and Ireland, this projected supply was considerably greater than the actual supply at the time the forecast was made. In addition, the firm's analysts estimated the quantity of fresh salmon that would be demanded three years ahead, using the sorts of techniques described in previous chapters. Their results showed that if the price of salmon remained unchanged over the next three years, the quantity supplied would exceed the quantity demanded by about 15 percent at the end of the three-year period.

The firm's analysts also estimated the price elasticity of demand for fresh salmon to be about −1.5. This estimate too was based on the sorts of techniques described in previous chapters. Like the other estimates presented above, it was regarded as being rough, but useful.

If you were a consultant to this firm, and if you were asked to use these estimates to forecast the change in the salmon price over the next three years, what would be your forecast? (The firm's analysts believed that the quantity supplied three years hence would be approximately equal to their estimates, regardless of whatever changes occurred in price during this three-year period.)

*This section is based on an actual case, although the numbers and situation have been disguised somewhat.

put, we note that since the firm's total variable cost equals $6Q + 2Q^2$, its average variable cost equals

$$AVC = \frac{6Q + 2Q^2}{Q} = 6 + 2Q.$$

Thus, if $Q = 6$, average variable cost equals $6 + 2(6)$, or $18, which is less than the price of $30.

Producer Surplus in the Short Run

In Chapter 4, we examined consumer surplus and we saw that consumer surplus equals the difference between the price consumers pay for a good or service, and the price they were willing to pay (their reservation price). Now we can introduce a parallel idea, called producer surplus, which derives from the supply side of the market. Producer surplus is the difference between the price received by the producer and the price the producer is willing to receive for the good or service (her reservation price). As we have just shown in our analysis of a perfectly competitive market, a producer's reservation price is the marginal cost of producing the good or service. Panel A of Figure 10.5 shows this surplus (the shaded area). The firm's profit before accounting for fixed cost (its variable cost profit) is just total revenue (P^*Q^*) minus variable cost. But variable cost is just the area under the marginal cost curve up to output Q^*. This variable cost profit is also the shaded area in Panel A of Figure 10.5. Note the difference between profit (P^*BCD) and producer surplus. To arrive at producer surplus, managers only subtract variable costs from revenues, while to get their profit, they subtract both fixed and variable costs. Thus, producer surplus and variable cost profit are one in the same. Because the perfectly competitive firm's MC represents its supply curve, we can view producer surplus as the difference between the supply curve and the price received for the good (area b in Panel B of Figure 10.5).

Figure 10.6 shows the market equilibrium. Just as market demand for a product is the horizontal summation of individuals' demand curves for the product, market supply for a product is the horizontal summation of individual firms' supply curves of the product. Combining the results for consumer surplus (Chapter 4), we can see from Figure 10.6 that the market equilibrium price of P^* yields a consumer surplus of A and a producer surplus of B.

The sum of A and B, the total surplus, is the economist's measure of social welfare of the market equilibrium at the price P^* and quantity Q^*. To understand this idea, think about the total benefit and cost that consumers and producers assign to the goods in the market. For consumers, this is the area beneath the demand curve, left of the equilibrium quantity, that is, the total amount consumers are willing to pay for the goods. For producers, the total variable cost of supplying the equilibrium quantity of goods is the area beneath the supply curve, left of the equilibrium quantity. In the market, consumers pay and producers receive P^*. Yet, P^* is less than the total benefit, and greater than the total cost of the goods. In this sense, the market exchange generates value for the participants, represented by consumer, producer, and total surplus. Clearly, the magnitude of the total surplus, and its distribution between consumers and producers, depends on the shape of the demand and supply curves. But the thing to remember is that market exchanges, generally speaking, provide opportunities for gains, and as we'll see later, savvy managers can devise ways to capture a greater share of those gains for their firms.

FIGURE
10.5

Producer Surplus and Variable Cost Profit

Producer surplus for the firm is its variable cost profit, or, total revenue minus variable cost. Producer surplus for the market is the area above the supply curve but below the price received for the good.

FIGURE
10.6

Market Social Welfare (A + B) of Perfectly Competitive Price Policy, P*

Societal welfare at a given price (P*) is measured by the sum of the consumer surplus (A) and the producer surplus (B).

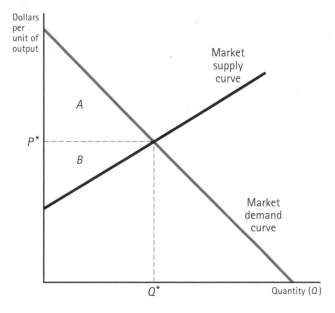

Long-Run Equilibrium of the Firm

In the long run, how much will a competitive firm produce? The long-run equilibrium position of the firm is at the point at which its long-run average total costs equal price. If price is in excess of average total costs for any firm, economic profits are being earned and new firms will enter the industry. This will increase supply, thereby driving down price and hence profits. If price is less than average total costs for any firm, that firm will eventually leave the industry. As firms exit, supply falls, causing price and profits to rise. Only when economic profits are zero (which means that long-run average cost equals price) will a firm be in long-run equilibrium.

Recall from Chapter 1 that economic profits are not the same as accounting profits. Economic profits are profits above and beyond what the owners of the firm could obtain elsewhere from the resources they invest in the firm. Thus, long-run equilibrium occurs when the owners receive no more (and no less) than they could obtain elsewhere from these resources.

More specifically, price must be equal to the *lowest value* of long-run average total cost. That is, firms must be producing at the minimum point on their long-run average cost curves. To see why, note that if firms maximize their profits, they must operate where price equals long-run marginal cost. Also, we have just seen that they must operate where price equals long-run average cost. But if both of these conditions are satisfied, it follows that long-run marginal cost must equal long-run average cost. And we know from Chapter 9 that long-run marginal cost is equal to long-run average cost only at the point at which long-run average cost is a minimum. Consequently, this point must be the equilibrium position of the firm.

To illustrate this equilibrium position, consider Figure 10.7. When all adjustments are made, price equals *G*. Since price is constant, the demand curve is horizontal, and therefore the marginal revenue curve is the same as the demand curve, both being *GG'*. The equilibrium output of the firm is *V*, and its optimal-sized plant is described by the short-run average and marginal cost curves, *AA'* and *MM'*. At this output and with this plant, we see that long-run marginal cost equals short-run marginal cost equals price. This ensures that the

FIGURE
10.7

Long-Run Equilibrium, Perfectly Competitive Firm

In long-run equilibrium, the firm produces an output of *V*, and price = marginal cost (both long-run and short-run) = average cost (both long-run and short-run).

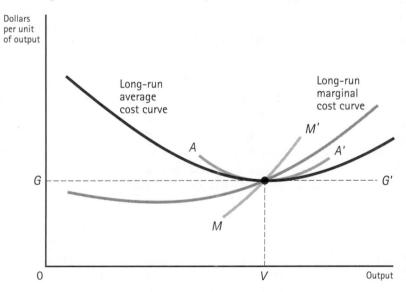

firm is maximizing profit. Also, long-run average cost equals short-run average cost equals price: this ensures that economic profits are zero. Because the long-run marginal cost and long-run average cost must be equal, the equilibrium point is at the bottom of the long-run average cost curve.

For example, suppose that the Milton Company's long-run average cost curve is

$$AC = 200 - 4Q + 0.05Q^2, \tag{10.5}$$

where AC is long-run average cost (in dollars), and Q is the firm's output per day. Since the Milton Company is a perfectly competitive firm, its output in the long run will equal the value of Q that minimizes AC. To determine this value of Q, we obtain the derivative of AC with respect to Q:

$$\frac{dAC}{dQ} = -4 + 0.10Q.$$

Setting dAC/dQ equal to zero, we find that $Q = 40$. Thus, if the firm maximizes profit, its output in the long run will equal 40 units per day.

As indicated above, average cost will equal marginal cost at this output. To see this, note that since total cost equals Q times AC,

$$TC = Q(200 - 4Q + 0.05Q^2)$$
$$= 200Q - 4Q^2 + 0.05Q^3,$$

where TC is total cost. Taking the derivative of TC with respect to Q,

$$MC = \frac{dTC}{dQ} = 200 - 8Q + 0.15Q^2,$$

where MC equals marginal cost. Since $Q = 40$,

$$MC = 200 - 8(40) + 0.15(40)^2 = 120.$$

Also, inserting 40 for Q in equation (10.5),

$$AC = 200 - 4(40) + 0.05(40)^2 = 120.$$

Thus, marginal cost equals average cost when $Q = 40$. (Both marginal cost and average cost equal \$120.)

The Long-Run Adjustment Process:
A Constant-Cost Industry

Having looked at the behavior of the perfectly competitive firm in the short and long runs, we turn to the long-run adjustment process of a perfectly competitive industry. To begin with, we assume that the industry is a *constant-cost industry*, which means that expansion of the industry does not result in an increase in input prices. Figure 10.8 shows long-run equilibrium under conditions of constant cost. The left-hand panel shows the short- and long-run cost curves of a typical firm in the industry. The right-hand panel shows the demand and supply curves in the market as a whole, D being the original demand curve and S being the original short-run supply curve. It is assumed that the industry is in long-run equilibrium, with the result that the price ($6 per unit) equals the minimum value of long-run (and short-run) average cost.

Suppose now that the demand curve shifts to D_1. In the short run, with the number of firms fixed, the price of the product will rise from $6 to $7 per unit; each firm will expand output from 5,000 to 6,000 units per day; and each firm

---

FIGURE 10.8

Long-Run Equilibrium: Constant-Cost Industry

A constant-cost industry has a horizontal long-run supply curve, as shown in panel B. If demand shifts upward from D to D_1, the consequent increase in price (to $7 per unit) results in the entry of firms, which shifts the supply curve to the right (to S_1), thus pushing the price back to its original level ($6 per unit).

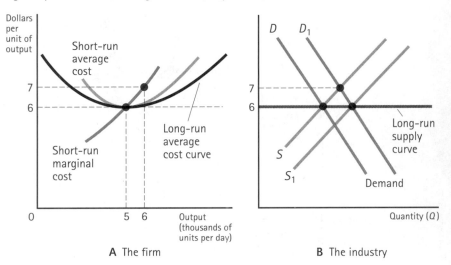

A The firm

B The industry

will be making economic profits since the new price, $7, exceeds the short-run average costs of the firm when output is 6,000 units per day. The result is that firms will enter the industry and shift the supply curve to the right. In the case of a constant-cost industry, the entrance of the new firms does not influence the costs of the existing firms. The inputs used by this industry are used by many other industries as well, and the appearance of the new firms in this industry does not bid up the price of inputs and hence raise the costs of existing firms. Neither does the entry of the new firms reduce existing firms' costs.

Thus, a constant-cost industry *has a horizontal long-run supply curve.* Since output can be increased by increasing the number of firms producing 5,000 units of output per day at an average cost of $6 per unit, the long-run supply curve is horizontal at $6 per unit. So long as the industry remains in a state of constant costs, its output can be increased indefinitely. If price exceeds $6 per unit, firms would enter the industry; if price were less than $6 per unit, firms would leave the industry. Thus, long-run equilibrium can only occur in this industry when price is $6 per unit. And industry output can be raised or lowered, in accord with demand conditions, without changing this long-run equilibrium price.

The Long-Run Adjustment Process: An Increasing-Cost Industry

Not all industries are constant-cost industries. Next, let's consider the case of an *increasing-cost industry,* which occurs when the expansion of the industry results in an increase in input prices.[4] An increasing-cost industry is shown in Figure 10.9. The original conditions are the same as in Figure 10.8, *D* being the original demand curve, *S* being the original supply curve, $6 per unit being the equilibrium price, and *LL'* and *AA'* in the left panel being the long- and short-run average cost curves of each firm. As in Figure 10.8, the original position is one of long-run equilibrium, since the price equals the minimum value of long-run (and short-run) average cost.

Assume now that the demand curve shifts to D_1, with the result that the price of the product goes up and firms earn economic profits, thus attracting new entrants. More and more inputs are needed by the industry, and in an increasing-cost industry, the price of inputs goes up with the amount used by the

---

[4]Besides constant-cost and increasing-cost industries, there are also decreasing-cost industries, which are the most unusual case, although quite young industries may fall into this category. External economies, which are cost reductions that occur when the industry expands, may be responsible for the existence of decreasing-cost industries. For example, the expansion of an industry may lead to an improvement in transportation that reduces the costs of each firm in the industry. A decreasing-cost industry has a negatively sloped long-run supply curve.

FIGURE
10.9

Long–Run Equilibrium: Increasing–Cost Industry

An increasing-cost industry has a positively sloped long-run supply curve, as shown in panel B. After long-run equilibrium is achieved, increases in output require increases in the price of the product.

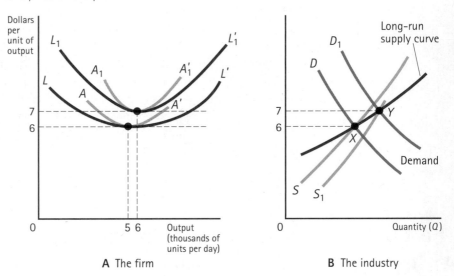

A The firm

B The industry

industry. Thus, the cost of inputs increases for the established firms as well as the new entrants and the average cost curves are pushed up to $L_1L'_1$ and $A_1A'_1$.

If each firm's marginal cost curve is shifted to the left by the increase in input prices, the industry supply curve will tend to shift to the left. But this tendency is more than counterbalanced by the effects of the increase in the number of firms, which shifts the industry supply curve to the right. The latter effect must more than offset the former effect because otherwise there would be no expansion in total industry output. (No new resources would have been attracted to the industry.) The process of adjustment must go on until a new point of long-run equilibrium is reached. In Figure 10.9, this point is where the price of the product is $7 per unit and each firm produces 6,000 units per day;[5] the new short-run supply curve is S_1.

An increasing-cost industry *has a positively sloped long-run supply curve*. That is, after long-run equilibrium is achieved, increases in output require increases in the price of the product. For example, points X and Y in Figure 10.9 are both on the long-run supply curve for the industry. The difference between

---

[5]We cannot be sure that the firm's new output exceeds its old output as shown in Figure 10.9. It is possible for its new output to be less than or equal to its old output.

constant-cost and increasing-cost industries is as follows: *In constant-cost industries, new firms enter in response to an increase in demand until price returns to its original level, whereas in increasing-cost industries, new firms enter until the minimum point on the long-run average cost curve has increased to the point where it equals the new price.*[6]

Finally, some industries are neither constant-cost nor increasing-cost industries; they are decreasing-cost industries. Their long-run supply curve is negatively sloped. For further discussion of these industries, which are less frequently encountered than constant-cost or increasing-cost industries, see footnote 4.

How a Perfectly Competitive Economy Allocates Resources

It is very important for managers to understand how a competitive economy allocates resources. Without such an understanding, they cannot interpret or anticipate the fundamental changes that occur in many industries. To illustrate this allocation process, let's take a simple case: Consumers become more favorably disposed toward corn and less favorably disposed toward rice than in the past. What will happen in the short run? The increase in the demand for corn increases the price of corn, and results in some increase in the output of corn. However, the output of corn cannot be increased very substantially because the capacity of the industry cannot be expanded in the short run. Similarly, the fall in the demand for rice reduces the price of rice, and results in some reduction in the output of rice. But the output of rice will not be curtailed greatly because firms will continue to produce as long as they can cover variable costs. Because of the increase in the price of corn and the decrease in the price of rice, corn producers are earning economic profits and rice producers are showing economic losses. Producers will reallocate resources to correct this imbalance.

When short-run equilibrium is achieved in both the corn and rice industries, the reallocation of resources is not yet complete since there has not been enough time for producers to build new capacity or liquidate old capacity. In particular, neither industry is operating at minimum average cost. The corn producers may be operating at greater than the output level where average cost is a minimum; and the rice producers may be operating at less than the output level where average cost is a minimum.

---

[6]This is not the only way in which equilibrium can be achieved in increasing-cost industries. It is also possible that the increase in input prices (due to the expansion of industry output) raises average cost more than the increase in demand raises average revenue. Thus firms may experience losses, some may leave the industry, and the remaining firms may produce at a bigger scale.

What will occur in the long run? The shift in consumer demand from rice to corn will result in greater adjustments in output and smaller adjustments in price than in the short run. In the long run, existing firms can leave rice production and new firms can enter corn production. As firms leave rice production, the supply curve shifts to the left, causing the price to rise above its short-run level. The transfer of resources out of rice production will cease when the price has increased, and costs have decreased, to the point where losses no longer occur.

Whereas rice production is losing resources, corn production is gaining them. The short-run economic profits in corn production will stimulate the entry of new firms. The increased demand for inputs will raise input prices and cost curves in corn production, and the price of corn will be depressed by the movement to the right of the supply curve because of the entry of new firms. Entry stops when economic profits are no longer being earned. At that point, when long-run equilibrium is achieved, there will be more firms and more resources used in the corn industry than in the short run.

Price and Output Decisions under Monopoly

Let's turn now from perfect competition to monopoly. An unregulated monopolist, if it maximizes profit, will choose the price and output at which the difference between total revenue and total cost is largest. For example, if a monopolist's total revenue and total cost curves are as shown in Table 10.4, it will choose an output rate of either 5 or 6 units per time period and a price of $331 or $311. Figure 10.10 shows the situation graphically.[7]

Under monopoly, the firm will maximize profit if it sets its output rate at the point at which marginal cost equals marginal revenue. Table 10.5 and Figure 10.11 show that this is true in this example. It is easy to prove that this is generally a necessary condition for profit maximization. If TR is the monopolist's total revenue and TC is its total cost, the monopolist's profit equals

$$\pi = TR - TC,$$

and

$$\frac{d\pi}{dQ} = \frac{dTR}{dQ} - \frac{dTC}{dQ}.$$

[7]If the monopolist can produce a fractional number of units per time period and if the monopolist's total cost curve and total revenue curve are linear between 5 and 6 units per time period, profits will be maximized if the monopolist produces 5 or 6 units per time period—or any output in between.

TABLE 10.4

Cost, Revenue, and Profit of a Monopolist

Output	Price (dollars)	Total revenue (dollars)	Total cost (dollars)	Total profit (dollars)
2	360	720	640	80
3	350	1,050	790	260
4	$342\frac{1}{2}$	1,370	960	410
5	331	1,655	1,150	505
6	311	1,866	1,361	505
7	278	1,946	1,590	356
8	250	2,000	1,840	160

FIGURE 10.10

Total Revenue, Total Cost, and Total Profit of a Monopolist

To maximize profit, the monopolist will choose an output rate of 5 or 6 units per period of time.

TABLE 10.5

Marginal Cost and Marginal Revenue of a Monopolist

Output	Marginal cost* (dollars)	Marginal revenue* (dollars)	Total profit (dollars)
3	150	330	260
4	170	320	410
5	190	285	505
6	211	211	505
7	229	80	356
8	250	54	160

*These figures pertain to the interval between the indicated quantity of output and 1 unit less than the indicated quantity of output.

FIGURE 10.11

Marginal Revenue and Marginal Cost of a Monopolist

At the monopolist's profit-maximizing output (5 or 6 units), marginal cost equals marginal revenue.

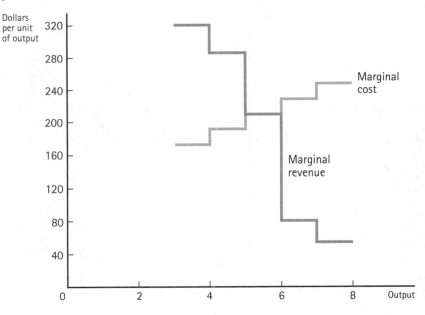

Setting $d\pi/dQ = 0$ to obtain the conditions under which profit is a maximum, we find that

$$\frac{dTR}{dQ} = \frac{dTC}{dQ}. \tag{10.6}$$

Thus, marginal revenue must equal marginal cost when profits are maximized, since the expression on the left-hand side is marginal revenue and the expression on the right-hand side is marginal cost.

It is easy to represent graphically the price and output decisions of the monopolist. Figure 10.12 shows the demand curve, the marginal revenue curve, the marginal cost curve, and the average total cost curve faced by the firm. To maximize profit, it should produce the output, Q, where the marginal cost curve intersects the marginal revenue curve. If the monopolist produces Q units, the demand curve shows that it must set a price of P. It is important to recognize that since the monopolist is the only member of the industry, the demand curve for the output of the monopolist is the industry demand curve. Thus, in contrast to perfect competition where the demand curve for the output of an indi-

FIGURE
10.12

Output and Price Decisions of a Monopolist

In equilibrium, the monopolist produces Q units of output and sets a price of P. (Note that, in contrast to perfect competition, the demand curve slopes downward to the right.)

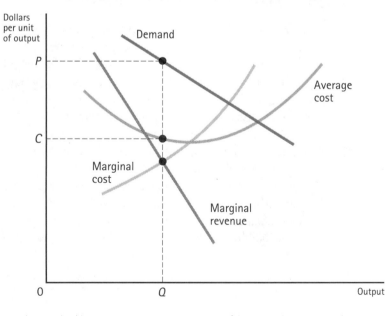

vidual firm is horizontal, the demand curve for the monopolist's output slopes downward to the right, as shown in Figure 10.12.

If an industry is monopolized, it generally will set a higher price and lower output than if it is perfectly competitive. The perfectly competitive firm operates at the point at which price equals marginal cost, whereas the monopolist operates at a point at which price exceeds marginal cost. To see that the monopolist's price exceeds marginal cost, recall from equation (3.16) that

$$MR = P\left(1 + \frac{1}{\eta}\right),$$

where MR is marginal revenue, P is price, and η is the price elasticity of demand. Since the monopolist sets marginal revenue equal to marginal cost, MC, it follows that at the point where profit is maximized,

$$MC = P\left(1 + \frac{1}{\eta}\right),$$

so that
$$P = MC \div \left(1 + \frac{1}{\eta}\right).$$

Thus, since $\eta < 0$, it follows that $(1 + 1/\eta) < 1$, which means that P must exceed MC.[8]

The Newspaper Industry in Detroit

Relatively few cities in the United States have rival newspapers that are separately owned and commercially independent. Take the case of Detroit. In early 1989, the *Detroit Free Press* and the *Detroit News* obtained approval from the U.S. Court of Appeals to establish a newspaper monopoly in Detroit. Arguing that the *Free Press* was a failing newspaper, they took advantage of a special exemption from antitrust law, permitted under the Newspaper Preservation Act of 1970. (This exemption was created to keep alive competing editorial voices in major cities.) The two newspapers were allowed to continue to print newspapers under their own names, but all commercial operations would be merged.

Because the merged newspapers were legally permitted to fix prices and allocate markets as they pleased, they would constitute a monopoly, even though their newspapers were printed under two different names. The result would be a very substantial increase in profit. Before they combined, each lost more than

---

[8]Not only is $\eta < 0$, but for a monopolist, $\eta < -1$. We will discuss cost-plus pricing at length in Chapter 13.

$10 million a year; after they combined, experts estimated that they would make more than $150 million a year. This is eloquent testimony to the effect of monopoly on profit.

The reasons for this increase in profit were summarized as follows by the *New York Times:* "The formation of the monopoly enterprise would end an all-out war for control of advertising and circulation dollars, sending . . . rates skyrocketing for readers and advertisers."[9] This, of course, is entirely consistent with our discussion in the previous section. A monopolist, free from the constraints imposed by direct competition, can set a higher price—and obtain a higher profit level—than it could if it had to compete with rival firms.

However, even a monopoly is not guaranteed a profit. In July 1995, about 2,500 reporters, editors, press operators, drivers, and other workers of the *Detroit Free Press* and *Detroit News* struck over job cuts, wages, and work rules. This strike continued for over 18 months, and cut heavily into the profits of the merged newspapers.[10]

The Raleigh Company: A Numerical Example

To illustrate how price and output can be chosen to maximize profit, consider the Raleigh Company, a monopolist producing and selling a product with the demand curve

$$P = 30 - 6Q, \tag{10.7}$$

where P is price (in thousands of dollars), and Q is the firm's output (in thousands of units). The firm's total cost function is

$$TC = 14 + 3Q + 3Q^2, \tag{10.8}$$

where TC is total cost (in millions of dollars).

From the demand curve in equation (10.7), we can determine the firm's total revenue (in millions of dollars), which is

$$TR = PQ = (30 - 6Q)Q = 30Q - 6Q^2.$$

Thus, marginal revenue equals

$$\frac{dTR}{dQ} = \frac{d(30Q - 6Q^2)}{dQ} = 30 - 12Q.$$

[9]*New York Times*, September 18, 1988.
[10]*New York Times*, February 20, 1997.

ANALYZING MANAGERIAL DECISIONS

Franchiser versus Franchisee?

What happens when a franchiser with monopoly power has a different objective from a franchisee's? Consider the case of McDonald's where the franchiser makes its money by collecting a percentage of each store's sales, or total revenues. Thus, the franchiser wants to maximize the total revenue from the sales of its hamburgers by having each store maximize its total revenues (and by adding more stores). We'll assume that franchisees wish to maximize their profits. To do so, the franchisee would set $MR = MC$ (in the elastic range of demand where $\eta_D < -1$). But maximizing total revenue requires that $MR = 0$ (and that $\eta_D = -1$). Since the objectives of the franchiser and the franchisee can't be accomplished with the same pricing policy, they are in conflict. The situation is depicted in the figure below.*

Revenue Maximization vs. Profit Maximization

A monopolist will produce at $P_{Franchisee}$, $Q_{Franchisee}$ as dictated by marginal revenue equals marginal cost. A revenue maximizer will produce where marginal revenue is zero ($P_{Franchiser}$, $Q_{Franchiser}$), i.e., where $\eta = -1$.

Note that this conflict exists in other situations such as book publishing. Authors generally receive a percentage of book sales as a royalty. Thus, authors would like publishers to maximize total revenues. Publishers, on the other hand, want to maximize profits.

*Business Week, June 2, 1997.

CONCEPTS IN CONTEXT

Using Patents to Maintain Market Power

The U.S. government often tries to break up monopolies, but one government institution, the patent system, is designed to grant firms monopoly power on their inventions and product innovations. The government grants companies patents for twenty years. This gives the patent holder the exclusive rights to their invention or new product for the life of the patent. Because companies apply for a patent before the product is on the market, the effective life of a patent can be significantly less than twenty years. For drugs, the effective patent protection is about twelve years.

Because of the monopoly granted by the patent system (and the anticipated monopoly profits from a popular product), drug companies are willing to invest significant funds in research and development (R and D). It is estimated that a successful new drug averages approximately $350 million in development costs. Without patent protection, it is doubtful whether drug companies would undertake highly problematic and expensive R and D.

What do drug companies do price-wise with their patent-generated monopoly power? One test is to compare the price of drugs just as drugs come off patent with the price of the generics that presently appear on the market. Bristol-Meyers Squibbs's heart drug Capoten sold for 57 cents per pill and the generic sold for 3 cents. This suggests at least a 19 times markup.

*Source: "With Patents Expiring on Big Prescription Drugs, Drug Industry Quakes," *Wall Street Journal*, August 12, 1997.

From the total cost function in equation (10.8), we can determine marginal cost, which is

$$MC = \frac{dTC}{dQ} = \frac{d(14 + 3Q + 3Q^2)}{dQ} = 3 + 6Q.$$

Setting marginal revenue equal to marginal cost,

$$30 - 12Q = 3 + 6Q.$$

This means that $Q = 1.5$. Inserting 1.5 for Q in the demand curve in equation (10.7), we find that $P = 30 - 6(1.5)$, or 21. Thus, to maximize profit, the Raleigh Company should set a price of $21 thousand and produce and sell 1.5 thousand units. If it does so, its profit equals $[30(1.5) - 6(1.5)^2] - [14 + 3(1.5) + 3(1.5)^2] = 6.25$ million dollars.

Two-Part Tariffs

A monopolist sometimes requires the consumer to pay an initial fee for the right to buy its product as well as a usage fee for each unit of the product that he or she buys. This is known as a *two-part tariff*. There are many cases in which this pricing technique is used. For example, telephone companies charge a basic monthly fee for telephone service plus an amount for message units.

If a monopolist uses this pricing technique, it must determine how high the initial fee must be, as well as the size of the usage fee. Clearly, the lower the initial fee, the greater the number of consumers that will purchase the right to buy the product. Thus, lower initial fees are likely to result in greater profits from the sales of the product. But this may not be best for the firm, since it also receives profits from the initial fees it charges—and if it lowers the initial fee, these profits will fall. Consequently, the monopolist would be expected to choose the initial fee and usage fee so that its total profit—from both the sales of the product and from initial fees—is a maximum.

To illustrate the use of a two-part tariff, consider Disneyland, the California amusement park cited in Chapter 1. Disneyland used to charge each person a price to enter the park and an extra amount for each ride he or she went on. In the early 1980s, Disneyland eliminated the fee for individual rides and raised the entrance fee. Presumably, Disneyland's managers felt that this would increase the park's profits.

Bundling

Consumers often encounter bundling, when firms offer distinct goods or services together at a package price. Economists distinguish between pure bundling, when the goods are offered only in the package, and mixed bundling, when the goods have packaged prices as well as stand-alone prices. Examples abound. Fast-food restaurants practice mixed bundling when they offer "value meals" comprised of items that may also be purchased separately. Entertainers as diverse as professional sports teams and opera companies also commonly practice mixed bundling, offering tickets to individual performances, as well as season tickets, subscriptions of tickets to multiple performances, and other bundles. On the other hand, Columbia bundles 12 songs of Mary Chapin Carpenter on a CD, and you must buy the CD to obtain the several songs you want (and hence obtain more songs that you don't want). They sell their product only as a pure bundle.

Why is bundling so common? One reason is that it can increase a firm's profits, if their customers have varied tastes. To see this, consider the University of Pittsburgh football team, which several years ago was playing home games versus Penn State University and Temple University. The Pittsburgh team

CONCEPTS IN CONTEXT

Verizon Local Calling Plans

Telephone service is a classic example of a two-part tariff. A subscriber pays the phone company a monthly fee for the privilege of receiving a dial tone. This fee must be paid regardless of whether there are zero, ten, or hundreds of incoming or outgoing calls per month. It is an entry fee for having service available (although one could avoid this entry fee by using the pay phone on the corner—albeit at a high use fee for local outgoing calls).

But phone companies have become even more sophisticated in their utilization of two-part tariffs.

Consider Verizon's (a local northeastern company) local calling plans. Because they don't know individual demands, to emulate the theoretical two-part tariff, they offer a menu of entry fees and use fees (which are available only if you've paid the dial tone fee). And they let the customer decide what plan is best for them, and, by doing so, the customer reveals what demand category he is in).

Verizon offers four local calling plans in the Philadelphia area:

	Monthly Rate
Local calling with a $0.25 allowance	$0.00
Local calling with a $4.00 allowance	$2.60
Unlimited calling to local area	$8.85
Metropolitan area—unlimited calling	$21.00

Note: The use fee is $0.02 per message unit (a minute of use or fraction thereof. Thus, plan 1 entails 12.5 "free" message units.)

Plan 1 is a no-entry fee, all-use fee plan (the allowance is for "lifeline" emergency calls). Plan 2 has a higher entry fee, a certain number of local calls (200 message units) with a $0 use fee and thereafter a $0.02 use fee per message unit. Plans 3 and 4 have no use fee and are all-entry fee. Light users and those who only receive calls choose plan 1. Moderate users choose plan 2. Heavy users choose plans 3 or 4 (depending on where they are making their local calls).

Source: Verizon letter to residential customers, August 2000.

at the time was not that powerful, Penn State was a national power, and Temple was one of the worst teams in the nation. Pittsburgh traditionally did not sell out its games. Not only did Penn State sell out its home games but its fans traveled to away games to cheer their team on. Temple fans did not attend their home games, much less go to the team's away games.

For simplicity, we'll assume that there are two types of football fans: those whose main objective is to see the Penn State game (type *A*) and those whose objective is to see the Temple game—because they want to see a Pittsburgh win (type *B*). To further simplify things, we'll assume an equal number of fans of each category. Table 10.6 shows the maximum price that each type of fan would pay to see each game.

We'll assume that it costs Pitt a constant $5 per fan to hold a football game. If the games are sold separately, the best price that can be charged for the Penn

TABLE
10.6

Maximum Price That Each Fan Type Would Pay for Tickets to Two Games, Sold Separately or as a Bundle (Case Where Bundling Is Profitable)

Game	Reservation prices by fan type (in dollars)	
	Type *A*	Type *B*
Pitt–Penn State	50	19
Pitt–Temple	6	27
Bundle (both games combined)	56	46

State game is $50, and the best price that can be charged for the Temple game is $27. Why? Because if Pitt sets prices lower than these, they won't make as much money. If the Penn State game sells for $50, they'll sell 1 ticket and make $45. If it sells for $19, they'll sell 2 tickets but since they make only $14 from each ticket, they'll make $28. With analogous calculations, they'll make $22 by selling the Temple tickets at $27 (versus $2 if they sell the tickets at $6).

But what if Pitt insists that fans buy tickets to *both* games? Type *A* (the Penn State fan) will be willing to pay $56 for both tickets and type *B* (the Pitt fan) will be willing to pay $46 for both tickets. If they charge $56 for a bundle of both tickets, Pitt will net $46 but sell only one bundle of tickets. If they charge $46 for the bundle of tickets, they'll net $36 per bundle but sell 2 bundles for a profit of $72.

Clearly, bundling the tickets at $46 (yielding a profit of $72) is better than selling Penn State tickets separately at $50 each and Temple tickets separately at $27 each (yielding a profit of $67).

While this example is stylized, it's indicative of what Pitt did. They bundled the tickets. Both games were nominally sellouts, even though many seats were empty for the Temple game.[11] Why did they do it? Because they made more money via bundling than selling tickets separately.

Managers at Pitt will find it more profitable to sell tickets to the two games as a bundle, relative to pricing them separately, as long as there is an inverse relationship between the amount a fan is willing to pay for the Penn State game and the amount he is willing to pay for the Temple game (as long as the costs of holding a game are not too high relative to the reservation prices of fans for the games). An inverse relationship exists if one type of fan highly values the

---

[11]Ironically, Pitt gave Penn State a great game, in which Penn State won in the last minutes of play, and Temple beat Pitt in a thrilling game.

FIGURE
10.13

Alternative Relationships between the Maximum Amount a Fan Would Pay for a Penn State Ticket and the Maximum Amount a Fan Would Pay for a Temple Ticket

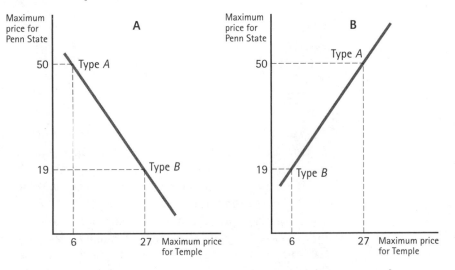

Penn State game, but doesn't really care too much for the Temple game, while another type of fan has just the reverse preference. (Panel A of Figure 10.13 shows that the relationship stated in Table 10.6 is, in fact, inverse). If there is a positive association in fan preference (see Panel B of Figure 10.13), there is no advantage to using a bundling strategy.

For example, if the reservation prices of fan types are as shown in Table 10.7, the highest price Pitt managers could charge for the Penn State game is $50, and the highest price they could charge for the Temple game is $27. Given the fixed cost of $5 for holding a game, Pitt would realize revenues of $77 and profits of $67. These amounts are identical to those generated by a bundling strategy. (Panel B of Figure 10.13 shows why this is true—fan preference for the two games is positively associated.)

However, a third strategy remains for Pitt managers. They could sell tickets for the two games as a bundle and also sell them individually. This strategy is called mixed bundling. It basically lets the fans decide whether to purchase tickets for the two games as a bundle, or simply purchase tickets for a single game. Mixed bundling strategies are commonly used by managers. For examples, customers can go to McDonald's and order a value meal (consisting of a sandwich, fries, and a drink), or they can individually order a sandwich, fries, or a drink.

TABLE 10.7

Maximum Price That Each Fan Type Would Pay for Tickets to Two Games, Sold Separately or as a Bundle (Case Where Bundling Is Not Profitable)

	Reservation Prices by Fan Type	
Game	Type A	Type B
Pitt–Penn State	50	19
Pitt–Temple	27	6
Bundle (both games combined)	77	25

The bundle's price is less than what it would cost to individually order the components of the bundle, but if a customer only wants two of the three components, then it is cheaper to purchase them individually.

The optimal mixed bundle pricing package is somewhat tricky to calculate. In fact, there is no formula to help managers derive the optimal pricing scheme. The procedure is more of trial and error than derivation. The mixed bundle pricing package will consist of prices for individual components, and then a single price for the product (or service) bundle. This pricing strategy can involve having the prices of individual components and/or the bundled product be different from the reservation prices of consumers. Whether this occurs or not depends on trade-offs from both the consumer and the producer. We see this in the following example.

Consider the scenario shown in Table 10.8. There are three consumers—A, B, C (or consumer groups, for simplicity, with an equal number of demanders in each group and each demander wanting no more than one of each good) and two goods—X and Y. The best price separately prices are shown in bold in

TABLE 10.8

Consumer Reservation Prices for Good X and Good Y (in dollars)*

	Consumer A	Consumer B	Consumer C
Good X	5.33	12.00	3.00
Good Y	8.00	3.00	11.00
Bundle	13.33	15.00	14.00

*Each good costs $4/unit to make.

TABLE 10.9

Best Price Separately Strategy

Price of X	Cost/Unit	Profit/Unit	Number of units	Profit
5.33	4	1.33	2	2.66
12	4	8	1	8
3	4	−1	3	−3

Price of Y	Cost/Unit	Profit/Unit	Number of units	Profit
8	4	4	2	8
3	4	−1	3	−3
11	4	7	1	7

Table 10.9. Thus, the best price separately price is to price X at $12 and price Y at $8 and make a profit of $16. The best pure bundle price is shown in Table 10.10. Thus, the best pure bundle price is $13.33, which yields a profit of $15.99.

Consider now a mixed bundle with a bundle price of $13.33, a price of good X at $10.32, and a price of good Y at $10.32. It might first appear that all would buy the bundle at $13.33 (because B gets consumer surplus of $15 − $13.33 = $1.67 and C gets a consumer surplus of $14 − $13.33 = $0.67). But if the price of X is $10.32, consumer B gets a consumer surplus of $12 − $10.32 = $1.68 > $1.67, and if the price of good Y is $10.32, consumer C gets a consumer surplus of $11 − $10.32 = $0.68 > $0.67. But consumer B doesn't get to consume good Y if she doesn't buy the bundle and consumer C doesn't get to consume good X if he doesn't buy the bundle—doesn't that count? Yes— but they are still better off with the larger consumer surplus from consuming just one good, as we will see below.

Consider consumer B. Suppose consumer B has $15. If she buys the bundle for $13.33, she'll have consumer surplus of $1.67 and both goods. But if she

TABLE 10.10

Best Pure Bundling Strategy

Price of bundle	Cost of bundle	Profit of bundle	Number of bundles	Profit
13.33	8	5.33	3	15.99
15	8	7	1	7
14	8	6	2	12

TABLE 10.11

Best Mixed Bundling Strategy

Price of bundle	Cost of bundle	Profit of bundle	Number of bundles	Profit
13.33	8	5.33	1 (buyer A)	5.33

Price of X	Cost of X	Profit/Unit	Number of units	Profit
10.32	4	6.32	1 (buyer B)	6.32

Price of Y	Cost of Y	Profit/Unit	Number of units	Profit
10.32	4	6.32	1 (buyer C)	6.32

buys just good X for $10.32, she'll have good X and $4.68 left over. She'll have $1.68 in consumer surplus from good X and while she does not have good Y, she has $4.68 in cash (that isn't part of the consumer surplus from good X). But $4.68 in cash instead of good Y is attractive since good Y is worth only $3 to her. Thus, $4.68 in cash and good X is a better position for consumer B than $1.67 in cash and both goods (which is worth only $4.67 to her). Analogously, consumer C, starting off with $14, is better off with $3.68 in cash and good Y rather than having $0.67 in cash and both goods (because good X is worth $3 to him).

How does the firm do with such a mixed bundle? Table 10.11 demonstrates the profit improvement:

So profits total $17.97 via this mixed bundle, which dominates the $16 available from pricing separately and the $15.99 from pure bundling. As you can see, mixed bundling does not have to charge reservation prices of a consumer for the items and thus is "tricky." But we see a lot of mixed bundling in the market—so it is important to know that experimentation plays an important role and that pure bundling and pricing separately aren't always the best pricing strategies.

Monopolistic Competition

Having taken up perfect competition and monopoly, let's turn now to monopolistic competition. The central feature of monopolistic competition is *product differentiation*. Unlike perfect competition, in which all firms sell an identical product, firms under monopolistic competition sell somewhat different products. In many parts of retail trade, producers try to make their product a little different, by altering the product's physical makeup, the services they offer, and other such variables. Eddie Bauer's shirts are not *exactly* the same as Land's End's, but they are not too dissimilar either. Because of the differences among their products, producers have some control over their price, but it usually is small, because the products of other firms are very similar to their own.

Under perfect competition, the firms included in an industry are easy to determine because they all produce an identical product. But if product differentiation exists, it is no longer simple to define an industry, because each firm produces a somewhat different product. Nevertheless, it may be useful to group together firms that produce similar products and call them a **product group.** We can formulate a product group called "neckties" or "toothbrushes" or "shirts." The process by which we combine firms into product groups must be somewhat arbitrary, since there is no way to decide how close a pair of substitutes must be to belong to the same product group. But it is assumed that meaningful product groups can be established. Clearly, the broader the definition of the product group, the greater the number of firms included.

In addition to product differentiation, other conditions must be met for an industry to qualify as a case of monopolistic competition. (1) *There must be a large number of firms in the product group.* The product must be produced by perhaps 50 to 100 or more firms, with each firm's product a fairly close substitute for the products of the other firms in the product group. (2) *The number of firms in the product group must be large enough so that each firm expects its actions to go unheeded by its rivals and is unimpeded by possible retaliatory moves on their part.* Hence, when formulating their own policies with regard to price and output, they do not explicitly concern themselves with their rivals' responses. If there are a large number of firms, this condition will normally be met. (3) *Entry into the product group must be relatively easy, and there must be no collusion, such as price fixing or market sharing, among firms in the product group.* If there are a large number of firms, it generally is difficult, if not impossible, for them to collude.

Price and Output Decisions under Monopolistic Competition

If each firm produces a somewhat different product, it follows that the demand curve facing each firm slopes downward to the right. That is, if the firm raises its price slightly, it will lose some, but by no means all, of its customers to other firms. And if it lowers its price slightly, it will gain some, but by no means all, of its competitors' customers.

Figure 10.14 shows the short-run equilibrium of a monopolistically competitive firm. The firm in the short run will set its price at P_0 and its output rate at Q_0, since this combination of price and output will maximize its prof-

FIGURE
10.14

Short-Run Equilibrium, Monopolistic Competition

The firm will set price at P_0 and its output rate at Q_0, since marginal cost equals marginal revenue at this output. It will earn a profit of $P_0 C_0$ per unit of output.

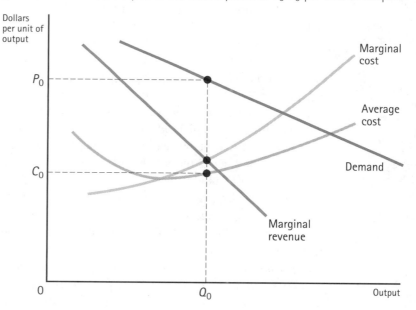

its. We can be sure that this combination of price and output maximizes profit because marginal cost equals marginal revenue at this output rate. Economic profits will be earned because price, P_0, exceeds average total cost, C_0, at this output rate.

One condition for long-run equilibrium is that each firm be making no economic profits or losses, since entry or exit of firms will occur otherwise—and entry and exit are incompatible with long-run equilibrium. Another condition for long-run equilibrium is that each firm be maximizing its profits. At what price and output will both these conditions be fulfilled? Figure 10.15 shows that the long-run equilibrium is at a price of P_1 and an output of Q_1. The zero-economic-profit condition is met at this combination of price and output, since the firm's average cost at this output equals the price, P_1. And the profit-maximization condition is met, since the marginal revenue curve intersects the marginal cost curve at this output rate.[12]

---

[12]The seminal work in the theory of monopolistic competition was E. Chamberlin, *The Theory of Monopolistic Competition* (Cambridge, Mass.: Harvard University Press, 1933).

FIGURE
10.15

Long-Run Equilibrium, Monopolistic Competition

The long-run equilibrium is at a price of P_1 and an output of Q_1. There are zero profits, since long-run average cost equals price. Profits are being maximized, since marginal cost equals marginal revenue at this output.

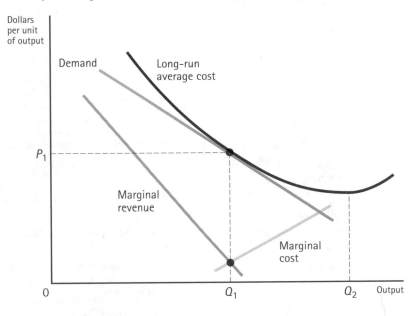

Advertising Expenditures: A Simple Rule

Firms under monopolistic competition, as well as other market structures, spend huge amounts on advertising. How much should a profit-maximizing firm spend on advertising? In this section, a simple rule is derived that helps to answer this question.[13] The quantity that a firm sells of its product is assumed to be a function of its price and the level of its advertising expenditure. There are assumed to be diminishing marginal returns to advertising expenditures, which means that beyond some point, successive increments of advertising outlays will yield smaller and smaller increases in additional sales. (Table 10.12 shows an illustrative case in which successive increments of $100,000 in advertising outlays result in smaller and smaller increases in quantity sold. For example,

---

[13] This rule, put forth by R. Dorfman and P. Steiner, applies to monopolistic or oligopolistic firms, as well as to monopolistically competitive firms. However, since monopolistically competitive firms spend large amounts on advertising, this is a good place for this discussion.

TABLE
10.12

Relationship between Advertising Expenditures and Quantity

Advertising expenditures (millions of dollars)	Quantity sold of product (millions of units)
0.8	15.0
0.9	17.0
1.0	18.5
1.1	19.5
1.2	20.0

the quantity sold increases by 2.0 million units when advertising expenditures rise from $800,000 to $900,000, but by only 1.5 million units when they rise from $900,000 to $1 million.)

Let P be the price of a unit of the product and MC be the marginal cost of production. If we assume that neither price nor marginal cost will be altered by small changes in advertising expenditures, the firm receives an increase in gross profit of $(P - MC)$ from each additional unit of the product that it makes and sells. Why is this the *gross* profit of making and selling an additional unit of output? Because it takes no account of whatever additional advertising expenditures were required to sell this extra unit of output. To obtain the *net* profit, the firm must deduct these additional advertising outlays from the gross profit.

For its total net profits to be a maximum, a firm must set its advertising expenditures at the level where an extra dollar of advertising results in extra gross profit equal to the extra dollar of advertising cost. Unless this is the case, the firm's total net profits can be increased by changing its advertising outlays. If an extra dollar of advertising results in more than a dollar increase in gross profit, the extra dollar should be spent on advertising (since this will raise total net profits). If an extra dollar (as well as the last dollar) of advertising results in less than a dollar increase in gross profit, advertising outlays should be cut.[14] Thus, if ΔQ is the number of extra units of output sold as a result of an extra dollar of advertising, the firm should set its advertising expenditures so that

$$\Delta Q(P - MC) = 1, \qquad (10.9)$$

[14]For simplicity, we assume that the gross profit resulting from an extra dollar spent on advertising is essentially equal to the gross profit resulting from the last dollar spent. This is an innocuous assumption.

because the right-hand side of this equation equals the extra dollar of advertising cost, and the left-hand side equals the extra gross profit resulting from this advertising dollar.

If we multiply both sides of equation (10.9) by $P/(P - MC)$, we obtain

$$P\Delta Q = \frac{P}{P - MC}. \qquad (10.10)$$

Because the firm is maximizing profit, it is producing an output where marginal cost (MC) equals marginal revenue (MR). Thus, we can substitute MR for MC in equation (10.10), the result being

$$P\Delta Q = \frac{P}{P - MR}. \qquad (10.11)$$

Using equation (3.16), it can be shown that the right-hand side of equation (10.11) equals $-\eta$, negative price elasticity of demand for the firm's product.[15] The left-hand side of equation (10.11) is the marginal revenue from an extra dollar of advertising (since it equals the price times the extra number of units sold as a result of an extra dollar of advertising). Thus, to maximize profit, the firm should set its advertising expenditure so that

Marginal revenue from an extra dollar of advertising $= -\eta$. (10.12)

This rule can be very helpful to managers.[16] Consider the Solomon Corporation, which knows that the price elasticity of demand for its product equals -1.6. To maximize profit, this firm must set the marginal revenue from an extra dollar of advertising equal to 1.6, according to this rule. Suppose Solomon's managers believe that an extra \$100,000 of advertising would increase the firm's sales by \$200,000, which implies that the marginal revenue from an extra dollar of advertising is about \$200,000/\$100,000, or 2.0 rather than 1.6. Because the marginal revenue exceeds the negative price elasticity, Solomon will increase its profit if it does more advertising.[17] To maximize profit, it should in-

---

[15]Recall from equation (3.16) that $MR = P(1 + 1/\eta)$. Thus $1 + 1/\eta = MR/P$, and $-1/\eta = 1 - MR/P$; this means that

$$-\eta = \frac{1}{1 - MR/P} = \frac{P}{P - MR}.$$

which is the right-hand side of equation (10.11).

[16]However, this rule is based on many simplifying assumptions and is not a complete solution to this complex problem, which is considered further in Chapter 13.

[17]Had Solomon's managers believed that the marginal revenue from an extra dollar of advertising was *less* than the price elasticity of demand, a *reduction* in the firm's advertising expenditures would increase profit.

crease its advertising up to the point where the marginal revenue from an extra dollar of advertising falls to 1.6, negative the value of the price elasticity of demand.

Using Graphs to Help Determine Advertising Expenditure

A simple graphical technique can be used to see how much a firm, if it uses the above rule, should spend on advertising. Take the case of the Brady Chemical Company. Curve *A* in Figure 10.16 shows the relationship between the price elasticity of demand of this firm's product and the amount it spends on advertising. With little or no advertising, this firm's product would be regarded by consumers as similar to lots of other products; hence, its price elasticity of demand would be very high.

But since appropriate advertising can induce consumers to attach importance to this product's distinguishing features, increases in advertising expen-

Optimal Advertising Expenditure

The firm's optimal advertising expenditure is *R* if the marginal revenue curve is *B* (or *S* if the marginal revenue curve is *B'*).

diture reduce its price elasticity considerably (by decreasing the product's perceived substitutability with other goods).[18] At each level of advertising expenditure, the *B* curve shows the marginal revenue from an extra dollar of advertising. Since the *A* curve intersects the *B* curve when Brady's advertising expenditure is *R* dollars, this, on the basis of equation (10.12), is the level of advertising expenditures that maximizes Brady's profits.

A firm's optimal advertising expenditure depends on the position and shape of its *B* curve and its *A* curve. For example, suppose Brady's *B* curve shifts rightward to *B'*, as shown in Figure 10.16. Such a shift might occur if the firm or its advertising agency found ways to increase the effectiveness of its advertisements. An increase in the optimal level of the firm's advertising expenditures (to *S* dollars in Figure 10.16) would be the result.

Advertising, the Price Elasticity of Demand, and Brand Loyalty: The Case of the Retail Coffee Market

Many firms, such as retail stores, advertise changes in the prices of selected products. One effect of advertising such price changes is likely to be an increase in the price elasticity of demand for the product whose price is changed. Why? Because more consumers will be aware of the price change under these circumstances. To illustrate, consider a study carried out by Berkeley's Michael Katz and Carl Shapiro of the purchases of coffee by 935 households from 1980 to 1982.[19] For each purchase, information concerning the time of purchase, the store in which it was made, the price paid, and the use of either manufacturer or retailer coupons was obtained. (A coupon allows the buyer to obtain coffee at a lower price.) In all, about 50,000 purchase events were included in their sample. These events occurred in Pittsfield, Massachusetts.

Using regression analysis (discussed in Chapter 5), Katz and Shapiro estimated the price elasticity of demand for each of four brands of coffee—Chock Full o' Nuts, Maxwell House, Folgers, and Hills Brothers—during periods when price changes for these brands were advertised and during periods when they were not advertised. As shown in Table 10.13, the price elasticity of demand tended to be higher during the former periods than during the latter periods. For example, the price elasticity of Hills Brothers coffee was about −6.3 during periods when price changes were advertised, but only about −4.2 during periods when they were not advertised.

---

[18]This is true for some products, but not for others. In some cases, the price elasticity of demand is directly, not inversely, related to the amount spent on advertising.

[19]M. Katz and C. Shapiro, "Consumer Shopping Behavior in the Retail Coffee Market," in *Empirical Approaches to Consumer Protection Economics*, eds. P. Ippolito and D. Scheffman (Washington, D.C.: Federal Trade Commission, 1986).

TABLE 10.13

Price Elasticities of Demand, Periods of Advertised and Unadvertised Price Changes

| | Price elasticity of demand | |
Brand	Advertised price change	Unadvertised price change
Chock Full o' Nuts	−8.9	−6.5
Maxwell House	−6.0	a
Folgers	−15.1	−10.6
Hills Brothers	−6.3	−4.2

[a]Not significantly different from zero.

Source: Katz and Shapiro, "Consumer Shopping Behavior in the Retail Coffee Market."

Katz and Shapiro also studied how frequently consumers switched from brand to brand, rather than remained loyal to a particular brand. One simple measure of brand loyalty is the percentage of customers buying a particular brand today who will buy this brand again when next they buy this sort of product. Table 10.14 shows the value of this measure for the four coffee brands studied by Katz and Shapiro. For example, about 62 percent of the buyers of Maxwell House coffee today will buy this same brand when next they buy coffee.

From the data in Table 10.14, one can conclude that brand loyalty tends to be rather high among coffees, but it varies from one brand to another. In particular, consumers tend to be less loyal to Hills Brothers than to the other three brands. Also, brand loyalty tends to be lower for consumers who purchase coffee with a coupon than for those who do not use a coupon. For example, 55 percent of consumers using a coupon to buy Maxwell House coffee were repeat

TABLE 10.14

Percentage of Customers That Are Repeat Buyers of the Same Brand

	Chock Full o' Nuts	Maxwell House	Folgers	Hills Brothers
All purchasers	62	62	63	42
Coupon users	49	55	56	14
Purchasers not using coupons	63	70	65	44

Source: Katz and Shapiro. "Consumer Shopping Behavior in the Retail Coffee Market."

buyers, whereas 70 percent of those not using coupons to buy Maxwell House coffee were repeat buyers. The fact that coupon users tend to have relatively low brand loyalty is of importance to firms. If the probability of repeat purchases by coupon users is low enough, the profitability of issuing coupons may be substantially impaired. The analysis of data of this sort concerning brand switching and brand loyalty has been very helpful to managers.

Summary

1. A perfectly competitive firm will set its output so that price equals marginal cost. If there exists an output rate where price exceeds average variable cost, it will pay the firm to produce in the short run, even though price does not cover average total costs. But if there does not exist an output rate where price exceeds average variable cost, the firm is better off to produce nothing at all. In the long run, the firm will produce at the minimum point on its long-run average total cost curve. Price tends to be at the level where the market demand curve intersects the market supply curve.

2. A constant-cost industry has a horizontal long-run supply curve; an increasing-cost industry has a positively sloped long-run supply curve. If a constant-cost industry expands, there is no increase (or decrease) in input prices; if an increasing-cost industry expands, there is an increase in input prices.

3. Under monopoly, a firm will maximize profit if it sets its output rate at the point where marginal revenue equals marginal cost. It does not follow that a firm that holds a monopoly over the production of a particular product must make a profit. If the monopolist cannot cover its variable costs, it, like a perfectly competitive firm, will shut down, even in the short run.

4. If an industry is monopolized, it generally will set a higher price and lower output than if it is perfectly competitive. The perfectly competitive firm operates at the point at which price equals marginal cost, whereas the monopolist operates at a point at which price exceeds marginal cost.

5. A monopolist sometimes requires the consumer to pay an initial fee for the right to buy its product as well as a usage fee for each unit of the product he or she buys. This is known as a two-part tariff. Another pricing technique sometimes used by monopolists is bundling, which occurs if a firm requires customers that buy one of its products to buy another of its products as well.

6. In contrast to perfect competition, where all firms sell an identical product, firms under monopolistic competition sell somewhat different products. Producers differentiate their product from that of other producers. Thus, the demand curve facing each firm slopes downward to the right—and is not horizontal, as it would be under perfect competition. Each firm will set marginal revenue equal to marginal cost if it maximizes profit.

7. Monopolistically competitive firms spend very large amounts on advertising. To maximize its profits, a firm should set its advertising so that the marginal revenue from an extra dollar of advertising equals the negative of the price elasticity of demand (under the conditions discussed above).

8. Advertising of price changes may make the price elasticity of demand for the product whose price is changed more elastic. This is because the advertising makes consumers more aware of the price changes. Measures of brand loyalty are useful in guiding decisions concerning promotional activities to increase sales of particular brands.

Problems

1. The Hamilton Company is a member of a perfectly competitive industry. Like all members of the industry, its total cost function is

$$TC = 25{,}000 + 150Q + 3Q^2,$$

where TC is the firm's monthly total cost (in dollars), and Q is the firm's monthly output.

   a. If the industry is in long-run equilibrium, what is the price of the Hamilton Company's product?

   b. What is the firm's monthly output?

2. In 2001, the box industry is perfectly competitive. The lowest point on the long-run average cost curve of each of the identical box producers is $4, and this minimum point occurs at an output of 1,000 boxes per month. The market demand curve for boxes is

$$Q_D = 140{,}000 - 10{,}000P,$$

where P is the price of a box (in dollars per box), and Q_D is the quantity of boxes demanded per month. The market supply curve for boxes is

$$Q_S = 80{,}000 + 5{,}000P,$$

where Q_S is the quantity of boxes supplied per month.

   a. What is the equilibrium price of a box? Is this the long-run equilibrium price?

   b. How many firms are in this industry when it is in long-run equilibrium?

3. The Burr Corporation's total cost function (where TC is the total cost in dollars, and Q is quantity) is

$$TC = 200 + 4Q + 2Q^2.$$

   a. If the firm is perfectly competitive and if the price of its product is $24, what is its optimal output rate?

   b. At this output rate, what are its profits?

4. The supply and demand curves for pears are:

$$Q_S = 10,000P$$
$$Q_D = 25,000 - 15,000P,$$

where Q_S is the quantity (tons) supplied, Q_D is the quantity (tons) demanded, and P is the price per pear (in hundreds of dollars per ton).
   a. Plot the supply and demand curves.
   b. What is the equilibrium price?
   c. What is the equilibrium quantity?

5. Harry Smith is the owner of a metals-producing firm that is an unregulated monopoly. After considerable experimentation and research, he finds that its marginal cost curve can be approximated by a straight line, $MC = 60 + 2Q$, where MC is marginal cost (in dollars), and Q is output. The demand curve for the product is $P = 100 - Q$, where P is the product price (in dollars), and Q is output.
   a. If he wants to maximize profit, what output should he choose?
   b. What price should he charge?

6. The White Company is a member of the lamp industry, which is perfectly competitive. The price of a lamp is $50. The firm's total cost function is

$$TC = 1,000 + 20Q + 5Q^2,$$

where TC is total cost (in dollars), and Q is hourly output.
   a. What output maximizes profit?
   b. What is the firm's economic profit at this output?
   c. What is the firm's average cost at this output?
   d. If other firms in the lamp industry have the same cost function as this firm, is the industry in equilibrium? Why or why not?

7. The long-run supply curve for a particular type of kitchen knife is a horizontal line at a price of $3 per knife. The demand curve for such a kitchen knife is

$$Q_D = 50 - 2P,$$

where Q_D is the quantity of knives demanded (in millions per year), and P is the price per knife (in dollars).
   a. What is the equilibrium output of such knives?
   b. If a tax of $1 is imposed on each knife, what is the equilibrium output of such knives? (Assume that the tax is collected by the government from the suppliers of knives.)
   c. After the tax is imposed, you buy such a knife for $3.75. Is this the long-run equilibrium price?

8. The Wilson Company's marketing manager has determined that the price elasticity of demand for its product equals -2.2. According to studies he

has carried out, the relationship between the amount spent by the firm on advertising and its sales is as follows:

Advertising expenditure	Sales
$100,000	$1.0 million
200,000	1.3 million
300,000	1.5 million
400,000	1.6 million

   a. If the Wilson Company is spending $200,000 on advertising, what is the marginal revenue from an extra dollar of advertising?
   b. Is $200,000 the optimal amount for the firm to spend on advertising?
   c. If $200,000 is not the optimal amount, would you recommend that the firm spend more or less on advertising?
9. The Coolidge Corporation is the only producer of a particular type of laser. The demand curve for its product is

$$Q_D = 8,300 - 2.1P,$$

and its total cost function is

$$TC = 2,200 + 480Q + 20Q^2,$$

where P is price (in dollars), TC is total cost (in dollars), and Q is monthly output.
   a. Derive an expression for the firm's marginal revenue curve.
   b. To maximize profit, how many lasers should the firm produce and sell per month?
   c. If this number is produced and sold, what will be the firm's monthly profit?
10. The Madison Corporation, a monopolist, receives a report from a consulting firm concluding that the demand function for its product is

$$Q = 78 - 1.1P + 2.3Y + 0.9A,$$

where Q is the number of units sold, P is the price of its product (in dollars), Y is per capita income (in thousands of dollars), and A is the firm's advertising expenditure (in thousands of dollars). The firm's average variable cost function is

$$AVC = 42 - 8Q + 1.5Q^2,$$

where AVC is average variable cost (in dollars).
   a. Can one determine the firm's marginal cost curve?
   b. Can one determine the firm's marginal revenue curve?

    c. If per capita income is $4,000 and advertising expenditure is $200,000, can one determine the price and output where marginal revenue equals marginal cost? If so, what are they?

*11. The Wilcox Company has two plants with the marginal cost functions

$$MC_1 = 20 + 2Q_1$$

and $$MC_2 = 10 + 5Q_2,$$

where MC_1 is marginal cost in the first plant, MC_2 is marginal cost in the second plant, Q_1 is output in the first plant, and Q_2 is output in the second plant.

    a. If the Wilcox Company is minimizing its costs and if it is producing 5 units of output in the first plant, how many units of output is it producing in the second plant? Explain.

    b. What is the marginal cost function for the firm as a whole?

    c. Can you determine from the above data the average cost function for each plant? Why or why not?

12. If the Rhine Company ignores the possibility that other firms may enter its market, it should set a price of $10,000 for its product, which is a power tool. But if it does so, other firms will begin to enter the market. During the next two years, it will earn $4 million per year, but in the following two years, it will earn $1 million per year. On the other hand, if it sets a price of $7,000, it will earn $2.5 million in each of the next four years, since no entrants will appear.

    a. If the interest rate is 10 percent, should the Rhine Company set a price of $7,000 or $10,000? Why? (Consider only the next four years.)

    b. If the interest rate is 8 percent, should the Rhine Company set a price of $7,000 or $10,000? Why? (Consider only the next four years.)

    c. The results in parts a and b pertain only to the next four years. How can the firm's managers extend the planning horizon?

13. During recessions and economic hard times, many people—particularly those who have difficulty getting bank loans—turn to pawnshops to raise cash. But even during boom years, pawnshops can be very profitable. Because the collateral that customers put up (such as jewelry, guns, or electric guitars) is generally worth at least double what is lent, it generally can be sold at a profit. And because the usury laws allow higher interest ceilings for pawnshops than for other lending institutions, pawnshops often charge spectacularly high rates of interest. For example, Florida's pawnshops charge interest rates of 20 percent or more *per month*. According to Steven Kent, an analyst at Goldman, Sachs, pawnshops make 20 percent gross profit on defaulted loans and 205 percent interest on loans repaid.

---

* This question pertains to the chapter appendix.

a. In late 1991, there were about 8,000 pawnshops in the United States, according to American Business Information. This was much higher than in 1986, when the number was about 5,000. Indeed, in late 1991 alone, the number jumped by about 1,000. Why did the number increase?

b. In a particular small city, do the pawnshops constitute a perfectly competitive industry? If not, what is the market structure of the industry?

c. Are there considerable barriers to entry in the pawnshop industry? (Note: A pawnshop can be opened for less than $125,000, but a number of states have tightened licensing requirements for pawnshops.)

14. In 1996, dairy farmers, hurt by a decade of low milk prices, began reducing their herds. Subsequently, Kenneth Hein, a Wisconsin farmer, said he was getting $16 per 100 pounds of milk, rather than $12, which he had gotten earlier.[20]

a. Why did the price increase?

b. Dairy cattle are often fed corn. When Mr. Hein got $16 per 100 pounds of milk, he paid $5 a bushel for corn; but when he got $12 per 100 pounds of milk, he paid $2.50 a bushel for corn. Does this mean that Mr. Hein made less money when the price of milk was $16 than when it was $12?

15. The reservation prices (in dollars) of three classes of demanders (classes A, B, and C) for Ricky Parton's (a Latin country-western singer) compact discs are given in the table below:

Class	CD 1	CD 2
A	11	5
B	8	9
C	9	10

It costs 4 dollars to produce and distribute each compact disc. The company can sell each CD separately, can put them together as a boxed set, i.e., as a pure bundle, or sell them in a mixed bundling format, i.e., offer the CDs both separately and as a boxed set. Assume that each demander wants only one of each of the CDs at their reservation price (or at any lower price) and that there are an equal number of demanders in each class. For simplicity, assume that the only costs are those mentioned above.

a. What pricing method would you advise Ricky's company to use?

b. How much better (profit-wise) is the best pricing method than the second most profitable pricing method?

16. The demand for diamonds is given by:

$$P_Z = 980 - 2Q_Z$$

[20]*Philadelphia Inquirer*, September 14, 1996.

where Q_Z is the number of diamonds demanded if the price is P_Z per diamond. The total cost (TC_Z) of the De Beers Company (a monopolist) is given by:

$$TC_Z = 100 + 50Q_Z + 0.5Q_Z^2$$

where Q_Z is the number of diamonds produced and put on the market by the De Beers Company. Suppose that the government could force De Beers to behave as if it were a perfect competitor, i.e., via regulation, force the firm to price diamonds at marginal cost.

a. What is social welfare when De Beers acts as a single price monopolist?

b. What is social welfare when De Beers acts as a perfect competitor?

c. How much does social welfare increase when De Beers moves from monopoly to competition?

Appendix: Allocation of Output among Plants

Many firms own and operate more than one plant. In this appendix, we show how the managers of these firms should allocate output among various plants. This is an important decision, and our results have major direct practical value. We consider the case of the Mercer Company, a monopolist, but our results are as valid for nonmonopolists as for monopolists.

The Mercer Company, a monopolist that makes a particular type of metal fixture, operates two plants with marginal cost curves shown in columns 2 and 3 of Table 10.15, output being shown in column 1. Clearly, if the firm decides to produce only 1 unit of output per hour, it should use plant I, since the marginal cost between 0 and 1 unit is lower in plant I than in plant II. Hence, for the firm as a whole, the marginal cost between 0 and 1 unit of output is $10 (the marginal cost between 0 and 1 unit for plant I). Similarly, if the firm decides to produce 2 units of output per hour, both should be produced in plant I, and the marginal cost between the first and second unit of output for the firm as a whole is $12 (the marginal cost between the first and second unit in plant I). If the firm decides to produce 3 units of output per hour, 2 should be produced in plant I and 1 in plant II, and the marginal cost between the second and third unit of output for the firm as a whole is $14 (the marginal cost between 0 and 1 unit of output for plant II). Alternatively, all 3 could be produced at plant I.

Going on in this way, we can derive the marginal cost curve for the firm as a whole, shown in column 4 of Table 10.15. To maximize profits, the firm should find that output at which marginal revenue equals the marginal cost of the firm as a whole. This is the profit-maximizing output level. In this case, it is 3 or 4 units per hour. Suppose that the firm picks 4 units. To determine what

TABLE
10.15

Costs of the Mercer Company

Output per hour	Marginal cost[a] Plant I (dollars)	Plant II (dollars)	Marginal cost for firm[a] (dollars)	Price (dollars)	Marginal revenue[a] (dollars)
1	10	14	10	40	–
2	12	18	12	30	20
3	14	22	14	26	18
4	20	26	14	23	14
5	24	30	18	20.8	12

[a] These figures pertain to the interval between the indicated output and 1 unit less than the indicated output.

price to charge, the firm must see what price corresponds to this output on the demand curve. In this case, the answer is $23.

At this point, we have solved most of the Mercer Company's problems, but not quite all. Given that it will produce 4 units of output per hour, how should it divide this production between the two plants? The answer is that it should set the marginal cost in plant I equal to the marginal cost in plant II. Table 10.15 shows that this means that plant I will produce 3 units per hour and plant II will produce 1 unit per hour. The common value of the marginal costs of the two plants is the marginal cost of the firm as a whole; this common value must be set equal to marginal revenue if the firm is maximizing profit.

Many firms have used this technique to allocate output among plants. For example, electric power companies have developed computer programs to facilitate the actual job of allocating electricity demand (or "load") among plants in accord with the above theoretical rule. These programs allow a central dispatcher, who is in constant communication with the plants, to compute quickly the optimal allocation among plants. The result has been millions of dollars in savings.

As a further illustration, consider the Anderson Company, which has plants at Altoona, Pennsylvania, and at High Point, North Carolina. The total cost function for the Altoona plant is

$$TC_A = 5 + 9Q_A + Q_A^2,$$

where TC_A is the daily total cost (in thousands of dollars) at this plant, and Q_A is its output (in units per day). The total cost curve for the High Point plant is

$$TC_H = 4 + 10Q_H + 0.5Q_H^2,$$

where TC_H is the daily total cost (in thousands of dollars) at this plant, and Q_H is its output (in units per day). Since the Anderson Company's demand curve is

$$P = 31 - Q,$$

its marginal revenue curve is

$$MR = \frac{dPQ}{dQ} = \frac{d(31Q - Q^2)}{dQ}$$
$$= 31 - 2Q$$

where $Q = Q_A + Q_H$ and where P is price and MR is marginal revenue (both in thousands of dollars per unit).

To maximize profit, the firm must choose its price and output so that

$$MC_A = MC_H = MR, \tag{10.13}$$

where MC_A is the marginal cost (in thousands of dollars) at the Altoona plant, and MC_H is the marginal cost (in thousands of dollars) at the High Point plant. To obtain MC_A and MC_H, we take the following derivatives:

$$MC_A = \frac{dTC_A}{dQ_A} = 9 + 2Q_A$$

$$MC_H = \frac{dTC_H}{dQ_H} = 10 + Q_H.$$

According to equation (10.13), MC_A must equal MC_H. Thus,

$$9 + 2Q_A = 10 + Q_H$$
$$Q_H = -1 + 2Q_A.$$

Also, because equation (10.13) states that MC_A must equal MR,

$$9 + 2Q_A = 31 - 2(Q_A + Q_H)$$
$$= 31 - 2(Q_A - 1 + 2Q_A)$$
$$= 33 - 6Q_A.$$

Consequently, $Q_A = 3$. And since $Q_H = -1 + 2Q_A$, it follows that $Q_H = 5$. Moreover, $P = 23$, because $P = 31 - (Q_A + Q_H)$. Put in a nutshell, the Anderson Company should charge a price of $23,000 per unit, and produce 3 units per day at its Altoona plant and 5 units per day at its High Point plant.

Oligopoly

An oligopoly is a market structure with a small number of firms. A good example of an oligopoly is the U.S. petroleum industry, in which a few firms have accounted in recent years for much of the industry's refining capacity. Each of the major oil firms must take account of the reaction of the others when it formulates its price and output policy, since its policy is likely to affect theirs. Thus, when Exxon raises its price of home heating oil by 1 or 2 cents per gallon, it has to anticipate what the reaction of other firms in the industry will be. If its rivals decide against such a price increase, it is likely that the price increase will have to be rescinded; otherwise its rivals will pull away a large number of Exxon customers.

Oligopolies abound in most countries. In the United States, the automobile industry is dominated by three domestic firms—General Motors, Ford, and Daimler-Chrysler—as well as a small number of foreign producers. There are many reasons for oligopoly, one being economies of scale. In some industries, the number of firms tends to be rather small because low costs cannot be achieved unless a firm is producing an output equal to a substantial percentage of the total available market.

We devote an entire chapter to oligopoly both because of its importance and because there is no single theory of oligopoly. In contrast to perfect competition or monopoly, for which there is a single unified model, many types of oligopoly models exist and are used. Each of these theories may be appropriate, depending on the circumstances. In the following chapter, we take up game theory, which is also used to analyze oligopoly.

The Emergence of Oligopolistic Industries[1]

Oligopolistic industries, like others, often (but not always) pass through a number of stages—introduction, growth, maturity, and decline.[2] As indicated in Figure 11.1, the industry's sales grow very rapidly in the introduction phase, less rapidly in the growth phase, and even less rapidly during maturity; in the stage of decline, the industry's sales fall. As an industry goes through these stages, the nature of competition often shifts.

During the early stages when industry sales are growing relatively rapidly, there frequently is a great deal of uncertainty about the industry's technology. Which product configuration will turn out to be best? Which process technology will be most efficient? Because of small production volume and the newness of the product, production costs tend to be higher than those that the industry will eventually achieve. The learning curve (recall Chapter 8) often is comparatively steep. Newly formed companies tend to be a larger percentage of the industry than in subsequent years. Many of these new firms may be started by personnel leaving other firms to start their own businesses. For example, many semiconductor firms were offshoots of Fairchild Camera and Instrument Corporation.

At these early stages of an industry's evolution, one of the major strategic questions facing managers is: Which markets for the industry's new product will tend to open up early, and which ones will open up relatively late? This question is important both because firms should allocate marketing efforts and R and D resources to relatively receptive markets and because the nature of the early markets can exert a significant influence on the way the industry evolves. To forecast which markets or market segments are likely to be most receptive to a new product, one should consider the following three factors.

---

[1]The discussion in this and the following section is based largely on M. Porter, *Competitive Strategy* (New York: Free Press, 1980).
[2]Whether industries are perfectly competitive, monopolistic, monopolistically competitive, or oligopolistic, they often go through the stages discussed here. However, we focus in this chapter on the evolution of oligopolistic industries.

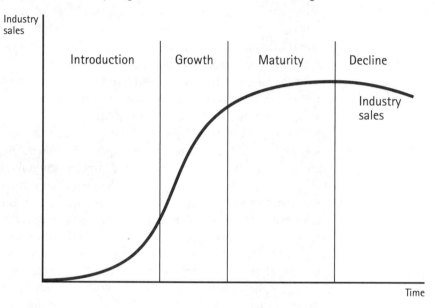

FIGURE
11.1

Typical Stages of the Evolution of an Industry

Industry sales grow at a rapid rate in the introduction and growth stages, more modestly in the maturity stage, and not at all in the decline stage.

First, the most receptive buyers tend to be those for which the new product is most profitable. For example, if a new robot is much more profitable in the railroad industry than in the agricultural equipment industry, it is more likely to be used first by railroads, not by agricultural equipment firms. Second, buyers who face a relatively low cost of product failure are likely to be quicker to adopt a new product than those for which the potential costs are very high. Thus, if this new robot could cause millions of dollars of losses in the auto industry but only minor losses in the steel industry, it is more likely that steel producers will take a chance on it than that auto firms will do so. Third, buyers who would experience relatively low costs in switching from old products to the new one sold by this industry are likely to be more receptive to this industry's product than buyers who would experience high changeover costs.

Maturity and Decline of Oligopolistic Industries

Eventually, most industries enter the maturity phase, when industry sales grow much more modestly than before. This is often a critical phase for many members of the industry. Since firms cannot maintain the growth rates to which they are accustomed merely by protecting their market share, there is often a tendency for firms to attack the market shares of their rivals in the same industry. For example, this occurred in the dishwasher business in the late 1970s, when GE and Maytag attacked Hobart in the higher-price segments of the market, which was becoming saturated. In this phase of an industry's evolution, firms often must alter their assumptions about how their competitors are likely to behave and react. The likelihood of interfirm warfare, based on price, service, or promotion, is high in this phase.

During the maturity phase, rivalry among firms often centers on cost and service, rather than new or greatly improved products. Because of slower growth, more knowledgeable customers, and greater technological maturity, competition tends to focus on cost and service, which may prompt a significant reorientation of firms that have competed on other grounds in the past. Also, as the industry adjusts to slower growth, there generally is a reduction in the additions to productive capacity. Often, firms do not realize that they have entered this maturity phase until after they have installed more capacity than is required. Thus, for a time, the industry suffers from overcapacity.

After the maturity phase, many industries enter a stage during which sales decline. One reason for such a decline may be that the product is being supplanted by a new one (as slide rules were supplanted by electronic calculators). Another reason may be a shrinkage in the size of the customer group that buys the product, perhaps because of demographic changes. Still another reason may be a change in buyers' tastes or needs.

Although firms in declining industries are often advised to curtail investment and get lots of cash out of the business as quickly as possible, this is not always the best strategy. Some industries, like some people, grow old more gracefully and profitably than others. Some firms have done well by investing heavily in a declining industry, thus making their businesses better "cash cows" later. Others have avoided losses subsequently experienced by their rivals by selling out before it was generally recognized that the industry was in decline.

Collusive Agreements

Conditions in oligopolistic industries tend to encourage collusion, since the number of firms is small and the firms are aware of their interdependence. The advantages to the firms of collusion seem clear: increased profits, decreased uncertainty, and a better opportunity to prevent entry. But collusive arrangements are often hard to maintain, since once a collusive agreement is made, any of the firms can increase its profits by cheating on the agreement. Moreover, in the United States, collusive arrangements generally are illegal.

If a collusive arrangement is made openly and formally, it is called a **cartel.** In many other countries, cartels have been common and legally acceptable; but in the United States, most collusive agreements, whether secret or open cartels, were declared illegal by the Sherman Antitrust Act (discussed in detail in Chapter 17), which dates back to 1890. But this does not mean that such agreements do not exist. For instance, there was widespread collusion among U.S. electric equipment manufacturers during the 1950s. Also, trade associations and professional organizations may sometimes perform functions somewhat similar to those of a cartel. Further, some types of cartels have had the official sanction of the U.S. government. Thus, airlines flying transatlantic routes have been members of the International Air Transport Association, which has agreed on uniform prices for transatlantic flights.

If a cartel is established to set a uniform price for a particular (homogeneous) product, what price will it charge? To answer this question, the cartel must estimate the marginal cost curve for the cartel as a whole. If input prices do not increase as the cartel expands, this marginal cost curve is the horizontal sum of the marginal cost curves of the individual firms. Suppose that the resulting marginal cost curve for the cartel is as shown in Figure 11.2. If the demand curve for the industry's product and the relevant marginal revenue curve are as shown there, the output that maximizes the total profit of the cartel members is Q_0. Thus, if it maximizes cartel profits, the cartel will choose a price of P_0, which is the monopoly price.

The cartel must also distribute the industry's total sales among the firms belonging to the cartel. If the purpose of the cartel is to maximize cartel profits, it will allocate sales to firms in such a way that the marginal cost of all firms is equal. Otherwise the cartel could make more money by reallocating output among firms so as to reduce the cost of producing the cartel's total output. If the marginal cost at firm A is higher than at firm B, the cartel can increase its total profits by transferring some production from firm A to firm B.

But this allocation of output is unlikely to take place, since allocation decisions are the results of negotiation between firms with varying interests and varying capabilities. This is a political process in which firms have different amounts of influence. Those with the most influence and the shrewdest negotiators are likely to receive the largest sales quotas, even though this raises total cartel costs. Also, high-cost firms are likely to receive bigger sales quotas than cost minimization would require, since they would be unwilling to accept the small quotas required by cost minimization. In practice, sales are often dis-

FIGURE
11.2

Price and Output Determination by a Cartel

The cartel chooses a price of P_0 and an output of Q_0.

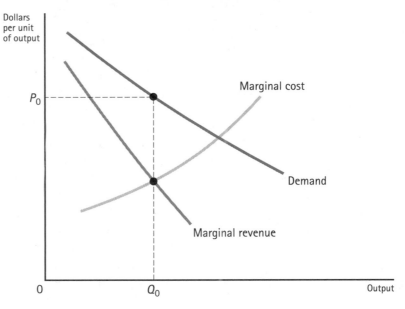

tributed in accord with a firm's level of sales in the past, or the extent of its productive capacity. Also, a cartel sometimes divides a market geographically, with some firms being given particular countries or regions and other firms being given other countries or regions.

The Breakdown of Collusive Agreements

One of the most important things a manager should understand about collusive agreements is that they tend to break down. To understand why firms are tempted to leave the cartel, consider the case of the firm in Figure 11.3. If this firm were to leave the cartel, it would be faced with a demand curve of DD' as long as the other firms in the cartel maintained a price of P_0. This demand curve is very elastic; the firm is able to expand its sales considerably by small reductions in price. Even if the firm were not to leave the cartel, but it granted secret price concessions, the same sort of demand curve would exist.

The firm's maximum profit if it leaves the cartel or secretly lowers price will be attained if it sells an output of Q_1 at a price of P_1, since this is the output at which marginal cost equals marginal revenue. This price would result in a

FIGURE
11.3

Instability of Cartels

If it leaves the cartel, the firm's profit equals $Q_1 \times BP_1$, which is higher than it would be if the firm adhered to the price and sales quota established by the cartel.

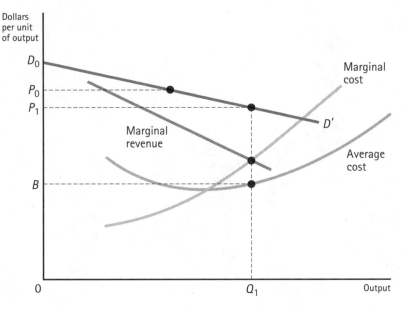

profit of $Q_1 \times P_1 B$, which is higher than the profit would be if the firm conformed to the price and sales quota dictated by the cartel. A firm that breaks away from a cartel—or secretly cheats—can raise its profits as long as other firms do not do the same thing and as long as the cartel does not punish it in some way. But if all firms do this, the cartel disintegrates.

Thus, there is a constant threat to the existence of a cartel. Its members have an incentive to cheat, and once a few do so, others may follow. Price concessions made secretly by a few "chiselers" or openly by a few malcontents cut into the sales of cooperative members of the cartel, who are induced to match them. Ultimately the cartel may fall apart.

Dissension in the OPEC Oil Cartel

To illustrate the difficulties in maintaining an effective cartel, consider the Organization of Petroleum Exporting Countries (OPEC), which consists of 12 ma-

CONCEPTS IN CONTEXT

Cartels Come in Many Shapes and Sizes

Every two weeks in Rutherford, New Jersey, twenty shipping line managers meet and discuss what they will charge to move cargo across the North Atlantic. While this meeting could be composed of the managers of a single ocean shipping line discussing pricing strategy, it is not. Rather, they are executives of twenty different companies. Exempt from the U.S. antitrust laws, they collusively set rates on tens of billions of dollars of cargo.

Their monopoly power is limited because the cartel has not been able to control the shipping capacity of members, and some ocean carriers are not members of the cartel. Nevertheless, it is estimated that the cartel is able to raise rates 18 to 19 percent above competitive rates.

Of course, the modern epitome of controlling supply and hence creating monopoly power is OPEC and the crude oil market. The ability to mark price up over marginal cost is substantial. A product that costs the most efficient producer several dollars to take out of the ground is marked up as much as twenty times.

The monopoly power is so substantial because of the strong demand for the product, the inelasticity of demand for the product, and the fact that the low-cost producers are members of the cartel, and although the cartel is not perfect (not all producers are members), those nonmembers are high-cost producers.

Others have tried to emulate the behavior of OPEC. Brazil and Columbia, major coffee producers, attempted a coffee cartel that failed. The major problem was that coffee has a fairly elastic demand. So when the Brazilians and Columbians withheld supply to raise prices, consumers switched to other beverages like tea and caffeinated colas. If you control supply in a market that has many close substitutes, your monopoly power is not likely to be significant.

Cartels don't have to exist for goods only. They can exist for services too. In Germany a wage-setting cartel exists which is constitutionally sanctioned between unions and corporations. The cartel keeps wages high and labor strife low and ends up costing Germans jobs. This is exactly what we'd expect a monopoly to do—raise prices (wages) and restrict output (jobs).

Sources: "As U.S. Trade Grows, Shipping Cartels Get a Bit More Scrutiny," *Wall Street Journal*, October 7, 1997; "German Wage Pact Ends Up Costing Jobs," *Wall Street Journal*, February 19, 1997.

jor oil-producing countries, including Saudi Arabia, Iran, Venezuela, Libya, Nigeria, and the United Arab Emirates. This cartel increased the price of crude oil dramatically during the 1970s, but by 1983, a decade after the first of its huge price increases, OPEC experienced problems in maintaining the price of oil, and by 1993, the price had fallen to below $15 per barrel. To some extent, the downward pressure on price was due to a leftward shift in the demand for oil brought about by conservation of oil and competition from other fuels (stemming partly from the great increases in the oil price in earlier years). Also, non-

OPEC oil production (in Mexico and the North Sea, for example) soared, thus putting additional pressure on OPEC.

But this is only part of the story. The price declines were also due to the fact that there was internal dissension and that individual members of the OPEC cartel refused to abide by the production quotas set by the cartel. Consider the meeting of OPEC oil ministers in early 1994. Iran and other OPEC countries criticized Saudi Arabia severely, arguing that it should reduce its huge output rate. The Saudis refused, saying that there would be little or no effect on price if they reduced their production, because other OPEC members would cheat and raise their own output correspondingly. Clearly, in cartels as in families, harmony may be hard to achieve.

By the late 1990s, oil prices had fallen to about $12 a barrel, fostering another round of production cuts and price increases. This time, non-OPEC countries such as Mexico and Norway, just as weary of the low prices as the OPEC members, agreed to reduce production. Oil prices skyrocketed, reaching $40 per barrel in early 2000. This led to production increases aimed at restoring prices to about $24–$25 per barrel.

Price Leadership

In many oligopolistic industries, one firm sets the price and the rest follow its lead. Examples of industries that have been characterized by such **price leadership** are steel, nonferrous alloys, and agricultural implements. In this section, we show how the price leader should set its price and output. We assume that the industry is composed of a large dominant firm—the price leader—and a number of small firms. It is also assumed that the dominant firm sets the price for the industry, but that it lets the small firms sell all they want at that price. Whatever amount the small firms do not supply at that price is provided by the dominant firm.

Under these circumstances, you can readily determine the price that the dominant firm will set if it maximizes profits. Since each small firm takes the price as given, it produces the output at which price equals marginal cost. Thus, a supply curve for all small firms combined can be drawn by summing horizontally their marginal cost curves. This supply curve is shown in Figure 11.4. The demand curve for the dominant firm can be derived by subtracting the amount supplied by the small firms at each price from the total amount demanded at that price. Thus, the demand curve for the output of the dominant firm, d, can be determined by finding the horizontal difference at each price between the industry demand curve and the supply curve for all small firms combined.

Price Leadership by a Dominant Firm

The dominant firm sets a price of P_1 and supplies Q_1 units of the product. Total industry output is D_1.

To illustrate how d is derived, suppose that the dominant firm sets a price of P_0. The small firms will supply R_0, and the total amount demanded will be V_0. Thus, the amount to be supplied by the dominant firm is $V_0 - R_0$ which is the quantity on the d curve at price P_0. In other words, d_0 is set equal to $V_0 - R_0$. The process by which the other points on the d curve are determined is exactly the same; this procedure is repeated at various levels of price.

Knowing the demand curve for the output of the dominant firm, d, and the dominant firm's marginal cost curve, M, you can readily determine the price and output that will maximize the profits of the dominant firm. The dominant firm's marginal revenue curve, R, can be derived from the dominant firm's demand curve, d, in the usual way. The optimal output for the dominant firm is the output, Q_1, where its marginal cost equals its marginal revenue. This output will be achieved if the dominant firm sets a price of P_1. The total industry output will be D_1, and the small firms will supply S_1 (= $D_1 - Q_1$).

ANALYZING MANAGERIAL DECISIONS

Price Cuts for Breakfast

In April 1996, the Kraft Food Division of Philip Morris cut prices on its Post and Nabisco brands of breakfast cereal by 20 percent. According to industry observers, this was because the cereal producers had become frustrated with stagnating demand, and consumers had become annoyed by escalating prices of cereal. Before this price cut, the market shares of the leading cereal producers were as follows:

Producer	Share of market for 52 weeks ending February 25, 1996
Kellogg	36
General Mills	26
Philip Morris	16
Quaker	8
Ralston	4
Other	10
Total	100

(a) By June 1996, Philip Morris's share of the market was more than 20 percent. Does it appear that the price cut worked? (b) Kellogg had products that are relatively similar to Philip Morris's. By June 1996, Kellogg's share of the market was 32 percent. Was it particularly affected by Philip Morris' price cut? (c) Subsequently, Kellogg announced a 19 percent cut in its own prices. It was estimated that this would reduce the firm's revenues by about $350 million. Why then did the price cut seem worthwhile?

SOLUTION (a) Yes. (b) Yes. (c) Apparently, Kellogg believed that it would incur an even greater loss if it did not cut its prices.

Source: New York Times, June 11, 1996.

Ajax, Inc.: A Numerical Example

To illustrate how a dominant firm can determine the price that will maximize its profits, consider Ajax, Inc., the dominant firm in a particular industry. The demand curve for this industry's product is

$$Q = 100 - 5P,$$

where Q is the quantity demanded, and P is the price. The supply curve for the small firms in this industry is

$$Q_S = 10 + P$$

ANALYZING MANAGERIAL DECISIONS

Cranberries: Where 34 Percent of the Market Producers Are Price Takers

The cranberry, that marvelous red berry that helps prevent bladder infections, has a lot of vitamin C, contains antioxidants, and has gained status in the medical and health conscious community, is dominated by a giant growers' cooperative—Ocean Spray.

Ocean Spray is the price setter. When Ocean Spray (with a 66 percent market share) sets its price for cranberries, the other (nonmember) producers fall into line. Each year, in late September and early October, Ocean Spray sets a price for sales to supermarkets per case of twenty-four 12-ounce bags. This price is based on anticipated and actual supply and demand conditions in the market.

Given the price that Ocean Spray sets, other producers must decide how much of the product they wish to harvest for sale, harvest to inventory, harvest but for use in other products (e.g., juice and juice blends), or leave in the bogs.

Thus, Ocean Spray is the price leader and the remaining 34 percent of the producers are follow-

ers. Whatever price is set by Ocean Spray, the followers take as given and optimize versus that price.

Source: New York Times, "The Case of the Vanishing Berries," November 12, 2000.

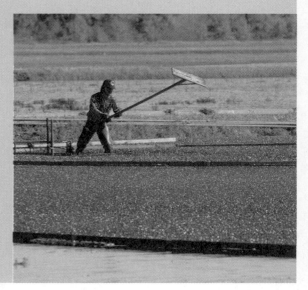

where Q_S is the total amount supplied by all these small firms combined. Ajax's marginal cost curve is

$$MC = 2Q_A, \tag{11.1}$$

where Q_A is Ajax's output.

To derive the demand curve for Ajax's output, we subtract Q_S from Q, the result being

$$Q_A = Q - Q_S = (100 - 5P) - (10 + P) = 90 - 6P.$$

Thus,
$$P = 15 - \frac{1}{6} Q_A. \tag{11.2}$$

Remembering that Ajax's total revenue equals PQ_A, Ajax's total revenue equals

$$TR = (15 - \frac{1}{6} Q_A)Q_A = 15 Q_A - \frac{1}{6} Q_A^2,$$

and marginal revenue equals

$$\frac{dTR}{dQ_A} = \frac{d(15Q_A - \frac{1}{6} Q^2{}_A)}{dQ_A} = 15 - \frac{1}{3}Q_A, \tag{11.3}$$

To maximize profit, Ajax must set marginal revenue, in equation (11.3), equal to marginal cost, in equation (11.1). Thus,

$$2Q_A = 15 - \frac{1}{3}Q_A,$$

so Q_A must equal $6\frac{3}{7}$. Consequently, from equation (11.2), it follows that $P = 13\frac{39}{42}$, or $13.93.

To sum up, if you were the chief executive officer of Ajax, and if you wanted to maximize profit, you would be well advised to charge a price of $13.93. This is the profit-maximizing price.

Summary

1. Oligopoly is characterized by a small number of firms and a great deal of interdependence, actual and perceived, among them. A good example of an oligopoly is the U.S. oil industry, in which a small number of firms account for the bulk of the industry's capacity.
2. Oligopolistic industries, like others, usually pass through a number of phases—introduction, growth, maturity, and decline. As an industry goes through these phases, the nature of firm behavior often shifts. During the early stages, there often is considerable uncertainty regarding the industry's technology and which markets will open up soonest. During the maturity phase, there frequently is a tendency for firms to attack the market shares of their rivals.

3. There is no single model of oligopoly. Instead, there are many models, depending on the circumstances. Conditions in oligopolistic industries tend to promote collusion, since the number of firms is small and firms recognize their interdependence. The advantages to be derived by the firms from collusion seem obvious: increased profits, decreased uncertainty, and a better opportunity to control the entry of new firms. However, collusive arrangements are often hard to maintain, since once a collusive agreement is made, any of the firms can increase its profits by cheating on the agreement. Also, firms may find it difficult to identify a course of action that is agreeable to all members of the industry.

4. Another model of oligopolistic behavior is based on the supposition that one of the firms in the industry is a price leader, because it is a dominant firm. We have shown how under these circumstances this firm should set its price to maximize its profits.

5. Statistical studies based on data pertaining to hundreds of firms suggest that the single most important factor influencing a business unit's profitability is the quality of its products and services, relative to those of rivals, and that market share and profitability are strongly related.

Problems

1. The Bergen Company and the Gutenberg Company are the only two firms that produce and sell a particular kind of machinery. The demand curve for their product is

$$P = 580 - 3Q,$$

where P is the price (in dollars) of the product, and Q is the total amount demanded. The total cost function of the Bergen Company is

$$TC_B = 410Q_B,$$

where TC_B is its total cost (in dollars), and Q_B is its output. The total cost function of the Gutenberg Company is

$$TC_G = 460Q_G,$$

where TC_G is its total cost (in dollars), and Q_G is its output.

a. If these two firms collude, and if they want to maximize their combined profits, how much will the Bergen Company produce?

b. How much will the Gutenberg Company produce?

c. Will the Gutenberg Company agree to such an arrangement? Why or why not?

2. The can industry is composed of two firms. Suppose that the demand curve for cans is

$$P = 100 - Q$$

where P is the price (in cents) of a can, and Q is the quantity demanded (in millions per month) of cans. Suppose that the total cost function of each firm is

$$TC = 2 + 15q,$$

where TC is total cost (in tens of thousands of dollars) per month, and q is the quantity produced (in millions) per month by the firm.

a. What are the price and output if the firms set price equal to marginal cost?

b. What are the profit-maximizing price and output if the firms collude and act like a monopolist?

c. Do the firms make a higher combined profit if they collude than they would if they set price equal to marginal cost? If so, how much higher is their combined profit?

3. An oligopolistic industry selling a particular type of machine tool is composed of two firms. The two firms set the same price and share the total market equally. The demand curve confronting each firm (assuming that the other firm sets the same price as this firm) is shown below, as well as each firm's total cost function.

Price (thousands of dollars)	Quantity demanded per day	Daily output	Total cost (thousands of dollars)
10	5	5	45
9	6	6	47
8	7	7	50
7	8	8	55
6	9	9	65

a. Assuming that each firm is correct in believing that the other firm will charge the same price as it does, what is the price that each should charge?

    b. Under the assumptions in part a, what daily output rate should each firm set?

4. James Pizzo is president of a firm that is the price leader in the industry; that is, it sets the price and the other firms sell all they want at that price. In other words, the other firms act as perfect competitors. The demand curve for the industry's product is $P = 300 - Q$, where P is the price of the product, and Q is the total quantity demanded. The total amount supplied by the other firms is equal to Q_r, where $Q_r = 49P$. (P is measured in dollars per barrel; Q, Q_r, and Q_b are measured in millions of barrels per week.)

    a. If Pizzo's firm's marginal cost curve is $2.96Q_b$, where Q_b is the output of his firm, at what output level should he operate to maximize profit?

    b. What price should he charge?

    c. How much will the industry as a whole produce at this price?

    d. Is Pizzo's firm the dominant firm in the industry?

5. The International Air Transport Association (IATA) has been composed of 108 U.S. and European airlines that fly transatlantic routes. For many years, IATA acted as a cartel: it fixed and enforced uniform prices.

    a. If IATA wanted to maximize the total profit of all member airlines, what uniform price would it charge?

    b. How would the total amount of traffic be allocated among the member airlines?

    c. Would IATA set price equal to marginal cost? Why or why not?

6. In late 1991, two firms, Delta Airlines and the Trump Shuttle, provided air shuttle service between New York and Boston or Washington. The one-way price charged by both firms was $142 on weekdays and $92 on weekends, with lower off-peak advance-purchase fares. In September 1991, Delta increased the per-trip shuttle mileage given to members of the Delta frequent-flier program from 1,000 to 2,000 miles, even though actual mileage from New York to either Boston or Washington is about 200 miles. Moreover, Delta also offered an extra 1,000 miles to frequent fliers who made a round-trip on the same day, raising a possible day's total to 5,000 miles. Almost simultaneously, Trump changed the frequent-flier mileage it gave shuttle passengers. (It participated in the One Pass frequent-flier program with Continental Airlines and some foreign carriers.) What sorts of changes do you think Trump made? Why?

7. Two firms, the Alliance Company and the Bangor Corporation, produce vision systems. The demand curve for vision systems is

$$P = 200,000 - 6(Q_1 + Q_2),$$

where P is the price (in dollars) of a vision system, Q_1 is the number of vision systems produced and sold per month by Alliance, and Q_2 is the number of vision systems produced and sold per month by Bangor. Alliance's total cost (in dollars) is

$$TC_1 = 8,000 \ Q_1;$$

Bangor's total cost (in dollars) is

$$TC_2 = 12,000 \ Q_2.$$

    a. If each of these two firms sets its own output level to maximize its profits, assuming that the other firm holds constant its output level, what is the equilibrium price?

    b. What will be the output of each firm?

    c. What will be the profit of each firm?

8. In Britain, price competition among bookshops has been suppressed for over 100 years by the Net Book Agreement (of 1900), which was aimed at the prevention of price wars. However, in October 1991, Waterstone and Company began cutting book prices at its 85 British shops. According to Richard Barker, Waterstone's operations director, the decision to reduce the price of about 40 titles by about 25 percent was due to price cuts by Dillons, Waterstone's principal rival.

    a. According to the president of Britain's Publishers Association, the price-cutting was "an enormous pity" that will "damage many booksellers who operate on very slim margins."[3] Does this mean that price-cutting of this sort is contrary to the public interest?

    b. Why would Dillons want to cut price? Under what circumstances would this be a good strategy? Under what circumstances would it be a mistake?

9. In the 1960s, Procter and Gamble recognized that disposable diapers could be made a mass-market product, and developed techniques to produce diapers at high speed and correspondingly low cost. The result: it dominated the market. According to Harvard's Michael Porter, who has made a careful study of this industry, the following were some ways in which Procter and Gamble might have signaled other firms to deter entry.[4]

---

[3]"British Book Shops in Price Skirmishes," *New York Times*, October 7, 1991.
[4]M. Porter, "Strategic Interaction: Some Lessons from Industry Histories for Theory and Antitrust Policy," in *Strategy, Predation, and Antitrust Analysis*, ed., S. Salop (Washington, D.C.: Federal Trade Commission, 1981); *New York Times*, April 15, 1993, and March 25, 1995; and *Business Week*, April 26, 1993, and September 19, 1994.

Tactic	Cost to Procter and Gamble	Cost to an entrant
1. Signal a commitment to defend position in diapers through public statements, comments to retailers, etc.	None	Raises expected cost of entry by increasing probability and extent of retaliation.
2. File a patent suit	Legal fees	Incurs legal fees plus probability that P and G wins the suit with subsequent cost to the competitor.
3. Announce planned capacity expansion.	None	Raises expected risk of price-cutting and the probability of P and G's retaliation to entry.
4. Announce a new generation of diapers to be introduced in the future.	None	Raises the expected cost of entry by forcing entrant to bear possible product development and changeover costs contingent on the ultimate configuration of the new generation.

a. In considering these possible tactics, why should Procter and Gamble be concerned about the costs to itself?

b. Why should it be concerned with the costs to an entrant?

c. By the 1990s Procter and Gamble had to compete with high-quality, private-label diapers (as well as with Kimberly-Clark, which successfully entered the market in the 1970s). In March 1993, its Pampers brand had about 30 percent of the market, and its Luvs brand had about 10 percent. The price of Luvs and Pampers exceeded that of discount brands by over 30 percent. Should Procter and Gamble have cut its price?

d. In 1993, Procter and Gamble sued Paragon Trade Brands, a private-label producer, alleging infringement of two patents. Are lawsuits of this kind a part of the process of oligopolistic rivalry and struggle?

10. Under which circumstances do firms find it profitable to increase the quality of their products? Do the benefits always exceed the costs? Why or why not?

11. The West Chester Corporation believes that the demand curve for its product is

$$P = 28 - 0.14Q,$$

where P is price (in dollars), and Q is output (in thousands of units). The firm's board of directors, after a lengthy meeting, concludes that the firm should attempt, at least for a while, to increase its total revenue, even if this means lower profit.

a. Why might a firm adopt such a policy?

b. What price should the firm set if it wants to maximize its total revenue?

c. If the firm's marginal cost equals $14, does the firm produce a larger or smaller output than it would if it maximized profit? How much larger or smaller?

Game Theory

In this chapter, we will discuss how game theoretic models can help managers make "better" pricing and output decisions. Because managers operate in interactive payoff environments, they need a framework that explicitly considers (and anticipates) the actions of others.

Game theory was developed in the early 1940s (in connection with war strategies) and is concerned with the formal study of rational decisions in strategic situations. Because payoffs are dependent on the actions (behavior) of all players, managers must form expectations about the behavior of others. Specifically, because payoffs are interactive, a manager's optimal decision depends on what she expects others to do. This means others are similarly guided so all are aware that each must form beliefs about what others believe you believe others believe and so forth. This is called the chain of reciprocal expectations. Good managers attempt to influence the behavior of others by systematically evaluating the variables subject to their control and using these variables to influence expectations.

What are management strategic games? At the very least, game theory provides a taxonomy that can classify strategic situations, much like the classification scheme biologists use to organize animal species, or the periodic tables of chemical elements. This game theory taxonomy can organize situations based on strategic characteristics, such as: trigger strategies, reputation building, pooling or separating equilibria, repeated games, entry deterrence strategies, and so on. There are a variety of generic games: prisoners' dilemma, chicken, battle of the sexes, to name a few. Many actual management problems can be reduced to these generic form games. Understanding how to win in these games helps you to understand and plan winning strategies in real management games.

Not only will applying game theory reasoning make you a better manager, but if I have to play your management games, I might as well play to win. How should I play? Game theoretic reasoning describes a decision rule or algorithm that predicts the strategy that players will select. For example, on page 451, we study a Cournot quantity game. The logic underlying Cournot strategies is that you want to choose your quantity decision based on the knowledge a rival is doing the same. The resulting games produce an equilibrium that is functionally equivalent to finding the intersection of the two reaction functions. Other equilibrium concepts (e.g., backward or forward induction) employ other types of decision rules.

Game theory is extremely helpful for making competitive sense of some of the most common strategic situations in the business world—situations where conflict interfaces with mutual dependence. Such games are common both within firms and in market actions between firms, for example, in price wars, new product introductions, strikes, negotiations, and divisional relationships. In these situations, players have conflicting objectives but also share a mutual dependence.

Understanding the principles of game theory will show the manager how game theoretic reasoning can improve managerial decision making.

Two-Person Games

Each player—a player may be a single person or an organization—is a decision-making unit with a certain amount of resources; the **rules of the game** describe how these resources can be employed. Thus, the rules of poker indicate how bets can be made and which hands are better than other hands. A **strategy** is a complete specification of what a player will do under each contingency in the playing of the game. For example, a corporation president might tell his subordinates how he wants an R and D program to start, and what should be done at subsequent times in response to various actions of competing firms. The game's outcome clearly depends on the strategies used by each player. A player's **payoff** varies from game to game: it is win, lose, or draw in checkers, and various sums of money in poker. For simplicity, we deal only with **two-person games,** games with only two players.

The relevant features of a two-person game can be shown by constructing

FIGURE
12.1

Payoff Matrix: R and D Programs

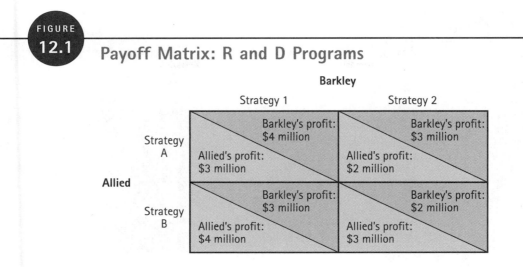

Barkley

		Strategy 1	Strategy 2
Allied	Strategy A	Barkley's profit: $4 million / Allied's profit: $3 million	Barkley's profit: $3 million / Allied's profit: $2 million
	Strategy B	Barkley's profit: $3 million / Allied's profit: $4 million	Barkley's profit: $2 million / Allied's profit: $3 million

a **payoff matrix.** To illustrate, suppose that two firms, the Allied Company and the Barkley Corporation, are about to stage rival R and D programs and that each firm has a choice of strategies. Allied can choose strategy A or B, and Barkley can choose strategy 1 or 2. The payoff, expressed in terms of profits for each firm, is shown in Figure 12.1 for each combination of strategies. For example, if Allied adopts strategy A and Barkley adopts strategy 2, Allied makes a profit of $2 million and Barkley makes a profit of $3 million.

In this game, there is a **dominant strategy** for each player. Regardless of whether Barkley adopts strategy 1 or 2, Allied will make more profit if it chooses strategy B rather than A. Thus, strategy B is Allied's dominant strategy. Similarly, regardless of whether Allied adopts strategy A or B, Barkley will make more profit if it chooses strategy 1 rather than 2. Thus, strategy 1 is Barkley's dominant strategy. The solution to this game is quite simple. Allied chooses strategy B, and Barkley chooses strategy 1. Allied's profit equals $4 million, and Barkley's profit equals $3 million. This is the best that either firm can achieve.

Nash Equilibrium

Not all games have a dominant strategy for every player. For example, suppose that the payoff matrix for Allied and Barkley is that shown in Figure 12.2. (This is the same as the payoff matrix in Figure 12.1 except that Barkley's profit is $4 million, not $2 million, if it adopts strategy 2 and Allied adopts strategy B.) Under these circumstances, Allied still has a dominant strategy: strategy B. Regardless of which strategy Barkley adopts, strategy B is Allied's best strategy. But Barkley no longer has a dominant strategy, since its optimal strategy depends on what Allied decides to do. If Allied adopts strategy A, Barkley will

FIGURE
12.2
Payoff Matrix: No Dominant Strategy for Barkley

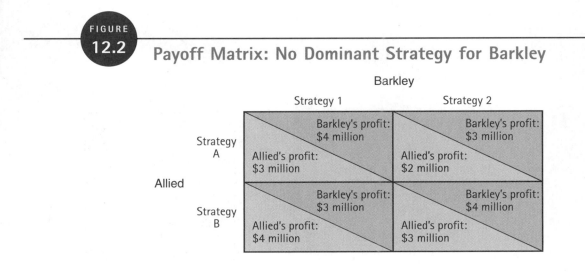

make more profit if it chooses strategy 1 rather than 2. If Allied adopts strategy B, Barkley will make more profit if it chooses strategy 2 rather than 1.

To determine what to do, Barkley must try to figure out what action Allied is likely to take. In other words, Barkley must put itself in Allied's place and see whether strategy A or strategy B is best for Allied. As pointed out in the previous paragraph, Allied's dominant strategy is strategy B. Since Barkley knows all the numbers in the payoff matrix, it can readily determine that this is the case. Thus, it will conclude that Allied will choose strategy B and that it should therefore pick strategy 2 (because strategy 2 is more profitable than strategy 1 if Allied adopts strategy B).

Thus, Allied would be expected to adopt strategy B, and Barkley would be expected to adopt strategy 2. This is the *Nash equilibrium* (named after Nobel laureate John F. Nash, a Princeton mathematician) for this game. A Nash equilibrium occurs if each player's strategy is optimal given the strategies chosen by the other player(s). Put differently, *a Nash equilibrium is a set of strategies (in this case, strategy B for Allied and strategy 2 for Barkley) such that each player believes (accurately) that it is doing the best it can given the strategy of the other player(s).* Taking the other firm's decision as given, both Allied and Barkley are pursuing their own best interests by adopting strategy B and strategy 2, respectively. Neither regrets its own decision or has any incentive to change it.

What is the difference between a Nash equilibrium and an equilibrium where each player has a dominant strategy (as in Figure 12.1)? If each player has a dominant strategy, this strategy is its best choice *regardless of what other players do*. In a Nash equilibrium, each player adopts a strategy that is its best choice *given what the other players do*. It is also important to recognize that some games do not have a Nash equilibrium and that some games have more

FIGURE
12.3

Payoff Matrix: Two Nash Equilibria

than one Nash equilibrium. Figure 12.3 contains the payoff matrix for a game with two Nash equilibria. If Allied adopts strategy A and Barkley adopts strategy 1, each is doing the best it can given the other's choice of strategy. Also, if Allied adopts strategy B and Barkley adopts strategy 2, each is doing the best it can given the other's choice of strategy. Hence, there are two Nash equilibria in this game.

Carpenter Company and Hanover Corporation: A Numerical Example

To illustrate further the concept of a Nash equilibrium, we consider a theory put forth by Augustin Cournot, a French economist. Although this theory is too simple to capture much of the richness of the oligopolistic situation, it has attracted considerable attention. Cournot considers the case in which there are two sellers, that is, the case of *duopoly,* but his model can easily be generalized to include the case of three or more sellers. To describe his model, it is convenient to assume that the two firms, the Carpenter Company and the Hanover Corporation, produce the same product, have the same cost functions, and are perfectly aware of the demand curve for their product, which is supposed to be linear.

Each firm assumes that, regardless of what output it produces, the other will hold its output constant at the existing level. Taking the other firm's output level as given, each firm chooses its own output level to maximize profit. Of course, the level of output that it chooses will depend on how much it thinks its rival will produce. For example, consider the situation in Figure 12.4, which

FIGURE
12.4

Optimal Output of Carpenter Company If Hanover Corporation Produces 0, 100, or 200 Units of Output per Month

Carpenter will produce and sell 150, 100, or 50 units, depending on whether it believes that Hanover will produce and sell 0, 100, or 200 units.

shows the demand curve for Carpenter's product, based on three alternative assumptions by Carpenter concerning Hanover's output.

1. *Carpenter thinks that Hanover will produce and sell nothing.* If this is what Carpenter thinks, the demand curve for Carpenter's product is believed to be the market demand curve, since Carpenter is expected to be the sole producer. The top panel of Figure 12.4 shows the demand curve and the corresponding marginal revenue curve. To maximize profit, Carpenter will choose the output where marginal revenue equals marginal cost; this output is 150 units per month. (For simplicity, we assume that marginal cost is constant in Figure 12.4.)

2. *Carpenter thinks that Hanover will produce and sell 100 units per month.* If this is what Carpenter thinks, the demand curve for Carpenter's product is believed to be the market demand curve *shifted to the left by 100 units.* Why? Because at each possible level of price Carpenter expects to sell the total amount demanded less the 100 units that Hanover is expected to produce and sell. The middle panel of Figure 12.4 shows this demand curve and the corresponding marginal revenue curve. To maximize profit, Carpenter will choose the output where marginal revenue equals marginal cost, this output being 100 units per month in this case (see the middle panel of Figure 12.4).

3. *Carpenter thinks that Hanover will produce and sell 200 units per month.* If this is what Carpenter thinks, the demand curve for Carpenter's product is believed to be the market demand curve *shifted to the left by 200 units,* since at each possible level of price, Carpenter expects to sell the total amount demanded less the 200 units that Hanover is expected to produce and sell. The bottom panel of Figure 12.4 shows this demand curve and the corresponding marginal revenue curve. To maximize profit, Carpenter will choose the output where marginal revenue equals marginal cost, this output being 50 units per month in this case (as shown in the bottom panel of Figure 12.4.)

Employing these results, it is a simple matter to draw a curve showing how Carpenter's output depends on how much it thinks that Hanover will produce and sell. In the previous three paragraphs, we derived three points on this curve. These three points are plotted in Figure 12.5. Other points on this curve could be derived in the same way. This curve is called Carpenter's *reaction curve,* because it shows how Carpenter will react, as a function of how much it thinks Hanover will produce and sell. Hanover also has a reaction curve, which is shown in Figure 12.5. Hanover's reaction curve shows how much Hanover will produce, as a function of how much it thinks that Carpenter will produce and sell. It can be derived in precisely the same way that we derived Carpenter's reaction curve.

According to the Cournot model, an equilibrium will occur at the point where the firms' reaction curves intersect. Thus, in Figure 12.5, an equilibrium will occur if both Carpenter and Hanover are producing and selling 100 units per month. Why is this a Nash equilibrium? *Because each firm's expectation con-*

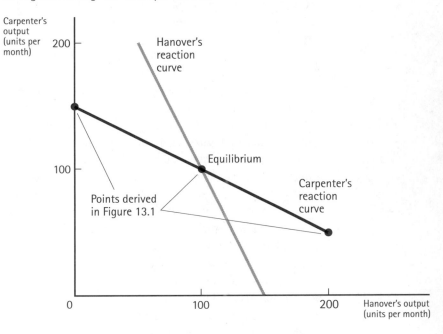

FIGURE
12.5

Reaction Curves of Carpenter Company and Hanover Corporation

Equilibrium occurs at the intersection of the reaction curves where each firm is producing and selling 100 units per month.

cerning the other's output is correct and because each firm is maximizing its profit (given that its rival's output is what it is). To see that each firm's expectation concerning the other's output is correct at this intersection point, note that at this point Carpenter expects Hanover to produce 100 units per month—and this in fact is what Hanover produces. Similarly, at this point Hanover expects Carpenter to produce 100 units per month—and this in fact is what Carpenter produces. Thus, there are no surprises, and equally important, there are no incentives for either firm to alter its behavior. Each firm is maximizing its profit, if (as is the case) the other produces 100 units per month.

While the Cournot model is useful in illustrating the concept of a Nash equilibrium, it has severe limitations as a representation of oligopoly behavior. For one thing, it provides no satisfactory description or explanation of the way in which firms move toward this equilibrium. Cournot's own explanation is naive in many respects and is rejected by most economists. The lack of any explanation of the dynamic adjustment process is regarded as a serious problem by many economists. In later sections, we will take up models that pay more attention to dynamic considerations and are far richer and more interesting.

The Prisoner's Dilemma

A specific type of game—the so-called **prisoner's dilemma**—is particularly useful in analyzing oligopolistic situations. To illustrate this type of game, consider a situation in which two stockbrokers, William Jones and Mary Mulloy, are arrested after making illegal use of inside information. The police lock each person in a separate room and offer each the following deal: "If you confess, while your partner does not confess, you will get a two-year jail term, while your partner will get ten years." Each person knows that if they both confess, each will get eight years (not ten years, because they cooperated with the police). If neither confesses, each will get only four years because the evidence against them is weak.

Both Jones and Mulloy have two possible strategies: to confess or not to confess. The four possible outcomes, depending on which strategy each person chooses, are shown in the payoff matrix in Figure 12.6. What strategy will Jones choose? If Mulloy does not confess, the better strategy for Jones is to confess, since Jones will serve less time (two years) than he would if he did not confess (four years). If Mulloy confesses, the better strategy for Jones is to confess, since Jones will serve less time (eight years) than he would if he did not confess (ten years). Thus, Jones will confess, since regardless of which strategy Mulloy adopts, Jones is better off to confess than not to confess. Similarly, Mulloy

FIGURE 12.6

Payoff Matrix: Jones and Mulloy

too will confess, since regardless of which strategy Jones adopts, Mulloy is better off to confess than not to confess.

Consequently, it appears that *both Jones and Mulloy will confess*. This is the dominant strategy for each person. However, it is important to recognize that each is doing worse than if neither of them confessed. If they could trust each other not to confess, each could serve four years rather than eight years. But they are trapped by their incentive to pursue their own interest: interestingly, even if they could meet and agree not to confess, each one would still have an interest in cheating on the agreement.

Does Cheating Pay?

To illustrate how the type of game discussed in the previous section can help to indicate the circumstances under which firms will tend to cheat (that is, secretly cut price) on a cartel agreement, suppose that the only two producers of a specialized type of scientific instrument—Acron, Inc., and the Farmer Company—form a cartel. Each firm has two possible strategies: to abide by the cartel agreement or to cheat. There are four possible outcomes, depending on which strategy each firm pursues. These are shown in Figure 12.7.

Which strategy should Acron choose? If Farmer sticks by the agreement, it appears that the better strategy for Acron is to cheat, since Acron's profits will be greater than they would be if it stuck by the agreement. If Farmer cheats, the better strategy for Acron seems to be to cheat as well, since Acron's profits will be higher than they would be if it stuck by the agreement. Thus, it appears that Acron will choose the strategy of cheating, since regardless of which

FIGURE
12.7

Payoff Matrix: Acron and Farmer

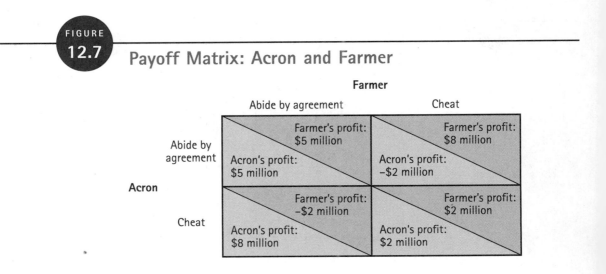

strategy Farmer adopts, Acron seems better off by cheating than abiding by the agreement.

Which strategy should Farmer choose? If Acron sticks by the agreement, the better strategy for Farmer seems to be to cheat, since Farmer's profits will be greater than they would be if it stuck by the agreement. If Acron cheats, the better strategy for Farmer appears to be to cheat as well, since Farmer's profits will be higher than they would be if it stuck by the agreement. Thus, it seems that Farmer will choose the strategy of cheating, since regardless of which strategy Acron adopts, Farmer is better off by cheating than abiding by the agreement.

Therefore, it appears that both firms will cheat. Like the game in Figure 12.6 involving Jones and Mulloy, this is an example of the prisoner's dilemma. Recall that because neither Jones nor Mulloy could trust the other not to confess, both wound up serving more time in jail (eight years versus four years) than they would have if they had trusted each other. Similarly, Acron and Farmer, because they do not trust each other to stick by their agreement, wind up with lower profits than they would if they both were to abide by the agreement ($2 million versus $5 million).

A More Sophisticated Analysis

Any manager worth his or her salt should recognize that there is an important difference between the situation facing Acron and Farmer and that facing Jones and Mulloy. In the case of Jones and Mulloy, if this was the only crime they performed together and if they did not intend to work together again, it might have been reasonable for each of them to assume that they would play this game only once. But for Acron and Farmer, such an assumption would not be reasonable. At every point in time, each of these firms must decide whether it will cheat. Since they are continually dealing with customers, they must continually decide whether to cut price secretly.

Since Acron and Farmer play this game repeatedly, the analysis in the previous section may not be correct. To understand this, suppose that Acron refuses to cheat the first time it must make such a decision and that it continues to abide by the agreement so long as Farmer does so. But if Farmer fails even once to cooperate, Acron will revert forever to the safe policy of cheating. If Farmer adopts the same sort of policy, then each can reap profits of $5 million. If either one cheats, that firm will increase its profit to $8 million for a brief period of time, but subsequently its profit will fall permanently to $2 million. Consequently, it will not be in the interest of either firm to cheat. Moreover, Acron and Farmer can achieve this outcome even if they do not collude or make any binding agreements. If each presumes that the other will have the intelligence to maintain the monopoly price, their presumptions will tend to be correct.[1]

Under these circumstances, a good strategy for each player may be "tit for tat," which means that each player should do on this round whatever the other player did on the previous round. If Acron pursues a tit-for-tat strategy, it should abide by the agreement on the first round. If Farmer also abides by it, Acron should continue to do so, but once Farmer cheats, Acron should retaliate by cheating as well. Experimental results, based on a computer analysis of the results of various strategies, suggest that this often is a very effective approach.[2]

Most-Favored-Customer Clauses[3]

To illustrate how game theory can help shed light on strategic behavior, suppose that Acron and Farmer both announce to their customers that they will grant them a **most-favored-customer clause.** Such a clause stipulates that if the firm reduces its price subsequent to a purchase, the early customer will get a rebate so that he or she will pay no more than those buying after the price reduction. On the surface, this may seem to be a generous policy; indeed, one might question whether it is a profitable policy for the firms. But it is easy to show that this may be a very smart move from Acron's and Farmer's points of view.

For simplicity, suppose that both firms can sell their product at either $2,000 or $1,000. Figure 12.8 shows the profits of each firm, depending on which price the firm sets. Since $2,000 is assumed to be the price that would be set if the two firms formed a cartel, and $1,000 is assumed to be the price that would be set by either of them if it cheated on such a cartel agreement, the payoff matrix in Figure 12.8 is the same as that in Figure 12.7. This is the payoff matrix before the announcement of the most-favored-customer clause. As indicated above, there is a temptation for both firms to cheat, although they may adopt a tit-for-tat strategy.

After the announcement by each firm of the most-favored-customer clause, the payoff matrix changes, as indicated in Figure 12.9. Now each firm's profit is $4 million, not $8 million, if it sets a price of $1,000 while the other firm

---

[1] We assume that each firm can readily detect whether the other firm is cheating. In reality, this may not be so easy. In some cases, trade associations have been authorized to collect detailed information concerning each firm's transactions; in this way, an attempt has been made to detect cheating quickly. Of course, the more quickly cheating is detected, the less profitable it is likely to be.

[2] R. Axelrod, *The Evolution of Cooperation* (New York: Basic Books, 1984).

[3] The discussion in this section is based on S. Salop, "Practices That (Credibly) Facilitate Oligopoly Coordination," in *New Developments in the Analysis of Market Structures,* J. Stiglitz and G. F. Mathewson, eds. (Cambridge, Mass.: MIT Press, 1986). For pedagogical reasons, Salop's analysis has been simplified.

FIGURE
12.8

Payoff Matrix before Most-Favored-Customer Clause

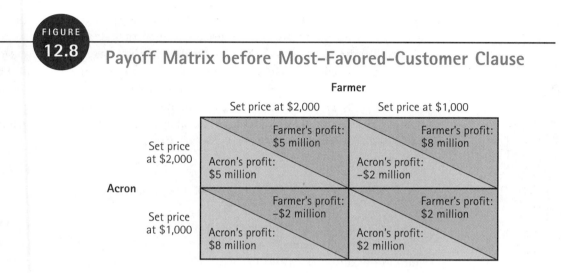

Farmer

	Set price at $2,000	Set price at $1,000
Set price at $2,000	Farmer's profit: $5 million / Acron's profit: $5 million	Farmer's profit: $8 million / Acron's profit: –$2 million
Set price at $1,000	Farmer's profit: –$2 million / Acron's profit: $8 million	Farmer's profit: $2 million / Acron's profit: $2 million

Acron

sets a price of $2,000. Why? Because, if $2,000 has been the price, it will have to give rebates to all of its old customers who paid $2,000.

Given this change in the payoff matrix, it is much more probable that both firms will adhere to the price of $2,000, since the payoff from price-cutting is less than before. Suppose Acron has the first move. Its managers are likely to think as follows: "If we establish a price of $2,000, Farmer's superior strategy is to do the same (rather than cut price to $1,000). On the other hand, if we establish a price of $1,000, Farmer's superior strategy is to follow our lead and cut price to $1,000. Thus, we are better off to establish a price of $2,000, since our profits will be greater ($5 million versus $2 million) than they would be if

FIGURE
12.9

Payoff Matrix after Most-Favored-Customer Clause

Farmer

	Set price at $2,000	Set price at $1,000
Set price at $2,000	Farmer's profit: $5 million / Acron's profit: $5 million	Farmer's profit: $4 million / Acron's profit: –$2 million
Set price at $1,000	Farmer's profit: –$2 million / Acron's profit: $4 million	Farmer's profit: $2 million / Acron's profit: $2 million

Acron

we charged only $1,000." Of course, Farmer's managers are likely to think the same way, with the result that the price will tend to stay at $2,000.

Thus, contrary to what one might believe at first, most-favored-customer clauses can be clever devices to discourage price-cutting. Using game theory, this fact is evident, whereas without the concepts of game theory, it is by no means obvious. General Electric and Westinghouse, among others, have adopted such clauses. The Justice Department has alleged that these clauses have facilitated tacit coordination between these two firms.

The Thrust and Parry of Oligopolistic Rivalry[4]

Previous sections have demonstrated that firms in oligopolistic industries continually face a dilemma. In a broad sense, it may be in their interest to cooperate in various ways with their rivals, but nonetheless they may pursue their narrow self-interest. For members of a cartel, this tension between self-interest and cooperation is reflected in the constant temptation to cheat. For firms that do not collude, this tension is reflected in the fact that firms, to avoid economic warfare with their rivals, may have to sacrifice some of their own potential profits.

Oligopolists, like boxers or chess players, must constantly look for ways to improve their position. Some moves that a firm can make are much less threatening to its rivals than others. Such moves have the important advantage that retaliation is much less likely if they, rather than more threatening moves, are carried out. Moves tend to be perceived as nonthreatening if rivals do not notice them or if they do not affect the level of performance of rivals (as they measure it). For example, when Timex entered the watch industry, its strategy was to produce a watch that was so cheap that it did not pay to have it repaired, and to sell it in drugstores rather than jewelry stores. The Swiss watchmakers, who dominated the industry at that time, did not view this move as threatening, since it did not affect their position as the leading producers of high-quality watches.

But managers cannot always make nonthreatening moves. In deciding whether to make a threatening move, you should consider how likely it is that retaliation will occur, how soon it is likely to come, and how effective (and painful) it will be. It frequently is possible to lengthen the time lag before your rivals are aware of a threatening move, either because the move is not revealed to them or because it is on the periphery of their centers of attention. For example, years after Timex began to take significant portions of the watch market away from Swiss and U.S. producers, its watch was still regarded by them as an inferior product not meriting retaliation.

---

[4]This and the following section are based on Porter, *Competitive Strategy*.

Retaliation to some kinds of threatening moves can be very fast. If you cut your price, your rivals can do the same in a matter of days or even hours. Take the case of Bristol-Myers, which introduced a new product, Datril, and promoted it as "just as good as Tylenol, only cheaper." Literally over a weekend, Johnson and Johnson, the maker of Tylenol, decided to mobilize its sales force and match Datril's price, the result being that it successfully countered Bristol-Myers' challenge.[5]

For other types of threatening moves, it may take years to retaliate. For example, Eastman Kodak had to work for over six years to develop the instant camera that it introduced in 1976 to compete with Polaroid's instant camera. In choosing which threatening moves to make, you should look carefully at your rivals' probable reaction times, and pick moves for which retaliation is likely to be slow and ineffective.

One reason why your rivals may be unable to retaliate effectively is that if they do retaliate, their action may backfire and hurt them as well. Thus, when the Swiss watch companies finally recognized that their financial and growth goals were being threatened by Timex, they found it very difficult to retaliate directly, because such retaliation would seem to legitimize the Timex concept and blur the Swiss product image.

Since, as managers, you must respond to threatening moves as well as make them, it is important to create situations in which it will appear to your rivals that threatening moves against your firm will not pay off. Although economic warfare sometimes is worthwhile, it frequently is better to arrange matters so that no battle takes place. To deter a threatening move, you should do what you can to ensure that competitors expect retaliation if they make such a move. Moreover, if such a move occurs, you would be well advised to retaliate fast and effectively, since this will help to deter such moves by your competitors in the future.

The Importance of Commitment

One of the central concepts in formulating and executing offensive and defensive moves is the concept of **commitment,** of which there are three major types. First, it frequently is important that you convince your firm's rivals that your firm is committed to a strategic move that it is making. If this can be done, it increases the probability that your rivals will become resigned to the new situation and not waste their time and resources trying to prevent its occurrence. If they feel that your firm is determined at all costs to make this move, they

---

[5]J. Hauser, "Theory and Application of Defensive Strategy," in L. G. Thomas, ed., *The Economics of Strategic Planning* (Lexington, Mass.: D. C. Heath, 1986).

CONSULTANT'S CORNER

Using a Price Announcement to Preempt a Market*

Texas Instruments once announced a price for random access memories to be available two years after the announcement. A week later, Bowmar announced that it would produce this product and sell it at a lower price than Texas Instruments. A few weeks later, Motorola said it too would produce this product and sell it at a lower price than Bowmar. Finally, a couple of weeks after this, Texas Instruments announced a price that was 50 percent below Motorola's, and the other two firms said that after reconsidering their decision, they would not produce the product.

The president of a machinery firm, having heard this story at a meeting of the board of directors, decided that his company should consider the sort of strategic move that Texas Instruments used so successfully. His machinery firm was about to develop a new product, which was scheduled for commercial introduction in about two years. This product, although its production costs would not be lower than those of all competitive products that would be introduced at the same time, was expected to be cheaper to produce than some of them. The firm's president believed that his firm should announce a very low price for its forthcoming product, with an eye toward inducing other firms to drop their plans to develop their own new products. He felt that there was very little risk in doing so, since his firm really did not have to abide by the announcement. (Announcements of this sort were not regarded as binding in this industry.)

If you were a consultant to this machinery firm, would you advise the firm's president to announce a very low price for the product his firm intended to introduce in two years?

*This section is based on an actual case. For further discussion, see Porter, *Competitive Strategy*.

may conclude that if they retaliate, your firm will fight back, and a mutually disadvantageous war may ensue.

Second, it frequently is important that you convince your firm's rivals that if they make particular moves, your firm is committed to retaliate swiftly and effectively. The more binding and irreversible this commitment is, the more seriously it will have to be taken by your rivals. Moreover, the greater the ability of your firm to retaliate, the more seriously this commitment will be taken. Thus, if your firm has already developed new products that it could quickly produce and market in such a way as to hurt your rivals, this fact might be leaked to them.

Third, it frequently is important that you convince your firm's rivals that your firm is committed to *not* make particular threatening moves against them. In business, as in all other walks of life, you have to build trust. This is not easy, particularly if your firm has not had an unblemished past record in this regard. The most persuasive evidence often is a demonstration that your firm can be trusted: if your firm continually lives up to its commitments, this will help.

Your firm's commitments must be credible. It is useless for your firm to commit itself to retaliate against a particular move by its rivals if it lacks the resources and know-how to do so. For example, suppose that your firm commits itself to match price reductions by its rivals, although it has no way to discover whatever secret price concessions they make. Obviously, this commitment lacks credibility.

To make a commitment credible, firms sometimes put themselves in a position where it would be difficult and costly, perhaps impossible, for them to violate their commitments. For example, a firm may make large investments in plant and equipment to produce a particular product, thus signaling to others that they have a long-run commitment to stay in the relevant market. Contracts can be signed with employees, suppliers, or customers that bind the firm to particular actions. In this way, firms enhance the credibility of their commitments. However, there are dangers in putting a firm in a position in which if it reneges on a commitment, it suffers substantial losses. Sometimes a firm has to violate a commitment, despite the consequences. Hence firms sometimes put themselves in a position in which it appears that they will suffer substantial losses if they violate a commitment, but like Houdini, they have a secret escape hatch. For example, it may be possible to renegotiate contracts and find alternative uses for plant and equipment.

When Is a Threat Credible?

Firms often transmit signals to one another to indicate their intentions, motives, and aims. Some signals are threats. Suppose, for example, that the Gelhart Company hears that the LIV Corporation, its principal rival, intends to lower its price. Gelhart may announce its intention of lowering its own price significantly, thus signaling to LIV that it is willing to engage in a price war if LIV goes ahead with its price cut. Indeed, some of Gelhart's executives may see to it that this message gets transmitted indirectly to some of LIV's managers.

However, not all threats are credible. If, for example, the payoff matrix is as shown in Figure 12.10, Gelhart's threat is not very credible. To understand why, let's compare Gelhart's profits if it sets a low price with its profits if it sets a high price. (For simplicity, we assume that price can be set at only these two levels.) If LIV sets a high price, Gelhart makes $11 million if it sets a high price and $3 million if it sets a low price. If LIV sets a low price, Gelhart makes $7 million if it sets a high price and $2 million if it sets a low price. Conse-

FIGURE
12.10

Payoff Matrix: Gelhart and LIV

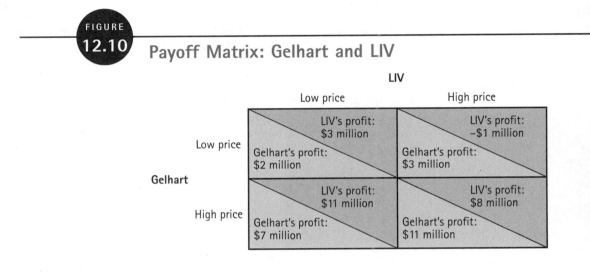

quently, regardless of whether LIV sets a high or a low price, Gelhart will do better if it sets a high price than if it sets a low price.

Since this is the case, it certainly seems unlikely that Gelhart will carry out its threat to cut its price to the low level. After all, as we've just seen, if LIV does cut its price to the low level, Gelhart will earn higher profits by keeping its price at the high level. Consequently, if LIV can be sure that Gelhart will take the course of action that maximizes Gelhart's profit, it can dismiss Gelhart's threat as no more than an empty gesture.

But if Gelhart can convince LIV that it is not going to take the course of action that maximizes its profit, it can make its threat credible. Specifically, if it can convince LIV that if LIV sets the low price, it will match it, *even though this lowers Gelhart's own profits*, LIV may decide not to set the low price. After all, LIV's profits are higher ($8 million versus $3 million) if it maintains a high price (and Gelhart does the same) than if LIV sets a low price (and Gelhart does the same).

How can Gelhart convince LIV that it will lower its price, even though this seems to be irrational? One way is for Gelhart's managers to develop a reputation for doing what they say, "regardless of the costs." They may have a well-publicized taste for facing down opponents and for refusing to back down, regardless of how irrational they may seem. Faced with the "crazy" Gelhart Company, the LIV Corporation may decide not to cut price. But if Gelhart cannot convince LIV of its "irrationality," LIV will rightly regard Gelhart's threat to lower price as not being credible.

The Importance of Entry

Up to this point, we have been concerned principally with oligopolistic behavior in the short run. In the long run, it may be possible for entry or exit of firms to take place. Whether the industry remains oligopolistic in the face of relatively easy entry depends on the size of the market for the product relative to the optimum size of firm. Above-average profits will attract new firms. If the market is small relative to the optimum size of a firm in this industry, the number of firms will remain sufficiently small so that the industry will still be an oligopoly. If the market is large relative to the optimum size of a firm, the number of firms will grow sufficiently large so that the industry will no longer be an oligopoly.

Easy entry also tends to erode collusive agreements. We saw in Figure 11.3 that existing firms are tempted continually to "cheat" on a collusive agreement, since they can attract business from their rivals by lowering prices. The situation is similar for entrants. They too are faced by a relatively elastic demand curve as long as existing firms adhere to collusive agreements to maintain price at its existing level. As long as profits exist in the industry, firms will be tempted to enter and take business away from the collusive group by lowering the price a bit. Once entry of this sort occurs, it becomes harder and harder to keep a cartel together.

The Deterrence of Entry

To understand how oligopolists try to deter entry, it is useful once again to apply game theory. Consider the Lotus Company, which faces the threat of entry by the Salem Company. Figure 12.11 shows the profits of each firm, depending on whether Salem enters the market and on whether Lotus resists Salem's entry (for example, by cutting price and increasing output).

Salem has the first move: it must decide whether to enter. If it enters, Lotus must decide whether to resist. On the basis of the payoff matrix in Figure 12.11, Lotus will not resist because its profits will be $1 million less (that is, $3 million rather than $4 million) if it resists than they will be if it does not resist. Knowing this, Salem will enter because its profits will be $3 million higher (that is, $12 million rather than $9 million) if it enters than they will be if it does not enter. Of course, Lotus may well threaten to resist, but given the nature of the payoff matrix in Figure 12.11, this threat is not credible. Why? Because resistance would lower Lotus' profits.

To deter Salem's entry into the market, Lotus can alter the payoff matrix. For example, it can build excess production capacity, which will be employed to increase output—and slash price—if Salem enters. Since it costs money to

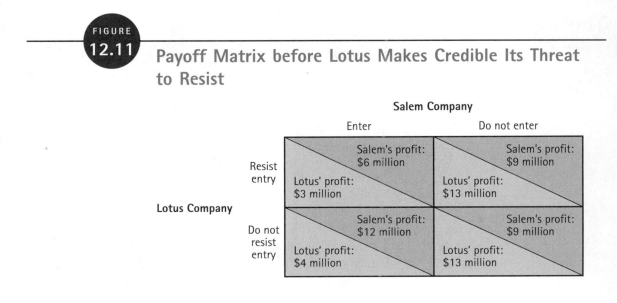

FIGURE
12.11

Payoff Matrix before Lotus Makes Credible Its Threat to Resist

keep excess capacity on hand, Lotus' profits are reduced by $2 million if it does not resist entry or if Salem does not enter. Consequently, the new payoff matrix is as shown in Figure 12.12. Now Lotus' profits if it resists are $1 million higher than they will be if it does not resist (that is, $3 million rather than $2 million). Thus, Lotus' threat to resist becomes credible, and Salem will not enter because its profits will be $3 million lower (that is, $6 million rather than $9 million) if it enters than they will be if it does not enter.

FIGURE
12.12

Payoff Matrix after Lotus Makes Credible Its Threat to Resist

ANALYZING MANAGERIAL DECISIONS

Difficulties in Formulating Effective Contracts

Suppose Dell Computer and General Electric are considering engaging in a joint venture. Each will have to invest $12 million in assets that are of no use or value outside this project. If both firms act in accord with their promises, the annual economic profit to each firm is $3 million. If one or both do not act in this way, the annual economic profit to each one is as shown below:

(a) If a contract can be formulated that will ensure that both firms act in accord with their promises, will this contract be drawn up and signed by both firms (if the attorneys' fees are nominal)? Why or why not? (b) If such a contract cannot be formulated, will either firm enter into the joint venture? Why or why not? (c) Why may it be very difficult to formulate an effective contract of this sort? (d) Is this an ordinary prisoner's dilemma game? If not, why not?

SOLUTION (a) Yes, because both firms will make an annual economic profit of $3 million (before deducting the attorneys' fees). Recall that an economic profit is profit above what could have been earned from alternative ways of investing the $12 million. (b) Without such a contract, each firm would have an incentive not to act in accord with its promises once both had invested in the joint venture. To see this, note that, whether or not Dell

acts in accord with its promise, General Electric would make more money by not acting in accord with its promise than by doing so. Similarly, whether or not General Electric acts in accord with its promise, Dell would make more money by not acting in accord with its promise than by doing so. Nonetheless, perhaps both would trust each other, but if they did so and one did not keep its promise, the relevant managers of the other firm might be vulnerable to criticism, perhaps dismissal. Thus, the relevant managers of one or both firms may not be willing to take the risks. (c) It is very difficult to foresee the full range of circumstances that may prevail in the future and to specify in a contract completely and unambiguously what action each firm is to take under each possible set of circumstances. Often it is impractical to attempt to formulate such a contract. (d) No. In this case both firms have the option of not playing the game.

Du Pont's Attempt to Deter Entry into the Titanium Dioxide Industry

To illustrate how firms sometimes build up productive capacity to deter entry, consider the case of Du Pont, the United States' largest chemical firm, which in the early 1970s accounted for about one-third of the nation's sales of titanium dioxide, a whitener used in paints and other products. Du Pont's top executives felt at that time that the demand for titanium dioxide would grow considerably, and that new government regulations would soon be instituted that would force Du Pont's rivals to shut down their plants. (Because Du Pont's facilities used a different technology and were located in areas different from those of its rivals, it would not have to shut down.) Thus, many of Du Pont's rivals would have to "enter" the industry with new plants.

Du Pont's managers decided to invest over a third of a billion dollars to increase the firm's capacity to produce titanium dioxide, the strategy (according to outside observers) being to install much more capacity than was immediately necessary in order to deter Du Pont's rivals from entering the market. By making this huge investment, Du Pont, like the Lotus Company in the previous section, made credible its intention to resist if entry occurred.

In fact, however, although this strategy seemed sound, many of Du Pont's forecasts turned out to be wrong, with unfortunate consequences for the firm. The actual increase in the demand for titanium dioxide was less than was forecasted, and because the government regulations were not enforced as strongly as expected, Du Pont's rivals did not have to shut down their plants. Also, Du Pont's actions led to an antitrust case in which Du Pont was charged with attempting to monopolize the titanium dioxide market. (This case is discussed at length in Chapter 17.) Nonetheless, the fact that things did not work as Du Pont expected does not deny that the model in the previous section helps to explain Du Pont's behavior.[6]

Advertising to Resist Entry: Maxwell House versus Folgers

As we have seen, price cuts and the construction of excess productive capacity can be used to forestall and resist entry. But they are not the only strategies that can be used. For example, advertising can be used to resist entry.

Take the case of Folgers Coffee, which began to market its product in areas of the eastern United States where it had not previously been active and where

[6]See P. Ghemawat, "Capacity Expansion in the Titanium Dioxide Industry," *Journal of Industrial Economics,* December 1984.

Maxwell House was the leading coffee seller. Maxwell House responded by substantially increasing its advertising, the purpose being to encourage consumers to stock up on Maxwell House Coffee and to make them less likely to pay attention to Folgers' ads asking them to try its new brand. Also, Maxwell House hoped that its additional advertising would enable it to absorb retailers' warehouse space that otherwise might be used to stock Folgers' new brand.

Specifically, Maxwell House established a target of out-advertising the entrant (Folgers) by 50 percent. Moreover, it developed advertising similar to that of Folgers to reduce the apparent novelty of Folgers' ads. If consumers were confused by the similarity, it was felt that this could help Maxwell House's sales because of greater consumer familiarity with the leading brand. The idea was to discourage potential buyers from trying Folgers Coffee and to prevent the sort of brand loyalty discussed in Chapter 10 from developing for Folgers. This is one way that an oligopolist can resist entry, and it can be effective.[7]

Preemptive Strategies: The Case of Wal-Mart Stores

Having studied various cases in which an oligopolist wants to deter entry, let's turn to cases in which an investment opportunity exists that has not been exploited by any firm, and the prize will go to the firm that exploits it first. For example, consider Wal-Mart stores, a very successful chain of discount retail stores. Sam Walton, the company's founder, established hundreds of such stores in small towns in the Southwest. Because the market in each such town was too limited to support more than one discount store, his strategy was to be the first to do so. In other words, his was a **preemptive strategy**—a strategy of setting up stores before another firm did so.

To see why such a strategy was sound, suppose that Wal-Mart and the Jones Brothers are both considering establishing a discount store in a small town in Oklahoma. Figure 12.13 shows the relevant payoff matrix. If Wal-Mart enters the town, but Jones Brothers does not, Wal-Mart will make $5 million and Jones Brothers will make nothing. If Jones Brothers enters the town, but Wal-Mart does not, Jones Brothers will make $5 million and Wal-Mart will make nothing. If *both* Wal-Mart and Jones Brothers enter the town, both *lose* $2 million.

There are two Nash equilibria in this game—one where Wal-Mart alone enters and one where Jones Brothers alone enters. Which one occurs depends on which firm acts first. If Wal-Mart acts first, it can enter and be confident that Jones Brothers is very unlikely to do the same (since Jones Brothers would lose

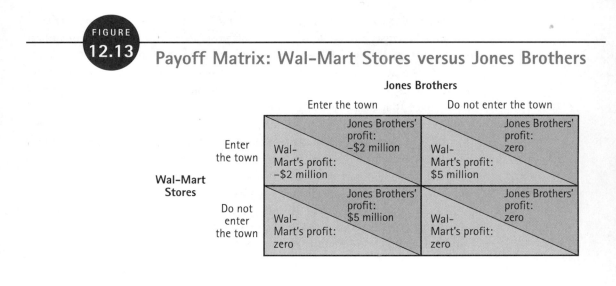

FIGURE
12.13 Payoff Matrix: Wal-Mart Stores versus Jones Brothers

$2 million if it entered). Thus, Wal-Mart, if it is fast on its feet, can be reasonably sure to garner the prize of $5 million in profits. In fact, Wal-Mart has been very fast indeed, as evidenced by its having established more than 1,600 stores. And the late Sam Walton was very successful, as evidenced by his estimated net worth of over $6 billion.

Representing Games with Game Trees

Throughout this chapter we have examined games in which players select their best strategies and move at the same time, but sometimes games have a sequential structure, in which case it may be helpful to represent the game with a game tree. Suppose that Compaq Computer Corporation and Hewlett-Packard Company each must decide whether to expand its productive capacity of a particular type and that Compaq will make its decision first. The game tree for this scenario appears in Figure 12.14. The tree consists of decision nodes and branches. Decision nodes are points at which a decision will be made by one of the players. The branches extending to the right of each decision node reflect the choices facing the player at the decision mode. The possible outcomes of the game are given by the payoffs on the right side of the tree. The left-most decision node in Figure 12.14 is Compaq's decision whether or not to expand production. Hewlett-Packard's decision comes next. There are two decision nodes for Hewlett-Packard because Compaq has two choices. If Compaq decides to expand, Hewlett-Packard faces the decision of the upper decision node; if Compaq decides not to expand, Hewlett-Packard faces the decision of the lower decision node. The four different payoffs correspond to the four possible out-

FIGURE
12.14 Game Tree: Compaq and Hewlett–Packard

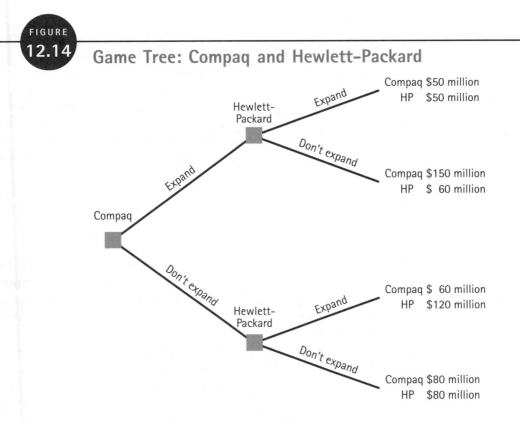

comes to the game: (1) Compaq expands and H-P expands; (2) Compaq expands and H-P doesn't expand; (3) Compaq doesn't expand and H-P expands; or (4) Compaq doesn't expand and H-P doesn't expand.

How do we solve this game? Compaq wants to make the choice that will lead to the best payoff, but of course, Compaq's payoff depends on H-P's decision. If Compaq expands, H-P will enter the game at its upper decision node, and face a payoff of $50 million if it expands and $60 million if it doesn't expand. Thus, if Compaq expands, it knows H-P will not expand and the payoff to Compaq will be $150 million. What if Compaq decides not to expand? Working from its lower decision node, H-P will then face a payoff of $120 million and if it expands and $80 million if it doesn't expand. Thus, if Compaq doesn't expand, it knows H-P will expand and the payoff to Compaq will be $60 million. Now Compaq can compare these different outcomes. Expanding leads to a payoff of $150 million; deciding not to expand leads to a payoff of $60 million. The game is solved. Compaq chooses to expand and H-P then chooses not to expand. The payoffs, reached by following Compaq's "Expand" branch and then H-P's "Don't Expand" branch, are $150 million to Compaq and $60 million to H-P.

A general principle emerges from this analysis. By evaluating the payoffs to H-P, Compaq can see how H-P will conclude the game at its two alternative decision nodes, and this in turn makes clear Compaq's payoffs for expanding or not expanding. The game is solved by reasoning backward from the various payoffs. Economists call this *backward induction*, and this is a general principle that applies to any strategic context. Whenever possible, players should identify the possible outcomes of a game and reason backward to determine their best strategies. If the game is sequential in nature, a good way to organize all the various outcomes and choices is with a game tree like the ones in Figure 12.14.

Summary

1. Game theory is often used to represent and analyze oligopolistic behavior. The relevant features of a two-person game can be shown by constructing a payoff matrix. If each firm has a dominant strategy, this strategy is its best choice regardless of what other firms do. Not all games have a dominant strategy for every firm.

2. In a Nash equilibrium, each firm adopts a strategy that is its best choice given what the other firms do. Some games do not have a Nash equilibrium; others have more than one Nash equilibrium. To illustrate the concept of a Nash equilibrium, we considered a very simple theory put forth by Augustin Cournot, a French economist.

3. The prisoner's dilemma is a type of game useful in analyzing oligopolistic situations, such as whether cartel members should cheat. If the game is played once, there are strong incentives to cheat, but if it is repeated, other strategies, such as tit for tat, may be better. Most-favored-customer clauses can be devices to discourage price-cutting.

4. In considering whether to make a move that threatens its rivals, an oligopolist should consider how likely it is that retaliation will occur, how soon it is likely to come, and how effective (and painful) it will be. It frequently is important that you convince your firm's rivals that your firm is committed to a strategic move it is making, that if they make particular moves, your firm is committed to retaliate swiftly and effectively, and that your firm is committed not to make particular threatening moves against them.

5. Oligopolists often fight hard to deter other firms from entering their market. Game theory is useful in analyzing how they go about deterring entry. Frequently they change the payoff matrix so as to make their threat to resist entry more credible. Game theory is also useful in analyzing preemptive strategies, like that of Wal-Mart stores.

Problems

1. Two soap producers, the Fortnum Company and the Maison Company, can stress either newspapers or magazines in their forthcoming advertising campaigns. The payoff matrix is as follows:

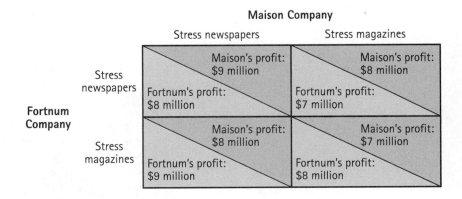

a. Is there a dominant strategy for each firm? If so, what is it?
b. What will be the profit of each firm?
c. Is this game an example of the prisoner's dilemma?

2. The Ulysses Corporation and the Xenophon Company are the only producers of a very sophisticated type of camera. They each can engage in either a high or a low level of advertising in trade journals. The payoff matrix is as follows:

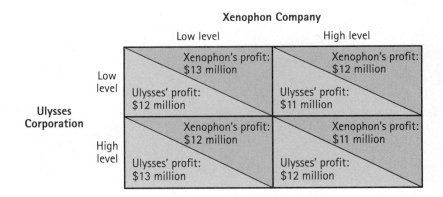

a. Will Ulysses engage in a high or a low level of advertising in trade journals?
b. Will Xenophon engage in a high or a low level of advertising in trade journals?
c. Is there a dominant strategy for each firm?

3. The Boca Raton Company announces that, if it reduces its price subsequent to a purchase, the early customer will get a rebate so that he or she will pay no more than those buying after the price reduction.

   a. If the Boca Raton Company has only one rival, and if its rival too makes such an announcement, does this change the payoff matrix? If so, in what way?

   b. Do these announcements tend to discourage price cutting? Why or why not?

4. Two soft drink producers, York Cola and Reno Cola, secretly collude to fix prices. Each firm must decide whether to abide by the agreement or to cheat on it. The payoff matrix is as follows:

   a. What strategy will each firm choose, and what will be each firm's profit?

   b. Does it matter whether this is a one-shot agreement or it is meant to continue for some time?

   c. Is this game an example of the prisoner's dilemma?

5. Two firms, the Martin Company and the Malone Corporation, make and sell electrical equipment. Martin can choose strategy A or B, and Malone can choose strategy 1 or 2. The payoff, expressed in terms of profits for each firm, is given below for each combination of strategies.

   a. What strategy will the Malone Corporation adopt? Why?

   b. What strategy will the Martin Company adopt? Why?

6. The Hogan Company receives information that its chief rival, the Cosgrove Corporation, intends to lower its price. The payoff matrix is as follows:

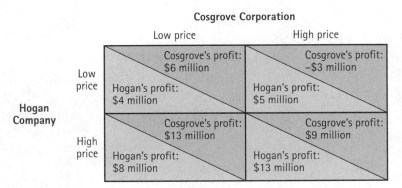

Cosgrove Corporation

		Low price	High price
Hogan Company	Low price	Cosgrove's profit: $6 million / Hogan's profit: $4 million	Cosgrove's profit: −$3 million / Hogan's profit: $5 million
	High price	Cosgrove's profit: $13 million / Hogan's profit: $8 million	Cosgrove's profit: $9 million / Hogan's profit: $13 million

The Hogan Company decides to announce its intention of lowering its own price significantly, thus indicating to Cosgrove that it is prepared to engage in a price war if Cosgrove carries out the price reduction. Is Cosgrove likely to doubt that Hogan really will cut its price? Why or why not?

7. The Beaumont Corporation and the Biltmore Company are both considering the establishment of a high-priced French restaurant in a small but affluent town in California. The payoff matrix is as follows:

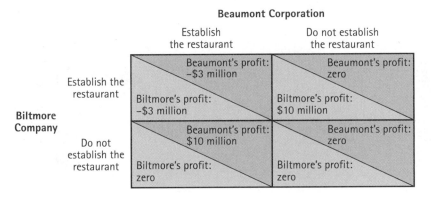

Beaumont Corporation

		Establish the restaurant	Do not establish the restaurant
Biltmore Company	Establish the restaurant	Beaumont's profit: −$3 million / Biltmore's profit: −$3 million	Beaumont's profit: zero / Biltmore's profit: $10 million
	Do not establish the restaurant	Beaumont's profit: $10 million / Biltmore's profit: zero	Beaumont's profit: zero / Biltmore's profit: zero

a. How many Nash equilibria are there?

b. What will determine the outcome?

8. The Rose Corporation is one of two sellers of paint. It pursues a tit-for-tat strategy. However, it has great difficulty in telling whether its rival is secretly cutting its price. What problems is this likely to cause?

9. Why is the concept of commitment so important? Why must a firm's commitments be credible?

10. How do oligopolists try to deter entry? Are all threats to resist entry credible? Why or why not?

Pricing
Techniques

In April 1992, Robert Crandall, chairman of American Airlines, dropped a bombshell on the travel business by drastically revising his firm's price structure. Specifically, he reduced a complex system of dozens of fares to four basic types. The result: a tidal wave of calls to all the airlines and to travel agents from customers wanting information and requesting changes in existing tickets. Although the previous chapters covered a considerable amount of material concerning pricing, they by no means included everything a manager like Crandall needs to know about this central topic.

In this chapter, we take up four additional topics regarding pricing. First, we describe and evaluate the commonly used practice known as cost-plus pricing. Because this practice is so widespread, its advantages and disadvantages should be understood. Second, we discuss the ways in which a multiproduct firm should set prices in order to maximize its profit. This is an important extension of the material presented in previous chapters, which assumed that the firm produces only one product.

Third, we describe and analyze price discrimination, a practice whereby a firm charges different prices to different customers. Because many firms use price discrimination to enhance their profits, any manager should understand how this practice works and the conditions under which it can be profitable. Fourth, this chapter takes up transfer pricing. If one division of a firm sells its product to another division of the same firm, the firm's top management must determine the price that the former division should charge the latter division. If this so-called transfer price is set incorrectly, the firm's profits will suffer. This chapter shows how this transfer price should be established.

Cost-Plus Pricing

In the past half-century, a great many surveys of business pricing practices have been carried out by academic researchers and others. The results, which have been surprisingly consistent from one survey to another, indicate that **cost-plus pricing** (sometimes called **full-cost pricing**) is a technique used by a large number of firms. Although there are many forms of cost-plus pricing, the typical form involves the following two steps. First, the firm estimates the cost per unit of output of the product. Since this cost will generally vary with output, the firm must base this computation on some assumed output level. Usually, firms use for this purpose some proportion of capacity, generally between two-thirds and three-quarters. Second, the firm adds a markup (generally put in the form of a percentage) to the estimated average cost. This markup is meant to include certain costs that cannot be allocated to any specific product and to provide a return on the firm's investment.

In terms of basic algebra, the percentage markup can be expressed:

$$\text{Markup} = \frac{\text{price} - \text{cost}}{\text{cost}}, \tag{13.1}$$

where the numerator—that is, (price − cost)—is the **profit margin.** Thus, if the cost of a paperback book is $4 and its price is $6,

$$\text{Markup} = \frac{6 - 4}{4} = 0.50,$$

or 50 percent. If we solve equation 13.1 for price, the result is

$$\text{Price} = \text{cost}(1 + \text{markup}), \tag{13.2}$$

which is the pricing formula described in the previous paragraph. In the case of the paperback book,

$$\text{Price} = 4(1 + 0.50)$$

$$= \$6,$$

since the markup is 50 percent.

Some firms have set up a **target return** figure that they hope to earn, which determines the markup. For example, General Electric at times has established a target rate of return of 20 percent. Under target-rate-of-return pricing, price is set equal to

$$P = L + M + K + \frac{F}{Q} + \frac{\pi A}{Q},$$ (13.3)

where P is price, L is unit labor cost, M is unit material cost, K is unit marketing cost, F is total fixed or indirect costs, Q is the number of units the firm plans to produce during the relevant planning period, A is total gross operating assets, and π is the desired profit rate on those assets. Thus, if a firm believes that its unit labor cost is \$2, its unit material cost is \$1, its unit marketing cost is \$3, its total fixed cost is \$10,000, its output will be 1,000 units, its assets are \$100,000, and its target rate of return is 15 percent, its price would be set at

$$P = 2 + 1 + 3 + \frac{10,000}{1,000} + \frac{0.15(100,000)}{1,000} = \$31.$$

For firms that produce more than one product, the charge for indirect cost, or overhead, is often established by allocating this cost among the firm's products on the basis of their average variable costs. Thus, if a firm's total annual indirect costs (for all products) are estimated to be \$3 million and the total annual variable costs (for all products) are estimated to be \$2 million, then indirect costs would be allocated to products at a rate of 150 percent of variable cost. For example, if the average variable cost of product Y is estimated to be \$10, the firm would add a charge of 1.50 × \$10, or \$15, for indirect cost. Adding this charge to the average variable cost, the firm obtains an estimated fully allocated cost of \$10 + \$15, or \$25. This figure would then be marked up to allow for profit. For example, if the markup is 40 percent, the price is 1.40 × 25, or \$35.

Cost-Plus Pricing at Computron, Inc.: A Case Study

Computron, Inc., a manufacturer of digital computers used in process control applications in chemical and other industries, adopted the following procedure to set the price for its 1000X computer. It calculated the average production cost, including indirect costs, and added on a $33\frac{1}{3}$ percent markup:

Factory cost	\$192,000
$33\frac{1}{3}$% markup on cost	64,000
U.S. list price	\$256,000

The company felt that it manufactured the best all-around computer of its type, as judged by dependability, precision, and flexibility. It did not try to sell the 1000X computer on the basis of price. Although the price that the company charged was frequently higher than that of its rivals, the high quality of its products enabled it to compete successfully, both in the United States and abroad. The firm's management felt that price-cutting "not only reduced profits, but also reflected unfavorably on the company's 'quality' image." Of course, such an aversion to price-cutting, if unjustified, can cost a company dearly.[1]

Cost–Plus Pricing at Internet Companies and Government–regulated Industries

Many online companies seem to have adopted a cost-plus pricing scheme. Consider Onsale, an online computer store. Its pricing policy is called "At Cost" and their claim is that they sell products based at the wholesale price plus a fixed transaction fee (the markup).[2] Online sellers in other product lines have adopted the same pricing scheme. 4Cost.com claims to sell major household appliances (GE, Hotpoint washers, dryers, refrigerators, and ovens) and electronics (RCA, Sony, TVs, and camcorders) at a cost-plus basis, where the purchaser is shown the wholesale price of the item they are interested in.[3] Many automobile dealers are also using this approach. However, auto dealer invoices contain some items such as "area allowances," which are hard for the novice consumer to interpret, and manufacturer give-backs are not included in the invoice. Thus, consumers are not seeing the true price that the dealer paid for the car. In addition, many customers are trading in their old vehicle. In dealing with a customer, the dealers are concerned with how much money they can make on the package—the trade-in plus the sale of the new vehicle. This makes dealing with the auto dealer harder than dealing with an appliance dealer (where trade-ins are nonexistent).

Government regulators have also used cost-plus pricing in industries that they regulate or control. For instance, the Coal Ministry in India recently allowed "Rajmahal" coal to be priced at cost plus Rs143 per tonne. This will allow the mining company, Eastern Coalfields Ltd., a margin of Rs143 per tonne after meeting production costs.[4] The danger of such a pricing scheme in a government-controlling industry is that when the profit is guaranteed, the firm may lose incentive to be cost efficient. This tends to create a larger government regulatory bureaucracy to monitor costs.

---

[1]E. R. Corey, *Industrial Marketing: Cases and Concepts* (3d ed.; Englewood Cliffs, N.J.: Prentice-Hall, 1983).
[2]*San Francisco Chronicle,* "Egghead Whips Up a $400 Million Deal With Onsale," July 15, 1997.
[3]4Cost Appliances and Electronics: Lowest Prices on the Web found at *www.4cost.com/.*
[4]Badal Sanyal, "Cost Plus Pricing Helps Raymahal Expansion," August 26, 1996 found at *www.hindubusinessline.com/1996/08/26/BLFP.08.html.*

Does Cost–Plus Pricing Maximize Profit?

On the basis of the previous discussion, it seems extremely unlikely that cost-plus pricing can result in the maximization of profits. Indeed, this pricing technique seems naive, because it takes no account, explicitly at least, of the extent or elasticity of demand or of the size of marginal, rather than average, cost. Nevertheless, if applied properly, cost-plus pricing may result in firms' coming close to maximum profits. To see this, it is important to note how little has been said about the factors determining the size of the percentage markup. (Even in the case of target-rate-of-return pricing, no explanation has been given for the target rate of return that a firm chooses.) For example, why was the paperback book cited on page 478 marked up by 50 percent? Why not 25 percent, or 150 percent? If the bookseller is maximizing profit, the markup is determined by the price elasticity of demand for the book.

To understand why this is true, recall from Chapter 3 that

$$MR = P\left(1 + \frac{1}{\eta}\right), \tag{13.4}$$

where MR is the product's marginal revenue, P is the price, and η is the price elasticity of demand. This, of course, is the basic relationship between price, marginal revenue, and price elasticity of demand that we emphasized on page 101. If the firm is maximizing profit, it must be setting marginal revenue equal to marginal cost, as we have often seen (beginning in Chapter 2). Thus, if the firm is maximizing profit, we can replace MR with MC in equation (13.4);

$$MC = P\left(1 + \frac{1}{\eta}\right), \tag{13.5}$$

where MC equals the product's marginal cost (recall that this result was discussed in Chapter 3).

Dividing both sides of equation (13.5) by $(1 + 1/\eta)$, we get

$$P = MC \, \frac{1}{1 + \dfrac{1}{\eta}}, \tag{13.6}$$

which means that to maximize profit, the firm should set the product's price so that it equals its marginal cost multiplied by

$$\frac{1}{1 + \dfrac{1}{\eta}}.$$

Glancing back at equation (13.2), you can see that according to cost-plus pricing, price is set equal to cost multiplied by (1 + markup). Thus, if marginal (not average) cost is the cost concept that is really being used here and if the markup equals

$$- \frac{1}{\eta + 1} \qquad (13.7)$$

cost-plus pricing results in the maximization of profit.

Put differently, a firm will maximize profit if it marks up marginal (not average) cost, and if the markup equals the value specified in (13.7). As (13.7) shows clearly, the markup under these circumstances depends entirely on the product's price elasticity of demand. Table 13.1 provides the profit-maximizing markup corresponding to particular values of the elasticity. If a product's price elasticity of demand equals 1.2, the optimal markup is 500 percent. If its price elasticity is 20, the optimal markup is only 5 percent. Table 13.1 should be studied carefully, since it provides interesting and useful information that can help you formulate and maintain an effective pricing policy.

Note that the optimal markup goes up as the price elasticity of demand for the product goes down. Table 13.1 shows this very clearly. In managerial economics as in other things, you ought to check whenever possible to make sure that what you're told makes sense. To see that the inverse relationship in Table 13.1 between the markup and the price elasticity is eminently reasonable, ask yourself the following question: If the quantity demanded of a product is not very sensitive to its price, should I set a relatively high or low price for this

TABLE
13.1

Relationship between Optimal Markup and Price Elasticity of Demand

Price elasticity of demand	Optimal percentage markup of marginal cost
−1.2	500
−1.4	250
−1.8	125
−2.5	66.67
−5.0	25
−11.0	10
−21.0	5
−51.0	2

product? Obviously, you should set a high price if you want to make as much money as possible. Since this is what Table 13.1 is telling us, it accords with common sense.

The Clawson Corporation: A Numerical Example

To illustrate how cost-plus pricing can be used to maximize a firm's profits, consider the Clawson Corporation, a seller of office furniture. One of Clawson's major products is a metal desk for which the company has to pay $76 per desk, including transportation and related costs. Although Clawson has a variety of overhead and marketing costs, these costs are essentially fixed, so marginal cost is approximately $76. Given that there are many firms in Clawson's geographic area that sell reasonably comparable desks, Clawson's marketing managers believe that the price elasticity of demand for its desks is fairly elastic—about −2.5. Thus, on the basis of Table 13.1, it should establish a markup of 67 percent if it wants to maximize profit.

According to equation (13.2), the optimal price is

$$\text{Price} = \text{cost}(1 + \text{markup})$$
$$= 76(1 + 0.667)$$
$$= \$126.67.$$

Consequently, to maximize profit, Clawson should set a price of approximately $127 per desk. However, this is spuriously precise. In fact, as we have seen in Chapters 5 and 9, firms very seldom can estimate their marginal costs or the price elasticity of demand with great precision. Nor is it worth what it would cost them to try to do so. Since Clawson's estimates are only approximate, so is the $127 figure. Recognizing that this is the case, Clawson's managers set a price of $127, but are prepared to push it up or down a bit in accord with their sense of what is most profitable.

The Multiple-Product Firm: Demand Interrelationships

Having discussed cost-plus pricing, we turn to the pricing problems of the multi-product firm. If a firm makes more than one product, it must recognize that a change in the price or quantity sold of one of its products may influence the demand for other products it produces. For example, if the Johnson Company produces and sells two products, X and Y, its total revenue (that is, sales) can be represented as

$$TR = TR_X + TR_Y, \tag{13.8}$$

ANALYZING MANAGERIAL DECISIONS

Pricing Steaks at the Palm Restaurant

If you want a steak in New York, a top-notch place to go is the Palm restaurant, owned by the Palm Management Corporation, which has 11 Palm restaurants in 10 cities, all with the same menu. The price of a steak at each of these 11 restaurants in 1993 was as shown below.

New York (2 restaurants)	$27.00	Chicago	$22.00
East Hampton	26.00	Houston	23.00
Philadelphia	24.00	Dallas	23.00
Washington	24.00	Las Vegas	25.00
Miami	24.50	Los Angeles	26.00

(a) According to Bruce Bozzi, the co-owner of the Palm Management Corporation, "People are very price-conscious in Chicago, and our manager there knows what we have to charge to be competitive." Assuming that the market for restaurant food is monopolistically competitive in each of these cities, is the demand curve for steak at the Palm restaurant in Chicago the same as at the Palm restaurant in New York? If not, how does it differ? (b) Mr. Bozzi also states that "Our labor costs are highest in New York. We figure labor at around $8 per customer. That's nearly double what we pay in some other cities. Utilities are also high. It costs us $7,000 a month for garbage removal for the two restaurants." Is the marginal cost curve for steak at the Palm restaurant in New York the same as at the Palm restaurant in Chicago? If not, how does it differ? (c) Why is the price higher in New York than in Chicago? (d) If marginal cost is 20 percent higher in New York than in Chicago, and if the price elasticity of demand is −3 in New York and −4 in Chicago, what would you expect to be the percentage price differential between New York and Chicago?

SOLUTION (a) No. On the basis of Mr. Bozzi's statement, the demand curve is more price elastic in Chicago than in New York. A 1 percent price increase is likely to reduce the quantity demanded by a larger percentage in Chicago than in New York. (b) No. The marginal cost curve is lower in Chicago than in New York. (c) As pointed out on page 478, the profit-maximizing price equals

$$P = MC \div \left(1 + \frac{1}{\eta}\right),$$

where MC equals marginal cost and η equals the price elasticity of demand.(This is true under any market structure.) Since MC is higher and η is less elastic in New York than in Chicago, the profit-maximizing price is higher in New York than in Chicago. (d) If P_C is the price in Chicago and P_N is the price in New York, MC_C is the marginal cost in

Chicago and MC_N is the marginal cost in New York, and η_C is the price elasticity of demand in Chicago and η_N is the price elasticity of demand in New York,

$$\frac{P_C}{P_N} = \frac{MC_C \div \left(1 + \frac{1}{\eta_c}\right)}{MC_N \div \left(1 + \frac{1}{\eta_N}\right)}$$

$$= \frac{MC_C \div \left(1 + \frac{1}{-4}\right)}{1.2 MC_C \div \left(1 + \frac{1}{-3}\right)} = 0.74.$$

Thus, the price in Chicago would be expected to be about 26 percent below the price in New York.*

*For further discussion, see *New York Times*, April 28, 1993. All prices refer to filet mignon.

where TR_X is its total revenue from product X, and TR_Y is its total revenue from product Y. The marginal revenue of each product is

$$MR_X = \frac{\partial TR}{\partial Q_X} = \frac{\partial TR_X}{\partial Q_X} - \frac{\partial TR_Y}{\partial Q_X} \tag{13.9a}$$

and

$$MR_Y = \frac{\partial TR}{\partial Q_Y} = \frac{\partial TR_Y}{\partial Q_Y} - \frac{\partial TR_X}{\partial Q_Y}. \tag{13.9b}$$

The last term in each of these equations represents the demand interrelationship between the two products. Thus, in equation (13.9a), the last term shows the effect of an increase in the quantity sold of product X on the total revenue from product Y. This effect can be either positive or negative. If products X and Y are complements, this effect will be positive, since an increase in the quantity sold of one product will increase the total revenue from the other product. On the other hand, if products X and Y are substitutes, this effect will be negative, since an increase in the quantity sold of one product will reduce the total revenue from the other product.

If you do not understand and pay proper attention to demand interrelationships of this sort among the products your firm sells, serious errors can result. For example, if product X is a fairly close substitute for product Y, and if the division of the Johnson Company producing product X launches a campaign to increase its sales, the results may be good for the division but bad for the company as a whole. Why? Because the resulting increase in product X's sales may be largely at the expense of product Y's sales.

Pricing of Joint Products: Fixed Proportions

Besides being interrelated on the demand side, a firm's products are often interrelated in production. For example, products sometimes are produced in a fixed ratio, as in the case of cattle, where beef and hide are gotten from each animal. In such a situation, there is no reason to distinguish between the products from the point of view of production or costs. Since they must be produced in fixed proportions, they are not separate products from a production point of view, but should be regarded as a bundle. Thus, one hide and two sides of beef might be such a bundle in the case of cattle, since they are produced from each animal. Because the products are produced jointly, there is no economically correct way to allocate the cost of producing each such bundle to the individual products.

To determine the optimal price and output of each such product, you must compare the marginal revenue of the output bundle with its marginal cost of production. If the total marginal revenue—that is, the sum of the marginal revenues gotten from each product in the package—is greater than its marginal cost, you should expand your output. Assuming that there are two joint products (A and B), Figure 13.1 shows the demand and marginal revenue curves for each, as well as the marginal cost curve for the bundle composed of these products in the fixed proportions in which they are produced.[5] The **total marginal revenue** curve is the **vertical** summation of the two marginal revenue curves for the individual products, since each bundle of output yields revenues from the sale of both products. Consequently, the profit-maximizing output in Figure 13.1 is Q, where the total marginal revenue equals marginal cost. The optimal price for product A is P_A, and the optimal price for product B is P_B.

It is important to note that the total marginal revenue curve coincides with the marginal revenue curve for product A at all outputs beyond Q_0 in Figure 13.1. This is because the firm would never sell an amount of product B where its marginal revenue is negative, since this would mean that greater revenues could be obtained if less were sold. Thus, if total output exceeds Q_0, the firm would sell only part of the product B produced; specifically, it would sell the amount corresponding to an output of Q_0 product bundles. Consequently, if

[5]For simplicity, we assume that the demand curve for product A is not influenced by the price of product B, and that the demand curve for product B is not influenced by the price of product A.

FIGURE

13.1

Optimal Pricing for Joint Products Produced in Fixed Proportions (Case 1)

The price of product A is set at P_A, the price of product B is set at P_B, and output is set at Q.

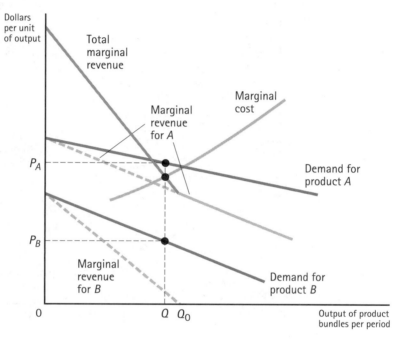

output exceeds Q_0, total marginal revenue equals the marginal revenue of product A alone.

What if the marginal cost curve intersects the total marginal revenue curve to the right of Q_0 in Figure 13.1? In particular, suppose that the situation is as shown in Figure 13.2, where the marginal cost curve is lower than in Figure 13.1 (but the other curves are the same). The profit-maximizing output is Q_1, where the marginal cost and total marginal revenue curves intersect. All of product A that is produced is sold, the price being P_A, but not all of product B is sold. Instead, the amount sold is limited to the amount in output Q_0, so that the price of product B is maintained at P_B. The "surplus" amount of product B must be thrown away and kept off the market to avoid depressing its price.

FIGURE
13.2

Optimal Pricing for Joint Products Produced in Fixed Proportions (Case 2)

The price of product A is set at P_A, the price of product B is set at P_B, and not all of product B is sold.

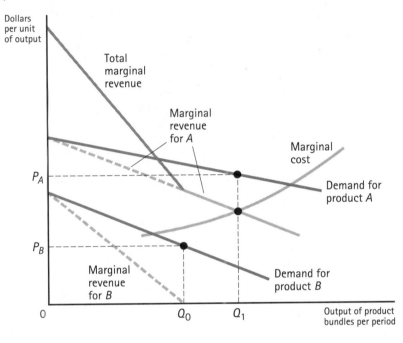

The Avtech Company: A Numerical Example

To illustrate the technique discussed in the previous section, consider the Avtech Company, which manufactures two goods, A and B, that are jointly produced in equal quantities. That is, for every unit of product A that is produced, the firm also produces a unit of product B (whether it wants it or not). Avtech's total cost function is

$$TC = 100 + Q + 2Q^2,\tag{13.10}$$

where Q is the number of units of output. (Each unit contains 1 unit of product A and 1 unit of product B.) The demand curves for the firm's two products are

$$P_A = 200 - Q_A\tag{13.11}$$

$$P_B = 150 - 2Q_B,\tag{13.12}$$

where P_A and Q_A are the price and output of product A, and P_B and Q_B are the price and output of product B.

How much of each product should Avtech produce and sell per period? What price should it charge for each? Avtech's total revenue equals the sum of the total revenues from its two products; thus,

$$TR = P_A Q_A + P_B Q_B. \tag{13.13}$$

Substituting the right-hand sides of equations (13.11) and (13.12) for P_A and P_B, respectively, it follows that

$$TR = (200 - Q_A)Q_A + (150 - 2Q_B)Q_B$$
$$= 200Q_A - Q_A^2 + 150Q_B - 2Q_B^2.$$

Assuming that Avtech sells all that it produces of both products, $Q_A = Q_B = Q$, since, as stressed above, a unit of one product is produced whenever a unit of the other product is produced. Thus,

$$TR = 200Q - Q^2 + 150Q - 2Q^2 = 350Q - 3Q^2. \tag{13.14}$$

To obtain Avtech's profit, π, we must subtract its total cost in equation (13.10) from its total revenue in equation (13.14).

$$\pi = (350Q - 3Q^2) - (100 + Q + 2Q^2)$$
$$= -100 + 349Q - 5Q^2.$$

Thus, the profit-maximizing output level is such that

$$\frac{d\pi}{dQ} = 349 - 10Q = 0$$
$$10Q = 349$$
$$Q = 34.9.$$

In other words, to maximize profit, Avtech should produce 34.9 units of each product per period of time.[6] To sell this amount, equation (13.11) tells us that the price of product A must be

$$P_A = 200 - 34.9 = \$165.10,$$

and equation (13.12) tells us that the price of product B must be

$$P_B = 150 - 2(34.9) = \$80.20.$$

[6]Note that there is no reason why Q must be an integer. Avtech can produce 34.9 units per period of time. How? By producing a total of 349 units during 10 periods.

At this point, it may seem that the analysis is finished—but it isn't. As indicated above, we have assumed that Avtech sells all that it produces of both products. To see whether this assumption is true, we must see whether, if $Q = 34.9$, the marginal revenues of both products are nonnegative. Only if this is the case will Avtech sell all that it produces of both products (recall Figure 13.2). From equations (13.11) and (13.12), we find that TR_A, the total revenue from product A, equals

$$TR_A = P_A Q_A = (200 - Q_A)Q_A = 200Q_A - Q_A^2,$$

and that TR_B, the total revenue from product B, equals

$$TR_B = P_B Q_B = (150 - 2Q_B)Q_B = 150Q_B - 2Q_B^2.$$

Thus, the marginal revenues of products A and B equal

$$MR_A = \frac{dTR_A}{dQ_A} = 200 - 2Q_A = 130.2 \quad \text{(when } Q_A = 34.9)$$

and

$$MR_B = \frac{dTR_B}{dQ_B} = 150 - 4Q_B = 10.4 \quad \text{(when } Q_B = 34.9).$$

Since both marginal revenues (MR_A and MR_B) are nonnegative when Q_A and $Q_B = 34.9$, the assumption underlying the above analysis is valid.[7]

Output of Joint Products: Variable Proportions

Having discussed the case where two joint products are produced in fixed proportions, let's turn to the case in which they are produced in variable proportions. This generally is the more realistic case, particularly if one is considering a fairly long period of time. Even in the case of cattle, the proportions of hides and beef can be altered because cattle can be bred to produce more or less beef relative to hide.

Suppose a firm produces and sells two products, A and B, and that each **isocost curve** (labeled TC) in Figure 13.3 shows the amounts of these goods that can be produced at the same total cost. Thus, the isocost curve labeled

---

[7]If one product's marginal revenue had been negative when Q_A and Q_B equaled 34.9, the optimal solution would have involved producing more of this product than is sold, as indicated in Figure 13.2. The firm would sell only the amount of this product where the marginal revenue is zero. The marginal revenue for the other product would be used to determine the optimal output level, as shown in Figure 13.2.

FIGURE
13.3

Optimal Outputs for Joint Products Produced in Variable Proportions

The optimal point, which must be at a point where an isorevenue line is tangent to an isocost curve, is at point *M*, where profit per day is $7,000.

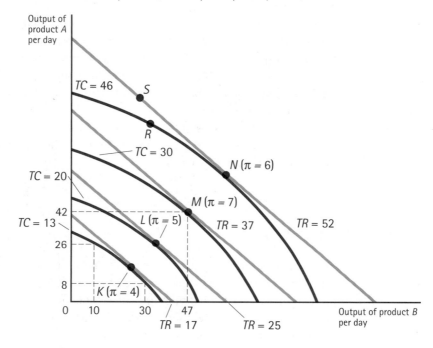

TC = 13 shows the various combinations of outputs—for example, 26 units of product *A* and 10 units of product *B*, or 8 units of product *A* and 30 units of product *B*—that can be produced at a total cost of $13,000 per day.

Also included in Figure 13.3 are **isorevenue lines** (labeled *TR*), each of which shows the combinations of outputs of the two products that yield the same total revenue. For example, the isorevenue line labeled *TR* = 52 shows the various combinations of outputs—such as those corresponding to points *S* or *N*—that yield a total revenue of $52,000 per day. Other isorevenue lines show the output combinations that yield total revenues of $17,000, $25,000, and $37,000, respectively.

The problem facing the firm is to determine how much of products *A* and *B* to produce. The first step toward solving this problem is to observe that if an output combination is at a point where an isorevenue line is *not* tangent to an isocost curve, it *cannot* be the optimal output combination. To see this, note that if an output combination is at a point where an isorevenue line is not tangent to an isocost curve (say point *R*), it is possible to increase revenue (without changing cost) by moving to the point (on the same isocost curve) where an isorevenue line *is* tangent to the isocost curve (say point *N*). Thus, any output combination that is not at a tangency point cannot be the profit-maximizing output combination, since we have indicated how profit can be increased if the firm is at such a nontangency point.

Given that this is the case, we can find the optimal output combination by comparing the profit level at each tangency point, and choosing the point where the profit level is highest. For example, four tangency points are shown in Figure 13.3—points *K*, *L*, *M*, and *N*. As indicated in Figure 13.3, the profit levels (labeled π) corresponding to these four points are $4,000, $5,000, $7,000, and $6,000, respectively. Thus, if we must choose among the output combinations on the isocost curves in Figure 13.3, the optimal output combination for this firm is point *M*, where the firm produces and sells 42 units of product *A* and 47 units of product *B* per day.

Price Discrimination

Price discrimination occurs when the same product is sold at more than one price. For example, an airline may sell tickets on a particular flight at a higher price to business travelers than to college students. Even if the products are not precisely the same, price discrimination is said to occur if very similar products are sold at prices that are in different ratios to marginal costs. Thus, if a firm sells boxes of candy with a label (cost of label: 2 cents) saying "Premium Quality" in rich neighborhoods for $12 and sells the same boxes of candy without this label in poor neighborhoods for $5, this is discrimination. The mere fact that differences in price exist among similar products is not evidence of discrimination; only if these differences do not reflect cost differences is there evidence of this kind.

For a firm to be able and willing to engage in price discrimination, the buyers of the firm's product must fall into classes with considerable differences among classes in the price elasticity of demand for the product, and it must be possible to identify and segregate these classes at moderate cost. Also, buyers must be unable to transfer the product easily from one class to another, since otherwise persons could make money by buying the product from the low-price classes and selling it to the high-price classes, thus making it difficult to maintain the price differentials among classes. The differences among classes of buyers in the price elasticity of demand may be due to differences among classes in income level, tastes, or the availability of substitutes. Thus, the price elasticity of demand for the boxes of candy cited above may be lower (in absolute value) for the rich than for the poor.

If a firm practices discrimination of this sort, it must decide two questions: How much output should it allocate to each class of buyer, and what price should it charge each class of buyer? Suppose that there are only two classes of buyers. Also, for the moment, assume that the firm has already decided on its total output, and consequently that the only real question is how it should be allocated between the two classes. The firm will maximize its profits by allocating the total output between the two classes in such a way that marginal revenue in one class is equal to marginal revenue in the other class. For example, if marginal revenue in the first class is $25 and marginal revenue in the second class is $10, the allocation is not optimal, since profits can be increased by allocating 1 less unit of output to the second class and 1 more unit of output to the first class. Only if the two marginal revenues are equal is the allocation optimal. And if the marginal revenues in the two classes are equal, the ratio of the price in the first class to the price in the second class will equal

$$\left(1 + \frac{1}{\eta_2}\right) \div \left(1 + \frac{1}{\eta_1}\right),$$

where η_1 is the price elasticity of demand in the first class, and η_2 is the price elasticity of demand in the second class.[8] Thus, it will not pay to discriminate if the two price elasticities are equal. Moreover, if discrimination does pay, the price will be higher in the class in which demand is less elastic.

Turning to the more realistic case in which the firm must also decide on its total output, it is obvious that the firm must look at its costs as well as demand in the two classes. Specifically, the firm will choose the output where the marginal cost of its entire output is equal to the common value of the marginal revenue in the two classes. To see this, consider Figure 13.4, which shows D_1, the demand curve in class 1; D_2, the demand curve in class 2; R_1, the marginal revenue curve in class 1; R_2, the marginal revenue curve in class 2; and the firm's marginal cost curve. The firm begins to determine its total output by summing horizontally over the two marginal revenue curves, R_1 and R_2. The curve representing the horizontal summation of the two marginal revenue curves is G. This curve shows, for each level of marginal revenue, the total output that is needed if marginal revenue in each class is to be maintained at this level. The optimal output is shown by the point where the G curve intersects the marginal cost curve, since marginal cost must be equal to the common value of marginal revenue in each class. If this were not the case, profits could be in-

---

[8]Recall from equation (13.4) that marginal revenue equals $P(1 + 1/\eta)$, where P is price, and η is the price elasticity of demand. Therefore, if marginal revenue is the same in the two classes, $P_1(1 + 1/\eta_1) = P_2(1 + 1/\eta_2)$. Hence $P_1/P_2 = (1 + 1/\eta_2)/(1 + 1/\eta_1)$.

FIGURE
13.4

Price Discrimination

To maximize profit, the firm will produce a total output of Q units, and set a price of P_1 in the class 1 market and a price of P_2 in the class 2 market.

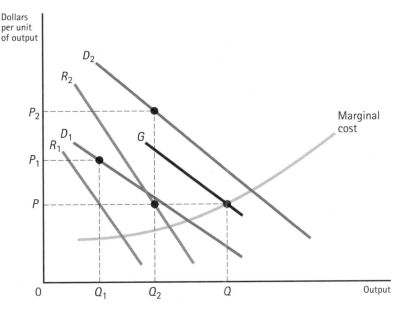

creased by expanding output (if marginal cost were less than marginal revenue) or by contracting output (if marginal cost were greater than marginal revenue). Thus, the firm will produce an output of Q units and sell Q_1 units in the class 1 market and Q_2 units in the class 2 market. Price will be P_1 in the class 1 market and P_2 in the class 2 market. This will result in higher profits than if the firm quoted the same price in both markets.

Airline Travel: A Case Study

Perhaps the most frequently cited example of price discrimination is the case of airline tickets. The airlines often charge a lower fare for essentially the same ticket if it is bought well in advance, if there is a penalty if the trip is canceled or changed, and if the trip includes a Saturday night stay. For example, in 2001, the price of a round-trip coach ticket from New York to San Francisco ranged from about $301 to over $850 for flights leaving and returning on similar dates.

One reason for these price differences is that the price elasticity of demand for business travel is much less elastic than that for vacation travel. Business travelers must meet with clients, suppliers, and associates at particular times, often as soon as possible. Regardless of the price of an air ticket (so long as it remains within reasonable bounds), many of these trips would be well worth making. On the other hand, vacation travelers often plan their trips well in advance, are relatively flexible with regard to the timing of their trips, and are sensitive to moderate differences in ticket price. From our discussion in the previous section, it seems likely that the airlines, to maximize profit, would like to set higher prices for business travelers than for vacation travelers. And this is the effect of the price differences cited above, since business travelers are much less likely than vacation travelers to buy their tickets well in advance or to include a Saturday night stay.

At the same time, it is also worth noting that because the airlines can reduce their costs if demand is more predictable (as a result of better scheduling of equipment and personnel), they may enjoy savings if travelers buy their tickets well in advance. Also, if a ticket is not refundable, it clearly is not the same as a ticket that is refundable, even though the penalty involved in changing it may be relatively small. Thus, the price differences are not due entirely to price discrimination, pure and simple.

Price Discrimination: A Pharmaceutical Example

To illustrate how price discrimination can be used, suppose a drug manufacturer sells a major drug in Europe and the United States. Because of legal restrictions, the drug cannot be bought in one country and sold in another. The demand curve for the drug in Europe is

$$P_E = 10 - Q_E, \tag{13.15}$$

where P_E is the price (in dollars per pound) in Europe, and Q_E is the amount (in millions of pounds) sold there. The demand curve for the drug in the United States is

$$P_U = 20 - 1.5Q_U, \tag{13.16}$$

where P_U is the price (in dollars per pound) in the United States, and Q_U is the amount (in millions of pounds) sold there. The total cost (in millions of dollars) of producing the drug for sale worldwide is

$$TC = 4 + 2(Q_E + Q_U). \tag{13.17}$$

The firm's total profit from both Europe and the United States is

$$\begin{aligned}
\pi &= P_E Q_E + P_U Q_U - TC \\
&= (10 - Q_E)Q_E + (20 - 1.5Q_U)Q_U - [4 + 2(Q_E + Q_U)] \\
&= -4 + 8Q_E - Q_E^2 + 18Q_U - 1.5Q_U^2.
\end{aligned} \tag{13.18}$$

To maximize π with respect to Q_E and Q_U, we find first derivatives of equation (13.18) with respect to Q_E and Q_U, and set them equal to zero.

$$\frac{\partial \pi}{\partial Q_E} = 8 - 2Q_E = 0.$$

$$\frac{\partial \pi}{\partial Q_U} = 18 - 3Q_U = 0.$$

Solving these equations for Q_E and Q_U, we find that 4 million pounds of the drug should be sold in Europe, and 6 million pounds should be sold in the United States.

To find the optimal prices in Europe and the United States, we substitute 4 for Q_E and 6 for Q_U in equations (13.15) and (13.16), the result being that the price in Europe should be $6 per pound, and the price in the United States should be $11 per pound. Substituting these values of P_E and P_U, as well as the foregoing values of Q_E and Q_U, into equation (13.18), we find that the firm's profit equals

$$\pi = -4 + 8(4) - 4^2 + 18(6) - 1.5(6^2) = 66,$$

or $66 million.

At this point, it is important to note that if we had used the graphical technique in the previous section, we would have obtained precisely the same results. Whether the graphical technique or the calculus is used, the answer will be the same.

Having obtained the above results, it is interesting and useful to determine how much additional profit the firm makes because it engages in price discrimination. If price discrimination were not possible, P_E would have to equal P_U. Letting this common price be P, it follows from equation (13.15) that $Q_E = 10 - P$, and from equation (13.16) that $Q_U = (1/1.5)(20 - P)$. Thus, the firm's total amount sold in Europe and the United States combined is

$$Q = Q_E + Q_U = 10 - P + \frac{1}{1.5}(20 - P) = 23\frac{1}{3} - \frac{5}{3}P,$$

which implies that

$$P = 14 - 0.6Q \tag{13.19}$$

for $P \leq 10$ or for $Q \geq 6^2/_3$. (For $P \geq 10$ or $Q \leq 6^2/_3$, $P = 20 - 1.5Q$). Thus, the firm's profit would be

$$
\begin{aligned}
\pi &= PQ - TC \\
&= (14 - 0.6Q)Q - (4 + 2Q) \\
\pi &= -4 + 12Q - 0.6Q^2.
\end{aligned} \tag{13.20}
$$

To find the value of Q that maximizes profit, we differentiate equation (13.20) with respect to Q and set the derivative equal to zero.

$$
\frac{d\pi}{dQ} = 12 - 1.2Q = 0.
$$

Solving for Q, we find that the firm, if it could not engage in price discrimination, should produce a total of 10 million pounds of the drug. Substituting 10 for Q in equation (13.19) and (13.20), it follows that

$$
P = 14 - 0.6(10) = 8
$$

$$
\pi = -4 + 12(10) - 0.6(10^2) = 56.
$$

Thus, if the firm could not engage in price discrimination, its profit would be $56 million, rather than the $66 million it can earn by price discrimination.

The Different Types of Price Discrimination

There are three basic types of price discrimination. Thus far we've discussed third-degree price discrimination, and now we will focus on **first- and second-degree price discrimination.** By examining price discrimination in a bit more detail, we can get a handle on all three types.

Consider the diagram of a simple monopoly profit maximizer shown in Figure 13.5. Consumers in segment AB of the demand curve are willing to pay more than the simple monopoly price of P_M. Consumers in the segment BC of the demand curve are willing to pay more for the good than it costs the producer to produce it, that is, the marginal cost.

The simple monopolist is making a variable cost profit of X as shown in Figure 13.5. (Recall that variable cost profit is profit less fixed cost; since fixed cost is fixed, if the firm maximizes its variable cost profit, it will maximize its profit.) This variable cost profit of X is the firm's total revenue (the area of the rectangle, $P_M Q_M$ in Figure 13.5) minus the firm's variable cost (M—the area under the firm's marginal cost).

Recall that the demand curve is made up of the reservation prices of consumers (the maximum amount that they would be willing to spend for each

FIGURE
13.5

Rationale for Price Discrimination

A manager can increase firm profits by using a price discrimination strategy relative to using a simple monopoly pricing strategy.

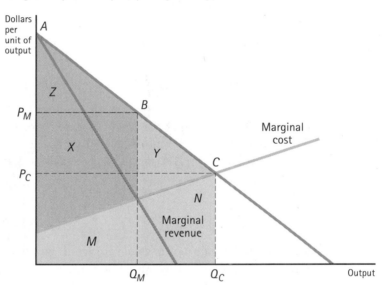

unit of that good). In segment AB of the demand curve in Figure 13.5, consumers' reservation prices exceed the simple monopoly price of P_M. In other words, those consumers are willing to pay more than P_M for the good but the firm is not asking them to do so. Thus, the firm is leaving consumer surplus (of amount Z) with those consumers. If the firm could price discriminate, it could capture the consumer surplus and turn it into producer surplus, or variable cost profit.

By discriminating in segment AB of the demand curve, the firm's variable cost profit becomes $X + Z$. But the firm can do better. By discriminating in the segment BC, the firm can earn an additional profit of Y since the reservation price of the consumers exceeds the additional cost of producing the units involved. Thus, by discriminating in both segments AB and BC, the firm has increased its profits by $Y + Z$. The potential for these additional profits gets creative managers thinking about pricing strategies to capture them.

If the firm is able to capture all of $Y + Z$, we say that they are practicing discrimination of the first degree. In essence, the firm is charging the reservation price for each unit of the good. Clearly the firm would be willing to do this up to Q_C units in Figure 13.5. The additional revenue the firm earns by selling an additional unit of product is the reservation price of the consumer. Managers will sell to that consumer as long as the reservation price (which they can charge and the consumer is willing to pay) exceeds the marginal cost of producing the good. In essence, under perfect discrimination, the firm's demand curve becomes the firm's marginal revenue curve. Thus, the firm will not sell the $Q_C + 1^{st}$ item because the marginal cost of producing it exceeds the revenue that it would generate for the firm (the reservation price of the $Q_C + 1^{st}$ good).

While first-degree discrimination captures all of area $Z + Y$, third-degree discrimination captures some of area Z and some of area Y—recall we raised prices in the United States (segment AB) and lowered prices in Europe (segment BC) from the simple monopoly price of $P_M = 8$. But we charged only a single price in the United States (not the reservation price of each U.S. consumer) and only a single price in Europe (not the reservation price of each European consumer).

Let's now view an example of first-degree discrimination versus simple monopoly pricing. Honest Sam sells used cars. The demand for used cars is $P = 12 - Q$, where P is the price in thousands and Q is the quantity of cars per month.

Sam has two ways of selling cars. He can set a price (like Saturn Motor Company) and merely pay a general manager to write up the paperwork. The total cost of selling each car under such an arrangement will be 2, so Sam's marginal cost is 2 (in thousands). Sam has a fixed cost of 5 (in thousands) per month.

To maximize profit under the simple monopoly pricing would entail setting marginal revenue ($MR = 12 - 2Q$) equal to marginal cost (2), or,

$$MR = 12 - 2Q = 2 = MC, \text{ or } Q = 5,$$

which implies that the posted price is 7.

Sam's total revenue per month is 35 ((7)(5)), variable costs are 10((2)(5)), and fixed costs are 5, resulting in a monthly profit of 20 by following simple monopoly pricing.

Sam could also sell cars the old-fashioned way—customers could haggle with salespeople. Sam can hire a sales force that is pretty slick. By chit-chatting with customers, the salesperson can pretty well estimate the customer's reservation price for a car. The general manager will still be needed to write up the paperwork, and the salespeople will be paid strictly on commission—$1 (thousand) for each car they sell. Thus, under this model of sales, Sam's marginal cost is $3 (thousand). The haggle model is first-degree price discrimination in action.

Under this model, Sam would sell cars up to the point where the reservation price equals marginal cost, or,

$$P = 12 - Q = 3 = MC, \text{ or } Q = 9$$

All consumer surplus (J in Figure 13.6) will be captured. Sam's profit is total revenue ($J + K$) less total cost (variable cost [K] plus fixed cost). In this case, total revenue is 67.5, variable cost is 27, and fixed cost is 5, resulting in a profit of 35.5.

Sam prefers the haggle model over the simple monopoly posted price model (since 35.5 > 20). Presumably this gives some explanation as to why most auto dealers have not switched to the Saturn posted price policy and continue with the haggling method of selling cars.

Note also that the two-part tariff discussed in Chapter 10 is yet another way of operationalizing first-degree price discrimination. With every demander having the same demand curve for the product, the optimal use fee in the two-part tariff is the firm's marginal cost, and the optimal entry fee is the consumer surplus. In Figure 13.6 (with the figure now representing an individual's demand curve), the use fee would be 3 and the entry fee would be $J = 40.5$. Thus, the two-part tariff can yield the same results as a discriminating monopolist of the first degree.

FIGURE
13.6

First-Degree Price Discrimination

The first-degree price discriminator captures all consumer surplus J and turns it into producer surplus (variable cost profit).

FIGURE 13.7

Second-Degree Price Discrimination

The company charges a different price (P_0, P_1, or P_2) depending on how much the consumer purchases, thus increasing its revenue and profits.

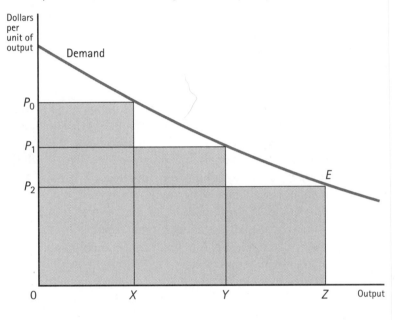

For first-degree price discrimination to occur, a firm must have a relatively small number of buyers, and it must be able to guess the maximum prices they are willing to accept. **Second-degree price discrimination** is much more common. Take the case of a gas company, each of whose customers has the demand curve shown in Figure 13.7. The company charges a high price, P_0, if the consumer purchases less than X units of gas per month. For an amount beyond X units per month, the company charges a medium price, P_1. For purchases beyond Y, the company charges an even lower price, P_2. Consequently, the company's total revenues from each consumer are equal to the shaded area in Figure 13.7, since the consumer will purchase X units at a price of P_0, $(Y - X)$ units at a price of P_1, and $(Z - Y)$ units at a price of P_2.[9]

The gas company, by charging different prices for various amounts of the commodity, is able to increase its revenue and profits considerably. After all, if it were permitted to charge only one price and if it wanted to sell Z units, it

[9]Of course, this assumes for simplicity that each consumer purchases Z units. Also, other simplifying assumptions (which need not concern us here) are made in this and the next paragraph.

would have to charge a price of P_2. Thus, the firm's total revenue would equal only the rectangle OP_2EZ, which is considerably less than the shaded area in Figure 13.7. By charging different prices, the firm is able to raise its profits. According to some authorities, second-degree price discrimination plays an important role in the schedules of rates charged by many public utilities—gas, water, electricity, and others.[10]

Using Coupons and Rebates for Price Discrimination

One way of implementing a price discrimination strategy is with coupons and rebates. Basically these devices reduce the price of products. But why don't managers simply reduce prices? Primarily, because coupons are used to price discriminate. Not all consumers use coupons. Of 291.9 billion coupons distributed in 1995, only 5.8 billion were redeemed. A certain segment (20 to 30 percent) regularly use coupons in buying goods and services. This demand segment is more price sensitive and is on the more elastic part of their demand curve. Hence, managers use coupons and rebates to price discriminate, because consumers on the less elastic part of their demand curve are willing to pay "higher prices" (without a coupon).

By estimating the elasticity of demand, managers can approximate how much coupons should be worth. Suppose the Barnegat Light Fish Company sells its product, a special blend of crab cake, in a market where they estimate two types of consumers exist—a more affluent group (R) with an estimated price elasticity for Barnegat Light crab cakes of -2 ($\eta_R = -2$) and a less affluent group (S) with an estimated price elasticity for Barnegat Light crab cakes of -5 ($\eta_S = -5$). The Barnegat Light Fish Company will put a posted price of a particular amount (P) on its product but issue a $X-off coupon in the local newspaper to the consumer types. Every buyer will pay the nominal price of P per unit for Barnegat Light crab cakes on the grocers' sales receipt but at the bottom of the sales receipt, a X credit will appear for those who tender a coupon. Thus, while all buyers nominally pay the same price P, in reality the noncoupon tenderers pay P while the coupon tenderers pay $P - X$. What should the values of P and X be? As we saw above, to maximize profits, marginal revenue in each market should be equal and they, in turn, should equal Barnegat Light's marginal cost (MC). Thus,

$$P\left(1 + \left[\frac{1}{\eta_R}\right]\right) = (P - X)\left(1 + \left[\frac{1}{\eta_S}\right]\right) = MC.$$

---

[10]R. Davidson, *Price Determination in Selling Gas and Electricity* (Baltimore: Johns Hopkins University Press, 1955), and C. Cicchetti and J. Jurewitz, *Studies in Electric Utility Regulation* (Cambridge, Mass.: Ballinger, 1975).

Suppose Barnegat Light's marginal cost was a constant 2. Thus,

$$P\left(1 - \left[\frac{1}{2}\right]\right) = 2, \text{ or } P = 4,$$

and

$$(4 - X)\left(1 - \left[\frac{1}{5}\right]\right) = 2,$$

or

$$3.2 - 0.8X = 2, \text{ or } X = 1.5.$$

Thus, Barnegat Light should price its crab cakes at $4 per unit and offer a $1.50-off coupon. The more affluent will pay $4/unit for the crab cakes and the less affluent will clip the coupon and pay (net) $2.50/unit for the same crab cakes. More elastic people (the less affluent in this case) will use coupons and the less elastic people (the affluent in this case) will not. Thus, by issuing coupons (and rebates too), firms can price discriminate (and increase their profits).

As a regular reader of a local newspaper and/or as the holder of a mailbox, you will become acquainted with many coupon offers per year. More price elastic consumers take the time to sort through all the coupons and clip the ones they are interested in using. The less elastic consumers can't be bothered with such activity for the $0.25- or $0.50-off that the coupons yield. The "transaction costs" of taking the time to sort and clip outweigh the monetary value of the coupon for such individuals. For small rebates, there are even more transaction costs—clip the UPC code from the product and mail it (postage is your expense) and the cash register receipt and wait six weeks for a very small check. As a result, the customer response rate to small-dollar-amount rebates is very low.

Tying at IBM, Xerox, and Microsoft

Tying is a pricing technique in which managers will sell a product, the use of which requires the consumption of a complementary product. The consumer is required, generally by contract, to buy the complementary product from the firm selling the product itself. For example, during the 1950s, customers who leased a Xerox copying machine had to buy Xerox paper, and customers who leased an IBM computer had to buy paper computer cards made by IBM. More recently, one charge the U.S. government leveled against Microsoft in its recent antitrust trial was that the firm used a tying strategy to force consumers to use their browser product (Internet Explorer) instead of a rival product (Netscape Navigator). Microsoft did this by tying their browser to the Windows operating system and then using their market power to force PC manufacturers to package only Internet Explorer on their products.

Successful implementation of a tying strategy generally requires the exercise of market power. For example, IBM, Xerox, and Microsoft all had market shares above 85 percent in their respective markets. There are several reasons why firms engage in tying practices. One reason is that it is a way of practicing price discrimination. By setting the price of the complementary product well above its cost, the firm can get what is in effect a much higher price from the customers who use its product intensely than from those who use it less often. For example, suppose that customer *A* uses a Xerox copier to make 10,000 copies per month, whereas customer *B* makes only 1,000 copies per month. It is hard for Xerox to price its machines to obtain more revenue from customer *A*, the more intensive user, than from customer *B*. But if Xerox can tie the sale of copying paper to the sale of its copier, it can get more profit from customer *A* than from customer *B* because it makes more on the copying paper. Polaroid has done the same thing with its cameras. The cameras are not expensive, but they require special Polaroid film, which comes at a premium.

Another reason firms use the strategy is to maintain their monopoly position. For example, Microsoft has held a market share of above 90 percent in the PC operating system market since 1991. Even a competitor the size of IBM was forced to quickly withdraw from the market after spending hundreds of millions of dollars on their OS/2 operating system. Netscape was a concern for Microsoft because its product threatened to reduce the number of application programs written for Windows. So Microsoft wanted to exclude Netscape's product. When asked the following question by a government lawyer, a Microsoft executive agreed with the lawyer's assessment:

> And all I am trying to establish is that the reason for that (packaging Internet Browser with Windows) was because you believed that if the customer had a choice of the two browsers side by side, the user would, in the vast majority of cases or in the majority of cases, pick Netscape for the reasons that you've identified, correct?[11]

This belief was reiterated in an internal Microsoft e-mail presented at the trial:

> It seems clear that it will be very hard to increase browser share on the merits of Internet Explorer alone. It will be more important to leverage the OS asset to make people—to make people choose Explorer instead of Navigator.[12]

In addition, managers will use a tying strategy to ensure that their product works properly and that its brand name is protected. To do so, it insists that customers use its complementary product. For example, Jerrold Electronics Corporation, which installed community antenna systems, required customers to accept five-year maintenance contracts to avoid breakdowns resulting from improper servicing of its equipment. And McDonald's franchises have had to buy their materials and food from McDonald's so that the hamburgers are uniform, and the company's brand name is not tarnished. McDonald's is in fact protect-

[11]From *www.microsoft/presspass/trial/transcript,* September 21, 1999, trial transcript.
[12]Ibid.

ing the franchise value of all franchisees by promoting a policy of "you know exactly what to expect" at every McDonald's.

Transfer Pricing

In previous sections, we have assumed that the firm was selling its product to outsiders. Although this generally is the case, many large firms are decentralized, and one division of a firm sells its product to another division of the same firm. For example, in the Ford Motor Company, the Engine and Foundry Division transfers its products to the Automobile Assembly Division, which in turn transfers its products to the Ford and Lincoln-Mercury Divisions. The price that the selling division charges the buying division for its product should be set so that the firm as a whole maximizes profit. In this and the following two sections, we show how this can be done.

CONCEPTS IN CONTEXT

Why Do Women Pay More?

Two individuals walk into a hair salon. They have equal length hair and want the same amount cut and the same hairstyle. Yet one pays more for the service than the other. The same two individuals walk into a dry cleaning establishment. One tenders a white silk dress shirt as does the other. Except in the latter case, the shirt is called a blouse. The bill for the first shirt is less than for the second. In some states, like Pennsylvania, Massachusetts, and California, state laws exist that prohibit price discrimination based on gender. A consumer advocacy group surveying Philadelphia business establishments found that women paid a premium at 4 of the 14 dry cleaners they randomly surveyed and at 18 of the 22 hair salons randomly surveyed. For the "same" shirt, the maximum difference for a standard shirt was $2.45. At hair salons, the difference could be double. A California study suggested that gender pricing could entail an additional expense of $1,351/woman/year for a total of $15 billion more than men.

The law, however, states that if the price differs, it must be for a reason other than gender. We must then ask this question: is the good or service exactly the same or not and, if not, do the price differences reflect the cost of service differences? Not surprisingly, those found not in compliance argued that women were more expensive to service than men—hence the price difference. Another explanation was that what currently is sold under a one-number rubric, like a haircut, is really a bundle of products. Were the law to be enforced, one hair salon owner stated that they'd just unbundle the product and charge separately for the actual cutting of the hair, the gelling, the blow drying, and the styling. Since many men get nothing more than the cutting and since many women get more than just the cutting, women would pay more than men.

Source: "Being a Woman: It Can Cost You In PA," *Philadelphia Inquirer,* March 5, 1999.

ANALYZING MANAGERIAL DECISIONS

Yield Management at American Airlines

In an article in Interfaces, three American Airline employees explain the goals of the carrier's yield management plan (the airline's politically correct way of referring to their practice of third-degree price discrimination). Terminology analogous to that used in this book such as the equality of marginal expected revenue (expected to allow for the probabilistic nature of demand) is used. This is not surprising because we'd expect marginal revenues to be set equal for all classes of demanders on a flight to maximize profit on the flight.*

While American pioneered yield management, they are not alone in utilizing it. Today, all airlines worldwide practice it. In fact, American was selling the product to other industries, like railroads, trucking companies, and hotels. Many hotel chains currently practice yield management. The room adjacent to yours and the same as yours, may be going for a much different rate than you are paying for tonight's stay.

United Airlines recently purchased the services of Deep Blue. This is the IBM computer that defeated Gary Kasparov, the world chess champion, in a recent match. United believes that the use of the computer will make them even better in determining the number of seats to allocate to a particular class of passenger on a particular flight so as to fill the maximum number of seats at the most profit. United describes this as not "another chance to squeeze another dollar out of you" but rather allowing United to get "more revenue by better utilization of our resources."

Simplistically speaking, yield management systems estimate the number of seats to be held off the market for the last-minute business traveler who has a very high reservation price versus the number of seats to be sold at deep discount off the "regular" coach fare to those potential passengers with low reservation prices.

How do the systems work? United has twenty years of past data showing when tickets were bought for a given flight relative to the flight date and at what price. This data gives United a basis for estimating demand. But such data is backward-looking. Each individual day and flight are different. So while yield management has made incredible strides in filling airline seats, the airlines still fly with approximately 25 percent empty seats—hence firms like Priceline and now the new airline joint venture to further sell unsold seats. (Note that an airline seat on flight X is a perishable commodity—if that flight takes off with no one in that seat, a revenue possibility has been forgone. Given that the flight is going, the marginal cost of putting a passenger in that seat approaches zero. Thus, an airline would prefer a passenger in that seat. However, putting a $100 passenger in that seat, as opposed to an $800 passenger, costs the airline $700 in opportunity costs. Yield management helps the airline make these decisions by predicting the likelihood that an $800 passenger will show up before the plane is scheduled to take off.)

Why did United want the services of Deep Blue? Because many flight itineraries entail multiple-trip legs. Given the hub nature of the air system today, a trip from A to C many times involves a trip from A to a hub airport at B and then a trip from B to C. The capacity of Deep Blue will be able to determine the probabilities and expected marginal revenues on all possible permutations of multilink flights and make yield management more precise. For United this means instead of looking at 3,000 flights, they'll look at 350,000 flight paths. United estimates that this improved yield management could generate $50 million to $100 million in additional revenue. Presumably, United wouldn't do this unless estimated benefits exceeded estimated costs. United spent $3.5 million on hardware and $17 million to get the system up and running. Thus benefits are estimated to be at least 2.5 to 5 times the costs.

United describes the system as being a win-win for United and its customers: "If we're more efficient, it turns into lower fares over time. Better utilization of seats benefits everyone." Do you think that this will happen?

*"Yield Management at American Airlines," *Interfaces* 22, 1992, pp. 8–31.

Source: "Deep Blue Turns Its Silicon Sights from Chess to the Airline Industry," *Philadelphia Inquirer*, December 11, 1997.

Assume that the Orion Corporation, a chemical firm, consists of two separate divisions, a production division and a marketing division. The production division manufactures the basic chemical, which is sold internally to the marketing division. The price at which this transfer takes place is called the **transfer price**. The marketing division packages the basic chemical into the final product and sells it to outside customers. In this section, we assume that there is no market for the basic chemical outside the firm. In the next section, we relax this assumption.

With no market outside the firm for the basic chemical, the marketing division is completely dependent on the production division for its supply of the basic chemical. Also, if no such market exists, the production division is not able to sell any amount of this chemical that the marketing division does not want. Thus, the quantity of the basic chemical manufactured by the production division must equal the amount sold by the marketing division.[13]

Figure 13.8 shows the optimal price and output for the firm as a whole. Looking at the two divisions combined, the marginal cost to the firm, MC, at any level of output is the sum of the marginal cost of production, MC_P, and the marginal cost of marketing, MC_M. Thus, as we stressed repeatedly in previous chapters, the firm will maximize profit by choosing the output Q, where marginal cost (MC) equals marginal revenue (MR_M). To sell this output, it should establish a price of P_M for its final product.

Knowing that this is the optimal output and price for the firm as a whole, at what level should the transfer price be set? In other words, how much should the production division charge the marketing division for the basic chemical?

---

[13]For simplicity, we assume that all the basic chemical produced during the period must be sold then. In other words, no inventories of the chemical can be carried over.

If each division maximizes its own divisional profit, the transfer price, P_t, should equal MC_P, the marginal production cost at the optimal output, Q. To see this, note that once this transfer price is set, the production division will encounter a horizontal demand curve for the basic chemical that it produces, and its marginal revenue will equal P_t. To maximize its profit, it will choose the output level where its marginal cost, MC_P, equals P_t. As shown in Figure 13.8, this output level is Q, which was shown in the previous paragraph to be the optimal output level for the firm as a whole.

Turning to the marketing division, if the transfer price is P_t, this division's marginal cost curve equals MC_t, which is the sum of the marginal marketing cost, MC_M, and the transfer price, P_t. This division will maximize its profits by setting its output level at Q, the point where its marginal cost, MC_t, equals its marginal revenue, MR_M. To sell this amount, it charges a price of P_M. Thus, this division, like the production division, acts to promote the firm's overall interests. It establishes the output level, Q, and the price, P_M, that maximize the firm's overall profit.

FIGURE
13.8

Determination of Transfer Price, Given No External Market for the Transferred Good

The optimal transfer price, P_t, equals the marginal production cost at the optimal output, Q.

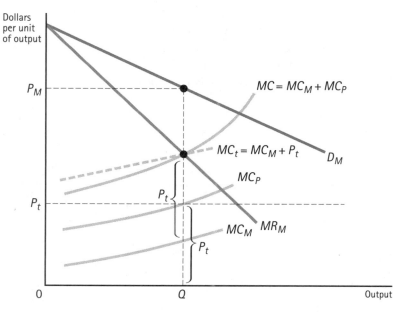

Transfer Pricing: A Perfectly Competitive Market for the Transferred Product

In many cases, there is a market outside the firm for the product that is transferred from one division to the other. If this is true in the case of the Orion Corporation, the output levels of the production and marketing divisions no longer have to be equal. If the marketing division wants more of the basic chemical than is produced by the production division, it can buy some from external suppliers. If the production division produces more of the basic chemical than the marketing division wants, it can sell some to external customers. Assuming that the market for the basic chemical is perfectly competitive, we can readily determine the way in which the firm should set the transfer price under these circumstances.

Figure 13.9 shows the optimal price and output for the firm as a whole. Since there is a perfectly competitive market for the basic chemical, the production division is confronted with a horizontal demand curve, D_P, for its output, where the price is P_t, the price of the basic chemical in the external market. To maximize profit, the production division should produce the output, Q_P, where the marginal production cost MC_P equals the price P_t. In this sense, the production division behaves like a perfectly competitive firm.

To maximize the firm's overall profit, the transfer price should equal P_t, the price of the basic chemical in the perfectly competitive market outside the firm. Since the production division can sell as much of the basic chemical as it wants to external customers at a price of P_t, it has no incentive to sell it at a price below P_t to the marketing division. Similarly, since the marketing division can buy as much of the basic chemical as it wants from external suppliers at a price of P_t it has no incentive to buy it from the production division at a price above P_t.

The marketing division, which must buy the basic chemical at a price of P_t regardless of where it comes from, has a marginal cost curve, MC_t, which is the sum of the marketing marginal cost MC_M and the price of the basic chemical, P_t. To maximize its own profit, the marketing division must choose that output level, Q_M, where its marginal cost, MC_t, equals its marginal revenue, MR_M. Since Figure 13.9 shows that the output of the marketing division, Q_M, is less than the output of the production division, Q_P, the optimal solution in this case calls for Orion's production division to sell part of its output (specifically, $Q_P - Q_M$ units) to outside customers.[14]

---

[14]Of course, it is not always true that Q_M is less than Q_P. Whether this is the case depends on the shape and position of the marginal cost curves (MC_M and MC_P) and the demand curve, as well as the price of the transferred product in the external perfectly competitive market.

Transfer Pricing in Practice Around the World

Transfer pricing is widespread. Many firms have policies whereby one division can buy another division's product, with the transfer price determined by various means. This observation found support in a 1992 survey of transfer pricing, which targeted Fortune 500 firms. For domestic interdivisional transfers, the most common pricing methods were the use of market prices, actual or standard full production costs, full production costs plus a markup, and negotiated prices. For international transfers, market-based transfer prices and full production costs plus a mark-up were the most commonly reported methods. Comparing the results from an earlier survey conducted in 1977, the shift has been

 CONCEPTS IN CONTEXT

Japan's Tax Man Leans on Foreign Firms

Japan's tax authority claims that foreign companies have a propensity to avoid the country's high corporate taxes by illegally shifting profits off their books in Japan.

The authority has filed claims against at least 50 multinationals totaling approximately $492.4 million in back taxes. Among the firms accused are Coca Cola, Goodyear Tire and Rubber, Proctor and Gamble, DaimlerChrysler, Roche Holding AG. DaimlerChrysler recently paid Japan an extra $45.87 million for taxes allegedly owed in Japan that werre shifted to Germany via transfer payments.

Japanese activity in this regard has become so large that Arthur Anderson has recently added 10 more transfer pricing specialists to their Tokyo office. While Japan isn't the only country that goes after firms that allegedly hide profits from local tax authorities, Japan's high taxes make Japan a tempting country in which to dodge taxes. In Japan, about 50 percent of yearly earnings go to national and local governments. The comparable tax burden is estimated to be 41 percent in the United States and 33 percent in the United Kingdom.

Japan believes that the non-Japanese parent company of a Japanese subsidiary overcharged the subsidiary for use of its products and/or trademarks and hence transferred profits out of Japan.

But Japan isn't the only one. In 1993, Nissan paid approximately $144 million to the United States Internal Revenue Service to settle a claim that Nissan had transferred part of its profits back to Japan. Nissan had a comparable problem in the United Kingdom. The auto industry has a reputation for using transfer pricing to minimize taxable profits.

The potential problem here is enormous. Approximately half of the world's trade is estimated to involve goods that are subject to transfer pricing. Over two-thirds of the world's multinationals have been investigated by tax authorities regarding their transfer pricing policies.

Sources: "Japan's Tax Man Leans on Foreign Firms," *Wall Street Journal,* November 25, 1996; "Transfer Pricing: Confusion over tax treatment," *Financial Tiimes,* September 2, 1997; "Daimler-Chrysler Japan Forced to Pay More Tax," *Financial Times,* October 10, 2000; and "Nissan's UK arm hit by tax charges," *Financial Times,* November 8, 2000.

to market-based prices from cost-based prices in both the domestic and international markets.[15]

Firms have used transfer pricing to shift profits from division to division to minimize tax liability. This has been done on a state by state and country by country basis and has caused government officials to investigate transfer pricing as a method to avoid taxation. A 1999 survey by Ernst and Young showed that the number one international tax issue is transfer pricing. Firms are concerned with double taxation and onerous penalties for noncompliance. Many countries have enacted new legislation enabling their tax agencies to intensify their transfer pricing inquiries and regulation enforcement. Items included in transfer pricing are goods, services, property, loans, and leases. Fortunately (and in line with the theory developed in this chapter), survey respondents note that "the most important factor shaping transfer pricing policies is maximization of operating performance, not optimizing tax arrangements.[16]

Just why have transfer prices become so important on the international level? Four basic reasons exist: increased globalization, different levels of taxation in various countries, increased scrutiny by tax authorities, and inconsistency in rules/laws in the various tax jurisdictions. Transfer price policies that seem to cause the least degree of problems in the international scenario are (1) comparable uncontrolled price, in which the prices are the same or similar to "arm's length" transaction prices, (2) cost plus prices, in which a markup used in arm's length transactions is added to the seller's cost of the good/service; and (3) resale price, in which the resale price is used as a base for determining an arm's length margin for the functions performed by the selling company.[17]

The Orion Corporation: A Numerical Example

To illustrate how a firm's managers can calculate the optimal output rates in the situation analyzed in the section before last, let's again consider the Orion Corporation, assuming that its demand and cost conditions are no longer those given in Figure 13.9. Suppose the demand curve for the finished product sold by Orion's marketing division is

$$P_M = 100 - Q_M, \qquad (13.21)$$

[15]Roger Tang, "Transfer Pricing in the 1990s," *Management Accounting,* 73(8), pp. 22–26. This 1992 survey replicated one conducted in 1977.

[16]"Multinationals Face Greater Transfer Pricing Scrutiny According to New Ernst & Young Survey," *Business Wire,* November 3, 1999.

[17]Brenda Humphreys, "International transfer pricing: More important than ever before!" *Cost & Management,* 68(4), 24–26.

FIGURE

13.9

Determination of Transfer Price, Given Perfectly Competitive External Market for the Transferred Product

The optimal transfer price, P_t, equals the market price of the transferred product.

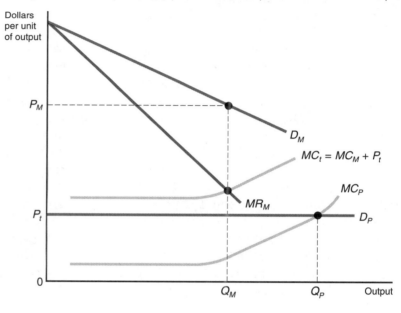

where P_M is the price (in dollars per ton) of the finished product, and Q_M is the quantity sold (in millions of tons per year). Excluding the cost of the basic chemical, the marketing division's total cost function is

$$TC_M = 200 + 10Q_M, \tag{13.22}$$

where TC_M is the division's total cost (in millions of dollars).

Turning to Orion's production division, its total cost function is

$$TC_P = 10 + 2Q_P + 0.5Q_P^2, \tag{13.23}$$

where TC_P is total production cost (in millions of dollars) and Q_P is the total quantity produced of the basic chemical (in millions of tons per year). As in-

CONSULTANT'S CORNER

Settling Some Strife over a Pricing Formula

An oil company consisted of two divisions, one involved in the production and sale of natural gas products and one involved in petrochemical production. The former division owned and operated about ten plants containing extraction units, which took the gas liquids out of the natural gas stream, and fractionators, which separated the gas liquid stream into particular gas liquids. The latter division, which had a variety of petrochemical plants, bought about half of the ethane it used from the former division.

The price that the gas products division charged the petrochemical division for ethane was determined by a formula that was designed to help the gas products division earn a 12 percent rate of return on its investment. This formula had evolved from negotiations between the former heads of the two divisions, but the present head of the gas products division felt that it should be abandoned because he could get much more for his ethane by selling it to buyers outside the firm. (The formula resulted in a price that was below the current market price of ethane.) On the other hand, the head of the petrochemical division pointed out that the ethane production facilities at the gas products division had been constructed to provide ethane for his division.

If you were a consultant to this firm, would you support the recommendation of the head of the gas products division? Explain why or why not.*

*For a much more complete account of a somewhat similar situation, see M. E. Barrett and M. P. Cormack, *Management Strategy in the Oil and Gas Industries: Cases and Readings* (Houston: Gulf, 1983).

dicated in the section before last, there is a perfectly competitive market for the basic chemical. Assume that its price in this market is $42 per ton.

Under these conditions, we can readily determine the optimal output rate for each division, as well as the proper transfer price for the basic chemical. The production division can sell all the basic chemical that it wants at $42 per ton. Thus, its marginal revenue equals $42. Since its marginal cost is the first derivative of TC_P [in equation (13.23)] with respect to Q_P, it follows that

$$MC_P = \frac{dTC_P}{dQ_P} = 2 + Q_P. \tag{13.24}$$

To find the output that maximizes the production division's profits, we must set its marginal revenue equal to its marginal cost:

$$42 = 2 + Q_P$$
$$Q_P = 40.$$

Thus, the production division should produce 40 million tons per year of the basic chemical.

The transfer price for the basic chemical should be its price in the perfectly competitive market outside the firm. Since this market price is $42 per ton, the transfer price should be the same. Also, we know from the section before last that the marketing division's marginal cost, MC_t, is the sum of its own marginal marketing cost, MC_M, and the transfer price. That is,

$$MC_t = MC_M + P_t.$$

Since $P_t = \$42$, and its own marginal marketing cost equals the first derivative of TC_M [in equation (13.22)] with respect to Q_M, it follows that

$$MC_t = \frac{dTC_M}{dQ_M} + 42 = 10 + 42 = 52. \qquad (13.25)$$

To maximize the marketing division's profit, we must set its marginal cost equal to its marginal revenue. Its total revenue is

$$TR_M = P_M Q_M = (100 - Q_M)Q_M$$
$$= 100Q_M - Q_M^2,$$

since its demand curve is as indicated in equation (13.21). Taking the first derivative of its total revenue with respect to Q_M, we obtain its marginal revenue:

$$MR_M = \frac{dTR_M}{dQ_M} = 100 - 2Q_M.$$

Setting this expression for its marginal revenue equal to its marginal cost [in equation (13.25)], we find that

$$100 - 2Q_M = 52$$
$$Q_M = 24.$$

Thus, the marketing division should sell 24 million tons per year of the basic chemical at a price of $76.

To sum up, the Orion Corporation's production division should produce 40 million tons per year of the basic chemical. Of this amount, 16 million tons should be sold externally at the market price of $42 per ton, and 24 million tons should be transferred to Orion's marketing division, the transfer price being the same as the market price, that is, $42 per ton.

Summary

1. Empirical studies indicate that cost-plus pricing is used by many firms. In this approach, the firm estimates the cost per unit of output of the product (based on some assumed output level) and adds a markup to include costs that cannot be allocated to any specific product and to provide a return on the firm's investment. On the surface, it is questionable whether this approach can maximize profit, but if marginal cost (not average cost) is really what is being marked up, and if the size of the markup is determined (in the appropriate way) by the product's price elasticity of demand, cost-plus pricing can result in profit maximization.

2. Firms generally produce and sell more than one product. It is important for them to recognize the demand interrelationships among the products they sell. Also, a firm's products are often interrelated in production. If two products are produced jointly in fixed proportions, the profit-maximizing output is where the total marginal revenue curve—the vertical summation of the marginal revenue curves for the individual products—intersects the marginal cost curve for the bundle of products (assuming that the marginal revenue of each product is nonnegative).

3. If two products are produced jointly in variable proportions, one can construct isocost curves, each of which shows the combinations of outputs that can be produced at the same total cost. Also, isorevenue lines can be constructed, each of which shows the combinations of outputs that yield the same total revenue. For an output combination to be optimal, it must be at a point where an isorevenue line is tangent to an isocost curve. To determine which output combination is optimal, one compares the profit levels at the tangency points. The tangency point where profit is highest is the optimal output combination.

4. Price discrimination occurs when the same product is sold at more than one price, or when similar products are sold at prices that are in different ratios to marginal cost. A firm will be able and willing to practice price discrimination if various classes of buyers with different price elasticities of demand can be identified and segregated, and if the product cannot be transferred easily from one class to another. If the total market is divided into such classes, a firm that discriminates will maximize its profits by choosing prices and outputs so that the marginal revenue in each class is equal to marginal cost.

5. Many large firms are decentralized, and one division of the firm sells its product to another division of the firm. To maximize the firm's overall profit, it is important that the price at which this transfer takes place—the so-called transfer price—be set properly. If there is no market outside the firm for the transferred product, the transfer price should equal the mar-

ginal production cost at the optimal output. If there is a perfectly competitive market for the transferred product outside the firm, the transfer price should equal the price of this product in that market.

Problems

1. The Hassman Company produces two joint products, X and Y. The isocost curve corresponding to a total cost of $500,000 is

$$Q_Y = 1,000 - 10Q_X - 5Q_X^2,$$

where Q_Y is the quantity of product Y produced by the firm, and Q_X is the quantity of product X produced. The price of product X is 50 times that of product Y.
    a. If the optimum output combination lies on this isocost curve, what is the optimal output of product X?
    b. What is the optimal output of product Y?
    c. Can you be sure that the optimum output combination lies on this isocost curve? Why or why not?

2. The Ridgeway Corporation produces a medical device, which it sells in Japan, Europe, and the United States. Transportation costs are a negligible proportion of the product's total costs. The price elasticity of demand for the product is -4.0 in Japan, -2.0 in the United States, and -1.33 in Europe. Because of legal limitations, this medical device, once sold to a customer in one country, cannot be resold to a buyer in another country.
    a. The firm's vice president for marketing circulates a memo recommending that the price of the device be $1,000 in Japan, $2,000 in the United States, and $3,000 in Europe. Comment on his recommendations.
    b. His recommendations are accepted. Sales managers send reports to corporate headquarters saying that the quantity of the devices being sold in the United States is lower than expected. Comment on their reports.
    c. After considerable argument, the U.S. sales manager agrees to lower the price in the United States to $1,500. Is this a wise decision? Why or why not?
    d. Can you be sure that the firm is maximizing profit? Why or why not?

3. The McDermott Company estimates its average total cost to be $10 per unit of output when it produces 10,000 units, which it regards as 80 percent of capacity. Its goal is to earn 20 percent on its total investment, which is $250,000.
    a. If the company uses cost-plus pricing, what price should it set?
    b. Can it be sure of selling 10,000 units if it sets this price?
    c. What are the arguments for and against a pricing policy of this sort?

4. The Locust Corporation is composed of a marketing division and a production division. The marginal cost of producing a unit of the firm's prod-

uct is $10 per unit, and the marginal cost of marketing it is $4 per unit. The demand curve for the firm's product is

$$P = 100 - 0.01Q,$$

where P is the price per unit (in dollars), and Q is output (in units). There is no external market for the good made by the production division.
a. What is the firm's optimal output?
b. What price should the firm charge?
c. How much should the production division charge the marketing division for each unit of the product?

5. Ann McCutcheon is hired as a consultant to a firm producing ball bearings. This firm sells in two distinct markets, one of which is completely sealed off from the other. The demand curve for the firm's output in the one market is $P_1 = 160 - 8Q_1$, where P_1 is the price of the product, and Q_1 is the amount sold in the first market. The demand curve for the firm's output in the second market is $P_2 = 80 - 2Q_2$, where P_2 is the price of the product, and Q_2 is the amount sold in the second market. The firm's marginal cost curve is $5 + Q$, where Q is the firm's entire output (destined for either market). The firm asks Ann McCutcheon to suggest what its pricing policy should be.
a. How many units of output should the firm sell in the second market?
b. How many units of output should it sell in the first market?
c. What price should it establish in each market?

6. The Morrison Company produces tennis rackets, the marginal cost of a racket being $20. Since there are many substitutes for the firm's rackets, the price elasticity of demand for its rackets equals about -2. In the relevant range of output, average variable cost is very close to marginal cost.
a. The president of the Morrison Company feels that cost-plus pricing is appropriate for his firm. He marks up average variable cost by 100 percent to get price. Comment on this procedure.
b. Because of heightened competition, the price elasticity of demand for the firm's rackets increases to -3. The president continues to use the same cost-plus pricing formula as before. Comment on its adequacy.

7. The Backus Corporation makes two products, X and Y. For every unit of good X that the firm produces, it produces 2 units of good Y. Backus' total cost function is

$$TC = 500 + 3Q + 9Q^2,$$

where Q is the number of units of output (where each unit contains 1 unit of good X and 2 units of good Y), and TC is total cost (in dollars). The demand curves for the firm's two products are

$$P_X = 400 - Q_X$$

and $$P_Y = 300 - 3Q_Y,$$

where P_X and Q_X are the price and output of product X, and P_Y and Q_Y are the price and output of product Y.

a. How much of each product should the Backus Corporation produce and sell per period of time?

b. What price should it charge for each product?

8. The Xerxes Company is composed of a marketing division and a production division. The marketing division packages and distributes a plastic item made by the production division. The demand curve for the finished product sold by the marketing division is

$$P_0 = 200 - 3Q_0,$$

where P_0 is the price (in dollars per pound) of the finished product, and Q_0 is the quantity sold (in thousands of pounds). Excluding the production cost of the basic plastic item, the marketing division's total cost function is

$$TC_0 = 100 + 15Q_0,$$

where TC_0 is the marketing division's total cost (in thousands of dollars). The production division's total cost function is

$$TC_1 = 5 + 3Q_1 + 0.4Q_1^2,$$

where TC_1 is total production cost (in thousands of dollars), and Q_1 is the total quantity produced of the basic plastic item (in thousands of pounds). There is a perfectly competitive market for the basic plastic item, the price being $20 per pound.

a. What is the optimal output for the production division?

b. What is the optimal output for the marketing division?

c. What is the optimal transfer price for the basic plastic item?

d. At what price should the marketing division sell its product?

9. The Lone Star Transportation Company hauls coal and manufactured goods. The demand curve for its services by the coal producers is

$$P_C = 495 - 5Q_C,$$

where P_C is the price (in dollars) per ton-mile of coal hauled, and Q_C is the number of ton-miles of coal hauled (in thousands). The demand curve for its services by the producers of manufactured goods is

$$P_M = 750 - 10Q_M,$$

where P_M is the price (in dollars) per ton-mile of manufactured goods hauled, and Q_M is the number of ton-miles of manufactured goods hauled (in thousands). The firm's total cost function is

$$TC = 410 + 8(Q_C + Q_M),$$

where T_C is total cost (in thousands of dollars).

a. What price should the firm charge to haul coal?

b. What price should the firm charge to haul manufactured goods?

c. If a regulatory agency were to require the firm to charge the same price to haul both coal and manufactured goods, will this reduce the firm's profits? If so, by how much?

10. Electric companies typically have five to ten different rate schedules for their main customer groups. The average price charged large industrial users may differ substantially from that charged residences. Moreover, many consumers pay a price for electricity that is based on the time of day they use it. For example, the prices charged by Consolidated Edison, a large New York electric utility, and Pacific Gas and Electric, a major California electric utility, are as follows:

Company and time of day of electricity use	Price (cents per kilowatt-hour)
Consolidated Edison	
8 AM–10 PM (peak hours)	27
10 PM–8 AM (off-peak hours)	4[a]
Pacific Gas and Electric	
Summer:	
Noon–6 PM (peak hours)	28.3
6 PM–noon (off-peak hours)	9.2
Winter:	
Noon–6 PM (peak hours)	11.3
6 PM–noon (off-peak hours)	8.0

[a]Approximate figure.

Electric utilities utilize their cheapest generators continuously and start up their more costly ones as demand goes up. Consequently, at 3 AM a utility might meet its requirements from a hydroelectric dam that produces electricity for 2 cents per kilowatt-hour. However, on a hot day in August when air conditioners are running full blast, demand would be so great that the utility would be forced to use its most costly generators, perhaps an oil-fired plant where electricity costs 7 cents per kilowatt-hour.

a. Does price discrimination occur in the market for electricity?

b. Why have some state regulatory commissions, including the Public Service Commission of New York, ordered that time-of-day rates be phased in for residential consumers?

c. In many areas, both residential and industrial consumers tend to pay a lower price per kilowatt-hour if they use more rather than less electricity.

MANAGERIAL ECONOMICS IN CONTEXT

A Rocky Road for Caterpillar Tractor

For decades, Caterpillar Tractor Company has been regarded as the leader in the world market for earth-moving equipment, a market dominated by relatively few firms. It makes products of very high quality. As one of its vice presidents once said, "Market share for us is not an objective. Building sophisticated, durable, reliable products and providing good support is." The firm also invests heavily in advanced automation to reduce its costs. Noted for its conservative financial policies, it has been well respected by Wall Street, its customers, and its competitors.

With regard to its pricing, Caterpillar traditionally charged more than its rivals. For example, in 1981, Lee Morgan, Caterpillar's chairman, compared his firm's prices with those of Komatsu (Caterpillar's leading rival) in the following terms: "Komatsu's products are priced at least ten to fifteen percent below Caterpillar's. That says clearly what they believe our value is versus theirs." In other words, Caterpillar's managers felt that their products were sufficiently superior to that of their rivals to warrant their charging a premium price.

In the early 1980s, the dollar became very strong relative to the Japanese yen, and as a result Komatsu, a Japanese firm, could sell its products at prices that Caterpillar found difficult to meet. Moreover, the recession in the United States caused Caterpillar's U.S. customers to emphasize its price disadvantage. As one of Caterpillar's cus-

tomers stated in 1982, "Work's going cheap in our business, so we're looking particularly hard at costs." For these and other reasons, Caterpillar's sales fell by about 29 percent in 1982, and it experienced a $180 million loss. As Lee Morgan put it, "It seemed like we were in a free fall. If I had any personal despair, it was coming in every morning and wondering if we would ever hit bottom."

In 1983, Caterpillar began to change its pricing policy. In order to become more competitive, it offered price discounts. Its rival, Komatsu, priced to expand market share, and operated with very tight profit margins (about 4 to 5 percent of sales). Caterpillar felt it had to become more competitive with respect to price. To do so, the firm embarked on a major cost-reduction program, including cuts in blue-collar and white-collar employment. During 1983–84, plans were announced to close six plants. By 1985, the company was back in the black (see table below).

In 1987, Caterpillar's chairman stated:

> We recognized that our industry was faced with substantial overcapacity, and that there would be tremendous price pressure on our products.... We've priced our products competitively on a value basis and offered special incentive programs to enhance the marketing effects of our dealers—perhaps at the sacrifice of some short-term profitability for longer-term improved results.

Sales and Profits, Caterpillar Tractor Company, 1981–1996 (Billions of Dollars)

	1996	1995	1993	1991	1989	1987	1985	1983	1981
Sales	16.5	16.0	11.6	10.2	11.1	8.2	6.7	5.4	9.2
Profits	1.4	1.1	0.7	−0.4	0.6	0.3	0.2	−0.3	0.6

During the late 1980s, Caterpillar continued its worldwide effort to improve productivity and cut costs. In 1987, the company started a $2.1 billion program to modernize its production facilities, called Plant with a Future. Flexible manufacturing systems (recall page 281) were installed. In 1990, Caterpillar eliminated layers of managers and organized itself into 17 profit centers. Nonetheless, because of the recession in the United States and elsewhere, as well as a strike and lockout at the firm, Caterpillar lost money in 1991 and 1992.

In 1993, the firm's sales rose considerably as a weak dollar made it hard for Komatsu to compete and as the U.S. economy recovered. Profits at Caterpillar increased greatly from 1993 to 1996. However, labor relations at the firm were a problem. Although the union (the United Auto Workers) returned to work in late 1995 after a tough 18-month strike, its members did not ratify the contract Caterpillar offered and in 1997 were working without a contract.

(a) What sort of market structure exists in the tractor industry?

(b) Does Caterpillar use cost-plus pricing? Why or why not?

(c) In 1981, did Caterpillar set its prices to deter entry?

(d) Was Caterpillar minimizing its cost in 1981 and 1982?

(e) According to Caterpillar's chairman, "New designs, new materials, new technology, and increased attention to 'manufacturability' are providing substantial cost reduction with further gains in quality and performance." Up to what point is it worthwhile to spend money on such technical improvements?

(f) As pointed out above, Caterpillar's chairman also stated that in pricing and marketing strategy, the company may have sacrificed "some short-term profitability for longer-term improved results." Is this always wise? Under what conditions is it wise policy?

(g) In 1991, the average hourly worker represented by the United Auto Workers at Caterpillar earned $31.74 per hour. The firm asked for wage concessions to reduce its costs. On November 4, 1991, the union struck two of the firm's plants; four days later, the firm closed several more. In April 1992, after a five-month strike the workers agreed to return to work on terms regarded as favorable to the firm. In 1994, the union struck once again, and managers, supervisors, and other white-collar employees began working on Caterpillar's assembly lines. Some observers said that the firm was trying to exert pressure on union leaders to force them to negotiate issues that would lower labor costs. What effect would this have on the firm's pricing?*

*For further discussion, see Bartlett, *Cases in Strategic Management;* Caterpillar's Annual Reports; *New York Times,* April 16, 1992, and June 24, 1994; and *Business Week,* July 4, 1994, and January 20, 1997.

Is this price discrimination? If so, what kind of price discrimination is it?

d. Explain why price discrimination is used by electric companies.*

11. The Breen Company makes a scientific instrument used in chemical laboratories. The price of the instrument is set at 180 percent of average variable cost. The firm's marketing manager receives a telephone call from a large chemical company offering to buy six of the instruments at $5,000 each. To meet the terms of the offer, Breen would have to manufacture the six instruments in the next three months, which would mean that Breen would lose orders for four instruments because of its limited production capacity. If fulfilled, these orders would be at the regular price of $7,200 per instrument. (Because the chemical firm was ordering six of the instruments, it wanted a reduced price of $5,000.)

a. Should the firm accept the offer from the chemical company? Why or why not?

b. If not, what is the minimum price it should ask the chemical company to pay?

c. If you were a consultant to Breen's chief executive officer, would you advise her to maintain or abandon the firm's cost-plus pricing policy? Why?

12. Knox Chemical Corporation has been one of the largest producers of isopropyl alcohol, or isopropanol, as it frequently is called. Isopropanol is used to produce acetone, an important industrial chemical; also, it is used to make various chemical intermediate products. Since Knox Chemical has produced both acetone and these chemical intermediates, it has used much of the isopropanol that it has made. One of the many tasks of Knox's product manager for isopropanol was to set transfer prices for isopropanol within the company.

a. Knox's product manager for isopropanol generally set the transfer price equal to the prevailing market price. Was this a sensible procedure?

b. When the production of phenol expanded rapidly, a great deal of acetone was produced because it was a by-product of the process leading to phenol. What effect do you think this had on the market price of isopropanol?

c. In producing a pound of phenol, 0.6 pound of acetone is produced. Are phenol and acetone joint products?

d. Are they produced in fixed proportions?†

---

*For further discussion, see W. Shepherd and C. Wilcox, *Public Policies toward Business* (Homewood, Ill.: Irwin, 1979), and *New York Times*, June 9, 1990.
†For further discussion, see Corey, *Industrial Marketing*.

PART

5

Risk, Uncertainty, and Incentives

Risk
Analysis

Most business decisions involve some risk or uncertainty. Having made a decision, the manager cannot be sure of the outcome. Chance, or the actions of others, may play a role. For example, marketing a new product involves risk since we cannot be sure of the level of demand. If demand is high, profit can be high; but if demand is lower than expected, profits may be negative. Investing in research and development for a new drug or new software is risky. Can we be sure that the investment will eventually result in a product that can be brought to market? The answer is usually "no." More innovative ideas offer the tantalizing possibility of high reward but they also offer great risk. Drilling a well for oil is risky. We cannot be sure in advance whether we will strike oil, or how much we will strike, or exactly what will be the costs of extraction of any oil we find. The inability to see the future can sometimes paralyze decision makers. However, there are managerial techniques that can help us see through the maze of possibilities and come to sensible decisions.

In this chapter, we will present a variety of tools for helping make decisions in the face of risk. We will start with the concept of expected value, which summarizes a set of possible outcomes into a single representative value. We will look at decision trees. Many decisions involve a myriad of possible outcomes, many of which are conditional on pure chance, or upon the actions of others. For example, a manager might pose questions such as: "If interest rates are low, and if my competitor keeps his prices high, then demand for my new product will be high—but what if interest rates rise, competitors' prices fall, or new entrants come into the market?" Decision trees give us a visual and intuitive guide through the web of possible consequences and allow us to structure decisions in a simple and sequential way.

We will also examine techniques to reduce uncertainty. Techniques and databases are available that enable us to improve our ability to forecast the future. For example, the designer of a new product can conduct market research on consumer acceptance and can analyze the performance of comparable products in order to provide more information about likely demand. The oil company can use geological models and satellite surveys to give a clearer picture of the drilling site and its likelihood of holding oil. In short, we can invest in information about the future. We will show how valuable such information is and how its quality depends on its reliability.

The other major concept we introduce here is the concept of expected utility. People react differently to risk, much as they have differing preferences for real goods. Given a choice between a safe investment with a low rate of return and a risky investment with a high *expected* return, some would choose the former, others the latter. This reflects their tolerance of risk. We will see how expected utility analysis can be used to build risk tolerance into managerial decisions.

Risk and Probability

In ordinary parlance, risk is a hazard or a chance of loss. Thus, if you invest $10,000 in a firm carrying out research and development in biotechnology, and if there is a very substantial chance that you will lose your money because the firm will not come up with a successful new product, such an investment is risky. Moreover, in ordinary parlance, the bigger the chance of loss, the more risky a particular course of action is. Thus, an investment in a firm doing biotechnology research is riskier than an investment in Treasury notes, since there is a relatively greater chance of loss from the former investment.

To analyze risk, it is necessary to define a probability. Suppose a situation exists in which one of a number of possible outcomes can occur. For example, if a gambler throws a single die, the number that comes up may be 1, 2, 3, 4, 5, or 6. A **probability** is a number that is attached to each outcome. It is the proportion of times that this outcome occurs over the long run if this situation exists repeatedly. Thus, the probability that a particular die will come up a 1 is the proportion of times this will occur if the die is thrown many, many times; and the probability that the same die will come up a 2 is the proportion of times this will occur if the die is thrown many, many times; and so on.

If a situation exists a very large number of times R, and if outcome A occurs r times, the probability of A is

$$P(A) = \frac{r}{R}. \tag{14.1}$$

Thus, if a die is "true" (meaning that each of its sides is equally likely to come up when the die is rolled), the probability of its coming up a 1 is 1/6, or 0.167, because if it is rolled many, many times, this will occur one-sixth of the time.

What we have just provided is the so-called **frequency definition of probability**. In some situations, this concept of probability may be difficult to apply because these situations cannot be repeated over and over. When the IBM Corporation introduced Warp, a new software package, in October 1994, this was an "experiment" that could not be repeated over and over again under essentially the same set of circumstances. Market and other conditions vary from month to month. If Warp had not been introduced that month, the types of software packages available from other firms (like Microsoft), the prices of these competing products, the advertising campaigns of other firms, and a host of other relevant factors would probably have been different.

In dealing with situations of this sort, managerial economists sometimes use a **subjective definition of probability**. According to this definition, the probability of an event is the degree of confidence or belief on the part of the decision maker that the event will occur. Thus, if the decision maker believes that outcome X is more likely to occur than outcome Y, the probability of X's occurring is higher than the probability of Y's doing so. If the decision maker believes that it is equally likely that a particular outcome will or will not occur, the probability attached to the occurrence of this outcome equals 0.50. The important factor in this concept of probability is what the decision maker believes.

Probability Distributions and Expected Values

In a particular situation, if all possible outcomes are listed, and if the probability of occurrence is assigned to each outcome, the resulting table is called a **probability distribution**. For example, suppose that Adept Technology, a San Jose, California, manufacturer of robots, believes that the probability is 0.6 that it can develop a new type of robot in one year, and that the probability is 0.4 that it cannot do so in this length of time. The probability distribution is as follows on the next page:

Event	Probability of occurrence
New robot is developed in one year	0.6
New robot is not developed in one year	<u>0.4</u>
	1.0

Note that the probabilities sum to 1, which must be the case if all possible outcomes or events are listed.

If Adept Technology will earn a profit of $1 million if it develops the new robot in one year, and if it will lose $600,000 if it does not develop the robot in one year, we can readily calculate the probability distribution of its profit from the new robot, which is:

Profit	Probability
$1,000,000	0.6
−600,000	0.4

Moreover, we can also calculate the **expected value** of the profit, which is

$$\$1,000,000(0.6) + (-\$600,000)(0.4) = \$360,000.$$

The expected value is the weighted average of the profits corresponding to the various outcomes, each of these profit figures being weighted by its probability of occurrence.

In general, the expected profit can be expressed by the equation

$$\text{Expected profit} = E(\pi) = \sum_{i=1}^{N} \pi_i P_i, \tag{14.2}$$

where π_i is the level of profit associated with the ith outcome, P_i is the probability that the ith outcome will take place, and N is the number of possible outcomes. Since $N = 2$, $\pi_1 = \$1,000,000$, $\pi_2 = -\$600,000$, $P_1 = 0.6$, and $P_2 = 0.4$ in the case of Adept Technology, equation (14.2) says precisely the same thing as the equation that precedes it above.

Comparisons of Expected Profit

To decide which of a number of courses of action to take, managers can compare the expected profit resulting from each one. For example, suppose that the Jones Corporation, a producer of automobile tires, is thinking of raising the price of its product by $1 per tire. On the basis of the firm's estimates, if it raises its price, it will experience an $800,000 profit if its current advertising campaign is successful and a $600,000 loss if the campaign is not successful. The firm believes that there is a 0.5 probability that its current advertising campaign will be successful and a 0.5 probability that it will not be successful.

Under these circumstances, the expected profit to the firm if it raises its price equals

$$\$800,000(0.5) + (-\$600,000)(0.5) = \$100,000.$$

As indicated above, the expected profit is the sum of the amount of money gained (or lost) if each outcome occurs times the probability of occurrence of the outcome. In this case, there are two possible outcomes: (1) the firm's current advertising campaign is successful, or (2) it is not successful. If we multiply the amount of money gained (or lost) if the first outcome occurs times its probability of occurrence, the result is $800,000(0.5). If we multiply the amount of money gained (or lost) if the second outcome occurs times its probability of occurrence, the result is $-$600,000(0.5). Summing these two results, we get $100,000, which is the expected profit if the firm raises its price.

What would be the expected profit if the Jones Corporation did *not* increase its price? Suppose that the firm's executives believe that if there were no price increase, the firm's profits would be $200,000. And for simplicity, let's assume that this profit level is regarded as certain if the price is not increased. Then, if the firm wants to maximize expected profit, it should not increase its price, because its expected profit equals $200,000 if it does not do so, but only $100,000 if it does. Later on in this chapter, we will discuss at length the circumstances under which it is rational to maximize expected profit—and how to proceed if it is not rational to do so.

How to Construct a Decision Tree

Any situation involving decision making under conditions of risk has the following characteristics. First, the decision maker must make a choice, or perhaps a series of choices, among alternative courses of action. Second, this choice leads to some consequence, but the decision maker cannot tell in advance the exact nature of this consequence because it depends on some unpredictable event, or series of events, as well as on the choice itself. For example, consider the case of the Jones Corporation, which must decide whether to increase the price of its automobile tires. The choice is between two alternatives: increase price or do not do so. The consequence of increasing price is uncertain, since the firm cannot be sure that its current advertising campaign will be successful.

To analyze any such problem, a decision tree is useful. A **decision tree** is a diagram that helps you visualize the relevant choices. It represents a decision problem as a series of choices, each of which is depicted by a fork (sometimes called a juncture or branching point). A **decision fork** is a juncture representing a choice where the decision maker is in control of the outcome; a **chance fork** is a juncture where "chance" controls the outcome. To differentiate between a decision fork and a chance fork, we will place a small square at the former juncture but not at the latter.

In Figure 14.1, we show the decision tree for the problem facing the Jones Corporation. Starting at the left-hand side of the diagram, the first choice is up to the firm, which can either follow the branch representing a price increase or the branch representing no such increase. Since this fork is a decision fork, it is represented by a square. If the branch representing no price increase is followed, the consequence is certain: the firm will have a profit of $200,000. Thus, $200,000 is shown at the end of this branch. If the branch representing a price increase is followed, we come to a chance fork, since it is uncertain whether the firm's current advertising campaign is successful. The upper branch following this chance fork represents the consequence that it is successful, in which case the firm will have a profit of $800,000, shown at the end of this branch.

FIGURE
14.1

Decision Tree, Jones Corporation

If the Jones Corporation increases its price, the expected profit is $100,000. If it does not increase its price, the expected profit is $200,000.

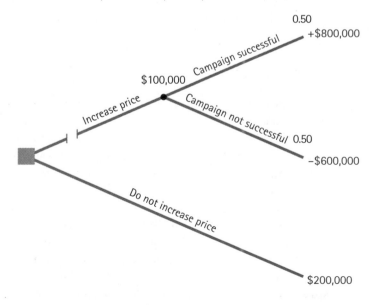

The lower branch following this chance fork represents the consequence that it is not successful, in which case the outcome is −$600,000 (a loss), shown at the end of this branch. The probability that "chance" will choose each of these branches is shown above the end of each branch; in both cases, this probability equals 0.50.

On the basis of such a decision tree, you can readily determine which branch the firm should choose in order to maximize expected profit. The process by which you can solve this problem, known as **backward induction**, requires that you begin at the right-hand side of the decision tree, where the profit figures are located. The first step is to calculate the expected profit when the firm is situated at the chance fork immediately to the left of these payoff figures. In other words, this is the expected profit to the firm given that "chance" will choose which subsequent branch will be followed. Because there is a 0.50 probability that the branch culminating in a profit of $800,000 will be followed, and a 0.50 probability that the branch culminating in a loss of $600,000 will be followed, the expected profit when situated at this chance fork is

$$0.50(\$800,000) + 0.50(-\$600,000) = \$100,000.$$

This number is written above the chance fork in question to show that this is the expected profit when the firm is located at that fork. Moving farther to the left along the decision tree, it is clear that the firm has a choice of two branches, one of which leads to an expected profit of $100,000, the other of which leads to a $200,000 expected profit. If the firm wants to maximize expected profit, it should choose the latter branch. In other words, it should not increase its price. Since the former branch (increase price) is nonoptimal, you place two vertical lines through it.

Of course, this graphic procedure for analyzing the Jones Corporation's pricing problem amounts to precisely the same thing as the calculations we made in the previous section. Recall that we compared the expected profit if the price was increased ($100,000) with the expected profit if it was not increased ($200,000) and followed the course of action that resulted in the larger of the two. Our procedure in Figure 14.1 is exactly the same.

Should Tomco Oil Corporation Drill a Well?

One major area where the concepts presented in the previous sections have been applied is oil exploration. Very large amounts of money have been, and are being, invested in oil exploration. Oil firms use these analytical tools as an aid to decision making. To illustrate how these concepts can be applied, consider the actual case of Tomco Oil Corporation, an oil producer that had to decide whether to drill a well at Blair West, a site in Kansas.[1] The firm had information concerning the cost of drilling and the price of oil, as well as geologists' reports concerning the likelihood of striking oil. Suppose the geologists' reports led the firm to believe that if the well was drilled, there was a 0.60 probability that no oil would be found, a 0.15 probability that 10,000 barrels would be found, a 0.15 probability that 20,000 barrels would be found, and a 0.10 probability that 30,000 barrels would be found.

Using these probabilities alone, the firm cannot decide whether to drill the well. In addition, information is needed concerning the profit (or loss) that will accrue to the firm if each of these outcomes occurs. Suppose the firm believes that if it drills the well, it will incur a $90,000 loss if it finds no oil, a $100,000 profit if it finds 10,000 barrels of oil, a $300,000 profit if it finds 20,000 barrels, and a $500,000 profit if it finds 30,000 barrels. Should the firm drill the well?

Assuming that the firm wants to maximize its expected profit, it can answer this question by constructing the decision tree shown in Figure 14.2. Starting at the left-hand side of the diagram, the first choice is up to the firm, which can follow the branch representing drilling the well or the branch representing not drilling. If the branch representing not drilling is followed, the expected profit is zero, which is shown at the end of this branch. (Why? Because the firm neither gains nor loses if it does not drill.) If the branch representing drilling the well is followed, we come to a chance fork, since it is uncertain whether the firm will strike oil and, if it does, how much oil it will find. The highest branch following this chance fork represents the consequence that no oil is found, in which case the firm loses $90,000, shown at the end of this branch. The second highest branch following this chance fork represents the consequence that 10,000 barrels are found, in which case the firm gains $100,000, shown at the end of this branch. Similarly, the second lowest and lowest branches following this chance fork represent respectively the consequences that 20,000 and 30,000 barrels are found; the number at the end of each of these branches is the corresponding profit to the firm.

Having constructed this decision tree, the firm's managers can compute the expected profit to the firm if it is situated at the chance fork immediately to the left of the profit (or loss) figures. If the firm is at this fork, there is a 0.60 probability that the branch culminating in a $90,000 loss will be followed, a 0.15 probability that the branch culminating in a $100,000 profit will be followed, a 0.15 probability that the branch culminating in a $300,000 profit will

---

[1]This case is described in detail in J. Hosseini, "Decision Analysis and Its Application in the Choice between Two Wildcat Oil Ventures," *Interfaces,* March–April 1986. For pedagogical reasons, we have simplified the analysis and the numbers involved. A general account of the use of decision trees in oil exploration is found in J. Pratt, H. Raiffa, and R. Schlaifer, "Introduction to Statistical Decision Theory," in *Managerial Economics and Operations Research,* Mansfield.

FIGURE
14.2

Decision Tree, Tomco Oil Corporation

If Tomco Oil drills the well, the expected profit is $56,000. If it does not, the expected profit is zero.

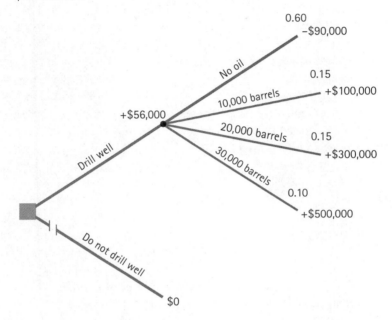

be followed, and a 0.10 probability that the branch culminating in a $500,000 profit will be followed. To obtain the expected profit if the firm is situated at this fork, the firm's managers should multiply each possible value of profit (or loss) by its probability, and sum the results. Thus, the expected profit if the firm is situated at this fork equals

$$0.60(-\$90,000) + 0.15(\$100,000) + 0.15(\$300,000)$$
$$+ 0.10(\$500,000) = \$56,000.$$

In Figure 14.2, this result is written above the chance fork in question to show that this is the expected profit if the firm is located at that fork.

Going farther along the decision tree to the left, the firm has a choice of two branches, one of which leads to an expected profit of $56,000, the other of which leads to an expected profit of zero. If the firm wants to maximize its expected profit, it should choose the former branch. That is, it should drill the well.

CONCEPTS IN CONTEXT

Bidding for the SS *Kuniang**

Prudent application of decision tree analysis can make you a winning manager even if your bid is second best, as one utility discovered in 1981. The New England Electric System is a public utility holding company that generates and delivers electricity to over one million customers in Massachusetts, Rhode Island, and New Hampshire. Because some of its oil-fired power stations were converted to coal, it decided to obtain ships to bring coal from Virginia to New England. In 1981, the SS *Kuniang* ran aground, and the ship's owners offered to sell the salvage rights by means of a sealed bid auction. The New England Electric System was interested in making a bid, since if the *Kuniang* could be restored, it would meet the company's needs very well.

To determine how much to bid, the company carried out a detailed analysis, based on a decision tree like that in Figure 14.1 or 14.2. It calculated the expected net present value of its earnings, given each amount it might bid. For example, if it bid $5 million, it calculated that the expected net present value would be $2.85 million. On the other hand, if it bid $7 million, it calculated that the net present value would be $3.05 million.

Why was the net present value higher if it bid $7 million rather than $5 million? Because the probability was higher that its bid would win. Obviously, the company could not be sure of this probability, but according to its best estimates, this probability would increase from about 1/6 to 1/2 if it bid $7 million rather than $5 million.

As a result of this analysis, the New England Electric System bid $6.7 million for the *Kuniang*, since this was the bid that maximized expected net present value. It came in second. The winning bid was $10 million. Of course, the fact that the company did not make the winning bid does not mean that the analysis was not useful. The point of the analysis was to determine how much it was worthwhile to bid. (If the company had made a high enough bid, it could have been reasonably sure of winning, but it would have lost money by doing so, the so-called winner's curse.) According to Guy W. Nichols, the company's chairman at that time, the analysis "was a useful contribution to our deliberations and to our decision regarding an appropriate bid for the ship."

*D. Bell, "Bidding for the S.S. *Kuniang*," *Interfaces*, March–April 1984, pp. 17–23.

The Expected Value of Perfect Information

Frequently, the decision maker can obtain information that will dispel (at least some of) the relevant risk. If the decision maker can get perfect information, how much is it worth? To answer this question, we define the expected value of perfect information as the increase in expected profit if the decision maker could obtain completely accurate information concerning the outcome of the relevant situation (but if he or she does not yet know what this information will be). Thus, in the case of the Jones Corporation (the firm that must decide whether to increase its tire price), this expected value is the increase in expected profit if the firm could obtain perfectly accurate information indicating whether its current advertising campaign will be successful.

To illustrate how one can compute the expected value of perfect information, let's return to the Jones case. We begin by evaluating the expected monetary value to the Jones Corporation if it can obtain access to perfectly accurate information of this sort. If it can obtain perfect information, it will be able to make the correct decision, regardless of whether or not its current advertising campaign is successful. If it is successful, the firm will be aware of this fact, and will increase the price. If it is not successful, the firm will be aware of this fact also, and will not increase the price. Thus, given that the firm has access to perfect information, the expected profit is

$$0.50(\$800,000) + 0.50(\$200,000) = \$500,000.$$

To understand why this is the expected profit if the Jones Corporation has access to perfect information, it is important to recognize that although it is assumed that the firm has access to perfect information, it *does not yet know what this information will be.* There is a 0.50 probability that this information will show that its advertising campaign is successful, in which case the Jones Corporation will increase its price and the profit will be $800,000. There is also a 0.50 probability that the information will show that it is not successful, in which case the Jones Corporation will not increase its price and its profit will be $200,000. Thus, as shown above, the expected profit if the firm has access to perfect information (that is not yet revealed to the firm) is $500,000.

At this point, we must recall that the expected profit if the firm bases its decision on existing information is $200,000 (as we saw on pages 528–31), not $500,000. The difference between these two figures—$500,000 minus $200,000, or $300,000—is the expected value of perfect information. It is a measure of the value of perfect information. *It shows the amount by which the expected profit increases as a consequence of the firm's having access to perfect information.*

In many circumstances, it is very important that the decision maker know how much perfect information would be worth. Business executives are continually being offered information by testing services, research organizations, news bureaus, and a variety of other organizations. Unless you know how much particular types of information are worth, it will be difficult to decide rationally whether they should be bought. The sort of analysis presented in this section is useful to guide such decisions, since it shows the maximum amount that the firm should pay to obtain perfect information.

TABLE
14.1

Expected Value of Perfect Information Concerning Factors Influencing Whether to Build New Chemical Plant

Factor	Expected value of perfect information (millions of dollars)
By-product quantity	6.2
Level of impurities	3.9
Raw material costs	0.3
Plant efficiency	0.0

Source: Spetzler and Zamora, "Facilities Investment and Expansion Problem."

Evaluating an Investment in a New Chemical Plant: A Case Study

To illustrate the usefulness of the expected value of perfect information, consider an actual case in which a decision tree was constructed to determine whether a major U.S. corporation should invest in a new plant. The major product of the new plant would be a brightener, but by using new processing methods, a valuable by-product could be made as well. The exact amounts of both products that would be produced were uncertain. Very small quantities of impurities in the raw materials used in the process could greatly influence the amounts of brightener and by-product produced. Also, there were uncertainties concerning the costs of raw materials and plant efficiency.

Table 14.1 shows the expected value of perfect information concerning by-product quantity, impurities, raw material costs, and plant efficiency. As you can see, the critical uncertainties were those regarding by-product quantity and the level of impurities. For example, perfect information concerning by-product quantity would have been worth up to $6.2 million. On the other hand, information regarding raw materials and plant efficiency was of much less importance for this decision. Indeed, the expected value of perfect information concerning plant efficiency was close to zero. On the basis of these results, the analysts advised the company to do some research to reduce the uncertainties regarding by-product quantity and the level of impurities before committing itself to the construction of the new plant.[2]

[2]C. Spetzler and R. Zamora, "Decision Analysis of a Facilities Investment and Expansion Problem," in *The Principles and Applications of Decision Analysis,* eds. R. Howard and J. Matheson (Menlo Park, Calif.: Strategic Decision Group, 1984).

CONSULTANT'S CORNER

Choosing Areas for Research Regarding Pollution Costs*

The National Academy of Sciences sponsored a study to examine emission control strategies for power plants. One purpose of this study was to determine the value of reducing the uncertainty concerning the pollution costs of various strategies. Efforts to reduce harmful emissions from coal-burning power plants focus on at least four strategies: (1) treating the coal to reduce its sulfur content, (2) using premium-priced, low-sulfur coal, (3) employing a tall stack and intermittent control systems, and (4) adopting a flue-gas desulfurization process. This study was concerned with the effects of various control alternatives on the total cost of electricity. Choosing among them is not easy, partly because it has been difficult to establish, with any certainty, the pollution costs of each strategy.

Because of the limitations of existing knowledge, the study found that there was considerable uncertainty regarding which of the alternative strategies was least costly. The expected value of perfect information, shown below, depended on whether the plant was in an urban or a remote area and whether low-sulfur coal was available.

	Low–sulfur coal available	Low–sulfur coal not available
Remote plant	$3.7 million	$2.4 million
Urban plant	1.3 million	2.8 million

If you were a consultant to the National Academy of Sciences, what conclusions could you draw concerning the kinds of plants for which further research of this sort would be most valuable?

*This section is based on an actual case. For further discussion, see S. Watson and D. Buede, *Decision Synthesis* (Cambridge, U.K.: Cambridge University Press, 1987) (which summarizes the work of D. North and M. Merkhofer).

Measuring Attitudes toward Risk: The Utility Approach

In discussing both the Jones Corporation's pricing decision and the Tomco Oil Corporation's drilling decision, we have assumed that the decision maker wants to maximize expected profit. In this and the following sections, we formulate a more realistic criterion. To understand why a decision maker may not want to maximize expected profit, consider a situation where a firm is given a choice between (1) a profit of $2,000,000 for certain and (2) a gamble in which there is a 50-50 chance of a $4,100,000 profit and a 50-50 chance of a $60,000 loss. The expected profit for the gamble is

$$0.50(\$4,100,000) + 0.50(-\$60,000) = \$2,020,000,$$

so the firm should choose the gamble over the certainty of $2,000,000 if it wants to maximize expected profit. However, it seems likely that many firms, particularly small ones, would prefer the certainty of $2,000,000, since the gamble entails a 50 percent chance that the firm will lose $60,000, a very substantial sum for a very small firm. Moreover, many people may feel that they can do almost as much with $2,000,000 as with $4,100,000, and therefore the extra profit is not worth the risk of losing $60,000.

Whether the firm's managers will want to maximize expected profit in this situation depends on their attitude toward risk. If they are elderly people of modest means, they may be overwhelmed at the thought of taking a 50 percent chance of losing $60,000. On the other hand, if they are the heads of a big corporation, the prospect of a $60,000 loss may be not the least bit unsettling, and they may prefer the gamble to the certainty of a mere $2,000,000 gain.

Fortunately, we need not assume that the decision maker wants to maximize expected profit. Instead, we can construct a **utility function** for the decision maker that measures his or her attitudes toward risk. This concept of utility should not be confused with that discussed in Chapter 4. As we shall see, it is a quite different sort of concept. From this utility function, we can then go on to find the alternative that is best for the decision maker, given his or her attitudes toward risk.

Constructing a Utility Function

A rational decision maker will *maximize expected utility*. In other words, the decision maker should choose the course of action with the highest expected utility. But what (in this context) is a utility? It is a number that is attached to a possible outcome of the decision. Each outcome has a utility. The decision maker's utility function shows the utility that he or she attaches to each possible outcome. This utility function, as we shall see, shows the decision maker's preferences with respect to risk. What is **expected utility?** It is the sum of the utility if each outcome occurs times the probability of occurrence of the outcome. For example, if a situation has two possible outcomes, A and B, if the utility of outcome A is 2 and the utility of outcome B is 8, and if the probability of each outcome is 0.50, the expected utility equals

$$0.50(2) + 0.50(8) = 5.$$

What is the expected utility if the Tomco Oil Corporation drills the well under the circumstances described on pages 531–33? It equals

$$0.60\,U(-90) + 0.15U(100) + 0.15U(300) + 0.10U(500),$$

where $U(-90)$ is the utility that the decision maker attaches to a monetary loss of $90,000, $U(100)$ is the utility attached to a gain of $100,000, $U(300)$ is the utility attached to a gain of $300,000, and so on. Since there is a 0.60 probability of a $90,000 loss, a 0.15 probability of a $100,000 gain, a 0.15 probability of a $300,000 gain, and a 0.10 probability of a $500,000 gain, this is the expected utility. What is the expected utility if the firm does not drill the well? It equals $U(0)$, since under these circumstances it is certain that the gain will be zero.

To find the utility that the decision maker attaches to each possible outcome, we begin by setting the utility attached to two levels of profit arbitrarily. The utility of the better consequence is set higher than the utility of the worse one. In the case of the decision maker in the oil-drilling problem, we might set $U(-90)$ equal to 0 and $U(500)$ equal to 50. It turns out that the ultimate results of the analysis do not depend on which two numbers we choose, as long as the utility of the better consequence is set higher than the utility of the worse one. Thus, we could set $U(-90)$ equal to 1 and $U(500)$ equal to 10. It would make no difference to the ultimate outcome of the analysis.[3]

Next, we present the decision maker with a choice between the certainty of one of the other levels of profit and a gamble where the possible outcomes are the two profit levels whose utilities we set arbitrarily. Thus, in the oil-drilling case, suppose we want to find $U(100)$. To do so, we ask the decision maker whether he or she would prefer the certainty of a $100,000 gain to a gamble where there is a probability of P that the gain is $500,000 and a probability of $(1 - P)$ that the loss is $90,000. We then try various values of P until we find the one at which the decision maker is indifferent between the certainty of a $100,000 gain and this gamble. Suppose that this value of P is 0.40.

If the decision maker is indifferent between the certain gain of $100,000 and this gamble, it must be that the expected utility of the certain gain of

---

[3]The utility function we construct is not unique. Because we set the two utilities arbitrarily, the results will vary, depending on the values of the utilities that are chosen. If $X_1, X_2, \ldots, X_n$ are the utilities attached to n possible monetary values, $(\alpha + \beta X_1), (\alpha + \beta X_2), \ldots, (\alpha + \beta X_n)$ can also be utilities attached to them (where α and β are constants, and $\beta > 0$).

ANALYZING MANAGERIAL DECISIONS

Should Maxwell House Have Increased Its Price?

When coffee was first marketed in keyless containers, most consumers who tried it seemed to prefer the new can to the old one. Maxwell House, the nation's largest producer of coffee, developed its own keyless container (which operated on the tear-strip opening principle). One important decision that Maxwell House had to make before introducing its new can was whether to raise the per-pound price of coffee in the new can by 2 cents. Coffee in the quick-strip can was expected to cost an average of 0.7 cent per pound more than in the old container.

According to Joseph Newman, who studied this case, if Maxwell House raised its price by 2 cents per pound, it might have been reasonable to expect (1) a 0.25 probability that its market share would decline by 1.5 percentage points, (2) a 0.25 probability that its market share would remain constant, (3) a 0.25 probability that its market share would increase by 1.0 percentage point, and (4) a 0.25 probability that its market share would increase by 2.5 percentage points. The change in Maxwell House's profits corresponding to each change in its market share is given in the table below.

According to Newman, if Maxwell House did not raise its price, it might have been reasonable to expect (1) a 0.1 probability that its market share would decline by 0.6 percentage point, (2) a 0.2 probability that its market share would remain constant, (3) a 0.5 probability that its market share would increase by 1.0 percentage point, and (4) a 0.2 probability that its market share would increase by 2.8 percentage points. The change in Maxwell House's profits corresponding to each of these market-share changes is provided in the table below.

Price per pound held constant		Price per pound increased by 2 cents	
Change in market share (percentage points)	Change in profit (thousands of dollars)	Change in market share (percentage points)	Change in profit (thousands of dollars)
+2.8	4,104	+2.5	11,939
+1.0	−591	+1.0	6,489
0	−840	0	2,856
−0.6	−1,218	−1.5	−1,050

$100,000 equals the expected utility of the gamble. (Why? Because the decision maker maximizes expected utility.) Thus,

$$U(100) = 0.40\,U(500) + 0.60\,U(-90).$$

And since we set $U(500)$ equal to 50 and $U(-90)$ equal to 0, it follows that

$$U(100) = 0.40(50) + 0.60(0) = 20.$$

That is, the utility attached to a gain of $100,000 is 20.

(a) Construct a decision tree representing Maxwell House's pricing problem. (b) If Maxwell House wanted to maximize the expected profit, should it have increased the price per pound of coffee in its new can by 2 cents?

SOLUTION (a)

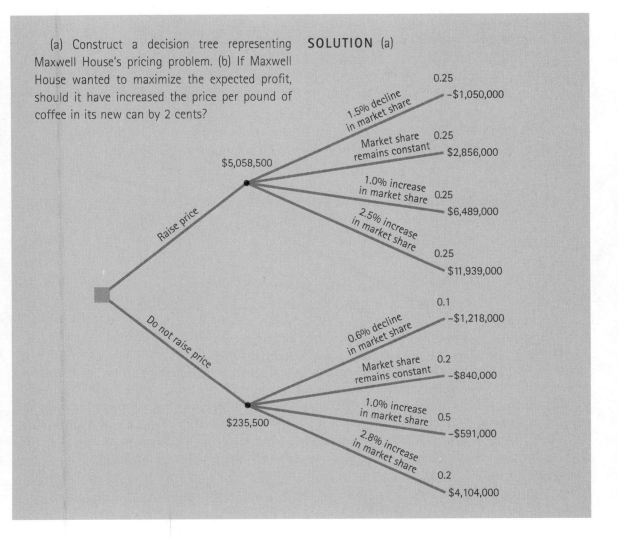

Using the same procedure, we can find $U(300)$ and $U(0)$, the other utilities required to calculate the expected utility if the oil company drills the well and the expected utility if it does not drill it. For example, to obtain $U(300)$, we ask the decision maker whether he or she would prefer the certainty of a $300,000 gain to a gamble where there is a probability of P that the gain is $500,000 and a probability of $(1 - P)$ that the loss is $90,000. Then we try various values of P until we find the one where the decision maker is indifferent between the certainty of a $300,000 gain and this gamble. Suppose this value of P is 0.80. Then the expected utility of a certain gain of $300,000 must equal the expected utility of this gamble; this means that

$$U(300) = 0.80\,U(500) + 0.20\,U(-90).$$

And since $U(500)$ equals 50 and $U(-90)$ equals 0, it follows that $U(300)$ equals 40.

FIGURE
14.3

Utility Function

The decision maker's utility function is useful in indicating whether particular gambles should be accepted.

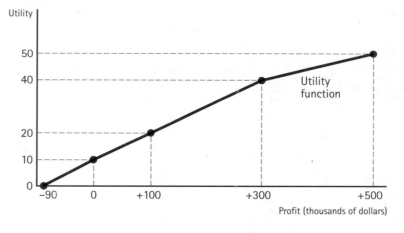

The decision maker's utility function is the relationship between his or her utility and the amount of his or her profit (or loss). On the basis of our evaluation of $U(-90)$, $U(100)$, $U(300)$, and $U(500)$ in previous paragraphs, we can identify four points on the decision maker's utility function, as shown in Figure 14.3. By the repeated use of the procedure described above, we can obtain as many such points as we like. (According to Figure 14.3, $U(0) = 10$.)

Using a Utility Function

Once a manager's utility function has been constructed, it can be used to indicate whether he or she should accept or reject particular gambles. Consider the actual case of Thomas Blair, president of the Tomco Oil Corporation. Using the above procedures, a managerial economist constructed Mr. Blair's utility function.[4] Suppose the result is as shown in Figure 14.3, and Mr. Blair must decide whether to drill the well described on pages 531–33. He should drill the well if his expected utility if the well is drilled exceeds his expected utility if it is not drilled. As pointed out in the previous section, his expected utility if the well is drilled equals

$$0.60U(-90) + 0.15U(100) + 0.15U(300) + 0.10U(500).$$

[4]Hosseini, "Decision Analysis." The utility function in Figure 14.3 is hypothetical, but adequate for present purposes. As noted above, this case has been simplified in various ways for pedagogical reasons.

If his utility function is as shown in Figure 14.3, this expression can be evaluated. Since $U(-90)$ equals 0, $U(100)$ equals 20, $U(300)$ equals 40, and $U(500)$ equals 50, his expected utility if the well is drilled is

$$0.60(0) + 0.15(20) + 0.15(40) + 0.10(50) = 14.$$

If the well is not drilled, Mr. Blair's expected utility equals $U(0)$, which is 10, according to Figure 14.3. Thus, he should drill the well. Why? Because if he does not drill it, his expected utility is 10, whereas if he drills it, his expected utility is 14. Since he should maximize expected utility, he should choose the action with the higher expected utility, which is to drill.

In fact, Tomco Oil Corporation did drill a well at Blair West. Subsequently, Mr. Blair stated, "Before we actually used decision-tree analysis to aid in our selection of drilling sites, we were skeptical as to the application of decision-tree analysis in oil exploration and field development decisions. Now we find it helpful, not only in choosing between two or more drilling sites, but also in making decisions subsequent to the choice of a drilling site."[5]

Attitudes toward Risk: Three Types

Although one can expect that utility increases with monetary gain, the shape of the utility function can vary greatly, depending on the preferences of the decision maker. Figure 14.4 shows three general types of utility functions. The one in panel A is like that in Figure 14.3 in the sense that utility increases with profit, but *at a decreasing rate*. In other words, an increase in monetary gain of \$1 is associated with *smaller and smaller* increases in utility as the monetary gain increases in size. Managers with utility functions of this sort are *risk averters*. That is, when confronted with gambles with equal expected profits, they prefer a gamble with a more certain outcome to one with a less certain outcome.[6]

Panel B of Figure 14.4 shows a case in which utility increases with profit, but *at an increasing rate*. In other words, an increase in monetary gain of \$1 is associated with *larger and larger* increases in utility as the monetary gain increases in size. Managers with utility functions of this sort are **risk lovers.** That is, when confronted with gambles with equal expected profits, they prefer a gamble with a less certain outcome to one with a more certain outcome.[7]

---

[5]Hosseini, "Decision Analysis."

[6]Consider a gamble in which there is a probability of P that the gain is π_1, and a probability of $(1 - P)$ that the loss is π_2. A person is a risk averter if the utility of the gamble's expected profit, $U[P\pi_1 + (1 - P)\pi_2]$, is greater than the expected utility of the gamble, $PU(\pi_1) + (1 - P)U(\pi_2)$.

[7]Consider the gamble described in footnote 6. A person is a risk lover if the utility of the gamble's expected profit, $U[P\pi_1 + (1 - P)\pi_2]$, is less than the expected utility of the gamble, $PU(\pi_1) + (1 - P)U(\pi_2)$.

Three Types of Utility Functions

Utility functions assume a variety of shapes. In panel A, the decision maker is a risk averter; in panel B, he or she is a risk lover; and in panel C, he or she is risk neutral.

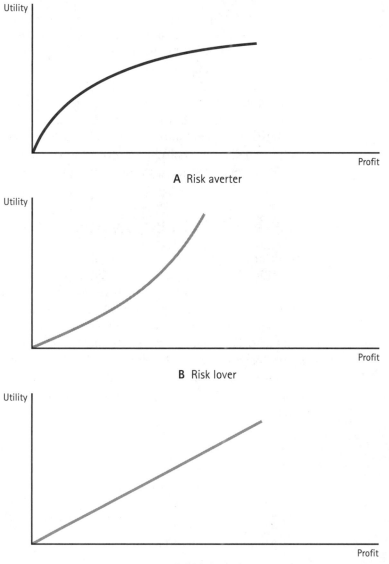

A Risk averter

B Risk lover

C Risk neutral

Finally, panel C shows a case where utility increases with profit and *at a constant rate*. In other words, an increase of $1 in monetary gain is associated with a *constant* increase in utility as the monetary gain grows larger and larger. Stated differently, utility in this case is a linear function of profit:

$$U = a + b\pi, \tag{14.3}$$

where U is utility, π is monetary gain, and a and b are constants (of course, $b > 0$). People with utility functions of this sort are **risk neutral**.[8] In other words, they maximize expected profit, regardless of risk. It is easy to prove that this is true. If equation (14.3) holds,

$$E(U) = a + bE(\pi), \tag{14.4}$$

where $E(U)$ is expected utility, and $E(\pi)$ is expected profit.[9] Consequently, since expected utility is directly related to expected profit, it can only be a maximum when expected profit is a maximum.

The Standard Deviation and Coefficient of Variation: Measures of Risk

The concept of risk is not easy to measure, but it is generally agreed that the riskiness of a given decision is directly related to the extent of the dispersion of the probability distribution of profit resulting from the decision. For example, suppose the Jones Corporation must decide whether to invest in a new plant. If the probability distribution of profit resulting from the new plant is as shown in panel A of Figure 14.5, the decision to invest in the new plant is more risky than it would be if this probability distribution were as shown in panel B. Why? Because the profit resulting from the new plant is more uncertain and variable in panel A than in panel B.

---

[8]A person can be a risk averter under some circumstances, a risk lover under other circumstances, and risk neutral under still other circumstances. The utility functions in Figure 14.4 are "pure" cases in which the person is always only one of these types, at least in the range covered by the graphs.

[9]To illustrate that equation (14.4) is correct, suppose that π can assume two possible values, π_1 and π_2, and that the probability that π_1 occurs is P and the probability that π_2 occurs is $(1 - P)$. Then, if $U = a + b\pi$,

$$E(U) = P(a + b\pi_1) + (1 - P)(a + b/\pi_2)$$
$$= a + b[P\pi_1 + (1 - P)\pi_2]$$
$$= a + bE(\pi),$$

since $E(\pi)$ equals $P\pi_1 + (1 - P)\pi_2$.

FIGURE

14.5

Probability Distribution of Profit from Investment in New Plant

The probability distribution in panel A shows more dispersion than that in panel B.

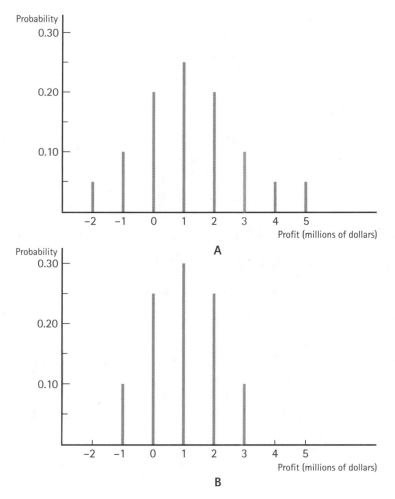

As a measure of risk, we often use the **standard deviation,** σ, which is the most frequently used measure of the dispersion in a probability distribution.[10] To calculate the standard deviation of profit, we begin by computing the expected value of profit, $E(\pi)$ [recall equation (14.2)]. Next, we subtract this ex-

---

[10]While the standard deviation often is a useful measure of risk, it may not always be the best measure. Our discussion here and in subsequent sections of this chapter is necessarily simplified. The measures and techniques we describe are rough, but many analysts have found them useful.

pected value from each possible profit level to obtain a set of deviations about this expected value. [The ith such deviation is $\pi_i - E(\pi)$.] Then we square each deviation, multiply the squared deviation by its probability of occurrence (P_i), and sum these products:

$$\sigma^2 = \sum_{i=1}^{N} [\pi_i - E(\pi)]^2 P_i.$$

Taking the square root of this result, we obtain the standard deviation

$$\sigma = \left(\sum_{i=1}^{N} [\pi_i - E(\pi)]^2 P_i \right)^{0.5} \tag{14.5}$$

As an illustration, consider a company that must decide whether to invest in a flexible manufacturing system. According to the company's engineers, there is a 0.3 probability that such an investment will result in a \$1 million profit, a 0.4 probability that it will result in a \$0.2 million profit, and a 0.3 probability that it will result in a \$0.6 million loss. Thus, the expected value of the profit from this investment is

$$E(\pi) = 1(0.3) + 0.2(0.4) + (-0.6)(0.3) = 0.2,$$

or \$0.2 million. And, based on equation (14.5), the standard deviation is

$$\sigma = [(1 - 0.2)^2(0.3) + (0.2 - 0.2)^2(0.4) + (-0.6 - 0.2)^2(0.3)]^{0.5}$$
$$= (0.384)^{0.5} = 0.62$$

or \$0.62 million.

A larger standard deviation tends to mean a larger amount of risk. Thus, if the standard deviation of the levels of profit resulting from the investment in the flexible manufacturing system were \$2 million, rather than \$0.62 million, there would be less certainty concerning its profitability. In other words, there would be a greater likelihood that its profitability would depart greatly from its expected value.

However, when we use the standard deviation as a measure of risk, we are implicitly assuming that the scale of the project is held constant. If one investment is twice as big as another, it would be expected that the standard deviation of its profits would be greater than that of the other investment. To take account of the scale of the project, a measure of relative risk is required. Such a measure is the **coefficient of variation,** defined as

$$V = \frac{\sigma}{E(\pi)}. \tag{14.6}$$

ANALYZING MANAGERIAL DECISIONS

Deciding Whether to Buy an Option on a New Flight-Safety System

Cutler-Hammer, Inc., an electronic equipment manufacturer in Milwaukee, Wisconsin, was offered the option to purchase a license to produce and sell a new flight-safety system. Because of pending legislative action, the market for the product was very uncertain. A team of Cutler-Hammer personnel and outside analysts carried out an analysis to help the company decide whether to purchase the option to obtain this license.

According to this team, if Cutler-Hammer purchased this option, there was a 0.29 probability that it would not obtain the license, in which case it would lose $125,000, and a 0.71 probability that it would obtain the license. If the company obtained such a license, the team estimated that there was a 0.85 probability that it would not obtain a defense contract, in which case it would lose $700,000, and a 0.15 probability that it would obtain a defense contract, in which case it would gain $5.25 million.

(a) Construct the decision tree. (b) If Cutler-Hammer wanted to maximize expected profit, should it have purchased the option? (c) Cutler-Hammer also analyzed the consequences of another course of action: waiting and seeking a sublicense. The team estimated that such a course of action would result in the following probability distribution of profit:

Profit Profitability	(thousands of dollars)
0.94	0
0.06	830

After considerable discussion, a unanimous decision was made by the firm's decision-making group (the president and his vice presidents for business development and operations) to adopt this course of action. Can you rationalize this graph decision?

For example, in the case of the investment in the flexible manufacturing system, the coefficient of variation for the profit levels is 0.62/0.2, or 3.1.

Adjusting the Valuation Model for Risk

According to the basic valuation model discussed in Chapter 1, a firm's managers must continually be concerned with the effects of their decisions on the present value of the firm's future profits, defined as

$$PV = \sum_{t=1}^{n} \frac{\pi_t}{(1 + i)^t}.$$ (14.7)

But the firm's managers do not know with certainty what the firm's profits in year t (that is, π_t) will be. The best that they can do is use the expected profit

SOLUTION (a) See graph below.
(b) Yes. (c) The expected profit from this course of action is $49,800, which is considerably less than it would be if the firm purchased the option ($100,425 according to part a). If the option is purchased, Cutler-Hammer has a 10.65 percent chance of making a large profit, but an 89.35 percent chance of ac-

tually losing money. If they wait, the profit may be smaller but they cannot lose money. So if Cutler-Hammer is sufficiently averse to the downside risk, it is preferable to wait and seek the sublicense.

*For further discussion, see J. Ulvila and R. Brown, "Decision Analysis Comes of Age," *Harvard Business Review*, reprinted in *Managerial Economics and Operations Research*, Mansfield.

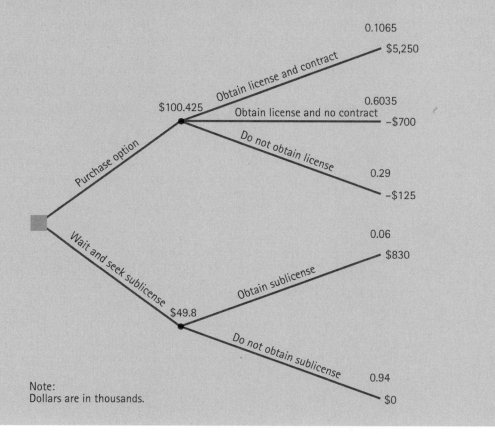

Note:
Dollars are in thousands.

[that is, $E(\pi_t)$] instead. How can they adjust the formula in equation (14.7) to take account of risk?

One way is to use the so-called certainty equivalent approach, which is related to the utility theory we developed in previous sections. For example, consider the manager of the firm considering the investment in the flexible manufacturing system. Suppose she is indifferent between the certainty of a $100,000 profit and the gamble involved in investing in this system. If so, the certainty equivalent ($100,000), rather than the expected profit ($200,000), should be used as π_t in equation (14.7). If the certainty equivalent is less than the expected profit, the decision maker is a risk averter; if it is more than the expected profit, she is a risk lover; and if it equals the expected profit, she is risk neutral.

On the basis of the decision maker's utility function, one can construct *indifference curves* of the sort shown in Figure 14.6. Each such indifference curve shows the certainty equivalent corresponding to various uncertain outcomes. Thus, Figure 14.6 shows that the manager is indifferent between the certainty of $100,000 and a gamble where the expected profit is $200,000 and the coefficient of variation is 3.1. Using such indifference curves, one can estimate the certainty equivalent of any uncertain situation. (In contrast to the indifference curves in Chapter 4 [other than on page 143], these indifference curves slope upward to the right. Why? Because the manager prefers less to more risk. In Chapter 4, the consumer preferred more of each commodity to less.)

In practice, of course, it is not easy to obtain such indifference curves, just as it is not easy to obtain the utility functions on which they are based. Because managers do not have unlimited time and patience, it may not be feasible to get more than a limited amount of information concerning their utility functions. Nor is it always clear which of a number of managers is the relevant

Manager's Indifference Curve between Expected Profit and Risk

The manager is indifferent between gambles with the expected profit and risk shown above. Thus, she is indifferent between the certainty of $100,000 and a gamble where the expected profit is $200,000 and the coefficient of variation is 3.1. Similar indifference curves exist for riskless amounts other than $100,000.

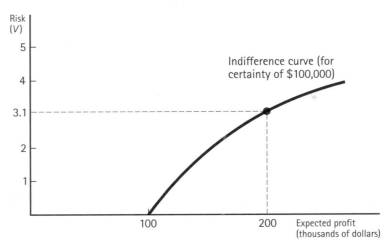

one. If many managers play an important role in coming to a particular decision, and if they have very divergent indifference curves, they may come to quite different conclusions. But this, of course, should be expected. Indeed, it would be strange if managers with diverse attitudes toward risk did not come to divergent conclusions when faced with a choice among alternatives entailing quite different amounts of risk.

Certainty Equivalence and the Market for Insurance

Consider an individual with initial wealth (W) of $900. This individual faces a 25 percent chance of a catastrophic event that will leave her with wealth of $400 (and likewise faces a 75 percent chance that nothing happens and her wealth remains at $900). This will be referred to as her gamble against nature. Her expected wealth is therefore

$$0.25(400) + 0.75(900) = 100 + 675 = 775.$$

The individual is risk averse with a utility (U) function of

$$U = W^{0.5}.$$

Thus, her expected utility from the situation that she faces is

$$0.25(400)^{0.5} + 0.75(900)^{0.5} = 0.25(20) + 0.75(30) = 5 + 22.5 = 27.5.$$

The certainty equivalent in this case is the amount of wealth the individual must have with perfect certainty that would render the individual the same expected utility as the gamble against nature which she faces, that is, 27.5,

$$U = W^{0.5} = 27.5.$$

Squaring both sides yields $W = \$756.25$. Thus, if the individual had wealth of $756.25 with perfect certainty, she'd have utility of 27.5, which is the same as her expected utility in the gamble against nature. So 756.25 is her certainty equivalent.

The LBI Insurance Company provides coverage to protect individuals against such catastrophic events. LBI offers full coverage insurance—it will cover the insured's entire loss (500 in this case). LBI is risk neutral.

What premium should LBI charge for this full coverage policy? LBI's expected payout is $125. They have a 25 percent chance of paying out $500 and a 75 percent chance of paying out $0. Thus, we'd expect at least a premium of $125 so that LBI would expect to at least break even on the policy. What is the maximum that the individual would pay for such a policy? That is where the certainty equivalent becomes relevant. By charging $143.75 for the policy, the individual would be left with $756.25 ($900 − $143.75) for sure (since there's a 75 percent chance that nothing happens, in which case she'd have $900 − $143.75 = $756.25 and a 25 percent chance that the catastrophic event occurs, in which case she'd have $900 − $143.75 − $500 + $500 = $756.25. With the policy, she'll always have wealth of $756.25 or utility of 27.5 for sure. Thus, she'll be indifferent between buying the full coverage insurance policy for $143.75 and facing the gamble against nature described above, because both give expected utility of 27.5.

The difference between the premium that will just cover LBI's expected pay-out ($125) and the maximum that the individual would pay ($143.75) is called the individual's risk premium, or the amount that the individual would be willing to pay the insurance company above the expected value of the loss. The risk premium is $18.75 in this case. A premium (P) between 125 and 143.75 will yield a situation where the individual would buy insurance (because utility of $900 − P > 27.5$) and the insurance company will sell the policy (because expected profit of $P − 125 > 0$) since both will gain.

The Use of Risk–Adjusted Discount Rates

Another way to introduce risk into the valuation model in equation (14.7) is to adjust the discount rate, i. This method, like that discussed in the previous section, is based on a manager's preferences with regard to risk. For example, suppose that Figure 14.7 shows a manager's indifference curve between expected rate of return and risk. As is evident from the fact that this curve slopes upward to the right, this manager is willing to accept greater risks if he obtains a higher expected rate of return. Specifically, he is indifferent between a riskless investment yielding an 8 percent return and a risky investment ($\sigma = 2$) yielding an expected 12 percent return. In other words, as risk rises, bigger expected profits are required to compensate for the higher risk.

The difference between the expected rate of return on a particular (risky) investment and that on a riskless investment is called the **risk premium** on this (risky) investment. For example, if the manager in Figure 14.7 can obtain an 8 percent rate of return from a riskless investment, he will require a risk premium of 4 percent (that is, 12 percent minus 8 percent) to compensate for the level of risk corresponding to $\sigma = 2$. This is the extra rate of return that is required to induce him to make such a risky investment. If he is offered less than this 4 percent risk premium, he will not make the investment.

Because the required rate of return depends on how risky the investment is, we can adjust the basic valuation model in equation (14.7) to take account of risk by modifying the discount rate, i. The adjusted version of equation (14.7) is

$$PV = \sum_{t=1}^{n} \frac{\pi_t}{(1 + r)^t},$$ (14.8)

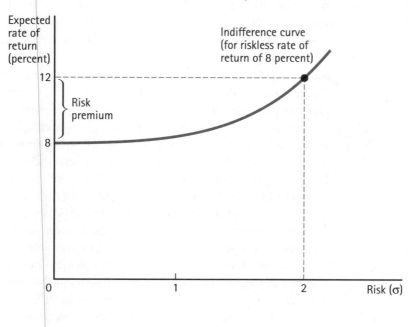

FIGURE 14.7

Manager's Indifference Curve between Expected Rate of Return and Risk

The manager is indifferent between a riskless rate of return of 8 percent and gambles with the expected rate of return and risk shown in the figure. Similar indifference curves exist for riskless rates of return other than 8 percent.

where r is the risk-adjusted discount rate. The risk-adjusted discount rate is the sum of the riskless rate of return and the risk premium required to compensate for the investment's level of risk. Thus, if the risk is such that $\sigma = 2$, the risk-adjusted discount rate would be 12 percent for the manager in Figure 14.7. This risk-adjusted rate equals 8 percent (the riskless rate) plus 4 percent (the risk premium).

Simulation Techniques

Confronted with decisions involving millions of dollars for which the risks are very substantial, managers frequently find simulation techniques to be useful. To illustrate the use of such techniques, suppose the officials of a chemical company must decide whether to build a new plant. The rate of return from the investment in this new plant depends on a number of factors—the cost of the plant, the plant's operating costs, the useful life of the plant, the size of the market for the product made by the plant, the price of this product, and this plant's share of the market. The firm's managers are uncertain concerning all these factors, but they and their staffs can provide probability distributions for the value of each factor. These probability distributions are shown in Figure 14.8.

Based on these probability distributions, a computer program can be developed to simulate what may occur. The computer picks one value at random from each of the probability distributions in Figure 14.8, and determines the rate of return from investing in the new plant (or the net present value) if these values prevail. For example, suppose that the computer picks a value of $2 million for the cost of the plant, $3 per pound for the plant's operating costs, five years for the useful life of the plant, $200 million for the market for the plant's product, $15 per pound for the price of this product, and 15 percent for this plant's share of the market. On the basis of these figures, the computer calculates the rate of return from the investment in this new plant.

This procedure is repeated over and over. The computer picks one set of values for the factors determining the rate of return from the investment, then a second set, then a third set, and so on. After picking each set of values, the computer calculates the rate of return from the investment. In this way, the computer builds up a frequency distribution of the rate of return. For example, the frequency distribution of the rate of return from this investment may be as shown in Figure 14.9. This frequency distribution can be of great use to managers because it summarizes concisely and effectively the extent of the risks involved in building the new plant. As was pointed out in previous sections, the standard deviation (or coefficient of variation) of this frequency distribution can be used as a rough measure of risk and, together with the mean, can be used in the sorts of analyses discussed in previous sections.

While simulation techniques of this kind are of great value, it is important to recognize that the results are no better than the original probability distributions fed into the computer. Thus, if the probability distributions in Figure 14.8 are wildly in error, it is foolish to expect the results in Figure 14.9 to be dependable. Because it frequently is expensive to obtain good estimates of the original probability distributions, this means that simulation studies of this kind, if carried out well, tend to be done to shed light only on major decisions, not minor ones.

A rougher procedure, called **sensitivity analysis,** is also worth considering. Rather than deriving the probability distributions in Figure 14.8, some analysts put together estimates of each factor (cost of plant, operating costs, and so on) that represent their best judgment of what will occur. Then they vary each of these values (within reasonable limits) to see how sensitive the rate of return is to each of them. The results indicate which factors are worth studying further, since there is little point in studying those factors that have only a minor effect on the results.

FIGURE
14.8

Probability Distributions for Factors Determining the Rate of Return from Investment in New Plant*

The computer picks one value at random from each of these probability distributions, and calculates the rate of return. This is repeated over and over.

*In contrast to Figure 14.5, these probability distributions are drawn as continuous curves. Depending on the circumstances, these variables can be regarded as continuous or discrete.

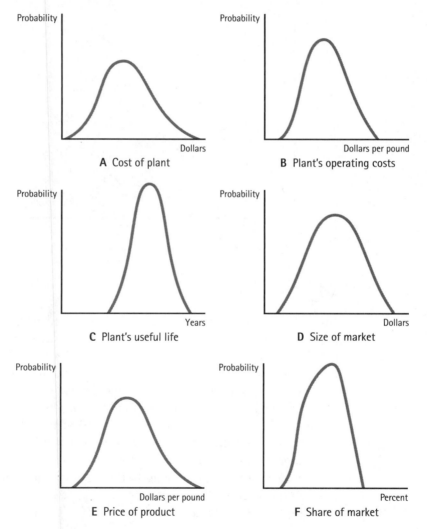

A Cost of plant

B Plant's operating costs

C Plant's useful life

D Size of market

E Price of product

F Share of market

Frequency Distribution of Calculated Rate of Return from Investment in New Plant

This is the frequency distribution resulting from the procedure described in Figure 14.8 being performed repeatedly.

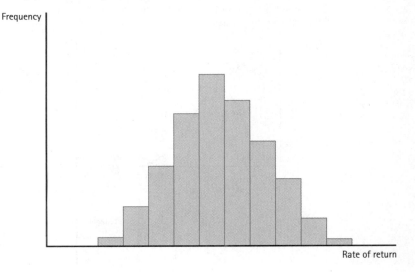

Application of the Maximin Rule

Throughout this chapter, we have been concerned with risk, not uncertainty. Risk occurs where the outcome is not certain, but where the probability of each possible outcome is known or can be estimated. **Uncertainty** refers to a situation where these probabilities are unknown. Although managerial economists have devised a number of types of rules to help a decision maker choose among alternative courses of action under conditions of uncertainty, none of these rules is universally considered to be preferable. All of them have disadvantages and difficulties. To illustrate the sorts of rules that have been proposed, and their limitations, we take up the *maximin rule*.[11]

The decision maker, according to this rule, should determine the worst outcome that can occur if each possible course of action is chosen, and should choose the course of action where this worst outcome is best. Consider a situation where the Jones Corporation, the hypothetical producer of automobile tires, must decide whether to move its production facilities from one location

---

[11]Frequently, this rule is referred to as the minimax rule; both names are in common use.

Using Simulation Techniques in the Computer Industry

In 1990, a major computer manufacturer was considering two investment projects. The first project involved a new technology requiring significant research. Because the technology was new and because it was hard to know whether the project would result in the desired results, there were considerable risks involved. The second project was based on existing technology. It called for incremental changes in technology and operations, and was felt to be less risky than the first project.

To compare projects of this sort, this firm has generally used analytical techniques that pay limited attention to the riskiness of the project. Using these techniques, the firm's analysts found that the two projects seemed to be about equally attractive. However, the firm's management was concerned about the large number of unknowns hidden in the sales, cost, and profit estimates for the first project.

Eventually, it was decided to use a simulation study to compare the attractiveness of the two projects. For each project, probability distributions of sales and costs were estimated. The computer then picked one value of sales at random from the probability distribution of sales and one value of costs at random from the probability distribution of costs. Then the computer calculated the discounted profit. This calculation was carried out repeatedly, first for one project and then for the other. Based on these calculations, a frequency distribution of discounted profit for each project was constructed; the results are shown below.

On the basis of these results, it was clear that the probability of a substantial loss was much higher with the first project than with the second project, as the firm's management had thought. Indeed, this probability was so high that the firm decided to reject the first project in favor of the second project. This is a good example of how the simulation techniques described on pages 553 to 554 have actually been used.

It is also a good illustration of the importance of taking proper account of risk. As Sandy Kurtzig, former head of ASK Computer Systems, put it, "Charting the future in business can be like one of those game shows where you have to choose from door #1, door #2, or door #3. You can as easily walk away with the set of carving knives as the trip to Hawaii."*

*S. Kurtzig, with T. Parker, *CEO: Building a $400 Million Company from the Ground Up* (New York: Norton, 1991).

TABLE 14.2

Jones Corporation's Gains (or Losses), with or without a Tax Increase, If a Tax Increase Does or Does Not Occur

Course of action	Outcome	
	Tax increase	No tax increase
Firm moves facilities	−$5 million	$20 million
Firm does not move facilities	zero	zero

to another. The Jones Corporation is concerned that if the tax authorities in the new location were to raise taxes, such a move might cut its profits considerably. As shown in Table 14.2, the Jones Corporation believes that if it moves its facilities and a tax increase occurs, it will lose $5 million. If it moves its facilities and a tax increase does not occur, it will gain $20 million. And if it does not move its facilities, it will gain (and lose) nothing.

The Jones Corporation, if it applies the maximin rule, should determine the worst outcome under each course of action. There are two possible courses of action: the firm can move its facilities or not move them. Regardless of which course of action is chosen, there are two possible outcomes: a tax increase can occur or not. If these facilities are moved, the worst outcome is a $5 million loss that will result if a tax increase occurs. If these facilities are not moved, the worst (and only) outcome is a zero gain. Thus, if the Jones Corporation applies the maximin rule, it should not move its facilities. Why? Because the worst outcome if these facilities are not moved is preferable to the worst outcome if they are moved.

Whether a tax increase will occur at the new location will not be determined by a rival or competitor who is out to inflict damages on the Jones Corporation. Instead, it will be determined by a host of political, economic, social, and other factors that have little to do with this particular firm. For this and other reasons, the maximin rule has been criticized as being overly conservative. Because there is no reason why the firm should assume that the relevant political, economic, social, and other factors are out to hurt it, there is no reason why it should pay attention only to the worst outcome that can occur if each course of action is taken.

Many rules other than the maximin rule have been proposed to help people make decisions under conditions of uncertainty.[12] However, each of these

---

[12]Some examples are Bayes's rule, the maximax rule, the Hurwicz rule, and L. J. Savage's minimax regret rule. See W. Baumol, *Economic Theory and Operations Analysis,* and M. Shubik, "A Note on Decision-Making under Uncertainty," in *Managerial Economics and Operations Research,* Mansfield.

rules has its problems and limitations. Which, if any, is appropriate depends on the attitudes toward risk and the financial resources of the decision maker, as well as on the other aspects of the situation. There is no single rule that can be applied universally to decision making under uncertainty. The truth is that in situations in which the probability of each outcome cannot be estimated (even roughly), it is very difficult to provide managers with general guidelines for decision making.

Summary

1. The probability of an event is the proportion of times that this event occurs over the long run. Expected profit is the sum of the amount of money gained (or lost) if each outcome occurs times the probability of occurrence of the outcome.

2. A decision tree is a graphical representation of a decision problem as a series of choices, each of which is depicted by a decision fork or a chance fork. A decision tree can be used to determine the course of action with the highest expected profit. A variety of examples were discussed, including Tomco Oil Corporation's decision of whether to drill an oil well at a site in Kansas.

3. The expected value of perfect information is the increase in expected profit if the decision maker could obtain completely accurate information concerning the outcome of the relevant situation (but he or she does not yet know what this information will be). This is the maximum amount that the decision maker should pay to obtain such information. Methods have been provided to enable you to calculate the expected value of perfect information.

4. Risk is often measured by the standard deviation or coefficient of variation of the probability distribution of profit. Whether a decision maker wants to maximize expected profit depends on his or her attitude toward risk. The decision maker's attitude toward risk can be measured by his or her utility function.

5. To construct such a utility function, we begin by setting the utility attached to two monetary values arbitrarily. Then we present the decision maker with a choice between the certainty of one of the other monetary values and a gamble in which the possible outcomes are the two monetary values whose utilities we set arbitrarily. Repeating this procedure over and over, we can construct the decision maker's utility function.

6. One way to adjust the basic valuation model for risk is to use certainty equivalents in place of the expected profit figures in equation (14.7). To do this, you construct indifference curves (based on the decision maker's utility function) showing the certainty equivalent corresponding to various uncertain outcomes.

7. Another way to introduce risk into the valuation model is to adjust the discount rate. To do this, you construct indifference curves between expected rate of return and risk, based on the decision maker's utility function. Using such indifference curves, you can estimate the risk premium (if any) that is appropriate.

8. Uncertainty refers to a situation in which the relevant probabilities cannot be estimated. According to the maximin rule, the decision maker under uncertainty should choose the course of action for which the worst possible outcome is least damaging. There are important problems with this rule, as well as with others proposed to handle the situation of uncertainty.

Problems

1. The president of the Martin Company is considering two alternative investments, X and Y. If each investment is carried out, there are four possible outcomes. The present value of net profit and probability of each outcome is shown below.

	Investment X			Investment Y	
Outcome	Net present value	Probability	Outcome	Net present value	Probability
1	$20 million	0.2	A	$12 million	0.1
2	8 million	0.3	B	9 million	0.3
3	10 million	0.4	C	16 million	0.1
4	3 million	0.1	D	11 million	0.5

a. What is the expected present value, standard deviation, and coefficient of variation of investment X?

b. What is the expected present value, standard deviation, and coefficient of variation of investment Y?

c. Which of these investments is riskier?

d. The president of the Martin Company has the utility function

$$U = 10 + 5P - 0.01P^2$$

where U is utility and P is net present value. Which investment should she choose?

2. William J. Bryan is the general manager of an electrical equipment plant. He must decide whether to install a number of assembly robots in his plant. This investment would be quite risky, since both management and the workforce have no real experience with the introduction or operation of such

robots. His indifference curve between expected rate of return and risk is as shown below.

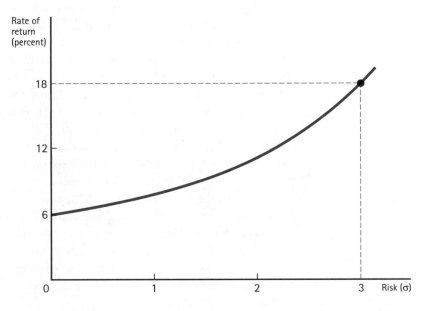

a. If the riskiness (σ) of this investment equals 3, what risk premium does he require?

b. What is the riskless rate of return?

c. What is the risk-adjusted discount rate?

d. In calculating the present value of future profits from this investment, what interest rate should be used?

3. The Zodiac Company is considering the development of a new type of plastic. Whether the plastic will be successful depends on the outcome of a research project being carried out at a major university. Zodiac's executives have no reasonably reliable means of estimating the university research team's probability of success. Zodiac's gains (or losses), depending on the outcome of the university research project, are as follows:

Action	Outcome of university research project	
	Success	Failure
Zodiac develops plastic	$50 million	−$8 million
Zodiac does not develop plastic	0	0

a. If the firm's executives use the maximin rule, should they develop the new type of plastic?

b. What are the disadvantages of the maximin rule?

    c. On the basis of the information given, can you calculate the expected value of perfect information? Why or why not?

4. The Electro Corporation, which manufactures television sets, has a fixed cost of $1 million per year. The gross profit from each TV set sold—that is, the price less the average variable cost—is $20. The expected value of the number of sets the company sells per year is 100,000. The standard deviation of the number of sets sold per year is 10,000.

    a. What is the expected value of the firm's annual profit?

    b. What is the standard deviation of the firm's annual profit?

    c. What is the coefficient of variation of the firm's annual profit?

5. Richard Miller, a Wall Street trader, says he is risk neutral. Suppose we let 0 be the utility he attaches to $100,000 and 1 be the utility he attaches to $200,000. If what he says is true, what is the utility he attaches to (a) $400,000? (b) $40,000? (c) −$20,000?

6. The chief executive officer of a publishing company says she is indifferent between the certainty of receiving $7,500 and a gamble where there is a 0.5 chance of receiving $5,000 and a 0.5 chance of receiving $10,000. Also, she says she is indifferent between the certainty of receiving $10,000 and a gamble where there is a 0.5 chance of receiving $7,500 and a 0.5 chance of receiving $12,500.

    a. Draw (on a piece of graph paper) four points on the utility function of this publishing executive.

    b. Does she seem to be a risk averter, a risk lover, or risk neutral? Explain.

7. The Oahu Trading Company is considering the purchase of a small firm that produces clocks. Oahu's management feels there is a 50-50 chance, if Oahu buys the firm, that it can mold the firm into an effective producer of washing machine parts. If the firm can be transformed in this way, Oahu believes that it will make $500,000 if it buys the firm; if it cannot be transformed in this way, Oahu believes that it will lose $400,000.

    a. Construct a decision tree to represent Oahu's problem.

    b. What are the decision forks? (Is there more than one?)

    c. What are the chance forks? (Is there more than one?)

    d. Use the decision tree to solve Oahu's problem. In other words, assuming that the firm wants to maximize expected extra profit, should Oahu buy the firm or not?

    e. Before Oahu makes a decision concerning the purchase of the firm, Oahu's president learns that if the clock producer cannot be made into an effective producer of washing machine parts, there is a 0.2 probability that it can be resold to a Saudi Arabian syndicate at a profit of $100,000. (If the firm cannot be resold, Oahu will lose $400,000.)

       (1) Does this information alter the decision tree?

       (2) Can you think of three mutually exclusive outcomes if Oahu buys the firm?

(3) What is the probability of each of these outcomes?

(4) What is the monetary value to Oahu of each of these outcomes?

f. Use your results in part e to solve Oahu's problem under this new set of conditions. In other words, on the basis of this new information, should Oahu buy the firm or not?

g. Oahu's executive vice president discovers an error in the estimate of how much Oahu will gain if it buys the clock manufacturer and turns it into an effective producer of washing machine parts.

(1) Under the circumstances in part d, how big would this error have to be to reverse the indicated decision?

(2) Under the circumstances in part e, how big would the error have to be to reverse the indicated decision?

8. According to Cal Tech's Nobel Prize–winning physicist the late Richard Feynman, the National Aeronautics and Space Administration (NASA) estimated the probability of a crash of the space shuttle to be 1 in 100,000, whereas the probability was in fact closer to about 0.01 to 0.02. If a decision tree had been used to determine whether to attempt a launch of the shuttle, what difference, if any, would this have made?

9. The *East Chester Tribune* must decide whether to publish a Sunday edition. The publisher thinks the probability is 0.6 that a Sunday edition would be a success and 0.4 that it would be a failure. If it is a success, she will gain $100,000. If it is a failure, she will lose $80,000.

a. Construct the decision tree corresponding to the problem, and use backward induction to solve the problem. (Assume that the publisher is risk neutral.)

b. List all forks in the decision tree you constructed, and indicate whether each is a decision fork or a chance fork, and state why.

10. Roy Lamb has an option on a particular piece of land, and must decide whether to drill on the land before the expiration of the option or give up his rights. If he drills, he believes that the cost will be $200,000. If he finds oil, he expects to receive $1 million; if he does not find oil, he expects to receive nothing.

a. Construct a decision tree to represent Lamb's decision.

b. Can you tell whether he should drill on the basis of the available information? Why or why not?

Mr. Lamb believes that the probability of finding oil if he drills on this piece of land is 1/4, and that the probability of not finding oil if he drills here is 3/4.

c. Can you tell whether he should drill on the basis of the available information? Why or why not?

d. Suppose Mr. Lamb can be demonstrated to be a risk lover. Should he drill or not? Why?

e. Suppose Mr. Lamb is risk neutral. Should he drill or not? Why?

Auctions

chapter 15

Revenues from online auctions in 2000 increased from

$650 million in 1998 to over $6.5 billion. Some estimate revenue from these auctions will have doubled by 2004. This dramatic increase in auction usage has caught the attention of federal officials who purchase over $200 billion worth of goods each year. They are currently experimenting with small online auctions, but want to create agency-wide e-commerce acquisition processes whose centerpiece will be online markets, including auctions. But, like the private sector, the government is uncertain about how the use of these auctions will alter the procurement process. As Dennis Rabkin of acquisition policy at General Services Administration (GSA) says, "We don't know all the answers yet. We don't really know where you can't go or shouldn't go with the tool (online auctions), and I don't know how far or broadly the tool should be defined. We want some feedback."[1]

[1]Douglas Brown, "Feds Seek Advice on Reverse Auctions," *E-Commerce News*, November 16, 2000. See www.zdnet.com/e-commerce/stories.

To obtain this feedback, in October of 2000 the government issued Special Notice #2712, which asks private companies and individuals for their advice on an e-commerce acquisition process. Of particular interest to the government are issues of auction structure—mechanism, price transparency, auction length, and ownership. Or, as the report states, "How are pricing models, discounts, and volume pricing contracts established and maintained within an eCommerce/service provider/exchange relationship?"[2] These questions are echoed by managers in the private sector as they see the use of B2B auction sites explode in number. Over $100 billion in revenue was generated worldwide by these sites in 2000; some estimate this number will double by 2003.

B2C auction sites are following a similar growth trajectory. Online auction sales to consumers totaled over $7 billion in 2000 and are expected to grow to over $12 billion in 2004. The message is clear: Auction markets will play an integral role in the next twenty years, and those managers who understand them best will realize added value from their use. Managers who don't understand them run the risk of being closed out of these fast-growing markets, or, even worse, seeing an erosion of firm value, as rivals use auctions to gain competitive advantages.

And e-commerce is not the only area experiencing an increase in auctions. Auction use is increasing in corporate acquisition activities and electronic trading markets.

This chapter examines structural parameters of auctions and shows how managers can manipulate them to affect revenue generation. All auctions, like markets, are governed by rules and procedures. Managers who understand these rules can design auctions to increase generated revenues. We focus on auction mechanism, for as you will see, this parameter can significantly influence the behavior of auction participants. We also show that managers do not have to abandon the sophisticated pricing strategies discussed earlier just because they employ an auction format. Performance-enhancing strategies like price discrimination are still feasible even within this format.

Also, managers will find a firm understanding of auction theory is helpful in other areas. The theory is used to help develop behavioral implications in negotiations and monopoly markets. And, since much of auction theory is game theoretical in nature, many of the principles we discussed in Chapter 12 can be applied to auction settings.

---

[2]United States Department of Commerce, Special Notice #2712, October 24, 2000.

A Short History of Auctions

The first written record of an auction was the annual Babylonian marriage market as described by Herodotus, "the father of history." The socially aware Babylonians actually structured the auction to ensure that all women who wanted husbands found them. The most beautiful women were auctioned first, their bidders being the rich who could afford to pay for beauty. More modest-looking women then participated in a negative bid auction. The man with the lowest negative bid received the woman and his bid price. This price was paid from the funds generated by the beautiful women. Not only did this ensure that all willing women were married; it also provided the newlyweds with financial support.

Auctions were used in ancient Greece to award mineral rights and by Roman authorities to collect debts owed by individuals. Cicero reports a court case in 80 B.C. involving the auctioning of goods to satisfy a debt. In 1556, the French monarch appointed an officer to appraise and auction all property left by those executed by the state. Pepys reports on a candle auction of 1660. Candle auctions gave bidders a limited time to bid (until the candle burned out); they are the forerunner of today's timed auctions on eBay.

Auctions almost caused the continuation of the War of 1812. During the war, English goods were prohibited from being imported to the United States. The end of the war saw British merchants flooding the United States with goods to satisfy the pent-up demand. The goods were sold via auction because of the speed by which goods could be allocated (this also being one reason auctions and the Internet are such a good match). American manufacturers claimed the British were dumping the goods (selling below cost) and tried to get the auctions outlawed. Newspapers and U.S. trade organizations led a spirited fight to get state legislatures to abolish auctions. The fight even extended to the U.S. Congress where the Ways and Means Committee actually introduced a bill to ban auctions. Fortunately, Congress never passed the bill.

Though markets grew quicker than auctions, auctions played a major role in the allocation of fruits and vegetables, fish, furs, tobacco, and livestock. By the 1980s, auctions were used to sell over $5 billion of goods yearly.

Auction use continued to increase and virtually exploded in the late 1990s with the increase in e-commerce. This exponential increase in use will continue, for the Internet is to auctions what mass retailing was to posted prices—a highly productive marriage of technology and allocation mechanism. Internet use significantly decreases organizational costs—a binding constraint on auction revenue. In most auctions, if I'm the seller, "the more the merrier" (this idea is shown more formally later in the chapter). Expected revenue never decreases with increases in the number of bidders. So any technology that decreases the costs of bringing individuals together should increase auction use.

Types of Auction Mechanisms

All auctions involve a bidding process. In most auctions, a service or product is made available, and buyers bid for the ownership rights. Reverse auctions occur when a buyer announces the need for a product or service and sellers bid for the right to sell the buyer the good or service. Whether using a normal or reverse auction, managers primarily use one of four auction mechanisms: the English or ascending-bid auction, the Dutch or descending-bid auction, the sealed-bid auction, and the second-price sealed-bid auction.

English or Ascending-Bid Auction

In these auctions, the initial price is set at the seller's reservation price (called the **reserve price**). Buyers then bid against each other with a succession of increasingly higher prices until only one bidder remains. This final bidder receives the good or service at her final stated price. There are several ways to manage this bidding procedure. An auctioneer can orally call out bids, bidders signal their acceptance of the price with a shake of their head or a wave of their bidding card. This method is used often by the large auction houses like Christie's and Sotheby's. Another method is for bidders themselves to call out their bids. This method is used by many commodity exchanges. Individual commodities are assigned their own area, called a pit; traders of a commodity gather in the pit and call out the price at which they are willing to buy (sell) the commodity. If others wish to sell (buy) at that price, they do so. English auctions are also conducted electronically. Here, the highest present bid is posted; if others want to bid higher they are free to do so, and their bid then becomes the current high bid. Many Internet auction sites, including eBay, use this electronic format.

Two special cases of an ascending-bid auction are the Japanese auction and the ascending-bid timed auction. Much theoretical work has centered on the Japanese auction. In these auctions, bidders bid until the price exceeds their reservation price. They then drop out of the bidding process and do not return. Remaining bidders can thus determine who has dropped out and who remains. In the ascending-bid timed auction, the bidding continues for a specified period of time. The high bidder at the end of this period receives the good or service (assuming the bid is greater than the seller's reserve price). These timed auctions are used extensively by Internet auction sites.

Dutch or Descending-Bid Auction

In these auctions, initial prices are very high. This price is announced and then a set time passes (for example, 15 seconds). If no bidder accepts the good at that price, the price is lowered a set interval (for example, a dollar) and then the procedure repeats itself. The price is lowered until one bidder accepts the announced price. The descending bid is often called a Dutch auction because it is used to sell flowers in the Netherlands. Here, auction halls larger than ten football fields are used daily to auction thousands of flowers. Current offered prices are shown on a large screen, and bidders accept the price by pushing electronic buttons. The process is very quick, with over 500 transactions every hour. (The photograph on the first page of this chapter shows a scene from the Dutch flower auction.)

Sealed-Bid Auction

In these auctions, each bidder submits a price bid that is known only to themselves. So, unlike an English auction, bidders do not know the valuation of others. In a first-price sealed-bid auction, bids are opened at a pre-announced time, and the high valuation bidder receives the item at his stated price. Sealed-bid auctions are often used for procurement of goods and services. So a state may submit a bid for highway construction, with the winning bidder being the one with the lowest bid.

Second-Price Sealed-Bid Auction

This auction is a variant of the sealed-bid type of auction. In a second-price auction, the highest bidder receives the good or service at the bid of the second-highest bidder. These auctions are also called Vickrey auctions after William Vickrey who wrote a seminal paper on the subject in the 1960s, which later led to his award of the 1996 Nobel Prize in economics. As we shall see, second-price auctions have characteristics conducive to bidders truthfully revealing their valuations.

Auction Mechanism and Revenue Generation

Similar to market settings, in auctions, managers want to maximize profit. And, as differences in structural parameters like differentiation, entry barriers, and location explain variance in market power (and profitability), auction rules explain variance in generated revenues. An advantage for auctions is that relative to markets, it is easier (and less costly) for managers to influence structural parameters through auction rules. Hence, it pays for managers to recognize how auction design influences revenues. We will examine the effect of auction rules on revenue by first looking at a simplified model. We then relax some model assumptions to show how rules affect revenue.

Our baseline case assumes that bidders are symmetric, risk neutral, and that bids are based on independent signals drawn from a commonly known distribution. The behavioral implications of these assumptions are explained below:

Bidders are symmetric. Think of a bidder as selecting a valuation (bid) from a distribution of possible bids. Symmetric bidders use similar distributions commonly known to all. So bidders with identical reservation prices and observing the same signal will submit equivalent bids. We emphasize that (as in the real world) differences in reservation prices across bidders is not constrained by this symmetry.

Bidders are risk neutral. That is, bidders bid to maximize expected values and not risk-adjusted utility. Most assume individuals are risk averse; however, evidence shows that when individuals "decide" as corporate agents, behavior resembles that of risk neutrality. That said, we later show how risk-averse bidders can be strategically exploited.

Signals are independent. Signals are independent in one of two ways. In **private-value auctions**, reservation prices are a function of information and utility. Since signals depend on the information space, valuation is constrained to one's own signal. So let's say you find yourself standing next to me at an art auction. Are differences in how we value a painting a function of our own personal experience, or does what happens to you (but is unknown to me) affect my valuation? The former sounds more plausible. This describes a private-value auction with independent signals.

In **common-value auctions**, all bidders value the good similarly. What is not known, though, is the true value of the good for which they bid. Consider the rights for minerals under a piece of land. Whatever is down there is worth about the same for all (given world-wide commodity markets), but none knows perfectly what is there. So each bidder measures and forms beliefs about the true value. If signals are independent, then what I estimate does not depend on the estimate of others, though the distribution of signals is commonly known.

For any auction format, let b = bid and p = price paid by auction winner. So expected profit is simply $(b - p)(Pr_w)$, with Pr_w = probability of winning the auction, conditional on bid level. Since managers want to maximize profits, optimal bids depend on valuations (reservation prices). Therefore, expected profits for any b, Pr_w combination is given by:

$$U(Pr_w, b, p) = (Pr_w)(b - p).$$

We can compare these profit functions across auction formats to determine how surplus $(b - p)$ is split between buyer and seller. We can show that the slope of the profit function is equal to the conditional probability of winning for any given bid. So auction formats with identical surplus functions (conditional on valuation) offer the same probability of winning at any given bid and hence recommend the same optimal strategies.

This relationship is the foundation for what is called the **revenue equivalence theorem.** The theorem shows that whether a manager chooses an English, Dutch, sealed-bid, or second-price sealed-bid auction, her choice does not affect the expected total surplus generated by the auction and hence does not affect the expected revenues of the seller. The theorem can even be extended to other auction formats. As long as the format ensures an efficient allocation of goods and gives zero profit to any bidder holding zero value ($0) for the good, then surplus functions are identical and hence so are the recommended bidding strategies across formats. For example, lobbying efforts can be modeled as an "all-pay" auction. All bidders pay for the good, but only the highest bidder receives it. Because this auction satisfies the stated conditions, its expected surplus is the same as any of the four standard auction formats.

Bidding Strategies

So what are the optimal bidding strategies across the four auction formats? Of the four standard formats, only English auctions give bidders an opportunity to learn more about the reservation price of others. In the sealed-bid format, bids of others are not revealed until after the bidding period is closed. In Dutch auctions, once a bidder reveals his reservation price (by accepting the current price) the auction is over. But, because of the ascending nature of the English auction and the public nature of bidding, bidders learn more about the reservation price of others. Unfortunately, this information is of limited value to the strategic bidder, for optimal behavior in these auctions is defined by a dominant strategy. And, if you remember, smart strategists don't worry about the behavior of others in using a dominant strategy, since it lacks strategic value. So optimal behavior in an ascending auction never changes. The bidder should always be willing to bid up to his reservation price.

Basically, this rule maximizes profit $(b - p)$. Clearly, you never bid above your reservation price unless you wish to suffer negative profit. Because profit always decreases with an increase in bid, why bid higher than necessary? After all, the winner in an ascending auction only has to pay the slightest bit (i.e., epsilon) higher than the reservation price of the second-highest bidder. Any bid above this amount is inefficient (and suggests badly trained managers, not to mention an inefficient format). The difference between the reservation prices of the top and second-highest bidders defines available surplus and thus, profits. If we want to maximize profits, then we must capture all available surplus.

The auction's dominant strategy helps managers reduce the complexity of strategic thought. Consider the strategy as a decision rule: You listen to any bid. If the bid is lower than your reservation price, you bid incrementally higher.

If higher, don't bid. The simplicity of the procedure highlights one component of a dominant strategy's value: process efficiencies. Managers do not have to consider what others might do in choosing their optimal strategy. So managers can focus (and simplify) strategic effort, trusting the completeness of dominance.

So, in any ascending price auction, be willing to bid to your reservation price. If everyone follows this strategy, then the item is sold at the reservation price of the second-highest bidder (well, actually, an epsilon higher). It is sold to the highest bidder, and her expected revenue is the total available surplus, defined as the reservation price differential between the two highest valuation bidders.

Now, some may ask, is it true, in first-price ascending auctions, that the highest bidder receive the item at the reservation price (plus epsilon) of the second-highest bidder? If the auction is efficient he does, and furthermore we shall show how this holds true across all four auction mechanisms.

So, in an ascending auction, the highest bidder claims the item at the reservation price of the second-highest bidder. We previously noted this is the same prediction of the Vickrey auctions (those sealed-bid affairs in which the highest bidder claims the item at the reservation price of the second-highest bidder). So both English and second-price sealed-bid auctions are ruled by the same dominant strategy. Though the two auctions differ in process, game theorists predict similar results. Of course, the latter format is more transparent than the former.

Anyway, let's see how the difference in bidding rules affects the decision rule of the dominant strategy. The two auctions differ in bidding rules. In English auctions the rules allow you to publicly bid multiple times; in the sealed-bid auction you bid once privately. English auctions let you respond to the bids of others; sealed-bid auctions don't. Because the bidder in a sealed-bid auction has only one chance to bid, he should bid his reservation price. Negative payoffs are nonexistent, as zero becomes his worst possible payoff. And, if he does win, he guarantees himself all the available surplus. So while the dominant strategy remains the same—be willing to bid up to your reservation price—the bidding rules of the second-price sealed bid require a slight revision of our managerial decision rule: **Bid your reservation price.** Managers who do so guarantee themselves the highest expected surplus. Don't worry about others (it does you no good); focus on your own preferences and think hard about your reservation price. Then bid it.

Second-price sealed-bid auctions are also a good example of how auction rules can change bidding behavior. The rules encourage all bidders to tell the truth. In fact, you are better off if you tell the truth. In a later discussion, we call such rules **incentive compatible.** These are rules that encourage individuals to reveal their true preferences.

Next, let's consider the descending (Dutch) and first-price sealed-bid auctions. Though the two operate with different bidding rules, they are strategically similar. In fact, consider them as identical twins that behave differently, for their behavior (as governed by their rules) is the only way to tell them apart. If we model them in their reduced normal form (matrix form), they have identical strategy sets and payoffs. That is, any given bid will yield the same payoff in either auction, as a function of the bids of others. And, unlike the ascending or second-price formats, neither has a dominant strategy. In the Dutch or first-price sealed-bid auctions, one must consider what others will bid. Let's see how this affects a manager's bid choice.

As we explained earlier, bidders learn little about the valuations of others in either of these first-price auctions because bids are private until the auction is completed. But, because bidders are symmetric, all know the distribution of valuations. This information gives bidders the ability to anticipate the bidding strategy of others. Note that it does not give them the ability to predict the bids of others, just what others would bid conditional on some privately known information.

Each bidder is faced with an identical decision. If her bid is not the highest, she receives and pays nothing, so her surplus is zero. If she bids her reservation price and her bid is the highest, surplus is still zero. A bid higher than her reservation price results in zero surplus (if she is lucky and loses the auction), or negative surplus if she wins. And, she knows there is some positive probability that her bid is the highest. So what should she bid?

Unlike the previous types of auctions, the set of possible strategies approaches infinity in the descending and first-price sealed-bid auctions. That is, dominant strategies exist for ascending and second-price sealed-bid, but not for Dutch or first-price sealed-bid auctions. Managers now must consider what others will bid. Bidding strategies become conditional on bidding strategies of others. The world becomes more complex.

So how does one reduce the complexity? If you can't get the feasible set reduced to one, how about at least a finite number? Since all bidders face the same complexity, can bidders help themselves via some constraint on bidding behavior? Well, economists believe they can by being rational. Rational players only consider those outcomes in which each player is maximizing given the actions of others. Unless we are all doing our best given the actions of others, why should anyone agree to it? And, if we do adopt this rule, then no individual has an incentive to cheat by changing her strategy.

As mentioned in Chapter 12, in **Nash equilibria,** all correctly anticipate the actions of others and choose those actions that maximize expected surplus. Often its use reduces feasible strategies to a handful and aids in managerial efficiency. Note that the Nash is not a promise that under some conditions your expected surplus is higher than that of all others. It simply

ANALYZING MANAGERIAL DECISIONS

Auction Design at Freemarkets, Inc.

FreeMarkets is an example of how managers use on-line auctions to generate additional revenue. The company is a global provider of e-sourcing software and service solutions, and operates the world's largest sourcing market. It is a major player in B2B Internet auctions and has been conducting them since 1995. As of September 30, 2001, the firm has conducted more than $25 billion worth of volume for goods and services. Managers estimate they have helped their customers identify over $5.2 billion in savings. Auctions are held for goods and services in over 190 supply verticals on a global basis. Firms, including Emerson Electric and Eaton Corp., use FreeMarkets as part of their purchasing process and report significant savings. For example, managers at global giant GlaxoSmithKline (GSK) estimate cost savings of 10 percent. So how does FreeMarkets achieve such results?

The company combines web-based software, in-depth supply market information, market operations, and expert sourcing services to create value-added markets for their customers. Let's examine more closely how they fashion markets to generate cost savings for their customers.

FreeMarkets e-source technology is designed to meet the needs of large industrial customers, many with global operations. These buyers use FreeMarkets to conduct real-time interactive auctions with selected suppliers. The auction format is that of descending price; suppliers bid for the right to supply, generally, with the low bidder declared the winner (see chart). The company identifies several areas of expertise: coordination, design, and services.

AUCTION COORDINATION All online markets are controlled from a central location. This guarantees that the markets will operate correctly during the bidding process. FreeMarkets reduces software learning costs by using easily understood graphics and giving first-time bidders simulated trading sessions prior to the actual auction. Support is given to all bidders during the actual auction (in over thirty languages).

FreeMarkets has developed and enforces auction rules. For example, trade in many industrial markets is decided by factors other than low cost, like quality control or delivery logistics. FreeMarkets managers work with buyers to determine the qualification of the bidding pool Their managers talk with those in the buying organizations about specifications, logistics, and quality. For example, all bidders could be required to be ISO-9000 certified and able to deliver within five days. Then FreeMarkets handles bidder certification. This reduces the transaction costs to the buyer and the risk that winning (low-cost) suppliers cannot deliver promised supplies. This certification feature also helps bidders decide whether the auction is best suited to their resource base.

FreeMarkets creates a customer care center for all auctions. Here, bidders can find such services as surrogate bidding. By agreeing to act as if they were a bidder's agent, FreeMarkets eases the transaction costs of bidders.

AUCTION DESIGN The auction software is flexible to address the unique needs of different industrial markets. For example, some auctions are of the multi-currency type. This feature helps reduce the risks of both seller and buyer to currency fluctuations during the life of a long-term contract. The software is also easy to integrate into a

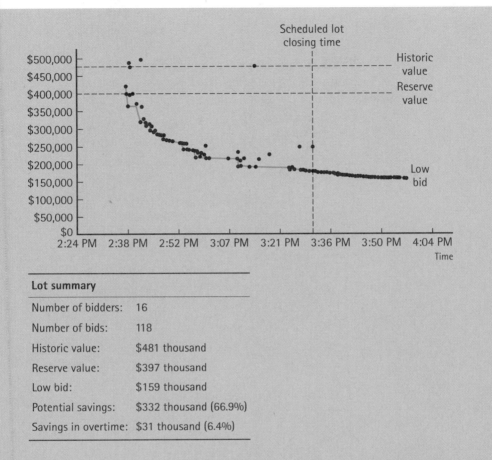

Lot summary

Number of bidders:	16
Number of bids:	118
Historic value:	$481 thousand
Reserve value:	$397 thousand
Low bid:	$159 thousand
Potential savings:	$332 thousand (66.9%)
Savings in overtime:	$31 thousand (6.4%)

buyer's ERP/MRP systems, which reduces the switching costs of buyers.

AUCTION SERVICES FreeMarkets gives advice to buyers about optimal auction lotting, strategies, and design. They will identify, recruit, and screen potential suppliers, reducing the risk that only qualified suppliers will compete in the auc-tion. Buyers are given post-auction briefings by FreeMarkets to analyze results and make suggested changes for the future. Free-Markets has a global network of over 150,000 regis-tered suppliers in 70 countries. They also supply filters for searching their supplier database and maintain performance statistics on all suppliers.

Source: FreeMarkets OnLine, Inc. 1997

Note: Each dot represents a distinct bid for the lot by an individual supplier.

states that given your attributes and those of others, you are doing the best you possibly can.

So what is the Nash solution to the descending and first-price sealed auctions? What should we assume others are doing, and then what is our optimal response to their actions? Well, we've already seen that we don't want to bid our reservation price because our highest possible payoff is then zero. But what if everyone thinks about their reservation price and then they discount back from that? And, the discount is equal to what their expectations are of the reservation price of the second-highest bidder. Then if our bid is the highest, we receive positive surplus; if it is not, we receive zero and lose nothing. As in the ascending and second-price auction, we must consider our reservation price, but in addition, we now must consider what others will bid and then base our bid on this expectation. So our decision rule is to estimate the reservation price of the second-highest bidder, and bid that.

Note that our beliefs about the reservation price of the second-highest bidder are influenced by the number of bidders. Basically, the greater the number of bidders, the closer to our reservation price we should bid. We can be even more precise if we assume the distribution of bids is uniform. Then our optimal bidding strategy is:

$$b = v - ((v - L)/n),$$

where v is the bidder's reservation price, L is the lowest possible bid, and n is the number of bidders. For example, assume our own valuation of an item is $3, and we believe the bids will be evenly distributed between $0 and $15. Then our optimal bid if there is only one other bidder is:

$$b = 3 - ((3 - 0)/2) \text{ or } \$1.50.$$

If there are two other bidders, then our optimal bid is:

$$b = 3 - ((3 - 0)/3) \text{ or } \$2.00.$$

And so we end where we began. It doesn't matter what auction format we use because expected revenues are identical across them. The optimal response of bidders in each produces the same expected revenue. We bid up to our reservation price in ascending and second-price auctions because the rules say if we are the high bidder, then we only have to pay the reservation price of the second-highest bidder. In descending and first-price sealed auctions, we consider our reservation price and then discount because the rules say the high bidder receives the item at her bid. But, the expected revenue is the same because the auction should yield revenue equal to the reservation price of the second-highest bidder.

Strategies for Sellers

Now we turn to sellers. These days, many managers use auctions to sell goods, services, and assets. In these circumstances, good managerial decisions follow the standard economic rule: Maximize profits with marginal revenue equal to marginal cost. Of course, some adjustments for the bidding rules must be made.

In markets, managers want to produce where $MR = MC$. This is a quantity decision and it determines the pricing point. But auctions are used to sell items few in quantity (often, one). So the notion of quantity holds little strategic value when quantity is so limited. What does determine the optimal pricing point is the distribution of reservation prices across bidders. So managers want to focus on this distribution.

This is a subtle but important difference realized by the strategic manager. Consider an ascending auction. Managerial action in this format is similar to third-degree price discrimination in markets. Recall that efficient allocation is defined as equality of marginal revenues across markets (the infamous $P_1/P_2 = (1 + [1/n_1])/(1 + [1/n_2])$). That is, managers maximize profits by ensuring sale to the consumers who value the product or service the most. Total output is determined by the horizontal summation of the marginal revenue curves and its intersection with marginal cost (see Figure 5.1).

Sellers want to use a similar strategy in auctions. Consider an auction selling a unique item. The seller will maximize profits by selling to the bidder with the highest reservation price. Because the seller's marginal costs remain constant to any change in price, the higher the winning bid, the greater the surplus. The expected revenue generated by a given price is simply that price times the probability it is the winning bid. This of course is determined by the distribution of reservation prices across bidders. Consider bidder i, and the distribution $F(b)$. Given $F(b)$, we determine the probability that any bid b is the winning bid. This is simply $1 - F(b)$ as shown in Figure 15.1. Function b acts as a demand curve in the following way. Each point on b tells us the probability of that point being the winning bid. So if the seller were to offer the item at price b, we could predict the expected demand at b. Expected revenue then is $b(1 - F(b))$ or the area under the marginal revenue function for any b. Let b^* be the actual winning bid (the reservation price of the second highest bidder). Mathematically we can show that b^* represents the expected revenue to the seller and the expected marginal revenue to the winning bidder. That is, in ascending bid auctions, they are equal.

What does this mean to the seller? As in third-degree price discrimination markets, managers need to sell to high reservation price bidders (buyers). And, because they want to maximize surplus in both situations, they definitely can't sell at any price below marginal costs. In auctions, consider marginal cost as being the value at which the seller refuses to sell. The price at which the seller says, "if that's all others are willing to pay, I'll keep it myself." So sellers need

FIGURE
15.1

Relationship between Seller's Expected Revenue and the Winning Bidder's Expected Marginal Revenue

If b^* is the winning bid, the seller's expected revenue is equal to the horizontally shaded box. This is also equal to the expected marginal revenue of the bidder.

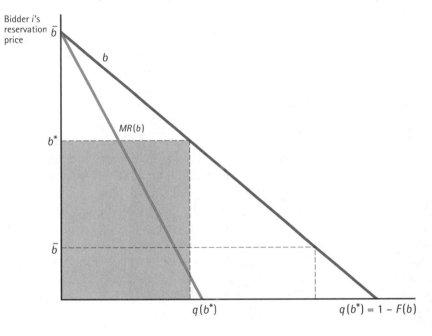

to set a reserve price (or begin bidding at their reserve price) for the auction. And, what should this reserve price be? It should be the bid when the bidder's marginal revenue is equal to the seller's marginal cost. (Recall that the bidder's marginal revenue is also equal to the auction's expected revenue.) Hence, under general conditions, managers should consider the following decision rule in setting a reserve price:

optimal reserve price = the value of the object being auctioned off, if it does not sell plus managerial estimates of the highest reservation price divided by 2.

For example, if the object's value is $0 if it is not sold, and a manager believes the highest reservation price is $300, then she should set a reserve price of

$150. After that, sellers should sit back and relax. Let the ascending bid mechanism work for you, as it maximizes your expected surplus. Unlike monopoly pricing, but similar to third-degree price discrimination, auctions are often more efficient than a posted price scheme. Unlike a posted price scheme, auctions guarantee the highest reservation price at which consumers will still purchase the good. We note that the managerial similarity to third-degree price discrimination is not confined to ascending auctions. All formats that are revenue equivalent to ascending auctions share this feature. The following example illustrates the efficiency of auctions.

Assume a seller has 4 units of output at a marginal cost of $0. There are 6 consumers in the market with reservation prices of $90, $60, $50, $40, $20, and $15. Table 15.1 shows the total available surplus broken down into consumer and seller surplus if sellers use an auction. Table 15.2 shows the total surplus if sellers post a $40 price.

At any posted price other than $40, total available surplus decreases. And while available surplus remains constant with a price of $40, sellers get a lower percentage of this relative to an auction ($160 versus $174). Auction usage increases seller surplus because of its price discriminatory property. The mechanism itself gets consumers to reveal their reservation prices.

Value of Information

The preference-revealing nature of auctions not only guarantees the highest reservation price at which consumers buy (at their higher values), but it gets buyers to identify themselves when demand is unknown. Managers can use

TABLE
15.1 Auction

Consumers	Reservation price	Win bid
1	$40	$21
2	20	
3	15	
4	90	61
5	60	51
6	50	41
Total consumer surplus		66
Total seller surplus		174
Total available surplus		240

TABLE
15.2
Posted price

Consumers	Reservation price	Price paid
1	$40	$40
2	20	
3	15	
4	90	40
5	60	40
6	50	40
Total consumer surplus		80
Total seller surplus		160
Total available surplus		240

auctions to gather more information about demand, before announcing their price schedule.

Repurchase Tender Offers

A primary example of this use of auctions is repurchase tender offers (RTO). The RTO is used by managers to buy back stock shares from current shareholders. Because shareholders are not required to sell, to induce selling, RTOs generally offer a premium above current market price. Until 1981, just about every RTO was fixed in price. Managers would announce the buy back price/share, and wait to see shareholder demand at that price. Since 1981, modified Dutch auction RTOs is the mechanism of managerial choice. And, it is easy to see why—relative to a fixed price RTO, the modified Dutch variety generally acquires shares at a lower total cost. Several studies show the average premium paid for fixed price tendered shares is 15 percent to 20 percent while those in modified Dutch auctions average 10 percent to 15 percent.

Unlike a fixed price RTO where one price is announced, in a modified Dutch one, managers announce a price range at which they are willing to repurchase tendered shares. Generally, the minimum price is at a slight premium to market, while the maximum approaches that of a fixed price RTO. Any shareholder willing to tender reveals her valuations, as she sends managers her pricing schedule (how many shares to tender at $X). Managers then take the schedules of individual shareholders and they construct a market supply schedule. They then determine how many shares they need and set the share price. All sellers who value the shares below that price receive the stated price. Again, note the timing differential between the fixed price and modified Dutch auction RTO. In the fixed price, managers set a price before knowing the supply schedule; in the modified Dutch, they set the price after seeing the supply schedule.

Citizens First Financial Corp. (CFFC) is a savings and loan holding company with headquarters in Bloomington, Illinois. The company has roughly $325 million in assets. Its managers recently wanted to repurchase 391,000 shares of its stock from shareholders. On October 31, 2000, managers announced a modified Dutch auction RTO. (The share price that day was $14). They set a price range of $15 to $17 per share, a premium above market of 7.1 percent to 21.4 percent. Shareholders had until December 1 to tender their shares. On December 11, 2000, CFFC managers announced they had purchased 391,096 shares at a price of $16 (a premium of 14.3 percent above market).

Let's look at the situation as CFFC managers may have viewed it. Many times managers will repurchase shares because they believe the stock is undervalued. An RTO is used by managers to distribute company value to shareholders. RTOs annually distribute over $4 billion to shareholders. Assume CFFC managers believe their stock will be worth $20 per share in the near future. They want to buy back some shares now but they don't know the valuations of shareholders. After stating their beliefs, managers construct Table 15.3 to summarize them. It shows how many shares will be tendered at different prices in three possible supply scenarios—strong, medium, and weak—and the generated value associated with each price-supply scenario. Profit is equal to the difference between a tender price and the expected future value of $20.

If managers choose a fixed price RTO, they must set price before knowing the supply schedule. They might then choose a price based on an expected value basis:

$$EB(\$15) = \$2,000,000(.40) + \$1,550,000(.30) + \$1,400,000(.30) = \$1,685,000;$$

$$EB(\$16) = \$1,660,000(.40) + \$1,600,000(.30) + \$1,260,000(.30) = \$1,522,000;$$

$$EB(\$17) = \$1,800,000(.40) + \$1,245,000(.30) + \$1,200,000(.30) = \$1,453,000.$$

TABLE 15.3

Shareholder Supply Schedule

Price	Strong	Profit	Medium	Profit	Weak	Profit
$15	400,000	$2,000,000	310,000	$1,550,000	280,000	$1,400,000
16	415,000	1,660,000	400,000	1,600,000	315,000	1,260,000
17	600,000	1,800,000	415,000	1,245,000	400,000	1,200,000
	.40		.30		.30	

Probability of shareholder's willingness to tender

ANALYZING MANAGERIAL DECISIONS

The Use of Sophisticated Pricing within an Auction Format

Priceline.com is a good example of how managers can use sophisticated pricing policies within an auction format. The company was launched in April 1998 after Priceline managers had helped develop software for a computer reservation system. The software gave airline managers the ability to make real-time adjustments to prices based on various factors, like unoccupied seats or competitor prices. Each airline only sees its own prices, but managers at Priceline are able to see prices across all member airlines.

Airline seats are perishable goods: once the plane departs, empty seats are worthless since they cannot be used again. And the marginal cost of flying a plane with one more passenger is almost zero, so any price is profitable for the airline. As Brian Ek of Priceline.com states, "The airlines fly with up to 700,000 empty seats a day. Naturally they would love to sell those seats if they could without affecting their retail fare structure." Priceline.com developed an auction mechanism to allow airlines to do just that. The company has sold over 5 million airline tickets since 1998.

Priceline.com uses a reverse auction mechanism. In reverse auctions, buyers name the price they are willing to pay for a good or service. The seller then decides whether to accept or reject this price. Priceline's auction operates as follows: A consumer specifies a departure date, the departing and destination airport, the price they are willing to pay for a ticket, and a credit card number. All sales are final. If Priceline finds a ticket at or below that price, the consumer is obligated to purchase it. After receiving a consumer's price, man-

agers at Priceline examine their database to determine if any airline is offering tickets at or below that price. If there are tickets, Priceline buys them. The profit to Priceline is the difference between what the consumer is willing to pay for the ticket and the price Priceline was charged.

Though Priceline claims they have increased the market power of consumers (since they are free to name their own price), many disagree with the claim. Basically, Priceline's reverse auction allows the firm to practice price discrimination. Like airlines, Priceline sells tickets on the same airplane at different prices depending on the price quoted by the consumer. Let's say I submit a price of $300 for a ticket from New York to Chicago. If my friend submits a price of $250, she would buy an identical product at a cheaper price (assuming airlines were willing to sell tickets for $250). Basically, Priceline's reverse auction gets consumers to name their reservation price, then Priceline charges them this price. So the reserve auction does not guarantee that consumers will receive a product at the lowest price, it simply guarantees them the chance to purchase a product at *their* reservation price.

Priceline's price-discriminating auction also improves on the traditional price discrimination schemes by making discounts less transparent to both consumers and rivals. Airlines do not have to post any special rates, which reduces the probability that rivals could engage in a disastrous price war. Also, the company is able to practice price discrimination selectively. For example, there is some evidence that Priceline will accept lower prices from first-time customers. When those consumers subsequently bid the same price for the same product, they find their bids are rejected.

Airlines that work with Priceline also receive demand information that helps them in their pricing decisions. The company compiles all bidding information (both successful and unsuccessful) and gives this information to airlines on a weekly basis. As Ek states, "They can see all of the demand, every consumer's price offer for every route, going all the way down to $1 . . . It's a great way for the airlines to privately move more inventory that was likely to go unsold through their retail sales channels."

If CFFC managers had used such an analysis, they might have set a tender price of $15 (and subsequently they would have fallen short of getting shareholders to tender 391,000 shares).

Now, how might they have increased firm value by structuring their RTO as a modified Dutch auction? If they use the auction, they will not select a tender price until after they know the supply schedule. So what is the expected value of the auction strategy? We use expected value because when CFFC managers announce their Dutch RTO on October 11, they will not know the supply schedule. So, if the willingness to tender is high, they will announce a price of $15; if it is medium, they will announce a price of $16; and if it is weak, a price of $15. Hence, the expected value of a modified Dutch auction RTO is:

$$EB(\text{auction}) = \$2,000,000(.40) + \$1,600,000(.30) + \$1,400,000(.30);$$
$$= \$1,700,000.$$

So managers are generally better off using a modified Dutch auction RTO. They get shareholders to reveal their valuations, and hence can buy back shares at a lower price than if they used a fixed price. This creates value for the remaining shareholders since some shares are retired at a lower cost.

Risk Aversion

As we've seen in Chapter 14, most individuals are risk averse. So what are the effects of risk aversion on bidding behavior? In second-price auctions, risk preferences do not influence bidding strategy. Bidders in these auctions should always bid up to their reservation price. However, risk preference does affect bidding behavior in first-price auctions.

Consider the choices facing a risk averse bidder in a first-price auction. The prevailing uncertainty in one's mind is: Will my bid win the auction? Since first-price auctions have no dominant strategies, managers must anticipate the bids of others, and hence only partially control this uncertainty. Their controlling mechanism is the bid price itself. Relative to any arbitrary benchmark, a higher bid increases the probability of winning. Since a risk averse bidder will pay to avoid loss, she simply raises her bid by the amount of this "bidding insurance." So, relative to risk-neutral bidders, risk averse ones bid higher. Their rush toward certainty is tempered, however, as higher bids also reduce expected surplus.

If bidders are risk averse, risk neutral managers can increase performance through the use of auction rules. If bidders are likely to be risk averse, then managers want to use a first-price auction. This allows the seller to capture profits generated by risk preference differences.

Now what if roles were reversed, bidders are risk neutral, and sellers are risk averse, how should this affect managerial actions? Here too, the seller prefers first-price auctions. Though we know that the expected revenues from the four auction formats are equal, there is more risk in second-price auctions. That is, though the means of the revenue distribution are equal, there is greater spread in possible revenues for second-price auctions. Because risk averse managers prefer to avoid risk, they should use first-price auctions.

Number of Bidders

We have seen that in all auction formats the expected bid is given by the reservation price of the second highest bidder. So managers should consider actions to increase these prices, as they similarly do in market settings. One possible variable that seems easily controlled is the number of bidders.

Let's consider how markets work. As the number of sellers increase (other factors held constant), the equilibrium price is pushed downward toward marginal cost (or the seller's reservation price). And, in perfectly competitive markets, the long-run equilibrium price is identical to marginal cost. In these markets there are many sellers, selling the same good or service to consumers. Auctions are the reflection of this—many buyers and one (or few) sellers. What works on the supply side must also work on the demand side. The entry of more bidders (buyers) into a market must push the demand curve rightward, and hence increases price. So the more bidders a manager can induce to enter the auction, the greater is the expected surplus.

So, are 1,000,001 bidders better than 1,000,000? No, that's not quite the case, though it may be true. For it turns out that auctions are efficient, under most conditions, so even a moderate number of bidders will result in seller revenue approaching that expected for maximum valuation (conditional on the probability function). You wouldn't want to pay much to attract the 1,000,000th bidder to your auction, but the first score or so is important. The following example assumes the reservation price of bidders is uniformly distributed, with the highest price being $100. A seller's expected revenue in English auctions is then given by:

$$B = ((N - 1)/(N + 1))(\text{reservation price of bidders}),$$

where N = the number of bidders. Figure 15.2 shows how a seller's expected revenue increases as the number of bidders increase.

Intuitively, the expected revenue of the seller increases because of the increased competition caused by additional bidders. In placing bids, bidders must consider the trade-off between the probability of winning the auction and the level of consumer surplus (bid price − reservation price) they will realize. A lower bid gives a bidder higher surplus but a decreased probability of winning, for one loses an auction if only one bidder bids higher. As more bidders join the auction the probability of someone bidding higher than you increases quickly. Hence, as more bidders join the auction, bids must approach the reservation price of bidders (and seller revenue increases). Note, too, that a seller's expected revenue approaches its maximal level with less than 30 bidders.

Winner's Curse

In some auctions, the value of the object or service being auctioned off is not known with certainty, though it has common value to all bidders. For example, the U.S. government auctions off the mineral rights to tracts of federally owned land. When the seller uses a sealed-bid first-price auction in these situations, bidders are exposed to what is known as the **winner's curse**. The bidder with the highest estimated value bids the highest and wins the auction, but

FIGURE 15.2

Expected Revenue versus Number of Bidders

As the number of bidders increases, the expected revenue of the seller increases.

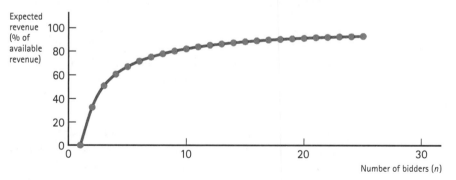

ANALYZING MANAGERIAL DECISIONS

The Winner's Curse in Bidding for Oil Rights

During their careers, many managers will find themselves in a competitive bidding situation. These might entail bidding for the services of a qualified job applicant, for production inputs, to acquire another company, or to obtain a contract for corporate or personal services. When the bidding is conducted as a sealed-bid auction and it involves an object of common value, managers must be aware of the winner's curse.

An example of how costly this curse can be is shown in the following table, which compiles the **actual bids** (in millions of dollars) of oil companies for the right to drill for oil on two tracts of government-owned land. Bids are listed in descending order of magnitude.

The table clearly shows the range of estimates regarding how much oil is present within these tracts of land. For tract 1, the winning bid is 87 percent higher than the second highest bid; for tract 2, this percentage increases to 181 percent. If we examine the ratio of the high bid to the low bid in each auction, we see for tract 1 the high bid is 10 times that of the low bid; for tract 2, this ratio is 109.

The natural tendency for managers is to in-

Bids to drill for oil on federal land (in millions of dollars)

Tract 1	Tract 2
32.5	43.5
17.7	15.5
11.1	11.6
7.1	8.5
5.6	8.1
4.1	5.6
3.3	4.7
	2.8
	2.6
	0.7
	0.7
	0.4

crease their bids when more bidders enter the auction. But, in these types of auctions, managers need to reduce their bids, not increase them. Obviously, the manager who submitted the winning bid for tract 2 didn't follow our recommendations. In both these auctions, the winning bidder did suffer the winner's curse. Neither of the firms realized a positive return from these tracts of land.

the amount he bids may be greater than the true value of the object. If this occurs, then the bidder wins the auction but pays a price that is higher than the object's true value. Let's see why this is true.

All bidders face the same decision problem. They must estimate the value of the object without knowing the estimates of others. Suppose each bidder makes an estimate, and on average, their estimates are approximately correct. Then the distribution of bids might resemble that shown in Figure 15.3. An unbiased estimate of the true value, if you knew the bids of others, would be the mean shown by the dotted line. Now given this distribution of values across

FIGURE
15.3

The Winner's Curse

If the value of the item being auctioned is uncertain, then bidders with extreme beliefs about the value can bid higher than the item's true value.

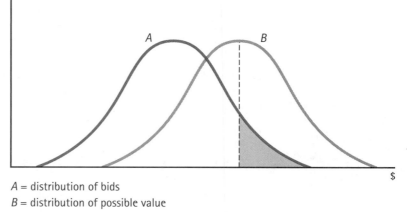

A = distribution of bids
B = distribution of possible value

bidders, the distribution of bids would lie to the right, say as distribution *A*. As you can see, those bidders with extreme estimates (in the right tail of *A*) will bid values that exceed the best estimate of the true value. The key is that they do not know their estimates are extreme (because they do not know the estimates of others). Hence, they are likely to win the auction but they pay a price that is greater than the object's true value.

The winner's curse is a robust phenomenon; it has been documented in many situations (see Box on facing page). While there are sophisticated algorithms for bidding behavior in these types of auctions, they are too complex to discuss in this text. However, managers should consider the following issues when contemplating their bids:

How much information do you have relative to others about the object's true value? The less information you have relative to others, the more you want to lower your bid.

How confident are you in your estimate of the object's true value? The less confident you are, the more you want to lower your bid.

How many others are bidding against you? The greater the number of bidders in the auction, the more you want to lower your bid.

Summary

1. There are four types of auction mechanisms—English, Dutch, and first- and second-price sealed-bid.
2. In common value auctions with symmetric, risk neutral bidders and independent signals, the auction mechanism chosen makes no difference. All mechanisms generate the same expected revenues.
3. There is no need to consider the bidding strategies of others in English and second-price auctions. In English auctions, managers should bid up to their reservation price. In second-price auctions, managers want to bid their reservation price.
4. Dutch and sealed-bid auctions have no dominant strategy. Optimal behavior in these auctions is conditional on beliefs about the strategies of others. In each auction, bidders must consider the reservation price of the second-highest bidder (assuming you are the highest bidder). Then bid this price.
5. Sellers want to set a reserve price according to the following rule:

   optimal reserve price = the value of the object being auctioned off, if it does not sell + managerial estimates of the highest reservation price divided by 2.

6. Auctions are often more efficient than posted pricing schemes because they can better discriminate among consumers with differing reservation prices. Most auction designs ensure that the highest reservation price consumers "win" the auction.
7. Auctions are useful if demand is unknown. They can be used to induce consumers to reveal their preferences before managers set price. By knowing demand before setting price, managers will increase revenues.
8. When bidding in sealed-bid, common value auctions, managers need to recognize the tendency to bid too high. This tendency results in the winner's curse, where the high bidder wins the auction but pays a price higher than the object's true value.

Problems

1. Consultant.com is an Internet startup. The company employs business professors as virtual consultants who supply answers to other companies' problems. Consultant.com wants to raise funds via a private equity issue. Unfortunately, because of fluctuations in the stock market, they are uncertain about demand for their offering. They hoped to issue the stock at ei-

ther $45 or $50. They categorized demand into four possible scenarios. The following table shows demand for each scenario-price combination along with their beliefs regarding the probability of each possible state. Consultant.com must pay 10 percent of the generated funds to the investment bank that helped them identify potential investors. The company wants to maximize funds raised.

Price/share	State 1	State 2	State 3	State 4
$45	1,750	1,975	2,220	2,445
$50	1,200	1,415	2,001	2,305
Probability	.35	.20	.30	.15

What is the expected value of the stock offering if consultant.com sets its price without knowing the future demand state? If consultant.com can determine the future demand state by using a modified Dutch auction, what is their expected profit? If someone approached consultant.com and told them she could tell them the future demand state, how much would that information be worth to them?

2. Your company is planning to auction off a manufacturing plant in Asia. You are asked to determine the auction design that will generate the highest revenues for the company. You believe that bidders will value the plant independently. Which design would you choose and why?

3. There are 100 bidders in an English auction. A random sample of 30 bidders shows the following reservation prices.

Number of bidders	Reservation price
1	$10
3	$20
6	$30
5	$40
8	$50
6	$60
7	$70
3	$80
1	$100

Assume the bidding distribution is normal.
a. What is the mean value of bids across the 100 bidders?
b. What is the probability of a bid being less than $80?

4. Your company is bidding for a service contract in a first-price sealed-bid auction. You value the contract at $12 million. You believe the distribution of bids will be uniform, with a high value of $16 million and a low value of $3 million. What is your optimal bidding strategy with:
   a. 5 bidders?
   b. 10 bidders?
   c. 20 bidders?

5. The Philadelphia Eagles of the NFL are building a new stadium. One revenue source for the new stadium is a personal seat license (PSL). A personal seat license is a one-time up-front payment that is charged to season ticketholders before the stadium is built. It gives the buyer the right to purchase tickets for a particular seat.

   The Eagles are uncertain about demand for seats in the new stadium. They have selected three price points for PSLs ($6,000, $7,000, and $8,000). Management also has estimated that demand for PSLs could be low, medium, or high. Their beliefs are reflected in the table below:

Price	Low demand Probability = 0.4	Medium demand Probability = .35	High demand Probability = 0.25
$6,000	24,500 PSLs sold	28,000 PSLs sold	40,000 PSLs sold
$7,000	21,500 PSLs sold	24,000 PSLs sold	32,000 PSLs sold
$8,000	17,500 PSLs sold	22,000 PSLs sold	25,000 PSLs sold

   Some of the stadium funding is provided by the city of Philadelphia. Because Eagle fans view PSLs as an attempt to take away consumer surplus, they resent them and have put pressure on the city government to limit their use. Therefore, the city has set a target of 25,000 seats assigned to PSLs. If the Eagles sell less than 25,000 PSLs, the city will grant them a tax benefit of $10/seat for each seat under 25,000. If the Eagles sell 25,000 or more PSLs, then no tax break is given. A consulting group has told the Eagles they are better off using a modified Dutch auction to sell their PSLs. The group has estimated the cost of running the auction as an additional $5.1 million. Eagles management has come to you for help. They want to know whether they should use an auction and what would be the expected benefits. What would you tell them?

6. Your company is bidding for a broadband spectrum license. You've been asked to submit an optimal bidding strategy. You expect that bidders will have independent private values for the licenses, since each bidder presently has a different structure in place. You believe the valuations for these licenses will be between $200 million and $700 million. Your own valua-

tion is $650 million. There is some uncertainty about the auction design that will be used, so you must suggest an optimal bidding strategy for the following auction designs:

a. second-price sealed-bid auction;
b. English auction; and
c. Dutch auction.

Moral Hazard
and Principal-
Agent Problems

Principal-Agent Problems

For most of this book we have looked at decision making in a firm as though the firm were a single person who wished to maximize personal wealth. For example, we have assumed that the firm makes a decision to maximize profit because profit is income to the firm's owner. But of course *firms* do not make decisions; *people* make decisions. In practice, the firm's operating decisions are made by paid managers, with some supervision by the board of directors. Are the managers' decisions always best for the shareholders, or do the managers often make decisions for their own benefit? This is the *principal-agent*, or *moral hazard*, problem: a conflict of interest that arises when one person, the agent, makes decisions on behalf of another, the principal. For example, in publicly held firms, managers (agents) make decisions that affect the wealth of shareholders (principals).

When the interests of the principal and agent are identical, we do not worry about this problem. For example, the captain and sailors on a ship in a storm need each other to save the ship. Because the sailors know the captain wishes to save his own life, the sailors may be confident he will make decisions that are also in the best interests of the sailors. Problems arise when the interests are not identical. For example, will a general, who is not on the battlefield, devise strategies that best serve the soldiers under his command? Generals may wish to win battles; soldiers wish to stay alive. Can we be sure that elected politicians really serve their constituents and are not nudged away from that goal by interest groups? Will a plaintiff's lawyer be tempted to advise her client to go to trial (which enhances the visibility of the lawyer) rather than to accept a good settlement offer? Will a doctor prescribe treatment that is best for his patient, or might the doctor use the patient to further a research agenda or prescribe treatment that leads to the highest payment for the doctor?

In this chapter, we will give examples of principal-agent problems, and show how such incentive conflicts can make everybody worse off. We will discuss how the problems can be anticipated and minimized. Many principal-agent problems arise under the umbrella of the firm. As mentioned, the most visible principal-agent problem we encounter here is between the firm's owners and its managers. In this chapter we will see how this problem is resolved through the use of bonuses, equity participation, and stock options. We will also show how incentive conflicts can arise between shareholders and creditors, which, if not anticipated and controlled, can prevent a firm from adopting investment projects despite their positive net present values. Finally, we will discuss how product liability law has evolved as a response to principal-agent problems between firms and their customers. Particularly, these laws provide incentives for firms to produce safe products. However, we will also show that, in the information age, product liability laws may not be necessary and the price mechanism may provide similar protections for consumers.

Owner–Manager Conflicts

One of the most important principal-agent problems encountered in business is that between the owners of a firm and its managers. The owners typically are shareholders who have purchased the stock as an investment, or who are simply investors who have bought shares in a mutual fund, or pensioners whose assets are invested in a large number of companies. Most investors probably are interested in maximizing the value of their investment, which means either maximizing the income that their assets yield or maximizing the value of those assets.

Shareholders are concerned about the value of their shares, but what are managers concerned with? Is it reasonable to assume that they are interested in the performance of the firm, because their reputations will be enhanced by high profits and a rising stock price. So, because both managers and owners prefer the same outcome, they share common interests. If we stopped the story here, the principal-agent problem would disappear. We would conclude that incentives were aligned and that managers would act in the best interests of shareholders. What is good for the one is good for the other. The problem is that managers may have other objectives in mind. Let us make a plausible, though not necessarily complete, list of managers' objectives.

MINIMIZING EFFORT Increasing profit often takes hard work. Many decisions involve a trade-off. How much harder is a manager prepared to work to make an extra dollar of profit for the owner? Given a choice between two activities—one involving a little more effort and the other a lot more effort—which would be chosen? The manager supplies the effort, while the owner reaps the profit. These examples suggest that many marginal decisions may tilt in favor of less effort rather than higher profit.

MAXIMIZING JOB SECURITY Many decisions involve risk, but sometimes risk is accompanied by high potential reward. Managers may be disinclined to make risky choices that could jeopardize their employment. Suppose that an investment decision carries a large probability of very high returns, and a small chance of failure that would cause the firm itself to fail. Shareholders, being diversified, might be inclined to accept this risk. Managers, however, might be more concerned with the downside (they do not share the upside profit and could lose their jobs given the downside risk), so they might be tempted to avoid such risky choices.

AVOIDING FAILURE Managers can be rewarded for good performance and penalized for bad results. If a risky project is undertaken, the manager will be rewarded if results (due somewhat to chance) are favorable and penalized if results are unfavorable. Often managers believe the bad results are much more likely to be noticed than good results. If so, they will be disinclined to take risks.

ENHANCING REPUTATION AND EMPLOYMENT OPPORTUNITIES Although we argue that sometimes reputation is promoted by doing things that benefit shareholders, this is not always so. For example, a CEO with ambitions to hold public office might be more concerned about showing himself to be a "good citizen" than maximizing the profits of the firm. Thus, prices charged might be lowered below their profit-maximizing level. Alternatively, a manager might conduct contract negotiations with another firm partly with a view to establishing a personal relationship that could be a springboard to a new job.

CONSUMING PERQUISITES Examples can include luxury travel, expensive artworks in the office, corporate donations to favorite charities, and employing favored people.

PAY Last and not least, the manager is presumably working for pay and, as we shall see, both the level and structure of the compensation package become important parts of the principal-agent story.

FIGURE 16.1

The Principal–Agent Problem

The principal employs an agent to undertake a task (product output for the principal). The agent must expend effort to produce output; the more effort, the more output. Because the principal cannot observe (and therefore cannot reward) effort, the agent will tend to "shirk," or reduce effort, which will, in turn, reduce output for the principal.

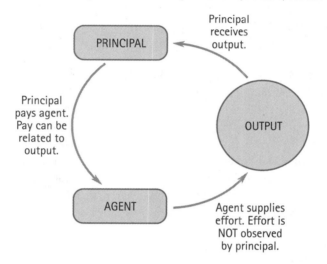

A Picture of the Principal-Agent Problem

Figure 16.1 shows a diagram of the principal-agent problem. The principal employs an agent who will perform a task that results in a benefit to the principal. The benefit is called *output*. The principal must pay the agent. This compensation can be a fixed sum or can depend on the output. The level of output will depend on the quantity and quality of the effort provided by the agent. If this effort were observable by the principal, the principal could simply require a certain level of effort, verify that this level of effort was provided, and compensate the agent accordingly. But effort is not always observable or measurable. The principal-agent problem is one in which effort cannot be monitored and measured by the principal and, therefore, cannot be directly rewarded. The solutions to this problem, as we will see, will require some alignment of interests of the two parties. In this way, even if the principal cannot see what the agent is doing, the principal still can be assured that what is good for the agent is also good for the principal.

Examples of Principal-Agent Problems

Principal-agent problems arise from conflicting incentives; they involve a "separation of ownership and control." One party, the agent, has the control and makes the decisions. The other party, the principal, bears the consequences of those decisions (i.e., has a stake in, or "owns," the outcome).

Principal-agent problems are sometimes referred to as *moral hazard*, a term usually associated with insurance. Suppose you have no insurance and you visit your doctor for a damaged wrist. Your doctor says it may be sprained or broken and she can do an x-ray which will cost $200 and/or an MRI, which will cost $1,500. She says the x-ray will almost certainly be sufficient to confirm a diagnosis and determine treatment, but there is a very small chance that the MRI will reveal something else that may cause a variation in treatment. Which will you choose? When paying ourselves, most would choose the x-ray, but what if you were insured? Many of us would also get the MRI because it is the insurance company, not us, that foots the bill. This tendency for people to spend more on medical treatment when insured is well documented and is another example of the separation of ownership and control. The agent, the patient, makes the decision, and the principal, the insurance company, pays the bill. Insurance also encounters prospective (ex ante) moral hazard. People who are insured may be tempted to take fewer precautions in protecting their homes (installation of burglar alarms, better locks, smoke alarms, and window shutters). Spending money on expensive safety devices saves the insurance company's money, rather than yours.

Returning to a more familiar theme in this book, we have spent a lot of time assuming that firms maximize profit. This seems reasonable because the firm's owners (shareholders) are clearly interested in the value of their shares, and this value rests on the long-run profitability of the firm. We would expect the shareholders to appoint a board of directors and management team that pursued the profit objective. However, corporate governance is more complex. A subject of considerable research attention is whether boards really do control managers or vice versa. What is clear is that, although managers are accountable in the long run to owners, they still have considerable discretion in making decisions. Consider some examples.

A life insurance company is thinking about selling its new products and has two choices about distribution channels. One alternative is to use an existing distribution channel: a network of independents agents who are paid commissions. This approach is safe but has a low expected profit. The other is to establish an electronic distribution system. This is new and untried but, if it succeeds, profits could be very high. If the expected profit is high enough for the e-business channel, one could argue that this system is best for the shareholders. Shareholders certainly benefit from the higher expected profit. Moreover, they probably are not too concerned about risk, because most shareholders hold a number of securities and can diversify the risk. However, managers might worry more about risk because, if the e-project is chosen and the firm has bad luck, the managers might lose their jobs. Thus, managers might be tempted to use the existing distribution network despite the fact that electronic distribution could be better for shareholders.

Many firms make charitable contributions, and it can be argued that some level of charity benefits the shareholders. This visibility might stimulate demand for the firm's products and cast the firm in a favorable light with legislators and regulators. Charity also might bring some benefit in courts. For example, a car manufacturer that donates considerable sums to university research on safety might find that this charitable giving is an important signal of its commitment to safety, which helps in the defense of lawsuits. Now consider a manager who has a personal agenda: he is a strong supporter of environmental causes. This manager not only increases the level of charitable giving above what is optimal for the shareholders, but he also redirects it to his favored environmental charity. This is a particularly stubborn problem because the firm might receive adverse publicity if it tried to discipline the manager and cut down on its charitable giving.

Finally, a firm that is inefficiently managed can become the target of a hostile takeover. Because the resources of the firm are not being managed effectively, the firm is generating lower profits than it otherwise would earn. If investors are aware of the inefficient management, this will lower the share price. This creates an opportunity for another firm to acquire the target firm and replace the management with one that is more competent or better motivated. If the new management is indeed better, or is perceived to be so by investors, the stock price will rise. Thus, shareholders benefit from the takeover if there is a reasonable expectation that management quality will increase. The problem is that shareholders need advice on whether to sell their shares to the potential acquirer. The board normally will provide this advice. Here the problems start. If the board had been effective, it previously would have addressed the management issue. The problem might be that the board is too much influenced by the management. If so, the shareholders are hardly likely to get good advice from managers and board members who will lose their positions if the takeover succeeds. More likely, shareholders will be advised to resist the takeover.

A Simple Model of the Principal–Agent Problem with No Risk

The Concept of "Effort"

We can summarize the idea of incentive conflict with the concept of *effort*. To achieve a target level of profit requires that managers incur some personal cost, which we will call effort. This effort might simply be the manager's time required to attain that level of output, and the cost to the manager is the value of that time. But time is not the only dimension. Certain tasks require less-pleasant work than others. Spending time with clients on the golf course may be valued differently by a manager than spending time bargaining with the union over wages. Managers may sacrifice other things to attain a profit goal. For example, to increase expected profits, a manager may cut down on perquisites and employ the best engineer, rather than giving the job to his favorite niece. In economist terms, the cost to the manager may be a direct cost or an opportunity cost. The personal cost to the manager of making a decision will reflect the quantity and quality of effort required. Given a choice between activities, managers can be expected to exert some bias toward those tasks that require lower effort.

In the next few sections, we will show how to resolve the principal-agent problem. To do so, we will be solving profit-maximizing equations similar to those in earlier chapters. We will show that profit is simply revenue minus costs, and we will try to maximize profit. However, in earlier chapters we were often trying to choose a quantity (and a price) for a given product that would maximize the profit, or perhaps some mix of inputs that would maximize profit. In the principal-agent problem, we will be choosing the *design of the manager's compensation* to maximize profits. In doing this, we must recognize that how we compensate the manager will, in turn, affect the manager's choice of effort.

We can now represent the principal-agent problem a little more precisely. The profit to the firm, Π, depends on the manager's effort, e. So we will write this function as $\Pi(e)$ to remind us of the impact of effort. We will use this device quite a lot in the next few pages. We write a variable $y(x)$, which simply says that y depends on, or is a function of, x. For the moment, we will pretend that the profit is not risky. Once the manager chooses effort, the profit can be forecast with certainty. However, profit is, of course, total revenue minus total costs, and the manager's effort affects profit by changing the total revenue. Thus, we will write revenue as $R(e)$, to show revenue as depending on effort. Finally, we will divide total cost between the manager's salary, S, and all other costs, C. So, profits can now be written as

$$\text{Profit} = \{\text{revenue}\} \text{ minus } \{\text{costs}\}$$
$$= \{\text{revenue}\} - \{\text{managerial compensation} + \text{other costs}\}$$
$$\Pi = \{R(e)\} - \{S + C\}$$

More effort on the part of the manager will result in higher revenue, so the derivative dR/de will be positive. However, for the moment we will assume that S is a flat salary and cannot change. We also will assume for simplification that other costs are not affected by the manager's effort. We could assume that managers could reduce costs if they tried harder. But this would complicate our analysis, and all the main ideas we develop in this chapter would be substantially the same anyway. Therefore, we will take the easiest route to our destination, which is to solve the principal-agent problem.

We can now state the profit before deducting the manager's salary as $R(e) - C$, and profit after deduction of salary, $\Pi(e) = R(e) - S - C$, will have the upward slope shown in Figure 16.2. If the owners were to choose the level of effort they wished the manager to supply, they would choose the highest feasible level. However, they cannot simply choose the level of effort, e, to maximize profit. It is the manager, not the owners, who must choose e. The manager has his (or her) own objectives and will choose a level of effort to maximize these personal objectives.

The objective of the manager is to maximize the net benefit of employment. The manager, first of all, obtains income from employment and will want this income to be high. To gain this income, the manager must supply effort. The cost to the manager of supplying effort is shown as the function $u(e)$. This can now be thought of as the *disutility of effort*. In Chapter 4, we talked of a basket of goods giving *utility* to the owner. In that context, the consumer enjoyed the goods, and utility was a measure of the satisfaction derived from those goods. Here, effort is not desirable; it is not a *good* to the manager but a *bad*. Therefore, the disutility of effort is a measure of the dissatisfaction to the manager from supplying effort. Naturally, more effort will involve more cost, or

FIGURE
16.2

The Principal–Agent Problem with a Flat Salary

Because the net benefit to the agent is the salary minus the disutility of effort, this benefit will decline as effort increases. Accordingly, the agent reduces effort, which reduces revenue.

The Principal–Agent Problem with Flat Pay

The owner pays the manager a flat pay. The manager chooses to minimize effort; therefore, revenue and profits fall.

Principal chooses pay to maximize

Agent chooses effort to maximize

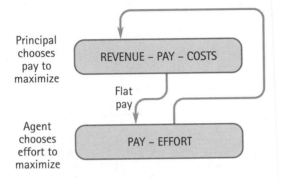

disutility, to the manager, so $u(e)$ slopes upward. The net benefit to the manager of working at a given level of effort is now shown as

$$B(e) = S - u(e).$$

Because the salary is constant and disutility increases with effort, the net benefit, $B(e)$, must slope downward, as in Figure 16.2. Thus the manager, who bears all of the cost of effort but gets none of the reward, is better off with as little effort as possible—in this case, zero effort. In contrast, the shareholders, who get all of the benefit of the manager's effort but pay none of the cost, want maximum effort from the manager.

The principal-agent problem with flat pay is summarized in Figure 16.3. At the top of the diagram, the principal wants to maximize profit but cannot control the manager's effort. The owner pays a flat salary. At the bottom of the picture, the manager wants to maximize the net benefit of employment, but, because the pay is flat, maximizing this benefit can be achieved only by reducing effort. This reduction in effort reduces revenue and thereby reduces profit.

Resolving the Incentive Conflict If Effort Is Observable

Can we improve this sad state of affairs? If owners were able to observe the effort provided by managers, the owners could simply reward managers directly in relation to the effort. To see where we are going, look at Figure 16.4. This is similar to Figure 16.3, except for the inclusion of incentive pay. The pay by

Motivating Managers When Effort Is Observable

The owner pays incentive compensation based directly on effort. Because the agent's pay increases with effort, the agent increases his effort. This in turn increases the firm's revenue. If the increase in revenue exceeds the increase in pay, profit increases.

Principal chooses pay to maximize

REVENUE – PAY – COSTS

Incentive pay

Agent chooses effort to maximize

PAY – EFFORT

the owners is scaled to the manager's effort. Now the manager's choice of effort is more complex. Although effort is unattractive in itself, it has the compensating advantage of increasing the manager's pay, so the manager is now persuaded to increase effort, which, in turn, increases revenue and profit.

To see how this works in more detail, let the owners structure the compensation in two parts. The first part, K, is a fixed amount, $U(e)$ is an additional amount that varies with managerial effort. So, $U(e)$ represents the reward paid by the firm for managerial effort, while the lower case, $u(e)$, represents the money value of the disutility of effort to the manager. When $U(e) = u(e)$, the manager will be fully compensated for effort, as we will see shortly. Because compensation now is a function of effort, we will write it as $S(e)$:

$$S(e) = K + U(e)$$

This is shown in Figure 16.5. The profit now is

$$\Pi(e) = R(e) - S(e) - C$$
$$= R(e) - (K + U(e)) - C,$$

which is shown in Figure 16.5. We can solve the desired level of profit (and thus of effort) for the shareholders by maximizing the profit function. Note that only $R(e)$ and $U(e)$ depend on effort, so the maximum is obtained by

$$\frac{d\Pi(e)}{de} = \frac{dR(e)}{de} - \frac{dU(e)}{de} = 0,$$

FIGURE 16.5

The Principal-Agent Problem with Pay as a Function of Effort

The manager is paid incentive compensation that increases with effort. Because this off-sets the disutility of effort for the manager, the manager will now expend more effort, which will increase revenue and profit.

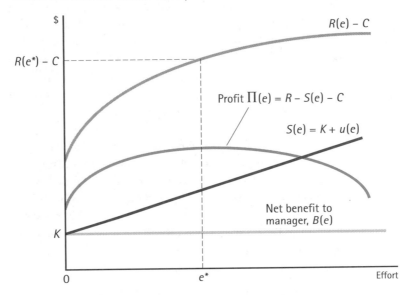

which simply says that the marginal benefit from effort [in terms of increased revenue $R(e)$] must equal the marginal cost of compensating managers for effort. Notice that profit does achieve a clear maximum in Figure 16.5 at effort level e^*. This is because profit reflects both the benefits to the shareholders and the costs to the manager for which the owners now have to pay him. The shareholders would wish to maximize profit at effort level e^*.

Now what does the manager wish to do? The manager receives a net benefit, $B(e)$, equal to compensation minus the cost of effort:

$$B(e) = S(e) - u(e)$$
$$= K + U(e) - u(e)$$

If that part of compensation designed to compensate the manager for effort, $U(e)$, is exactly equal to the disutility of effort, $u(e)$, then

$$B(e) = K.$$

The manager now is fully compensated for the effort supplied and is quite happy to supply any effort level. How can we get the manager to choose exactly e^*, which will maximize profit for the shareholders? The simple answer is for the shareholders to tell the manager to produce e^* in effort. This is fine in our little example because we made the assumption that the shareholders could observe the manager's effort. In practice, this assumption often is implausible.

In theory, the fact that managers and owners have inherently different interests would not be a problem if all managerial actions could be observed and evaluated without cost. If that were the case, the manager could be given very specific directions on what actions to take. For example, the owners allow a manager to consume *these* perquisites because they bring benefit to the owners, but she cannot consume *those* perks because they benefit the manager with no redeeming impact on profit. The manager is allowed to choose *this* risky investment project but not *that* one. She can lobby in Washington for *this* view, but not for *that* one, and so on. However, this ignores the main issue. Managers are appointed precisely because they, not shareholders, have the time and skill to make decisions. Shareholders do not have the time to micromanage every firm in which they own some shares, nor do they have expertise to evaluate each decision. Nor can a board of directors micromanage every decision. Managers must be invested with considerable discretion. In the long run, the impact of their stewardship of a firm will become visible. But the long run can be very long, and this permits managers considerable flexibility in balancing their own ambitions against those of the firm's owners. This discretion means that owners will not observe all the actions of the manager. In effect, the owners cannot always observe the manager's effort.

Resolving the Incentive Conflict If Effort Is Not Observable: Incentive Compatibility

The real nature of the principal-agent problem is that, when effort is not observable by the principal, effort cannot be rewarded or penalized directly. Thus, the agent has a degree of freedom to pursue his or her own objectives, instead of acting in the best interest of the principal.

There may be a way around this problem if the firm's revenue, $R(e)$, is riskless and is determined solely by the effort of the manager. The shareholders can ask the question *What level of effort is necessary to produce this level of revenue?* In this way shareholders deduce the level of effort by observing revenue. If $R(e)$ slopes upward, as we show in Figures 16.2 and 16.5, shareholders can read backward on the graph from a given R on the vertical axis to an implied level of e on the horizontal axis. For example, if shareholders observe output level, $R(e^*) - C$, then the effort level necessary to achieve this output must have been e^*.

Because shareholders can infer the level of effort, in this cosy little world, observing R is as good as observing e. We can now calculate what e must have been, so we can make the same compensation payment $S(e) = K + U(e)$ as before. However, there is one snag. This will ensure that the manager gets a *retrospective* payment that fully compensates him for effort *he has already provided.* Anticipating this reward for effort, the manager will be induced to work harder. But how can we be sure that he will choose in advance exactly the level of effort, e^*, that the shareholders desire?

We now need a simple but very important change to the manager's compensation; we need to give him a share, α, of profits, $\Pi(e)$. The new compensation is now $S(e) = U(e) + \alpha\Pi(e)$. We have replaced the fixed amount K with the profit-sharing bonus.[1] Naturally, the manager will have to wait until the end of the period before this element of pay will be finally settled. Therefore, we will decide on the level of bonus so that the overall package is competitive and will attract and retain skilled managers. We must be a little careful how we do our accounting here. First, let us divide the manager's compensation into two parts.

$$S(e) = (\text{salary}) + (\text{bonus})$$
$$= [U(e)] + [\alpha\Pi(e)]$$

Moreover, the bonus is a share of profit after the salary is paid. So the profit is now

$$\Pi(e) = R(e) - U(e) - C$$

This makes the bonus a real equity share in the firm.

The net benefit to the manager is now:

$$B(e) = S(e) - u(e)$$
$$= U(e) + \alpha\Pi(e) - u(e)$$
$$= \alpha\Pi(e)$$

The last step was taken by setting the monetary compensation for effort, $U(e)$, at a level sufficient to offset the disutility of effort, $u(e)$. We have a clear alignment of the interests of the managers, who get a net benefit of $\alpha\Pi(e)$, and the owners, who get the remainder $(1 - \alpha)(\Pi(e))$. Now, both are interested in maximizing the net profit, $\Pi(e)$.

Consider what level of effort the owners would want and what level the manager will choose. The owners get the portion of profit, $(1 - \alpha)\Pi(e)$, and the manager gets $\alpha\Pi(e)$, so whatever the level of α, both will be most happy if $\Pi(e)$ is maximized. We can think of the problem in two stages:

---

[1]Notice that we have set part of the compensation, $U(e)$, in relation to effort. Although effort is not directly observed, the principal can infer effort from the actual level of profit.

Stage 1. The manager chooses a level of effort to maximize $\Pi(e)$. This will be achieved where the marginal benefit of effort equals the marginal disutility of cost.

Stage 2. The firm's owners choose a level of α such that the compensation package is competitive.

We have now introduced an important concept: *incentive compatibility*. Because the agent and the owner share in the profits of the firm, their incentives are aligned and are compatible. We will refer to contracts that have this alignment of interests as *incentive-compatible contracts*.

Illustration of Optimal Compensation When Output Is Not Risky and Effort Is Not Observable

The weekly revenue, $R(e)$, of a retail store called Sporting Goods depends on the manager's effort, e; the more effort she provides, the higher the revenue. The effort is the number of hours worked. However, because many of the working hours are not in the store, the owner does not know directly how many hours the manager actually works. Assume that even if the manager supplies no effort, revenues would equal 3,500. Effort by the manager causes revenue to increase by $100e^{0.5}$. This revenue can be written as

$$R(e) = 3,500 + 100e^{0.5}.$$

But the manager incurs a disutility from supplying effort of:

$$u(e) = 853.55 + (7.07)e.$$

In addition to paying the manager's salary, the store must pay production costs of 1,000. In order to be persuaded to work for the store, the manager must receive a net benefit, $B(e)$, of 1,000. If she receives less, she will leave and take another job.

How much effort, e, will the manager supply?
How much weekly profit, $\Pi(e)$, will be made?
How much of this profit will be paid to the manager?

First, note that the owners of Sporting Goods can infer the level of effort provided by the manager from the week's revenue. This can be done by solving the revenue equation backward.

$$R(e) = 3,500 + 100e^{0.5}$$

$$\frac{R(e) - 3,500}{100} = e^{0.5}$$

$$e = \left(\frac{R(e) - 3,500}{100} \right)^2.$$

The owner can pay the manager a compensation package that includes

- a component $U(e)$ to compensate indirectly for effort and
- a bonus $\Pi(e)$ related directly to profit.

The profit is now

$$\Pi(e) = R(e) - U(e) - C.$$

If the compensation component $U(e)$ is enough to compensate the manager for disutility of effort, $U(e) = u(e)$, she will choose to maximize her bonus, which is the same as maximizing profit.

$$\frac{d\Pi(e)}{de} = \frac{dR(e)}{de} - \frac{dU(e)}{de}.$$

The solution to this type of problem is now familiar. The manager simply equates the marginal benefit and marginal cost:

$$\frac{dR(e)}{de} = 0.5(100)e^{-0.5} : \frac{dU(e)}{de} = 7.07.$$

Setting marginal benefit equal to marginal cost yields

$$0.5(100)(e)^{-0.5} = 7.07$$

so

$$e^{0.5} = 50/7.07$$

and

$$e = 50^2/7.07^2$$
$$= 2{,}500/50$$
$$= 50.$$

The manager works 50 hours per week. We can plug this effort level into the profit equation to give weekly profit:

$$\begin{aligned}
\Pi(e) &= R(e) - U(e) - C \\
&= (3{,}500 + 100e^{0.5}) - (853.55 + (7.07)e) - 1000 \\
&= (3{,}500 + 100(50)^{0.5}) - (853.55 + (7.07)(50)) - 1000 \\
&= (3{,}500 + 707) - (853.55 + 353.55) - 1000 \\
&= 2{,}000.
\end{aligned}$$

If the manager is to receive a net benefit, $B(e)$, of 1,000, clearly she must receive 50 percent of the profit, so $\alpha = 0.5$.

The Principal–Agent Problem: Output Is Risky and Effort Is Not Observable

Many of the most interesting principal-agent problems involve risk, and solutions are often compromises. These compromises are often summarized in the expression "there is a trade-off between risk sharing and efficiency." The main problems we have to deal with are how to account for risk and how to account for the fact that effort is not observable by the principal. The second of these problems is the crux of the principal-agent issue and is aggravated by the presence of risk. Without any risk, we could infer the level of effort from the firm's profit. However, when profit also is risky, we can never be sure whether high profits are due to high effort or simply good luck (a strong economy) and whether low profits are due to low effort or to bad luck. Poor management can occasionally result in high profits due to lady luck. Similarly, determined effort can sometimes come unstuck due to the vagaries of the market.

Risk Sharing

Executive compensation is usually designed around two competing ideas: risk sharing and efficiency. The efficiency idea has been dealt with previously. The manager will be inclined to attend to his or her own interests, so it becomes desirable for the firm's owners to align incentives with profit sharing bonuses, equity participation, stock options, and similar instruments. However, the firm's profits and its equity value are uncertain. Moreover, this volatility is partly outside the control of the managers and the owners. Profits and share prices are affected by macroeconomic factors such as changes in interest rates, changes in employment, inflation, changes in foreign exchange rates, and movements in stock market indices. Thus, bonus plans impose some risk on managers.

A competing view of how to design executive compensation is based on who can tolerate risk at least cost, or who is less risk averse. On this view, there is some value to be divided among the stakeholders, and this value is inherently risky. This value can be expressed as the periodic profits or as the value of the equity. As residual claimants, the shareholders normally will get the risky profit or equity, but first they must pay the managers. Should the shareholder take out a fixed sum (a flat salary) and pay this to the managers, or should they simply give the managers a share in the risky profit or equity? For the shareholders, the riskiness of profit may not be too problematic. Most shares are owned by individual investors or institutions who are quite diversified. Many individual investors hold several assets in their portfolios and are concerned, not with the riskiness of each stock, but with the risk in their whole portfolio. Unless the stocks are highly correlated, the risk in the portfolio can be quite modest. Thus, investors, being able to diversify, can tolerate the risk in an individual stock quite well. If, for example, the risk in one stock in her portfolio increased, the investor could offset this by spreading her capital over a few more stocks. Institutional investors are often much better diversified than individual investors and can very easily tolerate the risk for each individual stock.

In contrast, managers are usually much less well diversified. For the typical manager, the compensation received from his employer, and/or the equity stake he has in his employer, is a large proportion of his total wealth. Fluctuation in the value of his bonuses or stock options can have a very big impact on his net worth. Thus, we would expect managers to be quite averse to risk in their compensation plan. This does not mean that they will not accept a risky compensation plan. Rather, it means that they will need to be compensated for the risk; they will need a risk premium.

Comparing managers and shareholders, it seems that the riskiness of firms' profit and equity values can be absorbed at lower cost by the shareholders than by the managers. On this view, it appears that the optimal executive-compensation plan would be to place all risk on the shareholders—that is, to pay the managers a flat salary.

Two Executive-Compensation Schemes Based Solely on Risk Sharing

To illustrate this idea, the risky equity value of the firm (note that these values are before deduction of any compensation to the manager) is shown as

EQUITY = $10,000,000 (probability 0.5) or $20,000,000 (probability 0.5).

The manager is risk averse. We will represent the manager's attitude to risk by a utility function as shown in Chapter 15. To show risk aversion, we need to show a utility function such as that in Figure 15.4a, in which utility increases at a decreasing rate as wealth increases. This type of concave utility function can be represented by a square root function as follows:

$$\text{MANAGER'S UTILITY} = \sqrt{\text{WEALTH}} = (\text{WEALTH})^{0.5}$$

The manager's only wealth is derived from employment. To be competitive, the firm must offer the manager a compensation package that has an expected utility of 1,000; otherwise, the manager will leave and find other employment. In contrast to the manager, the shareholders are risk neutral and are interested only in the expected value of the equity.

FLAT SALARY OF $1,000,000 The manager has an expected utility that is sufficient to hold him in the job ($\sqrt{1,000,000} = 1,000$). The shareholders have expected equity stake, after paying the manager, of

0.5($10,000,000 − $1,000,000) + 0.5($20,000,000 − $1,000,000) = $14,000,000

BONUS OF A PROPORTION "x" OF EQUITY What proportion, x, of equity would be necessary to offer the manager an expected utility of 1,000? We can solve this by setting the expected utility from such a bonus equal to 1,000 (the manager will receive either x times 10 million or x times 20 million):

$$0.5(10,000,000x)^{0.5} + 0.5(20,000,000x)^{0.5} = 1,000$$

$$x^{0.5}[(10,000,000)^{0.5} + (20,000,000)^{0.5}] = 2,000$$

$$x^{0.5} = \frac{2,000}{7634.4}$$

$$x = 0.06863.$$

Notice that the expected dollar value of compensation is now 0.06863 times the expected value of equity.

expected value of compensation $= 0.06863(\$15,000,000) = \$1,029,450.$

This risky compensation offers the manager the same expected utility as a flat salary of $1 million, with the manager being paid a risk premium of $29,450 to compensate him for bearing the risk.

The expected value of equity remaining for the shareholders is

expected equity to shareholders $= \$15,000,000 - \$1,029,450 = \$13,970,550.$

Comparing the two compensation plans, both offer the manager an expected utility of 1,000, so the manager will be indifferent. However, the flat salary offers shareholders an expected residual equity of $14,000,000, whereas the bonus plan leaves them with an expected equity value of only $13,970,550. Therefore, looking only at risk sharing, the flat salary is clearly preferred.

Trading Off Risk Sharing and Efficiency

We now have two competing ideas about principal-agent problems. One says that we should align the interests of the principal and the agent—that is, make the contract incentive compatible. The other says we should assign risk to the party that can bear it most easily. How do we reconcile these ideas? First, we need to account for the fact that the revenue of the firm is risky. We will do this by dividing revenue into two parts. The first part, $R_1(e)$, depends on the effort of the manager; the higher the manager's effort, the higher is this component of revenue. The second part is beyond the control of the manager and depends on factors such as interest rates, economic movements, and so forth, and we will call this $\tilde{R}_2$. The tilde over the R shows that this component of revenue is risky. Thus:

$$R(e) = \qquad R_1(e) \qquad + \qquad \tilde{R}_2$$

under manager's   outside manager's

control   control

The compensation paid to the manager needs some modification. Because the principal cannot observe effort, nor can it be inferred from profit, then compensation cannot depend directly on effort. Thus, we will restate compensation(s) as combining a fixed element, E, which is independent of effort, and a bonus, $\alpha\Pi(e)$, which depends on profit.

$$S = E + \alpha\Pi(e)$$

and correspondingly, profit is (note that we only deduct the direct compensation from profit—the remaining compensation, the bonus, is a share of profit):

$$\Pi(e) = R(e) - E - C$$
$$= R_1(e) + \tilde{R}_2 - E - C.$$

The net benefit of employment for the manager also needs some changes because the manager will be exposed to risk if he or she receives a bonus. The net benefit now comprises two parts. The first shows the expected utility of the manager from wealth. We will show wealth as comprising only the manager's employment compensation, S.[2] The second element is the disutility of effort, $u(e)$.

$$B(e) = EU[S] - u(e)$$
$$= EU[E + \alpha\Pi(e)] - u(e)$$

The principal-agent problem can be presented now as:

Part 1: The principal's problem

The principal must design a contract to offer to the agent. The contract will specify the compensation to the agent. However, the principal knows that he will not be able to observe the agent's effort. Compensation cannot depend directly on effort. However, the principal does anticipate that the agent will choose effort after she sees the contract terms. Therefore, the principal will try to fashion the compensation to align his interest with that of the agent.

---

[2]It is easy to add in other components of wealth such as savings, financial assets, real assets, and so forth.

FIGURE
16.6

The Principal–Agent Problem When Effort Is Not Observable

The owner pays a bonus based on profit and flat pay. Because the expected value of the bonus will increase with expected effort, the agent increases effort, which, in turn, increases revenue. If the increase in revenue exceeds the increase in pay, then profit increases.

Principal chooses pay to maximize

PROFIT = Revenue – Pay – Costs

Bonus   Flat pay

Agent chooses effort to maximize

Bonus + Pay – Effort

Part 2: The agent's problem

Having seen the contract terms (particularly how she will be paid), the agent selects a level of output.

Part 3: Wrap-up

At the end of the contract, the output from the agent's activities is revealed. The agent is paid, and the remaining output is paid to the principal.

The overall effect is illustrated in Figure 16.6. The owner pays some flat pay to provide some certain income to the risk-averse manager. In addition, the manager is given a share of profits to ensure that the manager will increase effort, which will increase expected revenue and profit. Notice that there is no payment directly related to effort because this is not observable by the firm's owner. Instead, the bonus motivates the manager, because higher effort yields higher expected profit.

Illustration: Running the Family Farm

You inherit the family farm when you are halfway through your MBA degree. You plan to take a job in consulting and are not interested in, nor do you have the skills for, operating the farm yourself. However, because the farm has been in your family for generations, you do not wish to sell it. You want to pass it

TABLE
16.1

Profit and Managerial Effort

	Grain Low–Price (probability 0.5)	Grain High–Price (probability 0.5)
Low effort	$ 50,000	$150,000
High effort	$100,000	$200,000

on to your children, so you decide to hire a manager. Your neighbors tell you that the going salary for a good manager is $50,000, but you are worried that such a salary will not motivate the manager to run the farm to its potential. You estimate that a properly motivated manager could change the profit of the farm as shown in the following matrix. The figures shown in Table 16.1 are gross, so the manager's compensation must be paid from the profit figure.

Notice that, besides the manager's effort, profit is also sensitive to the price of grain. With low prices, profits will be low, but profit will increase if grain prices are higher. You have figured that with your investments and own career, the risk of the farm income is not critical to you, so you are interested in maximizing expected profit (after deducting the manager's compensation). The manager's only source of wealth is his compensation from the farm. Being undiversified, he is interested in maximizing expected utility. The manager's utility function if the manager supplies low effort is

$$U = W^{0.5}.$$

If the manager supplies high effort, it is

$$U = W^{0.5} - u(e)$$
$$= W^{0.5} - 46.3,$$

where U is utility and W is wealth. Notice utility is reduced by 46.3 for high effort. This represents the disutility of effort, $u(e)$.

Flat Salary

Consider first how the manager will behave if he is paid a flat salary.

$$\text{Utility with low effort} = (50,000)^{0.5} = 223.6$$
$$\text{Utility with high effort} = (50,000)^{0.5} - 46.3 = 177.3.$$

Naturally, the manager's expected utility is higher if he supplies low effort. Because the manager is not rewarded for high effort, he will not work hard.

Profit-Related Compensation

Because the local labor market for farm managers is competitive, you cannot offer the manager a package inferior to the flat salary of $50,000. Thus, you must offer him at least 223.6 in expected utility. What portion x of profit would achieve this? To be competitive, x should satisfy:

$$\begin{array}{c} \text{expected utility} \\ \text{with flat salary} \\ \text{and low effort} \end{array} = \begin{array}{c} \text{expected utility with} \\ \text{bonus of } x \text{ profit} \\ \text{and high effort} \end{array}$$

$$223.6 = (0.5)(100{,}000x)^{0.5} + (0.5)(200{,}000x)^{0.5} - 46.3$$
$$2(223.6 + 46.3) = x^{0.5}[(100{,}000)^{0.5} + (200{,}000)^{0.5}]$$
$$\frac{539.8}{763.4} = x^{0.5}$$
$$x = 0.5$$

Note that expected compensation would be $0.5(0.5(100{,}000) + 0.5(200{,}000)) = 75{,}000$. The extra $25,000 compensates the manager both for disutility of effort and for risk.

We have simply said that, if the manager is paid 50 percent of profit and works hard, he will be just as happy as with a flat salary of $50,000 and low effort. We still do not know whether the manager will choose to work hard when he gets 50 percent of profit. To see whether he will, we need to see whether the 50 percent bonus leads to higher expected utility with high than with low effort.

$$\text{EU with high effort} = (0.5)[0.5(100{,}000)]^{0.5} + [0.5(200{,}000)]^{0.5} - 46.3 = 223.6$$

$$\text{EU with low effort} = (0.5)[0.5(50{,}000)]^{0.5} + [0.5(150{,}000)]^{0.5} = 216$$

Therefore, the manager will choose to work hard.

The final question that needs answering is whether you, as owner, are better off paying the manager a flat $50,000 or 50 percent of profits. This is not a trivial question. If you pay the bonus, he will work harder and that will increase revenues. On the other hand, you will end up paying him more on average if you give the 50 percent bonus. To increase net profit, the extra expected revenue from high effort must exceed the additional expected compensation.

Your expected net profits will be as follows:

Flat salary:
$$E(\text{Profit}) = 0.5(50{,}000) + 0.5(150{,}000) - 50{,}000$$
$$= 50{,}000$$

Earnings related:
$$E(\text{Profit}) = 0.5(100{,}000) + 0.5(200{,}000) - 75{,}000$$
$$= 75{,}000$$

Thus, the new 50 percent of profits plan works for both the principal and for the agent.

Some Refinements of Executive Compensation

Figures 16.7 and 16.8 show how different compensation plans can be developed to motivate managers to supply high effort while imposing different levels of risk on the managers. In Figure 16.7, the higher utility function shows utility of wealth of the manager if he supplies low effort. The lower utility function represents utility when managers exert high effort. It is shifted downward to show that, for any level of wealth, high effort will lower utility. Thus, with a flat salary of B, the manager chooses low effort and has a utility level shown as $U(B)$.

MOTIVATING THE MANAGER WITH PROFIT SHARING Figure 16.7 shows how profit-sharing schemes can affect managerial effort. This is like that in the farm example—that is, a straight percentage of the firm's profits. The profits of the firm are

> 50 *times A*   with probability 0.4
> 50 *times C*   with probability 0.6.

FIGURE

16.7 The Effect of Compensation Schemes on Managerial Effort

The profit sharing gives the manager a 50–50 chance of pay levels A and C, which has an expected utility of EU when the manager supplies high effort. This profit-sharing plan is so designed that working hard gives the manager the same expected utility as a flat salary of B while supplying low effort.

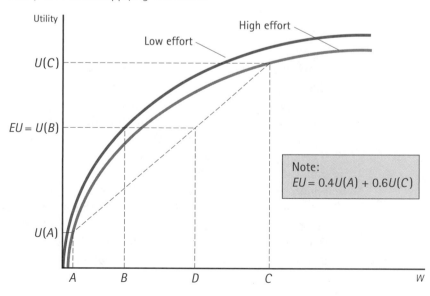

Note:
$EU = 0.4U(A) + 0.6U(C)$

In this case, the manager is paid 2 percent of profits, so his income will be either

A with probability 0.4 or
C with probability 0.6.

The expected value of this compensation is $(0.4)(A) + (0.6)(C) = D$ in the diagram. The purpose of this compensation is to get the manager to work hard. You will notice that the expected utility of this compensation with high effort (the lower utility curve) is $(0.4)U(A) + (0.6)U(C)$, which is labeled EU in the figure. This offers exactly the same expected utility as the flat salary of B and low effort, so the manager would be just as well off receiving the incentive compensation and working hard as having a flat salary and shirking. However, notice that the expected compensation has been increased from a flat value of B to an expected value of D. The difference, $D - B$, is the combined premium necessary to compensate the manager for the risk and disutility of effort.

MOTIVATING THE MANAGER WITH AN INCOME GUARANTEE AND STOCK OPTIONS Notice in particular that the manager is risking a 40 percent chance of a fall in income from B to A when he accepts the profit sharing plan. Can we achieve the same effect while protecting the manager from downside risk? Figure 16.8 shows how we can use stock options. Suppose we replace the incentive plan with a salary floor (i.e., a guaranteed minimum income) of E and a stock option which has a small chance of paying him a large amount of money, $E - F$.

The chances of the stock option paying off are 35 percent. Now the manager's income will be either

E with probability 0.65 or
F with probability 0.35,

which has an expected value of D (i.e., exactly the same as the previous profit sharing plan in Figure 16.7). Notice that the expected utility from this plan (if the manager works hard) is $0.65U(E) + 0.35U(F)$, which is exactly the same expected utility as he would get from the flat salary of B and shirking.

Why does this scheme reduce downside risk? First, the manager is paid a flat salary of E. This salary is riskless; it is paid regardless of performance. Second, the manager receives a call option on the firm's stock that is at risk. This option gives managers the right to purchase the firm's shares at some future date. Moreover, the price at which the stock can be purchased (the *striking price* or *exercise price*) is fixed in advance (see box). These call options may have a fairly modest value now but can be worth either nothing or a lot of money at maturity. Thus, they offer the firm a way of paying the manager a bonus that

FIGURE
16.8

Reducing Managerial Risk with Stock Options

The manager can be provided with minimum compensation and strong incentives for efficiency. A flat salary of *E* is paid together with a stock option, which will secure a gain of *F* minus *E* if the stock price rises sufficiently. This combination offers the manager the same expected utility as the simple profit sharing plan in Figure 16.7.

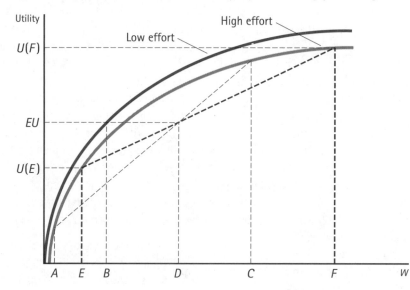

has modest current value and high risk, with fabulous payoffs to the manager if the stock price rises significantly.

INDEXED STOCK OPTIONS Both profit sharing and stock option plans motivate managers to give high effort; but even if they exert this greater effort, they are not guaranteed high payments. Factors they cannot control (e.g., interest rates) can affect firm performance. Hence, in introducing risk into executive compensation, the manager can be penalized for poor profit performance that is outside his control or rewarded simply because the market as a whole takes an upturn. Indeed, much of the impressive performance of executive compensation plans in the 1990s is due to the bull economy as much as to managerial effort and competence. Can we purge the performance yardstick of this external or exogenous risk?

One plan that has recently attracted attention is the indexed stock option.[3] Here the manager is given stock options, but the striking price is not fixed.

---

[3]These are discussed in Nicholas G. Carr, "Compensation: Refining CEO Stock Options," *Harvard Business Review*, 1998, vol. 76, pp. 15–18.

CONCEPTS IN CONTEXT

Call Options

A call option is a contract that gives the holder the right (but not an obligation) to purchase a given number of shares of stock in a firm at a preagreed price from a counterparty (the seller of the option). The fixed price is called the *striking price* or *exercise price*.

For example, suppose you have the right to buy *x* shares in six months' time (known as *maturity*) at a striking price of $50 per share. Suppose now that the actual market price of the stock in six months is $42 per share. You can, if you wish, *exercise your option* to buy the stock (which is now worth $42) for the striking price of $50, but that would be a silly thing to do. You can simply go to your broker and buy the stock anyway at the going market price of $42. Why use the option to pay more than the stock is worth?

Now suppose the stock rises in price so that, in six-months' time it is worth $74. You are sitting on a contract that allows you to buy the stock for $50, even though it is now worth $74. You would *exercise your option* to buy the stock for $50, thus clearing a profit of $24 per share.

The value of a call option, and thus its price, depends on several features. Most important are:

1. The lower the striking price, the higher the value of the option. The holder gets paid the difference between the market price at maturity and the striking price (if this difference is positive), thus a lower striking price increases the payoff and, therefore, increases the current value of the call option.
2. The higher the current price of the stock, the higher its value. The higher the current stock price, the more likely the price at maturity will be above the striking price.
3. The higher the risk or volatility of the stock price, the higher the option value. Increased risk enhances the possibility that the price at maturity will be very low (downside risk) or very high (upside risk). Increased downside risk does not hurt the option holder because the option will not be exercised, but increased upside risk, enhances the payoff at maturity. Thus, risk has a one-sided positive effect.

The methodology for pricing options was developed largely by Robert Merton and Myron Scholes, who won the 1998 Nobel Prize for their work.

In summary, the call option allows you to make a profit if the stock price rises above the striking price at the maturity date. However, if the stock price at maturity falls below the striking price, you can throw away the option and not lose anything. Thus the option gives you the chance of gain without the risk of loss. Naturally, such options are valuable, and you will have to pay a price to buy the option from the seller.

Rather it is expressed in relation to an index of stock prices, such as the Dow Jones. As the index rises, so does the striking price of the option. This ensures the manager is not rewarded simply because the market performs well. On the downside, the striking price will fall as the market index falls. This ensures the manager is not penalized for poor market performance. The net effect of all this is that the manager will be handsomely rewarded if the stock price rises relative to the market. This ensures the manager's compensation is more closely related to factors under his control.

Insurance and Moral Hazard

In insurance, the principal-agent problem is called *moral hazard*. If you are not insured against fire, car crashes, illness, and other of life's contingencies, you face the possibility of sudden and possible crippling financial losses. These uninsured risks should make you cautious. You should take care in your driving, look after your health, and protect your home by installation of smoke detectors and burglar alarms. Although these safety practices can be costly or inconvenient, you will be rewarded by a lowering of the probability, or intensity, of a financial loss. You bear the cost of safety (you pay for the smoke alarm), and you reap the reward (you avoid the costs of a fire). If you are insured, there is a separation of the costs and benefits of safety. The policyholder may incur the cost and inconvenience of safety devices and preventative behavior, but the main beneficiary is the insurance firm, which will now face lower expected losses.

Insurance moral hazard can be divided into two types: ex ante moral hazard and ex post moral hazard. Ex ante moral hazard refers to the tendency of insured people and firms to take less care to prevent future losses when they have insurance. The examples of the previous paragraph (absence of smoke alarms) relate to ex ante moral hazard. Ex post moral hazard is equally important, and this refers to the reluctance of policyholders who have already suffered some misfortune to keep the cost of the event under control. Consider a firm that has bought liability insurance against defective products and has now been sued by injured customers. The policy covers both the legal cost of defending the firm against the suit and the cost of compensating the victims. Because the insurer is paying both these costs, some managerial defendants want the settlement to be very generous. They see this as a way of buying back customer goodwill at the insurer's expense. Other defendants take the opposite view. Because the insurer is paying legal costs, they want the insurer to spend virtually unlimited amounts to defend the producer's reputation, even if it seems that liability is fairly clear.[4] Had the firm been without insurance, it might well have sought to balance the incremental costs of defending a claim with the costs of making a settlement offer to the injured customers.

---

[4]Although almost all insurance policies have limits on what they will pay for damages, some policies carry an unlimited obligation on the part of the insurer for legal defense costs.

ANALYZING MANAGERIAL DECISIONS

Do Directors Act on Behalf of Shareholders or Managers?

The board of directors should act on behalf of shareholders in resolving the principal agent problem. However, there is an ongoing debate about how much influence CEOs exert over the directors. The focus is on inside directors, who might be more easily influenced by the CEO. Recent studies show that agency problems are more severe in firms with inside directors. Newman and Moses found that when insiders are on the compensation committee (which designs the compensation for executives), the relationship between firm performance and CEO compensation is weaker.

Further work by Core, Larcker, and Holthausen is more specific. Their evidence shows that when the governance structure of the firm is weak, the CEO earns greater compensation and the firm's performance tends to be worse. These results stress the importance of the governance structures and the composition of the board of directors in resolving the agency problem. Influential CEOs can block efforts to resolve the agency problem and can redirect the focus of the board from protecting shareholders to favoring the management.

Sources: John E. Core, Robert W. Holthausen, and David F. Larcker, "Corporate Governance, Chief Executive Officer Compensation and Firm Performance," *Journal of Financial Economics,* 1999, vol. 51, pp. 371–406, and Harry A. Newman and Haim A. Moses, "Does the Composition of the Board Influence CEO Compensation Practices?" *Financial Management,* 1999, vol. 28, pp. 41–53.

Principal–Agent Problems between Shareholders and Creditors

Asset Substitution[5]

Our discussion has centered on stakeholders in a firm: the shareholders and the managers. But, there are other stakeholders under the corporate umbrella, and other principal-agent problems can arise. We consider now the problems that can occur between equity holders and creditors. To focus our attention, we will assume that the board of directors has taken control of managerial compensa-

---

[5]See Hayne Leland, "Agency Costs, Risk Management and Capital Structure," *Finance,* 53, 1213–43, and Neil Doherty, *Integrated Risk Management,* chaps. 7 and 8 (New York: McGraw-Hill, 2000).

tion and aligned the interests of the shareholders and managers. Therefore, we can be reasonably assured that the managers will act on behalf of the firm's owners. The new problem arises because shareholders have gained control (via their incentive-compatible schemes) of the decision making process, but creditors have not.

Consider a drug company with an existing product line that exposes the firm to some risk. Future earnings have an expected present value (PV) of either 100 or 200, each with a probability of 0.5. This risk could reflect different possible scenarios about consumer demand, or it could reflect the potential for the drug to have unforeseen side effects, which would result in a major lawsuit from injured customers. The firm has borrowed money under a bond issue, and this debt has a face value of 100 (the face value is the principal amount of the bond, also called the par value). Even under the worst-case scenario, the firm is worth 100 and can pay back its debt. Thus, there is no chance the firm will default. We can now see how much the equity and the bonds are worth.

The overall value of the firm is 0.5(100) + 0.5(200) = 150.

This value can be divided between the shareholders and the bondholders, with the bondholders' obligations being met first and only what is left (the residual claim) going to the shareholders. Therefore, if the firm is worth 100, the debt is paid off and nothing is left for equity. If the firm is worth 200, the debt is paid off, leaving the remaining 100 for the shareholders.

Value of bonds   0.5(100) + 0.5(100) = 100

Value of equity   0.5(0) + 0.5(100) = 50

The firm now faces a new investment decision. It can introduce a new hypertension drug. Its research has come up with two possible formulas. Formula *A* is moderately effective, has no adverse side effects, and is therefore unlikely to result in any consumer lawsuits. Formula *B* is a much more effective drug but has greater potential for unwanted side effects. If things go well, the firm could make much more money with formula B. However, if there were a lawsuit, the firm could lose a lot of money. The firm must choose which formula to produce. The capital cost of each project is 200 (as shown in Table 16.2), which will be financed by new borrowing. The third column shows the possible value that can be created. With project *A*, the present value, PV, of future earnings will be a certain 220. Thus, the net gain (Net Present

TABLE 16.2   Project Selection Using NPV

Capital cost	Present value of earnings	Expected net present value	
Project A	200	220	20
Project B	200	20; probability 0.5	
		or	−35
		310; probability 0.5	

Value or NPV) is $220 - 200 = 20$. In contrast, project B could earn a total of only 20 (if there were a lawsuit) or 310 (if there were no lawsuit).[6] The expected NPV is

$$0.5(20) + 0.5(310) - 200 = -35.$$

Which project should the firm choose? Well, clearly project A looks better because its NPV is a positive 20, whereas the NPV of B is a *negative* 35. However, we will see that the shareholders might look at the decision very differently.

Value of the Firm If Project A Is Chosen

Consider the total value of the firm with each project choice. With project A, the firm will have either 100 or 200 from existing operations, plus an additional 220 from the project. This gives a total value of either 320 or 420. This will be divided between the bondholders, to whom the firm owes a total of 300 (the original debt was 100, plus the firm borrowed 200 for the new project). We assume that the original 100 must be paid first (it is called senior debt) because it was borrowed first. The debt raised to fund the new project is junior and can be paid only after the original debt is paid.

Notice in Table 16.3 that the minimum value of the firm is 320, but it owes a total of 300. Therefore, there is always enough value to pay off the debt in full.

---

[6]The earnings from the projects are independent of those from existing operations.

TABLE

16.3

Firm Value If Project *A* Is Chosen

Value of the firm	0.5(320 + 420)	= 370
Old debt	0.5(100 + 100)	= 100
New debt	0.5(200 + 200)	= 200
Equity	0.5(20 + 120)	= 70

Value of the Firm If Project *B* Is Chosen

If project B is chosen, the total value can be either 100 or 200 from existing operations, plus either 20 or 310 from the project. This leaves possible total values of

$$100 + 20 = 120$$
$$100 + 310 = 410$$
$$200 + 20 = 220$$
$$200 + 310 = 510$$

The values of the firm and of debt and equity are as shown in Table 16.4.

Here is the problem. The firm borrows 200 to spend on one of these two projects. Then shareholders must choose which project to undertake. The choice should be clear. Shareholders are better off with project *B*, where their equity is worth 80, than with *A*, where their equity is worth only 70. How can this be? What seems like the worse project actually makes shareholders better off? The problem has to do with limited liability. If the firm undertakes *A*, it does not create any risk of defaulting on the debt. Shareholders would gain the full NPV of the new project of 20 (notice that before the project was undertaken, equity was worth 50; after project *A*, equity is worth 70). But if *B* is undertaken, there is a 50 percent chance that the project will fail, resulting only in a value of 20.

TABLE

16.4

Firm Value If Project *B* Is Chosen

Value of the firm	0.25(120 + 220 + 410 + 510)	= 315
Old debt	0.25(100 + 100 + 100 + 100)	= 100
New debt	0.25(20 + 120 + 200 + 200)	= 135
Equity	0.25(0 + 0 + 110 + 210)	= 80

If that happens, the firm will be bankrupt and unable to fully pay off the debt. On the other hand, if the project succeeds (is worth 310), the shareholders will reap a big reward. Therefore, when things go well, the shareholders keep all the upside risk; but when things go badly, the shareholders walk away from the debt. Shareholders are playing a "heads we win, tails bondholders lose" strategy.

This illustrates an important principal-agent problem. When firms have a significant amount of debt, the shareholders will tend to favor unusually risky investment decisions. It seems that the bondholders are the unwilling victims of these games. But let us look at the bondholders for a moment. Are they totally helpless? The answer is no. Bondholders must make the decisions of whether to lend to the firm and how much they wish to pay for the bonds. In this case, the firm is trying to issue bonds with a face value of 200 (the bonds contain a "promise" to pay back 200, assuming the firm is still solvent). If you were an investor looking at this firm, your thoughts might progress as follows:

> If I were to pay 200 to buy these bonds, what would the shareholders choose to do with the money? Well, the rational thing for the shareholders to do once they have my money is to choose project B, because the shares would then be worth 80 (compared with 70 for project A). In that case, I should anticipate that B would be chosen, and my new bonds would be very risky and would only be worth 135 (see the value of "new debt" in previous table when B is chosen). Consequently, I would not be willing to buy these bonds for 200, rather I would only pay 135 for them, which is what they are worth.

If we follow the logic a little further, we will see that the firm will be unable to undertake either project. Because rational bondholders would anticipate that B would be chosen, they would only be willing to pay 135 for the new debt issue, even though the face value is 200. Because the capital cost of project B is 200, the amount raised from the debt issue would be insufficient to fund the project. Thus, the firm would be unable to finance project B. Does that mean that A would be chosen? Suppose, indeed, that managers announced their intention to choose A. Unfortunately, investors buying the new debt issue would still rationally assume that, if they subscribed 200 for the issue, the shareholders would change their minds and use the 200 to fund project B. Thus, investors would still only subscribe 135 for the new bond issue. The firm is snookered. It is unable to undertake either project. Because bondholders anticipate the shareholders' temptation to choose the risky negative NPV project, the firm is unable to fund either project. It is forced to sacrifice not only the expropriatory project B, but also a project with a genuine positive NPV.

Representing the "Bait and Switch" in Game Theory

Figure 16.9 shows this problem in a game theory form. The shareholders must choose A or B. Bondholders must choose either to pay the full 200 for the new

FIGURE

16.9

Will Shareholders Pull the Bait and Switch?

If bondholders pay 200, they anticipate that shareholders will choose Project *B*.

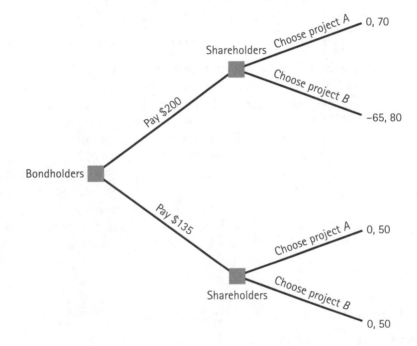

debt or to pay only 135. Because the firm cannot undertake either project un-less bondholders pay the full 200, shareholders will have only the original eq-uity value of 50 (from the existing product line). However, if the bondholders pay the full 200 to cover the project costs, the shareholders will have equity value of 70 from choosing *A* and 80 from choosing *B*. The bondholders' pay-off is the difference between what they pay for the bonds when they are issued and what they are worth. If the bondholders pay 200 and the firm chooses *A*, then the bonds are worth 200 and the net payoff is 0. If the bondholders pay 200 and the firm chooses *B*, then bonds are only worth 135, leaving a net pay-off of −65. If the bondholders anticipate the bait and switch, they will only pay what the bonds are worth and will have a net payoff of zero.

The game is a sequential one, with the bondholders making the first move. Bondholders anticipate that shareholders will choose *B* if they pay 200. There-fore, bondholders pay only 135, and shareholders cannot undertake either pro-ject and are left with equity of 50. Shareholders would like to make the following promise to bondholders: If you would pay 200, then we will promise to un-dertake project *A*. The problem is that the promise is not credible. Having received the 200, the shareholders would then have the incentive to change their minds. There is a credibility problem; shareholders have an incentive to pull the "bait and switch."

Possible Solutions to the Asset Substitution Problem

There are several ways managers can avoid or minimize this problem.

Fund with equity. The problem arose because managers tried to use debt to fund the project. If they can pay for the project by using internal funds or by making a new issue of shares, then the problem will be mitigated or disappear.

Establish a reputation for protecting creditors. If the firm makes a consistent habit of making decisions that preserve the interests of creditors, then a promise not to undertake risky projects in the future might be viewed as credible.

Precommit to hedge or insure risk. Another way this problem is sometimes tackled is that the firm voluntarily commits itself to insure the risks. The problem arose because project *B* was risky, and it was this risk that caused the possibility of default on the debt. If the risk were insured, then bondholders would be protected. Many debt instruments do carry a legal obligation for the firm to insure assets.

Product Liability and the Safety of Consumer Goods

Many countries have laws that protect consumers against the risks of injury from defective products. These laws serve two purposes. First, they provide compensation for the injured consumer. If a consumer is injured by a defective product, the firm has to pay compensation. Second, because the firm must pay compensation if products are defective, there is an incentive for the firm to make safer products. Safer products will result in fewer costly lawsuits. These laws are the solution to a principal-agent problem. The firm makes decisions on safety, but the consumer bears the costs if the product causes injury. The product liability law is incentive compatible because it aligns the interests of the principal (the consumer) and the agent (the producer).

How Safe Would Projects Be without a Product Liability Law?

We thought of the principal-agent problem earlier as one in which the agent chose a level of effort. The effort to consider here is how much the firm invests to make its products safer. We will use s to denote the expenditure undertaken by the firm to make its products safer. Thus, the cost of safety is s, and the marginal cost is simply 1.

$$\text{total cost of safety} = s$$
$$\text{marginal cost of safety} = \frac{ds}{ds} = 1$$

The benefit of safety is that it reduces the expected cost of injuries to consumers. Assume the expected cost of such injuries is

$$\text{expected cost of accidents} = 4{,}000 - 20s^{0.5}$$

It can be seen that the expected costs of accidents depend on the firm's choice of s. Moreover, as s increases, the expected costs will fall. This can be represented as the marginal benefit of safety (because the benefit of safety is a reduction in a cost, we must remember to change the sign):

$$\text{expected marginal benefit of safety} = \frac{d\left(-\left(4{,}000 - 20s^{0.5}\right)\right)}{ds} = \frac{10}{s^{0.5}}.$$

However, in the absence of a product liability law, the firm is not required to compensate consumers for injuries suffered, and these costs fall directly on customers. The expected benefit *to the firm* from safety is zero. Thus, the firm pays all the costs of safety and receives none of the benefits. The profit-maximizing firm will choose $s = 0$. In this case, products will be unusually dangerous.

Safety under a Product Liability Law

The product liability law can be rationalized as providing an incentive to managers to make safer products. To achieve this, the costs of accidents will be borne by the firm, which now must compensate the victims. Thus, the expected benefit *to the firm* from spending s on safety is now the reduction in the expected accident cost. The level of safety that is now optimal for the firm is that which equates marginal cost and marginal benefit.

$$\text{Marginal cost} = \text{marginal benefit}$$
$$1 = \frac{10}{s^{0.5}}$$
$$s = 100.$$

The introduction of the law increases the firm's choice of safety from 0 to 100. Consequently, the expected cost of accidents declines from 4,000 to (4,000 −

MANAGERIAL ECONOMICS IN CONTEXT

The Composition of CEO Pay

The composition of CEO pay is changing with increasing focus on incentives. In a recent survey of CEO compensation compiled for the *Wall Street Journal*, William M. Mercer Inc. found that, in 1999, salary and bonus represented just over one-third of total compensation, the other 63 percent being long-term incentives and notable stock options (another survey by Pearl Meyer and Partners put the proportion of long-term incentive compensation at 70 percent for the largest 50 companies). These figures compared with roughly 50 percent in salary and bonus and 50 percent in long-term incentives five years earlier. Mercer's Peter Chingos attributes this to companies working to bring pay and performance into closer alignment.

At the very top end of the CEO compensation scale, *Forbes* magazine recently examined 12 recently recruited CEOs with pay packages worth more than $100 million. The interesting fact is how little of this was salary and bonus. For example, Robert Knowling, who joined the then-private Covad Communications, accepted a salary and bonus of $650,000. In addition, he received stock shares equal to 5 percent of total equity. After six months on the job, Covac went public through an IPO (initial public offering). Following this IPO, Knowling's shares had a market value of $310 million.

Certainly, the 1990s bull market has had an enormous influence on these figures. However, they do illustrate dramatically the importance of incentive compensation.

Sources: Fay Hansen, "Currents in Compensation and Benefits," *Compensation and Benefits Review*, vol. 35, Sept/Oct. 2000, pp. 6–14, and *Forbes*, April 3, 2000, pp. 122–128.

20(100)) = 2,000. This clearly looks like a social benefit, but was the law really necessary to achieve this?

Optimal Safety under a Market Mechanism

Clearly, the product liability law was incentive compatible, but would an incentive-compatible solution evolve under private-market incentives? There is a marketplace for information. Specifically, information on the safety of products is widely disseminated in subscription magazines and newspaper articles. The volume of such information is increasing, and cost and access to information are improving as it becomes available over the Internet. Moreover, one might imagine that if there were not a product liability law, such information would be more valuable and more widely available. Without a product liability law, consumers would bear the costs of accidents themselves, and safety would be reflected in the demand for, and therefore the price of, products.

Suppose that our firm sells a product in a quantity of 1,000, and, to provide a reference point, customers would be willing to pay a price of 30 if they knew the product was perfectly safe. The firm's revenue would then be 30 ×

1,000 = 30,000. However, information is available about the safety of the product and customers are only willing to pay a price of

$$price = 30 - (4 - 0.02s^{0.5}).$$

Thus the total revenue is now

$$total\ revenue = 1,000[30 - (4 - 0.02s^{0.5})] = 30,000 - (4,000 - 20s^{0.5}).$$

Notice that the revenue is now discounted by exactly the expected cost of accidents. Further assume the firm has other costs of production of 10,000. The profit of the firm is now

$$\Pi = total\ revenue - cost\ of\ safety - other\ production\ costs$$
$$\Pi = 30,000 - (4,000 - 20s^{0.5}) - s - 10,000.$$

Now the firm must choose the level of safety that maximizes profit, so we can set the derivative to zero:

$$\frac{d\Pi}{ds} = \frac{10}{s^{0.5}} - 1 = 0.$$

Of course, this is exactly the same result we got with the product liability law. This should not be a surprise. With product liability, the firm ended up paying the full expected cost of accidents directly in lawsuits. Under the market mechanism, the firm ended up having its revenue reduced by the full expected cost of accidents. Either way, the firm internalized the full cost of accidents and had an incentive to reduce these costs by investing in safety.

What this example shows is that there might be very different ways of solving principal-agent problems. One way can be through the force of civil law, making firms responsible for defective products and, therefore, aligning interests of firms and their customers. The other way is by appealing to market mechanisms by which self-interested customers seek out information and use this information in their purchasing decisions. Customers reward (or punish) firms by varying the price they are willing to pay according to the level of product safety. Thus, the price mechanism becomes a way of aligning the interest of the firm and its customers.

Summary

1. A principal-agent relationship is one in which a principal employs an agent to undertake a task (shareholders employ managers to run a firm). The objectives of the principal and agent may be quite different. Shareholders like

a high profit and high share price. Managers like such things as prestige, income, pleasant work, and perquisites. More simply, managers may wish to do as little as possible for the greatest possible reward. Thus we use the term *effort* to describe when a manager forgoes his or her own objectives (the manager does not shirk) to attend the wishes of the shareholders. Thus, higher effort on the part of the manager can usually increase a firm's profit.

2. The problem for the principal is to motivate the agent to work, not on his or her own behalf, but for the benefit of the principal. Thus the shareholders seek to get managers to supply high effort and to maximize the firm's profits. If the shareholders could observe the effort of managers, this would not be a problem. The managers' compensation could be scaled to the managers' effort. However, if the shareholders don't know how hard managers work, they are hard-pressed to reward them for effort.

3. The full principal-agent problem arises because the firm's owners do not have the time or skill to observe all the actions of the manager. In other words, owners cannot observe the manager's effort. Nor can they infer the effort from the firm's revenue or profit if profit is risky. The solution recognizes that, on average, higher effort will result in higher profit. Managers will be motivated by being given a share of profit or an equity stake in the firm. However, this incentive compensation is risky for the manager. Profits can vary for reasons outside the manager's control. Thus, compensation usually has a fixed component and a profit-related piece.

4. A particularly powerful type of incentive compensation is the stock option. The manager is given an option to buy the firm's stock at some future date at a pre-agreed price. These options are very risky for the manager. If the stock price falls, the options are worth nothing, but a big increase in the stock price can bring fabulous returns. The manager is penalized severely for bad firm performance and rewarded handsomely for good performance. Given the bull stock market of the 1990s, stock option plans have brought great wealth to many CEOs.

5. Another type of principal-agent problem arises between shareholders and the firm's creditors. This is known as *asset substitution*. Limited liability means that when a firm is bankrupt, the shareholders can walk away rather than paying the creditors. This gives an incentive for the shareholders to take on very risky investments. Risk implies that there is a chance of a large upside gain and a chance of a large downside loss. If luck is favorable, the creditors can be paid off, and all the upside gain goes to the shareholders. But if things turn out badly, the shareholders can use bankruptcy law to default on the debt. Thus, high-risk projects have a "heads I win; tails you lose" quality for the shareholders. Of course, the risky projects will hurt the creditors. This tension may lead the firm into dysfunctional in-

vestment decisions, and the firm may be forced to limit its debt financing to resolve this type of agency problem.

Problems

1. Your business generates the following profits (these are stated before compensation is paid to the manager).

	Low demand (0.3)	Medium demand (0.4)	High demand (0.3)
Low effort	$5 million	$10 million	$15 million
High effort	$7 million	$12 million	$17 million

You will see that profit depends both on the level of effort chosen by the manager and on the level of demand. The demand is random, and probabilities of each demand level are shown. Thus, with low effort, expected profit is $10 million; with high effort, $12 million. The manager has a utility function which is either:

Utility = (Wealth)$^{0.5}$, if effort is low, or

Utility = −100 + (Wealth)$^{0.5}$, if effort is high.

Thus "minus-100" is the disutility of effort. You are interested in maximizing expected profit after deduction of compensation. You are considering three different compensation packages:

1. a flat salary of $575,000;
2. a payment of 6 percent of profits;
3. a flat payment of $500,000 plus half of any profits in excess of $15 million.

Which compensaion will you choose?

2. Suppose the typical Florida resident has wealth of $500,000, of which his home is worth $100,000. Unfortunately, he lives in hurricane alley, and it is believed there is a 10 percent chance of a hurricane which could totally destroy the house (i.e., a loss of $100,000). However, it is possible to retrofit the house with various protective devices (shutters, roof bolts, etc.) for a cost of $2,000. This will reduce the size of loss from a *10 percent chance of loss of $100,000 to a 5 percent chance of a loss of $50,000*. The homeowner must decide whether to retrofit and thereby reduce the expected loss.

The problem for an insurance company is that it does not know whether the retrofit will be chosen and therefore cannot quote a premium which is conditional on the policyholder choosing this action. Nevertheless, the insurance company offers the following two policies from which the homeowner can choose: (1) The premium for insurance covering total loss is $12,000; or (2) The premium for insurance covering only 50 percent of loss is $1,500. The typical homeowner has a utility function equal to the square root of wealth. Will the homeowner retrofit and which insurance policy will the homeowner buy? Will the insurance company make a profit (on average) given the homeowner's choice?

3. The expected profit of your firm is 1,000, plus 500 if the manager works hard. The value of the firm's equity (it has no debt) is the expected value of these profits discounted at 10 percent. The manager receives a flat salary of 100 plus a portion x of any equity value in excess of 13,000. The manager's utility function is

   EU = (compensation),$^{0.5}$ if she does not work hard.

   EU = [(compensation)$^{0.5}$ − 1], if she does work hard.

   What portion x must be paid to the manager to ensure that she chooses to work hard? This new compensation package must be competitive with the 100 flat salary.

4. A firm used to have productive assets that generated an income stream with a present value (PV) of 3,000. However, fire occurred and most of those assets were destroyed. The remaining, undamaged assets will produce an income stream that has a present value of only 1,000. Thus, the fire has led to reduction in the value of the firm from 3,000 to 1,000. The firm could undertake a reconstruction of the damaged assets for a capital cost of 1,500 which would restore the income stream to its pre-loss level (PV = 3,000). The firm has existing debt of 2,000 which is a senior claim. Would the shareholders choose to reinvest by issuing new equity to pay for the loss or are they better off walking away from the firm? Would the decision made by the shareholders be in the best interests of the bondholders? In answering this question remember that the shareholders have limited liability and therefore the share value cannot be negative.

5. CareLess Industries has two divisions. Divsion 1 makes cleaning products, and the net worth of this division (PV of cash flows) is 500. Division 2 makes a chemical product. The net worth of Division 2 is 300, absent any potential liability. However, there is a chance that division 2 could have a 700 liability for pollution damage. The potential victims have no contractual relationship with the firm. The probability of such a loss is $0.2/(1 + s)$

where s is the amount the firm spends on safety. The firm must choose the level of s. If you could sell off division 2, would you do so? What is the gain from splitting the firm in this way? Assume a separated Division 2 (as a stand-alone firm) is protected by limited liability. Note also the derivative of $a/(1 + s)$ with respect to s is $-a/(1 + s)^2$.

6. SubAquatics (SA) sells scuba diving equipment. Its clients typically read specialist journals and are very well informed about the price, reliability, and safety of SA products and of competitors' products. SA has estimated that, of 100,000 units sold each year, at a price of $100 each, there will be $4/(1 + s)$ or (4 divided by $1 + s$) fatal accidents due to defective equipment. The value s is the amount spent by SA on safety in millions of dollars.

   a. Assuming that SA is fully liable for such accidents and that the average settlement of each fatal accident is $1 million, how much should SA spend on safety?

   Now assume that SA can escape this liability by selling its product at a lower price under a sale contract which allocates all responsiblity for accidents to the purchaser (assume that courts will enforce such contracts). Now, if SA spends s (expressed in millions of dollars) on safety, the expected cost of accidents to any consumer is $\{4/(1 + s)\}(\$1m/100,000) = \$40/(1 + s)$. Noting that consumers were willing to pay $100 when all liability was assumed by SA (and assuming consumers are risk neutral),

   b. How much would consumers be willing to pay when they bear the cost of accidents?
   c. How much would SA spend on safety?
   d. Assuming that customers cannot observe the level of safety and there is no liability law, how much would SA spend on safety and how much would customers pay for the product?

7. A firm has existing operations that generate an earnings stream with a present value, PV, of 300 or 600 each with 0.5 probability. The firm has 250 existing debt. The firm wishes to undertake one of the following mutually exclusive new investments:

	Capital cost	PV of earnings	NPV
Project A	400	420	20
Project B	400	0; probability 0.5	−50
		or	
		700; probability 0.5	

The capital cost of each project (400) is financed with new junior debt (face value 400).

Is there an "asset substitution" problem? (Will shareholders try to choose the lower Net Present Value, NPV, project?) Now show whether any asset substitution problem would disappear if the new project were to be financed with an equity issue of 400 instead of new debt.

PART

6

Government-Business Relations and the Global Market

Government
and Business

17

Bill Gates, chairman of Microsoft, the computer software giant, is a billionaire, yet he and other top executives of Microsoft had to be concerned with the U.S. Department of Justice's investigation of the firm's competitive practices. The government prevailed, and Microsoft was found guilty of antitrust violations. This set into motion appeals of the verdict. The government and Microsoft ultimately reached a compromise settlement.

The government is a major player for business. Managers must be aware not only of the antitrust laws but also laws for fair trade, employment, safety, environmental issues, and securities. United States companies, who often complain of excessive government interference with their activities, are now complaining about a lack of rules in the developing countries of the world. The game of business cannot be played without rules, and it is the government that sets the rules.

In general, economic regulation has been decreased in the United States in the last twenty years. Transportation and banking are two prime examples. Previously, government agencies controlled which carriers could enter and exit from the transportation industries, the prices they charged, and whether they could merge or not. In banking, the range of services banks could provide was once heavily regulated; banks could provide banking services but not insurance or brokerage. After deregulation, transportation became like the restaurant industry—anyone could enter and charge what they wished.

Yet noneconomic regulation (which can have major economic costs) has grown in recent years. For instance, safety regulation and hours of service (number of hours on duty) regulation continue in the transportation industry. Laws are passed each year that impact how business is conducted.

Governments collect taxes that impact disposable income and the final prices of goods. Governments spend money that impacts the demand for goods. Tax laws impact corporate investment policy. Governments subsidize certain goods, like agricultural products, that increase their production. Governments certify whether and when certain goods can appear in the market, as in the case of drugs—both legal and illegal. Governments provide infrastructure, like roadways, which are an important part of many firms' production functions.

Thus, government activity is pervasive. It accounts for over a third of our gross national product. If you plan to move to the top of the executive ranks, you'd better be prepared to interact with your colleagues and your rivals but also with government agencies as well.

In this chapter, we discuss the nature and effects of public regulation, antitrust policy, and the patent system. Managers must not only understand the nature of public policy in these areas but they must understand what public policy is designed to achieve. Too frequently business executives lack the breadth of view and knowledge required to act effectively to promote their firms' interests in the public arena (although there are over 20,000 registered lobbyists, many of them corporate, in Washington).

Competition versus Monopoly

The Supreme Court has stated that "competition is our fundamental national policy." Many economists agree that competition is preferable to monopoly (or other serious departures from perfect competition), because it is likely to result in a better allocation of resources. As we saw in Chapter 10, a monopolist tends to restrict output, thus driving up price. These economists argue that, from the point of view of social welfare, it would be better if the monopolist raised its output to the competitive level. (Also, in their view, monopolists are likely to be less efficient than competitive firms.) While economists are by no means unanimous on this score, the majority seem to prefer competition over monopoly.

One way our society has tried to deal with these problems has been to establish government commissions like the Federal Communications Commission and the Interstate Commerce Commission (now abolished but with some residual authority retained in the Surface Transportation Board) to regulate the behavior of monopolists. In this way, as we will see in subsequent sections of this chapter, the government has tried to reduce the harmful effects of monopoly. In addition, Congress has enacted antitrust laws that are meant to promote competition and control monopoly. These laws too are discussed at length in this chapter. Any manager must be aware of the nature of these laws, since violating them may mean fines and jail sentences.

Although the United States has gone further in promoting competition than other major industrialized countries, this does not mean that our dedication to competition is complete. National policies are too ambiguous and rich in contradictions to be characterized so simply. The truth is that we as a nation have adopted many measures to promote monopoly and to limit competition. For example, this is the effect of the patent system, which is designed to promote invention and innovation. In later sections of this chapter, we will see why it is felt that the patent system is beneficial, despite the fact that it creates temporary monopolies.

Regulation of Monopoly

In some areas of the economy, such as the distribution of water, it is not economical for more than one firm to exist, because there are important economies of scale. In such industries, the single firm, a so-called **natural monopolist,** is in a position to charge a higher-than-competitive price for its product. Since such a price may lead to an inefficient allocation of society's resources, as well as to monopolistic profits regarded by the public as excessive and unjustifiable, government regulatory commissions often are established to set limits on the prices that a monopolist of this sort can charge.

Consider the Acme Water Company, whose demand curve, marginal revenue curve, average cost curve, and marginal cost curve are shown in Figure 17.1. Without regulation, the firm would charge a price of P_0, and would produce Q_0 units of the product. By setting a maximum price of P_1, the commission can make the monopolist increase output, thus pushing price and output to what they would be if the industry were organized competitively. If the commission imposes a maximum price of P_1, the firm's demand curve becomes P_1AD', its marginal revenue curve becomes P_1ABR', its optimum output becomes Q_1, and it will charge the maximum price of P_1. By setting the maximum price, the commission aids consumers who pay a lower price for more of the product. By the same token, the commission takes away some of the Acme Water Company's monopoly power.

Regulatory commissions often establish the price—or the maximum price—at the level at which it equals average total cost, including a "fair" rate of return on the company's investment. In Figure 17.2, the price would be set by the commission at P_2, where the demand curve intersects the average total cost curve. The latter curve includes what the commission regards as a fair profit

Regulation of Acme Water Company: Maximum Price

By setting a maximum price of P_1, a regulatory commission can make Acme increase output to Q_1.

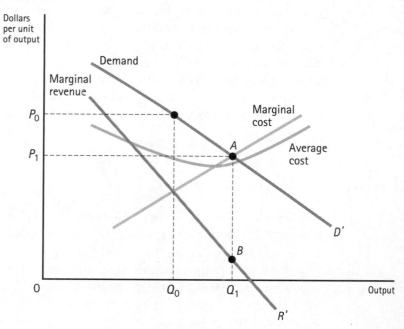

per unit of output. There has been considerable controversy over what constitutes a fair rate of return, as well as over what should be included in the company's investment on which the fair rate of return is to be earned.

To illustrate the workings of the regulatory process, consider the telephone industry in Michigan. The two organizations that have played a key role in the regulation of the telephone industry there are one firm, Michigan Bell Telephone System (a subsidiary of Ameritech), and one commission, the Public Service Commission in Michigan.[1] Although Michigan Bell is not the sole telephone company in the state, it is the dominant firm, and there is no direct competition between firms in the industry. The commission, composed of three people appointed by the governor, has had authority over the telephone industry for about half a century.

[1]Ameritech (American Information Technologies Corporation) is one of seven regional holding companies resulting from the breakup of the American Telephone and Telegraph Company (AT&T), which is discussed on pages 652–53.

FIGURE
17.2

Regulation of Acme Water Company: Fair Rate of Return

The regulated price is P_2, where the demand curve intersects the average total cost curve, which includes what the commission regards as a fair profit per unit of output.

General-rate cases play an important role in the regulatory process. Such cases are initiated by the firms and are based on company claims that earnings are too small and a higher price level is needed. Demand is generally assumed to be price inelastic; consequently, higher prices are assumed to result in greater revenues. The industry usually receives less than it requests (and commission decisions lag behind the industry's revenue requests). However, the fact that the commission does not approve all Bell requests does not imply that the company is constrained much by the commission, since the company may have asked for more than it thought it would receive.

The commission tries to regulate the industry so that earnings equal a "reasonable return on the value of a firm's existing plant." Yet there is a host of questions concerning what constitutes a "reasonable return" and what constitutes the "value of a firm's existing plant." The original cost or historical cost of the plant is the measure on which most commissions base their estimates of the value of the plant; but some permit firms to use replacement-cost valuations instead. In the early 1980s, regulated firms often asked for a rate of re-

ANALYZING MANAGERIAL DECISIONS

The Social Cost of Monopoly

Consider the figure below. A monopolist would set price at P_M and output at Q_M. Consumer surplus under monopoly would be A; producer surplus under monopoly would be $B + C$; and hence, social welfare under monopoly would be $A + B + C$.

If the market was perfectly competitive, price would equal marginal cost (P_C) and quantity would be Q_C. Consumer surplus under perfect competition would be $A + B + D$. Producer surplus would be $C + E$, and social welfare is $A + B + C + D + E$.

Thus, social welfare under perfect competition is $D + E$ greater than under monopoly. This is often called the social welfare triangle or deadweight loss triangle. The rationale for this welfare cost of monopoly is that the demanders along segment XY of the demand curve are willing to pay more than the marginal cost of producing the goods ($Q_C - Q_M$), yet the monopolist does not produce such socially beneficial goods (restricting output at Q_M).

Part of the rationale of antitrust policy and of regulation is to ensure that society captures part or all of this $D + E$ triangle.

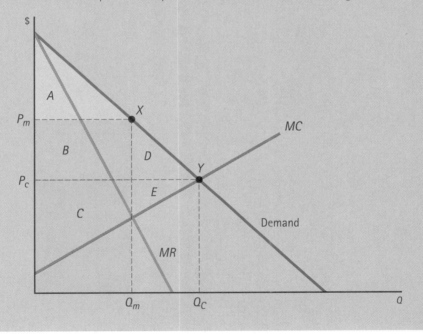

turn of about 10 to 15 percent; commissions in recent years have approved rates of return of about 6 to 10 percent.[2]

The Trenton Gas Company: A Numerical Example

To illustrate the workings of public utility regulation, consider the Trenton Gas Company, which has assets of $300 million. The State Public Utility Commission, after considering the extent of the risks assumed by the firm and the conditions in the financial markets, decides that a fair rate of return for the firm would be 10 percent. Thus, Trenton Gas is allowed to earn profits of 0.10($300 million) = $30 million per year. These profits are not economic profits; they are accounting profits. As stressed above, commissions try to allow firms to earn only a normal or fair rate of return, which tends to rule out economic profits (recall Chapter 1).

What price will the firm set, and what will its output be? To answer these questions, it is important to note that the demand curve for gas provided by the firm is

$$P = 30 - 0.1Q, \tag{17.1}$$

where P is the price per customer (in dollars), and Q is the number of customers served (in millions). The firm's total cost equals

$$TC = 10 + 5Q + 0.9Q^2, \tag{17.2}$$

where TC is total cost (in millions of dollars). Note that this concept of total cost does not include the opportunity cost of the capital invested in the firm by its owners. Thus, the firm's accounting profit equals

$$\begin{aligned} \pi &= (30 - 0.1Q)Q - (10 + 5Q + 0.9Q^2) \\ &= -Q^2 + 25Q - 10, \end{aligned} \tag{17.3}$$

where π is the firm's profit (in millions of dollars).

Since the commission has decided that the firm's accounting profit should equal $30 million, we set π equal to 30, which implies that

$$\begin{aligned} 30 &= -Q^2 + 25Q - 10 \\ Q^2 - 25Q + 40 &= 0, \end{aligned} \tag{17.4}$$

---

[2]See R. Noll and B. Owen, eds., *The Political Economy of Regulation* (Washington, D.C.: American Enterprise Institute, 1983); W. Shepherd and C. Wilcox, *Public Policies toward Business* (6th ed.; Homewood, Ill.: Irwin, 1979); and W. Shepherd, ed., *Public Policies toward Business: Readings and Cases* (Homewood, Ill.: Irwin, 1979).

which is an equation of the form $aQ^2 + bQ + c = 0$. We can use the following equation to solve for the roots of this equation:

$$Q = \frac{-b \pm (b^2 - 4ac)^{0.5}}{2a}$$

$$= \frac{25 \pm [(-25)^2 - 4(1)(40)]^{0.5}}{2(1)}$$

$$= \frac{25 \pm (465)^{0.5}}{2}$$

$$= \frac{25 \pm 21.56}{2}$$

$$= 1.72 \text{ or } 23.28.$$

Because commissions generally want public utilities to serve as many customers as possible, the larger figure, $Q = 23.28$, is the relevant one. Thus, price will be set as follows:

$$P = 30 - 0.1(23.28)$$
$$= 27.67.$$

To sum up, the Trenton Gas Company's price will be $27.67, and it will serve 23.28 million customers.

The Lone Star Gas Company: A Case Study

As a further illustration of how regulatory commissions work, let's look at an actual case. In 1978, the Lone Star Gas Company, which provides gas to 1.1 million residential and commercial customers in the Dallas–Fort Worth area, requested an increase in its price. The Texas Railroad Commission is the state regulatory body with authority over the rates that gas companies can charge. To decide whether an increase should be granted, the commission began by determining the appropriate rate base. The company's assets that were "used and useful" were identified, and valued at historical cost. After allowing for accumulated depreciation, the original cost of invested capital was calculated to be $185 million.

To establish the rate of return that Lone Star Gas should earn on this invested capital, the cost of both debt and equity capital and the percent of each to total capitalization were estimated. The cost of capital was estimated to be 13.87 percent for common equity, 9.75 percent for preferred equity, 8.59 percent for long-term debt, and 9.98 percent for short-term debt. After weighting each of these costs of capital by the percent of total capitalization it represented, the result was 11.1 percent. Thus, the commission concluded that Lone Star Gas should earn an 11.1 percent return on its invested capital of $185 million.

To earn this return, the firm should make an annual profit of 0.111 ($185 million), or $20.535 million. Since the firm's actual profit was only about $9.8 million, the commission decided to allow the firm to raise its price to the extent necessary to bring its profit up to the "reasonable" level of $20.535 million.[3]

Effects of Regulation on Efficiency

Regulators try to prevent a monopoly from earning excessive profits. As we have seen in previous sections, the firm is permitted only a "fair" rate of return on its investment. One difficulty with this arrangement is that the firm is guaranteed this rate of return, regardless of how well it performs. If the regulators decide that the Acme Water Company should get a 9 percent rate of return on its investment, this is the rate of return it will get regardless of whether the Acme Water Company is managed well or poorly. Why is this a problem? Because unlike a competitive firm, there is no incentive for the firm to increase its efficiency.

The regulatory process is characterized by long delays, which, ironically, may go partway toward encouraging efficiency in regulated firms. In many regulated industries, a proposed rate increase or decrease may be under review for months before a decision is made by the commission. In cases in which such a price change is hotly contested, it may take years for the required hearings to take place before the commission and for appeals to be made subsequently to the courts. Such a delay between a proposed price change and its ultimate disposition is called a **regulatory lag.** Long regulatory lags are often criticized by people who would like the regulatory process to adapt more quickly to changing conditions and to yield more timely decisions. But one advantage of regulatory lags is that they result in some penalties for inefficiency and rewards for efficiency.

To illustrate, consider a regulated company whose price is established so that the firm can earn a rate of return of 9 percent (which is what the commission regards as a "fair" rate of return). The firm develops and introduces some improved manufacturing processes that cut the firm's costs, thus allowing it to earn 11 percent. If it takes 15 months for the commission to review the prices it approved before and to modify them to take account of the new (lower) cost levels, the firm earns a higher rate of return (11 percent rather than

---

[3]For further discussion, see M. E. Barrett and M. P. Cormack, *Management Strategy in the Oil and Gas Industries: Cases and Readings* (Houston: Gulf, 1983). The present treatment is simplified for pedagogical reasons.

CONSULTANT'S CORNER

A Dispute Over a Requested Gas Rate Increase

The Boston Gas Company's request for a $17 million rate increase was examined at hearings conducted by the Massachusetts Department of Public Utilities. One consumers' group, which opposed the rate increase, argued that the gas company should be allowed a 10.5 percent rate of return, while the company asked for a 12.46 percent rate of return. The company also argued that because of regulatory lag, it was receiving considerably less than the 12 percent return it was allowed by the commission. Since previous rate increases had not become effective until almost a year after they were requested, the company earned about 9 percent, not 12 percent.

At the hearing, an economist testifying for the consumers' group argued that the company's cost of equity capital was about 12 percent, whereas an economist hired by the company testified that it was about 16 percent. This was an important issue in the case. Both economists used the following equation,

$$k_t = \frac{D_1}{W} + g$$

where k_t is the required cost of capital at time t, D_1 is the dividend paid next year, W is the firm's capitalized value, and g is the annual rate of growth in the corporate dividend, to estimate the company's cost of equity capital, but the economist hired by the consumers' group assumed that the annual rate of dividend growth, g, would equal 0.01, whereas the company's economist assumed that it would equal 0.05.

If asked to advise this firm, what suggestions would you make concerning ways to reduce the adverse effects of regulatory lag on the company's earnings? What sorts of analyses would you carry out to determine which of the two estimates of the cost of equity capital is closer to the truth?*

*For further discussion, see Barrett and Cormack, *Management Strategy in the Oil and Gas Industries.*

9 percent) during these 15 months than it would if it had not developed and introduced the improved manufacturing processes.

While the regulatory lag does restore some of the incentives for efficiency (and some of the penalties for inefficiency), it does not result in as strong a set of incentives as do competitive markets. One of the fundamental problems with regulation is that if a regulatory commission prevents a firm from earning higher-than-average profits, there may be little incentive for the firm to increase its efficiency and to introduce innovations.

The Concentration of Economic Power

Government regulatory commissions are not the only device used by society to deal with the problem of monopoly; another device is the nation's antitrust laws. The antitrust laws reflect a feeling that there is excessive power in the hands of relatively few firms. According to the latest available figures, the 100 largest manufacturing firms control about half of all manufacturing assets in the United States, and this percentage seems to have increased considerably since the end of World War II. Although bigness is not the same as monopoly power, there is a widespread feeling that economic power is concentrated in relatively few hands.

The antitrust laws are aimed at promoting competition and limiting monopoly. As was stressed above, many economists believe that competition is preferable to monopoly because competition tends to result in a more effective allocation of resources. To measure how close a particular industry is to being perfectly competitive (or monopolized), economists have devised the **market concentration ratio**, which shows the percentage of total sales or production accounted for by the industry's four largest firms. The higher the percentage, the more concentrated the industry.

Table 17.1 shows the market concentration ratios for selected industries. These ratios vary widely from industry to industry. In the automobile industry, the concentration ratio is very high—90 percent. In the commercial printing industry, it is very low—7 percent. The concentration ratio is only a rough measure of an industry's market structure, which must be supplemented with data on the extent and type of product differentiation in the industry, as well as on

TABLE 17.1

Concentration Ratios in Selected Manufacturing Product Markets

Industry	Market share of four largest firms (percent)
Automobiles	90
Photographic equipment	77
Tires	69
Aircraft	72
Blast furnaces and steel plants	44
Electronic computers	43
Petroleum refining	32
Bread and cake	34
Pharmaceuticals	22
Radio and TV equipment	37
Newspapers	25
Commercial printing (lithographic)	7

Source: U.S. Department of Commerce.

barriers to entry. Even with these supplements, it is still a crude measure because, for one thing, it takes no account of competition from foreign suppliers. Nonetheless, the concentration ratio has proved to be a valuable tool, although its limitations must be recognized.

Another measure of concentration is the **Herfindahl–Hirschman index** (HHI), which equals the sum of the squared market shares of the firms in the market. For example, if two firms exist in a market, and each has 50 percent of the market, this index equals $50^2 + 50^2 = 5,000$. The Herfindahl-Hirschman index was used by the Justice Department in its 1992 merger guidelines. According to the department, if this index (after the merger) was less than 1,000, the merger was unlikely to be challenged. If it was between 1,000 and 1,800, a merger that changed the index by less than 100 points probably would not be challenged. If it was greater than 1,800, a merger that changed the index by less than 50 points probably would not be challenged. Note that this latter requirement may be hard to satisfy. For instance, if a firm with a 49 percent share wanted to merge with a firm with a 1 percent share, the HHI would increase by 99 points and a firm with a 25 percent share merging with a firm with a 1 percent share would raise the HHI by 51 points.

The Sherman Act

The first federal antitrust law, the Sherman Act, was passed by Congress in 1890. While the common law had long outlawed monopolistic practices, it seemed to many Americans in the latter part of the nineteenth century that legislation was needed to discourage monopoly and to preserve and encourage competition. The formation of trusts—monopolistic combines that colluded to raise prices and restrict output—brought the matter to a head. The essence of the Sherman Act lies in the following two sections:

> Sec. 1. Every contract, combination in the form of trust or otherwise, or conspiracy, in restraint of trade or commerce among the several states or with foreign nations, is hereby declared to be illegal. Every person who shall make any such contract or engage in any such combination or conspiracy, shall be deemed guilty of a misdemeanor. . . .
>
> Sec. 2. Every person who shall monopolize, or attempt to monopolize or combine or conspire with any other person or persons, to monopolize any part of the trade or commerce among the several States, or with foreign nations shall be deemed guilty of a misdemeanor.

In 1974, the Sherman Act was amended, making violations felonies rather than misdemeanors. Corporations can now be fined up to $1 million, and individuals can be fined up to $100,000 and can receive prison terms of up to three years. Besides criminal fines and jail sentences, firms and individuals can be sued for triple damages in civil suits brought by those hurt by an antitrust violation.

It is important to recognize that if executives of two or more firms in a particular industry talk about prices and agree to fix them, this is a violation of Section 1 of the Sherman Act. To illustrate this point, consider Robert Crandall, chief executive officer of American Airlines, who was discussed on page 477. He called Howard Putnam, chief executive officer of Braniff Airways, on February 21, 1982, and proposed that they raise prices. The telephone call, which (unknown to Crandall) was taped, went as follows:

> Putnam: Do you have a suggestion for me?
> Crandall: Yes, I have a suggestion for you. Raise your goddamn fares 20 percent. I'll raise mine the next morning.
> Putnam: Robert, we . . .
> Crandall: You'll make more money and I will, too.
> Putnam: We can't talk about pricing!
> Crandall: Oh [expletive deleted], Howard. We can talk about any goddamn thing we want to talk about.[4]

After finding out about the call, the Justice Department filed a suit accusing Robert Crandall of breaking the antitrust laws by proposing to fix prices. But because there had been no agreement to fix prices, Section 1 had not been violated. Nonetheless, the court decided that a proposal of this sort could be an attempt to monopolize part of the airline industry, which is forbidden by Section 2 of the Sherman Act. American Airlines said that it would not do such a thing again.

The Clayton Act, the Robinson–Patman Act, and the Federal Trade Commission Act

During its first 20 years, the Sherman Act was not regarded by its supporters as being very effective. The ineffectiveness of the Sherman Act led Congress in 1914 to pass two other laws—the Clayton Act and the Federal Trade Commission Act. The Clayton Act attempted to be more specific than the Sherman Act in identifying certain practices that were illegal because they would "substantially lessen competition or tend to create a monopoly."

[4]*New York Times*, February 24, 1983.

The Clayton Act outlawed unjustified price discrimination, which (as you will recall from Chapter 13) is a practice whereby one buyer is charged more than another buyer for the same product. However, discrimination resulting from differences in the quality or quantity of the product sold, or resulting from differences in cost or competitive pressures, was allowed. In 1936, the Robinson-Patman Act amended the Clayton Act. It prohibited charging different prices to different purchasers of "goods of like grade and quality" where the effect "may be substantially to lessen competition or tend to create a monopoly in any line of commerce, or to injure, destroy, or prevent competition with any person who either grants or knowingly receives the benefit of such discrimination, or with customers of either of them." The Robinson-Patman Act was aimed at preventing price discrimination in favor of chain stores that buy goods in large quantities. The small independent retailers felt threatened by the chain stores, and pushed hard for this law.

The Clayton Act also outlawed the use of tying contracts that reduce competition. As Chapter 13 indicated, tying contracts make buyers purchase other items to get the product they want. For a long time, IBM rented, but would not sell, its machines and insisted that customers buy IBM punch cards and use IBM maintenance services. The Supreme Court required IBM to end its tying contracts. However, not all tying contracts have been prohibited. If a firm needs to maintain control over complementary goods and services to make sure that its product works properly, this can be an adequate justification for a tying contract. Also, if the tying arrangements are voluntary and informal, there is no violation of the law. Thus, if a customer bought IBM punch cards because he or she felt that they worked best on IBM equipment, this was no violation of the law, so long as this customer did not have to buy IBM punch cards.

Further, the Clayton Act outlawed mergers that substantially lessen competition; but since it did not prohibit one firm's purchase of a competitor's plant and equipment, it really could not stop mergers. In 1950, this loophole was closed by the Celler-Kefauver Antimerger Act. However, this does not mean that mergers have become less prevalent. On the contrary, there was an epidemic of mergers in the 1980s, as we shall see below.

The Federal Trade Commission Act was aimed at preventing undesirable and unfair competitive practices. It established the Federal Trade Commission to investigate unfair and predatory practices and to issue cease-and-desist orders. The act stated that "unfair methods of competition in commerce are hereby declared unlawful." The commission—composed of five commissioners, each appointed by the president for a term of seven years—was given the formidable task of defining exactly what was "unfair." Eventually, the courts took away much of the commission's power; but in 1938, the commission acquired the function of outlawing untrue and deceptive advertising. Also, the commission has authority to investigate various aspects of the structure of the U.S. economy.

The Interpretation of the Antitrust Laws

The real impact of the antitrust laws depends on how the courts interpret them, and the judicial interpretation of these laws has varied substantially from one period of time to another. Typically, charges are brought against a firm or group of firms by the Antitrust Division of the Department of Justice, a trial is held, and a decision is reached by the judge. In major cases, appeals are made that eventually reach the Supreme Court.

In 1911, as a consequence of the first major set of antitrust cases, the Standard Oil Company and the American Tobacco Company were forced to give up a large share of their holdings of other firms. The Supreme Court, in deciding these cases, put forth and used the famous **rule of reason**—that only unreasonable combinations in restraint of trade, not all trusts, required conviction under the Sherman Act. In 1920, the rule of reason was employed by the Supreme Court in its finding that U.S. Steel had not violated the antitrust laws even though it had tried to monopolize the industry—since the court said the company had not succeeded. U.S. Steel's large size and its potential monopoly power were ruled beside the point, since "the law does not make mere size an offense. It . . . requires overt acts."

In the 1920s and 1930s, the courts, including the conservative Supreme Court, interpreted the antitrust laws in such a way that they had little impact. While Eastman Kodak and International Harvester controlled very substantial shares of their markets, the court, using the rule of reason, found them innocent on the grounds that they had not built up their near-monopoly position through overt coercion or predatory practices.

During the late 1930s, this situation changed dramatically, with the prosecution of the Aluminum Company of America (Alcoa). This case, decided in 1945 (but begun in 1937), reversed the decisions in the *U.S. Steel* and *International Harvester* cases. Alcoa had achieved its 90 percent of the market by means that would have been regarded as "reasonable" in the earlier cases—keeping its price low enough to discourage entry, adding capacity to take care of increases in the market, and so forth. Nonetheless, the court decided that Alcoa, because it controlled practically all the industry's output, violated the antitrust laws.

Frustrating as it sometimes may be to managers, the antitrust laws are rather vague and ambiguous, and consequently it is not easy to tell whether certain actions are permissible. Take the case of two breweries, Pabst and Blatz, which wanted to merge in 1958. The government objected to this merger even though the two firms together accounted for less than 5 percent of the nation's beer sales. What troubled the government was that they accounted for about 24 percent of beer sales in Wisconsin. The district court judge, agreeing with Pabst and Blatz that Wisconsin should be viewed as only part of the relevant market, dismissed the complaint, but the Supreme Court ruled against the firms. This case shows how difficult it can be to establish even the boundaries of the relevant market.

Antitrust Policy during the 1960s and 1970s

The 1960s and 1970s generally were vigorous decades from the viewpoint of antitrust. In 1961, the major electrical equipment manufacturers were convicted of collusive price agreements. Executives of General Electric, Westinghouse, and other firms in the industry admitted that they met secretly and communicated in order to maintain prices, share the market, and eliminate competition. Some of the executives were sentenced to jail on criminal charges, and the firms had to pay large amounts to customers to make up for the overcharges. There were 1,800 triple-damage suits against the firms, which resulted in payments estimated at about $0.5 billion.

During the 1960s, horizontal mergers—mergers of firms making essentially the same good—became increasingly likely to run afoul of the antitrust laws. In the *Von's Grocery* case in 1965, the court disallowed a merger between two supermarkets that together had less than 8 percent of the Los Angeles market. Also, vertical mergers—mergers of firms that supply or sell to one another—were viewed with suspicion by the courts. For example, in the *Brown Shoe* case, the Supreme Court said that the merger of Brown with R. G. Kinney would mean that other shoe manufacturers would be frozen out of a substantial part of the retail shoe market. Another leading problem confronting the Justice Department was conglomerate mergers—mergers of firms in unrelated industries. However, this problem diminished in importance in the late 1960s, when the conglomerates began to show relatively disappointing earnings.

In 1969, the Antitrust Division sued IBM Corporation under Section 2 of the Sherman Act, thus beginning one of the biggest and most expensive antitrust cases in history. The government alleged that IBM held a monopoly and that the firm's 360 line of computers was introduced in 1965 in a way that eliminated competition. IBM's defense was that its market position resulted from its innovative performance and economies of scale, that its pricing was competitive, and that its profit rate really had not been high. After the trial began in 1975, it took the government almost three years to present its case. In early 1982, the Reagan administration dropped the IBM case, on the grounds that it was "without merit and should be dismissed."

In 1974, the government brought an antitrust suit against the American Telephone and Telegraph Company (AT&T), which was settled on the same day in 1982 as the IBM case. According to the settlement, AT&T divested itself of 22 companies that provide most of the nation's local telephone service, and kept its Long Lines Division, Western Electric, and the Bell Laboratories. The

Federal Communications Commission estimated that long-distance rates dropped 38 percent after the divestiture. (For example, the cost of a 10-minute call from New York to Boston fell from $4.09 in December 1983 to $2.34 in December 1988.) But the cost of local telephone service rose substantially, according to some estimates, and divestiture seemed to cause a great deal of confusion among customers and costly adjustments within AT&T. Nonetheless, many observers believe that AT&T is a leaner and more dynamic firm, and that new technologies and services will be introduced more rapidly than in the past.

Antitrust Policy during the 1980s and 1990s

The 1980s were not a period of intense antitrust activity. Antitrust officials felt they should attack conspiracies to fix prices, but they were less concerned than their predecessors about many kinds of mergers. While critics argued that antitrust enforcement was too lax, the Reagan administration maintained that it was enforcing the laws in ways that advanced, rather than hindered, competition.

There was an epidemic of mergers during the 1980s. For example, Chevron took over Gulf Oil, and General Electric took over RCA. In many cases, the acquiring firm bypassed the target corporation's management and tried to purchase a controlling interest directly from the target's stockholders. For example, Saul Steinberg, a prominent investor, tried to acquire the Walt Disney Company (page 5) in this way. A continuing debate has gone on concerning the social costs and benefits of this wave of takeovers. Without question, mergers can have substantial benefits; for example, they can result in economies of scale, the more accurate valuation of particular resources, or the substitution of a more efficient management for a less efficient one. However, these benefits are not assured. A firm may be less efficient, not more so, after a merger than before.

The Bush administration was more actively involved in antitrust than its predecessor. The Justice Department filed suit against the American Institute of Architects on the grounds that it unreasonably restrained price competition among architects. Also, the Federal Trade Commission complained that Capital Cities–ABC Inc. and the College Football Association had illegally conspired to limit the number of football games shown on television. Nonetheless, many observers feel that, for better or worse, antitrust activity during the early 1990s was not particularly aggressive.

The Clinton administration promised to put more emphasis on antitrust enforcement. It indicated that the Justice Department would look closely at mergers, business conduct, alleged price-fixing, and foreign compliance with U.S. antitrust laws. Cases were brought against firms in the flat-glass, milk, cellular communications, and computer software industries, among others. One of the most prominent actions was taken against General Electric and deBeers, described on page 676.

Du Pont's Titanium Dioxide Pigments: A Case Study

To understand the nature of antitrust law, it is useful to look closely at particular cases. Consider the case involving the chemical giant Du Pont, which produces titanium dioxide, a white chemical pigment used to make paint. In 1970, because of its development of the ilmenite chloride process for manufacturing titanium oxide, Du Pont held a substantial cost advantage (16 cents per pound versus 21 cents per pound) over its rivals. From 1972 to 1977, Du Pont increased its capacity and raised its market share from about 30 to 42 percent. (Recall our discussion of Du Pont's huge investment program in Chapter 12.) In 1978, the government charged that Du Pont had used unfair methods of competition and unfair acts and practices by using its dominant position in an attempt to monopolize the production of titanium dioxide (TiO2) pigments. The Federal Trade Commission described the situation as follows:

> Du Pont's growth strategy consists of three interrelated elements: a) expansion of capacity by construction of a large-scale plant; b) exploitation of its cost advantage by pricing its products high enough to finance its own expanded capacity, yet low enough to discourage rivals from expanding; and c) refusal to license its cost-saving ilmenite chloride technology with which rivals could learn to take advantage of the economies of scale inherent in the low-grade ore technology. In addition, the allegedly strategic behavior of Du Pont consisted of premature expansion of its TiO2 capacity and exaggerated announcements of its expansion intentions, all for the primary purpose of preempting competitors' expansion plans.

> Complaint counsel contend that this conduct amounted to exclusionary and anticompetitive behavior insulating Du Pont's cost advantage from competitive erosion since the ilmenite chloride technology actually changes as the scale of operation increases and, without large-scale operations, no competitor will be able to reduce or eliminate Du Pont's cost advantage through "learning-by-doing" ilmenite chloride technology. The inevitable result of this strategy, according to complaint counsel, will be to give Du Pont the power to raise prices at will, restrict output and prevent competition. Indeed, complaint counsel argue that Du Pont's expansion plan "made no sense unless it results in a monopoly."

> Du Pont admits that it sought to capitalize on its cost advantage in order to capture or serve the major portion of the growth in demand for TiO2 well into the 1980's. Even so, it denies that the cost advantage was "fortuitous," claiming instead that it was due to its costly innovations in low-grade ilmenite chloride technology in earlier years. It further denies that its capacity expansion had any purpose other than to satisfy the expected increase in demand for TiO2. Du Pont also denies that it engaged in an unlawful strategic pricing strategy, contending that its pricing during the period was attributable to market forces beyond its control. Indeed, Du Pont asserts

that complaint counsel failed to prove that its prices were not profit-maximizing under the prevailing economic conditions.

Furthermore, Du Pont claims that it was under no duty to license its ilmenite chloride technology to any competitor, and contends that its competitors, all large corporations engaged in TiO2 manufacture, are not prevented from developing their own low-grade ore technology or constructing large-scale plants if they choose to make such investments. Finally, Du Pont points to its failure to achieve the anticipated growth in its market share and denies that it could attain monopoly power in the TiO2 market.[5]

What was the outcome of this case? In 1980, the complaint was dismissed on the following grounds:

Du Pont engaged in conduct consistent with its own technological capacity and market opportunities. It did not attempt to build excess capacity or to expand temporarily as a means of deterring entry. Nor did respondent engage in other conduct that might tip the scales in the direction of liability, such as pricing below cost, making false announcements about future expansion plans, or attempting to lock up customers in requirements contracts to assure the success of its growth plans. In short, we find Du Pont's conduct to be reasonable.[6]

One point that should be recognized is that Du Pont's strategy did not work very well, since demand did not grow as rapidly as the company had forecast, with the result that there was considerable excess capacity in the industry. But whether or not Du Pont's strategy worked, it won the antitrust case, which is our primary interest here.

The Patent System

While the antitrust laws are designed to limit monopoly, not all public policies have this effect. The patent system is a good example. The United States patent laws have granted the inventor exclusive control over the use of an invention for twenty years (from initial filing), in exchange for his or her making the invention public knowledge. Not all new knowledge is patentable. In separate cases, courts have ruled that a patentable invention "is not a revelation of something which existed and was unknown, but the creation of something which did not exist before,"[7] and that there "can be no patent upon an abstract philosophical principle."[8] A patentable invention must have as its subject matter a

---

[5]Federal Trade Commission, *In the Matter of E. I. Du Pont de Nemours and Company*, docket no. 9108, October 20, 1980.
[6]Ibid., p. 51.
[7]*Pyrene Mfg. Co. v. Boyce*, C.C.A.N.J., 292 F.480.
[8]*Boyd v. Cherry*, 50 F.279, 282.

physical result or a physical means of attaining some result, not a purely human means of attaining it. Moreover, it must contain a certain minimum degree of novelty. "'Improvement' and 'invention' are not convertible terms. . . . Where the most favorable construction that can be given . . . is that the article constitutes an improvement over prior inventions, but it embodies no new principle or mode of operation not utilized before by other inventors, there is no invention."[9]

Three principal arguments are used to justify the existence of the patent laws. First, these laws are regarded as an important incentive to induce the inventor to put in the work required to produce an invention. Particularly in the case of the individual inventor, it is claimed that patent protection is a strong incentive. Second, patents are regarded as a necessary incentive to induce firms to carry out the further work and make the necessary investment in pilot plants and other items that are required to bring the invention to commercial use. If an invention became public property when made, why should a firm incur the costs and risks involved in experimenting with a new process or product? Another firm could watch, take no risks, and duplicate the process or product if it was successful. Third, it is argued that because of the patent laws, inventions are disclosed earlier than otherwise, the consequence being that other inventions are facilitated by the earlier dissemination of the information.

Unlike most other goods, new technological knowledge cannot be used up. A person or firm can use an idea repeatedly without wearing it out, and the same idea can serve many users at the same time. No one need be getting less of the idea because others are using it too. This fact creates an important difficulty for any firm that would like to make a business of producing knowledge. For an investment in research and development to be profitable, a firm must be able to sell its results, directly or indirectly, for a price. But potential customers would be unwilling to pay for a commodity that, once produced, becomes available to all in unlimited quantity. There is a tendency to let someone else pay for it, since then it would become available for nothing.

The patent laws, which are a way of addressing this problem, make it possible for firms to produce new knowledge and to sell or use it profitably. But the patent system has the disadvantage that new knowledge is not used as widely as it should be, because the patent holder, who attempts to make a profit, will set a price sufficiently high so that some people who could make productive use of the patented item will be discouraged from doing so. From society's point of view, everyone who can use the idea should be allowed to do so at a very low cost, since the marginal cost of their doing so is often practically zero. However, this would be a rather short-sighted policy because it would provide little incentive for invention.

---

[9]*William Schwarzwaelder and Co. v. City of Detroit*, 77 F.886, 891.

Without question, the patent system enables innovators to appropriate a larger portion of the social benefits from their innovations than would be the case without it, but this does not mean that patents are very effective in this regard. Contrary to popular opinion, patent protection does not make entry impossible, or even unlikely. Within four years of their introduction, 60 percent of the patented successful innovations included in one study were imitated.[10] Nonetheless, patent protection generally increases imitation costs. In the above study, the median estimated increase in imitation cost (the cost of developing and commercially introducing an imitative product) was 11 percent. In the drug industry, patents had a bigger impact on imitation costs than in the other industries, which helps to account for the fact that patents are regarded as more important in drugs than elsewhere. The median increase in imitation cost was about 30 percent in drugs, in contrast to about 10 percent in chemicals and about 7 percent in electronics and machinery.

Patents and the Rate of Innovation

One of the most important and controversial questions concerning the patent system is: What proportion of innovations would be delayed or not introduced at all if they could not be patented? To shed light on this question, carefully designed surveys have been carried out to determine the proportion of their patented innovations that firms report they would have introduced (with no appreciable delay) if patent protection had not been available. According to the firms in one such study, about one-half of the patented innovations would not have been introduced without patent protection. The bulk of these innovations occurred in the drug industry. Excluding drug innovations, the lack of patent protection would have affected less than one-fourth of the patented innovations in the sample.

Patents frequently are not regarded as crucial because they often have only a limited effect on the rate at which imitators enter the market. For about half of the innovations in the above study, the firms believed that patents had delayed the entry of imitators by less than a few months. Although patents generally increased the imitation costs, they did not increase the costs enough in these cases to have an appreciable effect on the rate of entry. But although patent protection seems to have only a limited effect on entry in about half of the cases, it seems to have a very important effect in a minority of them. For about 15 percent of the innovations, patent protection was estimated to have delayed the time when the first imitator entered the market by four years or more.

[10]E. Mansfield, M. Schwartz, and S. Wagner, "Imitation Costs and Patents: An Empirical Study," *Economic Journal*, December 1981.

In another study based on a random sample of 100 firms from 12 industries (excluding very small firms) in the United States, the results indicate that patent protection was judged by the firms to have been essential for the development or introduction of 30 percent or more of the inventions commercialized in two industries—pharmaceuticals and chemicals.[11] In another three industries (petroleum, machinery, and fabricated metal products), patent protection was estimated to be essential for the development and introduction of about 10 to 20 percent of their inventions. In the remaining seven industries (electrical equipment, office equipment, motor vehicles, instruments, primary metals, rubber, and textiles), patent protection was estimated to be of much more limited importance in this regard. Indeed, in office equipment, motor vehicles, rubber, and textiles, the firms were unanimous in reporting that patent protection was not essential for the development or introduction of any of their inventions during the period studied.

This does not mean, however, that firms make little use of the patent system. On the contrary, even in those industries in which practically all inventions would be introduced without patent protection, the bulk of the patentable inventions seem to be patented. And in such industries as pharmaceuticals and chemicals, in which patents are important, over 80 percent of the patentable inventions are reported to have been patented. Clearly, firms generally prefer not to rely on trade secret protection when patent protection is possible. Even in industries like motor vehicles, in which patents are frequently said to be relatively unimportant, about 60 percent of the patentable inventions seem to be patented.

Regulation of Environmental Pollution

Having looked briefly at antitrust policy and the patent system, let's return to the topic of government regulation. Government agencies regulate many aspects of economic life, not just the prices charged by electric, telephone, or transportation companies. Managers of firms in a wide variety of industries, ranging from steel or chemicals to paper or petroleum, must understand and cope with a huge number of government regulations to protect the environment. To illustrate the situation, consider the Reserve Mining Company, which produces iron pellets from taconite rock. For every ton of iron pellets it manufactures, Reserve also produces 2 tons of waste taconite tailings, which for over a decade were dumped into Lake Superior. In 1969, Reserve found itself in a court battle, one of the most hotly debated matters being the discovery of asbestoslike fibers in the water supply of Duluth, Minnesota. When the legal

[11]E. Mansfield, "Patents and Innovation: An Empirical Study," *Management Science*, February 1986.

battle was resolved in 1977, Reserve was granted the necessary permits to begin construction of a new dumping facility, which cost about $400 million. The price was high, but asbestos levels in Lake Superior seem to have dropped substantially.

In the following sections, we explain why our economy, in the absence of government action, is likely to generate too much pollution. Then we discuss the optimal level of pollution control and describe the various forms of government regulation. In view of the importance of the environment both to managers and to the public at large, this discussion should be of considerable interest.

External Economies and Diseconomies

To understand why our economy is likely to generate too much pollution, you must know what is meant by an external economy and an external diseconomy. An *external economy* occurs when an action taken by a firm or individual results in uncompensated benefits to others. Thus, a firm may train workers who eventually go to work for other firms that do not have to pay the training costs. Or a firm may carry out research that benefits other firms that do not have to pay for the research. In general, there is a tendency for activities resulting in external economies to be underperformed from society's point of view. If a firm or individual takes an action that contributes to society's welfare but receives no payment for it, the firm or the individual is likely to take this action less frequently than would be socially desirable.

An *external diseconomy* occurs when an action taken by a firm or individual results in uncompensated costs or harm to others. Thus, a firm may generate smoke that harms neighboring families and businesses, or a person may fail to keep up his or her property, thus reducing the value of neighboring houses. In general, there is a tendency for activities resulting in external diseconomies to be overperformed from society's point of view. If a firm or individual takes an action that results in costs borne by others, the firm or individual is likely to take this action more frequently than is socially desirable.

The Genesis of the Pollution Problem

The key to understanding why our economy generates too much pollution (from society's point of view) is the concept of an external diseconomy. When firms and individuals pollute our waterways and atmosphere, they are engaged in activities resulting in external diseconomies. For example, a firm may pollute a river by pumping out waste materials, or it may pollute the air with smoke or materials. These activities generate external diseconomies, and as pointed out above, they are likely to be overperformed from a social viewpoint.

In a competitive economy, resources tend to be used in their socially most valuable way because they are allocated to the people and firms that find it worthwhile to bid most for them, assuming that prices reflect true social costs. Suppose, however, that because of the presence of external diseconomies, people and firms do not pay the true social costs for certain resources. In particular, suppose that some firms or people can use water or air for nothing, but that other firms or people incur costs as a consequence of this prior use. In this case, *the price paid by the user of water or air is less than the true cost to society.* In a case like this, users of water and air are guided in their decisions by the prices they pay. Since they pay less than the true social costs, water and air are artificially cheap for them, so that they will use too much of these resources, from society's point of view.

The Optimal Level of Pollution Control

Managers, like other members of society, should be able to look at matters from a social, as well as private, standpoint. They should be sensitive to the effects of their actions on society as a whole, as well as on their firm's interests. An industry generally can vary, at each level of output, the amount of pollution it generates. For instance, it may install pollution control devices like scrubbers to lower the amount of pollution it generates at each level of output. In this section, we determine the socially optimal level of pollution control.

The total social cost of each level of discharge of an industry's wastes, holding constant the industry's output, is shown in Figure 17.3. The more untreated waste the industry discharges into the environment, the greater the total costs. Figure 17.4 shows the costs of pollution control at each level of discharge of the industry's wastes. The more the industry reduces the amount of wastes it discharges, the higher are its costs of pollution control. Figure 17.5 shows the sum of these two costs—the cost of pollution and the cost of pollution control—at each level of discharge of the industry's wastes.

From society's point of view, the industry should lower its discharge of pollution to the point where the sum of these two costs—the cost of pollution and the cost of pollution control—is a minimum. Specifically, the optimal level of pollution in the industry is B in Figure 17.5. To see why this is the optimal level, note that if the industry discharges *less* than this amount of pollution, a 1-unit increase in pollution will lower the cost of pollution control by more than it will increase the cost of pollution, whereas if the industry discharges *more* than this amount of pollution, a 1-unit reduction in pollution will lower the cost of pollution by more than it will increase the cost of pollution control.

Figure 17.6 shows the marginal cost of an extra unit of discharge of waste, at each level of discharge of the industry's wastes; this is designated by UU'. Figure 17.6 also shows the marginal cost of reducing the industry's discharge

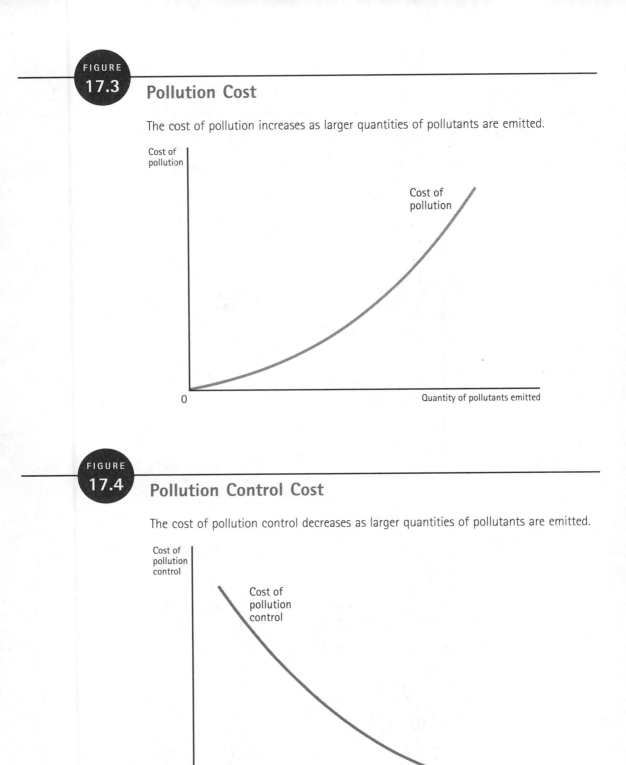

FIGURE

17.3

Pollution Cost

The cost of pollution increases as larger quantities of pollutants are emitted.

Cost of
pollution

Cost of
pollution

0   Quantity of pollutants emitted

FIGURE

17.4

Pollution Control Cost

The cost of pollution control decreases as larger quantities of pollutants are emitted.

Cost of
pollution
control

Cost of
pollution
control

0   Quantity of
                                                     pollutants emitted

Sum of Pollution Cost and Pollution Control Cost

From the point of view of society as a whole, the optimal level of pollution in this industry is *B*.

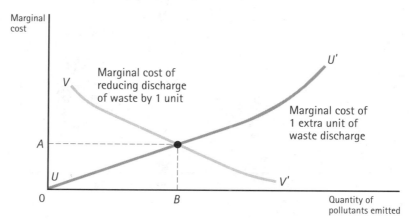

Marginal Cost of Pollution and Marginal Cost of Pollution Control

At the socially optimal level of pollution, *B*, the cost of an extra unit of pollution is equal to the cost of reducing pollution by an extra unit.

of waste by 1 unit; this is designated by VV'. The socially optimal level of pollution for the industry is at the point where the two curves intersect. At this point, the cost of an extra unit of pollution is just equal to the cost of reducing pollution by an extra unit. Regardless of whether we look at Figure 17.5 or 17.6, the answer is the same: B is the socially optimal level of pollution.

Forms of Government Regulation

Because it does not pay all of the social costs of its pollution, the industry in Figure 17.6 will not find it profitable to reduce its pollution level to B. One way that the government can establish incentives for firms to reduce their pollution is by direct regulation. For example, the government may decree that this industry is to limit its pollution to B units. Direct regulation of this sort is relied on in many sectors of the U.S. economy.

Another way to induce firms to reduce pollution is to establish effluent fees. An **effluent fee** is a fee that a polluter must pay to the government for discharging waste. For instance, in Figure 17.6, an effluent fee of A per unit of pollution discharge might be charged. If so, the marginal cost of an additional unit of pollution discharge to the industry is A, with the result that it will cut back its pollution to the socially optimal level, B units. To maximize their profits, the firms in the industry will reduce pollution to B units because it will be profitable to cut back pollution so long as the marginal cost of reducing pollution by a unit is less than A—and, as you can see from Figure 17.6, this is the case when the pollution discharge exceeds B.

To illustrate the usefulness of effluent fees, take the case of Germany's Ruhr Valley, a highly industrialized area with limited water supplies. Effluent fees have been used in the Ruhr to help maintain the quality of the local rivers, and the results have been highly successful. But this does not mean, of course, that direct regulation is not useful too. Some ways of disposing of certain types of waste are so dangerous that the only sensible thing to do is to ban them. Also, it sometimes is not feasible to impose effluent fees—for example, in cases in which it is very difficult to meter the amount of pollutants emitted by various firms and households.

Yet another way that the government can reduce the amount of pollution is to issue **transferable emissions permits,** which are permits to generate a particular amount of pollution. These permits, which are limited in total number so that the aggregate amount of pollution equals the level the government decides on, are allocated among firms. They can be bought and sold. Firms that find it very expensive to curb pollution are likely to buy these permits; firms that find it cheap to do so are likely to sell them. The Clean Air Act of 1990 called for the use of such permits to reduce the emission of sulfur dioxide, and the Chicago Board of Trade has voted to create a market for these permits (see problem 2 on page 672).

Consider another way of solving the problem. It's attributable to Richard Coase who recently won the Nobel Prize in Economics for his contributions (including this one) to economics. The Haddonfield Brewery (a micro brewery) is located downstream from the Cherry Hill Chemical Company. Cherry Hill dumps its effluent into the river. Haddonfield requires clean water to brew its beer and must, therefore, filter the river water before using it. This filtering costs Haddonfield $50,000 and their current profits are $200,000. Cherry Hill's current profits are $500,000. It is possible for Cherry Hill to refine their effluent before discharging it into the river so that the river water meets all standards for beer brewing. To install and operate such a refining system would cost Cherry Hill $40,000. Coase viewed the process on controlling pollution and its costs as one that could be solved without government intervention.

Suppose that there are no government laws regarding pollution. Cherry Hill can pollute at will. The value of society's output as we initially view the situation above is $700,000, or $200,000 + $500,000.

Note that if Haddonfield paid $40,000 to Cherry Hill to refine their outflowing water, Haddonfield could save $10,000 and increase their profits to $210,000 and hence increase societal welfare to $710,000. Pollution would be eliminated and societal welfare would be increased and only private entities would be involved.

However, such a solution could be thwarted by negotiation costs. Suppose negotiation costs for an agreement between Haddonfield and Cherry Hill are $11,000. Cherry Hill has no reason to negotiate or to pay negotiation costs. Haddonfield has $10,000 to gain but if they must bear $11,000 in negotiation costs, they will choose not to do so. Suppose that we impose the basic common law on the above situation—not a law against pollution per se, but a law that says one is liable for the damage one causes to another. Cherry Hill's effluent causes $50,000 in damages to Haddonfield (if Haddonfield had clean water, they wouldn't have to spend $50,000 on filtering and their profit would increase to $250,000). Given liability for the damages they cause, Cherry Hill could shut down and hence stop polluting. But they are very profitable, and shutting down would be foolish because they'd be depriving society of their output. A better solution would be to pay Haddonfield $50,000 for the damages caused to Haddonfield—they'd still have $450,000. Still a better solution is to install the refining system and incur a cost of $40,000—they'd still have $460,000. This eliminates any liability on Cherry Hill's part (because the water is now not polluted).

Notice, in the first case where there was no law (and no negotiation costs) and Cherry Hill could do as they wished, the ultimate solution was for Haddonfield to pay Cherry Hill to put in water refining equipment. In the latter situation where there was a liability law, the ultimate solution was for Cherry Hill to install the refining equipment without any payment from Haddonfield. With or without the law, the private sector installed the cheapest method to eliminate the pollution problem. In either case, societal welfare is $710,000.

The difference between the two situations is the distribution of welfare between Haddonfield and Cherry Hill. Under liability, Cherry Hill gets $500,000 − $40,000 = $460,000 and Haddonfield gets $250,000. With no liability, Cherry Hill gets $500,000 + $P − $40,000 = $460,000 + $P and Haddonfield gets $250,000 − $P, where $50,000 > $P > $40,000. Above we assumed that Haddonfield paid Cherry Hill's cost of installing the refining equipment, but with no liability laws, Cherry Hill does not have to abate its pollution. Clearly Cherry Hill must receive at least $40,000 (the cost of the refining equipment) from Haddonfield; since getting rid of the pollution is worth $50,000 to Haddonfield, Cherry Hill could hold out for a payment P that is greater than $40,000 (but Haddonfield would never pay more than $50,000).

Thus, under the nonlaw scenario, Cherry Hill would get between $500,000 and $510,000, and Haddonfield would get between $210,000 and $200,000. Cherry Hill prefers the nonliable scenario and Haddonfield prefers liability.

Effects of Regulation–Induced Cost Increase on Price and Output

Regardless of how the government induces firms to reduce pollution, the result is an increase in firms' costs, as in the case of the Reserve Mining Company discussed above. (Du Pont is reported to have spent about $500 million on environmental equipment in 1991 alone.[12]) It is important to recognize this fact, and to see how you can determine the extent to which this cost increase will be passed on to consumers in the form of a price increase—and the extent that it will be borne by the firms. In this section, we learn how this can be done.

Suppose a new regulation is enacted that says that paper mills must use new methods to reduce water pollution. Assuming that the paper industry is perfectly competitive, we can compare the situation in the industry after the regulation's enactment with that prior to its enactment. Before the regulation, the marginal cost function of each paper producer is assumed to be

$$MC = 20 + 40Q, \tag{17.5}$$

where Q equals the number (in thousands) of tons of paper produced per week. Thus, if the price is P, the firm, to maximize profit, will set price equal to marginal cost, which means that

$$P = 20 + 40Q,$$

or
$$Q = -0.5 + 0.025P.$$

---

[12]"How Clean-Air Bill Will Force Du Pont into Costly Moves," *Wall Street Journal*, May 25, 1990.

Buying and Selling the Right to Emit Nitrogen Oxides

Nitrogen oxides help to produce smog and aggravate asthma and other respiratory problems. On March 16, 1994, Public Service Electric and Gas, headquartered in Newark, New Jersey, announced that it would reduce its emissions of nitrogen oxides during the next five years by 2,400 more tons than the law requires, probably by altering a coal-fired plant in Jersey City. Northeast Utilities, which operates in Connecticut, Massachusetts, and New Hampshire, said it would purchase the rights to emit 500 of those tons. This was the first use of transferable emissions permits for an air pollutant that affects human health directly. Previous deals of this sort centered on sulfur dioxide, which helps cause acid rain.

The Clean Air Act of 1990 authorized a market in emissions permits. Firms finding it relatively expensive to cut down on their nitrogen oxide emissions are likely to buy pollution permits because such permits cost less than cutting down on their emissions. On the other hand, firms finding it relatively cheap to cut down on their nitrogen oxide emissions are likely to sell pollution permits because their costs of reducing the emissions are less than what they can sell the permits for. Thus, the reduction in the total emission of nitrogen oxides will occur at relatively low cost.

For such a scheme to work, firms must be able to buy and sell permits. In this case, Public Service Electric and Gas will sell the permits to a broker, the Clean Air Action Corporation of Tulsa, Oklahoma, at cost. Clean Air Action Corporation will sell them to Northeast Utilities and others at whatever the market price turns out to be. This price will be set by the supply and demand curves for permits.*

*For further discussion, see *New York Times*, March 16, 1994, and *Philadelphia Inquirer*, March 16, 1994.

If there are 1,000 paper producers, all with the same cost function, the industry's supply curve is

$$Q_S = 1,000(-0.5 + 0.025P) = -500 + 25P. \qquad (17.6)$$

Assuming that the market demand curve for paper is

$$Q_D = 3,500 - 15P, \qquad (17.7)$$

we can find the equilibrium price and output of paper by setting the quantity demanded, in equation (17.7), equal to the quantity supplied, in equation (17.6):

$$3,500 - 15\,P = -500 + 25P$$
$$40P = 4,000$$
$$P = 100.$$

Thus, the quantity demanded equals

$$Q_D = 3,500 - 15P = 3,500 - 15(100) = 2,000.$$

And the quantity supplied equals the same amount:

$$Q_S = -500 + 25P = -500 + 25(100) = 2,000.$$

In other words, before the new regulation, the price of paper is $100 per ton, and 2,000 thousands of tons are produced per week.

What is the effect of the new regulation on the price and output of paper? Suppose the regulation raises the marginal cost of producing paper by 25 percent. Thus, after the regulation, the marginal cost function of each paper producer is

$$MC = 1.25\ (20 + 40Q)$$
$$= 25 + 50Q.$$

To maximize profit, each firm sets marginal cost equal to price, which means that

$$25 + 50Q = P,$$

or $$Q = -0.5 + 0.02P.$$

Thus, the industry's postregulation supply curve is

$$Q'_S = 1,000(-0.5 + 0.02P)$$
$$= -500 + 20P, \qquad (17.8)$$

if all 1,000 of the paper producers stay in the industry. (Some may drop out if they cannot avoid losses. Recall Chapter 11.) To find the equilibrium price af-

ANALYZING MANAGERIAL DECISIONS

Auctioning Off Spectrum Rights: Australia and the United States

In 1995, the Federal Communications Commission (FCC) completed the first auction for broadband personal communications services (PCS) licenses. In designing its auction, both the FCC and its economic advisers were aware auctions could backfire, as illustrated by a famous case in Australia. In April 1993, two licenses for satellite television service were auctioned off in Australia. When the sealed bids were received, the winners were Hi Vision Ltd. and Ucom Pty. Ltd.; their winning bids were about $140 million and $120 million, respectively. Because these bids were arger than expected and because these firms were not among the major players in the Australiar television industry, the Australian government announced that the auction ushered in a "whole new era."

To the government's dismay, both Hi Vision and Ucom defaulted on their highest bids. Thus, the licenses had to be reawarded at the next-highest levels, which were also theirs. It soon became clear that each firm had submitted a large number of bids, each about $5 million higher than the next. After defaulting on a number of ts bids, Ucom eventually paid about $80 million for one license and $50 million for the other. An Australian politician called it "one of the world's great media license fiascos," and Bob Collins, Australia's communications minister, almost was fired.

(a) What are the advantages of auctions over other schemes to choose who gets licenses? (b) What was the fundamental flaw in Australia's auction of licenses? (c) To help avoid such flaws, the FCC stipulated that firms had to make downpayments to the FCC, and that, if a high bidder were to withdraw its bid during the auction, it would be liable for the difference between its bid and the price ultimately obtained for the license. (For bids withdrawn after the auction, there would be a supplementary penalty of 3 percent.) Why would these stipulations help to avoid such flaws?

SOLUTION (a) Auctions tend to reduce the costs and delays in choosing licenses. Hearings and lotteries, which are the principal alternative ways to allocate licenses, use up a great deal of resources, particularly the time of economic, engineering, and legal consultants. (b) The fundamental flaw in Australia's auction was the lack of a penalty for default, which implied that bids were really not meaningful. (c) These stipulations were aimed at preventing bidders from defaulting without penalty on their bids.*

*For further discussion, see John McMillan, "Selling Spectrum Rights," *Journal of Economic Perspectives*, Summer 1994.

ter the enactment of the new regulation, we set the quantity demanded in equation (17.7) equal to the quantity supplied in equation (17.8):

$$3,500 - 15P = -500 + 20P$$
$$35P = 4,000$$
$$P = 114.29$$

Thus, the postregulation quantity demanded equals

$$Q_D = 3,500 - 15P = 3,500 - 15(114.29) = 1,785.71.$$

And the quantity supplied equals the same amount:

$$Q'_S = -500 + 20P = -500 + 20(114.29) = 1,785.71.$$

In other words, after the new regulation, the price of paper is $114.29 per ton, and 1,785.71 thousands of tons of paper are produced per week.

Clearly, the new regulation results in an increase in price (from $100 to $114.29 per ton) and a reduction in output (from 2,000 to 1,785.71 thousands of tons per week). This will typically be the effect of such regulations, but the extent of the price increase (and the output reduction) will depend on the price elasticity of demand for the product. If the price elasticity is very low in absolute value, the price increase will be greater (and the output reduction will be smaller) than it would be if the price elasticity were very high in absolute value.

Public Goods

Besides regulating the environment and the behavior of monopolists, the government performs a wide variety of economic functions, including the provision of goods and services. For example, the government is responsible for the provision of national defense, a critically important product in any society. Why does the government provide some goods and not others? One important reason is that some goods—so-called public goods—are unlikely to be produced in sufficient amounts by the private (nongovernmental) sector of the economy. Thus, the government is given the task of providing these goods. Before concluding this chapter, we must describe briefly what a public good is and why the private sector is unlikely to provide a public good in sufficient amounts.

A major hallmark of a public good is that *it can be consumed by one person without diminishing the amount that other people consume of it*. Public goods tend to be relatively indivisible; they often come in such large units that they cannot be broken into pieces that can be bought or sold in ordinary markets. Also, *once such goods are produced, there is no way to bar citizens from consuming them*. Whether or not citizens contribute toward their cost, they benefit from them. Obviously, this means that it would be very difficult for any firm to market them effectively.

National defense is a public good. The benefits of expenditure on national defense apply to the entire nation. Extension of the benefits of national defense to an additional citizen does not mean that any other citizen gets less of these benefits. Also, there is no way of preventing citizens from benefiting from them, whether they contribute to their cost or not. Thus, there is no way to use ordinary markets (such as exist for wheat, steel, or computers) to provide for national defense. Since it is a public good, national defense, if it is to reach an

Entrance Fees to National Parks

The United States has many national parks, such as Yellowstone, and there are frequent complaints that they are overcrowded. Some economists, such as Allen Sanderson of the University of Chicago, have suggested that the solution is to raise entrance fees. They point out that, when the National Park Service was set up in 1916, a family of five arriving by car could gain admission to Yellowstone for $7.50; in 1995, the price was only $10. If the 1916 price had risen in accord with the general rate of inflation, the 1995 fee would have been about $120.

According to Sanderson, "We are treating our national and historical treasures as free goods when they are not. We are ignoring the costs of maintaining these places and rationing by congestion—when it gets too crowded no more visitors are allowed—perhaps the most inefficient way to allocate scarce resources."*

*New York Times, September 30, 1995, p. 19.

adequate level, must be provided by the government—similarly with flood control, environmental protection, and other such services.

However, it is important to recognize that although these services are provided by the government, this does not mean that they must be produced entirely by the government. The U.S. Air Force does not produce the B-2 Stealth Bomber; Northrop Corporation (now part of Northrop Grumman) does. The U.S. Navy does not produce the F-14 fighter; Grumman (now also part of Northrop Grumman) does. Firms play a central role in developing and producing the weapons systems on which our military establishment relies, although national defense is a public good.

Government agencies have a major influence over a wide variety of industries, not just defense contractors like Northrop or Grumman. This chapter has described in detail many of the activities of government agencies that are of most importance to managers. Much more will be said on this score in the following chapter, which deals with managerial economics in a global context.

Summary

1. Commissions regulating public utilities often set price at the level at which it equals average total cost, including a "fair" rate of return on the firm's investment. One difficulty with this arrangement is that since the firm is guaranteed this rate of return (regardless of how well or poorly it performs), there is no incentive for the firm to increase its efficiency. Although regulatory lag results in some incentives of this sort, they often are relatively weak.

2. The Sherman Act outlaws any contract, combination, or conspiracy in restraint of trade and makes it illegal to monopolize or attempt to monopolize. The Clayton Act outlaws unjustified price discrimination and tying contracts that reduce competition, among other things. The Robinson-Patman Act was aimed at preventing price discrimination in favor of chain stores that buy goods in large quantities. The Federal Trade Commission Act was designed to prevent undesirable and unfair competitive practices.

3. The real impact of the antitrust laws depends on the interpretation placed on these laws by the courts. In its early cases, the Supreme Court put forth and used the famous rule of reason—that only unreasonable combinations in restraint of trade, not all trusts, required conviction under the Sherman Act. The situation changed greatly in the 1940s when the court decided that Alcoa, because it controlled practically all the nation's aluminum output, was in violation of the antitrust laws. In the early 1980s, two major antitrust cases—against American Telephone and Telegraph and the IBM Corporation—were decided.

4. The patent laws grant the inventor exclusive control over the use of an invention in exchange for his or her making the invention public knowledge. The patent system enables innovators to appropriate a larger portion of the social benefits from their innovations than would be the case without it, but it frequently has only a limited effect on the rate at which imitators appear. Nonetheless, firms continue to make extensive use of the patent system.

5. An external economy occurs when an action taken by a firm or individual results in uncompensated benefits to others. An external diseconomy occurs when an action taken by a firm or individual results in uncompensated costs or harm to others. When firms and individuals pollute our waterways and atmosphere, they are engaged in activities resulting in external diseconomies.

6. The socially optimal level of pollution (holding output constant) is at the point where the marginal cost of pollution equals the marginal cost of pollution control. In general, this will be at a point where a nonzero amount of pollution occurs. To formulate incentives that will lead to a more nearly optimal level of pollution, the government can establish effluent fees, issue transferable emissions permits, or enact direct regulations, among other things.

7. Regulations (and other measures) designed to reduce pollution tend to increase the costs of the regulated firms. The price of their product generally goes up, and industry output tends to go down. If the price elasticity of demand is relatively low in absolute value, more of the cost increase can be passed along to consumers in the form of a price increase than would be the case if the price elasticity of demand were relatively high in absolute value.

8. A public good can be consumed by one person without diminishing the amount of it that other people consume. Also, once a public good is pro-

duced, there is no way to bar citizens from consuming it. Public goods, such as national defense, are unlikely to be produced in sufficient quantities by the private (nongovernmental) sector of the economy. Thus, the government often is given the task of providing these goods.

Problems

1. In 1985, United Airlines purchased Pan Am's Pacific Division for $750 million. The Department of Justice opposed the purchase, but it was approved by the U.S. Department of Transportation. The percentage of total passengers carried across the Pacific by each airline in 1984 was as follows:

Firm	Percentage	Firm	Percentage
Northeast	27.5	United	7.3
JAL	21.9	China Airlines	6.8
Pan Am	18.5	Singapore Airlines	2.9
Korean Air	9.3	Other	5.8

   a. What was the concentration ratio before the purchase? Was it relatively high?
   b. What was the concentration ratio after the purchase?

2. The Chicago Board of Trade has voted to create a private market for rights to emit sulfur dioxide. The Clean Air Act of 1990 established a limit, beginning in 1995, on total emissions of sulfur dioxide from 110 power plants. Firms finding it relatively expensive to cut down on their sulfur dioxide emissions are likely to buy pollution permits because such permits cost less than cutting down on their emissions. Given that firms can exceed their legal limits and pay fines of $2,000 per ton, do you think that the price of a right to emit a ton of sulfur dioxide will exceed $2,000? Why or why not?

3. The Harrison Electric Company is engaged in a rate case with the local regulatory commission. The demand curve for the firm's product is

$$P = 1,000 - 2Q,$$

   where P is price per unit of output (in dollars), and Q is output (in thousands of units per year). Its total cost (excluding the opportunity cost of the capital invested in the firm by its owners) is

$$TC = 50 + 0.25Q,$$

   where TC is expressed in millions of dollars.

    a. The Harrison Electric Company has requested an annual rate (that is, price) of $480. If the firm has assets of $100 million, what will be its rate of return on its assets if this request is granted?

    b. How much greater would the firm's accounting profits be if it were deregulated?

4. The cost of pollution (in billions of dollars) originating in the paper industry is

$$C_P = 2P + P^2,$$

where P is the quantity of pollutants emitted (in thousands of tons). The cost of pollution control (in billions of dollars) for this industry is

$$C_C = 5 - 3P.$$

    a. What is the optimal level of pollution?

    b. At this level of pollution, what is the marginal cost of pollution?

    c. At this level of pollution, what is the marginal cost of pollution control?

5. There are seven firms that produce kitchen tables. Suppose their sales in the year 2000 are as follows:

Firm	Sales (million of dollars)
A	100
B	50
C	40
D	30
E	20
F	5
G	5

    a. What is the concentration ratio in this industry?

    b. Would you regard this industry as oligopolistic? Why or why not?

    c. Suppose that firm A merges with firm G. What now will be the concentration ratio in this industry?

    d. Suppose that after they merge, firms A and G go out of business. What now will be the concentration ratio in this industry?

6. The cost of pollution emanating from the chemical industry (in billions of dollars) is

$$C_P = 3P + 3P^2,$$

where P is the quantity of pollutants emitted (in thousands of tons). The cost of pollution control (in billions of dollars) is

$$C_C = 7 - 5P.$$

a. What is the optimal effluent fee?

b. If the cost of pollution control falls by $1 billion at each level of pollution, does this alter your answer to part a?

7. In the cardboard box industry, the minimum value of average cost is reached when a firm produces 1,000 units of output per month. At this output rate, average cost is $1 per unit of output. The demand curve for this product is as follows:

Price (dollars per unit of output)	Quantity (units demanded per month)
3.00	1,000
2.00	8,000
1.00	12,000
0.50	20,000

a. Is this industry a natural monopoly? Why or why not?

b. If the price is $2, how many firms, each of which is producing an output such that average cost is a minimum, can the market support?

8. The Kravis Company, which sells engines, has a uniform price of $500, which it charges all its customers. But after its competitors begin to cut their prices in the California market to $400, Kravis reduces its price to $400.

a. Does this tend to violate the Clayton Act?

b. If the Kravis Company had cut its price to $300, might this tend to violate the Clayton Act?

c. Suppose the Kravis Company decides to purchase enough of the stock of competing firms so that it can exercise control over them and see to it that the price-cutting in the California market stops. Is this legal? If not, what law does it violate?

9. Bethlehem and Youngstown, two major steel producers, accounted for about 21 percent of the national steel market in the late 1950s, when they proposed to merge.

a. Should the two steel companies have been allowed to merge? Why or why not?

b. According to the companies, Bethlehem sold most of its output in the East, whereas Youngstown sold most of its output in the Midwest. Was this fact of relevance? Why or why not?

c. In fact, the district court did not allow Bethlehem and Youngstown to merge. Yet in 1985 (as we saw on page 672), the Department of Transportation allowed United Airlines (with about 7 percent of the service between Japan and the U.S. mainland) to acquire Pan Am's Pacific Division (with about 19 percent). How can you explain this?

10. One of the most celebrated antitrust cases of recent years involved Eastman Kodak and Berkey Photo. Eastman Kodak has long been a dominant producer of cameras and film. Berkey Photo competed with Kodak as photofinisher, and less successfully (until 1978) as a camera manufacturer. Berkey bought much of its film and photo finishing equipment and supplies from Kodak. In 1973, Berkey filed suit, saying that Kodak had violated the antitrust laws when in 1972 it introduced its new 110 "Pocket Instamatic" camera. Because the camera was introduced with no advance notice to Kodak's competitors, Berkey could not introduce its own version of the new camera until late 1973, and did not reach a substantial sales volume until 1974. Berkey claimed that Kodak's failure to disclose the innovation to its competitors before introducing it violated Section 2 of the Sherman Act. Does withholding from others advance knowledge of a firm's new products ordinarily constitute valid and legal competitive conduct?

11. On August 28, 1991, the New York State Electric and Gas Corporation filed a request for a 10.7 percent increase in electric revenues. The reasons given to justify the increase were that the value of the firm's plant and equipment had increased by $140 million, that operating costs had increased, and that investors required a higher rate of return.
    a. Why should an increase in the value of the firm's plant and equipment result in an increase in the amount of revenue allowed by the Public Service Commission?
    b. Why should an increase in operating costs have the same effect?
    c. Why should the attitude of investors regarding what they require as a rate of return be relevant here?

12. During the 1990s, an enormous amount of attention was devoted to global warming. According to many scientific theories, increases in carbon dioxide and other so-called greenhouse gases may produce significant climatic changes over the next century. To cope with this potential problem, it has been suggested that firms reduce energy consumption and switch to non-fossil fuels. William Nordhaus, a leading expert on this topic, has estimated that the worldwide costs (in 1989 U.S. dollars) of various percentage reductions in the quantity of greenhouse gases emitted into the atmosphere would be as follows on the next page:

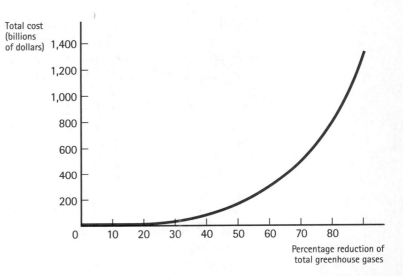

Source: R. Dornbusch and J. Poterba, eds., *Global Warming: Economic Policy Responses* (Cambridge, Mass.: MIT Press, 1991), p. 50.

a. Does this graph show the cost of pollution or the cost of pollution control?

b. Can this graph alone indicate the socially optimal amount of greenhouse gases that should be emitted into the atmosphere? Why or why not?

c. If world output is about $20 trillion, by what percentage would world output be reduced if the countries of the world agreed to cut greenhouse gas emission by 50 percent?

d. The single most common policy that is proposed to decrease greenhouse gas emission is a so-called carbon tax, a tax on fossil fuels in proportion to the amount of carbon they emit when burned. Why would such a tax have the desired effect?

13. On February 17, 1994, the Justice Department filed a criminal indictment against General Electric and deBeers, which are the dominant producers of industrial diamonds. According to the Justice Department, in November 1991, Peter Frenz of General Electric faxed price increases that his firm proposed to make to Philippe Liotier of Diamant Boart, a Belgian firm that is owned by Sibeka, which is 20 percent owned by deBeers. (Also, deBeers produces its industrial diamonds through a 50-50 joint venture with Sibeka.) In December 1991, Mr. Liotier provided Mr. Frenz with deBeers's proposed price increases. Subsequently, the two men met. According to Anne Bingaman, at that time chief of the Justice Department's antitrust division, "The division will not tolerate . . . sophisticated schemes that are used to fix prices and to disguise criminal activity."[13]

---

[13]*Wall Street Journal*, February 22, 1994.

a. About $600 million of industrial diamonds, used in cutting tools for construction and oil drilling, are sold per year, and General Electric and deBeers account for 80 percent of total sales. Is this the kind of market where collusion is relatively likely? Why or why not?

b. What law did the Justice Department charge the firms with violating?

c. This investigation by the federal government was stimulated by Edward Russell, a discharged General Electric executive, who alleged antitrust violations by General Electric and sued the company for improperly firing him. A day before the Justice Department's indictment, Mr. Russell settled his suit against General Electric. He received part of his legal costs and a package of benefits, and signed a statement that he hadn't "any personal knowledge" of antitrust violations. What effect did this have on the strength or weakness of the government's case?

d. According to the New York Times, "The government's case depended on proving that Mr. Liotier was acting not as a General Electric customer, but for deBeers, which owned part of Diamant Boart's parent company."[14] Why did the case hinge on this issue?

e. General Electric chairman John F. Welch called the charges "outrageous." Was the Justice Department able to win the case?

[14]*New York Times*, December 6, 1994, p. D2.

Managerial Economics: Taking a Global View

CHAPTER 18

Managers are conducting business in increasingly global environments. Many large firms are multinationals. Even small firms source their production overseas. Overseas firms are producing their products here. The supply chain for many goods is global. United States firms are acquiring firms abroad and non-U.S. firms are acquiring U.S. firms.

As an example, the U.S. auto market has changed dramatically in the last thirty years. The U.S. market was dominated by the big three domestic producers (General Motors, Ford, and Chrysler). But in short period of time, imports (primarily from Japan) had 25 percent of the market. Even when the U.S. firms caught up with the Japanese in quality and fuel efficiency, they could not reverse the market share numbers. As the exchange rate changed and protectionism in the U.S. increased, Japanese auto firms set up production facilities in the United States. In the last several years mergers or alliances have occurred between Daimler Benz and Chrysler, Ford and Volvo, Renault and Nissan, and General Motors and Fiat.

Forty years ago, virtually all television sets and stereos consumed in the United States were manufactured in the United States. Today not a single TV is manufactured in the United States. The imbalance of maritime container traffic (net empty moving westbound from the west coast of the United States) between the Far East and the United States is indicative of the trade activity and its direction. Most drug companies are multinationals, and oil companies are becoming multinational. Large commercial jet aircraft are produced by only two companies—an American company (Boeing) and Airbus (a joint French, English, German, and Spanish company). Smaller (regional) jet aircraft are dominated by two companies—Bombardier of Canada and Embraer of Brazil. Airlines from all over the world use their products. Governments may offer considerable aid to major industries. Boeing and Airbus have spent many years accusing the other of receiving unfair advantages from their home government. Brazil and Canada have had a long-running dispute on export credits involving Embraer and Bombardier before the World Trade Organization.

Governments also influence international trade flows through the use of tariffs, quotas, and embargoes. Managers playing the international market game must understand the relevant aspects of international economics. We will take up the factors influencing whether a country will import or export a particular product, the determinants of exchange rates, and the nature and effects of tariffs, quotas, and strategic trade policy. We will also discuss the factors that managers should consider in deciding whether to build a plant abroad, where to build it, and how quickly, and in choosing whether—and, if so, how to transfer technology abroad. Today, these topics are of central importance, when advances in transportation and communication have truly made this a shrinking world.

Foreign Trade

First, it is important to recognize that foreign trade is of great importance to the United States. As Table 18.1 shows, we exported about $900 billion in goods and services in 1999 and were exporting at a seasonally adjusted rate of almost $1.1 billion in 2000. About $700 billion was exports of goods (in 1999), much of it being capital goods and industrial supplies. We imported over $1.24 billion in goods and services in 1999 and were importing at a seasonally adjusted rate of over $1.45 billion in 2000. About $1.05 billion was imports of goods (in 1999), much of it being capital goods, consumer goods, and autos. As Table 18.2 shows, about half of our export transactions went to Western Europe and Canada in 1999, and over half of our imports were from Western Europe and Canada, and Japan.

Why does trade occur among countries? As economists have pointed out for over a century, *trade permits specialization, and specialization increases output.* Because the United States can trade with other countries, it can specialize in the goods and services it produces well and cheaply. Then it can trade

TABLE
18.1

U.S. Goods—Exports and Imports, 1999

| | Exports | | Imports | |
| | Amount | | Amount | |
Product	(billions of dollars)	Product	(billions of dollars)
Food, feed, and beverages	45.5	Food, feed, and beverages	43.6
Industrial supplies	141.8	Industrial supplies	148.6
Capital goods	311.8	Capital goods	297.1
Autos and parts	75.8	Autos and parts	179.4
Consumer goods	80.8	Consumer goods	239.6
Other	43.6	Other	72.5
Total	699.2	Total	1,048.6

Source: Survey of Current Business, September, 2000, Table 4.3, p. D3.

them for goods and services that other countries are particularly good at producing. The result: both we and our trading partners can benefit.

International differences in resource endowments, and in the relative quantity of various types of human and nonhuman resources, are important bases for specialization. Consider countries with lots of fertile soil, little capital, and much unskilled labor. They are likely to find it advantageous to produce agricultural goods, while countries with poor soil, much capital, and highly skilled labor will probably do better to produce capital-intensive, high-technology goods. However, the bases for specialization do not remain fixed over time. In-

TABLE
18.2

Geographical Distribution of U.S. Exports and Imports, 1999

| | Percentage distribution | |
Area	Exports	Imports
Japan	8.3	12.7
Western Europe	23.9	20.7
Canada	24.5	19.7
Eastern Europe	0.8	1.1
Others	42.5	45.7

Source: Economic Report of the President, 2000, Table B-103, p. 425.

stead, as technology and the resource endowments of various nations change, the pattern of international specialization changes as well. For example, the United States specialized more in raw materials and foodstuffs a century ago than it does now.

Comparative Advantage

Even if one country is able to produce everything more cheaply than another country, it still is likely that they both can benefit from specialization and trade. This proposition, known as the *law of comparative advantage,* must be understood. Suppose that the United States is twice as efficient as China in producing computers and 50 percent more efficient than China in producing textiles. In particular, suppose that the United States can produce 2 computers or 6,000 pounds of textiles with 1 unit of resources, and China can produce 1 computer or 4,000 pounds of textiles with 1 unit of resources. In this case, the United States is a more efficient producer of both computers and textiles, but it has a comparative advantage in computers, not textiles. In other words, its efficiency advantage over China is greater in computers than in textiles, so its comparative advantage lies in computers. (Why is its efficiency advantage greater in computers than in textiles? Because it can produce twice as many computers, but only 50 percent more textiles, from a unit of resources than China can.)

If countries specialize in producing goods and services in which they have a comparative advantage and trade with one another, each country can improve its standard of living. Figure 18.1 shows the *production possibilities curve* in the United States—the curve that shows the maximum number of computers that can be produced, given various outputs of textiles. The United States must give up 1 computer for every additional 3,000 pounds of textiles it produces; thus, the slope of the U.S. production possibilities curve is −1/3,000. Also, Figure 18.1 shows China's production possibilities curve. Since China must give up 1 computer for every additional 4,000 pounds of textiles it produces, the slope of its production possibilities curve is −1/4,000.

Suppose that the United States has 1,000 units of resources and uses all of them to produce computers, while China has 800 units of resources and uses all of them to produce textiles.[1] In other words, the United States operates at point *G* on its production possibilities curve and China operates at point *M* on its production possibilities curve. Then suppose that the United States trades its

---

[1]By resources we mean here a combination of labor, capital, and other types of inputs, not just labor alone, so it is realistic to suppose that the United States has more resources than China. Note too that it generally is more realistic to assume that production possibilities curves are curvilinear, rather than linear (as in Figure 18.1). Usually, the slope of a production possibilities curve becomes steeper as one moves to the right along the horizontal axis. However, for present purposes, we assume that these curves are linear to keep the analysis as simple as possible.

FIGURE
18.1

Production and Trading Possibilities Curves, United States and China

Each country's trading possibilities curve lies above its production possibilities curve. This means that both countries can have more of both commodities by specializing and trading than by trying to be self-sufficient.

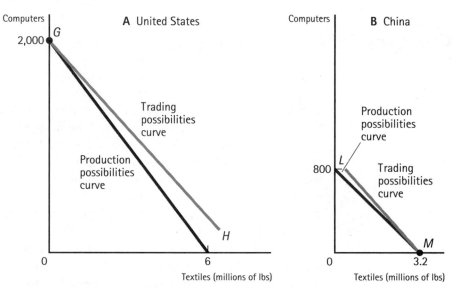

computers for China's textiles. The line *GH* in panel A of Figure 18.1 shows the various amounts of computers and textiles the United States can end up with if it specializes in computers and trades them for Chinese textiles. The line *GH* is called the *trading possibilities curve* of the United States. The slope of *GH* is

$$- \frac{\text{Price of textiles (per pound)}}{\text{Price of a computer}},$$

which (in absolute value) equals the number of computers the United States must give up to get a pound of Chinese textiles. Similarly, the line *LM* in panel B of Figure 18.1 shows China's trading possibilities curve. That is, *LM* represents the various amounts of computers and textiles China can wind up with if it specializes in textiles and trades them for U.S. computers. The slope of the line will be somewhere between −1/3,000 and −1/4,000 depending on the supply and demand curves for computers and textiles.

The big point to note about both panels of Figure 18.1 is that *each country's trading possibilities curve—GH* in panel A and *LM* in panel B—lies above its production possibilities curve. This means that both countries can have more of both commodities by specializing and trading than by trying to be self-sufficient—even though the United States is more efficient than China at producing both commodities. Moreover, firms in the United States can make money by producing computers and selling them in both countries, and firms in China can make money by producing textiles and selling them in both countries.

Changes in Comparative Advantage

Any good manager must recognize that if a country has a comparative advantage in the production of a particular commodity, it cannot count on this situation to last indefinitely. To illustrate, consider the case of watches. In 1945, Switzerland produced about 90 percent of the world's watches and watch movements. The production of watches was labor intensive; about 60 percent of the production cost of a watch went for labor. The Swiss firms concentrated on making high-quality, expensive watches (so-called jewel-levered watches). Their watches were sold largely in jewelry stores (and some department stores), where profit margins were typically about 50 percent. During the 1950s and 1960s, Switzerland's share of world watch output declined, in part because Timex, a U.S. firm, successfully produced and marketed inexpensive watches that were popular and because the Japanese became a bigger factor in the watch market. (Recall page 461 of Chapter 12.) Nonetheless, the Swiss still produced about half the world's watches in 1970.

During the 1970s, the technology of watchmaking was revolutionized, resulting in the quartz watch. This new technology permitted the design of watches that were very accurate; also, it allowed miniaturization and the digital display of time. For analog quartz watches (those with the traditional face and hands), average variable production costs fell by about 83 percent between 1974 and 1979. By 1979, direct labor accounted for less than 20 percent of the production cost of an analog quartz watch. In the case of digital quartz watches, many semiconductor firms, often in the United States or Hong Kong, constructed fully automated production processes to make them.

By 1980, Switzerland no longer had a comparative advantage in watch manufacture. It produced only about 15 percent of the world's watches, less than Hong Kong or Japan. The leading producer was Hong Kong, where most watches were made by semiconductor firms, not the traditional watch manufacturers. What happened to the Swiss watch industry? It shrank. In 1980, it contained about half as many firms—and employed about half as many employees—as in 1970.

Clearly, the managers of any firm selling largely to foreign markets (or competing against foreign rivals in domestic markets) must constantly be on their guard against the loss of comparative advantage. In some cases, if such a loss occurs, the answer is to locate the firm's factories in some other part of the world where costs are lower. For example, Timex produced overseas many of the watches it sold in the United States. In other cases, the firm may be best off to get out of the business and invest its resources elsewhere. Thus, as pointed out in Chapter 2, John Welch, chairman of General Electric, decided to sell its aerospace business to Martin Marietta Corporation.[2]

Using Demand and Supply Curves to Determine Which Country Will Export a Product

How can a manager tell whether his or her country has a comparative advantage in the production of a particular product? One important indicator is whether this country's firms can make money by producing and exporting the product. Consider the Wilton Company, maker of a new product produced and sold only in Germany and the United States, the only two countries where this product has a significant market. In the United States, the demand curve for this product is such that[3]

$$Q_D^U = 100 - 2P_U, \tag{18.1}$$

and the supply curve is such that[4]

$$Q_S^U = 5 + 2.6P_U, \tag{18.2}$$

where P_U is the price of the product (in dollars) in the United States, Q_D^U is the quantity demanded (in millions of units) per month in the United States, and

---

[2]For further discussion, see D. Yoffie, *International Trade and Competition* (New York: McGraw-Hill, 1990).

[3]As was pointed out in Chapter 3, the demand curve for a product is an equation where price is on the left-hand side of the equation and quantity demanded is on the right-hand side. To derive equation (18.1) [and equation (18.3)], we move price to the right-hand side and quantity demanded to the left-hand side.

[4]As pointed out in Chapter 10, the supply curve for a product is an equation where price is on the left-hand side of the equation, and quantity supplied is on the right-hand side. To derive equation (18.2) [and equation (18.4)], we move price to the right-hand side and quantity supplied to the left-hand side.

Q_S^U is the quantity supplied (in millions of units) per month in the United States. In Germany, the demand curve for this product is such that

$$Q_D^G = 120 - 4P_G, \qquad (18.3)$$

and the supply curve is such that

$$Q_S^G = 2 + 2P_G, \qquad (18.4)$$

where P_G is the price of the product (in German marks) in Germany, Q_D^G is the quantity demanded (in millions of units) per month in Germany, and Q_S^G is the quantity supplied (in millions of units) per month in Germany.

Since this new product is now being introduced for the first time in Germany and the United States, managers and analysts in both countries would like to predict whether, after markets in both countries settle down, this product will be exported, and if so, by which of these two countries. To answer this question, we must begin by noting that if the cost of transporting this product from the United States to Germany (or back) is zero, the price of this product must be the same in both countries. Why? Because if it were different, a firm could make money by purchasing it in the country where its price is lower and selling it in the country where its price is higher. As this continued, the price would rise in the former country and fall in the latter country, until eventually the price in both countries would be equal.

But what do we mean by the prices in both countries being equal? Prices in the United States are quoted in dollars; prices in Germany are quoted in marks. What we mean is that, based on prevailing exchange rates, the prices in the two countries are the same. If the U.S. dollar exchanges (at banks and elsewhere) for 1.6 German marks, a price of $10 in the United States is equivalent to a price of 16 marks in Germany. Consequently, if this is the exchange rate, what we mean when we say that the prices in the two countries are the same is that

$$P_G = 1.6P_U, \qquad (18.5)$$

If there is no government intervention in the market for this product and if this market is competitive, the price of this product will tend to be at the level where the total world demand for the product equals the total world supply. In other words, in equilibrium,

$$Q_D^U + Q_D^G = Q_S^U + Q_S^G. \qquad (18.6)$$

Using equations (18.1) to (18.4), we can express each of the Qs in equation (18.6) as a function of P_U or P_G. Substituting each of these functions for each of the Qs in equation (18.6), we obtain

$$(100 - 2P_U) + (120 - 4P_G) = (5 + 2.6P_U) + (2 + 2P_G).$$

And substituting $1.6P_U$ for P_G we find that

$$(100 - 2P_U) + (120 - 4 \times 1.6P_U) = (5 + 2.6P_U) + (2 + 2 \times 1.6P_U),$$

or

$$220 - 8.4P_U = 7 + 5.8P_U$$
$$213 = 14.2P_U$$
$$P_U = \$15.$$

And since $P_G = 1.6P_U$, $P_G = 1.6(15) = 24$ marks. In other words, the price of the product will be $15 in the United States and 24 marks in Germany.

Given these prices, we can determine whether Germany or the United States will be an exporter of the product. Based on equation (18.1), the monthly demand in the United States will be $100 - 2P_U = 100 - 2(15) = 70$ millions of units. Based on equation (18.2), the amount supplied per month in the United States will be $5 + 2.6P_U = 5 + 2.6(15) = 44$ millions of units. Thus, the United States will import $70 - 44 = 26$ millions of units per month. Based on equation (18.3), the monthly demand in Germany will be $120 - 4P_G = 120 - 4(24) = 24$ millions of units. Based on equation (18.4), the amount supplied per month in Germany will be $2 + 2P_G = 2 + 2(24) = 50$ million units per month. Thus, Germany will export 26 million units per month.

In sum, the answer is that Germany will be the exporter of this new product—and that its exports will be 26 million units per month.

Analyzing the Gains from Trade

Let's now view the gains from trade for both the United States and for Germany in the above example. To do so, we'll use the concepts of consumer surplus (introduced in Chapter 4) and producer surplus (introduced in Chapter 9). Figure 18.2 shows the situation in the United States.

Before trade with Germany, the price of the product was approximately $20.65 and approximately 58.70 units were transacted. This left U.S. consumers with a consumer surplus of A and U.S. producers with a producer surplus of $B + D$. Because of the lower price ($15) after trade, consumers gain consumer surplus (now $A + B + C_1 + C_2$). Thus, consumers gain $B + C_1 + C_2$. Prior to trade, U.S. producers received producer surplus of $B + D$. The lowering of price reduces producer surplus to D. Thus, U.S. producers lose B in producer surplus because of the trade. The sum of the consumers gain and the producer surplus loss ($C_1 + C_2$) is the gains from trade. Its magnitude is $C_1 + C_2 = 0.5(\$20.65 - \$15)26 = \$73.45$. Society is better off because societal welfare has increased from $A + B + D$ to $A + B + D + C_1 + C_2$, or, by $C_1 + C_2$. While the producers

FIGURE
18.2

U.S. Demand and Supply and Gains from Trade*

The U.S. gain in consumer surplus is $B + C_1 + C_2$ and the U.S. loss in producer surplus is B, for a net societal gain of $C_1 + C_2$.

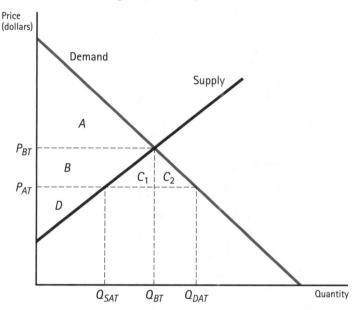

*P_{AT} = price after trade; P_{BT} = price before trade; Q_{SAT} = quantity supplied after trade; Q_{DAT} = quantity demanded after trade; Q_{BT} = quantity demanded and supplied before trade.

have lost, in theory there are enough gains that they could be more than compensated for their loss.

For example, suppose that the government wrote the producers a check for $B + C_1$. Producers now have gained C_1 ($B + D - B + B + C_1 = B + D + C_1$ versus $B + D$ before trade). Where did the government get the money to pay the producers? By taxing the recently better-off consumers. However, even after being taxed $B + C_1$, consumers are still better off because they have $A + B + C_1 + C_2 - (B + C_1) = A + C_2$, as compared to the A they had before trade. Thus, trade makes a country better off, and, depending on how the gains are distributed, can make both consumers and producers better off. Figure 18.3 shows the situation in Germany.

Before trade, the good sold for 19.67 marks and 41.33 units of the good transacted. German consumers enjoyed a consumer surplus of $W + X$ while German producers had a producer surplus of Z for a total German social welfare of $W + X + Z$.

FIGURE
18.3

German Demand and Supply and Gains from Trade

German loss in consumer surplus is X, and German gain in producer surplus is X + Y for a net societal gain of Y.

*P_{AT} = price after trade; P_{BT} = price before trade; Q_{SAT} = quantity supplied after trade; Q_{DAT} = quantity demanded after trade; Q_{BT} = quantity demanded and supplied before trade.

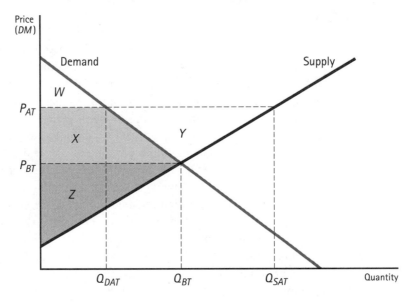

After trade, the price increases to 24 marks. This price increase hurts German consumers and consumer surplus falls to W (a loss of X). However, the price increase benefits German producers, and producer surplus increases to X + Y + Z (a gain of X + Y). The producers gain more than offsets the consumer loss (by Y). Social welfare is now W + X + Y + Z (it's up by Y). As measured above, Y is $Y = 0.5(24 - 19.67)26 = 56.33$ marks or 56.33($1.6) = $90.13. Note that the gains in each country don't have to be equal and in this case, Germany has gained much more from trade than has the US—but the point is that both have gained, giving each side incentive to join in trade.

One thing that must be true however in this two-good trading world—the U.S. imports (26) must equal the German exports (26). The 26 units imported is the U.S. physical trade deficit. The fiscal trade deficit is the 26 units multiplied by the "world" price of $15, or, 26($15) = $390. Germany, on the other hand, is running a physical trade surplus of 26 and a fiscal trade surplus of 26(24) = 624 marks (or 624/1.6 = $390).

How does the United States obtain the marks to import goods from Germany? We can receive marks from Germans who use marks as payment when they import a good from the United States; from German tourists, who spend money in the United States; and from Germans who buy U.S. securities, services, and real estate. Alternatively, we also have reserves of marks which were accrued in the past.

Exchange Rates

Practically any manager of a large firm (and many managers of small firms) must be concerned with exchange rates. For example, suppose that a U.S. firm wants to buy a machine tool from a German firm. To buy the machine tool, it must somehow get German marks to pay the machine tool maker, since this is the currency in which the machine tool maker deals. Or, if the machine tool maker agrees, the U.S. firm might pay in dollars; but the German firm would then have to exchange the dollars for marks; since its bills must be paid in marks. Whatever happens, either the U.S. firm or the German firm must somehow exchange dollars for marks, since international business transactions, unlike transactions within a country, involve two different currencies.

As was pointed out in the previous section, *the exchange rate is the number of units of one currency that exchanges for a unit of another currency.* In November 2000, a U.S. dollar exchanged for about 2.3049 marks; thus, this was the exchange rate between these two currencies. Exchange rates can vary considerably over time; for example, in 1985, a dollar exchanged for about 2.9420 marks, and in late 1995, a dollar exchanged for about 1.4321 (see Figure 18.4). To a large extent, exchange rates, like any prices in a competitive market, are determined by demand and supply.[5]

In the case of German marks, what would be the exchange rate if the demand and supply curves were as represented in Figure 18.5? The demand curve shows the amount of German marks that people with dollars will demand at various prices of a mark. The supply curve shows the amount of German marks that people with marks will supply at various prices of a mark. Since the amount

---

[5]Prior to 1973, exchange rates generally were fixed by government agreements. The International Monetary Fund was established to maintain a stable system of fixed exchange rates and to ensure that when exchange rates had to be changed because of significant trade imbalances, disruption was minimized. This system, set up at the end of World War II, broke down and was replaced by flexible exchange rates in 1973.

However, governments still intervene to some extent in the currency markets. That is, they step in to buy and sell their currency. Thus the United States has agreed that "when necessary and desirable," it would support the value of the dollar. Also, some European countries have attempted to maintain fixed exchange rates among their own currencies, but to float jointly against other currencies.

FIGURE
18.4

Number of German Marks that Could Be Bought for a U.S. Dollar (1973–2000)

The exchange rate between the dollar and the mark has varied greatly in the last twenty-seven years.

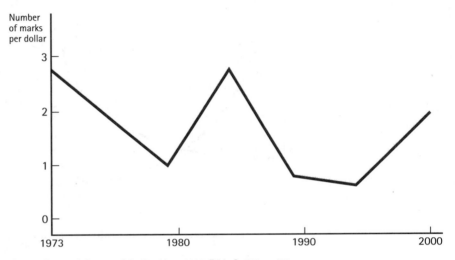

Source: *Economic Report of the President*, 2000, Table B-108, p. 430.

of German currency supplied must equal the amount demanded in equilibrium, the equilibrium price (in cents) of a German mark is given by the intersection of the demand and supply curves. In Figure 18.5, this intersection is at 45 cents.

Changes in exchange rates can have a big effect on practially any firm. For example, if the dollar goes up relative to other currencies, this means that U.S. goods and services go up in price, relative to those of our foreign rivals. Consequently, it is harder for U.S. firms to sell abroad and easier for foreign producers to sell in the United States. In the early 1980s (peaking in 1985), the dollar went up relative to other major currencies (see Figure 18.6), and U.S. firms complained bitterly of the difficulties they were experiencing as a consequence of selling abroad and competing with imports. Recall the plight of Caterpillar Tractor, which had great difficulties in meeting the prices charged by its Japanese rival, Komatsu (see page 520).

To understand why changes in exchange rates occur, we must look in more detail at the demand and supply curves in Figure 18.5. On the demand side of the market are firms that want to import German goods into the United States, people who want to travel to Germany (where they'll need German money),

FIGURE
18.5

Demand and Supply Curves for German Marks

The equilibrium price of a mark is 45 cents.

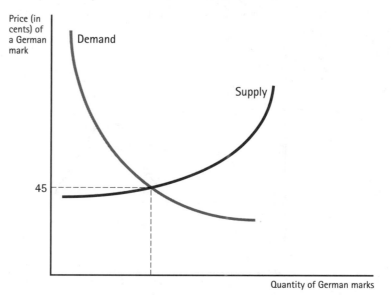

firms that want to invest in facilities in Germany, and others with dollars who want German currency. The people on the supply side of the market are those who want to import U.S. goods into Germany, Germans who want to travel in the United States (where they'll need U.S. money), firms with marks that want to invest in facilities in the United States, and others with marks who want U.S. currency.

When U.S. firms and individuals demand more German goods and services, thus causing the demand curve in Figure 18.5 to shift upward and to the right, the price (in cents) of the German mark will tend to increase. For example, if the demand curve for marks shifts as shown in Figure 18.7, the result will be an increase in the equilibrium price of the mark from 45 cents to 50 cents. On the other hand, when the Germans demand more U.S. goods and services, thus causing the supply curve in Figure 18.5 to shift downward and to the right, the price (in cents) of the German mark will tend to decrease.

Why does an increase in German demand for U.S. goods and services cause the supply curve in Figure 18.5 to shift downward and to the right? Because this supply curve shows the amount of marks that will be supplied at each price of a mark. Since an increase in German demand for U.S. goods and services would be expected to result in a greater amount of marks being put forth at a

FIGURE
18.6

Value of U.S. Dollar in Terms of Major Foreign Currencies (Real Effective Exchange Rate), 1976–1998

The value of a dollar rose greatly (relative to other major currencies) in the early 1980s.

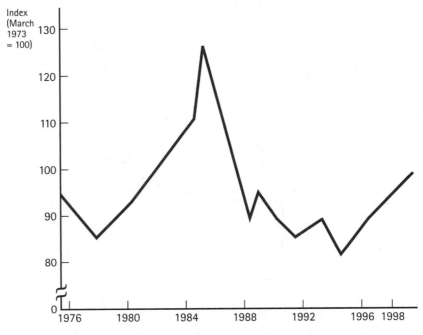

Source: Economic Report of the President, 2000, Chart 6-9, p. 234.

given price of the mark, it would be expected to shift this supply curve downward and to the right.

Determinants of Exchange Rates

Having pointed out that exchange rates are determined by supply and demand, we must now go on to cite some of the major factors that determine the position of these supply and demand curves. In the long run, according to the so-called purchasing power parity theory of exchange rate determination, the exchange rate between any two currencies may be expected to reflect differences in the price levels in the two countries. To see why, suppose that Germany and the United States are the only exporters or importers of automobiles

FIGURE
18.7

Effect of Rightward Shift of the Demand Curve for German Marks

Because of the rightward shift of the demand curve, the equilibrium price of a mark shifts from 45 to 50 cents.

and that automobiles are the only product they export or import. If an automobile costs $10,000 in the United States and a comparable automobile costs 20,000 marks in Germany, what must be the exchange rate between the dollar and the mark? Clearly, a mark must be worth $0.50, because otherwise the two countries' automobiles would not be competitive in the world market. If a mark were set equal to $0.60, this would mean that a German automobile would cost $12,000 (that is 20,000 times $0.60), which is more than what a U.S. automobile would cost. Thus, foreign buyers would obtain their automobiles in the United States.

On the basis of this theory, one would expect that *if the rate of inflation in Country A is higher than in Country B, Country A's currency is likely to fall in value relative to Country B's.* Suppose that costs double in the United States, but increase by only 50 percent in Germany. After this burst of inflation, an automobile costs $20,000 (that is, 2 times $10,000) in the United States and 30,000 marks (that is, 1.50 times 20,000 marks) in Germany. Thus, based on the purchasing power parity theory, the new value of the mark must be $0.67, rather than the old value of $0.50. (Why $0.67? Because this is the exchange rate that makes the new cost of an automobile in the United States, $20,000, equivalent to the new cost of an automobile in Germany, 30,000 marks.) Because the rate of inflation is higher in the United States than in Germany, the dollar falls in value relative to the mark.

While relative price levels may play an important role in the long run, other factors tend to exert more influence on exchange rates in the short run. In particular, *if one country's rate of economic growth is higher than the rest of the world's, its currency is likely to depreciate* (that is, fall in value relative to other countries' currencies). If a country's economy is booming, this tends to increase its imports. If there is a boom in the United States, Americans will tend to make more money and buy more of all goods, including foreign-made goods. If a country's imports tend to grow faster than its exports, its demand for foreign currency will tend to grow more rapidly than the amount of foreign currency that is supplied to it. Consequently, its currency is likely to depreciate.

Furthermore, if the rate of interest in Germany is higher than in the United States, banks, multinational corporations, and other investors in the United States will sell dollars and buy marks in order to invest in the high-yielding Germany securities. Also, German investors (and others) will be less likely to find U.S. securities attractive. Thus, the mark will tend to appreciate (that is, rise in value) relative to the dollar, since the demand curve for marks will shift to the right and the supply curve for marks will shift to the left. In general, *an increase in a country's interest rates leads to an appreciation of its currency, and a decrease in its interest rates leads to a depreciation of its currency.* In the short run, interest rate differentials can have a major impact on exchange rates, since huge amounts of money are moved from country to country in response to differentials in interest rates.

Tariffs and Quotas

When an industry is threatened by foreign competition, it sometimes presses for a *tariff,* a tax that the government imposes on imports. The object of a tariff is to reduce imports in order to protect domestic industry and workers from foreign competition. Obviously, if foreign firms are faced with a tariff, they will cut down on the amount they export to this country. Indeed, if the tariff is high enough (a so-called prohibitive tariff), foreign firms will find it unprofitable to export to this country at all.

For example, during the early 1950s, watches imported from Switzerland rose from 38 to 58 percent of the U.S. market. In 1954, U.S. watch manufacturers petitioned the federal government to increase tariffs on Swiss watches. They argued that the Swiss had a cost advantage because of lower wage rates and that watch manufacturing technology was important to national defense. The government agreed to increase tariffs by 50 percent on watches with 1 to 17 jewels.

Besides tariffs, other barriers to free trade are *quotas*, which are limits that many countries impose on the quantities of certain commodities that can be imported annually. In many cases, a quota insulates local industry from foreign competition even more effectively than a tariff does. Foreigners, if their costs are low enough, can surmount a tariff barrier; but if a quota exists, there is no way they can exceed the quota. The United States has imposed quotas on the imports of sugar and steel, among other commodities. In the case of sugar, imports in 1990 were limited to 1.6 million tons. In the case of steel, quotas were instituted in 1984, after U.S. steel firms experienced substantial losses in the early 1980s and turned to the government for help. By 1989, steel imports were limited to about 20 percent of the U.S. market. In early 1992, the Bush administration, citing the improved position of U.S. steel firms, allowed the steel import quotas to expire.

While economists traditionally have argued for free trade, there are circumstances in which, from society's point of view, tariffs and quotas make sense. If a particular industry is essential for national defense, it may be reasonable to protect it in this way. Also, if an industry is young (a so-called *infant industry*), it may be sensible for the government to shelter it temporarily from the rigors of international competition, thus enabling it to develop to the point where it becomes strong and viable. However, even if there is a legitimate case on such grounds for protecting a domestic industry, government subsidies may be a more straightforward means to do so than tariffs or quotas.

The Effects of a Quota: The Case of the Wilton Company's Product

To illustrate the effects of a quota, let's return to the Wilton Company, producer of the new product produced and sold only in Germany and the United States. According to the analysis presented earlier in this chapter, Germany would be expected to export 26 million units of this product to the United States per month. Suppose that the Wilton Company and other U.S. producers of the product succeed in getting the federal government to establish a quota of 3 million units per month on imports of this product from Germany. What will be the effect on the price of this product in the United States?

Since Q_D^U is the quantity demanded in the United States and Q_S^U is the quantity supplied in the United States, our imports of this product from Germany equal

$$Q_D^U - Q_S^U = (100 - 2P_U) - (5 + 2.6P_U) = 95 - 4.6P_U. \qquad (18.7)$$

CONCEPTS IN CONTEXT

Sweetening with Corn, Not Sugar*

The Archer-Daniels-Midland Company, a huge manufacturer of agricultural products, made an estimated profit in 1994 of about $290 million from its corn sweeteners, which are used as a substitute for sugar. The world price for raw sugar has been about half of the domestic price in the United States, but because of sugar quotas only a limited amount of sugar has been imported. Thus, corn sweetener, which costs about 12 cents a pound, has found a ready market in making candy and soft drinks.

The U.S. Department of Commerce has estimated that the quotas and other devices that keep relatively cheap imported sugar out of the United States cost about $3 billion a year. Consequently, critics say that Archer-Daniels's profit comes at a considerable cost to consumers. In rebuttal, it has been claimed that makers of candy and soft drinks would not pass along the savings from cheaper sweeteners to consumers.

*"It's Dwayne's World," *New York Times*, January 16, 1996, p. D1.

And since the quota says that these imports must not exceed 3 million units, it follows that

$$95 - 4.6P_U = 3,$$

which means that

$$P_U = 20.$$

Thus, the price of this product will be $20 in the United States, not $15 as it was before the quota. Clearly, this increase in price is a welcome development for the Wilton Company and other U.S. producers of the product, but not for U.S. consumers.

The Presence of Protectionism

During most of the period since World War II, the United States has pushed for reductions in tariffs, quotas, and other barriers to global trade. In 1947, the United States and 22 other countries signed the General Agreement on Tariffs and Trade (GATT), which calls for all participating parties to meet periodically to negotiate bilaterally on tariff cuts. Any tariff cut negotiated in this way will be extended to all participating countries. During the 1960s, the "Kennedy Round" negotiations took place among 40 countries in an effort to reduce taxes;

CONCEPTS IN CONTEXT

Why Bridgestone Paid $2.6 Billion for Firestone

The Bridgestone Tire Company is the biggest tire producer in Japan and the second largest tire producer in the world. During the 1970s and 1980s, its sales grew rapidly, both in Japan and in the rest of the world. Because its tires are part of the original equipment on exported Japanese cars, many of its tires enter foreign markets with little or no effort on its part. But direct exports of its tires are also important, and Bridgestone's management wanted to expand its export sales.

In 1988, Bridgestone surprised many observers by buying Firestone Rubber, a major U.S. producer. Bridgestone paid Firestone $2.6 billion, for which it received five tire plants in North America (which provided at that time about 40 percent of the tires for North American cars built by Ford and 20 percent of those built by General Motors), and other plants in Europe and South America, as well as Firestone's nontire business.

To understand this key decision, you must look carefully at two topics emphasized in this chapter—the imposition by governments of tariffs and quotas, and the movements of exchange rates. With regard to tariffs and quotas, Bridgestone's decision was influenced by actual and potential limitations by the U.S. government on U.S. imports of Japanese automobiles. These limitations led four major Japanese auto producers to start making cars in the United States, and all of them put U.S.-made tires on their U.S.-made cars. Clearly, the purchase of Firestone's plants enabled Bridgestone to elude many of the effects of these limitations.

Turning to the movement of exchange rates,

Bridgestone's decision was also influenced by its need to keep its costs competitive with those in the United States. During the early 1980s, Bridgestone's costs were no higher than its U.S. competitors' (despite its much higher transportation costs) because of the low value of the yen relative to the U.S. dollar. But in the late 1980s the value of the yen increased, so that the price of tires in the United States, when expressed in yen, fell below Bridgestone's unit costs. By buying Firestone's plants, Bridgestone could prevent increases in the value of the yen from increasing the cost of its tires to its U.S. customers.

Further, its purchase of these plants reduced very significantly Bridgestone's transportation costs in serving the U.S. market. Because the cost of shipping a tire to the United States is relatively high ($3 to $12 per tire for Bridgestone), there are obvious problems in trying to sell tires in the United States except as part of original vehicle equipment. By buying Firestone's plants, Bridgestone cut its transportation costs greatly.

Returning to the central point here, you can't understand why Bridgestone made this huge investment in Firestone unless you understand the nature and effects of import restrictions like tariffs and quotas and unless you understand the implications for firms of changes in exchange rates.*

*For further discussion, see J. Daniels and L. Radebaugh, *International Business: Environments and Operations* (5th ed.; Reading, Mass.: Addison-Wesley, 1989). Information provided by Bridgestone/Firestone, Inc. is gratefully acknowledged.

and during the 1970s over 100 countries met in Tokyo to further reduce tariffs and promote free global trade. Lastly, after 7.5 years of discussion and debate, 125 nations signed the Uruguay Round in 1994. This agreement brought the greatest reform in free world trade since GATT. Besides reducing tariffs and import duties, this agreement also set up a dispute settlement system and a trade policy review mechanism. By 1999, tariffs on industrial products averaged less than 4 percent across industrial countries.

Despite this support for free trade, protectionism sentiment still exists in most countries, including the United States. For example, in the 1980s hundreds of petitions were filed by industry and labor, appealing to the federal government for protection from imports. Strong lobbying by the auto manufacturers and unions caused many on Capitol Hill to support mandatory restrictions on the number of autos imported into the United States. This led the Japanese auto manufacturers to voluntarily limit exports to the United States at 1.68 million units per year. As with most protectionist policies, consumers were burdened with the costs. Since the Japanese manufacturers restricted their supply, they could charge a higher price per auto. This in turn allowed U.S. manufacturers to increase their prices. Some economists estimated that each saved auto worker job cost U.S. consumers about $160,000 per year.

One reason U.S. manufacturers felt so much pressure from their foreign rivals during this time was because of the strength of the U.S. dollar. As shown in Figure 18.4, the value of the dollar (relative to other major currencies) increased by over 50 percent between 1980 and 1985. Besides making U.S. goods more expensive to foreigners, which hurt our exports, this made foreign goods less expensive in the United States.

Though the dollar's strength has lessened in recent years, there is still sentiment for protectionism in certain industrial segments, despite economic evidence of a strong link between free trade and economic growth. Segments demanding this protection are generally concerned about their own performance, not the effect on the national economy or consumers. For example, in 1999 the steel industry strongly lobbied Congress to impose highly restrictive quotas on imported steel, despite the fact that U.S. steel mills shipped 102 million tons of steel in 1998 (the second highest total in over 20 years), that these mills supplied over 66 percent of the steel used in the United States, and that 11 of the 13 largest steel producers were profitable. Some economists estimate these protectionist efforts cost consumers about $60 billion per year in higher prices.

Strategic Trade Policy

Traditionally, economists have tended to argue that free trade is the best policy to promote the interests of society as a whole. Thus, they generally applauded the lowering of tariffs in the 1960s and early 1970s, and they generally looked with disfavor on the growth of protectionism during the 1980s. But some economists have begun to dispute these traditional beliefs. In their view, the U.S. government should control the access of foreign firms to our domestic markets, as well as promote the activities of our firms in foreign markets. For example, if particular high-technology industries result in large technological benefits to other domestic industries, the government may be justified in using subsidies or tariffs to protect and promote these industries. And if economies of scale mean that only two highly profitable producers can exist in the world market for a particular product, the government may be justified in using subsidies or tariffs to increase the chances that a U.S. firm will be one of the lucky pair.

According to these economists, there are strategic industries that, from the point of view of a particular country, are worth protecting in this way. However, it is very difficult to identify which industries fall into this category and to estimate how much the country would gain from such policies. Consequently, critics of such strategic trade policies worry that special-interest groups will use such policies to advance their own interests, not those of the nation as a whole. Given the vagueness of the criteria for identifying which industries should be protected, many industries could use these ideas to justify protection for themselves and their allies, regardless of whether it was merited.[6]

Airbus versus Boeing: Strategic Trade Policy in Action

To illustrate the workings of strategic trade policy, suppose that only two firms, Airbus and Boeing, are capable of producing a new 150-seat passenger aircraft. Each firm must decide whether or not to produce and market such a plane. Because Boeing has a head start, it will be able to make this decision first. Table 18.3 shows the payoff matrix for the two firms.[7] If either firm is the sole producer of the plane, it will make $120 million, but if both firms decide to produce and market such a plane, both will lose $8 million. Clearly, Boeing, which has the first move in this game, will decide to produce the plane; and Airbus, once it realizes that Boeing is committed to this course of action, will decide not to produce it.

But Boeing is a U.S. firm, while Airbus is a joint venture of French, British, German, and Spanish aerospace firms (with their governments' blessings and participation). If European governments decide to pay Airbus a subsidy of $10

---

[6]P. Krugman, *Journal of Economic Perspectives*, Fall 1987.
[7]The concept of a payoff matrix is discussed in detail from pages 447 to 451.

TABLE 18.3

Payoff Matrix: Airbus and Boeing

Possible strategies for Airbus	Possible strategies for Boeing	
	Produce the new plane	Do not produce the new plane
Produce the new plane	Airbus's profit: −$8 million Boeing's profit: −$8 million	Airbus's profit: $120 million Boeing's profit: zero
Do not produce the new plane	Airbus's profit: zero Boeing's profit: $120 million	Airbus's profit: zero Boeing's profit: zero

million if it will produce the plane, the game has quite a different outcome. Since the payoff matrix is now as shown in Table 18.4, it is clear that Airbus will produce the plane, regardless of whether Boeing commits itself to produce it. Thus, Boeing, recognizing that this will be Airbus's decision, will not find it profitable to produce it. Instead, Boeing will decide against production of the plane.

In effect, the European governments have taken the profit of $120 million away from Boeing and bestowed it on Airbus. Admittedly, they have to pay a subsidy of $10 million, but this is relatively small. Without question, this example seems to indicate that government intervention of this sort can pay off. But things are not so simple. For one thing, such government actions are likely to provoke retaliation. Thus, the U.S. government may retaliate by granting a $10 million subsidy to Boeing to produce the plane, with the result that both firms may produce it, although this is not economically desirable.

TABLE 18.4

Payoff Matrix after Subsidy to Airbus

Possible strategies for Airbus	Possible strategies for Boeing	
	Produce the new plane	Do not produce the new the new plane
Produce the new plane	Airbus's profit: $2 million Boeing's profit: −$8 million	Airbus's profit: $130 million Boeing's profit: zero
Do not produce the new plane	Airbus's profit: zero Boeing's profit: $120 million	Airbus's profit: zero Boeing's profit: zero

International Trade Disputes

Many U.S. industries are influenced in an important way by international trade disputes. For example, the semiconductor industry has been involved in a series of disputes with the Japanese. Among other things, the semiconductor firms have charged that the Japanese have *dumped* chips (that is, sold them at a lower price than in Japan, and perhaps below cost) in the United States and that the Japanese have not allowed U.S. firms to gain access to Japanese markets.

In 1974, Congress passed major legislation relating to international trade, often referred to as the 1974 Trade Act. Section 301 of this act gave the president of the United States the authority to take action to remove foreign trade barriers. In 1988, the Omnibus Trade and Competitiveness Act gave the U.S. trade representative the authority to determine whether a foreign trade practice was unfair. The trade representative, subject to presidential direction, could then choose what action to take.

These pieces of legislation have given the president considerable leeway in deciding what sorts of retaliatory action to take against other countries. The president can suspend or withdraw any trade concessions, can impose tariffs or other restrictions on imports from the countries involved, and can retaliate against goods or services other than those cited in the complaints. Section 301 can be invoked if U.S. firms file a complaint with the trade representative or if the trade representative on his or her own decides to do so.

In 1985, the semiconductor firms filed a petition with the federal government asking for the use of Section 301 against the Japanese. The trade representative expressed support for the semiconductor firms' position. The Japanese then agreed to increase their purchase of foreign-made chips and to have their government monitor export prices on semiconductor products to prevent their going below fair market value in the United States and elsewhere. The United States in turn agreed to drop the 301 case. But problems continued. The semiconductor firms have complained repeatedly that the Japanese have violated this and other agreements.[8]

International trade disputes of this sort are very hard to resolve. Despite its obvious economic, political, and military strength, the United States cannot dictate to the rest of the world. Indeed, despite its superpower status, the United States sometimes has remarkably little influence over other countries' economic policies. Moreover, as in all disputes, there are two sides of the story, and it would be naive to believe that the United States has a monopoly on righteousness.

In late 1994, Congress approved an agreement to extend GATT. This agreement, which included over 100 countries, created a World Trade Organization, which was meant to enforce the accord. Reduction in tariffs (including agri-

---

[8]See Yoffie, *International Trade and Competition*. Also, see D. Yoffie and B. Gomes-Casseres, *International Trade and Competition*, (2^d ed.; New York: McGraw-Hill, 1994).

ANALYZING MANAGERIAL DECISIONS

Is Airbus Playing by the Rules?

In March 1986, European and U.S. officials met in Geneva, Switzerland to discuss allegations by both sides of unfair competitive practices, including an allegation by the United States about Airbus subsidies. There were rumors that the Reagan administration was considering a Section 301 case against Airbus, and the governments of France, Germany, and the United Kingdom (the biggest governments involved in the Airbus program) asked for the meeting.

The U.S. government charged that "direct program subsidies by [France, Germany, and the United Kingdom] . . . are leading to trade distortions in large transport aircraft. The United States believes that continued support of this type will result in increased trade tensions in the area of civil aircraft—a sector that has generally been one of cooperation in trade."* According to the president of Boeing's commercial aircraft unit, these governments had put about $10 billion into Airbus without regard to profit.

By 1990, the conflict had intensified, as Airbus's share of the world aircraft market rose to about 30 percent, as shown below. By 2001, there was virtual parity between the two companies.

Company	Percent of passenger jet market (based on orders)	
	1988	1990
Airbus	15	34
Boeing	59	45
McDonnell Douglas	22	15
Other	4	6
	100	100

(a) Why does the U.S. government say that it is unfair for the European governments to subsidize Airbus in this way? (b) The European governments retort that U.S. firms like Boeing also receive large government subsidies, since the work they do for the Department of Defense under government contracts yields great benefits to their civilian business. Is this true? (c) If the U.S. aircraft manufacturers feel that Airbus constitutes unfair competition, why hasn't a Section 301 case been brought against Airbus?

SOLUTION (a) In the U.S. view, Airbus is selling its airplanes at well under their true cost, which the European governments refuse to divulge. (b) Yes. However, the United States points out that there was not direct U.S. government support for commercial aircraft programs, and it argues that there were "only negligible" indirect benefits to U.S. civil aircraft manufacturers from their defense work. (The latter argument is often challenged.) (c) Neither Boeing nor McDonnell Douglas filed a petition, because they feared that sanctions could disrupt the market. Many of the components of their aircraft are produced abroad, and many of their customers are in Europe. They feared that if the United States tried to get tough, the Europeans might retaliate.[†]

*U.S. press release, March 21, 1986, quoted by Yoffie, *International Trade and Competition*, p. 352.
†For further information, see J. Pierce and R. Robinson, *Cases in Strategic Management* (2d ed.; Homewood, Ill.: Irwin, 1991); Yoffie, *International Trade and Competition;* and *New York Times*, June 23, 1991.

cultural tariffs) and quotas were called for under the agreement. Also, all countries agreed to protect intellectual property. However, there was no agreement on limiting government subsidies to civil aircraft producers, and shipping, steel, and telecommunications were largely exempted.

Making Direct Investments Abroad

To survive and prosper, many firms must produce and sell in a number of countries. One of the most important questions faced by a variety of industrial managers is whether—and if so, where—to establish sales outlets, manufacturing facilities, and R and D laboratories abroad. In other words, what sorts of direct investments should be made in other countries?

Many firms are multinational; that is, they already have facilities in other countries (recall the case of Bridgestone, described on page 698). In some industries like aluminum and oil, firms have established overseas facilities to control foreign sources of raw materials. Frequently, firms have invested overseas in an attempt to defend their competitive position. In many cases, firms have set up foreign branches to exploit a technological lead. That is, after exporting a new product to a foreign market, a firm may decide to establish a plant overseas to supply that market. Once a foreign market is large enough to accommodate a plant of minimum efficient size, this decision does not conflict with economies of scale. Moreover, transport costs often can be reduced in this way; and in some cases, the only way a firm can introduce its innovation into a foreign market is by establishing a production facility there.

What factors are important in deciding where to locate a new plant? Firms seem to be particularly interested in the size of the local market, both because a large local market tends to reduce freight and delivery costs and because it means lower tariffs (since much of the plant's output will be sold within the country where the plant is located). Another important factor is the country's investment and political climate—whether the country allows foreign ownership, whether its government is reasonably stable, and whether profits can be taken out of the country. Still another major factor is the availability of skilled labor and relevant technology or know-how in the country.

Establishing a Plant Abroad: Time-Cost Trade-offs

If a firm decides to establish a plant overseas, there often is a time-cost trade-off that is somewhat similar to that which pertains to industrial innovation (recall Chapter 8). That is, if the firm decides to design and construct this plant in a relatively short period of time, the costs often will be higher than if more

FIGURE
18.8

Time–Cost Trade-off in Design and Construction of Overseas Plant

The optimal duration of the project is Y months, since this is the value of t where the present value of net profit is highest.

time is taken to do the work. As additional engineers are brought on to the project to speed the design work, diminishing returns can generally be expected. Attempts to reduce project time by speeding equipment procurement can also be expected to increase project costs. The available evidence indicates that the relationship between C, the present value of the costs of establishing the plant, and t, the number of months it takes to establish the plant, is generally like that shown in Figure 18.8.[9]

To determine how quickly to do the design and construction work, the firm must estimate, for each value of t, the present value of gross profit if the duration of the project is t months. If the results are as shown in Figure 18.8, the optimal duration of the project is Y months, since this is the value of t where the present value of net profit is highest. To see that this is true, note that the present value of *net profit* at each value of t is the vertical distance between the present value of *gross profit* (given by the gross profit curve in Figure 18.8)

[9]E. Mansfield, A. Romeo, M. Schwartz, D. Teece, S. Wagner, and P. Brach, *Technology Transfer, Productivity, and Economic Policy* (New York: Norton, 1982).

and the present value of the *costs* (given by the cost curve in Figure 18.8). Clearly, this vertical distance is greatest when the duration of the project is Y months.

Channels of International Technology Transfer

In today's global economy, international technology transfer is of vital importance in many industries. Firms want both to make profitable use of their technology in other countries and to obtain technology at minimum cost from foreign firms, universities, and other sources. Thus, international technology transfer is a two-way street. To understand the nature of international technology transfer, it is necessary to describe the principal ways in which technology can be transferred across national borders.

EXPORT OF GOODS The mere existence or availability of a good in a foreign country may result in the transfer of technology, since the good may provide information to the importers of the good. Thus, the export of advanced computers to a particular country may result in technology transfer. In addition, the importing country may gain technology because the exporters of the good, to promote their sales, may help the importing country's personnel to use the good efficiently—and this training is a form of technology transfer. Also, if the country that imports the good is able to reverse-engineer it (that is, take it apart to discover how it is constructed), there is the opportunity for further technology transfer.

DIRECT INVESTMENT IN WHOLLY OWNED SUBSIDIARIES Another way of transferring technology is through direct investment in overseas subsidiaries. For example, firms like IBM and Hewlett-Packard have established global networks of facilities. They train foreign operatives and managers, communicate information and capabilities to foreign engineers and technicians, help the foreign users of their products to use them more effectively, and help foreign suppliers to upgrade their technology.

LICENSING AGREEMENTS Firms with significant new products or processes often engage in licensing agreements with foreigners covering patents, trademarks, franchises, technical assistance, and so on. Licensing agreements often call for the licensee to pay a certain percentage of its sales to the licensor, plus, in some cases, a flat fee for technical help. Some licensing agreements also require the licensee to buy certain inputs from the licensor.

JOINT VENTURES Technology can also be transferred to other countries through the formation of a joint venture, an operation owned jointly by the

ANALYZING MANAGERIAL DECISIONS

Seagram Makes Vodka in Ukraine

In 1992, the Seagram Company, a leading liquor producer, established a plant to produce vodka in Ukraine. Attracted by low labor costs, a competent labor force, and a large market for vodka in Russia and Ukraine, Edgar Bronfman, CEO of Seagram, felt that this overseas investment was promising. Moreover, the Ukrainian government, in its original foreign investment law of 1992, offered a variety of tax breaks, and stipulated that the conditions would not change for five years.

(a) After more than a year of negotiations, the Ukrainian government refused to give Seagram permission to produce for export markets. In its view, the export of spirits is a state monopoly. What effect did this have on the prospective profitability of Seagram's investment? (b) In December 1993, the Ukrainian government suddenly increased the excise tax on Seagram's vodka so that its price rose by about 150 percent. The aim was to increase government revenue, but the result has been an upsurge in the amount of liquor smuggled into the country. Why did smuggling increase? What was the effect of this tax increase on the quantity sold of Seagram's Ukrainian vodka? (c) In 1994, the price level rose by about 100 percent per month in Ukraine. What effect did this have on the efficiency of Seagram's operations there? (d) For-

eign business executives in Ukraine charge that widespread corruption exists. According to their statements, unless one contributes to the "minister's pension fund," government officials will not give permits needed to keep a business functioning. What difficulties does this produce for firms operating in Ukraine?

SOLUTION a) The prospective profitability of Seagram's investment was reduced considerably because Seagram had intended to export from Ukraine into Russia, which is a very large market for vodka. (b) Smuggling increased because the price of vodka rose sharply and it became more profitable to smuggle it into Ukraine. Because it raised the price of Seagram's vodka, the tax increase reduced the quantity sold of Seagram's Ukrainian vodka. (c) Very rapid inflation makes it very difficult for firms to minimize costs and maximize profit because no one knows what the prices of various inputs and outputs will be, even a month or two ahead. (d) According to Walter Kish, Seagram's manager in Ukraine (and like Mr. Bronfman, of Ukrainian descent), "It is now impossible to do business in Ukraine legally and make a profit."*

*For further discussion, see New York Times, January 27, 1994.

firm with the technology and a firm or agency of the host country. The joint venture generally produces a good or service based on the technology in question. Joint venture agreements are often made by smaller firms that need capital to complement their technology.[10]

---

[10]There are other ways that technology is transferred. For example, scientists and engineers exchange information at international meetings, and one country's scientists and engineers read the publications of other countries' scientists and engineers. Also, emigration can sometimes be an important channel of international technology transfer.

Choice among Transfer Channels

Which of these means of transferring their technology do firms generally prefer? According to the available evidence, direct investment in wholly owned subsidiaries is generally preferred if firms can obtain the necessary resources and if they believe that licensing will give away valuable know-how to foreign producers who are likely to become competitors in the future. Of course, the longer the estimated life of the innovation, the less inclined a firm is to enter into a licensing agreement. Also, firms prefer direct investment over licensing when the technology is sophisticated and foreigners lack the know-how to assimilate it or when a firm is concerned about protecting quality standards. For example, if a firm licenses technology to a less-than-capable foreign firm, and the foreign firm produces defective merchandise, it may reflect adversely on the firm whose technology was used (or abused).

On the other hand, licensing is often preferred when the foreign market is too small to warrant direct investment, when the firm with the technology lacks the resources required for direct investment, or when advantages accrue through cross-licensing. Also, in some countries, direct investment has been discouraged by the government. (Particularly in the developing countries, there has sometimes been considerable hostility toward multinational firms. Some governments feel that their sovereignty is threatened by the great power of the multinational firm over their national economies.) Turning to joint ventures, they have advantages with regard to forging good relations with host countries, but they have disadvantages and problems in operation, personnel matters, and division of profits.

To the host country's government, the choice among these alternative means of obtaining technology looks quite different than it does to the firm with the technology. To the host government, direct investment creates many problems because the wholly owned subsidiary of a foreign firm is partly outside the government's control. The direct investor is only partly responsive to the host country's economic policies. The investor can draw on funds and resources outside the host country. Moreover, the investor has a global strategy, which may be at odds with the optimal operation of the subsidiary from the viewpoint of the host government. Joint ventures may overcome some of these disadvantages of direct investment, but they have the disadvantage that the host country must invest more capital. Licensing arrangements eliminate many of the problems of control, but they have the disadvantage that the firm with the technology has little commitment or incentive to help the licensee with managerial and technical problems.

The choice of the channel of technology transfer may in fact depend on the age of the technology being transferred. Consider the case of petrochemicals. When various important petrochemicals were relatively new, direct investment was the dominant form of technology transfer, but as they became mature, li-

CONSULTANT'S CORNER

Reorganizing a Firm's Global R and D Network*

Boehringer Ingelheim was the first German pharmaceutical firm to establish subsidiaries in the United States and Japan. The U.S. subsidiary (in Ridgefield, Connecticut) began to carry out research and development in about 1975; the Japanese subsidiary began to do so in the early 1980s. Decision making regarding R and D was completely decentralized. The head of research and development of each subsidiary could develop products for his or her own geographical markets. Thus, the U.S. subsidiary could develop a new product for the U.S. market, and the Japanese subsidiary could develop a new product for the Japanese market. This seemed to be the best way for Boehringer Ingelheim to expand its market share in the U.S. and Japanese markets.

In the late 1980s, however, the firm's top managers became convinced that this was not the optimal way to manage its global network of R and D laboratories. Too much money was being spent on developing products that could not be transferred from one market to another. Given the very high costs of developing a new drug, there were obvious advantages in being able to spread these costs over a number of markets, not just one.

If you were a consultant to Boehringer Ingelheim, what changes would you recommend in the organization and administration of its global R and D activities?

*This case is based on material in P. Roussel, K. Saad, and T. Erickson, *Third Generation R and D* (Boston: Harvard Business School Press, 1991).

censing became dominant. One reason for this sort of pattern lies in the changes over time in the relative bargaining positions of the innovating firm and the country wanting the technology. When the technology is quite new, it is closely held, and countries wanting the technology are under pressure to accept the firm's conditions, which often are a wholly owned subsidiary. But as time goes on, the technology becomes more widely known, and the host country can take advantage of competition among technologically capable firms to obtain joint ventures or sometimes licenses. Eventually, the technology may become available in plants that can be acquired by the host country on a turnkey basis from independent engineering firms.

Strategic Alliances

In recent years, more and more firms have been forming strategic alliances with firms in other countries (as well as firms in their own countries). In the auto industry, major companies have cooperated in joint development and supply of complete vehicles, engines, and transmissions. For example, during the 1980s,

FIGURE
18.9

Global Network of Auto Producers

Practically all the major firms in the auto industry are involved in a global cooperative network.

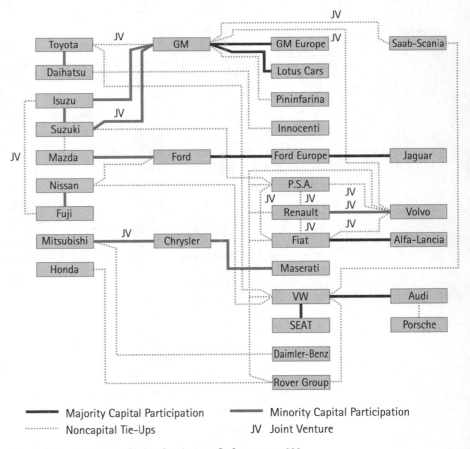

Source: Clark and Fujimoto, *Product Development Performance,* p. 326.

Renault, a French firm, jointly produced transmissions with Volkswagen (Germany), gasoline engines with Volvo (Sweden) and Peugeot (France), and diesel engines with Fiat (Italy). Practically all the major firms in the auto industry are involved in this global cooperative network. Figure 18.9 shows the various links between the leading firms. As you can see, U.S. firms like General Motors have ties with a variety of Japanese and European auto producers.[11]

[11]K. Clark and T. Fujimoto, *Product Development Performance* (Boston: Harvard Business School Press, 1991).

Many strategic alliances involve the sharing of technological information. In the semiconductor industry, U.S. firms often trade design information regarding their products for information concerning Japanese firms' production techniques. (There is evidence that Japanese firms tend to devote a larger proportion of their industrial R and D to processes than do U.S. firms.) For example, in the alliance between VLSI Technology (United States) and Hitachi (Japan), VLSI Technology traded design technology for Hitachi's process technology in integrated circuits.[12]

Strategic alliances of this sort can be of considerable value, since they enable firms to gain access to technology that is complementary to their own technology and help them to enter new markets or defend existing market positions. But they also can be hazardous. If a firm provides valuable technology to others and gets little in return, such an alliance can be very costly. Unfortunately, some firms have had this happen. It is important that a firm's managers be clear as to exactly what benefits an alliance of this sort will bring—and how they can be reasonably sure that these benefits will be forthcoming.

Summary

1. If countries specialize in producing goods and services in which they have a comparative advantage, and trade with one another, each country can improve its standard of living. Whether a particular country has a comparative advantage in the production of a given product depends on the country's resource endowments and technological expertise. Managers must constantly be on their guard against the loss of comparative advantage.

2. The exchange rate is the number of units of one currency that exchanges for a unit of another currency. To a large extent, exchange rates currently are set by supply and demand. The value of a country's currency (relative to other currencies) tends to fall if its inflation rate or economic growth rate is high or if its interest rates are comparatively low.

3. A tariff is a tax imposed by the government on imports, the aim being to protect domestic industry and workers from foreign competition. Quotas are another major barrier to free trade. While tariffs and quotas can sometimes be justified (for example, on the basis of national security considerations), economists traditionally have felt that a tariff or quota tends to cost the general public more than the protected industry (and its workers and suppliers) gains.

4. In recent years, some economists have begun to argue that countries should adopt strategic trade policies. In their view, the U.S. government should control the access of foreign firms to our domestic markets, as well as pro-

---

[12]D. Methé, *Technological Competition in Global Industries* (New York: Quorum Books, 1991).

mote the activities of our firms in foreign markets. If particular high-technology industries result in large technological benefits to other domestic industries, these economists believe that the government may be justified in using subsidies, tariffs, or quotas to protect and promote these industries.

5. The 1974 Trade Act and the 1988 Omnibus Trade and Competitiveness Act gave the president considerable leeway in deciding what retaliatory action to take against foreign trade practices that are regarded as unfair. The president can suspend or withdraw any trade concessions, impose tariffs or other restrictions on imports from the countries involved, and retaliate against goods and services other than those cited in the complaints.

6. Many firms must decide whether—and if so, where—to establish facilities abroad. Whether a firm locates a plant in a particular country depends on the size of the market in that country, the country's investment climate, and the availability of skilled labor there. If a firm decides to build a plant overseas, there often is a time-cost trade-off.

7. International technology transfer is of vital importance to many firms. There are four principal ways by which technology can be transferred across national borders: export of goods, direct investment in wholly owned foreign subsidiaries, licensing agreements, and joint ventures. Direct investment is often preferred by firms if they can obtain the necessary resources and if they believe that other methods of transfer will give away valuable know-how to foreign producers who are likely to become competitors in the future.

8. In recent years, more and more firms have been forming strategic alliances with firms in other countries (as well as firms in their own countries). Many strategic alliances involve the sharing of technological information. It is important that a firm's managers be clear as to exactly what benefits an alliance of this sort will bring—and how they can be confident that these benefits will be obtained.

Problems

1. Donald R. Keough, president of the Coca-Cola Company, has said, "Our single and relentless focus has been internationalizing this business."[13] In 1991, Coke had pushed the international contribution to its profits to 80 percent from 50 percent in 1985. By the year 2000, the United States may account for no more than 10 percent of the firm's profits.

   a. In the United States, per capita consumption of soft drinks made by Coca-Cola equals 292 eight-ounce servings per year, whereas it equals

---

[13]"For Coke, World Is Its Oyster," *New York Times*, November 21, 1991.

MANAGERIAL ECONOMICS IN CONTEXT

NAFTA: A Historic Agreement

For decades, there was talk about a free trade agreement for North America. All tariffs and quotas would be eliminated on trade among Canada, Mexico, and the United States. The result would be the world's largest free market, with about 400 million consumers and a total output of $6 trillion (about 25 percent larger than the European Community). During the 1980s, this talk became much more serious. Indeed, in 1988, the Canada–U.S. Free Trade Agreement was signed by Prime Minister Brian Mulroney and President Ronald Reagan.*

According to some estimates, this agreement was supposed to create an additional 750,000 jobs in the United States and 150,000 in Canada. On both sides of the U.S.–Canadian border, there were misgivings about the agreement. On the Canadian side, people were concerned that they would lose their cultural identity and be overwhelmed by the economic and political juggernaut to their south. On the U.S. side, some people were worried that they would lose production and jobs to Canada. Nonetheless, on January 1, 1989, the historic agreement went into operation. All bilateral tariffs were to be removed in ten equal, annual steps, which began on that date (except for those cases where the relevant industries agreed to a faster phaseout of the tariffs).

In late November 1990, Presidents George Bush and Carlos Salinas de Gortari met to launch trade talks between Mexico and the United States. Mexico wanted to weaken U.S. quotas on textiles and steel and to open U.S. markets to its fruits and vegetables. The United States wanted Mexico to allow foreign investment in its oil industry. (Such investment was prohibited by the Mexican constitution.) As these talks continued, alarm bells went off among U.S. labor leaders, who feared the export of jobs to Mexico. Also, environmentalists warned that Mexico could degrade clean-air and toxic-waste standards across the continent. Industries that might be hurt by free trade with Mexico also were concerned. For example, Bill Becker, chairman of the Florida Citrus Commission, warned that the removal of the U.S. tariff on orange juice would "wipe out the Florida industry. We can't compete with our environmental constraints, labor constraints, and the other regulations."[†]

Actually, many of the barriers to trade between Mexico and the United States had already been torn down. Take the important case of automobiles. In 1991, Mexico produced over 1 million vehicles. With a North American Free Trade Agreement, many auto executives think that Mexican output could hit 3 million by the year 2000. But even if such an agreement had not been signed, many auto executives think that Mexican auto output could have hit 2 million.

Many of these cars are made by Ford, Chrysler, and General Motors. For example, at Ramos Arizpe, General Motors makes the Buick Century and the Chevrolet Cavalier for export and for local sale. At Hermosillo, Ford makes Tracers and Escorts for export to California and elsewhere. At Toluca, Chrysler's plant exports Shadows and Spirits. But Mexico is not the home of only U.S. auto producers; France's Renault, Japan's Nissan, and Germany's Volkswagen, among others, have plants there.

*For background, see Daniels and Radebaugh, *International Business.*
[†]*Business Week,* May 27, 1991, p. 33.

Why have auto producers moved into Mexico? One reason is low wages. An experienced welder at Chrysler's Toluca plant has made about $1.75 per hour, much less than the $16 an hour earned by experienced welders at Chrysler's Michigan plant. However, this is only part of the story. Surprising as it has been to many observers, the quality of the cars produced is high. Within two years after its start-up in 1987, Ford's Hermosillo plant was winning quality awards. Ramos Arizpe, only five years old, is General Motors' top plant of its kind, outscoring other plants in Oklahoma City and Quebec.

According to auto executives, Mexico's young workers learn new industrial methods more quickly than their older counterparts in the United States. For example, the labor force at Ramos Arizpe quickly learned Japanese-style manufacturing techniques. Highly trained workers in small teams can substitute for one another and effectively monitor quality. In contrast, many U.S. plants still have rigid work rules. At Hermosillo, Ford provides trainees with a seven-week program where they study statistics and economics.

While U.S. auto companies are enthusiastic about their experiences in Mexico, the United Auto Workers (UAW) has been protesting loudly. Indeed, the UAW tried to torpedo the North American Free Trade Agreement. According to Owen Bieber, president of the UAW, the agreement means "you can kiss the jobs and livelihoods of thousands of Americans goodbye."[†]

On August 13, 1992, the United States, Canada, and Mexico announced a free trade agreement, which subsequently was ratified by lawmakers in the three countries. According to William Ethier of the University of Pennsylvania, the most important effect of this action was on Mexico. It is "a way for the current [Mexican] president to set in concrete the dramatic economic reforms that

have been made in Mexico. [He] . . . wants to make sure that there is no backsliding in the future and an international agreement is one way of doing that."[§]

In late 1994, the value (in dollars) of the Mexican peso (Mexico's currency) dropped dramatically, from about 29 cents to about 20 cents. To help restore investor confidence in Mexico, President Clinton expanded U.S. financial support for Mexico to $20 billion. This support included loan guarantees backed by claims on the proceeds from Mexican oil exports. Support of this sort was not dictated by the free trade agreement. In the words of President Clinton's Council of Economic Advisers, "The United States is providing support to Mexico because we have a stake in the stability of a country with whom we share a 2,000-mile border and important commercial ties. There is no commitment under NAFTA to do so."[||]

(a) Does it appear that the United States has lost its comparative advantage in the production of automobiles? Is the evidence clear-cut?

(b) On February 12, 1992, the U.S. Customs Service ruled that Honda Motor Company had to pay tariffs of about $180 per car on the Civics it shipped from its plant in Alliston, Ontario, to the United States because, in its view, too little of these cars were produced in North America to allow them to enter the United States duty-free. Some leading Canadians said Canada should abrogate its free trade agreements with the United States. Why were they so concerned?

(c) Have Ford, General Motors, and Chrysler transferred technology to Mexico? If so, through

[†]*Business Week*, March 16, 1992, p. 100.
[§]"An Economist's View of NAFTA," *Penn Arts and Sciences*, Winter 1994, p. 5.
[||]*Economic Report of the President* (Washington, D.C.: Government Printing Office, 1995), p. 224.

what channels have they done so? Why have they chosen these channels?

(d) Florida has produced 95 percent of the winter tomato crop in the United States. According to Paul DiMare, whose family oversees a big Florida farm, field hands are paid $3 a day in Mexico whereas U.S. farm workers make $50 a day (plus Social Security and other benefits). As a result of NAFTA, Mexican producers have shipped tomatoes into the United States for sale at $3 to $5 for a 25-pound box, compared with the $8 to $10 it costs DiMare to grow and ship the same amount.# Should this be allowed?

(e) A study published by the University of California at Los Angeles in late 1996 concluded that the near-collapse of the Mexican economy in 1995 had a much bigger effect on the number of trade-related jobs in the United States than did NAFTA.**

Philadelphia Inquirer, March 16, 1996, p. D1.
** *New York Times*, December 19, 1996, p. D1.

Did it increase or decrease the number of jobs among U.S. exporters?

(f) Environmentalists cite the sludge in the Rio Grande river and the smog over Mexico City. (The lower Rio Grande is the most polluted river in the United States.) How can one tell whether existing levels of pollution in these cases are excessive? If they are excessive, what can the government of Mexico and the United States do to reduce pollution?

Ford's Mexico plant

48 in France and 112 in Japan. Does this help to account for the fact that Coke's unit sales are growing at an annual rate of 8 to 10 percent overseas, as compared with 3.5 percent in the United States? If so, how?

b. Mr. Keough has said, "When I think of Indonesia—a country on the Equator with 180 million people, a median age of 18, and a Moslem ban on alcohol, I feel I know what heaven looks like." Why was he so enthusiastic about Indonesia? (Note: Indonesia's per capita consumption of soft drinks made by Coca-Cola equals 4 eight-ounce servings per year.)

c. In some countries, like Britain and Taiwan, Coke has used joint ventures with bottlers to enter foreign markets; in others, like France, it has established wholly owned bottling operations. What factors influence Coke's decision in this regard?

d. Coke's principal rival, Pepsi Cola, obtains less than 20 percent of its profits from outside the United States. Whereas Coke has about 40 percent of the domestic soft drink market as compared with Pepsi's figure of about a third, it outsells Pepsi 4 to 1 outside the United States. According to some analysts, this helps to explain why Coke makes 3 or 4 times as much profit per gallon sold in many overseas markets as in the United States. Why do they think that this is the explanation?

2. In 1991, local cement makers in Florida filed a complaint against Venezuelan firms, charging that they were dumping cement in Florida. According to U.S. law, dumping occurs when foreigners set their price below "fair market value," which is defined as either the price they establish at home or their cost of production. More than half of Florida's cement is supplied by local firms, such as a subsidiary of Texas-based Southdown Inc. The rest comes from overseas. The price of cement is roughly $60 in both Florida and Venezuela.[14]

   a. Why is it profitable for Venezuelan firms to enter the Florida cement market? (Hint: Ocean transportation is cheap relative to railroads or trucks.)

   b. If transportation and storage add about $10 to $15 per ton to the cost of sending Venezuelan cement to Florida, does it appear that the Venezuelan firms are selling cement at a lower price in Florida than in their home markets?

   c. According to Kenneth Clarkson of the University of Miami and Stephen Morrell of Barry University, both consultants for the Venezuelan firms, Florida consumers would pay over $600 million more for cement in the period 1991 to 1996 if foreign firms were no longer permitted to ship into the Florida market. If this is true, should foreign firms be allowed to continue selling cement at $60 per ton in Florida?

3. Suppose that Japan and the United States are the only producers and consumers of a particular sort of flashbulb. The demand and supply curves for this flashbulb in the United States are as follows:

Price (dollars)	Quantity demanded (millions)	Quantity supplied (millions)
5	10	4
10	8	6
15	6	8
20	4	10

[14]"Cement Shoes for Venezuela," *New York Times*, September 25, 1991.

The demand and supply curves for this flashbulb in Japan are:

Price (expressed in dollar equivalent of Japanese price)	Quantity demanded (millions)	Quantity supplied (millions)
5	5	2
10	4	6
15	3	10
20	2	14

a. Suppose that there is free trade in these flashbulbs. What will be the equilibrium price?

b. Which country will export flashbulbs to the other country?

c. How large will be the exports?

d. Suppose that the United States imposes a tariff of $10 per flashbulb. What will happen to exports and imports?

4. According to a (hypothetical) government report, the United States can produce 3 computers or 3,000 cases of wine with 1 unit of resources, while Germany can produce 1 computer or 5,000 cases of wine with 1 unit of resources.

a. If this report is accurate, will specialization increase world output of computers and wine?

b. If the maximum number of computers that can be produced per year in the United States is 1,000, draw the U.S. production possibilities curve on the graph below:

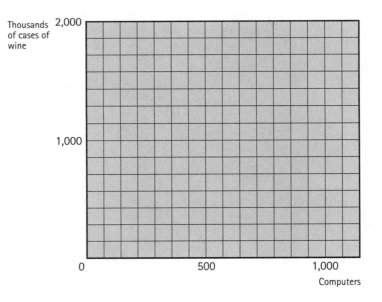

   c. In the diagram above, draw the trading possibilities curve if the United States produces only computers and trades them for German wine (at a price for each computer that is equivalent to 2,000 cases of German wine). Does this curve lie above the production possibilities curve?

   d. If the maximum number of cases of wine that can be produced per year in Germany is 2 million, draw the German production possibilities curve below.

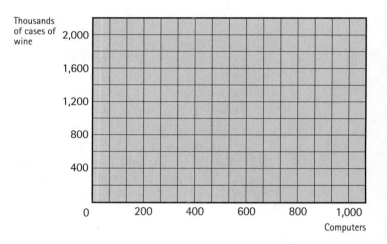

   e. In the diagram above, draw the trading possibilities curve if Germany produces only wine and trades it for U.S. computers (at a price for each computer that is equivalent to 2,000 cases of German wine). Does this curve lie above the production possibilities curve?

5. If labor is the only input, a study indicates that two countries, Honduras and Panama, can produce the following amounts of two commodities, bananas and coffee, with a day of labor.

	Bananas (lbs.)	Coffee (lbs.)
Honduras	20	6
Panama	10	8

   a. In order for both countries to gain from trade with one another, between what limits must the ratio of the prices lie?

   b. Suppose that there is free trade and the price of bananas increases relative to the price of coffee. Is this change in relative prices to the advantage of Honduras or Panama?

6. The supply curve for Japanese cameras to the U.S. market is shown on the next page for two periods of time.

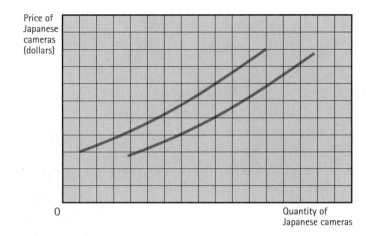

a. One curve is before a depreciation of the dollar relative to the yen; one curve is after it. Which curve is which? Why?
b. What will be the effect of the depreciation on the dollar price of Japanese cameras?
c. What will be the effect on U.S. expenditures (in dollars) for Japanese cameras if the demand for them in the United States is price elastic?
d. What will be the effect on U.S. expenditures (in dollars) for Japanese cameras if the demand for them in the United States is price inelastic?

7. The demand curve in Italy for U.S. computers is as shown below.

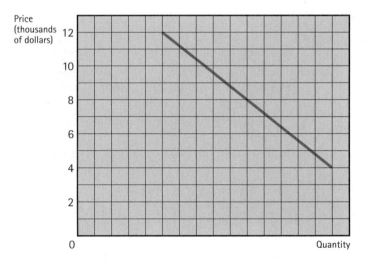

a. If the Italian lira depreciates relative to the U.S. dollar, will the quantity of computers sold in Italy at a dollar price of $8,000 rise or fall?
b. Under these circumstances, will the demand curve rise or fall?

8. The demand and supply curves for the Swiss franc are as follows:

Price of franc (dollars)	Millions of francs demanded	Millions of francs supplied
0.80	600	800
0.70	640	740
0.60	680	680
0.50	720	620
0.40	760	560

a. What is the equilibrium rate of exchange for the dollar?
b. What is the equilibrium rate of exchange for the Swiss franc?
c. How many dollars will be bought in the market?
d. How many Swiss francs will be bought in the market?

9. The demand curve for British pounds is as follows:

Price of British pound (dollars)	Millions of pounds demanded
2.00	400
2.10	380
2.20	360
2.30	340
2.40	320
2.50	300

a. Suppose that the British government tries to maintain the exchange rate at $2.40 and that the quantity of pounds supplied at this exchange rate is 360 million pounds. Will the British government have to buy or sell pounds? If so, how many?
b. If the British government has to buy pounds with dollars, where will it get the dollars?

10. The Liverous Company is the maker of a new product made and bought only in Japan and the United States. In the United States, the demand curve for this product is such that

$$Q_D^U = 20 - 2P_U,$$

and the supply curve is such that

$$Q_S^U = 5 + 3P_U,$$

where P_U is the price of the product (in dollars) in the United States, Q_D^U is the quantity demanded (in thousands of units) per week in the United States, and Q_S^U is the quantity supplied (in thousands of units) per week in the United States. In Japan, the demand curve for this product is such that

$$Q_D^J = 45.5 - 3P_J,$$

and the supply curve is such that

$$Q_S^J = -5 + 2P_J,$$

where P_J is the price of the product (in yen) in Japan, Q_D^J is the quantity demanded (in thousands of units) per week in Japan, and Q_S^J is the quantity supplied (in thousands of units) per week in Japan. Assume that a U.S. dollar exchanges for 130 Japanese yen.

   a. What will be the price of this product in Japan? In the United States?

   b. How much of this product will each country supply?

   c. Will the United States be an importer or an exporter of this product?

11. During the 1980s, Black and Decker (B&D), the manufacturer of power tools, encountered a number of problems. The recession of the early 1980s hurt B&D's sales, as did the subsequent strength of the U.S. dollar. Its rival, Japan's Mikita Electric Works, reduced its costs and was able to nearly equal B&D's 20 percent share of the world market. In part, B&D's problems were of its own making, according to some observers, for reasons given below.

By 1982, B&D operated 25 manufacturing plants in 13 countries on six continents. It had three operating groups, as well as the headquarters in Maryland. Each group had its own staff. In addition, B&D companies, such as B&D of West Germany, operated autonomously in each of the more than 50 countries where B&D sells and services products. The company's philosophy had been to let each country adapt products and product lines to fit the unique characteristics of each market. The Italian firm produced power tools for Italians, the British subsidiary made power tools for the British, and so on.

As a result, countries did not communicate well with each other. Successful products in one country often took years to be introduced in others. In order to meet the tailor-made specifications of different markets, design centers were not being used efficiently. At one point, eight design centers around the world had produced 260 different motors, even though it was determined that the firm needed fewer than ten different models.[15]

If you were asked by B&D's top managers to recommend changes to improve this situation, what advice would you give?

---

[15]J. Daniels and L. Radebaugh, *International Business* (5th ed.; Reading, Mass.: Addison-Wesley, 1989), pp. 449–50.

Discounting and Present Values

When a manager chooses between two courses of action, A and B, he or she is choosing between the cash flows resulting if A is chosen and the cash flows when B is chosen. These cash flows generally occur over a number of periods. For example, if A is chosen, the firm may experience an outflow of $1 million this year and an inflow of $300,000 during each of the next five years. On the other hand, if B is chosen, the firm may experience an outflow of $1 million this year and an inflow of $250,000 for each of the next six years. How can a manager compare these two alternatives?

To answer this question, it is convenient to begin by pointing out one of the basic propositions in managerial economics: *A dollar received today is worth more than a dollar received a year from today.* Why? Because one can always invest money that is available now and obtain interest on it. If the interest rate is 6 percent, a dollar received now is equivalent to $1.06 received a year hence. Why? Because if you invest the dollar now, you'll get $1.06 in a year. Similarly, *a dollar received now is equivalent to $(1.06)^2$ dollars two years hence.* Why? Because if you invest the dollar now, you'll get 1.06 dollars in a year, and if you reinvest this amount for another year at 6 percent, you'll get $(1.06)^2$ dollars.

More generally, suppose that you can invest at a compound rate of i percent per year. What is the *present value*—that is, the value *today*—of a dollar received n years hence? Based on the foregoing argument, its present value is

$$\frac{1}{(1 + i)^n}.$$

(A.1)

Thus, if the interest rate is 0.10 and if $n = 4$ (which means that the dollar is received in four years), the present value of a dollar equals

$$\frac{1}{(1 + 0.10)^4} = \frac{1}{1.4641} = \$0.683.$$

In other words, the present value of the dollar is 68.3 cents.

To see that this answer is correct, let's see what would happen if you invested 68.3 cents today. As shown in Table A.1, this investment would be worth 75.1 cents after one year, 82.6 cents after two years, 90.9 cents after three years, and 1 dollar after four years. Thus, 68.3 cents is the present value of a dollar received four years hence, because if you invest 68.3 cents today, you will have exactly 1 dollar in four years.

Appendix Table 1 shows the value of $1/(1 + i)^n$, for various values of i and n. For example, according to this table, the present value of a dollar received ten years hence is 46.3 cents if the interest rate is 0.08. To see this, note that the figure in Appendix Table 1 corresponding to $n = 10$ and $i = 0.08$ is 0.46319.

Using this table, you can readily determine the present value of any amount received n years hence, not just 1 dollar. If you receive R_n dollars n years hence, the present value of this amount is

$$\frac{R_n}{(1 + i)^n}.$$

(A.2)

TABLE
A.1

Value of 68.3 Cents Invested at 10 Percent Interest

Number of years hence	Return received	Value of investment
1	68.301(0.10) = 6.830¢	68.301 + 6.830 = 75.13¢
2	75.131(0.10) = 7.513¢	75.131 + 7.513 = 82.64¢
3	82.643(0.10) = 8.264¢	82.645 + 8.265 = 90.91¢
4	90.907(0.10) = 9.091¢	90.909 + 9.091 = 100.00¢

Thus, to determine the present value of R_n, all that you have to do is multiply R_n by $1/(1 + i)^n$. Since Appendix Table 1 provides us with the value of $1/(1 + i)^n$, this is a simple calculation.

To illustrate, suppose you will receive $10,000 ten years hence and the interest rate is 0.12. According to equation (A.2), the present value of this amount equals $10,000[1/(1 + i)^n]$. Since Appendix Table 1 shows that $1/(1 + i)^n = 0.32197$ when $n = 10$ and $i = 0.12$, the present value of this amount is $10,000(0.32197) = $3,219.70$.

Present Value of a Series of Payments

As pointed out at the beginning of this appendix, managers generally must consider situations in which cash flows occur at more than a single time. For example, investment in a new machine tool is likely to result in a cash outflow now and a series of cash inflows in the future. To determine the present value of such an investment, it is convenient to begin by considering the simple case in which you receive $1 per year for n years, the interest rate being i. More specifically, the n receipts of $1 occur one year from now, two years from now, . . . , and n years from now. The present value of this stream of $1 receipts is

$$\frac{1}{1 + i} + \frac{1}{(1 + i)^2} + \cdots + \frac{1}{(1 + i)^n} = \sum_{t=1}^{n} \frac{1}{(1 + i)^t}. \tag{A.3}$$

For example, the present value of $1 to be received at the end of each of the next five years, if the interest rate is 0.10, is

$$\sum_{t=1}^{5} \frac{1}{(1 + 0.10)^t} = \frac{1}{(1 + 0.10)} + \frac{1}{(1 + 0.10)^2} + \frac{1}{(1 + 0.10)^3}.$$

$$+ \frac{1}{(1 + 0.10)^4} + \frac{1}{(1 + 0.10)^5} = 0.90909 + 0.82645$$

$$+ 0.75131 + 0.68301 + 0.62092 = $3.79. \tag{A.4}$$

To obtain each of the terms on the right in equation (A.4), we use Appendix Table 1. For example, the final term on the right is 0.62092, which is the present value of a dollar received five years hence (if the interest rate is 0.10), according to Appendix Table 1.

Table A.2 shows that $3.79 is indeed the present value of $1 to be received at the end of each of the next five years, if the interest rate is 0.10. As you can see, if you invest $3.79 at 10 percent interest, you will be able to withdraw $1 at the end of each year, with nothing left over or lacking. Since analysts fre-

Demonstration that $3.79 (Invested at 10 Percent Interest) Provides Exactly $1 at the End of Each of the Next Five Years

Number of years hence	Return received	Amount withdrawn	Net value of investment
1	$3.790(0.10) = $.3790	$1.00	$3.790 + 0.3790 − 1.00 = $3.169
2	3.169(0.10) = .3169	$1.00	3.169 + 0.3169 − 1.00 = 2.486
3	2.486(0.10) = .2486	$1.00	2.486 + 0.2486 − 1.00 = 1.735
4	1.735(0.10) = .1735	$1.00	1.735 + 0.1735 − 1.00 = .909
5	0.909(0.10) = .0909	$1.00	0.909 + 0.0909 − 1.00 = 0

quently must calculate the present value of a dollar received at the end of each of the next n years, the expression in equation (A.3),

$$\sum_{t=1}^{n} 1/(1 + i)^t,$$

has been tabled; the results are shown in Appendix Table 2. For example, if you receive $1 at the end of each of the next ten years, and if the interest rate is 0.06, the present value is $7.36. To see this, note that the figure in Appendix Table 2 corresponding to $n = 10$ and $i = 0.06$ is 7.3601.

More generally, if you receive R dollars at the end of each of the next n years, and if the interest rate is i, the present value is

$$\sum_{t=1}^{n} \frac{R}{(1 + i)^t} = R \sum_{t=1}^{n} \frac{1}{(1 + i)^t}. \tag{A.5}$$

Thus, the present value of $5,000 to be received at the end of each of the next five years, if the interest rate is 0.08, is $5,000(3.9927) = $19,963.5, since Appendix Table 2 shows that the value of $\sum_{t=1}^{n} 1/(1 + i)^t = 3.9927$, when $n = 5$ and $i = 0.08$.

Finally, we must consider the case in which there is a series of unequal, not equal, payments. Suppose that a payment is received at the end of each of the next n years, that the amount received at the end of the tth year is R_t, and that the interest rate is i. The present value of this series of unequal payments is

$$\sum_{t=1}^{n} \frac{R_t}{(1 + i)^t}. \tag{A.6}$$

TABLE
A.3

Present Value of Stream of Unequal Payments, Where $i = 0.10$ and $n = 3$

Number of years hence	(1) Amount received R_t	(2) $\dfrac{1}{(1 + 0.10)^t}$	(1) × (2) Present value of amount received
1	$3,000	0.90909	$2,727.27
2	2,000	0.82645	1,652.89
3	1,000	0.75131	751.31
			Total $5,131.48

Appendix Table 1 can be used to help carry out this computation. For example, suppose that $i = 0.10$, that $n = 3$, and that the amount received at the end of the first year is $3,000, the amount received at the end of the second year is $2,000, and the amount received at the end of the third year is $1,000. Table A.3 shows how to calculate the present value of this series of unequal payments, which in this case equals $5,131.48.

The Use of Periods Other Than a Year

Thus far, we have assumed that the interest or return from an invested amount is paid annually. In other words, we have assumed that a dollar invested at the beginning of a year earns interest of i percent at the end of that year. In many situations, this is not correct. Instead, interest, dividends, or other returns from an investment may be received semiannually, quarterly, monthly, or even daily. Because you earn a return in the next period on the return received in this period, the results differ from those given in previous sections of this appendix.

If interest is received *semiannually*, the present value of a dollar received n years hence is

$$\frac{1}{(1 + i/2)^{2n}}, \tag{A.7}$$

where i is the annual interest rate. To understand this expression, note that the interest rate for each semiannual period is $i/2$, and that there are $2n$ semiannual periods in n years. Bearing this in mind, this expression can be derived in the same way as expression (A.1).

If interest is received *quarterly*, the present value of a dollar received n years hence is

$$\frac{1}{(1 + i/4)^{4n}},$$

(A.8)

where i once again is the annual interest rate. To see why this is true, note that the interest rate for each quarterly period is $i/4$, and that there are $4n$ quarterly periods in n years. Bearing this in mind, this expression can be derived in the same way as expression (A.1).

More generally, suppose that interest is received c times per year. Under these circumstances, the present value of a dollar received n years hence is

$$\frac{1}{(1 + i/c)^{cn}}.$$

(A.9)

Appendix Table 1 can be used to determine present values under these circumstances. To evaluate expression (A.9), let the interest rate be i/c, and let the number of years be cn; using these values, Appendix Table 1 gives the correct answer. Thus, the present value of 1 dollar to be received 3 years hence, where the interest rate is 8 percent paid quarterly, can be obtained by finding in the table the present value of 1 dollar to be received 12 years hence where the interest rate is 2 percent. Specifically, the answer is 78.849 cents.

Determining the Internal Rate of Return

Previous sections of this appendix have been concerned entirely with determining the present value of a stream of cash flows. While this is of great importance in managerial economics, it also is important to calculate the internal rate of return—the interest rate that equates the present value of the cash inflows with the present value of the cash outflows. Put differently, the internal rate of return is the interest rate that makes the present value of a stream of cash flows equal zero. In other words, we want to find i where

$$R_0 + \frac{R_1}{1 + i} + \frac{R_2}{(1 + i)^2} + \cdots + \frac{R_n}{(1 + i)^n} = 0,$$

or

$$\sum_{t=0}^{n} \frac{R_t}{(1 + i)^t} = 0.$$

(A.10)

To solve equation (A.10) for i, it often is necessary to use trial and error (if you do not have access to a computer or calculator). The first step is to make a rough estimate of the value of i that will satisfy equation (A.10). The second step is to adjust this estimate. If the present value based on the original estimated rate of interest is *positive*, *increase* the value of i. If the present value based on the original estimated rate of return is *negative*, *reduce* the value of i. The third step is to continue to adjust this estimate until you find the value of i that will satisfy equation (A.10).

As an illustration, consider the following stream of cash flows: $R_0 = -\$5,980$, $R_1 = \$3,000$, $R_2 = \$2,000$, and $R_3 = \$2,000$. As a first step, we estimate (roughly) that the internal rate of return is in the neighborhood of 8 percent. As Table A.4 shows, the present value of this stream of cash flows, given that the interest rate is 8 percent, is $100.12, which is positive. Thus, a higher value of i must be tried. We choose 9 percent. As Table A.4 shows, the present value of this stream of cash flows, given that the interest rate is 9 percent, is virtually zero. Thus, the internal rate of return is 9 percent.

If the cash flows (in years other than year 0) are all equal, there is a simpler way to determine the internal rate of return. Under these circumstances, equation (A.10) can be written:

$$R_0 + \sum_{t=1}^{n} \frac{R}{(1 + i)^t} = 0,$$

where R is the cash flow in years 1 to n. Thus,

$$\sum_{t=1}^{n} \frac{1}{(1 + i)^t} = \frac{-R_0}{R}. \tag{A.11}$$

TABLE
A.4

Determination of the Internal Rate of Return

Year t	Cash flow R_t	$i = 8$ percent		$i = 9$ percent	
		$\dfrac{1}{(1 + i)^t}$	Present value	$\dfrac{1}{(1 + i)^t}$	Present value
0	−$5,980	1.00000	−$5,980	1.00000	−$5,980
1	$3,000	0.92593	$2,777.78	0.91743	$2,752.29
2	2,000	0.85734	1,714.68	0.84168	1,683.36
3	2,000	0.79383	1,587.66	0.77228	1,544.37
Total			100.12		0.02

Since we are given the value of $-R_0/R$, we can find the value of i in Appendix Table 2 where the entry in the nth row equals $-R_0/R$. This value of i is the internal rate of return.

To illustrate, suppose that a machine tool costs $10,000, and that it will result in a cash inflow of $2,500 for each of the next six years. Since $R_0 = -\$10,000$ and $R = \$2,500$, the value of $-R_0/R$ is 4. Looking in the row of Appendix Table 2 where $n = 6$, we look for the interest rate where the entry in the table is 4. Since the entry is 3.9976 when $i = 13$ percent, the internal rate of return is about 13 percent.

Finally, it is worth pointing out that if an investment yields an infinite series of equal cash flows, the present value of this series is

$$\sum_{t=1}^{\infty} \frac{R}{(1 + i)^t} = R \sum_{t=1}^{\infty} \frac{1}{(1 + i)^t} = \frac{R}{i}. \tag{A.12}$$

For example, if an investment yields a perpetual annual return of $4,000 per year, and if the interest rate is 8 percent, the present value of this perpetual stream of returns equals $4,000/0.08 = \$50,000$.

APPENDIX

B

The Normal, *t*, and *F* Distributions

The formula for the probability distribution of a variable with a normal distribution is

$$f(x) = \frac{1}{(2\pi)^{0.5}\sigma} e^{-1/2[(x-\mu)/\sigma]^2}, \tag{B.1}$$

where μ is the variable's mean, σ is its standard deviation, e is approximately 2.718 and is the base of the natural logarithms, and π is approximately 3.1416. This is often called the **normal curve**.

Although normal curves vary in shape because of differences in mean and standard deviation, all normal curves have the following characteristics in common:

1. *All normal curves are symmetrical about the mean.* In other words, the height of the normal curve at a value that is a certain amount *below* the mean

A-9

Comparison between Any Normal Curve (When Distance from Mean Is Measured in Units of σ) and the Standard Normal Curve

is equal to the height of the normal curve at a value that is the same amount *above* the mean. Besides being symmetrical, the normal curve is *bell shaped,* as in Figure B.1. (Note that a normal variable can assume values ranging from $-\infty$ to $+\infty$.)

2. Regardless of its mean or standard deviation, the probability that the value of a normal variable will lie within *one* standard deviation of its mean is 68.3 percent, the probability that it will lie within *two* standard deviations of its mean is 95.4 percent, and the probability that it will lie within *three* stan-

dard deviations of its mean is 99.7 percent. Panel B of Figure B.1 shows the distance from the mean, μ, in units of the standard deviation, σ. Clearly, almost all the area under a normal curve lies within three standard deviations of the mean.

3. The location of a normal curve along the horizontal axis is determined entirely by its mean, μ. For example, if the mean of a normal curve equals four, it is centered at four; if its mean equals 400, it is centered at 400. The amount of spread in a normal curve is determined *entirely* by its standard deviation, σ. If σ increases, the curve's spread widens; if σ decreases, the curve's spread narrows.

If one expresses any normal variable as a deviation from its mean, and measures these deviations in units of its standard deviation, the resulting variable, called a **standard normal variable**, has the probability distribution shown in panel A of Figure B.1. This probability distribution is called the **standard normal curve**.

If any normal variable is expressed in standard units (that is, if it is expressed as a deviation from its mean, and measured in units of its standard deviation), its probability distribution is given by the standard normal curve. Thus, if a firm's sales are normally distributed and if we express them in standard units, their probability distribution is given by the standard normal curve. Put more formally, if X is a normally distributed variable, then

$$Z = \frac{X - \mu}{\sigma} \tag{B.2}$$

has the standard normal distribution regardless of the values of μ and σ.

Appendix Table 3 shows the area under the standard normal curve from zero to the positive number (z) given in the left-hand column (and top) of the table. In other words, this table provides the probability that a standard normal variable lies between zero and z. Thus, the probability that a standard normal variable lies between zero and 1.10 equals 0.3643. Because of the symmetry of the normal curve, this is also the probability that it lies between zero and $-z$. Thus, the probability that a standard normal variable lies between zero and -1.10 equals 0.3643.

The t Distribution   The t distribution is really a family of distributions, each of which corresponds to a particular number of degrees of freedom. From a mathematical point of view, the number of degrees of freedom is simply a parameter in the formula for the t distribution. The shape of the t distribution is rather like that of the standard normal distribution. Figure B.2 compares the t distribution (with 2 degrees of freedom) with the standard normal distribution. As you can see, both are symmetrical, bell shaped, and have a mean of zero. The t distribution is somewhat flatter at the mean and somewhat higher in the

FIGURE
B.2

Comparison between Normal and *t* Distributions

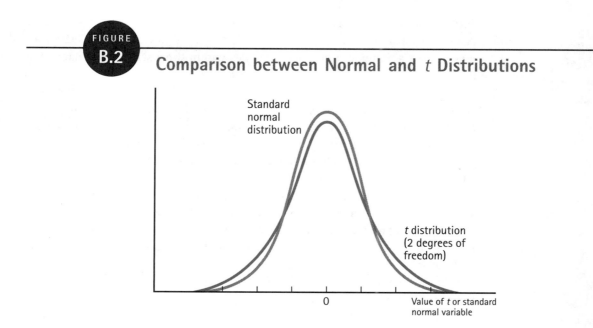

tails than the standard normal distribution. As the number of degrees of freedom becomes larger and larger, the *t* distribution tends to become exactly the
same as the standard normal distribution. The *t* distribution is often called Student's *t* distribution because the statistician W. S. Gosset, who first derived this
distribution, published his findings under the pseudonym Student.

To find the probability that the value of *t* exceeds a certain number, we can
use Appendix Table 4. As you can see, each row of this table corresponds to a
particular number of degrees of freedom. The numbers in each row are the numbers that are exceeded with the indicated probability by a *t* variable. For example, the first row indicates that if a *t* variable has 1 degree of freedom, there
is a 0.40 probability that its value will exceed 0.325, a 0.25 probability that its
value will exceed 1.000, a 0.05 probability that its value will exceed 6.314, a
0.01 probability that its value will exceed 31.821, and so on. Since the *t* distribution is symmetrical, it follows that if a *t* variable has 1 degree of freedom,
there is a 0.40 probability that its value will lie below -0.325, a 0.25 probability that its value will lie below -1.000, and so on.

The *F* Distribution   The *F* distribution, like the *t* distribution, is in reality a
family of probability distributions, each corresponding to certain numbers of
degrees of freedom. But unlike the *t* distribution, the *F* distribution has two
numbers of degrees of freedom, not one. Figure B.3 shows the *F* distribution
with 2 and 9 degrees of freedom. As you can see, the *F* distribution is skewed
to the right. However, as both numbers of degrees of freedom become very
large, the *F* distribution tends toward normality. Once again, it should be em-

FIGURE
B.3

The *F* Probability Distribution, with 2 and 9 Degrees of Freedom

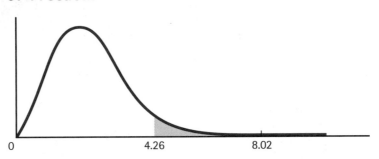

phasized that any *F* random variable has *two* numbers of degrees of freedom. Be careful to keep these numbers of degrees of freedom in the *correct order,* because an *F* distribution with v_1 and v_2 degrees of freedom is not the same as an *F* distribution with v_2 and v_1 degrees of freedom.

Tables are available that show the values of *F* that are exceeded with certain probabilities, such as 0.05 and 0.01. Appendix Table 5 shows, for various numbers of degrees of freedom, the value of *F* that is exceeded with probability equal to 0.05. For example, if the numbers of degrees of freedom are 2 and 9, the value of *F* that is exceeded with probability equal to 0.05 is 4.26. Similarly, Appendix Table 6 shows, for various numbers of degrees of freedom, the value of *F* that is exceeded with probability equal to 0.01. For example, if the numbers of degrees of freedom are 2 and 9, the value of *F* exceeded with probability equal to 0.01 is 8.02. (In Appendix Tables 5 and 6, the first number of degrees of freedom is labeled "Degrees of freedom for numerator," and the second number is labeled "Degrees of freedom for denominator.")

Brief Answers to Odd-Numbered End-of-Chapter Questions and Problems

Chapter 1

1. **a.** Yes. **b.** Yes. Yes.

3. They tend to exacerbate it, since the executive's pay is not so directly related to his or her effectiveness in raising the firm's profits.

5.
Number of years in the future	Profit (millions of dollars)	$\dfrac{1}{(1 + i)^t}$	Present value
1	8	0.90909	7.27272
2	10	0.82645	8.26450
3	12	0.75131	9.01572
4	14	0.68301	9.56214
5	15	0.62092	9.31380
6	16	0.56447	9.03152
7	17	0.51316	8.72372

Number of years in the future	Profit (millions of dollars)	$\dfrac{1}{(1 + i)^t}$	Present value
(cont'd)			
8	15	0.46651	6.99765
9	13	0.42410	5.51330
10	10	0.38554	3.85540
			Total 77.55056

Thus, the answer is $77.55056 million.

7. a. He will receive 80(50)($5) = $20,000, from which he must pay $3,000 for the umbrellas and 3($3,000) = $9,000 for rent. Thus, his accounting profit equals $20,000 − $3,000 − $9,000, or $8,000.

   b. Since he could earn $4,000 doing construction work, his economic profit is $8,000 − $4,000 = $4,000. (For simplicity, we ignore the fact that he could have earned interest on the money he invested in this business during the summer.)

9. No. No. The first group emphasized the demand side while the second group emphasized the supply side.

11. a. If the price were $65, the weekly operating profit would be $80,000, so it would take $8 million/$80,000 = 100 weeks for the operating profits to cover the $8 million investment. If the price were $75, the weekly operating profit would be $165,000, so it would take $8 million/$165,000 = 48.5 weeks for the operating profits to cover the $8 million investment. But note that it would take longer for the investors to get any return on their investment.

   b. Given that about two-thirds of Broadway shows have not broken even, investors in such shows obviously assume considerable risk.

   c. They do not take into account the likelihood that *Showboat* will play outside Broadway. Also, there may be profits from cast albums and other spin-offs from the show.

   d. Yes.

Chapter 2

1. a. Since the cost per patient-day (*Y*) = *C/X*, the desired relationship is

$$Y = \frac{4,700,000}{X} + 0.00013X.$$

   b. To find the value of *X* that minimizes the value of *Y*, we set the derivative of *Y* with respect to *X* equal to zero:

$$\frac{dY}{dX} = -\frac{4,700,000}{X^2} + 0.00013 = 0.$$

Thus, $X = \left(\dfrac{4,700,000}{0.00013}\right)^{0.5}$ or approximately 190,141.6476 patient-days.

   c. Since $d^2Y/dX^2 = 2(4,700,000)/X^3$, d^2Y/dX^2 must be positive (since X is positive). Thus, Y must be a minimum, not a maximum, at the point where $dY/dX = 0$.

3. a. $\$5,000. - \$3,000.$

   b. 7 units per day.

   c. No, because profit is higher at 9 units per day than at 7 units per day.

5. a. Since marginal cost equals $4 + 16Q$, it is 164 when $Q = 10$.

   b. $4 + 16(12) = 196.$

   c. $4 + 16(20) = 324.$

7. a. 6

   b. $24X$

   c. $48X^2$

   d. $8/X^3$

9. a. 2

   b. $12X^2$

   c. $0.8Z^{0.2}\,X^{-0.2} = 0.8\dfrac{Y}{X}$

   d. $-3Z/(4 + X)^2$

11. a. $\partial C/\partial X_1 = -3 + 4X_1 + X_2 = 0$

        $\partial C/\partial X_2 = -4 + 6X_2 + X_1 = 0.$

    Solving these two equations simultaneously,

    $X_1 = 14/23$ and $X_2 = 13/23.$

   b. The answer will not change.

13. a. The Lagrangian function is $L_{TC} = 7X_1^2 + 9X_2^2 - 1.5X_1X_2 + \lambda(10 - X_1 - X_2)$. Thus,

    $\partial L_{TC}/\partial X_1 = 14X_1 - 1.5X_2 - \lambda = 0$

    $\partial L_{TC}/\partial X_2 = 18X_2 - 1.5X_1 - \lambda = 0$

    $\partial L_{TC}/\partial \lambda = 10 - X_1 - X_2 = 0$

    From the first two of these equations, it follows that

    $X_1 = (195/155)X_2,$

    which, together with the third equation, implies that $X_1 = 195/35$ and $X_2 = 155/35.$

   b. Yes.

   c. If we substitute 195/35 for X_1, and 155/35 for X_2 in either of the first two equations, we find that $\lambda = 71.36$, which is the marginal cost of a rug at the cost-minimizing combination of types that total ten rugs per day.

Chapter 3

1. a. If $Q = 20$, $P = 2,000 - 50(20) = 1,000$. Thus, price would have to equal $\$1,000.$

  b. Since $500 = 2,000 - 50Q$, $Q = 1,500/50 = 30$. Thus, it will sell 30 per month.

  c. Because $Q = (2,000 - P)/50 = 40 - 0.02P$, $dQ/dP = -0.02$. Thus,

$$\left(\frac{P}{Q}\right)\left(\frac{\partial Q}{\partial P}\right) = -0.02\frac{500}{30} = -0.33.$$

  d. If $-0.02 \dfrac{P}{(2,000 - P)/50} = -1,$

$$-0.02\frac{50P}{2,000 - P} = -1,$$

$$P = 2,000 - P$$

$$= 2,000/2 = 1,000.$$

  Thus, if price equals \$1,000, the demand is of unitary elasticity.

3. a. $\dfrac{\partial Q}{\partial P}\left(\dfrac{P}{Q}\right) = \dfrac{-3(10)}{500 - 3(10) + 2(20) + 0.1(6,000)}$

$$= \frac{-30}{500 - 30 + 40 + 600} = \frac{-30}{1,110}.$$

  b. $\dfrac{\partial Q}{\partial I}\left(\dfrac{I}{Q}\right) = \dfrac{0.1(6,000)}{1,110} = \dfrac{600}{1,110}.$

  c. $\partial\dfrac{Q}{\partial P_r}\left(\dfrac{P_r}{Q}\right) = \dfrac{2(20)}{1,110} = \dfrac{40}{1,110}.$

  d. Population is assumed to be essentially constant (or to have no significant effect on Q, other than via whatever effect it has on per capita disposable income).

5. Yes.

7. a. Because there are lots of very close substitutes for a particular brand, but not for cigarettes as a whole. It appears that the elasticity was less than -2.

  b. No. More will be said about estimating demand functions in Chapter 5.

9. No. The fact that the elasticity of demand with respect to advertising is relatively low (0.003) does not necessarily mean that an additional dollar spent on advertising would not be profitable, or that the last dollar spent was not profitable.

11. a. -3.1.

  b. Decreases.

  c. 2.3.

  d. 0.1.

  e. The quantity demanded will increase by 10 percent. (Note that Q in this problem is defined as quantity demanded *per capita*.)

13. a. Price should be set equal to

$$MC\frac{1}{1 + 1/\eta} = 18\frac{1}{1 - 1/3} = \$27.$$

  b. \$18.

Chapter 4

1. a. His or her indifference curves are as follows:

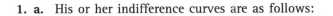

b. No. Indifference curves seldom are straight lines.

3.

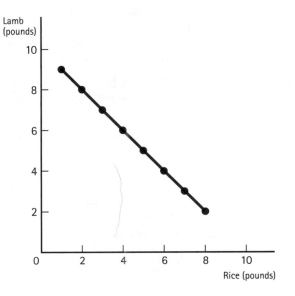

5. His budget line is as follows:

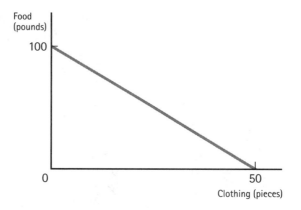

7. Maria will maximize utility at point *A*, where she purchases 15 units of both chips and salsa. Note that her indifference curves are 90-degree angles.

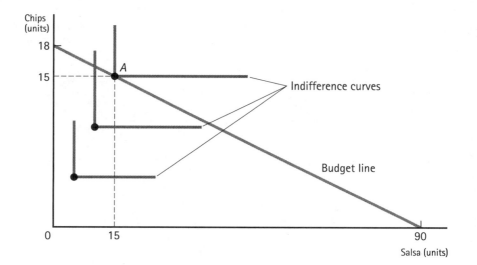

9. Since her marginal rate of substitution of opera tickets for movie tickets equals 5, and since the ratio of the price of an opera ticket to the price of a movie ticket is 10, it is impossible for her to set the marginal rate of substitution equal to the price ratio. She can increase satisfaction by substituting movie tickets for opera tickets because she is willing to give up only 5 movie tickets to get an extra opera ticket, but she has to give up 10 movie tickets to get an extra opera ticket. Thus, she will spend the entire $300 on movie tickets; she will buy 50 of them.

11. a. 150 miles   **b.** 300 miles   **c.** Yes. −0.5.   **d.** $3 billion.

Chapter 5

1. a. The evidence appears to be very strong that increases in the firm's advertising expenditure do have a positive effect on the quantity demanded of the firm's product.

b. $Q = -104 + 3.2(5,000) + 1.5(20) + 1.6(1,000) - 2.1P$
$= 17,526 - 2.1P.$

Thus,

$P = \dfrac{17,526 - Q}{2.1} = 8,346 - 0.476Q.$

c. From the answer to part b,

$Q = 17,526 - 2.1P.$

Thus, if $P = 500$,

$Q = 17,526 - 2.1(500) = 16,476.$

d. Since R^2 equals 0.89, the regression equation seems to fit the data quite well. However, we have no way of knowing (from the information given here) whether the error terms are serially correlated or a nonlinear equation fits significantly better.

3. a. Let profit equal Y and sales equal X. Plotting Y against X, we get the following:

$\Sigma X = 30.0$; $\Sigma Y = 0.94$; $\Sigma X^2 = 248.72$; $\Sigma XY = 8.307$; $n = 7$;
$\Sigma Y^2 = 0.3030.$

$b = \dfrac{7(8.307) - (30)(0.94)}{7(248.72) - 30^2} = \dfrac{58.149 - 28.200}{1,741.04 - 900} = \dfrac{29.949}{841.04} = 0.0356.$

$a = 0.134 - (0.0356)(4.286) = 0.134 - .153 = -0.019.$

The regression line is $\hat{Y} = -0.019 + 0.0356X.$

    b. $-0.019 + 0.0356(2) = -0.019 + 0.071 = 0.052$. Thus, the answer is about 0.05 billion dollars.

    c. No. Prices and costs will be different in 2001 than in 1980.

5. a. 40.833.

    b. -1.025.

    c. 0.006667.

    d. 0.916.

    e. 1.361.

    f. Less than 0.001.

    g. Less than 0.001.

    h. 0.244.

    i. The average relationship is $C1 = 40.8 - 1.02\ C2 + 0.00667\ C3$. This relationship seems to fit the data quite well, R^2 being 0.916. There is a very small probability that the estimated effect of C2 (price) is due to chance, but a much higher probability (0.244) that the effect of C3 (disposable income) could be due to chance.

7. a. Let General Electric's profits be Y and gross domestic product be X. If we plot Y against X, we get the following graph:

To calculate a and b, we can compute the following:

X	Y	X²	Y²	XY
688	355	473,344	126,025	244,240
753	339	567,009	114,921	255,267
796	361	633,616	130,321	287,356
868	357	753,424	127,449	309,876
936	278	876,096	77,284	260,208
982	363	964,324	131,769	356,466
1,063	510	1,129,969	260,100	542,130

	X	Y	X²	Y²	XY
(cont'd)					
	1,171	573	1,371,241	328,329	670,983
	1,306	661	1,705,636	436,921	863,266
	1,407	705	1,979,649	497,025	991,935
	1,529	688	2,337,841	473,344	1,051,952
	1,706	931	2,910,436	866,761	1,588,286
Sum	13,205	6,121	15,702,585	3,570,249	7,421,965
Mean	1,100.42	510.08			

The results are

$$b = \frac{12(7,421,965) - (13,205)(6,121)}{12(15,702,585) - 13,205^2}$$

$$= \frac{89,063,580 - 80,827,805}{188,431,020 - 174,372,025}$$

$$= \frac{8,235,775}{14,058,995} = 0.586$$

and

$$a = 510.08 - (0.586)(1,100.42) = 510.08 - 644.85 = -134.77.$$

Thus, the slope equals 0.586, and the intercept equals -134.77 millions of dollars.

b. On the average a \$1 increase in the GDP seems to be associated with a \$0.000586 increase in General Electric's profits (recalling that GDP is measured in billions of dollars, while General Electric's profits are measured in millions of dollars).

c. The forecast equals $-134.77 + 0.586(2,000) = -134.77 + 1,172 = 1,037.23$. That is, it equals 1,037.23 million dollars.

d. $r^2 = 0.90$.

e. No. No. A nonlinear relationship might be as good or better.

f. If nothing else is available, this model may be serviceable, but it is so crude that it is difficult to believe that the analyst could not improve upon it by taking other independent variables into account.

9. a. Taking antilogs,

$$Q = 102P^{-0.148}Z^{0.258}$$

$$\partial Q/\partial P = -0.148(102P^{-1.148}Z^{0.258}) = -0.148 \ Q/P.$$

Since the price elasticity of demand equals $(\partial Q/\partial P)(P/Q)$, it follows that the price elasticity of demand equals -0.148.

b. $\partial Q/\partial Z = 0.258(102P^{-0.148}Z^{-0.742}) = 0.258Q/Z$.

Since the cross elasticity of demand equals $(\partial Q/\partial Z)(Z/Q)$, it follows that the cross elasticity of demand equals 0.258.

c. The regression seems to provide a good fit. The fact that $\bar{R}^2$ equals 0.98 means that 98 percent of the variation in log Q can be explained by the regression (see the chapter appendix). See Figure 5.6.

11. a. No.

b. The market supply curve for wine.

Chapter 6

1. a. Yes. Room occupancy in August tends to be about 57 percent greater than in January.

   b. There are more tourists in the summer than in the winter. Because of the recession, there may have been fewer tourists, and hence the seasonal variation may have been less pronounced during the recession than before it.

   c. It might be of use in scheduling labor inputs and in ordering supplies. Certainly, the manager would want to take proper account of this seasonal variation in his or her hiring and purchasing decisions.

3. a. Because the seasonal index shows by what percent sales for a particular month tend to be above or below normal.

   b. Deseasonalized sales are as follows:

January	2.5/0.97 = $2.58 million
February	2.4/0.96 = $2.50 million
March	2.7/0.97 = $2.78 million
April	2.9/0.98 = $2.96 million
May	3.0/0.99 = $3.03 million
June	3.1/1.00 = $3.10 million
July	3.2/1.01 = $3.17 million
August	3.1/1.03 = $3.01 million
September	3.2/1.03 = $3.11 million
October	3.1/1.03 = $3.01 million
November	3.0/1.02 = $2.94 million
December	2.9/1.01 = $2.87 million

   c. Because they want to see how sales are changing, when the seasonal factor is deleted.

5. a. Yes. Yes.

   b. Yes. Yes.

7. a. $S_t = -5,744 + 2.9143t$.

   b. The forecast would have been $-5,744 + 2.9143(1991) = 58.4$ billion dollars, so the forecasting error would have been about 2 percent.

   c. The forecast would have been $-5,744 + 2.9143(1992) = 61.3$ billion dollars, so the forecasting error would have been about 17 percent.

9. a. Let $t' = 0$ when $t = 1963$. Let y be General Electric's sales.

t'	y	t'^2	y^2	$t'y$
−13	2.2	169	4.84	−28.6
−12	2.6	144	6.76	−31.2
−11	3.0	121	9.00	−33.0
−10	3.5	100	12.25	−35.0
−9	3.3	81	10.89	−29.7
−8	3.5	64	12.25	−28.0

	t'	y	t'^2	y^2	$t'y$
(cont'd)					
	-7	4.1	49	16.81	-28.7
	-6	4.3	36	18.49	-25.8
	-5	4.2	25	17.64	-21.0
	-4	4.5	16	20.25	-18.0
	-3	4.2	9	17.64	-12.6
	-2	4.5	4	20.25	-9.0
	-1	4.8	1	23.04	-4.8
	0	4.9	0	24.01	0.0
	1	4.9	1	24.01	4.9
	2	6.2	4	38.44	12.4
	3	7.2	9	51.84	21.6
	4	7.7	16	59.29	30.8
	5	8.4	25	70.56	42.0
	6	8.4	36	70.56	50.4
	7	8.8	49	77.44	61.6
	8	9.6	64	92.16	76.8
	9	10.5	81	110.25	94.5
	10	11.9	100	141.61	119.0
	11	13.9	121	193.21	152.9
	12	14.1	144	198.81	169.2
	13	15.7	169	246.49	204.1
Sum	0	180.9	1,638	1,588.79	734.8
Mean	0	6.7			

$$b = \frac{734.8 - (180.9)(0)}{1,638 - (0)(0)} = \frac{734.8}{1,638} = 0.449.$$

$a = 6.7 - (0.449)(0) = 6.7.$

Thus, the trend is $6.7 + 0.449t'$.

b. The graph is as follows:

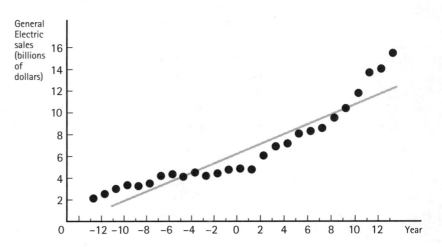

    c. It appears from the graph that the trend may be curvilinear, and that an exponential or quadratic trend might do better.

    d. The forecast would be $6.7 + 0.449(31) = 20.619$ billion dollars, which was only about 30 percent higher than actual sales in 1976. In fact, GE's sales were about \$60 billion in 1994, which indicates how poor linear extrapolations of this sort can be, particularly when one is using them to forecast many years (18 years in this case) into the future.

Chapter Appendix

1. a. Let S_0 be the smoothed value for 1989, S_1 be the smoothed value for 1990, and so on.

$S_0 = 2.$
$S_1 = (1/4)(4) + (3/4)(2) = 2.50.$
$S_2 = (1/4)(8) + (3/4)(2.50) = 3.88.$
$S_3 = (1/4)(12) + (3/4)(3.88) = 5.91.$
$S_4 = (1/4)(20) + (3/4)(5.91) = 9.43.$
$S_5 = (1/4)(28) + (3/4)(9.43) = 14.07.$
$S_6 = (1/4)(38) + (3/4)(14.07) = 9.50 + 10.55 = 20.05.$
$S_7 = (1/4)(50) + (3/4)(20.05) = 12.50 + 15.04 = 27.54.$
$S_8 = (1/4)(70) + (3/4)(27.54) = 17.50 + 20.66 = 38.16.$
$S_9 = (1/4)(90) + (3/4)(38.16) = 22.50 + 28.62 = 51.12.$

b. $S_0 = 2.$
$S_1 = (1/2)(4) + (1/2)(2) = 3.00.$
$S_2 = (1/2)(8) + (1/2)(3.00) = 5.50.$
$S_3 = (1/2)(12) + (1/2)(5.50) = 8.75.$
$S_4 = (1/2)(20) + (1/2)(8.75) = 14.38.$
$S_5 = (1/2)(28) + (1/2)(14.38) = 21.19.$
$S_6 = (1/2)(38) + (1/2)(21.19) = 29.60.$
$S_7 = (1/2)(50) + (1/2)(29.60) = 39.80.$
$S_8 = (1/2)(70) + (1/2)(39.80) = 54.90.$
$S_9 = (1/2)(90) + (1/2)(54.90) = 72.45.$

c. $S_0 = 2.$
$S_1 = (3/4)(4) + (1/4)(2) = 3.50.$
$S_2 = (3/4)(8) + (1/4)(3.50) = 6.88.$
$S_3 = (3/4)(12) + (1/4)(6.88) = 10.72.$
$S_4 = (3/4)(20) + (1/4)(10.72) = 17.68.$
$S_5 = (3/4)(28) + (1/4)(17.68) = 25.42.$
$S_6 = (3/4)(38) + (1/4)(25.42) = 28.50 + 6.36 = 34.86.$
$S_7 = (3/4)(50) + (1/4)(34.86) = 37.50 + 8.72 = 46.22.$
$S_8 = (3/4)(70) + (1/4)(46.22) = 52.50 + 11.56 = 64.06.$
$S_9 = (3/4)(90) + (1/4)(64.06) = 67.50 + 16.02 = 83.52.$

Chapter 7

1. a. To see whether 400 hours of skilled labor and 100 hours of unskilled labor are the optimal input combination, recall from equation (7.11) that to minimize cost, the Elwyn Company should pick an input combination where

$$\frac{MP_S}{P_S} = \frac{MP_U}{P_U},$$

where MP_S is the marginal product of skilled labor, MP_U is the marginal product of unskilled labor, P_S is the price of skilled labor, and P_U is the price of unskilled labor. Since $P_S = 10$, $P_U = 5$, and

$$MP_S = \frac{\partial Q}{\partial S} = 300 - 0.4S$$

$$MP_U = \frac{\partial Q}{\partial U} = 200 - 0.6U,$$

it follows that the Elwyn Company should pick an input combination where

$$\frac{300 - 0.4S}{10} = \frac{200 - 0.6U}{5},$$

or

$1,500 - 2S = 2,000 - 6U$

$S = -250 + 3U.$

Thus, 400 hours of skilled labor and 100 hours of unskilled labor are not the optimal input combination, because, if $S = 400$ and $U = 100$, this equation does not hold.

b. If a total of $5,000 is spent on skilled and unskilled labor,

$10S + 5U = 5,000,$

since $P_S = 10$ and $P_U = 5$. From the answer to part a, we know that

$S = -250 + 3U.$

Solving these two equations simultaneously, $S = 392.9$ and $U = 214.3$. Thus, to maximize output, Elwyn should hire about 393 hours of skilled labor and about 214 hours of unskilled labor.

c. From equation 7.4, we know that $MP_U \bullet P$ must equal P_U, where P is the price of the product. (Under present circumstances, the marginal revenue product of unskilled labor equals $MP_U \bullet P$, and the marginal expenditure on unskilled labor equals P_U.) Thus, since

$P = 10$, $P_U = 5$, and $MP_U = 200 - 0.6U,$

$10(200 - 0.6U) = 5$

$\qquad\qquad U = 332.5.$

To maximize profit, Elwyn should hire 332.5 hours of unskilled labor. (Note that we no longer assume that a total of $5,000 is spent on labor. Thus, the answer is different from that in part b.)

3. a. No.

    b. 50 pounds, since half of these amounts (that is, 50 pounds of hay and 125.1 pounds of grain) results in a 25-pound gain.

    c. $-(125.1 - 130.9)/(50 - 40) = 0.58$.

    d. No, because it is impossible to tell (from the information given in the question) how much hay and grain can be used to produce a 25-pound gain after the advance in technology.

5. a. No.

    b. General farms.

    c. No.

7. a. and b. The average and marginal products of grain when each amount is used are calculated as follows:

Amount of grain	Average product	Marginal product
1,200	$5,917/1,200 = 4.93$	$\dfrac{7,250 - 5,917}{1,800 - 1,200} = 2.22$
1,800	$7,250/1,800 = 4.03$	$\dfrac{8,379 - 7,250}{2,400 - 1,800} = 1.88$
2,400	$8,379/2,400 = 3.49$	$\dfrac{9,371 - 8,379}{3,000 - 2,400} = 1.65$
3,000	$9,371/3,000 = 3.12$	

    c. Yes. The marginal product of grain decreases as more of it is used.

9. a. To minimize cost, the firm should choose an input combination where $MP_L/P_L = MP_K/P_K$, where MP_L is the marginal product of labor, MP_K is the marginal product of capital, P_L is the price of labor, and P_K is the price of capital. Since

$$MP_L = \frac{\partial Q}{\partial L} = 5K \quad \text{and} \quad MP_K = \frac{\partial Q}{\partial K} = 5L,$$

it follows that,

$$\frac{5K}{1} = \frac{5L}{2},$$

or $K = L/2$. Since $Q = 20$, $K = 4/L$. Thus,

$$\frac{L}{2} = \frac{4}{L} \quad \text{or} \quad L^2 = 8,$$

which means that the firm should use $2(2)^{0.5}$ units of labor and $(2)^{0.5}$ units of capital.

    b. If the price of labor is \$2 per unit, the optimal value of K is 2, and the optimal value of L is 2. Thus, output per unit of labor is 20/2, or 10, whereas it formerly was $20/2 \times 2^{0.5}$ or $10/2^{0.5}$. Thus, output per unit of labor will rise.

    c. No, because a 1 percent increase in both K and L results in more than a 1 percent increase in Q.

11. a. Total annual cost equals $C = 40L/2 + (8,000)(1,000)/L$. Thus, $dC/dL = 20 - 8,000,000/L^2$, and the optimal lot size is

$$632.5 = \left(\frac{8,000 \times 1,000}{20}\right)^{0.5} = (400,000)^{0.5}$$

b. The optimal lot size is $2,000 = \left(\dfrac{8,000 \times 10,000}{20}\right)^{0.5} = (4,000,000)^{0.5}$

c. The optimal lot size is $6,324.6 = \left(\dfrac{8,000 \times 100,000}{20}\right)^{0.5} = (40,000)^{0.5}$

13. a. All other things equal, it often is less expensive to focus inputs in a particular area, rather than to spread them out.

b. The quicker cars are produced, the sooner the firm will sell them and receive the profit.

c. It costs money to maintain inventories, and reductions in inventories cut these costs.

Chapter 8

1. a. $\dfrac{200,000}{10(20,000) + 0.02(50,000) + 5(10,000)} = \dfrac{200,000}{251,000} = 0.797.$

b. $\dfrac{300,000}{10(30,000) + 0.02(100,000) + 5(14,000)} = \dfrac{300,000}{372,000} = 0.806.$

c. The base year is 2000.

3. a. $\log C = 5.1 - 0.25 \log 100$

$= 5.1 - 0.25(2)$

$= 4.6.$

Thus, $C = 39,811$.

b. $\log C = 5.1 - 0.25 \log 200$

$= 5.1 - 0.25\,(2.30)$

$= 4.525.$

Thus, $C = 33,497$.

c. $1 - 33,497/39,811 = 16$ percent.

5. $9.6 million. $7.68 million.

7. a. 0.5($1 million) + 0.5($2 million) = $1.5 million.

b. 0.75($1 million) + 0.25($2 million) + $150,000 = $1.4 million. This assumes that whether each approach costs $1 million or $2 million is independent of what the other approach costs. Also, the total cost figure for each approach, if adopted, includes the $150,000. Thus only the $150,000 spent on the aborted approach is lost. The $150,000 spent on the approach that is adopted is part of the total cost figure given in the problem.

c. Comparing the answers to parts a and b, parallel approaches result in lower expected cost.

9. a. 0.6($5 million) + 0.4($3 million) = $4.2 million.
   b. 0.7($3 million) + 0.3($5 million) = $3.6 million.
   c. 0.18($5 million) + 0.82($3 million) + $500,000 = $3.86 million.

Chapter 9

1. a. It is the cheapest of these three ways of making steel. Using this method, cost per ton is $310.34, as compared with $368.86 and $401.73 with the other methods.
   b. If the price of scrap rises, the cost of producing steel based on the electric-furnace continuous-casting route will increase, because this route uses scrap. Thus, the cost advantage of this route will be reduced if the price of scrap goes up.
   c. It suggests that U.S. steel producers may have a hard time competing with steel producers in low-wage countries.
   d. If each figure is the minimum value of long-run average cost for a particular technique, it also equals the long-run marginal cost for the technique, since marginal cost equals average cost when the latter is a minimum.

3. a. If Q is the sales volume,
   $Q(\$200) - \$5,000 = \$10,000$,
   so Q must equal 75.
   b. Since $Q(\$250) - \$5,000 = \$10,000$, Q must equal 60.
   c. Since $Q(\$265) - \$5,000 = \$10,000$, Q must equal 56.6.

5. The table is as follows:

Total fixed cost	Total variable cost	Average fixed cost	Average variable cost
50	0	—	—
50	25	50	25
50	50	25	25
50	70	$16^2/_3$	$23^1/_3$
50	85	$12^1/_2$	$21^1/_4$
50	100	10	20
50	140	$8^1/_3$	$23^1/_3$
50	210	$7^1/_7$	30

7. a. Yes. Since $(\partial TC/\partial Q)(Q/TC) = \alpha_1$, this is true.
   b. Yes. If $\alpha_1 < 1$, a 1 percent increase in output results in a less than 1 percent increase in total cost, so average cost falls with increases in output; in other words, there are economies of scale. If $\alpha_1 > 1$, a 1 percent increase in output results in a more than 1 percent increase in total cost, so average cost increases with increases in output; in other words, there are diseconomies of scale.

  c. If we assume that a 1 percent increase in both P_L and P_K will result in a 1 percent increase in TC, $\alpha_2 + \alpha_3 = 1$. Thus,

$$\frac{TC}{P_K} = \alpha_0 Q^{\alpha_1} \left(\frac{P_L}{P_K} \right)^{\alpha_2},$$

and

$$\log \left(\frac{TC}{P_K} \right) = \log \alpha_0 + \alpha_1 \log Q + \alpha_2 \log \left(\frac{P_L}{P_K} \right).$$

If this is treated as a regression equation, one can estimate the αs, using the regression technique discussed in Chapter 5, subject to the caveats concerning various kinds of possible errors cited there.

9. a. Since marginal cost equals $dTVC/dQ$, it equals

$$MC = 50 - 20Q + 3Q^2.$$

It is a minimum when

$$\frac{dMC}{dQ} = -20 + 6Q = 0, \quad \text{or} \quad Q = 20/6.$$

  b. Average variable cost equals

$$AVC = \frac{TVC}{Q} = 50 - 10Q + Q^2.$$

It is a minimum when

$$\frac{dAVC}{dQ} = -10 + 2Q = 0, \quad \text{or} \quad Q = 5.$$

  c. If $Q = 5$, average variable cost equals $50 - 10(5) + 5^2 = 25$. Marginal cost equals $50 - 20(5) + 3(5^2) = 25$. Thus, marginal cost equals average variable cost at this output level.

11. a. Using equation (9.7), $S = (23,000 + 11,000 - 30,000)/30,000 = 0.13$.

  b. Production facilities used to make one product sometimes can be used to make another product, and by-products resulting from the production of one product may be useful in making other products.

Chapter 10

1. a. Since average cost (AC) must be a minimum, and since

$$AC = \frac{25,000}{Q} + 150 + 3Q,$$

$$\frac{dAC}{dQ} = \frac{-25,000}{Q^2} + 3 = 0.$$

Thus, $Q = \left(\frac{25,000}{3} \right)^{0.5} = 91.3$, and

$AC = 25,000/91.3 + 150 + 3(91.3) = 697.7$

so the price must be $697.7, since in long-run equilibrium, price equals the minimum value of average cost.

  b. 91.3 units.

3. a. Marginal cost equals

$$MC = \frac{dTC}{dQ} = 4 + 4Q.$$

Setting marginal cost equal to price, we have

$$4 + 4Q = 24$$
$$4Q = 20$$
$$Q = 5.$$

Thus, the optimal output rate is 5.

   b. Profit equals total revenue minus total cost. Since total revenue equals $24Q$, profit equals

$$\pi = 24Q - 200 - 4Q - 2Q^2 = -200 + 20Q - 2Q^2.$$

Because $Q = 5$,

$$\pi = -200 + 20(5) - 2(5)^2 = -200 + 100 - 50 = -150.$$

Thus, the firm loses $150 (which is less than if it shuts down).

5. a. Marginal revenue $= 100 - 2Q$; marginal cost $= 60 + 2Q$. Thus, if marginal revenue equals marginal cost, $100 - 2Q = 60 + 2Q$, so $Q = 10$.

   b. Since $P = 100 - Q$, P must equal 90 if $Q = 10$. Thus, he should charge a price of $90.

7. a. Since the equation for the supply curve is $P = 3$, the long-run equilibrium output can be determined by finding the value of Q_D if $P = 3$. (This is the value where the supply and demand curves intersect.) Thus, since $Q_D = 50 - 2P$, the equilibrium output is $50 - 2(3)$, or 44 million knives per year.

   b. A tax of $1 will raise the supply curve by $1; this means that its equation will be $P = 4$. (To see why, note that producers, to have the same amount left over after the tax, must charge $1 more.) Thus, the long-run equilibrium output can be determined by finding the value of Q_D if $P = 4$. (This is the value where the demand curve intersects the new supply curve.) Thus, since $Q_D = 50 + 2P$, the equilibrium output is $50 - 2(4)$, or 42 million knives per year.

   c. No.

9. a. Since $P = (8,300 - Q)/2.1 = 3,952 - 0.476Q$,

$$MR = 3,952 - 0.952Q.$$

   b. $MC = 480 + 40Q$. If $MC = MR$,

$$480 + 40Q = 3,952 - 0.952Q$$
$$40.952Q = 3,472$$
$$Q = 84.8.$$

Thus, the firm would produce 84.8 lasers per month. If $Q = 84.8$, $P = 3,952 + 0.476(84.8) = 3,912$. Thus, the price should be $3,912.

   c. The firm's monthly profit equals

$$84.8(3,912) - [2,200 + 480(84.8) + 20(84.8)^2] = \$145,012.80.$$

11. a. If the firm is producing 5 units in the first plant, the marginal cost in the first plant equals $20 + 2(5)$, or 30. Thus, if the firm is minimizing costs, marginal cost in the second plant must also equal 30; this means that

$$10 + 5Q_2 = 30$$
$$Q_2 = 4.$$

Thus, the second plant must be producing 4 units of output.

b. Since $MC_1 = MC_2 = MC$ and the firm's output, Q, equals $Q_1 + Q_2$,

$$Q_1 = (MC_1/2) - 10$$
$$Q_2 = (MC_2/5) - 2$$
$$Q = Q_1 + Q_2 = 0.7MC - 12$$
$$MC = (1/0.7)(Q + 12).$$

c. No, because we do not have information concerning the fixed costs of each plant. But you can determine average variable cost.

13. a. It probably tended to increase because high profits induced entry. Also, the 1990–91 recession may have resulted in more demand for the services of pawnshops.

b. No. It is likely to be an oligopoly, since there generally is not a very large number of pawnshops in a small city.

c. Apparently not, but licensing requirements may exist.

15. Consider the price separately pricing system. The following table evaluates the profitability of each price separately price. Note that we only have to consider one demander in each class because if there were X demanders per class, profits would just be X times higher–but the largest profit for 1 would still be the largest profit if X demanders/class existed.

Price$_{CD1}$ $	Cost$_{CD1}$	Π/CD1	No. of CD1 demanded	Π from CD1
11	4	7	1	7
8	4	4	3	12 ← best
9	4	5	2	10

Chapter 11

1. a. They would want to set marginal revenue equal to the marginal cost of each firm, but this is impossible since Bergen's marginal cost is $410 and Gutenberg's marginal cost is $460. Because Bergen's marginal cost is always less than Gutenberg's, it will produce all the output. Equating its marginal cost to marginal revenue (MR),

$$MR = 580 - 6Q = 410,$$

so $Q = 170/6$. This is the output Bergen would produce.

b. Nothing.

c. Not unless Gutenberg receives an attractive share of the profit from Bergen's output even though it produces nothing.

3. a. $9,000. **b.** 6.

5. a. To find the profit-maximizing price, the IATA should construct the marginal cost curve for the cartel as a whole. Then, as shown in Figure 11.2, it should determine the amount of traffic (which is the output of this industry) where marginal revenue equals marginal cost. The price that will elicit this amount of traffic is the profit-maximizing price.

b. If IATA wants to maximize profit, it will allocate this traffic among the airlines in such a way that the marginal cost of all airlines is equal. (However, for reasons discussed on page 432, it may not want to maximize profit.)

c. No. This would not maximize profit.

7. a. Letting Alliance's profit be π_1,

$\pi_1 = Q_1[200,000 - 6(Q_1 + Q_2)] - 8,000\ Q_1$.

Letting Bangor's profit be π_2,

$\pi_2 = Q_2[200,000 - 6(Q_1 + Q_2)] - 12,000\ Q_2$.

If Alliance maximizes its profit, assuming that Bangor will hold its output constant,

$$\frac{\partial \pi_1}{\partial Q_1} = 192,000 - 6Q_2 - 12Q_1 = 0.$$

If Bangor maximizes its profit, assuming that Alliance will hold its output constant,

$$\frac{\partial \pi_2}{\partial Q_2} = 188,000 - 6Q_1 - 12Q_2 = 0.$$

Solving these equations simultaneously, $Q_1 = 196,000/18, = 10,888.89$, and

$Q_2 = (188,000 - 196,000/3)/12 = 122,667/12 = 10,222.22$,

so

$P - 200,000 - 6(10,888.89 + 10,222.22) = 73,333.33$ dollars.

b. Alliance's output is 10,888.89, and Bangor's output is 10,222.22.

c. Alliance's profit is 10,888.89(73,333.33 - 8,000), or approximately $711.41 million.

Bangor's profit is

10,222(73,333.33 - 12,000), or approximately $626.96 million.

9. a. Obviously, Procter and Gamble must be concerned with its own costs. If it adopts a tactic that is far more costly to itself than to a potential entrant, it may cost more than it is worth. If the costs of the strategy outweigh the benefits, Procter and Gamble, on net, will lose.

b. The point of these tactics is to raise the cost to a potential entrant, thus discouraging entry.

c. Whether Procter and Gamble should have cut its price depends on whether the discount brands (and Kimberly-Clark, which had become a major rival) would cut their prices in response, and by how much. In fact, Procter and Gamble did reduce its price substantially (by 16 percent in the case of Luvs). According to the chairperson of Procter and Gamble, "We believe our profits are going to grow because we're going to get volume back."

    d. Yes. Procter and Gamble wanted to reduce what it regarded as improper imitation of its technology. On the other hand, firms that are sued often regard such suits as attempts to intimidate them.

11. a. The size of a firm is often measured by its total revenue. Perhaps a firm might feel that a higher total revenue would make the firm more visible to investors and customers. Also, its managers may be more interested in the growth of the firm than in profits. (However, they are likely to feel that profits should not fall below some minimum level.)

    b. To maximize its total revenue, it should set

$$\frac{d(PQ)}{dQ} = \frac{d(28Q - 0.14Q^2)}{dQ} = 28 - 0.28Q = 0.$$

Thus, Q should equal 100, and P should equal $14.

    c. If it maximizes profit, it sets

$$MR = 28 - 0.28Q = 14 = MC$$

so $Q = 50$. Consequently, the firm produces 50,000 units more than it would if it maximized profit.

Chapter 12

1. a. Yes. Fortnum should stress magazines, and Maison should stress newspapers.

    b. Fortnum's profit will be $9 million, and Maison's profit will be $8 million.

    c. No.

3. a. Yes. See pages 458 to 460.

    b. Yes. See page 463.

5. a. Strategy 1.

    b. Strategy B.

7. a. Two.

    b. The outcome will depend on which firm acts first.

9. See pages 461 to 463.

Chapter 13

1. a. The slope of the isocost curve is $dQ_Y/dQ_X = -10 - 10Q_X$. If total revenue equals a constant (K),

$$P_X Q_X + P_Y Q_Y = K;$$

this means that

$$Q_Y = \frac{K}{P_Y} - \frac{P_X Q_X}{P_Y}.$$

Thus, the slope of the isorevenue curve is $-P_X/P_Y$, or -50. If the isorevenue curve is tangent to the isocost curve,

$$-10 - 10Q_X = -50, \quad \text{or} \quad Q_X = 4.$$

b. $Q_Y = 1{,}000 - 10(4) - 5(4^2) = 880$.

c. No. There is no evidence that this is true.

3. a. To earn 20 percent on its total investment of $250,000, its profit must equal $50,000 per year. Thus, if it operates at 80 percent of capacity (and sells 10,000 units), it must set a price of $15 per unit. (Since average cost equals $10, profit per unit will be $5, so total profit per year will be $50,000.)

b. From the information given, there is no assurance that it can sell 10,000 units per year if it charges a price of $15 per unit.

c. Unless the markup bears the proper relationship to the price elasticity of demand, the firm probably is sacrificing profit.

5. a. $MR_1 = 160 - 16Q_1$

$MR_2 = 80 - 4Q_2$

$MC = 5 + (Q_1 + Q_2)$.

Therefore

$160 - 16Q_1 = 5 + Q_1 + Q_2$

$80 - 4Q_2 = 5 + Q_1 + Q_2$.

Or

$155 - 17Q_1 = Q_2$

$75 - 5Q_2 = Q_1$.

Thus,

$155 - 17(75 - 5Q_2) = Q_2$

$155 - 1{,}275 + 85Q_2 = Q_2$

$84Q_2 = 1{,}120$

$Q_2 = 1{,}120/84 = 13\frac{1}{3}$

It should sell $13\frac{1}{3}$ units in the second market.

b. $Q_1 = 75 - 5Q_2$

$= 75 - 5(1{,}120/84)$

$= 75 - 5{,}600/84$

$= 75 - 66\frac{2}{3}$

$= 8\frac{1}{3}$.

It should sell $8\frac{1}{3}$ units in the first market.

c. $P_1 = 160 - 8(8\frac{1}{3}) = 93\frac{1}{3}$.

$P_2 = 80 - 2(13\frac{1}{3}) = 53\frac{1}{3}$.

7. a. Backus' total revenues equal

$TR = P_X Q_X + P_Y Q_Y = (400 - Q_X)Q_X + (300 - 3Q_Y)Q_Y$, and since $Q_Y = 2Q_X$,

$TR = (400 - Q_X)Q_X + (300 - 6Q_X)(2Q_X)$
$= 400Q_X - Q_X^2 + 600Q_X - 12Q_X^2 = 1,000Q_X - 13Q_X^2$.

Thus, the firm's profit equals

$\pi = 1,000Q_X - 13Q_X^2 - 500 - 3Q_X - 9Q_X^2$
$= -500 + 997Q_X - 22Q_X^2$

Setting $d\pi/dQ_X = 997 - 44Q_X = 0$, we find that the profit-maximizing value of $Q_X = 997/44 = 22.66$. Thus, Backus should produce and sell 22.66 units of product X and 45.32 units of product Y per period of time.

b. The price of product X must be $400 - 22.66 = \$377.34$, and the price of product Y must be $300 - 3(45.32) = \$164.05$.

We have assumed that Backus sells all that it produces of both products. The marginal revenue of product X equals $400 - 2(22.66) = 354.68$, and the marginal revenue of product Y equals $300 - 6(45.32) = 28.09$. Since both are nonnegative, this assumption is true if Backus maximizes profit.

9. a. The firm's profit equals $P_CQ_C + P_MQ_M - TC$, or

$\pi = (495 - 5Q_C)Q_C + (750 - 10Q_M)Q_M - 410 - 8(Q_C + Q_M)$.

Thus,

$\dfrac{\partial \pi}{\partial Q_C} = 495 - 10Q_C - 8 = 0$

$\dfrac{\partial \pi}{\partial Q_M} = 750 - 20Q_M - 8 = 0$.

Consequently, $Q_C = 48.7$ and $Q_M = 37.1$, so
$P_C = 495 - 5(48.7) = 251.5$.

b. $P_M = 750 - 10(37.1) = 379$.

c. Yes. Under these circumstances,

$Q_C = \dfrac{495 - P}{5}$ and $Q_M = \dfrac{750 - P}{10}$,

so

$Q = Q_C + Q_M = 174 - 0.3P$

and

$P = (174 - Q)/0.3 = 580 - {}^{10}/_3 Q$.

Thus,

$\pi = (580 - {}^{10}/_3 Q)Q - 410 - 8Q$
$= -410 + 572Q - {}^{10}/_3 Q^2$.

If π is a maximum,

$\dfrac{\partial \pi}{dQ} = 572 - {}^{20}/_3 Q = 0$,

so $Q = 572(3/20) = 85.8$. Consequently,

$\pi = -410 + 572(85.8) - {}^{10}/_3(85.8^2) = 24,129$,

which compares with

$$\pi = [495 - 5(48.7)]48.7 + [750 - 10(37.1)]37.1 - 410$$
$$- 8(48.7 + 37.1)$$
$$= 251.5(48.7) + 379(37.1) - 1,096.4$$
$$= 12,248.05 + 14,060.9 - 1,096.4 = 25,213,$$

the value of profits when price discrimination is allowed.
So profits decrease by $1,084.

11. **a.** No, the Breen Company should not accept the offer from the chemical company. The Breen Company sets price ($7,200) at 1.8 times average variable cost, or $P = 1.8(AVC)$. Thus, $7,200 = 1.8(AVC)$ or $AVC = $4,000$. Breen's total revenue from selling to the chemical company would be $5,000(6) = $30,000$. Breen's total variable cost from selling to the chemical company would be $4,000(6) = $24,000$. Thus, Breen's variable cost profit from selling to the chemical company would be $30,000 - $24,000 = $6,000.

If the Breen Company sold the four instruments that it would lose by serving the chemical company, its total revenue would be $7,200(4) = $28,800 and its total variable cost would be $4,000(4) = $16,000. Thus, the Breen Company's variable cost profit from selling the four instruments at normal price would be $28,800 - $16,000 = $12,800. Since $12,800 > $6,000, the Breen Company should not sell to the chemical company.

b. The chemical company would have to pay a price so that the Breen Company would make at least as much variable cost profit as it would by selling the four instruments at the regular price, $12,800. Call this price X. Thus, $(X - $4,000)6 = $12,800$ or $6X - $24,000 = $12,800$ or $4X = $36,800$ or $X = $6,133.33$. Thus, Breen should ask the chemical company to pay at least $6,133.33 per instrument for each of the six instruments.

c. There is only limited information with which to answer this part of the question. If Breen is to charge only a single price for its instrument, they should set a price compatible with marginal revenue equaling marginal cost. It's possible that this might occur where the price equals 1.8(AVC), but we don't have information to support or deny this. As the text points out, AVC is sometimes a bad proxy for marginal cost. But for a constant cost scenario, $AVC = MC$ and AVC is a perfect proxy for MC. Using $MC = AVC$ and the markup information from this chapter, if the demand elasticity is -2.25, then marking price 1.8 times marginal cost is optimal for single-price ($7,200) profit maximization.

Clearly, there are buyers with different reservation prices for Breen's product. This suggests the possibility of a policy of price discrimination (which would require the dropping of a single-markup pricing policy).

Chapter 14

1. **a.** The expected present value is $10.7 million, the standard deviation is $5.06 million, and the coefficient of variation is 47 percent.
   b. The expected present value is $11.0 million, the standard deviation is $1.95 million, and the coefficient of variation is 18 percent.
   c. Investment X.
   d. Investment Y, since she is a risk averter (as indicated by the fact that U increases at a decreasing rate as P rises). Investment Y has both a higher expected present value and a lower standard deviation than investment X and because $E(U_X) = 62.099 < 63.752 = E(U_Y)$, i.e., X's expected utility is less than Y's.

3. **a.** No.
   b. It is very conservative, as discussed on pages 558 to 559.
   c. No, because no probability distribution of the outcome can be given.

5. **a.** 3. **b.** -0.6. **c.** -1.2.

7. **a.**

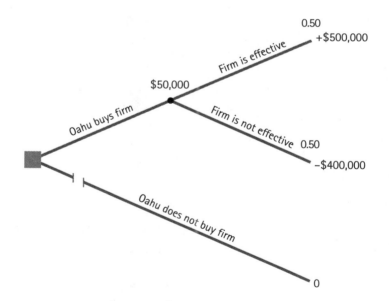

   b. There is only one: whether to buy the firm.
   c. There is only one: whether the firm becomes an effective producer of washing machine parts or not.
   d. Yes, it should buy the firm.
   e. (1) Yes.
      (2) Three mutually exclusive outcomes are: (a) The firm becomes an effective producer of washing machine parts. (b) The firm does not

become an effective producer of washing parts and is sold to the Saudis. (c) The firm does not become an effective producer of washing machine parts and cannot be sold to the Saudis.

(3) The probability of the first outcome (in part 2) is 0.5, the probability of the second outcome is 0.5(0.2), or 0.1, and the probability of the third outcome is (0.5)(0.8), or 0.4.

(4) The extra profit to Oahu from the first outcome is $500,000; the extra profit from the second outcome is $100,000; the extra profit from the third outcome is −$400,000.

f. Oahu should buy the firm. The expected extra profit if it does so is 0.5($500,000) + 0.1($100,000) + 0.4(−$400,000) = $100,000.

g. (1) If the extra profit if the firm is made into an effective producer of washing machine parts is $400,000 or less, the decision will be reversed. Put differently, if the *error* was an *overstatement* of this extra profit by $100,000 or more, the decision will be reversed.

(2) If the extra profit if the firm is made into an effective producer of washing machine parts is $300,000 or less, the decision will be reversed. Put differently, if the *error* was an *overstatement* of this extra profit by $200,000 or more, the decision will be reversed.

9. a.

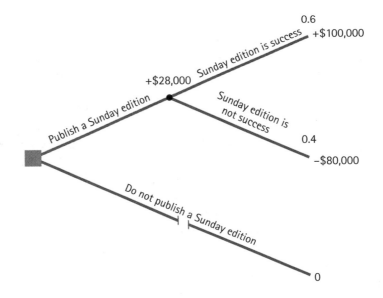

If the publisher is risk neutral, she wants to maximize expected profit. Thus, she should publish the Sunday edition.

b. Whether to publish the Sunday edition is a decision fork. Whether it is a success, if published, is a chance fork.

Chapter 15

1. Expected Value or EV($45) = 1,750($4.05)(.35) + 1,975($4.05)(.20) + 2,220($4.05)(.30) + 2,445($4.05)(.15).
   EV($45) = $2,480.63 + $1,599.75 + $2,697.30 + $1,485.34 or $8,263.02.
   EV($50) = 1,200($4.50)(.35) + 1,415($4.50)(.20) + 2,001($4.50)(.30) + 2,305($4.50)(.15).
   EV($50) = $1,890 + $1,273.50 + $2,701.35 + $1,555.88 or $7,420.73
   EV(auction) = $2,480.63 + 1,599.75 + 2,701.35 + 1,555.88 = $8,337.61.
   The value of information would be worth,
   EV($45) = 1,750($4.05)(.35) + 1,975($4.05)(.20) + 2,220($4.05)(.30) + 2,445($4.05)(.15).
   EV($45) = **$2,480.63 + $1,599.75** + $2,697.30 + $1,485.34 or $8,263.02.
   EV($50) = 1,200($4.50)(.35) + 1,415($4.50)(.20) + 2,001($4.50)(.30) + 2,305($4.50)(.15).
   EV($50) = $1,890 + $1,273.50 **+ $2,701.35 + $1,555.88** or $7,420.73
   EV(auction) = $2,480.63 + 1,599.75 + 2,701.35 + 1,555.88 = $8,337.61.
   So, the value of information = $8,337.61 − $8,263.02 or $74.59.
3. a. The mean value is 67.91.
   b. (80 − 67.91)/(63.64 = .04573; z score of .04573 = .4820. Hence the probability of a reservation price being less than 80 is approximately 19 percent.
5. If they choose to price their PSLs at $6,000, their expected revenue is: $58,802,000 + $58,800,000 + **$60,000** = $177,602,000. If they choose to price their PSLs at $7,000, their expected revenue is: **$60,214,000** + 58,803,500 + 56,000,000 = 175,017,500. If they choose to prices their PSLs at $8,000, their expected revenue is: $56,030,000 + **$61,610,500** + $50,000,000 = $167,640,500. So, if they set the price and don't use an auction, they should charge $6,000/PSL. If the Eagles use a modified Dutch auction, then their expected revenue is: $60,214,000 + **$61,610,500** + $60,000 = $181,824,500. So relative to setting a price of $6,000/PSL, the auction would increase expected revenue by $4,222,500. But since auction costs are $5,100,000, the Eagles are better off pricing the PSLs at $6,000.

Chapter 16

1. a. Flat salary:
   If effort is low, utility = 758.29. If effort is high, utility = 658.29. The manager chooses low effort since it gives higher expected utility. Your expected profit will be 0.3($5 million) + 0.4($10 million) + 0.3($15 million) − $0.575 million = $9.425 million.

b. Six percent of profit:

Expected utility of manager with

Low effort is $0.3\sqrt{0.06(\$5 \text{ million})} + 0.4\sqrt{0.06(\$10 \text{ million})} + 0.3\sqrt{0.06(15 \text{ million})} = 758.76$.

High effort is $-100 + 0.3\sqrt{0.06(\$7 \text{ million})} + 0.4\sqrt{0.06(\$12 \text{ million})} + 0.3\sqrt{0.06(\$17 \text{ million})} = 736.82$.

The manager chooses low effort since it gives higher expected utility. Given the manager's choice of low effort, your expected profit will be the expected profit of $10 million minus 6 percent which is $\{0.3(\$5 \text{ million}) + 0.4(\$10 \text{ million}) + 0.3(\$15 \text{ million})\}$ $(1 - 0.06) = \$9.4\text{m}$.

c. Five hundred thousand dollars plus half of profits in excess of $15 million:

Expected utility of manager with

Low effort is $\sqrt{(\$0.5 \text{ million})} = 707.11$.

High effort is $-100 + 0.7\sqrt{(\$0.5 \text{ million})} + 0.3\sqrt{^1/_2(\$17 \text{ million} - \$15 \text{ million}) + \$0.5 \text{ million}} = 762.40$.

The manager chooses high effort since it gives higher expected utility. Your expected profit will be the expected profit of $12 million minus expected compensation which is $\{\$0.5\text{m} + 0.3(0.5(\$2\text{m}))\} = \$800,000$.

$\{0.3(\$7\text{m}) + 0.4(\$12\text{m}) + 0.3(\$17\text{m})\} - \$0.8\text{m} = \$11.2\text{m}$.

You will choose the third plan (c) since it gives highest profit after deducting the manager's compensation.

3. If the manager does not work hard, she will receive,

$[100]^{0.5} = 10$.

If the manager works hard, she will receive

$[100 + x(15,000 - 13,000)]^{0.5} - 1$.

To calculate the minimum level of x necessary to ensure that expected compensation will be higher with hard work, set the expected utility with hard work equal to that without hard work:

$[100 + x(15,000 - 13,000)]^{0.5} - 1 = 10$

$[100 + x(15,000 - 13,000)]^{0.5} \qquad = 11$ (square both sides to get)

$[100 + x(15,000 - 13,000)] \qquad = 11^2 = 121$

$x = \dfrac{121 - 100}{15,000 - 13,000} = 0.0105$

Thus, if the manager gets a little over 0.105 times equity in excess of 13,000 she will work hard.

5. Total value of firm:

$$V = 500 + 300 - 700\,\frac{0.2}{1 + s} - s = 800 - \frac{140}{1 + s} - s.$$

To calculate the value of s that maximizes total value, set the derivative of value with respect to s equal to zero:

$$\frac{dV}{ds} = \frac{140}{(1+s)^2} - 1 = 0.$$

So, $S = 10.83$.

Therefore, the value of firm is

$$800 - \frac{140}{11.83} - 10.83 = 777.3.$$

Division 1 is riskless and has a stand-alone value of 500. Since all the risk comes from division 2, we must consider the chosen level of safety of this unit as a stand-alone entity. In calculating this value recollect that its value is 300 if no liability arises. However, if a loss of 700 occurs, it simply cannot pay more than the original 300 stand-alone value (because of limited liability). So, the stand-alone value of division 2 is:

$$300 - 300\,\frac{0.2}{1+s} - s = 300 - \frac{60}{1+s} - s$$

Set the derivative equal to zero to maximize the division 2 stand-alone value:

$$\frac{dV}{ds} = \frac{60}{(1+s)^2} - 1 = 0. \text{ So, } s = 6.746.$$

So, the stand-alone value of division 2 is:

$$300 - \frac{60}{7.746} - 6.746 = 285.5.$$

Total value with split up

$500 + 285.5 = 785.5$.

So the gain from split up is $785.55 - 777.34 = 8.21$.

7. There is an asset-substitution problem. To show this, we should value the firm as a whole, and each of the stakeholders' claims, first assuming A is chosen then assuming B is chosen. We can then see which project selection leads to the higher value of equity. This is the one share-holders would naturally favor.

Value of the firm if project A is chosen:

First, note that the value of the firm will be either 720 (300 from existing operations and 420 from the new project) or 1020 (600 from existing operations and 420 from the new project) depending on the success of existing operations. This value must be divided up by first paying off old debt, next new debt, and finally equity.

Value of the firm $0.5(720 + 1020) = 870$

Old debt $0.5(250 + \ \ 250) = 250$

New debt $0.5(400 + \ \ 400) = 400$

Equity $0.5(70) + \ \ 370) = 220$

Value of the firm if project B is chosen

The value of the firm will be either 300, 600, 1000, or 1300. These figures come from the different combinations of the two possible values for the existing operations (300 and 600) and the two values for the new project (0 and 700).

Value of the firm $0.25(300 + 600 + 1000 + 1300) = 800$
Old debt $0.25(250 + 250 + 250 + 250) = 250$
New debt $0.25(50 + 350 + 400 + 400) = 300$
Equity $0.25(0 + 0 + 350 + 650) = 250$

Shareholders would like to choose B after they had creditors' money. But since investors would pay only 300 for new debt, this cannot be funded. So neither project can be undertaken if debt financing is used. The analysis can be repeated using equity financing for the new project. The values of the firm will be the same as above, but these will be allocated first to the existing debt (for which 250 is owing) and any residual will accrue to equity.

Value of the firm if project A is chosen

Value of the firm $0.5(720 + 1020) = 870$
Old debt $0.5(250 + 250) = 250$
Equity $0.5(470 + 770) = 620$

Value of the firm if project B is chosen

Value of the firm $0.25(300 + 600 + 1000 + 1300) = 800$
Old debt $0.25(250 + 250 + 250 + 250) = 250$
Equity $0.25(50 + 350 + 750 + 1050) = 550$

Now, shareholders will naturally choose the higher Net Present Value project A since it has the higher equity value. The asset-substitution problem is solved.

Chapter 17

1. **a.** It equaled $27.5 + 21.9 + 18.5 + 9.3 = 77.2$ percent. Yes.
   b. It was $27.5 + 21.9 + (18.5 + 7.3) + 9.3 = 84.5$ percent if we simply combine United's and Pan Am's shares to approximate United's post-purchase share.

3. **a.** If $P = 480$, $Q = 260$, according to the demand curve. Thus, the firm's total revenue equals 260(480) thousand dollars, or $124,800,000$. The firm's total cost equals $50 + 0.25(260) = 115$ million dollars. Thus, the firm's accounting profit is $9,800,000$; this means that its rate of return is 9.8 percent.
   b. If it were deregulated, it would maximize
   $$\pi = (1/1,000)[Q(1,000 - 2Q)] - 50 - 0.25Q$$
   $$= -50 + 0.75Q - 0.002Q^2.$$
   Setting $d\pi/dQ = 0.75 - 0.004Q = 0$, $Q = 187.5$. Thus, under deregulation,
   $$\pi = -50 + 0.75(187.5) - 0.002(187.5^2) = \$20.3125 \text{ million.}$$
   So, the difference is $\$20.3125 - \$9.8 = \$10.5125$ million.

   5. a. 220/250 = 88 percent.
     b. Yes, because it is dominated by a few firms.
     c. 225/250 = 90 percent.
     d. 140/145 = 97 percent.
   7. a. No. If price is $1, 12 firms of optimal size can exist in the market.
     b. Eight.
   9. a. The district court ruled against the merger.
     b. The court held that transportation costs were small enough so that competition on a national basis was practical.
     c. Obviously, the views of courts and government agencies change over time. The prevailing climate of opinion was quite different in the 1980s than in the 1950s.
   11. a. Because the commission tries to provide the firm with a "fair" rate of return on its investment.
     b. Because this increase reduced the firm's profit.
     c. See pages 645 to 646.
   13. a. Yes. If there are only a very few sellers, collusion is much more likely than if there are many sellers.
     b. Sherman Act.
     c. It weakened the case.
     d. There is nothing wrong with G.E. discussing price increases with a customer.
     e. No. On December 5, 1994, District Court Judge George Smith ruled that there was not enough evidence to warrant sending the case to a jury.

Chapter 18

   1. a. Yes. Since consumption levels are much less in other countries, there appears to be far more room for growth than in the United States.
     b. Because the conditions in Indonesia seem to be very favorable to the consumption of soft drinks, and at present, Coca-Cola is selling relatively little there, it appears that great sales growth there is quite possible.
     c. Trade barriers and regulatory considerations are important. So are costs and local custom.
     d. Because Coke does not have to compete so aggressively against Pepsi, it can spend much less on marketing than domestically and thus increase its profits abroad.
   3. a. $10.
     b. Japan.
     c. 2 million flashbulbs.
     d. They will cease.

5. **a.** The price of a pound of bananas must be between $^3/_{10}$ and $^8/_{10}$ of the price of a pound of coffee.
   b. Honduras.
7. **a.** It will fall.
   b. It will fall.
9. **a.** Buy; 40 million pounds.
   b. From its reserves.
11. Basically, much more effort should be devoted to coordinating the work and planning of B&D's farflung (and largely uncoordinated) subsidiaries.

Brief Answers to "Consultant's Corner"

Planning to Meet Peak Engineering Requirements (Chapter 2)

The firm wanted an estimate of when the number of engineers required to carry out this project would reach a maximum. Since $a = 18$ and $b = 1$,

$$Y = 18t - t^2$$

and

$$\frac{dY}{dt} = 18 - 2t.$$

Setting dY/dt equal to zero,

$$18 - 2t = 0$$
$$t = 9.$$

Thus, Y reaches a maximum when $t = 9$. (Because $d^2Y/dt^2 = -2$, we can be sure that this is a maximum, not a minimum.)

The firm also wanted an estimate of the maximum number of engineers that would be required to carry out this project. To obtain such an estimate, we find the value of Y when $t = 9$.

$$Y = 18(9) - (9)^2 = 81.$$

Thus, when engineering requirements for this project reach their peak, 81 engineers will be needed.

To sum up, the engineering requirements for this project will reach their peak nine months after the project begins, when 81 engineers will be needed.

Estimating the Demand for Rail Passenger Business by Amtrak (Chapter 3)

(a) Disposable personal income: the quantity demanded for service is influenced by how well the economy is doing. As the economy does better, there is more business and leisure travel. As the note already implies, the sign of the coefficient is positive.

Amtrak fare: the quantity demanded for a service is influenced by its price. We would expect that fare would have a negative sign.

Amtrak fare/airline fare: air travel is a major competitor for Amtrak (even in the short-haul northeast corridor market between New York and Boston and between New York and Washington, DC). We expect that this variable will have a negative sign, indicating that if Amtrak's fare relative to its air competitor becomes higher, more travelers will opt for air travel.

Gasoline prices: another major competitor for Amtrak is the automobile, and the major "fare" of driving is the price of fuel. As the price of fuel increases, we expect more people to use the train, and hence, this variable would have a positive sign.

Dummies: while we don't have all the dummies used, we would expect increased traffic over the holidays and during bad weather. In addition, leisure travel increases in the summer season (because children are out of school and because many vacations are scheduled then).

(b) Since revenues are price times quantity, with the quantity estimate provided by the regression, multiplying the quantity estimate by the average rail fare (price) will give the estimate of systemwide revenues. **(c)** Income elasticity is $\eta_1 = \Delta Q/\Delta I$ so if ΔI is 1% and if ΔQ is 1.8 percent, the implied income elasticity is 1.8. If disposable personal income per capita increases from \$24,000 to \$25,000, this is a 4.17% increase. Thus, an estimate of %ΔQ is $(\eta_1)(\%\Delta I) = 1.8*4.17\% = 7.5\%$. Elasticities account for only small percentage changes in the denominator. The 4.17% change in per capita disposable personal income isn't very small, so we wouldn't expect our estimate to be 100% accurate. In addition, since regression analysis uses past data, the model is only good if the future is going to be like the past. Major structural changes in how a market behaves may render this condition inappropriate. **(d)** As disposable personal income has risen, it's had a positive impact on air and auto travel also. Air fares for leisure travel have increased below the increase in the Consumer Price Index (so the real price of leisure air travel has decreased). Automobile acquisitions have increased such that there are now more registered passenger vehicles and light trucks (SUVs, pickups, vans), than there are licensed drivers in the United States. On a real price basis (except for a spike in late 1999 through early 2000 and in spring of 2001), gasoline prices have been as inexpensive as they ever have been. Cheap gas and air prices and auto availability at all point to an explosion in travel by these modes.

The Trade-off between Risk and Return (Chapter 4)

These indifference curves slope *upward* to the right because this investor prefers less risk to more risk when the expected return is held constant. If there is an increase in risk, she must receive a higher expected return if she is to maintain the same level of satisfaction. She must choose some point on line RT. The point on this line which is on the highest indifference curve (and which therefore maximizes her satisfaction) is point S, where the expected return is 7.5 percent, which indicates that she invests half in U.S. government securities and half in common stocks. (Recall that the expected return from U.S. government securities is 5 percent and the expected return from common stocks is 10 percent.)

Marketing Plans at the Stafford Company (Chapter 5)

If the total market is 10,000 units, the relationship between price and quantity demanded is as follows:

Price	Quantity demanded
$ 800	10,000 (0.110) = 1,100
900	10,000 (0.102) = 1,020
1,000	10,000 (0.092) = 920
1,100	10,000 (0.084) = 840
1,200	10,000 (0.075) = 750
1,300	10,000 (0.066) = 660
1,400	10,000 (0.056) = 560

To obtain a simple equation expressing quantity demanded as a function of price, regression analysis can be used, the independent variable being price and the dependent variable being quantity demanded. The resulting regression equation is

$$Y = 1822 - 0.8964X,$$

where Y is the quantity demanded and X is price (in dollars). The equation seems to be reliable in the sense that it fits the above data very well, as indicated by the fact that $r^2 = 0.999$. However, the above data may or may not be very reliable, depending on how thoroughly the market research department did its job. It is risky to extrapolate a regression equation beyond the range to which the data apply. Thus, the firm cannot safely assume that this equation can predict quantity demanded if price is $1,500 or $1,600.

Without data on the costs of producing and marketing the electrical drive, one cannot say what the price should be.

Deciding Whether to Finance the Purchase of an Oil Field (Chapter 6)

In deciding whether to approve this loan application, the bank's forecasts of the price of oil are very important. Yet the simple extrapolation technique that is used is very crude. It is clear from the figures that this forecast was the result of a simple trend extrapolation that assumed a steady increase, beginning at $25 in 1986 and reaching $49 in 1998. Econometric models based on a more sophisticated analysis of the demand and supply of oil might be more effective. In fact, the bank's forecasts were very poor. For example, the price was about $13, not $25, in 1986, and about $20, not $31, in 1989.

Choosing the Size of an Oil Tanker (Chapter 7)

The company should build an oil tanker of 200,000 tonnes, not 20,000 tones. Because of the large economies of scale in tanker construction and operation, costs decrease as the size of the tanker increases. For example, a 280,000-tonne tanker costs roughly $75 million to construct. A 28,000-tonne tanker costs over $15 million to construct. Operating expenses show similar savings. For example, to operate a 280,000-tonne tanker does not require a crew size 10 times that of a 28,000-tonne tanker.

How Robots Spread in Japan and the United States (Chapter 8)

Holding π_{ij} and D_{ij} constant in the two countries, the rate of diffusion of robots tends to be higher in the United States than in Japan, since the top figure in brackets in equation (8.12)—which pertains to Japan—is less than the bottom figure in brackets—which pertains to the United States. But this does not mean that the rate of diffusion of robots was no greater in Japan than in the United States. The results in equation (8.12) pertain entirely to the rate at which firms *begin* to use robots. According to the President's Commission on International Competitiveness, Japan has been quicker than the United States to use robots in large numbers.

Mr. Martin Gets Chewed Out by the Boss (Chapter 9)

All the president's points are relevant. The fact that the product mix changes with increases in output may be quite important. It may be misleading to lump all three products together as the accountant did. Also, contrary to the assumption that the total cost curve is linear, the marginal cost of the first type of desk would increase with increases in output. Further, the price used for the second type of desk is not the relevant one.

Forecasting the Price of Salmon (Chapter 10)

If the quantity supplied three years ahead is in accord with the firm's estimate, regardless of whatever price changes occur, the quantity demanded must increase by about 15 percent to close the gap between the quantity supplied and the quantity demanded. Since the price elasticity of demand is about -1.5, a 10 percent decrease in price would increase the quantity demanded by about 15 percent. Thus, a very rough estimate would be that the price would fall by about 10 percent.

Using a Price Announcement to Preempt a Market (Chapter 12)

It seems doubtful that such a price announcement would have the desired effect. Since this firm will not be the lowest-cost producer of the next generation of products, it will not be able to announce a price that is low enough to make it unprofitable for all its rivals to enter the market. Unless it announces a price that is so low that it, as well as its rivals, would lose money, it is unlikely to induce its rivals to drop their plans to develop their own new products of the relevant kind. Moreover, even if it did announce a price at which it would lose money, it seems likely that its rivals would not take it too seriously, because announcements of this sort are not regarded as binding. Thus, such an announcement might well be regarded as a bluff. To be effective, an announcement must be credible. The firm's rivals would have to be convinced that the firm really would sell the product at a price that would impose unacceptable losses on them.

Settling Some Strife over a Pricing Formula (Chapter 13)

From our discussion of transfer pricing, we know that if there is a competitive market for ethane, the transfer price should equal the price in this market. However, it must be recognized that there can be heated disputes between divisions over transfer pricing. In this case, the petrochemical division may resist the increase in the transfer price of ethane because it will make the petrochemical division look less profitable—and make the division's managers appear less successful.

Choosing Areas for Research Regarding Pollution Costs (Chapter 14)

The expected value of perfect information seems to be greatest for a remote plant with low-sulfur coal available and least for an urban plant with low-sulfur coal available. However, this tells us nothing about the costs involved in obtaining perfect information. Unless you have some idea of these costs, it is very difficult to say much about the relative desirability of various areas of research.

A Dispute over a Requested Gas Rate Increase (Chapter 17)

To reduce the adverse effects of regulatory lag, you might suggest that the firm file for an interim rate increase (besides the permanent rate increase). The firm might promise to refund any difference between the interim rate and the permanent rate if the former turned out to be higher than the latter. (In fact, this is what the company proposed.) To see which of the two estimates of the cost of equity capital is closer to the truth, you might study the historical rate of growth of the firm's dividends, the object being to estimate g. Also, you might try to forecast the growth of the firm's dividends, based on various estimates published by brokerage firms as well as on statistical analysis.

Reorganizing a Firm's Global R and D Network (Chapter 18)

There are advantages in coordinating decisions regarding which products to develop with an eye toward the total world market, not just regional markets. In fact, Boehringer Ingelheim has altered its organization in this way. Decisions regarding which products to develop are now made centrally, but all the subsidiaries have a voice in these decisions, which are made by an International Steering Committee, composed of executives from all the major subsidiaries as well as from Germany.

Brief Answers to "Managerial Economics in Context"

Part 2 How to Forecast the Sales of Paper, According to McKinsey

a. Yes. One can calculate a regression where the quantity demanded of plain-paper copy paper is the dependent variable, while cents per copy and gross domestic product are the independent variables. However, in a time-series analysis of this sort, one must be careful to recognize that serial correlation may be present.

b. The multiple coefficient of determination.

c. On the basis of the graph on page 229, one cannot calculate the elasticity of demand for plain-paper copy paper with respect to cost per copy, because there are no numbers along the horizontal axis. But if these numbers were supplied, such a calculation could be made. This elasticity might be of use because it would indicate how sensitive the quantity demanded is to changes in cost per copy.

    d. Not necessarily. The annual rate of growth of the quantity demanded may have varied from one year to another. If an exponential curve fits well, the annual rate of growth is relatively constant from year to year.

    e. No. The procedures described on pages 205 to 209 might be used to calculate such a seasonal index. To make monthly or quarterly forecasts, a seasonal index would be useful.

    f. If the multiple regression described in the answer to question a were calculated, one would need forecasts of gross domestic product and of cents per copy to forecast quantity demanded. Econometric models might be used to forecast gross domestic product.

Part 4 A Rocky Road for Caterpillar Tractor

    a. Oligopoly.

    b. Caterpillar clearly has not maintained a constant percentage markup of price over average cost. During the 1980s, its profit margins often were less than in earlier years. As shown on page 520, its profits were negative in the early 1980s and early 1990s.

    c. No. It charged a price that was higher than that of its rivals in 1981.

    d. Faced with large losses, Caterpillar cut back on many expense items that would probably have not been cut so much otherwise. As was pointed out on page 520, the firm engaged in a major cost-reduction program in 1983 and 1984.

    e. It is worthwhile to spend money on them up to the point where the extra expenditure equals the extra savings. There are some technical improvements of this sort that require little expenditure relative to the savings they produce. Others require greater expenditure and yield smaller savings. Eventually one reaches a point where it is worthwhile to spend no more on such improvements, since the extra savings are less than the extra expenditures.

    f. No. It is wise only if the longer-term improved results are worth more than the short-term profits that are sacrificed. If a firm sacrifices $2 million in profits this year to obtain $1 million in profits five years from now, this is not a wise policy. Caterpillar estimated that the longer-term improved results were well worth the sacrifice.

    g. Cost reduction would allow the firm more latitude in keeping its prices down. However, bad labor relations can raise costs if productivity suffers.

Part 6 NAFTA: A Historic Agreement

    a. On the basis of the fact that U.S. auto plants have found it difficult to compete with the Japanese and others, some observers have argued that the United States has lost its comparative advantage, but it is a complex question, and more time is required to settle it.

b. Canadians felt that this ruling put their exporters at a disadvantage and that it would discourage investment in their country.

c. Yes. Direct investment in subsidiaries located in Mexico has been very important, for reasons cited in Chapter 18.

d. Florida tomato growers obviously are hurt by such imports, but U.S. consumers benefit.

e. It decreased the number of jobs.

f. In theory, one should carry out the sort of analysis shown in Figure 17.5, but in practice, it is very difficult to do this with any precision. They can use transferable emissions permits, effluent fees, and/or direct regulation.

ANSWERS

Appendix Tables

APPENDIX TABLE 1

Value of $\dfrac{1}{(1 + i)^n}$

Value of i

n	1%	2%	3%	4%	5%	6%	7%	8%	9%	10%
1	.99010	.98039	.97007	.96154	.95233	.94340	.93458	.92593	.91743	.90909
2	.98030	.96117	.94260	.92456	.90703	.89000	.87344	.85734	.84168	.82645
3	.97059	.94232	.91514	.88900	.86384	.83962	.81639	.79383	.77228	.75131
4	.96098	.92385	.88849	.85480	.82270	.79209	.76290	.73503	.70883	.68301
5	.95147	.90573	.86261	.82193	.78353	.74726	.71299	.68058	.64993	.62092
6	.94204	.88797	.83748	.79031	.74622	.70496	.66634	.63017	.59627	.56447
7	.93272	.87056	.81309	.75992	.71063	.66506	.62275	.58349	.54705	.51316
8	.92348	.85349	.78941	.73069	.67684	.62741	.58201	.54027	.50189	.46651
9	.91434	.83675	.76642	.70259	.64461	.59190	.54393	.50025	.46043	.42410
10	.90529	.82035	.74409	.67556	.61391	.55839	.50835	.46319	.42241	.38554
11	.89632	.80426	.72242	.64958	.58468	.52679	.47509	.42888	.38753	.35049
12	.88745	.78849	.70138	.62460	.55684	.49697	.44401	.39711	.35553	.31683
13	.87866	.77303	.68095	.60057	.53032	.46884	.41496	.36770	.32618	.28966
14	.86996	.75787	.66112	.57747	.50507	.44230	.38782	.34046	.29925	.26333
15	.86135	.74301	.64186	.55526	.48102	.41726	.36245	.31524	.27454	.23939
16	.85282	.72845	.62317	.53391	.45811	.39365	.33873	.29189	.25187	.21763
17	.84436	.71416	.60502	.51337	.43630	.37136	.31657	.27027	.23107	.19784
18	.83602	.70016	.58739	.49363	.41552	.35034	.29586	.25025	.21199	.17986
19	.82774	.68643	.57029	.47464	.39573	.33051	.27651	.23171	.19449	.16354
20	.81954	.67297	.55367	.45639	.37689	.31180	.25842	.21455	.17843	.14864
21	.81143	.65978	.53755	.44883	.35894	.29415	.24151	.19866	.16370	.13513
22	.80340	.64684	.52189	.42195	.34185	.27750	.22571	.18394	.15018	.12285
23	.79544	.63414	.50669	.40573	.32557	.26180	.21095	.17031	.13778	.11168
24	.78757	.62172	.49193	.39012	.31007	.24698	.19715	.15770	.12640	.10153
25	.77977	.60953	.47760	.37512	.29530	.23300	.18425	.14602	.11597	.09230

APPENDIX
TABLE
1

Value of $\dfrac{1}{(1 + i)^n}$ (Continued)

Value of i

n	11%	12%	13%	14%	15%	16%	17%	18%	19%	20%	24%
1	.90090	.89286	.88496	.87719	.86957	.86207	.85470	.84746	.84043	.83333	.8065
2	.81162	.79719	.78315	.76947	.75614	.74316	.73051	.71818	.70616	.69444	.6504
3	.73119	.71178	.69305	.67497	.65752	.64066	.62437	.60863	.59342	.57870	.5245
4	.65873	.63552	.61332	.59208	.57175	.55229	.53365	.51579	.49867	.48225	.4230
5	.59345	.56743	.54276	.51937	.49718	.47611	.45611	.43711	.41905	.40188	.3411
6	.53464	.50663	.48032	.45559	.43233	.41044	.38984	.37043	.35214	.33490	.2751
7	.48166	.45235	.42506	.39964	.37594	.35383	.33320	.31392	.29592	.27908	.2218
8	.43393	.40388	.37616	.35056	.32690	.30503	.28478	.26604	.24867	.23257	.1789
9	.39092	.36061	.33288	.30751	.28426	.26295	.24340	.22546	.20897	.19381	.1443
10	.35218	.32197	.29459	.26974	.24718	.22668	.20804	.19106	.17560	.16151	.1164
11	.31728	.28748	.26070	.23662	.21494	.19542	.17781	.16192	.14756	.13459	.0938
12	.28584	.25667	.23071	.20756	.18691	.16846	.15197	.13722	.12400	.11216	.0757
13	.25751	.22917	.20416	.18207	.16253	.14523	.12989	.11629	.10420	.09346	.0610
14	.23199	.20462	.18068	.15971	.14133	.12520	.11102	.09855	.08757	.07789	.0492
15	.20900	.18270	.15989	.14010	.12289	.10793	.09489	.08352	.07359	.06491	.0397
16	.18829	.16312	.14150	.12289	.10686	.09304	.08110	.07073	.06184	.05409	.0320
17	.16963	.14564	.12522	.10780	.09293	.08021	.06932	.05998	.05196	.04507	.0258
18	.15282	.13004	.11081	.09456	.08080	.06914	.05925	.05083	.04367	.03756	.0208
19	.13768	.11611	.09806	.08295	.07026	.05961	.05064	.04308	.03669	.03130	.0168
20	.12403	.10367	.08678	.07276	.06110	.05139	.04328	.03651	.03084	.02608	.0135
21	.11174	.09256	.07680	.06383	.05313	.04430	.03699	.03094	.02591	.02174	.0109
22	.10067	.08264	.06796	.05599	.04620	.03819	.03162	.02622	.02178	.01811	.0088
23	.09069	.07379	.06014	.04911	.04017	.03292	.02702	.02222	.01830	.01509	.0071
24	.08170	.06588	.05322	.04308	.03493	.02838	.02310	.01883	.01538	.01258	.0057
25	.07361	.05882	.04710	.03779	.03038	.02447	.01974	.01596	.01292	.01048	.0046

APPENDIX
TABLE
2

Value of $\displaystyle\sum_{t=1}^{n} \frac{1}{(1+i)^t}$

Value of i

n	1%	2%	3%	4%	5%	6%	7%	8%	9%	10%
1	.9901	.9804	.9709	.9615	.9524	.9434	.9346	.9259	.9174	.9091
2	1.9704	1.9416	1.9135	1.8861	1.8594	1.8334	1.8080	1.7833	1.7591	1.7355
3	2.9410	2.8839	2.8286	2.7751	2.7233	2.6730	2.6243	2.5771	2.5313	2.4868
4	3.9020	3.8077	3.7171	3.6299	3.5459	3.4651	3.3872	3.3121	3.2397	3.1699
5	4.8535	4.7134	4.5797	4.4518	4.3295	4.2123	4.1002	3.9927	3.8896	3.7908
6	5.7955	5.6014	5.4172	5.2421	5.0757	4.9173	4.7665	4.6229	4.4859	4.3553
7	6.7282	6.4720	6.2302	6.0020	5.7863	5.5824	5.3893	5.2064	5.0329	4.8684
8	7.6517	7.3254	7.0196	6.7327	6.4632	6.2093	5.9713	5.7466	5.5348	5.3349
9	8.5661	8.1622	7.7861	7.4353	7.1078	6.8017	6.5152	6.2469	5.9852	5.7590
10	9.4714	8.9825	8.7302	8.1109	7.7217	7.3601	7.0236	6.7101	6.4176	6.1446
11	10.3677	9.7868	9.2526	8.7604	8.3064	7.8868	7.4987	7.1389	6.8052	6.4951
12	11.2552	10.5753	9.9589	9.3850	8.8632	8.3838	7.9427	7.5361	7.1601	6.8137
13	12.1338	11.3483	10.6349	9.9856	9.3935	8.8527	8.3576	7.9038	7.4869	7.1034
14	13.0088	12.1062	11.2960	10.5631	9.8986	9.2950	8.7454	8.2442	7.7860	7.3667
15	13.8651	12.8492	11.9379	11.1183	10.3796	9.7122	9.1079	8.5595	8.0607	7.6061
16	14.7180	13.5777	12.5610	11.6522	10.8377	10.1059	9.4466	8.8514	8.3126	7.8237
17	15.5624	14.2918	13.1660	12.1656	11.2740	10.4772	9.7632	9.1216	8.5435	8.0215
18	16.3984	14.9920	13.7534	12.6592	11.6895	10.8276	10.0591	9.3719	8.7556	8.2014
19	17.2201	15.2684	14.3237	13.1339	12.0853	11.1581	10.3356	9.6036	8.9501	8.3649
20	18.0457	16.3514	14.8774	13.5903	12.4622	11.4699	10.5940	9.8181	9.1285	8.5136
21	18.8571	17.0111	15.4149	14.0291	12.8211	11.7640	10.8355	10.0168	9.2922	8.6487
22	19.6605	17.6581	15.9368	14.4511	13.1630	12.0416	11.0612	10.2007	9.4424	8.7715
23	20.4559	18.2921	16.4435	14.8568	13.4885	12.3033	11.2722	10.3710	9.5802	8.8832
24	21.2435	18.9139	16.9355	15.2469	13.7986	12.5503	11.4693	10.5287	9.7066	8.9847
25	22.0233	19.5234	17.4181	15.6220	14.9039	12.7833	11.6536	10.6748	9.8226	9.0770

APPENDIX
TABLE
2

Value of $\sum_{t=1}^{n} \dfrac{1}{(1 + i)^t}$ (Continued)

Value of i

n	11%	12%	13%	14%	15%	16%	17%	18%	19%	20%	24%
1	.9009	.8929	.8850	.8772	.8696	.8621	.8547	.8475	.8403	.8333	.8065
2	1.7125	1.6901	1.6681	1.6467	1.6257	1.6052	1.5852	1.5656	1.5465	1.5278	1.4568
3	2.4437	2.4018	2.3612	2.3126	2.2832	2.2459	2.2096	2.1743	2.1399	2.1065	1.9813
4	3.1024	3.0373	2.9745	2.9137	2.8550	2.7982	2.7432	2.6901	2.6386	2.5887	2.4043
5	3.6959	3.6048	3.5172	3.4331	3.3522	3.2743	3.1993	3.1272	3.0576	2.9906	2.7454
6	4.2305	4.1114	3.9976	3.8887	3.7845	3.6847	3.5892	3.4976	3.4098	3.3255	3.0205
7	4.7122	4.5638	4.4226	4.2883	4.1604	4.0386	3.9224	3.8115	3.7057	3.6046	3.2423
8	5.1461	4.9676	4.7988	4.6389	4.4873	4.3436	4.2072	4.0776	3.9544	3.8372	3.4212
9	5.5370	5.3282	5.1317	4.9464	4.7716	4.6065	4.4506	4.3030	4.1633	4.0310	3.5655
10	5.8892	5.6502	5.4262	5.2161	5.0188	4.8332	4.6586	4.4941	4.3389	4.1925	3.6819
11	6.2065	5.9377	5.6869	5.4527	5.2337	5.0286	4.8364	4.6560	4.4865	4.3271	3.7757
12	6.4924	6.1944	5.9176	5.6603	5.4206	5.1971	4.9884	4.7932	4.6105	4.4392	3.8514
13	6.7499	6.4235	6.1218	5.8424	5.5831	5.3423	5.1183	4.9095	4.7147	4.5327	3.9124
14	6.9819	6.6282	6.3025	6.0021	5.7245	5.4675	5.2293	5.0081	4.8023	4.6106	3.9616
15	7.1909	6.8109	6.4624	6.1422	5.8474	5.5755	5.3242	5.0916	4.8759	4.6755	4.0013
16	7.3792	6.9740	6.6039	6.2651	5.9542	5.6685	5.4053	5.1624	4.9377	4.7296	4.0333
17	7.5488	7.1196	6.7291	6.3729	6.0472	5.7487	5.4746	5.2223	4.9897	4.7746	4.0591
18	7.7016	7.2497	6.8389	6.4674	6.1280	5.8178	5.5339	5.2732	5.0333	4.8122	4.0799
19	7.8393	7.3650	6.9380	6.5504	6.1982	5.8775	5.5845	5.3176	5.0700	4.8435	4.0967
20	7.9633	7.4694	7.0248	6.6231	6.2593	5.9288	5.6278	5.3527	5.1009	4.8696	4.1103
21	8.0751	7.5620	7.1016	6.6870	6.3125	5.9731	5.6648	5.3837	5.1268	4.8913	4.1212
22	8.1757	7.6446	7.1695	6.7429	6.3587	6.0113	5.6964	5.4099	5.1486	4.9094	4.1300
23	8.2664	7.7184	7.2297	6.7921	6.3988	6.0442	5.7234	5.4321	5.1668	4.9245	4.1371
24	8.3481	7.7843	7.2829	6.8351	6.4338	6.0726	5.7465	5.4509	5.1822	4.9371	4.1428
25	8.4217	7.8431	7.3300	6.8729	6.4641	6.0971	5.7662	5.4669	5.1951	4.9476	4.1474

Areas under the Standard Normal Curve

This table shows the area between zero (the mean of a standard normal variable) and z. For example, if $z = 1.50$, this is the shaded area shown below, which equals .4332.

z	.00	.01	.02	.03	.04	.05	.06	.07	.08	.09
0.0	.0000	.0040	.0080	.0120	.0160	.0199	.0239	.0279	.0319	.0359
0.1	.0398	.0438	.0478	.0517	.0557	.0596	.0636	.0675	.0714	.0753
0.2	.0793	.0832	.0871	.0910	.0948	.0987	.1026	.1064	.1103	.1141
0.3	.1179	.1217	.1255	.1293	.1331	.1368	.1406	.1443	.1480	.1517
0.4	.1554	.1591	.1628	.1664	.1700	.1736	.1772	.1808	.1844	.1879
0.5	.1915	.1950	.1985	.2019	.2054	.2088	.2123	.2157	.2190	.2224
0.6	.2257	.2291	.2324	.2357	.2389	.2422	.2454	.2486	.2517	.2549
0.7	.2580	.2611	.2642	.2673	.2704	.2734	.2764	.2794	.2823	.2852
0.8	.2881	.2910	.2939	.2967	.2995	.3023	.3051	.3078	.3106	.3133
0.9	.3159	.3186	.3212	.3238	.3264	.3289	.3315	.3340	.3365	.3389
1.0	.3413	.3438	.3461	.3485	.3508	.3531	.3554	.3577	.3599	.3621

APPENDIX TABLE 3

Areas under the Standard Normal Curve (Continued)

z	.00	.01	.02	.03	.04	.05	.06	.07	.08	.09
1.1	.3643	.3665	.3686	.3708	.3729	.3749	.3770	.3790	.3810	.3830
1.2	.3849	.3869	.3888	.3907	.3925	.3944	.3962	.3980	.3997	.4015
1.3	.4032	.4049	.4066	.4082	.4099	.4115	.4131	.4147	.4162	.4177
1.4	.4192	.4207	.4222	.4236	.4251	.4265	.4279	.4292	.4306	.4319
1.5	.4332	.4345	.4357	.4370	.4382	.4394	.4406	.4418	.4429	.4441
1.6	.4452	.4463	.4474	.4484	.4495	.4505	.4515	.4525	.4535	.4545
1.7	.4554	.4564	.4573	.4582	.4591	.4599	.4608	.4616	.4625	.4633
1.8	.4641	.4649	.4656	.4664	.4671	.4678	.4686	.4693	.4699	.4706
1.9	.4713	.4719	.4726	.4732	.4738	.4744	.4750	.4756	.4761	.4767
2.0	.4772	.4778	.4783	.4788	.4793	.4798	.4803	.4808	.4812	.4817
2.1	.4821	.4826	.4830	.4834	.4838	.4842	.4846	.4850	.4854	.4857
2.2	.4861	.4864	.4868	.4871	.4875	.4878	.4881	.4884	.4887	.4890
2.3	.4893	.4896	.4898	.4901	.4904	.4906	.4909	.4911	.4913	.4916
2.4	.4918	.4920	.4922	.4925	.4927	.4929	.4931	.4932	.4934	.4936
2.5	.4938	.4940	.4941	.4943	.4945	.4946	.4948	.4949	.4951	.4952
2.6	.4953	.4955	.4956	.4957	.4959	.4960	.4961	.4962	.4963	.4964
2.7	.4965	.4966	.4967	.4968	.4969	.4970	.4971	.4972	.4973	.4974
2.8	.4974	.4975	.4976	.4977	.4977	.4978	.4979	.4979	.4980	.4981
2.9	.4981	.4982	.4982	.4983	.4984	.4984	.4985	.4985	.4986	.4986
3.0	.4987	.4987	.4987	.4988	.4988	.4989	.4989	.4989	.4990	.4990

Source: This table is adapted from National Bureau of Standards, *Tables of Normal Probability Functions*, Applied Mathematics Series 23, U.S. Department of Commerce, 1953.

Values of t That Will Be Exceeded with Specified Probabilities

This table shows the value of t where the area under the t distribution exceeding this value of t equals the specified amount. For example, the probability that a t variable with 14 degrees of freedom will exceed 1.345 equals .10.

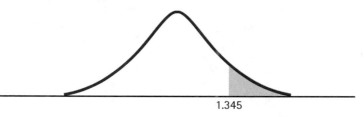

Degrees of freedom	Probability						
	.40	.25	.10	.05	.025	.01	.005
1	0.325	1.000	3.078	6.314	12.706	31.821	63.657
2	.289	0.816	1.886	2.920	4.303	6.965	9.925
3	.277	.765	1.638	2.353	3.182	4.541	5.841
4	.271	.741	1.533	2.132	2.776	3.747	4.604
5	0.267	0.727	1.476	2.015	2.571	3.365	4.032
6	.265	.718	1.440	1.943	2.447	3.143	3.707
7	.263	.711	1.415	1.895	2.365	2.998	3.499
8	.262	.706	1.397	1.860	2.306	2.896	3.355
9	.261	.703	1.383	1.833	2.262	2.821	3.250
10	0.260	0.700	1.372	1.812	2.228	2.764	3.169
11	.260	.697	1.363	1.796	2.201	2.718	3.106
12	.259	.695	1.356	1.782	2.179	2.681	3.055
13	.259	.694	1.350	1.771	2.160	2.650	3.012
14	.258	.692	1.345	1.761	2.145	2.624	2.977
15	0.258	0.691	1.341	1.753	2.131	2.602	2.947
16	.258	.690	1.337	1.746	2.120	2.583	2.921
17	.257	.689	1.333	1.740	2.110	2.567	2.898
18	.257	.688	1.330	1.734	2.101	2.552	2.878
19	.257	.688	1.328	1.729	2.093	2.539	2.861
20	0.257	0.687	1.325	1.725	2.086	2.528	2.845
21	.257	.686	1.323	1.721	2.080	2.518	2.831
22	.256	.686	1.321	1.717	2.074	2.508	2.819
23	.256	.685	1.319	1.714	2.069	2.500	2.807
24	.256	.685	1.318	1.711	2.064	2.492	2.797

APPENDIX
TABLE
4

Values of t That Will Be Exceeded with Specified Probabilities (Continued)

This table shows the value of t where the area under the t distribution exceeding this value of t equals the specified amount. For example, the probability that a t variable with 14 degrees of freedom will exceed 1.345 equals .10.

Degrees of freedom	Probability						
	.40	.25	.10	.05	.025	.01	.005
25	0.256	0.684	1.316	1.708	2.060	2.485	2.787
26	.256	.684	1.315	1.706	2.056	2.479	2.779
27	.256	.684	1.314	1.703	2.052	2.473	2.771
28	.256	.683	1.313	1.701	2.048	2.467	2.763
29	.256	.683	1.311	1.699	2.045	2.462	2.756
30	0.256	0.683	1.310	1.697	2.042	2.457	2.750
40	.255	.681	1.303	1.684	2.021	2.423	2.704
60	.254	.679	1.296	1.671	2.000	2.390	2.660
120	.254	.677	1.289	1.658	1.980	2.358	2.617
∞	.253	.674	1.282	1.645	1.960	2.326	2.576

Source: Biometrika Tables for Statisticians (Cambridge, U.K.: Cambridge University, 1954).

APPENDIX
TABLE
5

Value of an *F* Variable That Is Exceeded with Probability Equal to .05

		Degrees of freedom for numerator							
	1	2	3	4	5	6	7	8	9
1	161.4	199.5	215.7	224.6	230.2	234.0	236.8	238.9	240.5
2	18.51	19.00	19.16	19.25	19.30	19.33	19.35	19.37	19.38
3	10.13	9.55	9.28	9.12	9.01	8.94	8.89	8.85	8.81
4	7.71	6.94	6.59	6.39	6.26	6.16	6.09	6.04	6.00
5	6.61	5.79	5.41	5.19	5.05	4.95	4.88	4.82	4.77
6	5.99	5.14	4.76	4.53	4.39	4.28	4.21	4.15	4.10
7	5.59	4.74	4.35	4.12	3.97	3.87	3.79	3.73	3.68
8	5.32	4.46	4.07	3.84	3.69	3.58	3.50	3.44	3.39
9	5.12	4.26	3.86	3.63	3.48	3.37	3.29	3.23	3.18
10	4.96	4.10	3.71	3.48	3.33	3.22	3.14	3.07	3.02
11	4.84	3.98	3.59	3.36	3.20	3.09	3.01	2.95	2.90
12	4.75	3.89	3.49	3.26	3.11	3.00	2.91	2.85	2.80
13	4.67	3.81	3.41	3.18	3.03	2.92	2.83	2.77	2.71
14	4.60	3.74	3.34	3.11	2.96	2.85	2.76	2.70	2.65
15	4.54	3.68	3.29	3.06	2.90	2.79	2.71	2.64	2.59
16	4.49	3.63	3.24	3.01	2.85	2.74	2.66	2.59	2.54
17	4.45	3 59	3.20	2.96	2.81	2.70	2.61	2.55	2.49
18	4.41	3.55	3.16	2.93	2.77	2.66	2.58	2.51	2.46
19	4.38	3.52	3.13	2.90	2.74	2.63	2.54	2.48	2.42
20	4.35	3.49	3.10	2.87	2.71	2.60	2.51	2.45	2.39
21	4.32	3.47	3.07	2.84	2.68	2.57	2.49	2.42	2.37
22	4.30	3.44	3.05	2.82	2.66	2.55	2.46	2.40	2.34
23	4.28	3.42	3.03	2.80	2.64	2.53	2.44	2.37	2.32
24	4.26	3.40	3.01	2.78	2.62	2.51	2.42	2.36	2.30
25	4.24	3.39	2.99	2.76	2.60	2.49	2.40	2.34	2.28
26	4.23	3.37	2.98	2.74	2.59	2.47	2.39	2.32	2.27
27	4.21	3.35	2.96	2.73	2.57	2.46	2.37	2.31	2.25
28	4.20	3.34	2.95	2.71	2.56	2.45	2.36	2.29	2.24
29	4.18	3.33	2.93	2.70	2.55	2.43	2.35	2.28	2.22
30	4.17	3.32	2.92	2.69	2.53	2.42	2.33	2.27	2.21
40	4.08	3.23	2.84	2.61	2.45	2.34	2.25	2.18	2.12
60	4.00	3.15	2.76	2.53	2.37	2.25	2.17	2.10	2.04
120	3.92	3.07	2.68	2.45	2.29	2.17	2.09	2.02	1.96
∞	3.84	3.00	2.60	2.37	2.21	2.10	2.01	1.94	1.88

Degrees of freedom for denominator

Value of an *F* Variable That Is Exceeded with Probability Equal to .05 (Continued)

Degrees of freedom for numerator

	10	12	15	20	24	30	40	60	120	∞
1	241.9	243.9	245.9	248.0	249.1	250.1	251.1	252.2	253.3	254.3
2	19.40	19.41	19.43	19.45	19.45	19.46	19.47	19.48	19.49	19.50
3	8.79	8.74	8.70	8.66	8.64	8.62	8.59	8.57	8.55	8.53
4	5.96	5.91	5.86	5.80	5.77	5.75	5.72	5.69	5.66	5.63
5	4.74	4.68	4.62	4.56	4.53	4.50	4.46	4.43	4.40	4.36
6	4.06	4.00	3.94	3.87	3.84	3.81	3.77	3.74	3.70	3.67
7	3.64	3.57	3.51	3.44	3.41	3.38	3.34	3.30	3.27	3.23
8	3.35	3.28	3.22	3.15	3.12	3.08	3.04	3.01	2.97	2.93
9	3.14	3.07	3.01	2.94	2.90	2.86	2.83	2.79	2.75	2.71
10	2.98	2.91	2.85	2.77	2.74	2.70	2.66	2.62	2.58	2.54
11	2.85	2.79	2.72	2.65	2.61	2.57	2.53	2.49	2.45	2.40
12	2.75	2.69	2.62	2.54	2.51	2.47	2.43	2.38	2.34	2.30
13	2.67	2.60	2.53	2.46	2.42	2.38	2.34	2.30	2.25	2.21
14	2.60	2.53	2.46	2.39	2.35	2.31	2.27	2.22	2.18	2.13
15	2.54	2.48	2.40	2.33	2.29	2.25	2.20	2.16	2.11	2.07
16	2.49	2.42	2.35	2.28	2.24	2.19	2.15	2.11	2.06	2.01
17	2.45	2.38	2.31	2.23	2.19	2.15	2.10	2.06	2.01	1.96
18	2.41	2.34	2.27	2.19	2.15	2.11	2.06	2.02	1.97	1.92
19	2.38	2.31	2.23	2.16	2.11	2.07	2.03	1.98	1.93	1.88
20	2.35	2.28	2.20	2.12	2.08	2.04	1.99	1.95	1.90	1.84
21	2.32	2.25	2.18	2.10	2.05	2.01	1.96	1.92	1.87	1.81
22	2.30	2.23	2.15	2.07	2.03	1.98	1.94	1.89	1.84	1.78
23	2.27	2.20	2.13	2.05	2.01	1.96	1.91	1.86	1.81	1.76
24	2.25	2.18	2.11	2.03	1.98	1.94	1.89	1.84	1.79	1.73
25	2.24	2.16	2.09	2.01	1.96	1.92	1.87	1.82	1.77	1.71
26	2.22	2.15	2.07	1.99	1.95	1.90	1.85	1.80	1.75	1.69
27	2.20	2.13	2.06	1.97	1.93	1.88	1.84	1.79	1.73	1.67
28	2.19	2.12	2.04	1.96	1.91	1.87	1.82	1.77	1.71	1.65
29	2.18	2.10	2.03	1.94	1.90	1.85	1.81	1.75	1.70	1.64
30	2.16	2.09	2.01	1.93	1.89	1.84	1.79	1.74	1.68	1.62
40	2.08	2.00	1.92	1.84	1.79	1.74	1.69	1.64	1.58	1.51
60	1.99	1.92	1.84	1.75	1.70	1.65	1.59	1.53	1.47	1.39
120	1.91	1.83	1.75	1.66	1.61	1.55	1.50	1.43	1.35	1.25
∞	1.83	1.75	1.67	1.57	1.52	1.46	1.39	1.32	1.22	1.00

Degrees of freedom for denominator

Source: Biometrika Tables for Statisticians.

APPENDIX TABLE 6

Value of an *F* Variable That Is Exceeded with Probability Equal to .01

Degrees of freedom for numerator

		1	2	3	4	5	6	7	8	9
	1	4052	4999.5	5403	5625	5764	5859	5928	5982	6022
	2	98.50	99.00	99.17	99.25	99.30	99.33	99.36	99.37	99.39
	3	34.12	30.82	29.46	28.71	28.24	27.91	27.67	27.49	27.35
	4	21.20	18.00	16.69	15.98	15.52	15.21	14.98	14.80	14.66
	5	16.26	13.27	12.06	11.39	10.97	10.67	10.46	10.29	10.16
	6	13.75	10.92	9.78	9.15	8.75	8.47	8.26	8.10	7.98
	7	12.25	9.55	8.45	7.85	7.46	7.19	6.99	6.84	6.72
	8	11.26	8.65	7.59	7.01	6.63	6.37	6.18	6.03	5.91
	9	10.56	8.02	6.99	6.42	6.06	5.80	5.61	5.47	5.35
	10	10.04	7.56	6.55	5.99	5.64	5.39	5.20	5.06	4.94
	11	9.65	7.21	6.22	5.67	5.32	5.07	4.89	4.74	4.63
Degrees of freedom for denominator	12	9.33	6.93	5.95	5.41	5.06	4.82	4.64	4.50	4.39
	13	9.07	6.70	5.74	5.21	4.86	4.62	4.44	4.30	4.19
	14	8.86	6.51	5.56	5.04	4.69	4.46	4.28	4.14	4.03
	15	8.68	6.36	5.42	4.89	4.56	4.32	4.14	4.00	3.89
	16	8.53	6.23	5.29	4.77	4.44	4.20	4.03	3.89	3.78
	17	8.40	6.11	5.18	4.67	4.34	4.10	3.93	3.79	3.68
	18	8.29	6.01	5.09	4.58	4.25	4.01	3.84	3.71	3.60
	19	8.18	5.93	5.01	4.50	4.17	3.94	3.77	3.63	3.52
	20	8.10	5.85	4.94	4.43	4.10	3.87	3.70	3.56	3.46
	21	8.02	5.78	4.87	4.37	4.04	3.81	3.64	3.51	3.40
	22	7.95	5.72	4.82	4.31	3.99	3.76	3.59	3.45	3.35
	23	7.88	5.66	4.76	4.26	3.94	3.71	3.54	3.41	3.30
	24	7.82	5.61	4.72	4.22	3.90	3.67	3.50	3.36	3.26
	25	7.77	5.57	4.68	4.18	3.85	3.63	3.46	3.32	3.22
	26	7.72	5.53	4.64	4.14	3.82	3.59	3.42	3.29	3.18
	27	7.68	5.49	4.60	4.11	3.78	3.56	3.39	3.26	3.15
	28	7.64	5.45	4.57	4.07	3.75	3.53	3.36	3.23	3.12
	29	7.60	5.42	4.54	4.04	3.73	3.50	3.33	3.20	3.09
	30	7.56	5.39	4.51	4.02	3.70	3.47	3.30	3.17	3.07
	40	7.31	5.18	4.31	3.83	3.51	3.29	3.12	2.99	2.89
	60	7.08	4.98	4.13	3.65	3.34	3.12	2.95	2.82	2.72
	120	6.85	4.79	3.95	3.48	3.17	2.96	2.79	2.66	2.56
	∞	6.63	4.61	3.78	3.32	3.02	2.80	2.64	2.51	2.41

Value of an *F* Variable That is Exceeded with Probability Equal to .01 (Continued)

	Degrees of freedom for numerator									
	12	15	20	24	30	40	60	120	∞	
	6106	6157	6209	6235	6261	6287	6313	6339	6366	
	99.40	99.42	99.43	99.45	99.46	99.47	99.47	99.48	99.49	99.50
	27.23	27.05	26.87	26.69	26.60	26.50	26.41	26.32	26.22	26.13
	14.55	14.37	14.20	14.02	13.93	13.84	13.75	13.65	13.56	13.46
5	10.05	9.89	9.72	9.55	9.47	9.38	9.29	9.20	9.11	9.02
6	7.87	7.72	7.56	7.40	7.31	7.23	7.14	7.06	6.97	6.88
7	6.62	6.47	6.31	6.16	6.07	5.99	5.91	5.82	5.74	5.65
8	5.81	5.67	5.52	5.36	5.28	5.20	5.12	5.03	4.95	4.86
9	5.26	5.11	4.96	4.81	4.73	4.65	4.57	4.48	4.40	4.31
10	4.85	4.71	4.56	4.41	4.33	4.25	4.17	4.08	4.00	3.91
11	4.54	4.40	4.25	4.10	4.02	3.94	3.86	3.78	3.69	3.60
12	4.30	4.16	4.01	3.86	3.78	3.70	3.62	3.54	3.45	3.36
13	4.10	3.96	3.82	3.66	3.59	3.51	3.43	3.34	3.25	3.17
14	3.94	3.80	3.66	3.51	3.43	3.35	3.27	3.18	3.09	3.00
15	3.80	3.67	3.52	3.37	3.29	3.21	3.13	3.05	2.96	2.87
16	3.69	3.55	3.41	3.26	3.18	3.10	3.02	2.93	2.84	2.75
17	3.59	3.46	3.31	3.16	3.08	3.00	2.92	2.83	2.75	2.65
18	3.51	3.37	3.23	3.08	3.00	2.92	2.84	2.75	2.66	2.57
19	3.43	3.30	3.15	3.00	2.92	2.84	2.76	2.67	2.58	2.49
20	3.37	3.23	3.09	2.94	2.86	2.78	2.69	2.61	2.52	2.42
21	3.31	3.17	3.03	2.88	2.80	2.72	2.64	2.55	2.46	2.36
22	3.26	3.12	2.98	2.83	2.75	2.67	2.58	2.50	2.40	2.31
23	3.21	3.07	2.93	2.78	2.70	2.62	2.54	2.45	2.35	2.26
24	3.17	3.03	2.89	2.74	2.66	2.58	2.49	2.40	2.31	2.21
25	3.13	2.99	2.85	2.70	2.62	2.54	2.45	2.36	2.27	2.17
26	3.09	2.96	2.81	2.66	2.58	2.50	2.42	2.33	2.23	2.13
27	3.06	2.93	2.78	2.63	2.55	2.47	2.38	2.29	2.20	2.10
28	3.03	2.90	2.75	2.60	2.52	2.44	2.35	2.26	2.17	2.06
29	3.00	2.87	2.73	2.57	2.49	2.41	2.33	2.23	2.14	2.03
30	2.98	2.84	2.70	2.55	2.47	2.39	2.30	2.21	2.11	2.01
40	2.80	2.66	2.52	2.37	2.29	2.20	2.11	2.02	1.92	1.80
60	2.63	2.50	2.35	2.20	2.12	2.03	1.94	1.84	1.73	1.60
120	2.47	2.34	2.19	2.03	1.95	1.86	1.76	1.66	1.53	1.38
∞	2.32	2.18	2.04	1.88	1.79	1.70	1.59	1.47	1.32	1.00

Degrees of freedom for denominator

Source: Biometrika Tables for Statisticians.

Values of d_L and d_U for the Durbin–Watson

A. Significance level = .05

	k = 1		k = 2		k = 3		k = 4		
n	d_L	d_U	d_L	d_U	d_L	d_U	d_L	d_U	d_L
15	1.08	1.36	0.95	1.54	0.82	1.75	0.69	1.97	0.56	
16	1.10	1.37	0.98	1.54	0.86	1.73	0.74	1.93	0.62	2.
17	1.13	1.38	1.02	1.54	0.90	1.71	0.78	1.90	0.67	2.10
18	1.16	1.39	1.05	1.53	0.93	1.69	0.82	1.87	0.71	2.06
19	1.18	1.40	1.08	1.53	0.97	1.68	0.86	1.85	0.75	2.02
20	1.20	1.41	1.10	1.54	1.00	1.68	0.90	1.83	0.79	1.99
21	1.22	1.42	1.13	1.54	1.03	1.67	0.93	1.81	0.83	1.96
22	1.24	1.43	1.15	1.54	1.05	1.66	0.96	1.80	0.86	1.94
23	1.26	1.44	1.17	1.54	1.08	1.66	0.99	1.79	0.90	1.92
24	1.27	1.45	1.19	1.55	1.10	1.66	1.01	1.78	0.93	1.90
25	1.29	1.45	1.21	1.55	1.12	1.66	1.04	1.77	0.95	1.89
26	1.30	1.46	1.22	1.55	1.14	1.65	1.06	1.76	0.98	1.88
27	1.32	1.47	1.24	1.56	1.16	1.65	1.08	1.76	1.01	1.86
28	1.33	1.48	1.26	1.56	1.18	1.65	1.10	1.75	1.03	1.85
29	1.34	1.48	1.27	1.56	1.20	1.65	1.12	1.74	1.05	1.84
30	1.35	1.49	1.28	1.57	1.21	1.65	1.14	1.74	1.07	1.83
31	1.36	1.50	1.30	1.57	1.23	1.65	1.16	1.74	1.09	1.83
32	1.37	1.50	1.31	1.57	1.24	1.65	1.18	1.73	1.11	1.82
33	1.38	1.51	1.32	1.58	1.26	1.65	1.19	1.73	1.13	1.81
34	1.39	1.51	1.33	1.58	1.27	1.65	1.21	1.73	1.15	1.81
35	1.40	1.52	1.34	1.58	1.28	1.65	1.22	1.73	1.16	1.80
36	1.41	1.52	1.35	1.59	1.29	1.65	1.24	1.73	1.18	1.80
37	1.42	1.53	1.36	1.59	1.31	1.66	1.25	1.72	1.19	1.80
38	1.43	1.54	1.37	1.59	1.32	1.66	1.26	1.72	1.21	1.79
39	1.43	1.54	1.38	1.60	1.33	1.66	1.27	1.72	1.22	1.79
40	1.44	1.54	1.39	1.60	1.34	1.66	1.29	1.72	1.23	1.79
45	1.48	1.57	1.43	1.62	1.38	1.67	1.34	1.72	1.29	1.78
50	1.50	1.59	1.46	1.63	1.42	1.67	1.38	1.72	1.34	1.77
55	1.53	1.60	1.49	1.64	1.45	1.68	1.41	1.72	1.38	1 77
60	1.55	1.62	1.51	1.65	1.48	1.69	1.44	1.73	1.41	1.77
65	1.57	1.63	1.54	1.66	1.50	1.70	1.47	1.73	1.44	1.77
70	1.58	1.64	1.55	1.67	1.52	1.70	1.49	1.74	1.46	1.77
75	1.60	1.65	1.57	1.68	1.54	1.71	1.51	1.74	1.49	1.77
80	1.61	1.66	1.59	1.69	1.56	1.72	1.53	1.74	1.51	1.77
85	1.62	1.67	1.60	1.70	1.57	1.72	1.55	1.75	1.52	1.77
90	1.63	1.68	1.61	1.70	1.59	1.73	1.57	1.75	1.54	1.78
95	1.64	1.69	1.62	1.71	1.60	1.73	1.58	1.75	1.56	1.78
100	1.65	1.69	1.63	1.72	1.61	1.74	1.59	1.76	1.57	1.78

Values of d_L and d_U for the Durbin–Watson Test (Continued)

B. Significance level = .025

	k = 1		k = 2		k = 3		k = 4		k = 5	
n	d_L	d_U	d_L	d_U	d_L	d_U	d_L	d_U	d_L	d_U
15	0.95	1.23	0.83	1.40	0.71	1.61	0.59	1.84	0.48	2.09
16	0.98	1.24	0.86	1.40	0.75	1.59	0.64	1.80	0.53	2.03
17	1.01	1.25	0.90	1.40	0.79	1.58	0.68	1.77	0.57	1.98
18	1.03	1.26	0.93	1.40	0.82	1.56	0.72	1.74	0.62	1.93
19	1.06	1.28	0.96	1.41	0.86	1.55	0.76	1.72	0.66	1.90
20	1.08	1.28	0.99	1.41	0.89	1.55	0.79	1.70	0.70	1.87
21	1.10	1.30	1.01	1.41	0.92	1.54	0.83	1.69	0.73	1.84
22	1.12	1.31	1.04	1.42	0.95	1.54	0.86	1.68	0.77	1.82
23	1.14	1.32	1.06	1.42	0.97	1.54	0.89	1.67	0.80	1.80
24	1.16	1.33	1.08	1.43	1.00	1.54	0.91	1.66	0.83	1.79
25	1.18	1.34	1.10	1.43	1.02	1.54	0.94	1.65	0.86	1.77
26	1.19	1.35	1.12	1.44	1.04	1.54	0.96	1.65	0.88	1.76
27	1.21	1.36	1.13	1.44	1.06	1.54	0.99	1.64	0.91	1.75
28	1.22	1.37	1.15	1.45	1.08	1.54	1.01	1.64	0.93	1.74
29	1.24	1.38	1.17	1.45	1.10	1.54	1.03	1.63	0.96	1.73
30	1.25	1.38	1.18	1.46	1.12	1.54	1.05	1.63	0.98	1.73
31	1.26	1.39	1.20	1.47	1.13	1.55	1.07	1.63	1.00	1.72
32	1.27	1.40	1.21	1.47	1.15	1.55	1.08	1.63	1.02	1.71
33	1.28	1.41	1.22	1.48	1.16	1.55	1.10	1.63	1.04	1.71
34	1.29	1.41	1.24	1.48	1.17	1.55	1.12	1.63	1.06	1.70
35	1.30	1.42	1.25	1.48	1.19	1.55	1.13	1.63	1.07	1.70
36	1.31	1.43	1.26	1.49	1.20	1.56	1.15	1.63	1.09	1.70
37	1.32	1.43	1.27	1.49	1.21	1.56	1.16	1.62	1.10	1.70
38	1.33	1.44	1.28	1.50	1.23	1.56	1.17	1.62	1.12	1.70
39	1.34	1.44	1.29	1.50	1.24	1.56	1.19	1.63	1.13	1.69
40	1.35	1.45	1.30	1.51	1.25	1.57	1.20	1.63	1.15	1.69
45	1.39	1.48	1.34	1.53	1.30	1.58	1.25	1.63	1.21	1.69
50	1.42	1.50	1.38	1.54	1.34	1.59	1.30	1.64	1.26	1.69
55	1.45	1.52	1.41	1.56	1.37	1.60	1.33	1.64	1.30	1.69
60	1.47	1.54	1.44	1.57	1.40	1.61	1.37	1.65	1.33	1.69
65	1.49	1.55	1.46	1.59	1.43	1.62	1.40	1.66	1.36	1.69
70	1.51	1.57	1.48	1.60	1.45	1.63	1.42	1.66	1.39	1.70
75	1.53	1.58	1.50	1.61	1.47	1.64	1.45	1.67	1.42	1.70
80	1.54	1.59	1.52	1.62	1.49	1.65	1.47	1.67	1.44	1.70
85	1.56	1.60	1.53	1.63	1.51	1.65	1.49	1.68	1.46	1.71
90	1.57	1.61	1.55	1.64	1.53	1.66	1.50	1.69	1.48	1.71
95	1.58	1.62	1.56	1.65	1.54	1.67	1.52	1.69	1.50	1.71
100	1.59	1.63	1.57	1.65	1.55	1.67	1.53	1.70	1.51	1.72

Values of d_L and d_U for the Durbin–Watson Test (Continued)

C. Significance level = 0.01

n	k = 1		k = 2		k = 3		k = 4		k = 5	
	d_L	d_U	d_L	d_U	d_L	d_U	d_L	d_U	d_L	d_U
15	0.81	1.07	0.70	1.25	0.59	1.46	0.49	1.70	0.39	1.96
16	0.84	1.09	0.74	1.25	0.63	1.44	0.53	1.66	0.44	1.90
17	0.87	1.10	0.77	1.25	0.67	1.43	0.57	1.63	0.48	1.85
18	0.90	1.12	0.80	1.26	0.71	1.42	0.61	1.60	0.52	1.80
19	0.93	1.13	0.83	1.26	0.74	1.41	0.65	1.58	0.56	1.77
20	0.95	1.15	0.86	1.27	077	1.41	0.68	1.57	0.60	1.74
21	0.97	1.16	0.89	1.27	0.80	1.41	0.72	1.55	0.63	1.71
22	1.00	1.17	0.91	1.28	0.83	1.40	0.75	1.54	0.66	1.69
23	1.02	1.19	0.94	1.29	0.86	1.40	0.77	1.53	0.70	1.67
24	1.04	1.20	0.96	1.30	0.88	1.41	0.80	1.53	0.72	1.66
25	1.05	1.21	0.98	1.30	0.90	1.41	0.83	1.52	0.75	1.65
26	1.07	1.22	1.00	1.31	0.93	1.41	0.85	1.52	0.78	1.64
27	1.09	1.23	1.02	1.32	0.95	1.41	0.88	1.51	0.81	1.63
28	1.10	1.24	1.04	1.32	0.97	1.41	0.90	1.51	0.83	1.62
29	1.12	1.25	1.05	1.33	0.99	1.42	0.92	1.51	0.85	1.61
30	1.13	1.26	1.07	1.34	1.01	1.42	0.94	1.51	0.88	1.61
31	1.15	1.27	1.08	1.34	1.02	1.42	0.96	1.51	0.90	1.60
32	1.16	1.28	1.10	1.35	1.04	1.43	0.98	1.51	0.92	1.60
33	1.17	1.29	1.11	1.36	1.05	1.43	1.00	1.51	0.94	1.59
34	1.18	1.30	1.13	1.36	1.07	1.43	1.01	1.51	0.95	1.59
35	1.19	1.31	1.14	1.37	1.08	1.44	1.03	1.51	0.97	1.59
36	1.21	1.32	1.15	1.38	1.10	1.44	1.04	1.51	0.99	1.59
37	1.22	1.32	1.16	1.38	1.11	1.45	1.06	1.51	1.00	1.59
38	1.23	1.33	1.18	1.39	1.12	1.45	1.07	1.52	1.02	1.58
39	1.24	1.34	1.19	1.39	1.14	1.45	1.09	1.52	1.03	1.58
40	1.25	1.34	1.20	1.40	1.15	1.46	1.10	1.52	1.05	1.58
45	1.29	1.38	1.24	1.42	1.20	1.48	1.16	1.53	1.11	1.58
50	1.32	1.40	1.28	1.45	1.24	1.49	1.20	1.54	1.16	1.59
55	1.36	1.43	1.32	1.47	1.28	1.51	1.25	1.55	1.21	1.59
60	1.38	1.45	1.35	1.48	1.32	1.52	1.28	1.56	1.25	1.60
65	1.41	1.47	1.38	1.50	1.35	1.53	1.31	1.57	1.28	1.61
70	1.43	1.49	1.40	1.52	1.37	1.55	1.34	1.58	1.31	1.61
75	1.45	1.50	1.42	1.53	1.39	1.56	1.37	1.59	1.34	1.62
80	1.47	1.52	1.44	1.54	1.42	1.57	1.39	1.60	1.36	1.62
85	1.48	1.53	1.46	1.55	1.43	1.58	1.41	1.60	1.39	1.63
90	1.50	1.54	1.47	1.56	1.45	1.59	1.43	1.61	1.41	1.64
95	1.51	1.55	1.49	1.57	1.47	1.60	1.45	1.62	1.42	1.64
100	1.52	1.56	1.50	1.58	1.48	1.60	1.46	1.63	1.44	1.65

Source: J. Durbin and G. S. Watson, "Testing for Serial Correlation in Least Squares Regression," *Biometrika 38* (June 1951).

PHOTO CREDITS

INDEX